Introduction to

PUBLIC LAW

Sourcebook

SEVENTH EDITION

edited by

DAVID W. ELLIOTT

Department of Law
Carleton University

CANADIAN LEGAL STUDIES SERIES

Captus Press

Canadian Legal Studies Series
Introduction to Public Law: Sourcebook, 7th edition

Copyright © 1989–2007 by D.W. Elliott and Captus Press Inc.

First Captus Press edition, 1989
Seventh edition, 2007

Canada *We acknowledge the financial support of the Government of Canada through the Book Publishing Industry Development Program (BPIDP) for our publishing activities.*

Library and Archives Canada Cataloguing in Publication

Introduction to public law: sourcebook / edited by David W. Elliott — 7th ed.

(Canadian legal studies series)
Includes bibliographical references.
ISBN 978-1–55322–166–1

1. Public law — Canada — Textbooks. 2. Public law — Canada — Cases. I. Elliott, David W. (David William), date. II. Series.

KE4120.I57 2007   342.71   C2007–904223–6
KF4482.I57 2007

Captus Press Inc.
Units 14 & 15, 1600 Steeles Avenue West
Concord, Ontario
L4K 4M2, Canada
Telephone: (416) 736–5537
Fax: (416) 736–5793
Email: info@captus.com
Internet: http://www.captus.com

0 9 8 7 6 5 4 3 2 1
Printed and bound in Canada

Table of Contents

I

Law and Public Law

II

The Constitution

III
The Constitution Act, 1867

IV
Constitution Act, 1982
and After

Preface

What do fishing quotas, Aboriginal land claims, employment equity rules, hospital closing schemes, the *Quebec Secession Reference*, and neighbourhood zoning by-laws have in common? First, they involve the state and its relationship to society. Second, they involve the law, and they may well involve the courts of law. Third, they are aspects of a growing presence in modern Canadian life, the vast and vital field of public law.

These materials are intended to help provide an introduction to Canadian public law, with special emphasis on the role of courts. Just what is public law, and what role have courts played in it? What role do they play? What role should they play? How and where should public law be changed?

With questions such as these in mind, this volume starts with a brief general look at public law and then addresses some aspects of the federal system and constitutional reform. Theoretical public law issues, administrative law, civil liberties, and the impact of the *Charter* are explored in a companion volume, *Introduction to Public Law: Readings on the State, the Administrative Process, and Basic Values*, sixth edition, 2007, edited by D.W. Elliott.

Even in the fields it addresses, this is a selective volume. It should be supplemented by an introductory text on Canadian constitutional law (for example, one of those included in the general part of the Bibliography) and by additional readings chosen by the instructor. As well, students are urged to do as much reading as possible in history, philosophy, and the social sciences. For all their importance, public law and the courts are only one part of a larger and more complex social whole.

Ottawa, Ontario
July 2007

Acknowledgements

I gratefully acknowledge the helpful advice of my colleagues Christian Jaekl, Rosemary Warskett, and Vincent Kazmierski. Professor Warskett provided the basis for the introduction to the *Edwards* decision in Chapter 4. Ms. Pauline Lai and Ms. Lily Chu of Captus Press provided much help in preparing this edition for printing.

I thank the authors and publishers who gave permission to reproduce their works herein. Please note that the reproduced excerpts do not all contain the original footnotes, endnotes, or footnote and endnote numbering.

David W. Elliott
Ottawa, Ontario
2007

List of Abbreviations

Abbreviations are used for some references in this volume to other published works. The abbreviations and their full citations are as follows:

Brooks Stephen Brooks, *Canadian Democracy: An Introduction*, 4th ed. (Don Mills, Ont.: Oxford University Press, 2004)

Cheffins Ronald I. Cheffins & Patricia A. Johnson, *The Revised Canadian Constitution: Politics as Law* (Toronto: McGraw-Hill Ryerson, 1986)

Dyck Rand Dyck, *Canadian Politics: Critical Approaches,* 5th ed. (Toronto: Thomson Nelson, 2008)

Forcese Craig Forcese & Aaron Freeman, *The Laws of Government: The Legal Foundations of Canadian Democracy* (Toronto: Irwin Law, 2005)

Funston Bernard W. Funston & Eugene Meehan, *Canada's Constitutional Law in a Nutshell*, 3d ed. (Toronto: Carswell, 2003)

Hogg 2007 Peter W. Hogg, *Constitutional Law of Canada*, 4th ed.: 2007 student ed. (Toronto: Carswell, 2007)

MacIvor Heather MacIvor, ed., *Parameters of Power: Canada's Political Institutions*, 4th ed. (Toronto: Thomson Nelson, 2006)

Malcolmson Patrick Malcolmson & Richard Myers, *The Canadian Regime: An Introduction to Parliamentary Government in Canada*, 3d ed. (Peterborough: Broadview Press, 2005)

Milne David Milne, *The Canadian Constitution* (Toronto: James Lorimer and Company, 1991)

Monahan Patrick J. Monahan, *Constitutional Law*, 3d ed. (Toronto: Irwin Law, 2006)

Reesor Bayard Reesor, *The Canadian Constitution in Historical Perspective* (Scarborough: Prentice-Hall, 1992)

I

Law and Public Law

1

Elements of Public Law

(a) Public Law, the State, and the Courts

INTRODUCTION

Public law, the law relating to the state and its relationship to society, has always played a significant role in Canadian life. Today it is gaining even greater prominence. These are turbulent times. Constitutional law, administrative law, civil liberties, and other public law issues have moved from the back columns to the front pages of the Canadian consciousness.

At the same time, the focus has shifted within public law. In the past it shifted from legislatures to cabinets and first ministers. Now it is shared with another institution of government, the courts of law. Like public law itself, courts have a major impact on our lives, and this impact continues to grow.

One purpose of these materials is to help provide an introduction to Canadian public law, with a particular emphasis on the role of courts. What role have they played? What role do they play? What role should they play? Other purposes will depend on your individual instructor and your own interests.

PUBLIC LAW AND OTHER KINDS OF LAW

What Is Law?

Because public law is a form of law, it seems reasonable to approach it with some concept of law itself. As a start, we will define law tentatively as a body of rules enforceable in the courts.

This definition doesn't tell us that law operates in a social setting and is itself a social phenomenon.[1] It sheds no light on the ultimate purpose or purposes of law,[2] and begs the question of what rules the courts will or should enforce.

Yet the definition does isolate some key characteristics of law. It emphasizes that law is rule-based, normative, and enforceable. By noting the enforcement role of the courts, it suggests an important connection between law and government.[3] As long as we do not forget the social context of law, we should be able to limit our main focus to some of its distinctive features. As to law's purpose or purposes, the answers will vary with the vantage point and values of the individual observer. Here we will merely assume a general correlation between the stated goals of our system and its operation in practice, while acknowledging the likelihood of serious defects. Some readers may share this assumption; for others, it may require a temporary suspension of disbelief.

What Is Public Law?

The idea at the heart of public law is that of the state. The state — in the sense of government — is the institution that exercises sovereign power and purports to act on behalf of the "public" in a given geographical area.[4] This is the basis of our definition of public law as the law relating to the state and to the relationship between the state and society.[5] From here, we will define private law as the law relating to the actions of individuals and groups[6] in society.[7] But most law is created on behalf of the state, all law is subject to enforcement by the judicial branch of the state, and all law has some reference to private individuals. Our distinction is one of degree, not kind.

What Are the Other Main Kinds of Law?

Public law is only one of a number of general categories of law. Each of the others affects and interrelates with it.

At a general level, we can distinguish between various legal systems of the world.[8] Canada has both the common law system, applicable to public and private law matters outside Quebec, and the civil law system, applicable only to private law matters in Quebec. The common law system has an adversary procedure and is oriented toward case law. The civil law system has a more inquisitorial procedure and is based on legislative codes. Although Canadian public law is centred in the common law legal system, the civil law system may be relevant in cases involving private actions by public authorities in Quebec.

There is a distinction between common law and statute law. Common law is the body of rules and principles developed by the courts of law. Statute law, or primary legislation, is law enacted by the legislature. It includes constitutional statutes and ordinary statutes. Similar in effect to statute law is subordinate legislation, which consists of formal rules enacted by the executive branch of government, pursuant to statutory authority.[9] While statute law is explicit and consciously planned, common law develops haphazardly, depending on what is litigated. Although statute law prevails over common law in the event of a conflict, statute law is interpreted ultimately by courts, who apply common law principles when they interpret it.

Canadian public law can take the form of constitutional norms,[10] legislation or common law. Legal constitutional norms and legislation are interpreted by courts, and the common law is both created and interpreted by courts. Not surprisingly, then, some of the most significant questions in public law concern the strengths, weaknesses, and proper role of the courts of law.

We can also distinguish between criminal law, the law dealing with wrongs deemed serious enough to affect society as a whole, and other law, described in this context as civil law. Much of criminal law is found in a single systematic statute, the *Criminal Code*.[11] Criminal law's procedure is more inquisitorial than that of civil law. Its characteristic penalties are the fine and imprisonment. It has a public aspect, because the institution that represents the public as a whole is the state.

There is another distinction between municipal law and international law. In this context, municipal law is the internal law of a particular state, while international law addresses relations between different states and between citizens of different states.

Additional distinctions can be drawn between the systems of law of individual countries, and between the various subject areas of law, such as contract law, administrative law, and constitutional law. By our definition, all countries have some degree of public law, although it is less distinct in some than in others. Similarly, some subject matter areas are more closely concerned with the state than others. In Canada, these areas include constitutional law, administrative law, the law relating to civil liberties, and criminal law.

THE STATE

If we define public law in terms of the state, we must ask ourselves, just what *is* the state? What is the state in Canada? We have already described the state as the institution that exercises sovereign power and purports to act on behalf of the "public" in a given geographical area. Can we be more precise?

Composition of the Canadian State

The Canadian state is a collective entity. It includes a federal government that has responsibilities throughout Canada as a whole and represents Canada in formal relations with other states. It includes 10 provincial governments that have responsibilities within their respective regions. The remaining areas of the country are represented regionally by three territorial governments with provincial-type responsibilities in their respective regions, subject to federal government legislative power. Beyond this, there are municipal and/or regional governments exercising delegated provincial or territorial powers. There is even a National Capital Commission, which exercises delegated federal powers in the National Capital Region. Canada is truly a country of governments.

Each of the federal and provincial and territorial governments has three main branches:[12] a legislative branch,[13] an executive branch,[14] and a judicial branch.[15] The legislature's characteristic functions are three-fold: to represent the interests of the electorate, to monitor the executive branch, and to formally enact law. The executive's characteristic functions are to initiate and administer policy and law, and to manage the assets of the state. The judiciary's characteristic functions are resolving disputes according to law, and interpreting and developing law.

It is often hard to determine just where the state begins and ends. For example, the federal Department of Energy, Mines and Resources is clearly part of the state. Is the National Energy Board, a semi-independent regulatory agency, part of it? What about Canada Post Corporation, a Crown corporation organized partly on a private commercial model? What about Nav Canada, a privately incorporated body that operates Canada's civil air navigation system? What about a large "private" oil company incorporated pursuant to statute, subject to extensive construction and tariff regulations, and heavily dependent on sales to government or public subsidies?[16] Many of us would probably draw the state's outer boundary just outside Canada Post, but "stateness" in these cases is a matter of degree, not of kind. It often rests as much on traditional value judgments as on precise objective criteria.

To complicate things, the state's approximate boundaries are constantly shifting. Over the last two centuries, the executive branch has grown dramatically.[17] As this part of the state has expanded, so has the scope of public law. Even beyond the outer edge of the executive branch, the legislature has increasingly delegated statutory responsibilities to bodies that retain some private, non-governmental characteristics. Labour arbitrators, universities, and self-governing professional associations are all part of an emerging "quasi-state" with one foot in private law and another in public law. Even modern civil liberties statutory codes and constitutional safeguards designed to protect private individual and group rights involve an expanded enforcement role for members of the executive and judiciary. Ironically, the advent of the *Charter* adds a new dimension to the Canadian state.

Some Theoretical Approaches to the Concept of the State[18]

Most traditional concepts of the state appear to be related to one or more of the following four basic goals: pursuing collective action, protecting private rights, ensuring citizen control, and achieving equality.

Collective Action

A key feature of the state is its capacity to pursue collective action that would be difficult or impossible for individuals acting on their own.[19] Most philosophers seem to agree that this feature makes an institution such as the state necessary or desirable in any society.[20] One approach emphasizes this feature, and concentrates on the requisites of effective, strong collective action. Plato, for example, envisaged a three-part state of labourers, soldier-administrators, and "guardians" as the best way to meet human economic, external security, and general administrative needs, respectively.[21] For Thomas Hobbes, because individuals have a natural tendency to war and aggression when on their own, they consent to being ruled by a sovereign with power to maintain order by punishing wrongdoers.[22] Plato and Hobbes envisaged an authoritarian state, with few constraints on its collective action. Plato's guardians would administer the state as "philosopher-kings", drawing on their own wisdom and subject to control by no others. To maintain public order effectively, Hobbes' sovereign was to be all-powerful. Less authoritarian, but still in this tradition, is the wise, independent, élite member of Parliament envisaged by Edmund Burke.[23] Support for collective but non-authoritarian state action can be seen in the writings of many modern thinkers.[24]

Private Interests

A second approach emphasizes the need to protect interests of private individuals in concerns such as personal liberty or property. Some, like J.S. Mill[25] and Friedrich von Hayek,[26] have suggested that private interests are best protected by limiting state activities to the minimum necessary. Others, such as Cicero[27] and John Locke,[28] have said that people have natural rights that exist apart from the state, and have proposed forms of protection that may operate independently of the state. Locke argued that because people have entrusted the state with protecting their property and other interests, the state has a corresponding obligation to do so, and may be overturned if it shirks this basic obligation.[29] Still others have called for structural limitations on the state to protect private interests. Montesquieu, for example, said that "power should be a check to power."[30] He proposed that the liberty of the individual be protected by dividing the state's functions between a law-making branch, a law-implementing branch, and a law-interpreting branch.[31]

Citizen Control

Another tradition holds that those who are subject to state power should — as much as possible — direct it. It focuses less on protecting rights than on ensuring responsiveness and accountability in those who direct the affairs of state. Jean-Jacques Rousseau, for example, envisaged a sovereign somewhat similar to that of Hobbes, but one who should act pursuant to the "general will" of the people as a whole.[32] For John Stuart Mill and other utilitarians, the accountability of the state and its capacity to further the common good (for Mill, the greatest happiness of the greatest number) was enhanced by free discussion and an expanded electoral franchise.[33]

Equality

Yet another tradition emphasizes the goal of achieving greater equality. One strand here seeks substantive equality. Moderate socialists, such as the members of the British Fabian Society[34] and the Canadian League for Social Reconstruction,[35] advocated state collective action to put individuals in an equal position in relation to others, especially in economic matters. A more radical approach, with still more emphasis on economic interests, was that of Karl Marx. Marx believed that the capitalist state was dominated by the social class with control over the means of economic production.[36] He predicted that conflict between this class and the exploited working class would lead to basic change resulting in the formation of a quasi-egalitarian "dictatorship of the proletariat" and, ultimately, in a wholly egalitarian, classless society.[37]

Equality also has more formal meanings, requiring the state to afford all individuals equality of opportunity, and to deal equally with all individuals in comparable situations. The latter principle has been extended to require that individual members of the state should be as subject to the law as ordinary individuals.[38] Finally, a notion of equality is also behind the requirement that the law redress wrongs committed by individuals in proportion to the extent of these wrongs.[39]

Equality is also a basic element of the private interests and accountability approaches to the state. If all individuals are of equal worth, then each person's basic interests are entitled to equal protection against the state, and the state should be accountable equally to all its members.

State as Government or State as Society

In the approaches above, there is a spectrum of views as to whether the state is distinct from society on one hand and the government on the other. Greek philosophers such as Plato and Aristotle tended to regard the state and the whole political society or community as more or less interchangeable.[40] Where government was referred to separately,[41] it was as an instrument and part of both. Romans such as Cicero tended to distinguish the state as an abstract legal entity from society as a whole. They looked at the individual member of society as a person with interests separate from those of the state. This distinction was emphasized by modern writers such as John Locke, who contrasted the state (or government) sharply with the notion of the individual. More recently, some have suggested a more expansive picture of the state.[42] Others have focused on more encompassing concepts, such as class, hegemony or power.[43]

Canadian Concepts

Which, if any, of these theoretical approaches to the state has prevailed in Canada?

First, for reasons perhaps as much pragmatic as philosophical,[44] Canadians have looked traditionally[45] and increasingly to collective state action to help meet their needs and satisfy their aspirations.[46] Modern Canadian government extends far beyond the minimal functions of keeping order within and security without. Rather, it maintains a large system of social security, pursues cultural objectives, regulates many aspects of private enterprise, and carries on some enterprise itself. The Canadian positive state may not be everywhere, but it is a presence to be reckoned with.

Although Canadians have inherited strong executives[47] and have embraced the positive state, they seem to reject authoritarianism as a means of pursuing it. A would-be Hobbesian sovereign would feel out of place in modern Canada, but Canadians have reached little consensus on the best means of employing or controlling the state, or of combatting problems associated with it.

There is a strong tradition of asserting private rights. Canadians differentiate between government and the state on one hand, and the society as a whole and its members on the other. They tend to regard the "state" as synonymous with government,[48] and to draw a conceptual boundary between government and a sphere of protected freedoms[49] and interests.[50] Especially outside Quebec, the emphasis is on individual rights,[51] although private group rights have been gaining ground too.[52]

There is also a strong tradition of citizen control. A desire for greater accountability and local control helped precipitate the separation from British colonial control.[53] It helped to force the slow but ultimately successful expansion of the franchise.[54] Accountability in the form of parliamentary democracy is a key aspect of the "Constitution similar in principle to that of the United Kingdom" referred to in the *Constitution Act, 1867*;[55] it is supported in the "Democratic Rights" provisions of the *Charter*;[56] it is a major *raison d'être* of the legislative branch of government.[57] In a more general sense, accountability animates periodic calls for plebiscites and referenda. It was a key rallying cry of those who sought more grass roots control over the Meech Lake and Charlottetown constitutional processes.[58]

Of the major traditions, equality is perhaps the least well established in Canada. Despite labour unions,[59] equalization, progressive taxation, and many social welfare schemes, Canadians live in a country of considerable economic inequality. A few enjoy significant wealth while pensioners strain fixed incomes to meet monthly rent payments and the unemployed line up at food banks.[60] On the positive side, the principles of one-person-one-vote and universal adult suffrage are well established,[61] modern human rights legislation prohibits limited forms of discrimination in parts of the private sector,[62] and ss. 15 and 28 of the *Charter* impose equality requirements on government itself.[63] On the other hand, there is little agreement as to what equality requires of the state in individual cases, and serious disparities remain untouched.[64]

Canada, then, is home to at least four major philosophies of state,[65] with collective action, protection of private rights, and citizen control contending for primacy. As cabinet government has expanded, accountability and its traditional institutional forum, the legislature, have been overshadowed. Since 1982,[66] protection of rights has begun to challenge citizen control.[67] Although the two philosophies are not wholly contradictory, there is an unresolved tension between them. How the tension is resolved will determine whether we see the politician or the judge as the central figure of Canadian public law.

THE NATION-STATE

In his 1839 *Report on the Affairs of British America*, Lord Durham said, "I expected to find a contest between a government and people: instead I found two nations warring in the bosom of a single state...."[68] Indeed, it is possible to distinguish generally between the concept of a state, with sovereign, territorial, egalitarian, and inclusive aspects, and that of a nation, with cultural and often exclusive features.[69]

From this perspective, Canada is not just a state but a nation-state, and can be viewed differently according to whether these two aspects are thought to coincide. Those who see Canada as more than one nation may disagree as to which nation is most fundamental. Some of the possible contenders in the early 1990s were described as follows:

> One view of the country suggests that it is composed of ten equal provinces, with a strong central government, committed to the equality of all its citizens. A second vision sees Canada as the product of 'two founding nations', French and English. More recently, some have argued that Canada is composed of 'three nations': English, French, and Aboriginal. Each of these contradictory visions enjoys a measure of support and legitimacy in the country at present.[70]

These competing visions have both political and legal dimensions. While "state" describes a political reality, "nation" describes a sociological group that may or may not have political recognition. Canadian national group supporters tend to seek greater political status for their own group — either within or outside the Canadian state. Moreover, they tend to seek to achieve and protect this status through constitutional amendments or other changes with constitutional implications. Typically, others respond by proposing constitutional reforms to balance nationalist concerns with other interests. As a result, the struggle has the potential to generate additional responsibilities for the ultimate arbiters of public law — the courts.[71]

THE PUBLIC LAW/PRIVATE LAW DISTINCTION

An Elusive Boundary

Having considered the composition and general goals of the Canadian state, and its relationship to the concept of a nation, we can now return to the law that focuses on the state — public law. We noted earlier that the distinction between public law and private law is more one of degree than kind.[72] When we look specifically at the Canadian context, we can see at least four reasons why this is so.

Imprecision of State Boundaries

Having defined public law in terms of the state, we cannot expect the boundaries of public law to be any clearer than those of the state itself. We saw earlier that the state in Canada is complex, hazy-edged, and shifting. It is hardly surprising, then, that public law has these qualities too.

Varying Involvement of the State

The state's involvement in a social situation may vary considerably from case to case. This, in turn, can affect a decision to classify an issue as part of public or private law. Where the executive branch of government is the protagonist, the matter is generally regarded as one of public law. Where only the legislative or judicial branch is involved, public or private law may be involved, depending on the extent to which the subject matter is concerned solely with individuals. In the case of criminal law, the public element comes not from the accused, who is generally a private individual, but from the fact that the action alleged is considered serious enough to affect the public as a whole, and is usually prosecuted by the institution that represents the public: that is, the state.

Single Judicial Hierarchy

Canada lacks a separate system of courts for public law matters on one hand, and for private law matters on the other. In France, for example, private law matters are handled by a system of private law courts, culminating in a supreme private law court called the Cour de Cassation. For French public law, there is another distinct hierarchy culminating in a supreme public law court called the Conseil d'Etat.[73] Canada has a single judicial hierarchy. It culminates in a single Supreme Court of Canada, which decides both public and private law matters.[74]

Private Law Background

Another factor that works against a rigid separation between public and private law in Canada is the belief that state officers should be ultimately as accountable as the rest of us if they act outside authority conferred on them by the legislature. The general proposition is that "[e]very official, from the Prime Minister down to a constable or a collector of taxes, is under the same responsibility for every act done without legal justification as any other citizen."[75] Although our officers of state operate primarily in the realm of public law, principles of private law may lie in wait for them should they exceed their statutory power.

Need It Be Drawn?

If the distinction between public and private law is so difficult to draw, need one bother to try? Certainly, the distinction is sometimes unnecessary, and can be misleading.[76] On the other hand, some situations do require the distinction — or some variation of it — and in others the distinction may be convenient or even helpful.

Common and Civil Law in Quebec

In Quebec, the public/private law distinction helps determine which of our two main legal systems applies. If the subject matter is one of private law, the civil law system applies. If it is one of public law, the common law system normally applies. For these purposes, courts must now determine not only what is public law, but whether special public law rules are involved. In the classic Quebec case of *Roncarelli v. Duplessis*,[77] a majority of the Supreme Court of Canada treated damages proceedings as private law proceedings. For them, the case centred on an ordinary proceeding against a person acting as a private individual rather than on the preliminary question of whether a public authority had exceeded its power. Accordingly, the proper compensation remedy was through the Quebec *Civil Code* rather than common law torts. The Supreme Court affirmed this general approach in a more recent decision,[78] saying that under the more recent Quebec *Code of Civil Procedure*, the liability of public authorities in Quebec is governed by Quebec civil law, unless there is a particular public law to the contrary.[79] The distinction between public and private law in Quebec has its roots in British common colonial law respecting acquisition of territory and in the *Quebec Act*[80] of 1774, which provided that the French speaking inhabitants should be able to retain their own "property, usages and civil rights".

Exclusively Public Law Remedies

In all provinces, a number of legal remedies are normally available only in public law contexts. These include the prerogative writs of *certiorari*, prohibition, and *mandamus*, or their statutory equivalents, and the prerogative writ of *habeas corpus*.[81] In some respects, these remedies differ considerably from those available at private law. None of them, for example, can offer monetary compensation. Where this kind of relief is desired, it may be necessary to attempt to follow public law proceedings with a private law action for damages or with its Quebec counterpart in the *Civil Code*.

Scope of *Charter*

The *Canadian Charter of Rights and Freedoms* applies "to the Parliament and government of Canada in respect of all matters within the authority of Parliament," and "to the legislature and government of each province in respect of all matters within the authority of each province."[82] The courts have decided that this provision limits the binding effect of the *Charter* to the legislative and executive branches of government, to proceedings initiated for public purposes by courts, and to other actions implementing specific government policy.[83] The result is a new constitutional field restricted, in this special sense, to public law.

Convenience

In some situations, distinguishing public law areas can help us to isolate special features and problems that arise where the state is directly involved, and to devise principles that best reconcile the needs of the state with the needs of others. The state's unique size, power, and responsibilities suggest techniques of legal control different in at least some respects from those for private individuals. Common law tort, contract, and property notions may not be fully applicable — or appropriate — to a government body with a statutory mandate and statutory duties to discharge. In criminal law, there are special needs — such as balancing individual freedoms against public safety — that may call for distinct substantive and procedural laws. Important concepts, from the rules of natural justice to the principles for interpreting the division of legislative powers in the *Constitution Act, 1867*,[84] occupy the public law area, and have no private law counterparts. Distinctions of this kind are by no means sacrosanct, and should be kept no longer than useful, but they supply us with starting points for exploration and analysis: they are distinctions of convenience.

CANADIAN PUBLIC LAW AND THE JUDICIAL ROLE

As suggested above, Canadians have looked increasingly to government to help us meet our needs and fulfil our goals. In the constitutional field, we have asked government to help us resolve tensions between colonial and imperial interests, centralist and regional needs, and majority and minority cultural values. In the area of public administration, we have asked government to maintain a balance between doing its own job efficiently, on one hand, and meeting needs for fairness and accountability on the other. In the field of civil liberties, we have given government a key role in balancing public interests against those of individuals and groups, and in arbitrating clashes between different individuals and groups.

Government — in Canada, the governments of our federal system and municipal authorities — has responded to many of these needs by the use of law, in legislative or common law form. It has also responded institutionally, by vastly expanding its executive branch, and by transferring duties from the legislative branch to the executive and the judiciary.

By enlarging the written portion of our constitution in 1982, government further extended its reliance on law, and transferred wide new responsibilities to the judiciary. At the same time, government continued to submit fundamental constitutional questions to the courts in the form of references.[85]

How actively should the courts discharge their new responsibilities? How actively should courts be involved in the major public law fields? How should the fields themselves be changed? We will not be able to provide definitive answers. What we can do is explore some basic aspects of Canadian public law, examine the courts' existing role, and consider some proposals for the future. This should provide some useful introductory knowledge, and may assist us in the search for answers.

CANADIAN PUBLIC LAW AND THE PUBLIC

The past several decades have been difficult for the Canadian state. There was controversy over the patriation of the constitution. Friction over the Meech Lake and Charlottetown accords was followed by a wrenchingly close referendum on the secession of Quebec. There were fierce economic battles over Free Trade, the G.S.T., and the restraint measures of the 1990s. Both larger and smaller provinces are unsatisfied with federal–provincial financial arrangements. There have been recurring and sometimes violent confrontations with Aboriginal peoples. There have been security threats from both beyond and within, and peace-keeping and peacemaking dilemmas overseas. Canada's great natural resources have been ravaged by mass consumption and by widespread dumping of waste. SUVs and conveniences such as air conditioning have contributed to unprecedented smog and power shortages, and governments seem unable to grasp the inconvenient reality of global warming. Canada's public health care system, long a great source of pride, has been being plagued by long line-ups and massive public costs. Not surprisingly, there has been a feeling that problems such as these are sometimes too much for our elected politicians.

At the same time, though, there is a tendency to sit back and leave the problems of government — and of Canadian public law — to "experts". But apathy is surely a dead end. If we are concerned about the future of the Canadian state and Canadian public law, then we should learn about it, and do what we can to express our views. Canadian public law is not just a spectator sport, confined to our television screens. It affects us all, and we must all try to affect it too.

Notes

1. An aspect of law emphasized by Emile Durkheim, Max Weber, Roscoe Pound, Karl Llewellyn, and many others: see S. Vago, *Law and Society* (Englewood Cliffs, NJ: Prentice-Hall, 1981), ch. 2. In *The Sociology of Law: An Introduction*, 2d ed. (London: Butterworths, 1992) at 46, Roger Cotterrell attempts to incorporate the social aspect by defining state law as "the social rules and related doctrine created, adopted, interpreted and enforced by state agencies as a framework of general regulation within a politically organized society." Note, however, the prominence of the notion of the enforceable rule.

2. Is law a neutral mechanism that simply relays the will of society as a whole? Is it an instrument of repression at the service of ruling groups? Is it an aspect of power relationships that exist throughout society? Has it some other role? See Phil Harris, *An Introduction to Law*, 6th ed. (London: Butterworths, 2002), ch. 1; R.M. Unger, *The Critical Legal Studies Movement* (Cambridge, MA: Harvard University Press, 1986); S. Vago, *ibid.* at 12–14; M. Foucault, ed. by C. Gordon, *Power/Knowledge: Selected Interviews and Other Writings, 1972-1977* (Brighton, Sussex: Harvester Press, 1980); and E.P. Thompson, *Whigs and Hunters: The Origin of the Black Act* (New York: Pantheon Books, 1975), ch. 10.

3. The other branches of government are also closely connected to law. Most law outside the realm of contracts is initiated by the executive branch, and is enacted by or under the legislative branch.

4. *Cf.* Max Weber's description of the modern state as "a compulsory association with a territorial basis" that is regulated by an administrative and legal order and claims "to monopolize the [legitimate] use of force": *The Theory of Social and Economic Organization*, Introduction by T. Parsons (New York: Free Press, 1947) at 156.

5. In this context, we will use the term "society" to include both individuals and groups other than the state itself.

6. And not, primarily, to the state. Basing the distinction on the state leads us into formidable descriptive problems in identifying the "state" (see the discussion below), but may be less normative than starting with the assumption that certain areas (*e.g.*, sexual morality? contractual relations?) are necessarily inherently private.

7. See the note above about "society".

8. See R. David & J.E.C. Brierly, *Major Legal Systems in the World Today: An Introduction to Comparative Study of Law*, 3d ed. (London: Stevens, 1985); J.H. Merryman, *The Civil Law Tradition System: An Introduction to the Legal Systems of Western Europe and Latin America*, 2d ed. (Stanford: Stanford University Press, 1985); and A.T. von Mehren & J.R. Gordley, *The Civil Law System: An Introduction to the Comparative Study of Law*, 2d ed. (Boston: Little, Brown, 1977). See also N.J. Coulson, *A History of Islamic Law* (Edinburgh: University Press, 1964) (a major religious law system) and A.S. Diamond, *Primitive Law Past and Present* (London: Methuen, 1971) (traditional law systems).

9. Subordinate legislation must be authorized by an ordinary statute, whereas ordinary statutes are themselves subordinate to constitutional legislation such as the *Constitution Act, 1982* (itself a schedule to a British statute, the *Canada Act, 1982* (U.K.), 1982, c. 11).

10. A norm is a rule, principle or convention. Some norms are legislative in nature, some derive from common law, and still others are found in principles and conventions.

11. R.S.C. 1985, c. C–46. Other parts of the criminal law are found in the common law, and in the rights guaranteed by the *Canadian Charter of Rights and Freedoms*.

12. *Cf. Fraser v. Public Service Staff Relations Board*, [1985] 2 S.C.R. 455 at 469.

13. See Chapter 8 (and Chapter 3, 5, 6, and 7 on division of legislative powers and cooperative federalism).

14. See Chapter 8.

15. See Chapter 4.

16. On the connections between the modern state and the private sector, see W.T. Stanbury, "Business–Government Relations" in *Canada: Influencing Public Policy*, 2d ed. (Scarborough, Ont.: Nelson Canada, 1993); Alan C. Cairns, "The Past and Future of the Canadian Administrative State" (1990) 40 U.T.L.J. 319; J.K. Galbraith, *The New Industrial State* 3d ed., rev. (Boston: Houghton Mifflin, 1978); R. Presthus, *Elite Accommodation in Canadian Politics* (Cambridge, Eng.: University Press, 1974); R. Miliband, *The State in Capitalist Society: The Analysis of the Western System of Power* (London: Weidenfeld & Nicholson, 1973); and C. Reich, "The New Property" (1964) 73 Yale L.J. 733.

17. See, generally, Stanbury, *ibid.* Using an economic measure, Stanbury estimated that the proportion of government expenditures grew from 4 to 7% of the Canadian G.N.P. in 1867 to 45% in 1983: *ibid.* at 51. Despite significant downsizing in the 1990s, government expenditures accounted for 39.7% of Canada's gross domestic product in 2001: Bruce Little, "Study Unearths Spending Data" *The Globe and Mail* (21 April 2003) at B4. More recently, there have been major additions to government spending on health care.

18. For some other descriptions of the nature and functions of the state, see George W. White, *Nation, State, and Territory: Origins, Evolutions, and Relationships* (Lanham, MD: Rowman & Littlefield Publishers, 2004); T.V. Paul, G. John Ikenberry & John A. Hall, eds., *The Nation-state in Question* (Princeton, N.J.: Oxford: Princeton University Press, 2003); Phil Harris, *An Introduction to Law*, 6th ed. (London: Butterworths, 2002), chs. 2 and 4; Neil MacCormick, *Questioning Sovereignty: Law, State, and Practical Reason* (Oxford, New York: Oxford University Press, 1999); David Held, "Central Perspectives on the Modern State" in David Held et al., *States and Societies* (Oxford: Robertson in association with The Open University, 1983); Leonard Tivey, ed., *The Nation-state: The Formation of Modern Politics* (Oxford: M. Robertson, 1981); and Leo Panitch, *Canadian State: Political Economy and Political Power* (Toronto: University of Toronto Press, 1977).

19. For example, penalizing wrongdoers rather than relying on individual retribution; redistributing wealth rather than relying on individual charity; undertaking projects too large for private resources; and providing organized protection against external aggressors rather than leaving this to individual self-defence.

20. For John Locke, for example, the state provides a means of protecting property, personal security, and other personal rights more effectively than individuals can by themselves: Peter Laslett, ed., *John Locke, ed. Two Treatises of Civil Government* (1690), Rev. ed. (New York: New American Library, 1965) at 395.

21. Plato, *Republic*, Book V. See also G.H. Sabine & T.L. Thorson, eds., *A History of Political Theory*, 4th ed. (Hinsdale, IL: Dryden Press, 1973), ch. 4; R.C. Cross & A.D. Woozley, *Plato's Republic: A Philosophical Commentary* (London: Macmillan, 1964), ch. 5; and Bertrand Russell, *A History of Western Philosophy* (New York: Simon & Schuster, 1961 [1946]), Bk. 1, Pt. 2, ch. XIV.

22. *Leviathan*, 1651, esp. chs. 13, 14, and 17. See also Sabine & Thorson, *supra* note 21, ch. 24; F.S. McNeilly, *The Anatomy of Leviathan* (London: Macmillan, 1968), chs. 7 and 9; and Russell, *supra* note 21, Bk. 3, Pt. 1, ch. VIII.

23. H.V.F. Somerset, ed., *A Notebook of Edmund Burke* (Cambridge: Cambridge University Press, 1957). See also Sabine & Thorson, *supra* note 21 at 557–69.

24. For example, J. K. Galbraith, *The Affluent Society*, 4th ed. (Boston: Houghton Mifflin, 1984); N.H. MacCormick, *Legal Right and Social Democracy: Essays in Legal and Political Philosophy* (Oxford: Clarendon Press, 1982); and C.B. MacPherson, *The Real World of Democracy* (Toronto: Canadian Broadcasting Corp., 1965).

25. John S. Mill, *On Liberty*, 1859 (Everyman's Library, No. 482A), ch. 1: "... the only purpose for which power can be rightfully exercised over any member of a civilized community, against his will, is to prevent harm to others." However, in practice Mill was willing to concede considerable scope for government action: see Sabine & Thorson, *supra* note 21 at 643–54.

26. Friedrich A. von Hayek, *The Road to Serfdom* (Chicago: University of Chicago Press, 1944).

27. *De Legibus*, circa 52 B.C., Books I and II, C.W. Keyes, trans., 1982, where Cicero describes law and justice as natural phenomena, based not on the laws of governments, but on the "right reason" of man and the gods. See also Sabine & Thorson, *supra* note 21, ch. 10, especially at 161–64.

28. *Two Treatises of Civil Government* (1690), intro. by W.S. Carpenter (London: Dewt, 1966). *Cf.* Ronald Dworkin, *Law's Empire* (Cambridge, MA: Belknap Press, 1986); Ronald Dworkin, *Taking Rights Seriously* (Cambridge, MA: Harvard University Press, 1977).

29. *Two Treatises of Civil Government*, *ibid.*, Book II, chs. XVIII and XIX. See also Sabine & Thorson, *supra* note 21, ch. 27 and Russell, *supra* note 21, Bk. 3, Pt. 1, ch. XIV. The American constitution has been heavily influenced by the ideas of Locke. In Canada the enactment of the *Constitution Act, 1982* was a significant move in the Lockeian direction.

30. Baron de Montesquieu, *Spirit of the Laws*, 1648, Book XI, ch. IV. See also Sabine & Thorson, *supra* note 21 at 505–15.

31. *Spirit of the Laws*, *ibid. Cf.* Locke's approach in *Two Treatises of Civil Government*, *supra* note 29, Book II, ch. XII.

32. *Social Contract*, 1762. However, Rousseau's concept of the Social Contract and the general will was notoriously vague: see criticisms in Sabine & Thorson, *supra* note 21, ch. 29; Russell, *supra* note 21 at 669–74.

33. John S. Mill, *Considerations on Representative Government*, 1861, esp. chs. 3, 5, and 7. However, Mill was no supporter of universal suffrage; he was as worried about the tyranny of the majority as any tyranny of the state: C. Brinton, *English Political Thought in the Nineteenth Century* (Cambridge, MA: Harvard University Press, 1962 [1933]) at 97.

34. For example, Sydney and Beatrice Webb, and George Bernard Shaw.

35. For example, Francis R. Scott and Frank S. Underhill.

36. "... the State is the form in which the individuals of a ruling class assert their common interests...": Karl Marx in *German Ideology* (trans.), in T.B. Bottomore & M. Rubl, eds., *Karl Marx, Selected Writings in Sociology and Social Philosophy* (London: Watts, 1961) at 223. However, as most commentators note, Marx said relatively little about the state itself; he saw it as an instrument in a larger economic struggle.

37. K. Marx, *Das Kapital*, 1867. For a well-known post-Marxist approach, see W.L. Adamson, *Hegemony and Revolution: A Study of Antonio Gramsci's Political and Cultural Theory* (Berkeley: University of California Press, 1980) at 162–68, chs. 6 and 7, and Conclusion; and Quintin Hoare & Geoffrey Nowell-Smith, eds. and transl., *Selections from the Prison Notebooks of Antonio Gramsci* (London: Lawrence and Wishart, 1971) at 246–47 and 258–59.

38. This is one aspect of the "rule of law" (Chapter 2, Introduction). For an important exception, see the area explored in Law Reform Commission of Canada, *The Legal Status of the Federal Administration: Working Paper 40*, 1985.

39. The essence of the "corrective justice" of Aristotle: *Nichomachean Ethics*, trans. by H. Rackham, Book V. *Cf.* also the "proportionality" principle of fundamental justice invoked by Wilson J. in *Reference Re Section 94(2) of the Motor Vehicle Act* (1985), 24 D.L.R. (4th) 536 at 572 (S.C.C.).

40. W.W. Willoughby, *The Political Theories of the Ancient World* (Freeport, NY: Books for Libraries Press, 1969 [1903]) at 62–63.

41. As by Aristotle: *ibid.* at 167.

42. Alan C. Hutchinson, "Mice Under a Chair: Democracy, Courts, and the Administrative State" (1990) 40 U.T.L.J. 374.

43. See, respectively, Marx, *supra* note 36; Gramsci, *supra* note 37; and Foucault, *supra* note 2.

44. See, for example, R. Preece, "The Political Wisdom of Sir John Macdonald" (1984) Can. J. Pol. Sci. 459 (arguing that Macdonald's pragmatism was itself a philosophy); P.B. Waite, in M. Hamelin, ed., *The Political Ideas of the Prime Ministers of Canada* (Ottawa, Ont.: Editions de l'Universite d'Ottawa, 1969); and T.W.L. Macdermot, "The Political Ideas of John A. Macdonald" (1933) 14 Can. Historical Rev. 257. In the 19th century, religious and moral questions dominated: A.B. McKillop, *A Disciplined Intelligence: Critical Inquiry and Canadian Thought in the Victorian Era* (Montreal & Kingston: McGill-Queen's University Press, 1979); Mason Wade, *The French Canadians, 1760–1967*, Rev. ed., 2 vols. (Toronto: Macmillan, 1968); and J.A. Irving, "The Development of Philosophy in Central Canada from 1850 to 1900" (1950) 31 Can. Historical

Rev. 254. In the 20th century, economic depression and wars, not specific philosophies, played the major role in expanding government: Law Reform Commission of Canada, *Independent Administrative Agencies*, Working Paper 25, 1980, ch. 1; and Ronald I. Cheffins & R.N. Tucker, *The Constitutional Process in Canada*, 2d ed. (Toronto: McGraw-Hill Ryerson, 1976) at 51–56.

45. Gordon T. Stewart, *The Origins of Canadian Politics: A Comparative Approach* (Vancouver: UBC Press, 1986) argues that by the mid-19th century government played a more important role in Canada than in the United States or in Britain, and that subsequently the main challenge to the federal government came less from the ideologies of limited government than from the rival power of provincial governments.

46. See, for example, T.L. Powrie, *The Growth of Government*, in Tom C. Pocklington, ed., *Liberal Democracy in Canada and the United States* (Toronto: Holt, Rinehart and Winston of Canada, 1985), ch. 2; Economic Council of Canada, *Reforming Regulation*, 198; Law Reform Commission of Canada, *Independent Administrative Agencies*, Working Paper 25, 1980, ch. 1; and Dennis Olsen, *The State Elite* (Toronto: University of Toronto Press, 1980), ch. 11.

47. See, for example, G. Stewart, "The Origins of Canadian Politics and John A. Macdonald" in R. Kenneth Carty & W. Peter Ward, eds., *National Politics and Community in Canada* (Vancouver: UBC Press, 1986), ch. 2.

48. The concept of state is sometimes used to denote the political entity that represents the nation as a whole, but the narrower sense, equating it with "government", is probably more frequent. The term is normally used in this sourcebook in the narrower sense.

49. A "sphere of action in which society, as distinguished from the individual, has, if any, only an indirect interest" (John S. Mill, *Essay on Liberty*, 1859) was protected negatively before 1982, and now positively, in the fundamental freedoms provisions of the *Charter*: see Chapter 10.

50. For example, the ideas of private enterprise and property, and various other interests claimed by individuals or groups as rights and protected by such mechanisms as the Constitution Acts. See A. Abel, "The Dramatis Personae of Administrative Law" (1972) 10 Osgoode Hall L.J. 87.

51. For contrasts in the traditional approach in Quebec and elsewhere, see K. McRae, "The Structure of Canadian History" in L. Hartz, ed., *The Founding of New Societies* (New York: Harcourt, Brace & World, 1964) at 219. During the Meech Lake and Charlottetown constitutional processes, concern to safeguard the individual rights protections in the *Charter* was strongest outside Quebec.

52. For example, Aboriginal rights.

53. Responsible (and representative) government had a two-fold significance: (i) greater independence of British colonial authorities and (ii) greater accountability of elected Canadian legislatures to the Canadian electorate: Chapters 2 and 8.

54. See, generally, R. Kenneth Carty & W. Peter Ward, "The Making of a Canadian Political Citizenship" in Carty & Ward, *supra* note 47.

55. Chapter 3.

56. Chapter 10.

57. *Ibid.*

58. Chapter 10.

59. About 34% of Canada's non-agricultural paid labour force are members of labour unions: B.D. Palmer & T. McCallum, "Working-Class History" in James H. Marsh, ed., *The Canadian Encyclopedia*, Year 2000 ed. (Toronto: McClelland & Stewart, 1999) at 2543. At the political level, the socialist tradition is carried on mainly by the New Democratic party, formerly the Co-operative Commonwealth Federation.

60. See, for example, John Porter, *The Vertical Mosaic* (Toronto: University of Toronto Press, 1965); 1966 *Report of the Royal Commission on Taxation*; Olsen, *supra* note 46; and Linda McQuaig, *Behind Closed Doors* (Markham, Ont.: Viking, 1987). In 1935, the League for Social Reconstruction attacked "[t]he evils of inequality" and "the concentration of property in the hands of a small group of wealthy men": *Social Planning for Canada*, 1935, at xi and 242. Some of the League's proposals have been implemented, but significant economic inequalities remain. In May 1993, a United Nations Committee said that despite Canada's vast wealth, relatively little had been done in recent years to combat problems of homelessness and poverty.

61. Arguably, these are corollaries of the notion that individuals are of equal worth and dignity. See further, Dickson C.J.C. in *R. v. Big M Drug Mart Ltd.* (1985), 18 D.L.R. (4th) 321, 353, 361 (S.C.C.).

62. David W. Elliott, ed., *Introduction to Public Law: Readings on the State, the Administrative Process, and Basic Values*, 6th ed. (Concord, Ont.: Captus Press, 2007), ch. 7.

63. Chapter 10.

64. For example, in 2003, average earnings for full-time working females were 71% that of average male earnings: Statistics Canada, "Highlights" from *Women in Canada: A Gender-based Statistical Report*, 5th ed. (March 2005), catalogue no. 89-503-XPE, online: <http://www.statcan.ca/english/freepub/89-503-XIE/0010589-503-XIE.pdf> at p. 15. By way of comparison, in 1993, average earnings for full-time working females were 72% of average male earnings: M.P. Connelly, "Women in the Labour Force" in *The Canadian Encyclopedia*, *supra* note 59, 2530 at 2531. Aboriginal peoples have an unemployment rate of several times that for all Canadians: J.A. Price, F. Travato & M. Mills, *Native Peoples: Economic Conditions*, in *The Canadian Encyclopedia*, *ibid.* at 1580–81.

65. The number and nature of these philosophies vary with the criteria used to identify them. A common (but sometimes confusing) classification is between conservatism, liberalism, and socialism: see G. Horowitz, "Conservatism, Liberalism, and Socialism in Canada: An Interpretation" (1966) 32 Can. J. of Economics and Political Science 144. See also Murray Knuttila & Wendy Kubik, *State Theories: Classical, Global and Feminist Perspectives*, 3d ed. (Halifax: Fernwood Publishing, 2000) and Patrick Macklem, "Constitutional Ideologies" (1988) 20 Ottawa L. Rev. 117. Regional differences may yield further significant variations: see *supra* note 51.

66. Through the *Constitution Act, 1982*: Chapter 9. There was some protection of private group rights in the *Constitution Act, 1867*, but not on the scale of the *Constitution Act, 1982*. Although the division of legislative and executive powers in the *Constitution Act, 1867* limits the collective power of the state, this does not seem to have been a significant reason for creating the division in the first place: Chapter 9.

67. Both indirectly, as a rival approach to control of collective action, and directly, as means of protecting minority interests against the risks of a "tyranny of the majority".

68. Lord Durham, *British North America Report to the Queen's Most Excellent Majesty* (1839), in Gerald M. Craig, *Lord Durham's Report* (Toronto: McClelland & Stewart, 1963) at 23.

69. See, for example, Hannah Arendt, *The Origins of Totalitarianism* (London: Andre Deutch, 1985 [1951]), discussed in Peter Emberley, "Globalism and Localism: Constitutionalism in a New World Order" in Curtis Cook, ed., *Constitutional Predicament: Canada after the Referendum of 1992* (Montreal & Kingston: McGill-Queen's University Press, 1994) at 204–207. See also Philip Resnick, "'Canada's Three Sociological Nations" (October 1992) *Canadian Forum*. However, as Jürgen Habermas has pointed out, in the modern democratic

nation state, the common bond need not be exclusive: J. Habermas, "Citizenship and National Identity" from *Between Facts and Norms: Contributions to a Discourse Theory of Law and Democracy*, trans. W. Regh (Cambridge, MA: MIT Press, 1998) at 490, extracts reproduced below.

70. Patrick J. Monahan, "The Sounds of Silence" in Kenneth McRoberts & Patrick J. Monahan, eds., *The Charlottetown Accord, the Referendum, and the Future of Canada* (Toronto: University of Toronto Press, 1993) 222 at 329 (endnotes omitted).

71. In "The Fragmentation of Canadian Citizenship" in Alan C. Cairns, *Reconfigurations: Canadian Citizenship and Constitutional Change* (Toronto: McClelland & Stewart, 1995) 157 at 184–85, Alan Cairns said that sociological fragmentation is not an uncommon phenomenon in modern states, and pointed to the American experience. He added, though:

> The crucial Canadian difference is that our most serious fragmentation is structured around competing nationalisms and is also entangled with constitution. Hence our peril and our challenge are much greater.

72. We noted that all areas of law have some links with one or more of the branches of government, and that all law, including public law, necessarily affects relations between individuals.

73. See L.N. Brown & J.S. Bell, *French Administrative Law*, 5th ed. (Oxford: Clarendon Press, 1998).

74. See Chapter 4. (*Cf.* Alexander Pope, "The Rape of the Locke", cii, line 8.) Although the Ontario Divisional Court specializes in administrative law review and appeals, this "Court" is a division of the Ontario Superior Court of Justice, and appeals lie from the Divisional Court to the general appellate court for the province, the Ontario Court of Appeal. No other provincial superior court has its jurisdiction divided in this way, although the Federal Court of Canada deals mainly with administrative law matters.

75. Abbott J., in *Roncarelli v. Duplessis*, [1959] S.C.R. 121 at 184 (S.C.C.), quoting from Albert V. Dicey, *An Introduction to the Study of the Law of the Constitution*, 10th ed. (London: Macmillan, 1959), ch. IV. There are exceptions to this principle: see, for example, *supra* note 38.

76. Most criticisms of the distinction in (1982) 130 U. Pa. L. Rev. 1289–1608 attacked the assumptions (i) that certain spheres of life (e.g., the family and the workplace) are *inherently* private, and (ii) that they must be insulated from controls or safeguards normally applied to the activities of the state. See, however, (1982) 130 U. Pa. L. Rev. 1439–40. In "'Public and Private' in English Administrative Law" (1987) 103 L.Q.R. 34 at 35–37, J. Beatson noted that the designation "public" can result in special privileges as well as special burdens. Still, the distinction may obscure the fact that (notwithstanding Weber's description: *supra* note 4) the state has no monopoly on the abuse of power.

77. [1959] S.C.R. 121. (A majority decision: three judges dissented, and two suggested that liability might be based on either common law or civil law principles.)

78. *Prud'homme v. Prud'homme*, [2002] 4 S.C.R. 663. This effectively reversed the presumption in the earlier *Laurentide* decision, where the Supreme Court said that the liability of public authorities in the provinces was governed generally by the common law, except where there was public law authority to the contrary: *Laurentide v. Ville de Beauport*, [1989] S.C.R. 705.

79. The Court found a special public law rule here, but then held that in the circumstances of this case, this rule required private law/civil law standards! Note that the Court said the general criteria in *Laurentide* are subject to being overridden by otherwise valid statutes.

80. 14 Geo. III, c. 83 (1774).

81. See, for example, D.P. Jones & A.S. de Villars, *Principles of Administrative Law*, 4th ed. (Toronto: Carswell, 2004), Part IV.

82. Section 32: Chapter 9.

83. *RWDSU v. Dolphin Delivery*, [1986] 2 S.C.R. 573 at 598–600; *B.C. Government Employees' Union v. British Columbia*, [1988] 2 S.C.R. 214 at 244; *Eldridge v. British Columbia (A.G.)*, [1997] 3 S.C.R. 624 at paras. 41–43.

84. Chapter 3.

85. See, for example, *Re Resolution to Amend the Constitution of Canada*, [1981] 1 S.C.R. 753; *Re Secession of Quebec*, [1998] 2 S.C.R. 217.

(b) Citizenship and National Identity[†]

Jürgen Habermas

NOTE

Although statehood implies citizenship, citizenship can transcend statehood. In the following extracts, Jürgen Habermas reflects on the nature of the modern democratic constitutional nation-state. Ideally, he says, this kind of state is much more than a top-down, compulsory-membership ethnic community. Instead, it is based on a concept of citizenship that is active, voluntary, and open-ended. Through the medium of law, citizens in this kind of state can deliberate freely and equally on public

† From *Between Facts and Norms: Contributions to a Discourse Theory of Law and Democracy*, trans. W. Rehg (Cambridge, Mass.: MIT Press, 1998) at 490, 494–97, 500, 514–15. [Notes omitted.] Reproduced by permission of the publisher.

Cf. A.C. Cairns, *Reconfigurations: Canadian Citizenship and Constitutional Change*, ed. by D.E. Williams (Toronto: McClelland & Stewart, 1995).

issues, and can participate in the actions that affect them. Their participation is not coerced, says Habermas, and it is not limited by language or birth. Their citizenship is universal: it can pave the way for world citizenship.

EXTRACT

The history of the term "nation" reflects the historical genesis of the nation-state. For the Romans, *Natio* was the goddess of birth and origin. *Natio* refers, like *gens* and *populus* but unlike *civitas*, to peoples and tribes who were not yet organized into political associations; indeed the Romans often used it to refer to "savage", "barbaric", or "pagan" peoples. In this classical usage, then, nations are communities of people of the same descent, who are integrated geographically, in the form of settlements or neighbourhoods, and culturally by their common language, customs, and traditions, but who are not yet politically integrated through the organizational form of the state. This meaning of "nation" persisted through the Middle Ages and worked its way into the vernacular languages in the fifteenth century.... However, in the early-modern period a competing usage arose: the nation is the bearer of sovereignty. The estates represented the "nation" ... against the "king." Since the middle of the eighteenth century, these two meanings of "nation" — community of descent and "people of the state" — have intertwined. With the French Revolution, the "nation" became the source of state sovereignty, for example, in the thought of Emmanuel Sieyès. Each nation is now supposed to be given the right of self-determination. The intentional democratic community ... takes the place of the ethnic complex.

With the French Revolution, then, the meaning of "nation" was transformed from a prepolitical quantity into a constitutive feature of the political identity of the citizens of a democratic polity. At the end of the nineteenth century, the conditional relation between ascribed national identity and acquired democratic citizenship could even be reversed.... The nation of citizens finds its identity not in ethnic and cultural commonalities but in the practice of citizens who actively exercise their rights to participation and communication. At this juncture, the republican strand of citizenship completely parts company with the idea of belonging to a prepolitical community integrative on the basis of descent, shared tradition, and common language. Viewed from this end, the initial infusion of national consciousness with republican conviction only functioned as a catalyst.

... Ascribed nationality gave way to an achieved nationalism, that is, to a conscious product of one's own efforts. This nationalism was able to foster peoples' identification with a rule that demanded a high degree of personal commitment, even to the point of self-sacrifice; in this respect, general conscription was simply the flip side of civil rights....

However, this social-psychological connection does not mean that the two are linked at the conceptual level.... The nation-state sustained a close connection between "demos" and "ethos" only briefly. Citizenship was never conceptually tied to national identity.

The concept of citizenship developed out of Rousseau's concept of self-determination. "Popular sovereignty" was initially understood as a delimitation or reversal of royal sovereignty and was judged to rest on a contract between a people and its government. Kant and Rousseau, by contrast, did not conceive of popular sovereignty as the transfer of ruling authority from above to below or as its distribution between two contracting parties. For them, popular sovereignty signified rather the transformation of authority into *self-legislation*. A historical pact, the civil contract, is replaced here by the social contract, which functions as an abstract model for the way in which an authority legitimated only through the implementation of democratic self-legislation is *constituted*.... According to this idea, "only the united and consenting Will of all — ... by which each decides the same for all and all decide the same for each — can legislate."

This idea does not refer to the substantive generality of a popular will that would owe its unity to a prior homogeneity of descent or form of life. The consensus fought for and achieved in an association of free and equal persons ultimately rests only on the unity of a *procedure* to which all consent. This procedure of democratic opinion- and will-formation assumes a differentiated form in constitutions based on the rule of law. In a pluralistic society, the constitution expresses a formal consensus. The citizens want to regulate their living together according to principles that are in the equal interest of each and thus can meet with the justified assent of all....

. . . .

... In the democratic constitutional state, which understands itself as an association of free and equal persons, state membership depends on the principle of voluntariness....

13

. . . .

[Although constitutional democratic principles need to be grounded in the context of a common liberal and egalitarian political culture..., the] original thesis still stands: democratic citizenship need not be rooted in the national identity of a people....

. . . .

Only a democratic citizenship that does not close itself off in a particularistic fashion can pave the way for a *world citizenship*, which is already taking shape today in worldwide political communications. The Vietnam War, the revolutionary changes in eastern and central Europe, as well as the Gulf War, are the first *world-political* events in the strict sense. Through the electronic mass media, these events were brought instantaneously before a ubiquitous public sphere. In the context of the French Revolution, Kant made reference to the reactions of a participating public. At that time, he identified the phenomenon of a world public sphere, which today is becoming political reality for the first time in a cosmopolitan matrix of communication. Even the superpowers cannot ignore the reality of worldwide protests. The ongoing state of nature between bellicose states that have already forfeited their sovereignty has at least begun to appear obsolescent. Even if we still have a long way to go before fully achieving it, the cosmopolitan condition is no longer merely a mirage. State citizenship and world citizenship form a continuum whose contours, at least, are already becoming visible.

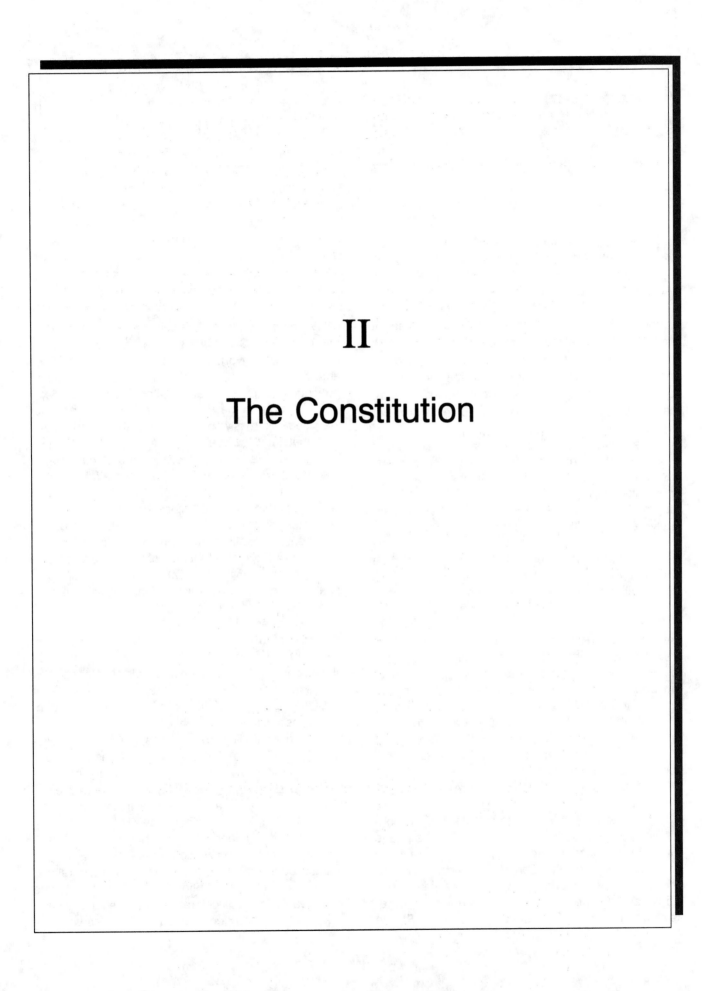

II

The Constitution

2   Elements of the Constitution

(a)   Introduction

A constitution is a collection of ground rules of government and society. These rules describe the basic structures of government, its main powers and their limits, and its general relationship to society. A constitution, then, is a foundation structure that provides support for the more detailed rules of everyday life.

The Canadian constitution has two main parts:[1] a formal part, and an informal part. The formal part is officially styled the "Constitution of Canada". The Constitution of Canada is declared to be the "supreme law of Canada".[2] Its provisions are generally enforceable in courts,[3] and they prevail over other forms of law.[4] Typically, they are also entrenched, in the sense that they cannot be changed by ordinary statutes.[5] The informal part, which will be described later, comprises all those ground rules of Canadian government and society — legal and non-legal — that are not included in the Constitution (with a capital "C") of Canada.

The Constitution of Canada includes the documents that are referred to expressly in s. 52(2) of the Constitution Act, 1982,[6] together with other documents and principles that the courts declare to be part of the Constitution of Canada.[7] The most important of the documents that are listed expressly in s. 52(2) are the Constitution Act, 1982[8] itself, its parent Canada Act 1982,[9] and the Constitution Act, 1867.[10] The Constitution Act, 1867 created Canada and its federal system, and served for over 130 years as the main formal part of our constitution.[11] Since 1982, it has shared centre stage with the Constitution Act, 1982. The Constitution Act, 1982 includes the Canadian Charter of Rights and Freedoms, Aboriginal and equalization provisions, and the formal amending formulas.[12] Other key documents in the schedule include the Statute of Westminster, 1931,[13] which ended British paramountcy over Canadian statutes except in regard to the British North America (Constitution) Acts, and the orders in council and statutes admitting provinces to Confederation after 1867.[14]

Although some constitutional norms are not identified expressly by s. 52(2), the courts have said that they too are components of the Constitution of Canada. So far, there are no documents in this group. However, the courts have attributed formal constitutional status to a number of "unwritten"[15] constitutional principles. These include the principles of federalism, democracy, the rule of law and constitutionalism, and the protection of minority rights;[16] the independence of the judiciary;[17] and parliamentary privilege.[18] Other principles or rules of this kind are the judicial doctrines of full faith and credit[19] and paramountcy,[20] and protection of political speech.[21]

The informal part of the Canadian constitution is a collection of norms that have constitutional significance but lie outside the official "Constitution of Canada" described in s. 52(2) of the Constitution Act, 1982. This group includes legal rules and principles as well as conventions. Among the legal rules and principles are statutes (such as the Parliament of Canada Act),[22] prerogative instruments,[23] and common law rules for interpreting constitutional documents[24] or for defining the royal prerogative power.[25] All are enforceable in law, but most do not prevail over ordinary laws.[26]

There is another group of norms in the informal part of the constitution that lacks even legal status. Constitutional conventions and their related principles are constitutional customs that are enforceable by political rather than legal means.[27] But constitutional conventions often serve very basic purposes. For example, they support key principles such as representative and responsible government that, in turn, support the general principle of democracy.[28] For example, both the convention that the Governor General acts on the advice of the Prime Minister and Cabinet and the convention that the Prime Minister and Cabinet must retain the confidence of the House of Commons support the principle of responsible government.

Constitutional common law rules, principles (both formal and conventional), and conventions can all be described as "unwritten" in the sense that they are not written in constitutional statutes or other constitutional texts. This makes them harder to identify than the texts. On the other hand, principles and conventions are far more flexible than texts. They help to adapt the constitution as a whole to continuous change.

The content of our constitution[29] is as complex as its components, but we can identity five general features that are especially important:

(i) parliamentary democracy;
(ii) federalism;
(iii) the rule of law and the principle of constitutionalism;
(iv) protection of basic and minority rights; and
(v) a complex amending process.

A democracy might be described as a system whose government is accountable to the people at large.[30] Our system of parliamentary democracy[31] tries to secure this accountability through a number of mechanisms, including the principles of representative and responsible government. Representative government is a principle by which the key part of the legislative branch of government is elected by, and is representative of, the general public. Responsible government is a principle by which the effective leadership of the executive branch of government must have the confidence of the elected part of the legislative branch.[32]

A federal system divides power between a government for the entire country and several relatively independent regional governments.[33] In Canada, these correspond to the federal government and the 10 provincial governments. The three territorial governments have provincial-type powers in some areas, but all their powers are subject to federal statutes.

The rule of law[34] is an imprecise goal with several possible meanings, but one common aspect is the idea that all public power should comply with law.[35] Other meanings are that all people, whether private individuals or government officials, should be subject to principles of law, and that there must be an actual positive order of law in place.[36] A subset of the rule of law is the principle of constitutionalism, which requires that all government action must comply with the Constitution.[37] All aspects of the rule of law assume the importance of the principle of the independence of the judiciary. This principle calls for independent courts, and requires that individual judges be impartial.[38]

Protection of basic and minority rights is important to ensure that everyone can benefit from and take part in a democracy.[39] Since 1982, many values regarded as important for individuals have been incorporated in the *Canadian Charter of Rights and Freedoms*, a part of the *Constitution Act, 1982*. For individuals, these include freedom of expression and conscience, the right to vote and participate in elections, and the right to equality before and under the law. The formal part of the constitution also includes a number of group rights, such as those relating to the official languages, denominational schools, and Aboriginal peoples. Rights are also protected by statutes, common law rules, political conventions, and — perhaps most important of all — the tolerance and goodwill of individual citizens.

Finally, the Constitution of Canada has a very complex formal amending process.[40] There are no fewer than four different formal amending procedures in the *Constitution Act, 1982*, with several additional variations. Outside the formal part of the constitution, change may be made by statute, by judicial interpretation, or by the evolution of constitutional conventions. As well, statutes (in some cases), judicial interpretation, and constitutional conventions can modify the formal amending process.

At the beginning of this discussion, we described a constitution as a foundation structure. In countries with strong informal and customary traditions, the constitutional foundation may lie partly below ground level, at a distance from public view. Before 1982, much of the Canadian constitution was like this. It was governed largely by conventions and political agreements. In that year, however, Canadian politicians responded to deep social and political concerns by redesigning the constitution. In doing so, they moved more law into the formal part of the constitution. They made both more defined, more visible, and more important. This development provoked informed debates and raised public consciousness. However, it also raised expectations, dramatized conflicts, and shifted responsibilities away from people who are elected and democratically accountable. More recently, this process of constitutionalization has been accompanied by an additional process, the legalization of the constitution. Constitutional principles outside written texts are now being given legal status as parts of the formal Constitution of Canada.

But these formal legal developments are not the whole story. Informal agreements, institutions, and practices still constitute a vital part of national efforts to respond to concerns, strengthen links, and build for the future.[41] In his oral submission in the *Quebec Secession Reference*, the Attorney General of Saskatchewan said that "[t]he threads of a thousand acts of accommodation are the fabric of a nation."[42] He might have added that many hundreds of these threads are informal.

Who can tell where these currents and countercurrents will lead? Who can predict the shape of the Canadian constitution three decades from now? Who can guarantee that there will be will be a Canada three decades from now? Canadian constitutional law does live with one certainty, though. That is the certainty of ongoing change!

Notes

1. Another distinction can be drawn between legal and non-legal constitutional norms, according to whether they are enforceable by courts. In 1981, for example, the Supreme Court summarized the Canadian constitution in a two-component equation, in which "constitutional conventions plus *constitutional law equal the total [c]onstitution of the country*": *Reference re Resolution to amend the Constitution*, [1981] 1 S.C.R. 753 at 884. As will be seen, not all legal constitutional norms are contained in the formal part of the Canadian constitution, and not all norms in the formal part are in statutes or other written texts. The more recent formal/informal distinction is a product of the constitutional changes of 1982 (Chapter 9, below).
2. *Constitution Act, 1982*, being Schedule B to the *Canada Act 1982* (U.K.), c. 11, s. 52(1). S. 52 is reproduced in part (b) of this chapter.
3. For an exception, see the equalization provision in s. 38 of the *Constitution Act, 1982*. This provision states a commitment to a principle instead of declaring an enforceable right. For another possible exception, see the constitutional duty to negotiate in regard to secession in *Reference re Secession of Quebec*, [1998] 2 S.C.R. 217. The Supreme Court has said that legal enforcement will be limited to the "framework", not the "political aspects", of these negotiations: *ibid.*, paras. 100–102
4. *Constitution Act, 1982*, s. 52(1): "any law that is inconsistent with the provisions of the Constitution is, to the extent of the inconsistency, of no force or effect."
5. For an exception, see s. 44 of the *Constitution Act, 1982*, which permits amendments to certain "internal" federal matters by Act of Parliament.
6. *Constitution Act*, 1982, *supra* note 2. Section 52(2) provides that:

    (2) The Constitution of Canada includes

    (a) the *Canada Act 1982*, including this Act;
    (b) the Acts and orders referred to in the schedule; and
    (c) any amendment to any Act or order referred to in paragraph (a) or (b).

7. Courts claim to be able to do this because s. 51(2) says the Constitution of Canada "includes" the documents to which the section refers. See *New Brunswick Broadcasting Co. v. Nova Scotia (Speaker of the House of Assembly)*, [1993] 1 S.C.R. 319 at 376, 378 (McLachlin J. for four judges; La Forest J. said he was "in general agreement" with McLachlin J.: 367–68); *Reference re Remuneration of Judges of the Provincial Court of Prince Edward Island*, [1997] 3 S.C.R. 3 at para. 92; *Reference re Secession of Quebec*, [1998] 2 S.C.R. 217 at para. 32.
8. *Supra* note 2.
9. (U.K.), 1982, c. 11. Note that the *Canada Act 1982* (and its schedule, the *Constitution Act, 1982*), and the *Constitution Act, 1867* — the central statutes of the Constitution of Canada — are both Acts of the Parliament of the United Kingdom. However, in the *Canada Act 1982*, the British Parliament renounced any authority to enact future laws having legal effect in Canada.
10. (U.K.) 30 & 31 Vict., c. 3. Although s. 52(2) does not refer to the *Constitution Act, 1867 (formerly called the British North America Act, 1867)* by name, it is the most important of "the Acts and orders referred to in the schedule" which are referred to directly in paragraph (b) of s. 52(2), *ibid.*
11. See Chapter 2.
12. See Chapter 9.
13. *Statute of Westminster, 1931* (U.K.), 22 Geo V, c. 4.
14. That is, the *Rupert's Land and North-Western Territory Order* (U.K.), June 23, 1870, transferring Hudson's Bay Company territory to Canada; the *Manitoba Act* (Can.), 333 Vict., c. 3 and (Can.), 32–33 Vict., c. 3, creating that province as part of Canada; the *British Columbia Terms of Union*, 1871 (U.K.), May 16, 1871, admitting that colony into Confederation as a province; the *Constitution Act, 1871* (U.K.), 34–35, Vict., c. 28, empowering Parliament to create new provinces from territories within Canada but outside existing provinces; the *Prince Edward Island Terms of Union* (U.K.), June 26, 1873, admitting that colony into Confederation as a province; the *Adjacent Territories Order* (U.K.), July 31, 1880, adding the northern Arctic islands into Canada; the *Alberta Act* (Can.), 4–5 Edw. VII, c. 3, and the *Saskatchewan Act* (Can.), 4–5 Edw. VII, c. 42, creating those provinces as parts of Canada, and the *Newfoundland Act* (U.K.), 12–13 Geo. VI, c. 22, admitting that colony into Confederation as a province. See also the *Constitution Act, 1930* (U.K.), 20–21 Geo. V, c. 26, confirming the *Natural Resources Transfer Agreements* of that year, which gave the prairie provinces control and ownership over natural resources within their boundaries on terms similar to those of the original provincial members of Confederation.

    Other key documents in the schedule include important amendments to the division of legislative powers. One such amendment was the *Constitution Act, 1940* (U.K.), 3–4 Geo. VI, c. 36, which gave Parliament jurisdiction over unemployment insurance.
15. That is, not derived from constitutional statutes or other legislative texts.
16. *Reference re Secession of Quebec*, [1998] 2 S.C.R. 217 at paras. 55–82.
17. *Reference re Remuneration of Judges of the Provincial Court of Prince Edward Island*, [1997] 3 S.C.R. 3 at paras. 105–109.
18. *New Brunswick Broadcasting Co. v. Nova Scotia (Speaker of the House of Assembly)*, [1993] 1 S.C.R. 319. *Quaere*, though, whether the privileges of provincial assemblies are included: *Reference re Remuneration of Judges of the*

Provincial Court of Prince Edward Island, [1997] 3 S.C.R. 3 at para. 93.

19. *Reference re Remuneration of Judges of the Provincial Court of Prince Edward Island*, [1997] 3 S.C.R. 3 at para. 97. This common law doctrine requires courts in one province to recognize the decisions of courts in other provinces.

20. *Ibid.* at 98. This common law doctrine requires courts to give precedence to federal statutes where they conflict with conflicting provincial legislation.

21. *Ibid.* at paras. 102–103. The Court said that judges have imposed limitations on the power of both provincial legislatures and Parliament to limit freedom of political speech, and have based this obligation on the recognition of parliamentary democracy in the Preamble of the *Constitution Act, 1867.*

22. R.S.C. 1985, c. P-1. Other examples include the pre-Confederation *Quebec Act, 1774*, which restored Quebec civil law in Quebec, but retained English criminal law: see M. Ollivier, *British North America Acts and Selected Statutes, 1867–1962* (Ottawa: Queen's Printer, 1962) at 17; the *Supreme Court Act*, R.S.C. 1985, c. Y-2; the *Federal Court Act*, R.S.C. 1985, c. F-7; the *Canadian Bill of Rights*, R.S.C. 1985, c. III; the *Northwest Territories Act*, R.S.C. 1985, c. N-27; the *Yukon Act*, S.C. 2002, c. 7; and the *Nunavut Act*, S.C. 1993, c. c-28; and statutes implementing Aboriginal land claims agreements. The latter include the *James Bay and Northern Quebec Native Claims Settlement Act*, S.C. 1977, c. 32; the *Western Arctic Inuvialuit Claims Act*, S.C. 1984, c. 24; the *Gwich'in Land Claim Settlement Act*, S.C. 1992, c. 53; the *Nunavut Land Claims Agreement Act*, S.C. 1993, c. 29; and the *Nisga'a Final Agreement Act*, S.C. 2000, c. 7. There is no comprehensive list of informal "constitutional" statutes. In individual cases, it may be unclear as to whether an individual statute is sufficiently important to relate to the ground rules of government and society. Courts have accorded human rights legislation an intermediate status, referring to them as quasi-constitutional: e.g., *Quebec (Commission des droits de la personne et de droits de la jeunesse) v. Montreal (City)*, [2000] S.C.J. No. 24 at para. 27.

23. For example, the *Royal Proclamation, 1763* (7 October 1763), in Chapter 2(c) below. For the royal prerogative power, see *infra* note 25, and Chapter 8.

24. For example, the "pith and substance" approach to classifying a law under the *Constitution Act, 1867.* See, for example, *R. v. Morgentaler*, [1993] 3 S.C.R. 463, in Chapter 6. Note, however, that some common law rules of constitutional interpretation, such as the doctrine of paramountcy, have been declared by the courts to be part of the Constitution of Canada: see *Reference re Remuneration of Judges of the Provincial Court of Prince Edward Island*, [1997] 3 S.C.R. 3 at paras. 97–104.

25. The royal prerogative is a power exercisable by the Crown and the Crown's representatives, independently of a grant of statutory power. This power is subject to common law definition as well as statutory restriction, and cannot be exercised in a legislative manner to impose obligations on individuals: Chapter 8. Key written documents regarding the exercise of prerogative power are the letters patent of 1947. These enable the Governor General to exercise, on the advice of relevant federal ministers, all the powers of the British Sovereign in regard to Canada: J.R. Mallory, *The Structure of Canadian Government*, Rev. ed. (Toronto: Gage, 1984), ch. 2.

26. Exceptions are statutes with provisions subject to the special amending requirements of ss. 38–43 of the *Constitution Act, 1982* (such as the composition provisions of the *Supreme Court Act*); the Aboriginal land claims agreement acts; and human rights statutes such as the *Canadian Bill of Rights*, which can prevail over other laws, unless they are expressly amended by statute (see, for example, *Winnipeg School Div. 1 v. Craton*, [1985] 2 S.C.R. 150 at

para. 4; *Quebec (Commission des droits de la personne et de droits de la jeunesse) v. Montreal (City)*, [2000] S.C.J. No. 24 at para. 27, and decisions referred to there).

27. The leading decision is *Reference re Resolution to amend the Constitution*, [1981] 1 S.C.R. 753, in Chapter 9. See pp. 883–84 of the *Reference*, and discussion of executive authority in Chapter 8.

28. Neither the specific conventions behind representative and responsible government, nor the principles themselves, have legal status. Yet democracy, a more general principle that these conventions and principles support, is now regarded as part of the "supreme law of Canada": *Reference re Secession of Quebec*, [1998] 2 S.C.R. 217 at paras. 32, 54, 61–69. This is a rather paradoxical result.

29. For another overview of key aspects of the Canadian constitution in a comparative work that examines 10 other constitutions as well, see James T. McHugh, *Comparative Constitutional Traditions* (New York: Peter Lang, 2002).

30. See the discussion of democracy in *Reference re Secession of Quebec*, [1998] 2 S.C.R. 217 at paras. 61–69.

31. Discussed in *Reference re Remuneration of Judges of the Provincial Court of Prince Edward Island*, [1997] 3 S.C.R. 3 at paras. 100–103.

32. At the federal level, this is the House of Commons. At the provincial level, it is the legislative assembly.

33. Federalism is discussed in *Reference re Secession of Quebec*, [1998] 2 S.C.R. 217 at paras. 70–78.

34. For key discussions of this concept, see *Roncarelli v. Duplessis*, [1959] S.C.R. 121 at 142; *Reference re Manitoba Language Rights*, [1985] 1 S.C.R. 721 at 749–50; *Reference re Secession of Quebec*, [1998] 2 S.C.R. 217 at paras. 70–78; *British Columbia v. Imperial Tobacco Canada Ltd.*, [2005] 2 S.C.R. 473, 2005 SCC 49 at 57–68; *Charkaoui v. Canada (Citizenship and Immigration)*, 2007 SCC 9, at para. 133–37; and *British Columbia (A.G.) v. Christie*, 2007 SCC 21 at 18–27.

35. "... [A]ll government action must comply with the law, including the Constitution": *Reference re Secession of Quebec, ibid.* at para. 72.

36. *Reference re Secession of Quebec, ibid.* at para. 71. In a more recent formulation, the Supreme Court has said that "**[t]**he first principle is that the 'law is supreme over officials of the government as well as private individuals, and thereby preclusive of the influence of arbitrary power' ... The second principle 'requires the creation and maintenance of an actual order of positive laws which preserves and embodies the more general principle of normative order' ... The third principle requires that 'the relationship between the state and the individual ... be regulated by law' ... ": *Christie, supra* note 34.

37. *Reference re Secession of Quebec, ibid.* at para. 72.

38. See *Reference re Remuneration of Judges of the Provincial Court of Prince Edward Island*, [1997] 3 S.C.R. 3 and *British Columbia v. Imperial Tobacco Canada Ltd.*, [2005] 2 S.C.R. 473.

39. Protection of minority rights is discussed in *Reference re Secession of Quebec*, [1998] 2 S.C.R. 217 at paras. 79–82. The Court refers to "individual and minority rights" as a general underlying constitutional principle at paras. 91 and 151.

40. Chapter 10.

41. These include the agreements on taxation, immigration, labour market training, internal trade, and the Social Union referred to in Chapters 8 and 11; the myriad interprovincial and interterritorial school, cultural, and sports exchanges; and national institutions as diverse as the Canadian Broadcasting Corporation, the Canadian Wildlife Association, the United Way-Centraide Canada, the Trans-Canada Highway, and the Trans-Canada Trail.

42. Quoted by the Court in *Reference re Secession of Quebec*, [1998] 2 S.C.R. 217 at para. 97.

(b)   The Constitution of Canada[†]

NOTE

As we have seen, the Canadian constitution has both a formal and an informal part. The formal part is a collection of legal materials that are included as part of the "Constitution of Canada", pursuant to s. 52(2) of the *Constitution Act, 1982*. Two of these documents are the *Canada Act 1982*, and the *Constitution Act, 1982* itself. The *Canada Act 1982* put an end to any further British role in legislating for Canada, while the *Constitution Act, 1982* defines the Constitution of Canada, includes the *Canadian Charter of Rights and Freedoms*, and details the procedures for making formal amendments.

Notice that s. 52(2) includes documents in "the schedule" as part of the Constitution of Canada. One of the 30 documents in this schedule is the *Constitution Act, 1867* (formerly called the *British North America Act, 1867*), the framework of the Canadian federal system. The *Constitution Act, 1867*, together with the *Canada Act 1982* and the *Constitution Act, 1982* are the central written documents of the *Constitution of Canada*. They will be considered in more detail in later chapters.

Section 52(2) includes "any amendment" to the Acts or orders to which it refers. Since 1982, there have been 10 formal amendments to the Constitution of Canada under the designation "Constitution Act", "Constitution Amendment", or "Constitution Amendment Proclamation".

While s. 52(2) relates to the content of the Constitution of Canada, ss. 52(1) and 52(3) relate to its status. By virtue of s. 52(1), the provisions of the Constitution of Canada are supreme law. Because they are law, they are legally enforceable. As supreme law, they prevail over other laws, such as ordinary federal and provincial statutes, subordinate legislation, common law, and prerogative enactments — to the extent of any inconsistency.

By virtue of s. 52(3), provisions in the Constitution of Canada can be amended only pursuant to the Constitution of Canada. In most cases, this makes them harder to amend than ordinary legislation.

EXTRACT

52.(1) The Constitution of Canada is the supreme law of Canada, and any law that is inconsistent with the provisions of the Constitution is, to the extent of the inconsistency, of no force or effect.

(2) The Constitution of Canada includes
(a) the *Canada Act 1982*, including this Act;
(b) the Acts and orders referred to in the schedule; and
(c) any amendment to any Act or order referred to in paragraph (a) or (b).

(3) Amendments to the Constitution of Canada shall be made only in accordance with the authority contained in the Constitution of Canada.

[†]   The Constitution of Canada is formally defined in section 52(1) of the Constitution Act, 1982, which is Schedule B to the *Canada Act, 1982* (U.K.) 1982 c. 11. The *Canada Act, 1982* and its schedules came into force on April 17, 1982. (Schedule A to the *Canada Act, 1982* is the *Constitution Act, 1982* in the French language.)

(c) The Constitution and Underlying Principles: *Quebec Secession Reference*†

NOTE

In 1995 the government of Quebec lost a referendum on separation from Canada, but the margin was barely more than a single percentage point. A total of 50.58% of those who voted said yes and 49.42% said no. The provincial government talked about holding another referendum. It claimed that all that would be needed to secede would be a simple majority vote, as this would be an expression of the democratic principle.

In the 1998 *Quebec Secession Reference* (considered more generally in Chapter 12), the Supreme Court said that democracy is not just a question of majority will, or of majority will in one region of the country, and that democracy is not the only important constitutional principle in Canada. However, the Court also said that in Canada, democracy and other constitutional principles can impose obligations on a government that wants constitutional change, and on other governments that would be affected by this change.

In the extract below, note how the Court stresses that the Canadian constitution comprises not just the text of the *Constitution Act, 1982* and other constitutional documents, but a variety of basic principles and conventions. Some of these principles, the Court says, have legal status as part of the "Constitution of Canada" identified in s. 52(2) of the *Constitution Act, 1982*. The Court identifies four sets of underlying legal-constitutional principles: federalism (considered in the next chapter), democracy, the rule of law and constitutionalism, and protection of basic and minority rights. What does the Court say about the content and context of the principle of democracy?

For other decisions on the unwritten legal constitutional principles, see *New Brunswick Broadcasting Co. v. Nova Scotia (Speaker of the House of Assembly*, [1993] 1 S.C.R. 319; *Reference re Remuneration of Judges of the Provincial Court (P.E.I.)*, [1997] 3 S.C.R. 3; *Lalonde v. Ontario (Commission de restucturation des services de santé)* (2001), 56 O.R. (3d) 505 (Ont. C.A.); *Babcock v. Canada (A.G.)*, [2002] 3 S.C.R. 3; *British Columbia v. Imperial Tobacco Canada Ltd.*, [2005] 2 S.C.R. 473; and *British Columbia (A.G.) v. Christie*, 2007 SCC 21. What unwritten legal constitutional principles have been identified so far? How do they differ from constitutional texts? What do these decisions — and the *Quebec Secession Reference* — say about how courts will interpret and enforce these principles?

EXTRACT

[THE COURT:]

[32] ... As we confirmed in *Reference re Objection by Quebec to a Resolution to amend the Constitution*, [1982] 2 S.C.R. 793, at p. 806, "The *Constitution Act, 1982* is now in force. Its legality is neither challenged nor assailable."

The "Constitution of Canada" certainly includes the constitutional texts enumerated in s. 52(2) of the *Constitution Act, 1982*. Although these texts have a primary place in determining constitutional rules, they are not exhaustive. The Constitution also "embraces unwritten, as well as written rules", as we recently observed in the *Provincial Judges Reference, supra*, at para. 92. Finally, as was said in the *Patriation Reference, supra*, at p. 874, the Constitution of Canada includes the global system of rules and principles which govern the exercise of constitutional authority in the whole and in every part of the Canadian state. [Editor's note: Because the *Patriation Reference* pre-dated the *Constitution Act, 1982*, the phrase "Constitution of Canada" here must be taken to mean the Canadian constitution in the broad sense, not only the "Constitution of Canada" designated by section 52(2) of the *Constitution Act, 1982*. The latter meaning would contradict the Supreme Court's reasoning below, which suggests that some non-textual rules and principles have entrenched legal status by virtue

---

† *Reference re Secession of Quebec*, [1998] 2 S.C.R. 217 at paras. 32–60. On the Canadian constitution and its components and sources, see also the following (some of which pre-date the *Quebec Secession Reference*): Dyck, ch. 2, "Principles of the Canadian Constitution"; Hogg 2007, ch. 1; MacIvor, ch. 2; Monahan, ch. 1; Forcese, ch. 2; Brooks, ch. 4; Funston, chs. 1 and 2; Reesor, ch. 4; Cheffins, chs. 1 and 2.

of their inclusion in the section 52(2) Constitution of Canada, and some do not.]

These supporting principles and rules, which include constitutional conventions and the workings of Parliament, are a necessary part of our Constitution because problems or situations may arise which are not expressly dealt with by the text of the Constitution. In order to endure over time, a constitution must contain a comprehensive set of rules and principles which are capable of providing an exhaustive legal framework for our system of government. Such principles and rules emerge from an understanding of the constitutional text itself, the historical context, and previous judicial interpretations of constitutional meaning. In our view, there are four fundamental and organizing principles of the Constitution which are relevant to addressing the question before us (although this enumeration is by no means exhaustive): federalism; democracy; constitutionalism and the rule of law; and respect for minorities....

. . . .

[49] What are those underlying principles? Our Constitution is primarily a written one, the product of 131 years of evolution. Behind the written word is an historical lineage stretching back through the ages, which aids in the consideration of the underlying constitutional principles. These principles inform and sustain the constitutional text: they are the vital unstated assumptions upon which the text is based. The following discussion addresses the four foundational constitutional principles that are most germane for resolution of this Reference: federalism, democracy, constitutionalism and the rule of law, and respect for minority rights. These defining principles function in symbiosis. No single principle can be defined in isolation from the others, nor does any one principle trump or exclude the operation of any other.

[50] Our Constitution has an internal architecture, or what the majority of this Court in *OPSEU* v. *Ontario (Attorney General)*, [1987] 2 S.C.R. 2, at p. 57, called a "basic constitutional structure". The individual elements of the Constitution are linked to the others, and must be interpreted by reference to the structure of the Constitution as a whole. As we recently emphasized in the *Provincial Judges Reference*, certain underlying principles infuse our Constitution and breathe life into it. Speaking of the rule of law principle in the *Manitoba Language Rights Reference*, *supra*, at p. 750, we held that "the princi-

ple is clearly implicit in the very nature of a Constitution". The same may be said of the other three constitutional principles we underscore today.

[51] Although these underlying principles are not explicitly made part of the Constitution by any written provision, other than in some respects by the oblique reference in the preamble to the *Constitution Act, 1867*, it would be impossible to conceive of our constitutional structure without them. The principles dictate major elements of the architecture of the Constitution itself and are as such its lifeblood.

[52] The principles assist in the interpretation of the text and the delineation of spheres of jurisdiction, the scope of rights and obligations, and the role of our political institutions. Equally important, observance of and respect for these principles is essential to the ongoing process of constitutional development and evolution of our Constitution as a "living tree", to invoke the famous description in *Edwards* v. *Attorney-General for Canada*, [1930] A.C. 124 (P.C.), at p. 136. As this Court indicated in *New Brunswick Broadcasting Co.* v. *Nova Scotia (Speaker of the House of Assembly)*, [1993] 1 S.C.R. 319, Canadians have long recognized the existence and importance of unwritten constitutional principles in our system of government.

[53] Given the existence of these underlying constitutional principles, what use may the Court make of them? In the *Provincial Judges Reference*, *supra*, at paras. 93 and 104, we cautioned that the recognition of these constitutional principles (the majority opinion referred to them as "organizing principles" and described one of them, judicial independence, as an "unwritten norm") could not be taken as an invitation to dispense with the written text of the Constitution. On the contrary, we confirmed that there are compelling reasons to insist upon the primacy of our written constitution. A written constitution promotes legal certainty and predictability, and it provides a foundation and a touchstone for the exercise of constitutional judicial review. However, we also observed in the *Provincial Judges Reference* that the effect of the preamble to the *Constitution Act, 1867* was to incorporate certain constitutional principles by reference, a point made earlier in *Fraser* v. *Public Service Staff Relations Board*, [1985] 2 S.C.R. 455, at pp. 462–63. In the *Provincial Judges Reference*, at para. 104, we determined that the preamble "invites the courts to turn those principles into the premises of a constitutional argument that culminates in the filling of gaps in the express terms of the constitutional text".

[54] Underlying constitutional principles may in certain circumstances give rise to substantive legal obligations (have "full legal force", as we described it in the *Patriation Reference, supra*, at p. 845), which constitute substantive limitations upon government action. These principles may give rise to very abstract and general obligations, or they may be more specific and precise in nature. The principles are not merely descriptive, but are also invested with a powerful normative force, and are binding upon both courts and governments. "In other words", as this Court confirmed in the *Manitoba Language Rights Reference, supra*, at p. 752, "in the process of Constitutional adjudication, the Court may have regard to unwritten postulates which form the very foundation of the Constitution of Canada". It is to a discussion of those underlying constitutional principles that we now turn.

Federalism

[For the Court's discussion of federalism, see Chapter 3].

. . . .

Democracy

[61] Democracy is a fundamental value in our constitutional law and political culture. While it has both an institutional and an individual aspect, the democratic principle was also argued before us in the sense of the supremacy of the sovereign will of a people, in this case potentially to be expressed by Quebecers in support of unilateral secession. It is useful to explore in a summary way these different aspects of the democratic principle.

[62] The principle of democracy has always informed the design of our constitutional structure, and continues to act as an essential interpretive consideration to this day. A majority of this Court in *OPSEU* v. *Ontario, supra*, at p. 57, confirmed that "the basic structure of our Constitution, as established by the *Constitution Act, 1867*, contemplates the existence of certain political institutions, including freely elected legislative bodies at the federal and provincial levels".... [T]he democracy principle can best be understood as a sort of baseline against which the framers of our Constitution, and subsequently, our elected representatives under it, have always operated. It is perhaps for this reason that the principle was not explicitly identified in the text of the *Constitution Act, 1867* itself. To have done so might have appeared redundant, even silly, to the framers. As

explained in the *Provincial Judges Reference, supra*, at para. 100, it is evident that our Constitution contemplates that Canada shall be a constitutional democracy. Yet this merely demonstrates the importance of underlying constitutional principles that are nowhere explicitly described in our constitutional texts. The representative and democratic nature of our political institutions was simply assumed.

[63] Democracy is commonly understood as being a political system of majority rule. It is essential to be clear what this means. The evolution of our democratic tradition can be traced back to the *Magna Carta* (1215) and before, through the long struggle for Parliamentary supremacy which culminated in the English *Bill of Rights of 1689*, the emergence of representative political institutions in the colonial era, the development of responsible government in the 19th century, and eventually, the achievement of Confederation itself in 1867. "[T]he Canadian tradition", the majority of this Court held in *Reference re Provincial Electoral Boundaries (Sask.)*, [1991] 2 S.C.R. 158, at p. 186, is "one of evolutionary democracy moving in uneven steps toward the goal of universal suffrage and more effective representation".

Since Confederation, efforts to extend the franchise to those unjustly excluded from participation in our political system — such as women, minorities, and aboriginal peoples — have continued, with some success, to the present day.

[64] Democracy is not simply concerned with the process of government. On the contrary, as suggested in *Switzman* v. *Elbling, supra*, at p. 306, democracy is fundamentally connected to substantive goals, most importantly, the promotion of self-government. Democracy accommodates cultural and group identities: *Reference re Provincial Electoral Boundaries*, at p. 188. Put another way, a sovereign people exercises its right to self-government through the democratic process....

[65] In institutional terms, democracy means that each of the provincial legislatures and the federal Parliament is elected by popular franchise. These legislatures, we have said, are "at the core of the system of representative government": *New Brunswick Broadcasting, supra*, at p. 387. In individual terms, the right to vote in elections to the House of Commons and the provincial legislatures, and to be candidates in those elections, is guaranteed to "Every citizen of Canada" by virtue of s. 3 of the *Charter*. Historically, this Court has interpreted democracy to mean the process of representative and responsible government and the right of citizens to partici-

pate in the political process as voters (*Reference re Provincial Electoral Boundaries, supra*) and as candidates (*Harvey* v. *New Brunswick (Attorney General)*, [1996] 2 S.C.R. 876). In addition, the effect of s. 4 of the *Charter* is to oblige the House of Commons and the provincial legislatures to hold regular elections and to permit citizens to elect representatives to their political institutions. The democratic principle is affirmed with particular clarity in that s. 4 is not subject to the notwithstanding power contained in s. 33.

[66] It is, of course, true that democracy expresses the sovereign will of the people. Yet this expression, too, must be taken in the context of the other institutional values we have identified as pertinent to this Reference. The relationship between democracy and federalism means, for example, that in Canada there may be different and equally legitimate majorities in different provinces and territories and at the federal level. No one majority is more or less "legitimate" than the others as an expression of democratic opinion, although, of course, the consequences will vary with the subject matter. A federal system of government enables different provinces to pursue policies responsive to the particular concerns and interests of people in that province. At the same time, Canada as a whole is also a democratic community in which citizens construct and achieve goals on a national scale through a federal government acting within the limits of its jurisdiction. The function of federalism is to enable citizens to participate concurrently in different collectivities and to pursue goals at both a provincial and a federal level.

[67] The consent of the governed is a value that is basic to our understanding of a free and democratic society. Yet democracy in any real sense of the word cannot exist without the rule of law. It is the law that creates the framework within which the "sovereign will" is to be ascertained and implemented. To be accorded legitimacy, democratic institutions must rest, ultimately, on a legal foundation. That is, they must allow for the participation of, and accountability to, the people, through public institutions created under the Constitution. Equally, however, a system of government cannot survive through adherence to the law alone. A political system must also possess legitimacy, and in our political culture, that requires an interaction between the rule of law and the democratic principle. The system must be capable of reflecting the aspirations of the people. But there is more. Our law's claim to legitimacy also rests on an appeal to moral values, many of which are imbedded in our constitutional structure. It would be a grave mistake to equate legitimacy with the "sovereign will" or majority rule alone, to the exclusion of other constitutional values.

[68] Finally, we highlight that a functioning democracy requires a continuous process of discussion. The Constitution mandates government by democratic legislatures, and an executive accountable to them, "resting ultimately on public opinion reached by discussion and the interplay of ideas" (*Saumur* v. *City of Quebec, supra*, at p. 330). At both the federal and provincial level, by its very nature, the need to build majorities necessitates compromise, negotiation, and deliberation. No one has a monopoly on truth, and our system is predicated on the faith that in the marketplace of ideas, the best solutions to public problems will rise to the top. Inevitably, there will be dissenting voices. A democratic system of government is committed to considering those dissenting voices, and seeking to acknowledge and address those voices in the laws by which all in the community must live.

[69] The *Constitution Act, 1982* gives expression to this principle, by conferring a right to initiate constitutional change on each participant in Confederation. In our view, the existence of this right imposes a corresponding duty on the participants in Confederation to engage in constitutional discussions in order to acknowledge and address democratic expressions of a desire for change in other provinces. This duty is inherent in the democratic principle which is a fundamental predicate of our system of governance.

Constitutionalism and the Rule of Law

[70] The principles of constitutionalism and the rule of law lie at the root of our system of government. The rule of law, as observed in *Roncarelli* v. *Duplessis*, [1959] S.C.R. 121, at p. 142, is "a fundamental postulate of our constitutional structure". As we noted in the *Patriation Reference, supra*, at pp. 805–6, "[t]he 'rule of law' is a highly textured expression, importing many things which are beyond the need of these reasons to explore but conveying, for example, a sense of orderliness, of subjection to known legal rules and of executive accountability to legal authority". At its most basic level, the rule of law vouchsafes to the citizens and residents of the country a stable, predictable and ordered society in which to conduct their affairs. It provides a shield for individuals from arbitrary state action.

[71] In the *Manitoba Language Rights Reference, supra*, at pp. 747–52, this Court outlined the ele-

ments of the rule of law. We emphasized, first, that the rule of law provides that the law is supreme over the acts of both government and private persons. There is, in short, one law for all. Second, we explained, at p. 749, that "the rule of law requires the creation and maintenance of an actual order of positive laws which preserves and embodies the more general principle of normative order". It was this second aspect of the rule of law that was primarily at issue in the Manitoba *Language Rights Reference* itself. A third aspect of the rule of law is, as recently confirmed in the *Provincial Judges Reference*, *supra*, at para. 10, that "the exercise of all public power must find its ultimate source in a legal rule". Put another way, the relationship between the state and the individual must be regulated by law. Taken together, these three considerations make up a principle of profound constitutional and political significance.

[72] The constitutionalism principle bears considerable similarity to the rule of law, although they are not identical. The essence of constitutionalism in Canada is embodied in s. 52(1) of the *Constitution Act, 1982*, which provides that "[t]he Constitution of Canada is the supreme law of Canada, and any law that is inconsistent with the provisions of the Constitution is, to the extent of the inconsistency, of no force or effect." Simply put, the constitutionalism principle requires that all government action comply with the Constitution. The rule of law principle requires that all government action must comply with the law, including the Constitution. This Court has noted on several occasions that with the adoption of the *Charter*, the Canadian system of government was transformed to a significant extent from a system of Parliamentary supremacy to one of constitutional supremacy. The Constitution binds all governments, both federal and provincial, including the executive branch (*Operation Dismantle Inc.* v. *The Queen*, [1985] 1 S.C.R. 441, at p. 455). They may not transgress its provisions: indeed, their sole claim to exercise lawful authority rests in the powers allocated to them under the Constitution, and can come from no other source.

[73] An understanding of the scope and importance of the principles of the rule of law and constitutionalism is aided by acknowledging explicitly why a constitution is entrenched beyond the reach of simple majority rule. There are three overlapping reasons.

[74] First, a constitution may provide an added safeguard for fundamental human rights and individual freedoms which might otherwise be susceptible to government interference. Although democratic government is generally solicitous of those rights, there are occasions when the majority will be tempted to ignore fundamental rights in order to accomplish collective goals more easily or effectively. Constitutional entrenchment ensures that those rights will be given due regard and protection. Second, a constitution may seek to ensure that vulnerable minority groups are endowed with the institutions and rights necessary to maintain and promote their identities against the assimilative pressures of the majority. And third, a constitution may provide for a division of political power that allocates political power amongst different levels of government. That purpose would be defeated if one of those democratically elected levels of government could usurp the powers of the other simply by exercising its legislative power to allocate additional political power to itself unilaterally.

[75] The argument that the Constitution may be legitimately circumvented by resort to a majority vote in a province-wide referendum is superficially persuasive.... [H]owever, it misunderstands the meaning of popular sovereignty and the essence of a constitutional democracy.

[76] Canadians have never accepted that ours is a system of simple majority rule. Our principle of democracy, taken in conjunction with the other constitutional principles discussed here, is richer. Constitutional government is necessarily predicated on the idea that the political representatives of the people of a province have the capacity and the power to commit the province to be bound into the future by the constitutional rules being adopted. These rules are "binding" not in the sense of frustrating the will of a majority of a province, but as defining the majority which must be consulted in order to alter the fundamental balances of political power (including the spheres of autonomy guaranteed by the principle of federalism), individual rights, and minority rights in our society. Of course, those constitutional rules are themselves amenable to amendment, but only through a process of negotiation which ensures that there is an opportunity for the constitutionally defined rights of all the parties to be respected and reconciled.

[77] In this way, our belief in democracy may be harmonized with our belief in constitutionalism. Constitutional amendment often requires some form of substantial consensus precisely because the content of the underlying principles of our Constitution demand it. By requiring broad support in the form of an "enhanced majority" to achieve constitutional change,

the Constitution ensures that minority interests must be addressed before proposed changes which would affect them may be enacted.

[78] It might be objected, then, that constitutionalism is therefore incompatible with democratic government. This would be an erroneous view. Constitutionalism facilitates — indeed, makes possible — a democratic political system by creating an orderly framework within which people may make political decisions. Viewed correctly, constitutionalism and the rule of law are not in conflict with democracy; rather, they are essential to it. Without that relationship, the political will upon which democratic decisions are taken would itself be undermined.

Protection of Minorities

[79] The fourth underlying constitutional principle we address here concerns the protection of minorities. There are a number of specific constitutional provisions protecting minority language, religion and education rights. Some of those provisions are, as we have recognized on a number of occasions, the product of historical compromises. As this Court observed in *Reference re Bill 30, An Act to amend the Education Act (Ont.)*, [1987] 1 S.C.R. 1148, at p. 1173, and in *Reference re Education Act (Que.)*, [1993] 2 S.C.R. 511, at pp. 529–30, the protection of minority religious education rights was a central consideration in the negotiations leading to Confederation. In the absence of such protection, it was felt that the minorities in what was then Canada East and Canada West would be submerged and assimilated. See also *Greater Montreal Protestant School Board* v. *Quebec (Attorney General)*, [1989] 1 S.C.R. 377, at pp. 401–2, and *Adler* v. *Ontario*, [1996] 3 S.C.R. 609. Similar concerns animated the provisions protecting minority language rights, as noted in *Société des Acadiens du Nouveau-Brunswick Inc.* v. *Association of Parents for Fairness in Education*, [1986] 1 S.C.R. 549, at p. 564.

[80] However, we highlight that even though those provisions were the product of negotiation and political compromise, that does not render them unprincipled. Rather, such a concern reflects a broader principle related to the protection of minority rights. Undoubtedly, the three other constitutional principles

inform the scope and operation of the specific provisions that protect the rights of minorities. We emphasize that the protection of minority rights is itself an independent principle underlying our constitutional order. The principle is clearly reflected in the *Charter*'s provisions for the protection of minority rights. See, e.g., *Reference re Public Schools Act (Man.)*, s. 79(3), (4) and (7), [1993] 1 S.C.R. 839, and *Mahe* v. *Alberta*, [1990] 1 S.C.R. 342.

[81] The concern of our courts and governments to protect minorities has been prominent in recent years, particularly following the enactment of the *Charter*. Undoubtedly, one of the key considerations motivating the enactment of the *Charter*, and the process of constitutional judicial review that it entails, is the protection of minorities. However, it should not be forgotten that the protection of minority rights had a long history before the enactment of the *Charter*. Indeed, the protection of minority rights was clearly an essential consideration in the design of our constitutional structure even at the time of Confederation: *Senate Reference*, *supra*, at p. 71. Although Canada's record of upholding the rights of minorities is not a spotless one, that goal is one towards which Canadians have been striving since Confederation, and the process has not been without successes. The principle of protecting minority rights continues to exercise influence in the operation and interpretation of our Constitution.

[82] Consistent with this long tradition of respect for minorities, which is at least as old as Canada itself, the framers of the *Constitution Act, 1982* included in s. 35 explicit protection for existing aboriginal and treaty rights, and in s. 25, a non-derogation clause in favour of the rights of aboriginal peoples. The "promise" of s. 35, as it was termed in *R.* v. *Sparrow*, [1990] 1 S.C.R. 1075, at p. 1083, recognized not only the ancient occupation of land by aboriginal peoples, but their contribution to the building of Canada, and the special commitments made to them by successive governments. The protection of these rights, so recently and arduously achieved, whether looked at in their own right or as part of the larger concern with minorities, reflects an important underlying constitutional value.

(d)   Unwritten Constitutional Principles: What is Going On?†

Beverley McLachlin, C.J.C., P.C.

NOTE

As we saw in the *Quebec Secession Reference*, the Supreme Court has said that the Constitution of Canada described by s. 52(2) of the *Constitution Act, 1982* is not limited to the legal documents expressly referred to there, but also includes a number of unwritten constitutional principles. As we have seen, in that reference, the Court identified democracy, federalism, the rule of law and constitutionalism, and protection of minority and basic rights as four sets of "underlying" unwritten constitutional principles. It is worth remembering that because of s. 52(1), these are not simply constitutional principles, but legal constitutional principles that are part of the supreme law of Canada. This suggests that when the principles conflict with government action, including statutes, they may be able to prevail. The idea that statutes might be overturned on the basis of concepts as potentially broad as federalism, democracy, and the rule of law raises basic questions about the nature of law and the proper role of the judiciary. Should our highest law be framed by elected politicians, or by unelected but independent judges? Or both? What role should be played by unwritten legal constitutional principles?

In the following speech, the Chief Justice of the Supreme Court delivers a powerful and eloquent defence of these principles. Do questions about life and human dignity relate more to reason or to morality? If they relate to morality, whose morality should prevail? The morality of elected politicians? Or the morality of judges? Do you agree with the Chief Justice's proposition that "the [real] debate is not about whether judges should ever use unwritten constitutional norms to invalidate [bad laws or state action], but rather about what norms may justify [doing this]." What happens if the bad law is an unwritten constitutional norm?

EXTRACT

... Whatever the cause, it is certainly clear that the post-Second World War period can properly be called the "age of rights." Clearly something is going on here; something that cannot be dismissed with a wave of the judicial hand. Tonight I would like to explore that question. Hence the title of my address: "Unwritten Constitutional Principles: What is Going On?"

I will suggest that actually quite a lot is going on, and that it is important. What is going on is the idea that there exist fundamental norms of justice so basic that they form part of the legal structure of governance and must be upheld by the courts, whether or not they find expression in constitutional texts. And the idea is important, going to the core of just governance and how we define the respective roles of Parliament, the executive and the judiciary.

. . . .

... First, unwritten constitutional principles refer to unwritten norms that are essential to a nation's history, identity, values and legal system. Second, constitutions are best understood as providing the normative framework for governance. Seen in this functional sense, there is thus no reason to believe that they cannot embrace both written and unwritten norms. Third — and this is important because of the tone that this debate often exhibits — the idea of unwritten constitutional principles is not new and should not be seen as a rejection of the constitutional heritage our two countries share.

... The contemporary concept of unwritten constitutional principles can be seen as a modern reincarnation of the ancient doctrines of natural law. Like those conceptions of justice, the identification of these principles seems to presuppose the existence of some kind of natural order. Unlike them, however, it does not fasten on theology as the source of the unwritten principles that transcend the exercise of state power. It is derived from the history, values

† Excerpt from 2005 Lord Cooke Lecture in Wellington, New Zealand, December 1, 2005. [Notes omitted.] Source: <www.scc-csc.gc.ca/aboutcourt/judges/speeches/UnwrittenPrinciples_e.asp>. Reproduced with the permission of the Supreme Court of Canada, 2007.

and culture of the nation, viewed in its constitutional context.

. . . .

This "rich intellectual tradition" of natural law seeks to give the law minimum moral content. It rests on the proposition that there is a distinction between rules and the law. Rules and rule systems can be good, but they can also be evil. Something more than the very existence of rules, it is argued, is required for them to demand respect: in short, to transform rules into law. The distinction between rule by law, which is the state of affairs in certain developing countries, and rule of law, which developed democracies espouse, succinctly captures the distinction between a mere rules system and a proper legal system that is founded on certain minimum values. The debate about unwritten constitutional principles can thus be seen as a debate about the nature of the law itself and what about it demands our allegiance.

Modern democratic theory, as espoused by most developed western democracies, combines two inherently contradictory doctrines. The first is what is often identified as the Diceyan doctrine that it is for Parliament and Parliament alone to establish the law, and, by implication, the fundamental norms upon which it rests. The second is the belief, widely accepted in developed modern democracies since World War II, that legal systems must adhere to certain basic norms. At a minimum they must allow citizens to vote for those who rule them, and they must not kill any (or many, depending on the state) of their citizens. This much we insist on since the Holocaust. Beyond this minimum, there is a variance, although still a solid core of agreement. States, most hold, should not torture their citizens. States should not discriminate on the basis of gender, race or religion. Finally, at the developing fringes of the new natural law, which goes by the name human rights, are other assertions. Not only should states not directly kill their citizens, they should avoid killing them indirectly by famine, medical neglect, and degradation of the environment.

Although cast in the language of religion, early natural law theories saw the manifestation of the divine in something that became the foundation of the Western world's conception of itself: human rationality. For Thomas Aquinas, it was human reason that allowed individuals to access, in some form, a deeper understanding of justice. Natural law was, he wrote, "something appointed by reason." And yet the limits of that reason made written law

incomplete in two important ways. On the one hand, lawmakers may abuse their power by deviating from reason and enacting unjust laws. On the other, because lawmakers can never imagine all possible circumstances under which their laws apply, just laws will become unjust in certain circumstances.

Today's fundamental norms are cast more clearly and exclusively in terms of reason [and] take at their heart the notion, in some form, of basic human dignity. There is no doubt that the norms I mentioned earlier — government by consent, the protection of life and personal security, and freedom from discrimination — can all be advanced by moral argument. It is worth noting, however, that they can also be supported by a democratic argument grounded in conceptions of the state and fundamental human dignity that we have developed since John Stuart Mill.

If the state, as we believe, exists as an expression of its citizens, then it follows that its legitimacy and power must be based on the citizens' consent. Hence, citizens must be given the right to vote their governments into and out of office. Similarly, as Canada's Secession Reference illustrates, transitions from one form of citizenship to another must be premised on democratic norms. This is so whether the right is written down or not; it flows from our conception of the democratic state. Similarly, if one agrees that the raison d'être of the modern state is to promote the interests of its citizens, it follows that states should not be allowed to exterminate entire sectors of the society. And if we accept equality based in the fundamental dignity of every human being, then it follows that states should not be able to single out innocent groups or individuals for torture or death. These precepts can be seen as the expression of unwritten constitutional principles based on the structure of democracy itself.

Thus the legitimacy of the modern democratic state arguably depends on its adhesion to fundamental norms that transcend the law and executive action. This applies to all of the branches of state governance — Parliament, the executive and the judiciary. For example, the Commonwealth Principles on the Accountability of and the Relationship Between the Three Branches of Government, which were based on the Latimer House Guidelines of 1998 and endorsed by heads of government in 2003, state in Article 1:

Each Commonwealth country's Parliaments, Executives and Judiciaries are the guarantors in their respective spheres of the rule of law, the promotion and protection of fundamental human rights and the entrenchment of good governance based on the highest standards of honesty, probity and accountability.

Rule of law. Human rights. Good governance. Principles that all branches of government, including the judiciary, must seek to uphold. Principles that may be written down, in some measure in some countries. But principles that the Commonwealth countries have asserted should prevail everywhere....

At this point, you will not be surprised to hear me declare my position. As a modern natural law proponent, I believe that the world was right, in the wake of the horrors of Nazi Germany and the Holocaust, to declare that there are certain fundamental norms that no nation should transgress. I believe that it was right to prosecute German judges in the Nuremberg Trials for applying laws that sent innocent people to concentration camps and probable deaths. I believe that the drafting and adoption of the *Universal Declaration of Human Rights* in 1948 was a giant step forward in legal and societal thinking. And I believe that judges have the duty to insist that the legislative and executive branches of government conform to certain established and fundamental norms, even in times of trouble....

The real debate, it seems to me, is not about whether judges should ever be able to rely on basic norms to trump bad laws or state action. At least in some circumstances they must be able to do this. If a state were to pass a genocidal law, for example, I think it would clearly be the duty of the judges to deny the law's validity on the ground that it offended the basic norm that states must not exterminate their people. It we agree on this — and I suspect most of us would — then the debate is not about whether judges should ever use unwritten constitutional norms to invalidate laws, but rather about what norms may justify such action.

The argument I have been advancing may dispose of the suggestion that, as a matter of principle, it is inherently wrong for judges to rely on unwritten constitutional norms, if constitutional is understood here in the sense of an overriding principle that can invalidate laws and executive acts. However, it does not dispose of the contradiction alluded to earlier between the theory that sees Parliament as the source of all law, and the idea that the law may include principles that Parliament has not made.

. . . .

The answer to the conundrum between justice as an expression of Parliamentary will and justice as an expression of fundamental principles, sometimes unarticulated, lies in the answer to three more particular problems that arise from the concept of underlying unwritten constitutional norms. The first is the problem of how unwritten norms can be squared with the precept that law should be set out in advance of its application. The second is the problem of how to identify these fundamental unwritten principles that are capable of trumping laws and executive action. The third is the problem of judicial legitimacy.

. . . .

[The Chief Justice said that law need not be set out in advance of its application. She cited the common law as an example of the way law evolves in the course of being applied. The basic requirement, she said, is that the law should provide a general idea of its consequences, and that these consequences should be justifiable in the light of existing law.]

. . . .

This brings us to the second problem: identifying those unwritten constitutional principles that can prevail over laws and executive action. At least three sources of unwritten constitutional principles can be identified: customary usage; inferences from written constitutional principles; and the norms set out or implied in international legal instruments to which the state has adhered.

. . . .

... The question of judicial legitimacy returns us to the conundrum I alluded to at the outset. To be legitimate, judges must conform to fundamental moral norms of a constitutional nature. But when they do, they risk going beyond what would appear to be their judicial functions. How is the conundrum to be resolved? The answer, I would suggest, is that the conundrum is a false one; that judges must be able to do justice and at the same time stay within the proper confines of their role.

The role of judges in a democracy is to interpret and apply the law. The law involves rules of different orders. The highest is the order of fundamental constitutional principles. These are the rules that guide all other law-making and the exercise of executive power by the state. More and more in our democratic states, we try to set these out in writing. But when we do not, or when, as is inevitable, the written text is unclear or incomplete, recourse must

29

be had to unwritten sources. The task of the judge, confronted with conflict between a constitutional principle of the highest order on the one hand, and an ordinary law or executive act on the other, is to interpret and apply the law as a whole — including relevant unwritten constitutional principles.

This presupposes that the constitutional principle is established having regard to the three sources just discussed — usage and custom; values affirmed by relevant textual constitutional sources; and principles of international law endorsed by the nation. Determining whether these sources disclose such principles is quintessential judicial work. It must be done with care and objectivity. It is not making the law, but interpreting, reconciling and applying the law, thus fulfilling the judge's role as guarantor of the Constitution.

How does the judge discharge this duty? First, it seems to me, the judge must seek to interpret a suspect law in a way that reconciles it with the constitutional norm, written or unwritten. Usually, this will resolve the problem. But in rare cases, it may not. If an ordinary law is clearly in conflict with a fundamental constitutional norm, the judge may have no option but to refuse to apply it.

. . . .

Judges must resist [the normalization that took place in Nazi Germany] — this making "law" out of what cannot be just, and hence, in a profound sense, cannot be legal. To do otherwise is to allow injustice to hide itself under the cloak of false legality.

Critics often concede the point, but suggest that this duty is narrow and limited. Professor Jeffrey Goldsworthy's landmark critique [in *The Sovereignty of Parliament: History and Philosophy* (Oxford: Clarendon Press, 1999)] of the judicial enforcement of unwritten principles, for example, allows that it may at times be proper, morally, for a judge to contradict Parliament in the face of injustice. At the same time, he argues that to turn this kind of moral obligation into a legal one is to confuse morality and legality. He goes on to argue that a view of the law that affirms its moral content is one that shows insufficient concern for the democratic consequences of this kind of judicial role:

> In a healthy democratic society, cases of clear and extreme injustice are rare; in most cases, whether or not a law violates some basic right is open to reasonable arguments on both sides. The whole point of having a democracy is that in these debatable cases the opinion of the majority

rather than of an unelected élite is supposed to prevail.

Goldsworthy's refutation, however, is a partial one. It applies only in a "healthy democratic society," where cases of "clear and extreme injustice are rare," and only to "debatable cases," where it is easy, and arguably right, to say that judges should leave the final resolution to the legislature or the executive. But what of unhealthy societies, less debatably wrong laws?

Interpreting and applying constitutional principles, written and unwritten, requires that the judge hold uncompromisingly to his or her judicial conscience, informed by past legal usage, written constitutional norms and international principles to which the nation has attorned. But judicial conscience is not to be confused with personal conscience. Judicial conscience is founded on the judge's sworn commitment to uphold the rule of law. It is informed not by the judge's personal views, nor the judge's views as to what policy is best. It is informed by the law, in all its complex majesty, as manifested in the three sources I've suggested.

In Robert Bolt's drama, "A Man For All Seasons," we encounter a scene in which Cardinal Wolsey, seeking to advance the King's interests, confronts the conscience of Sir Thomas More, not yet Lord Chancellor, who serves as symbol of the law and the constitution in the face of arbitrariness and the demands of politics. The Cardinal presents arguments of expedience, personal and public, for assisting the King, who requires a divorce. Appeals are made to More's "common sense" and he is implored to abandon the blinders of his "moral squint" to better see the political picture. But Thomas More cannot forsake a conscience grounded in deeper legal principles. He states his creed this way: "I believe, when statesmen forsake their own private conscience for the sake of their public duties ... they lead their country by a short route to chaos."

While Bolt's More speaks of "private conscience," it is clear that what he means is the legal conscience of a jurist who has considered the nature of the law. Indeed, the historical Thomas More viewed conscience as the foundation of law precisely because he did not see it as an expression of personal feeling or passion. Instead, what he termed "conscience" was what allowed all individuals, even traitors and tyrants, to access justice if they applied their reason. Never advocating open resistance by the masses in the face of unjust laws, and expressing concerns about lawlessness, More nevertheless understood that the positive laws did not define the boundaries of law. His correspondence with his daughter while imprisoned — in what would be his final days — reveals a man burdened by his own reasoned legal conscience. In what has been called More's "Dialogue on Conscience," he takes some comfort, even in prison and facing death, from his certainty that his conscience was clear and was the product of good faith, reason and diligence.

It is a similar conscience, grounded and schooled in custom and the law, that is the surest guide to upholding the fundamental principles upon which justice and democracy rest. Modern judges may not be called upon to exercise the courage of Thomas More, who described his choice as lying between "beheading and hell." But I do suggest that

a judge, if he or she is to take seriously the duties of the office, must apply his or her judicial conscience and reason, and that this may at times mean making decisions that are difficult or unpopular.

... [L]et me say again that the principles that guide these difficult decisions are not those of individual judges, but those implicit in the very system that gives the judges their authority. Ignoring one's judicial conscience is not about staying within one's role, but instead about abdicating one's responsibility to the law. There do indeed exist unwritten principles without which the law would become contradictory and self-defeating, and it is the duty of judges not only to discover them, but also to apply them. To forsake them, in Robert Bolt's phrase, is indeed to take the short route to chaos.

(e)   Democracy†

Paul Johnston and T.C. Pocklington

NOTE

Of all the unwritten constitutional principles, few are as vital as democracy. But like the other fundamental constitutional values, democracy is hard to pin down. In the introduction to this chapter, we referred to democracy as "a system whose government is accountable to the people." In the *Quebec Secession Reference*, the Supreme Court described democracy generally as "the sovereign will of the people" (paras. 62–66) and "[t]he consent of the governed": para. 67. In *Figueroa v. Canada (A.G.)*, [2003] 1 S.C.R. 912, the Court described it as "a form of government in which sovereign power resides in the people as a whole": para. 30. These phrases all recall the original Greek notion of rule by the people — direct majority rule — referred to by Johnston and Pocklington below.

Why *should* the people — all the people — rule? As Johnston and Pocklington suggest, the idea of equality is important here. If all are equal, all should rule. A second rationale is the general

notion of self-determination. This is the view that people should be able to shape their own lives, including the laws and other government actions that affect them. The Supreme Court touched on a third rationale in the *Secession Reference*, when it stressed the importance of "discussion" (para. 68) and a "marketplace of ideas" (*ibid.*). This is the rationale of diversity, championed by the 19th-century philosopher John Stuart Mill. Mill argued that just as the widest and most diverse range of opinion helps to ensure the best conclusions, the widest and most diverse range of citizen input helps ensure the best government: J.S. Mill, *On Liberty; Representative Government; The Subjection of Women: Three Essays*, Introduction by M.G. Fawcett (London, U.K.: Oxford University Press, 1960 [1859 and 1861]), especially 14–18, 57, 92–4, 186–198, and 290–91.

However, as Johnston and Pocklington tell us, direct rule by the people is rarely possible in modern society. Usually there are just too many people, with too many complex problems. As a result,

† From "Democracy and Representative Government," in *Representative Democracy: An Introduction to Politics and Government*, 2d ed., by T.C. Pocklington © 1994 (Toronto: Harcourt Brace, 1994) at 26–27. Reproduced with permission of Nelson, a division of Thomson Learning: www.thomsonrights.com. Fax: 800 730-2215

we have to rely heavily on elected representatives and on political and legal mechanisms to do our governing for us. The Supreme Court alluded to these tools of modern democracy when it spoke of "freely elected legislative bodies", "a political system of majority rule", "popular franchise", and "the process of representative and responsible government": *Secession Reference*, paras. 62–65.

How, then, could we re-state the concept of democracy in a modern context? One recent attempt was by the German philosopher Jürgen Habermas. Habermas suggested that the essence of democracy is the capacity of people to contribute, through free and equal discussion and agreement, to the laws that govern them: J. Habermas, *Between Facts and Norms: Contributions to a Discourse Theory of Law and Democracy*, trans. W. Regh (Cambridge, Mass.: MIT Press, 1998), especially chs. 3 and 4. Habermas' model captures the equality, self-determination, and diversity rationales mentioned above, and it illuminates the role of law in giving force and legitimacy to informal social consensus.

More work is needed, though, to accommodate specific modern challenges. For example, some social divisions may run too deep for unanimous agreement, even as a goal. For difficult cases, some writers ask only for overlapping consensus (John Rawls, *Political Liberalism* (New York: Columbia University Press, 1993), Lecture 4), for ongoing cooperation (James Bohman, *Public Deliberation: Pluralism, Complexity, and Democracy* (Cambridge, Mass.: The MIT Press, 1996)). Even the usual majority rule principle can be troublesome. For the sake of fairness and legitimacy, today's minority should have a reasonable hope of being tomorrow's majority. If not, or where fundamental interests are at stake, special enhanced majorities may be required. A federal state raises further problems: it requires special arrangements to determine *which* majorities should rule.

Clearly, Canada has all these challenges. To resolve them at both the theoretical and practical level, without losing the spark from the ancient Greeks, would be an extraordinary accomplishment.

EXTRACT

The idea of democracy is rooted in the general notion of rule by the people. (This understanding is, by the way, historically well founded. The word "democracy" is derived from two Greek words,

demos [the people] and *kratein* [to rule].) More specifically, but speaking still at a level of considerable generality, we see democracy as embodied in three broad principles: popular sovereignty, political equality, and majority rule (*cf.* Ranney and Kendall 1956). *Popular sovereignty* means that ultimate ruling authority is located in the entire body of citizens rather then one class or caste. *Political equality* means that citizens have an equal opportunity — within the limits imposed by the tendency of social systems to rank their members in categories of excellence — to influence public policy. *Majority rule* means that, when citizens disagree as to which measures should become public policy, the wishes of the larger number prevail over those of the smaller. Taken together, these three principles imply a fourth, which reflects the essence of democratic practice: that there should, as much as possible, always be widespread *popular consultation and participation* in making decisions about public concerns.

Our ideal of government by the people is direct democracy. (It should be noted that we use the term "ideal" here as equivalent to "perfect embodiment." We are not saying that we would prefer to live in a community in which direct democracy would be a practical proposition.) A direct democracy would embody popular sovereignty in the perfectly clear and straightforward sense that all citizens would be members of the sovereign assembly, in which all public issues would be decided. It would embody political equality in that all citizens would be entitled to advance proposals for public decision, to argue freely for or against proposals, to assemble freely to discuss proposals, and to have their votes counted equally with the votes of others in the disposition of proposals. A direct democracy would also adhere to the principle of majority rule in the most uncomplicated way possible, which is by abiding by the wishes of a simple majority whenever a proposal comes up for decision. Finally, a direct democracy would offer regular consultation among the citizenry in dealing with such matters and regularly involve its citizens in choosing appropriate courses of action.

Generally speaking, representative democracies are judged as more or less democratic to the extent that they exemplify the principles of direct democracy. Many contemporary representative democracies seem to fall short of fully implementing these basic principles and are rightly criticized when they do so in ways that might have been avoided. Needless to say, however, one cannot "deduct marks" from representative democracies for failing to do the impossible, such as holding referenda on all public issues or holding regular assemblies of the whole body of citizens. As Sartori has observed, "Between a face-to-face democracy and a large-scale democratic system, there is a huge, yawning gap" (Sartori 1987:15). But the issue of a government's responsiveness to its citizens' basic concerns is fundamental to both situations.

(f)　Responsible Government[1]

GENERAL CHARACTER

If individual human beings are of equal dignity and worth, then each person should be able to participate equally, directly, and effectively in governing public affairs. As suggested in the article above, this would be an ideal form of democracy, or rule by the people. But most of us lack the time, expertise, or inclination to participate directly in government, so it is carried on by only a portion of society as a whole. Indeed, the direction of government policy is in the hands of a relatively small number of people.

As a result, we need to ensure that those who do govern are accountable to the rest of us. In our system, one of the main means of securing accountability, or "citizen control", is the constitutional principle of responsible government. Stated generally, responsible government is the principle that the effective leadership of government must have the confidence of the people as a whole, through their elected representatives.

Embedded in the principle of responsible government is the notion of representative government. This is the principle that the legislative branch of government — or its key part — should be elected by and representative of the public as a whole. Taking a closer account of this elected element, we can define responsible government more precisely as *the principle by which the effective leadership of the executive branch of government must have the confidence of the elected part of the legislative branch, and must resign if it loses that confidence.*[2]

Responsible government requires three key links, each involving the main institutions of government. First, responsible government assumes a special relationship between the public at large and the elected legislators in the legislative branch of government. Second, the principle involves a special relationship between the political leaders — the effective leadership of the executive — and the elected legislatures. Third, responsible government assumes a special relationship between the formal leadership of the executive, the Governor General and the Lieutenant Governors on one hand, and the elected first ministers and their cabinets on the other hand.

Responsible government also has a "micro" aspect in regard to individual cabinet ministers. Cabinet ministers must be members of Parliament or the relevant legislative assembly; they are subject to special responsibilities in regard to their departmental portfolios;[3] and they have special obligations to the cabinet as a whole.[4]

RELATIONSHIP BETWEEN PUBLIC AND LEGISLATURES

The foundation of responsible government is the notion that ultimate control should be in the hands of the public, who act through democratically elected representatives. Under the principle of representative government, members of the legislative branch of government — or its key chamber[5] — are elected by and accountable to the public as a whole.

Clearly, the effectiveness of this concept depends heavily on the degree to which the public can participate in it. For a long time Canadians have had far less than universal adult suffrage. Women had no general right to vote in federal elections until 1918;[6] registered Indians, until 1960.[7] Even today our electoral system is still an imperfect representation mechanism.[8] It is periodic, generally functioning at four-year intervals. It offers no direct voice for supporters of losing candidates. The first-past-the-post system exaggerates the support of large parties. The largest number of votes may not produce the largest number of seats. Constituency boundaries tend to penalize voters in heavily populated areas. Meanwhile, Parliament and the legislative assemblies are dominated by their cabinets and first ministers. The legislative branch plays only a limited role in making legislation, offering some public criticism before conferring its official approval. Opposition parties have only limited access to the information resources of the administration.

Despite these problems, imperfect representation is better than none. The franchise is more nearly universal than ever before. (Paradoxically, though, as the franchise has expanded, voter turnout has contracted. In the latter part of the 19th century, federal voter turnout averaged 75%.[9] It fell to only 61% in the 2000 election.) Elected politicians still have important roles as constituency ombudsmen and spokespersons.[10] Unlike most other public officials, politicians can be removed at election time if they don't measure up to expectations. Representative government has another role, too. It is the main support for a second basic principle — responsible government.

RELATIONSHIP BETWEEN EFFECTIVE EXECUTIVE AND LEGISLATURES

All the elected MPs and MLAs of a legislative chamber would be too large and cumbersome a body to run the affairs of state directly. Instead, this responsibility goes to a relatively small number of elected politicians who become the effective leadership of the executive branch of government while retaining their status as elected legislators.

The effective leadership of the executive branch is generally given to the leader of the political party that has won a majority or plurality of the seats in the elected branch of the legislature.[11] This leader becomes the first minister (prime minister at the federal level and premier at the provincial level). He or she then chooses a cabinet of fellow party members, and this new leadership becomes the new "government in power". If a government in power loses a vote of confidence — a vote on a matter of major government policy such as a budget, the government is expected to resign or to request a dissolution of Parliament (or the legislature) to permit the calling of an election.[12] If the government loses an election, the political leader and cabinet must resign or risk being dismissed.[13]

RELATIONSHIP BETWEEN FORMAL AND EFFECTIVE EXECUTIVE HEADS

Elevation to the first minister's office, and the direction of the executive branch, is not an automatic process. Responsible government requires

a third element, a special relationship between (i) the political leader who has the support of the elected legislature and (ii) the formal head of the executive branch — the Governor General at the federal level and the Lieutenant Governor at the provincial level.[14] The Governor General has the power and responsibility to appoint as prime minister the individual who heads the political party with the most support in the House of Commons.[15] In most cases, the identity of this individual will be clear from election results, House of Commons votes, or inter-party agreement. Once a prime minister has been appointed, thereafter the Governor General must normally act only on the advice of the Prime Minister and his or her cabinet — as long as their government commands the support of the House of Commons.

Thus, the formal head of the executive normally acts on the direction of the effective head, as long as the latter commands the confidence of the public as measured by support in the elected House of Commons. A similar principle applies to Lieutenant Governors and their respective premiers in regard to the unicameral elected provincial legislatures.[16]

To help ensure that there is a prime minister or premier in office, and that the great power of the first minister is controlled ultimately by the public, the Governor General and Lieutenant Governors retain some residual controls.[17] If, for example, a first minister dies suddenly without a clear successor, the Governor General or Lieutenant Governor may have to exercise some personal discretion to appoint a successor, after consulting with the relevant political party.[18] Another example might arise if a first minister recommended a major appointment after having lost an election. Here, the Governor General or Lieutenant Governor would probably be justified in refusing to make the appointment.[19]

INDIVIDUAL ASPECTS

We have already seen that individual first ministers and their cabinet colleagues must be members of Parliament or the relevant provincial legislative assembly. Federal cabinet ministers should normally be elected members of the House of Commons, either at the time of appointment or within a reasonable period thereafter.[20]

In theory, ministerial responsibility requires that individual cabinet members are answerable to the elected legislatures for the general policy of the large government departments and ministries under their direction. Today, it is rare that a cabinet minister resigns for reasons other than personal error or wrongdoing.[21] On the other hand, cases of personal culpability are not uncommon, and a minister who fails to resign and escapes dismissal now may face a demotion later.[22] Moreover, a cabinet minister is still expected to explain and justify the general policy and record of the department under his or her responsibility.

Although ministers rarely resign to take general responsibility for departmental blunders, a more serious challenge to traditional ministerial responsibility may be the fact that large parts of the bureaucracy — Crown corporations and independent agencies — are largely beyond the control of individual cabinet ministers.[23]

Another individual aspect of responsible government is cabinet solidarity and confidentiality. Both are considered necessary to safeguard free cabinet discussion; the former helps ensure that the cabinet can be held collectively accountable to the legislature.[24]

HISTORICAL ASPECTS

Responsible government has an historical as well as a democratic significance.[25] In colonial times, as greater power was transferred to elected officials, greater power was also being transferred to Canadian officials. The Governor, Governor General, and Lieutenant Governor were for a long time appointees of the British government, while elected legislators were Canadian residents. As the formal executive officers delegated more and more effective power to the leaders of elected political parties, they were also delegating more and more effective power from Britain to Canada.

During the 1970s, there was a remarkably similar evolution of responsible government in the Yukon Territory. Simultaneously, this development permitted greater local electoral control and greater territorial government independence from the federal government.[26]

GENERAL ROLE

Virtually the entire process of responsible government has developed not by revolutions, nor by written constitutional enactments,[27] but by evolving political practice and constitutional conventions. Conversely, as will be seen in the *Constitution Amendment Reference*,[28] many of the most sig-

nificant constitutional conventions relate to the operation of responsible government. Responsible government has been aptly described as "probably the most important non-federal characteristic of the Canadian Constitution."[29] Flawed and rusty in places, responsible government is still a magnificent inheritance.

Notes

1. See also Hogg 2007, ch. 9 (Responsible Government); Monahan, ch. 2(A) to ch. 2(D) (historical development of representative and responsible government before 1867); Forcese, ch. 6(B); Malcolmson, ch. 3; Funston, ch. 2(9); Peter W. Hogg, *Constitutional Law of Canada*, 4th ed. (unabridged) (Toronto: Carswell, 1997), ch. 10 (The Crown); Reesor, chs. 2 and 4; Andrew Heard, *Canadian Constitutional Conventions: The Marriage of Law and Politics* (Toronto: Oxford University Press, 1991), chs. 2–4; Cheffins, ch. 3, at 25–33, and ch. 6 on "Executive Authority" (extracts in Chapter 8, below); J.R. Mallory, *The Structure of Canadian Government*, Rev. ed. (Toronto: Gage, 1984), chs. 1–3, 6, 7; *Re Amendment of the Constitution of Canada*, [1981] 1 S.C.R. 753, regarding conventions of responsible government.
2. For a similar description, see Hogg 2007, *supra* note 1, ch. 9.2.
3. The principle of ministerial responsibility.
4. The principle of cabinet solidarity, which requires individual ministers to support decisions of cabinet.
5. That is, the House of Commons in the case of the federal government. All provincial legislatures today are unicameral elected bodies.
6. See S.C. 1918, c. 20.
7. See S.C. 1960, c. 39.
8. For discussions see Dyck, chs. 11 to 16; Robert J. Jackson & Doreen Jackson, *Canadian Government in Transition: Disruption and Continuity* (Scarborough, Ont.: Prentice-Hall, 1996), chs. 7 and 11.
9. See J.R. Colombo, *The 2003 Canadian Global Almanac* (Toronto: Macmillan Canada, 2002) at 188.
10. See Dyck, ch. 23: "Roles of Members of Parliament", referring to MPs.
11. See part (d), below.
12. Heard, *supra* note 1 at 68–74. Want of confidence motions are rare: *ibid.* at 68. Hogg (4th ed. (unabridged), *supra* note 1 in ch. 9.4(b)) notes that federal governments have been defeated by loss of confidence of the House on only six occasions since Confederation. The last occasion was the defeat of the Clark minority Conservative government in 1979: *ibid.* Because of strict party discipline, loss of confidence is a greater threat to minority governments than those with majorities.

    A prime minister's request for a dissolution of Parliament for the calling of an election has been refused only once, in the "King-Bing" affair of 1926, discussed in Reesor at 65; E. Forsey, *The Royal Power of Dissolution in the British Parliament* (Toronto: Oxford University Press, 1943; reprinted 1968), chs. 5 and 6.
13. "No Canadian prime minister has faced dismissal but five provincial premiers have been dismissed [Quebec in 1878 and 1891; British Columbia in 1898, 1900, 1903]": Reesor, referring to J.T. Saywell, *The Office of Lieutenant-Governor: A Study in Canadian Government and Politics* (Toronto: University of Toronto Press, 1957), 112–44. See also Mallory, *supra* note 1, 57–58. The circumstances of the provincial dismissals varied. Regarding the contemporary situation, Heard, *supra* note 1, 29 says that "[t]he only dismissal that would be widely accepted, it appears, is the removal of a defeated government that tried to

remain in office." *Cf.* Hogg, 4th ed. (unabridged), *supra* note 1 at ch. 9(6)(c).

14. Technically, the head of the formal executive in Canada is the Queen, but virtually all her powers at the federal level are delegated to the Governor General, and the Lieutenant Governor acts on her behalf at the provincial level: see Cheffins & Johnson, Chapter 8, below.
15. See generally Heard, *supra* note 1 at 20–26.
16. See, for example, Bellamy *et al.*, eds., *The Provincial Political Systems* (Toronto: Methuen, 1975), ch. 20.
17. See generally, Heard, *ibid.*, ch. 3.
18. Reesor, citing three post-war examples from Quebec.
19. See Hogg, *supra* note 1 (4th ed. (unabridged), ch. 9(6)(e)), discussing Governor General Lord Aberdeen's refusal to make several senate and judicial appointments recommended by Prime Minister Tupper after the latter had been defeated in a general election.
20. A prime minister will not normally appoint more than one minister from the Senate, and cabinet ministers are not normally given departmental portfolios: Heard, *supra* note 1 at 50.
21. Heard, *supra* note 1 at 53–59.
22. *Ibid.* at 58.
23. This is one aspect of what political scientist Alan Cairns has called "fragmentation": see Alain C. Cairns, "The Past and Future of the Canadian Administrative State" (1990) 40 U.T.L.J. 1, 348–53. For an historical account of the growth of federal independent agencies, see Law Reform Commission of Canada, *Working Paper 25: Independent Administrative Agencies* (Ottawa: Supply and Services Canada, 1980), ch. 1.
24. Heard, *ibid.* at 64.
25. For the evolution of the principle in Canada, see J.R. Mallory, *The Structure of Canadian Government*, Rev. ed. (Toronto: Gage, 1984), ch. 1, Reesor, ch. 2. For the British historical experience, see J.P. Mackintosh, *The British Cabinet*, 3d ed. (London: Stevens, 1977), ch. 2.
26. Kenneth Coates & Judith Powell, *The Modern North: People, Politics, and the Rejection of Colonialism* (Toronto: Copp Clark Pitman, 1989) at 63–64. Thus far, the Northwest Territories government has followed a more non-partisan consensual model: *ibid.* at 69–73.
27. There is no definition or specific requirement of responsible government in the Constitution of Canada. The principle is implied in that part of the Preamble of the *Constitution Act, 1867* which refers to "a Constitution similar in Principle to that of the United Kingdom."
28. *Re Amendment of the Constitution of Canada (Nos. 1, 2, and 3)* (1981), 125 D.L.R. (3d) 1, 82–83 (S.C.C.), Chapter 9, below.
29. Hogg 2007 at 255.

III

The Constitution Act, 1867

3   Origins and Structure of the *Constitution Act, 1867*

(a)   Introduction

Federalism is the division of power between a government for the entire country and a number of relatively independent governments for parts of it. Federalism has been called "[t]he dominant principle of Canadian constitutional law."[1] Although the Canadian federation is in all respects a sovereign state,[2] neither the federal government nor any of the provincial governments has the capacity to exercise separately the full sovereign powers of the state, and each level of government has powers that cannot be repealed by the other. This structure contrasts with a unitary constitution, which provides for a single independent government for a country.

The legal framework of Canadian federalism is the *Constitution Act, 1867*.[3] This Act did seven main things:

(i) it united the colonies of Canada, Nova Scotia, and New Brunswick into the semi-self-governing colony of Canada;

(ii) it established one government for the whole colony and the provincial governments of Ontario, Quebec, Nova Scotia, and New Brunswick for its four regions, and provided for the admission of new provinces and territories after 1867;

(iii) it provided that the new colony was to have "a Constitution similar in principle to that of the United Kingdom";

(iv) it provided for the operation of the executive and judicial branches of government;

(v) it prescribed a detailed division of legislative powers between the two levels of government;

(vi) it divided property and natural resources between the two levels of government; and

(vii) it enshrined a number of language and educational rights, and provincial and sectoral safeguards.

Until 1982, the *Constitution Act, 1867* was the central formal part of the Canadian constitution; today it shares centre stage with another document, the *Constitution Act, 1982*.[4] Clearly, the *Constitution Act, 1867* is worth exploring further. What forces shaped it? What were its key elements? How did it evolve? How should it evolve?

The *Constitution Act, 1867* is worth considering from another perspective as well. From 1867 to 1949, the ultimate judicial authority for interpreting the Canadian constitution was a British tribunal, the Judicial Committee of the Privy Council. For most of their history, Canadian federalism and the *Constitution Act, 1867* were shaped by the Judicial Committee.

Many people believe that the Judicial Committee took a decentralist approach to interpreting our federal system.[5] This perception led critics to argue that the Judicial Committee misinterpreted what was intended to be a highly centralized federal constitution. Supporters, however, have claimed that the Committee responded faithfully to a relatively decentralist document. Others have argued that the Judicial Committee was an ivory tower institution, removed from Canadian economic and political realities.[6] Still another view is that the *British North America Act, 1867* was a complex and ambiguous document, responding to both centralist and decentralist pressures, and containing both centralist and decentralist elements.[7] What are the implications of these different possible interpretations for conclusions about the role of the Judicial Committee?

If we look at the historical factors at work in 1867 and in the following decades, we may gain some insight into these controversies, learn something about the Confederation bargain and how it evolved, and shed light on the role of courts in Canadian constitutional law. In subsequent chapters we will look at the judicial, legislative, and executive branches of government, and their relationship to Canadian federalism. In later chapters on constitutional reform, we will see that one of the most dominant themes is an old theme, the challenge of federalism.

Notes

1. *Re Amendment of the Constitution of Canada* (1981), 125 D.L.R. (3d) 1, 58 (S.C.C.). Although this comment was in a dissent, even the majority of the Supreme Court acknowledged "the essential federal character of the country": 47.
2. After the *Statute of Westminster, 1931* (U.K.) 20 & 23 Geo. V, c. 4, the Canadian state enjoyed full sovereignty except for the power to change provisions of the Constitution Acts, 1867 to 1930 that did not already permit amendment by Parliament or the provincial legislatures.

As a result of the *Canada Act, 1982* (U.K.), 1982, c. 11, this remaining restriction was removed, and the sovereignty was complete.

3. *Constitution Act, 1867* (U.K.) 30 & 31 Vict., c. 3. (formerly called *British North America Act, 1867*; re-named *Constitution Act, 1867* in 1982 by Item 1 of the Schedule to the *Constitution Act, 1982*, being Schedule B of the *Canada Act, 1982* (U.K.), 1982, c. 11).
4. Schedule B of the *Canada Act, 1982* (U.K.), 1982, c. 11, proclaimed in force on 17 April 1982.
5. For an analysis of criticisms of the Judicial Committee, see Chapter 7.
6. See, however, *Edwards v. Canada (A.G.)*, [1930] 1 D.L.R. 98 (J.C.P.C.: the *Persons* decision) in Chapter 4, a constitutional decision not involving the division of legislative powers.
7. See, for example, Peter W. Hogg & Wade K. Wright, "Canadian Federalism, the Privy Council and the Supreme Court: Reflections on the Debate About Canadian Federalism" (2005) 38 U.B.C. L. Rev. 329; Alan C. Cairns, "Comment on 'Critics of the Judicial Committee: The New Orthodoxy and an Alternative Explanation'" (1986) 19 Can. J. of Pol. Sci. 521; "Introduction" in Peter Russell, Rainer Knopff & Ted Morton, eds., *Federalism and the Charter: Leading Constitutional Decisions*, 3d ed. (Ottawa: Carleton University Press, 1982); Peter Russell, "Book Review of The Judicial Committee and the British North America Act by G.P. Brown" (March 1968) 49:1 Canadian Historical Review, 66–67.

(b) Federalism: *Quebec Secession Reference*†

NOTE

The *Quebec Secession Reference* is considered more generally in Chapter 12. The following extract contains some of the Court's comments on federalism, which was identified in the *Reference* as one of four fundamental principles underlying the Constitution of Canada.

EXTRACT

[THE COURT:]

[55] It is undisputed that Canada is a federal state. Yet many commentators have observed that, according to the precise terms of the *Constitution Act, 1867*, the federal system was only partial. See, e.g., K. C. Wheare, *Federal Government* (4th ed. 1963), at pp. 18–20. This was so because, on paper, the federal government retained sweeping powers which threatened to undermine the autonomy of the provinces. Here again, however, a review of the written provisions of the Constitution does not provide the entire picture. Our political and constitutional practice has adhered to an underlying principle of federalism, and has interpreted the written provisions of the Constitution in this light. For example, although the federal power of disallowance was included in the *Constitution Act, 1867*, the underlying principle of federalism triumphed early. Many constitutional

---

† *Reference re Secession of Quebec*, [1998] 2 S.C.R. 217 at paras. 55–60. See also: Dyck, ch. 18; Hogg 2007, ch. 5; MacIvor, ch. 10; Monahan, ch. 6(O); John Kincaid & G. Alan Tarr, eds., and John Kincaid, senior ed., *Constitutional Origins, Structure, and Change in Federal Countries* (Montreal & Kingston: McGill-Queen's University Press, 2005); Malcolmson, ch. 4; Brooks, ch. 5; Funston, ch. 4(1); G. Stevenson, "Federalism" in J.H. Marsh, ed., *The Canadian Encyclopedia*, Year 2000 ed. (Toronto: McClelland & Stewart, 1999) at 824–26; Cheffins, ch. 9. For general works on federalism, see P. King, *Federalism and Federation* (Baltimore: Johns Hopkins University Press, 1982); K.C. Wheare, *Federal Government*, 4th ed. (New York: Oxford University Press, 1964).

scholars contend that the federal power of disallowance has been abandoned (e.g., P.W. Hogg, *Constitutional Law of Canada* (4th ed. 1997), at p. 120).

[56] In a federal system of government such as ours, political power is shared by two orders of government: the federal government on the one hand, and the provinces on the other. Each is assigned respective spheres of jurisdiction by the *Constitution Act, 1867*. See, e.g., *Liquidators of the Maritime Bank of Canada* v. *Receiver-General of New Brunswick*, [1892] A.C. 437 (P.C.), at pp. 441–42. It is up to the courts "to control the limits of the respective sovereignties": *Northern Telecom Canada Ltd.* v. *Communication Workers of Canada*, [1983] 1 S.C.R. 733, at p. 741. In interpreting our Constitution, the courts have always been concerned with the federalism principle, inherent in the structure of our constitutional arrangements, which has from the beginning been the lodestar by which the courts have been guided.

[57] This underlying principle of federalism, then, has exercised a role of considerable importance in the interpretation of the written provisions of our Constitution. In the *Patriation Reference, supra,* at pp. 905–9, we confirmed that the principle of federalism runs through the political and legal systems of Canada. Indeed, Martland and Ritchie JJ., dissenting in the *Patriation Reference*, at p. 821, considered federalism to be "the dominant principle of Canadian constitutional law". With the enactment of the *Charter*, that proposition may have less force than it once did, but there can be little doubt that the principle of federalism remains a central organizational theme of our Constitution. Less obviously, perhaps, but certainly of equal importance, federalism is a political and legal response to underlying social and political realities.

[58] The principle of federalism recognizes the diversity of the component parts of Confederation, and the autonomy of provincial governments to develop their societies within their respective spheres of jurisdiction. The federal structure of our country also facilitates democratic participation by distributing power to the government thought to be most suited to achieving the particular societal objective having regard to this diversity. The scheme of the *Constitution Act, 1867*, it was said in *Re the Initiative and Referendum Act*, [1919] A.C. 935 (P.C.), at p. 942, was

not to weld the Provinces into one, nor to subordinate Provincial Governments to a central authority, but to establish a central government in which these Provinces should be represented, entrusted with exclusive authority only in affairs in which they had a common interest. Subject to this each Province was to retain its independence and autonomy and to be directly under the Crown as its head.

More recently, in *Haig* v. *Canada*, [1993] 2 S.C.R. 995, at p. 1047, the majority of this Court held that differences between provinces "are a rational part of the political reality in the federal process". It was referring to the differential application of federal law in individual provinces, but the point applies more generally. A unanimous Court expressed similar views in *R.* v. *S. (S.)*, [1990] 2 S.C.R. 254, at pp. 287–88.

[59] The principle of federalism facilitates the pursuit of collective goals by cultural and linguistic minorities which form the majority within a particular province. This is the case in Quebec, where the majority of the population is French-speaking, and which possesses a distinct culture. This is not merely the result of chance. The social and demographic reality of Quebec explains the existence of the province of Quebec as a political unit and indeed, was one of the essential reasons for establishing a federal structure for the Canadian union in 1867. The experience of both Canada East and Canada West under the *Union Act, 1840* (U.K.), 3–4 Vict., c. 35, had not been satisfactory. The federal structure adopted at Confederation enabled French-speaking Canadians to form a numerical majority in the province of Quebec, and so exercise the considerable provincial powers conferred by the *Constitution Act, 1867* in such a way as to promote their language and culture. It also made provision for certain guaranteed representation within the federal Parliament itself.

[60] Federalism was also welcomed by Nova Scotia and New Brunswick, both of which also affirmed their will to protect their individual cultures and their autonomy over local matters. All new provinces joining the federation sought to achieve similar objectives, which are no less vigorously pursued by the provinces and territories as we approach the new millennium.

(c) The Framework of Unity†

Edgar McInnis

In the opening years of the decade of the sixties the simultaneous emergence of a whole series of problems confronted the provinces of British North America with a crisis that called for prompt and effective action. The political and sectional deadlock within Canada, the growing urgency of the western problem, the unsolved and expanding problem of railways, the drastic change in the trade situation that seemed likely to follow the abrogation of the Reciprocity Treaty, the troublesome question of defense, all converged within this brief period. External factors weighed heavily in the situation. Britain, while placing strict limits on provincial autonomy, had followed her withdrawal of trade benefits by a retreat from the burden of imperial defense and seemed half willing to abandon her American possessions rather than undertake any serious effort on their behalf. The influence of the United States pervaded almost every aspect of the external difficulties. The threat to the West, the blow to trade, the complications that increased the gravity of the railway problem, all rose to no small extent from American attitudes and policies; and in addition there were the dangers embodied in the Fenian movement and the vociferous annexationist sentiment throughout the northern states.

These were problems which were largely beyond the competence of any single province to solve. Canada was far more vitally affected than the other provinces and more urgently impelled to a drastic effort at solution. Her internal difficulties had no parallel in the Maritimes, which were untroubled by serious racial divisions and whose political basis was not threatened with stultification by party instability. It was Canada that was most acutely concerned over the future of the West and most exposed to threats of attack from across the border. The other provinces, however, were not wholly indifferent to such matters and were directly involved in questions concerning trade and railways. A combination of circumstances gave unprecedented strength to the forces favoring unity and presented a unique opportunity.

But it was a fleeting situation, and the chance once missed might not soon recur. Canada's whole destiny was transformed by the men who seized this transient opportunity with boldness and decision and used it to weld the scattered communities with a population of less than 4,000,000 into a nation whose dominion should extend from sea to sea.

The idea of a union of British North America had been put forward as early as 1790 by Chief Justice William Smith. It was not until the 1850s, however, that a number of journalists and political leaders embarked on a serious effort to bring it about. Sectional difficulties in Canada motivated a search for some alternative basis other than a mere dissolution of the union. Federation was discussed during various negotiations over the Intercolonial Railway and was brought forward in connection with the agitation for control of the West. Galt pressed it in the debates of 1858 and made its acceptance a condition of his entry into the ministry in the autumn of that year. But although the matter was raised with the British government, no serious effort was made to secure its adoption. Galt's colleagues failed to share his enthusiasm. The Maritimes showed little interest, and the British Government was cold to the idea. There were leaders in the various provinces who preferred limited regional unions to a general federation. It took more urgent circumstances to bring the project into the forefront of the political scene.

Three developments were of special importance in precipitating the issue. The first was the outcome of the political deadlock in Canada. The fall of the Taché-Macdonald ministry in June 1864 brought prospects of a new election but little hope of any substantial change in the political balance. Only some new combination offered a promise of the way out of the impasse, and the key to any such combination was now George Brown.

Though Brown was unrivalled as the leader of the Upper Canada reformers, he had limited success in welding them into a coherent party. He had little

† From *Canada: A Political and Social History*, 3d ed. (Toronto: Holt, Rinehart and Winston of Canada Ltd., 1969) at 342–55. Copyright by Principal's Fund at Glendon College. Reproduced with permission.

See also Hogg 2007, chs. 2.4 and 2.5; Monahan, at 52–55; Funston, ch. 1(5); P.B. Waite, "Confederation" in J.H. Marsh, ed., *The Canadian Encyclopedia,* Year 2000 ed. (Toronto: McClelland & Stewart, 1999) at 541; Reesor, ch. 3; and Cheffins, at 33–40.

appreciation of politics as an art and little talent for the management of men. There were chronic divisions in the ranks — Grit radicals, Toronto liberals, right-wing moderates — and relations with the *Rouges* of Lower Canada were tenuous and uneasy at best. Yet no other figure commanded such personal loyalty or could have rallied a solid following in support of the great enterprise which was emerging through his own initiative.

By 1864 Brown had reached the conclusion that "rep by pop" was not by itself a practical solution for the difficulties of the Union. French Canada was adamantly opposed to being swamped by an English majority, and Brown had come to appreciate the legitimate desire of Lower Canada to maintain its own institutions and handle its own affairs. Yet the alternative of a simple dissolution of the Union was one to which he was utterly opposed. That left only federalism as the device for reconciling cultural duality with continued political unity. Powerfully reinforcing this view was his growing concern over the need to acquire the [West] for Canada, and to this end, a solution of Canada's political difficulties seemed essential. Federation might open the way to satisfying Lower Canada, to releasing Upper Canada from French political domination, and to securing the great western domain. "Let us endeavour," he pleaded in the *Globe*, "in carrying on the affairs of our common country to arrive at some basis on which we may all stand in peace and contentment."

It was with this aim that he secured in May 1864 the appointment of a legislative committee to examine the constitutional problem and to devise a remedy. On June 14 the committee reported a strong feeling "in favour of changes in the direction of a federative system, applied either to Canada alone or to the whole British North America Provinces." On the same day, the Taché-Macdonald ministry fell, leaving no assurance that the project would not expire with it.

In actual fact the crisis opened the way to its realization. Brown made it known that he would support any ministry that would sincerely try to solve the constitutional question. John Alexander Macdonald, though he had publicly dissented from the federal proposals of the committee, grasped at the prospect of a coalition that would avert the threatened breakdown of government. The governor general, Lord Monck, used his influence in favour of negotiation rather than dissolution of the Assembly, and helped to persuade a reluctant Brown that he must personally enter the ministry if it was to succeed. In the discussions Macdonald dropped his insistence on legislative union and agreed to seek a general federation, while Brown, though sceptical about the immediate prospects, consented to the attempt provided that a federation of the two Canadas was accepted as a possible alternative if the wider scheme should fail. With the entry of Brown and two of his supporters into the ministry, the Great Coalition came into being on June 30. This was the event that actually set in motion the process that led to the formation of the Dominion of Canada.

A second motivating force was provided by the Grand Trunk. Even the substantial help that it received from the government in 1862 had not brought salvation to the railway. Edward Watkin, sent out by the London financial interests to investigate, discovered that "the management of this railway is an organized mess — I will not say, a sink of iniquity." The appointment of a new manager, C.J. Brydges, brought some order into affairs, but the real need was for a fundamental change of basis. The hope of capturing the trade of the American West had fallen through. The Canadian West, toward which the eyes of Canadian business leaders had now turned, seemed to Watkin the new land of promise, where the Grand Trunk would find relief from its woes. The remedy for a railway that was too expensive for the existing population was to build a railway several times the existing length into regions that were still unpopulated. In addition to opening the West for settlement, a line to the Pacific would give access to the trade of the Orient and provide a fast military route between Britain and her possessions in the Far East. The old dream of Canada as the entrepôt between Europe and the interior of North America was replaced by the still more grandiose vision of British North America as the halfway house between Europe and Asia. Its realization involved not merely the construction of the long-deferred Intercolonial as well as of a transcontinental railway, but the political union of the provinces that would facilitate the acquisition of the West. In the end the Grand Trunk took no part in the tremendous construction project that was thus projected; but its influence was enlisted on the side of the new political departure, which seemed a necessary prelude, and was of no small importance in making it a reality.

The third development was the emergence of a scheme for Maritime union. Here, too, railways were an important factor. For a decade after the setback to the plan for the Intercolonial in 1852, the provinces continued to negotiate on the project and to seek the aid of the imperial government. By 1861, with the new influence of the Grand Trunk now enlisted and the *Trent* affair providing a fresh illustration of the military importance of the railway, the British government was persuaded to renew its earlier offer of a financial guarantee, and the construction of local lines in the Maritimes had diminished their earlier objections to the Robinson route. A conference in 1862 led to an agreement on the share of the cost to be borne by each province. It seemed that the building of the Intercolonial was at last assured, when Canada suddenly raised objections to that part of the financial provisions which provided for a sinking fund and which was a condition of the imperial guarantee. Once more the arrangements collapsed amid recriminations that added to the long-standing dislike and distrust of Canada in the Maritimes. The disappointment that gave rise to these emotions also lent an impetus to the idea of Maritime union, which had been tentatively put forward from time to time, and Nova Scotia in 1864 took the lead in initiating the first official discussion of the project. Even then the response of New Brunswick and Prince Edward Island showed little enthusiasm. The Nova Scotia resolution as originally drafted provided for the appointment of delegates to a conference to *arrange* a plan of union. The two other provinces agreed to meet to *consider* it, and even then they were in no haste to arrange the actual meeting.

They were jolted into action by a message from Canada. On June 30 a formal communication was sent by the governor, Lord Monck, asking whether a Canadian deputation might attend the forthcoming conference to present their wider proposals. The Maritimes agreed to accept an unofficial delegation and proceeded in a somewhat leisurely fashion to make definite arrangements for the conference to meet at Charlottetown on September 1. It was perhaps typical of the very casual interest aroused by the prospective discussions that, when the appointed date arrived, members of the Island government as well as the general public were less interested in the arrival of the delegations from the mainland than in the rare presence of a circus in Charlottetown. The delegates from Nova Scotia found no one to welcome them, and the reception to the Canadians took the form of a self-sacrificing provincial secretary rowing out in a small boat to meet the ship in which they arrived.

It was the Canadians who took the initiative in the discussions and whose proposals dominated the conference. Maritime union, which the meeting had officially been called to consider, received scant attention. It proved to have few strong advocates, and it encountered the rooted reluctance of Prince Edward Island to see its legislature abolished and a demand that in any case the capital should be at Charlottetown. Theoretically, Maritime union was quite compatible with the larger federation; but in practice, the broader scheme weakened still further the slender prospect of a merger of the three eastern provinces. After a few brief discussions, consideration was postponed until after the Quebec conference, and ultimately at a meeting in Toronto the plan was shelved indefinitely. Its vanishing wraiths trailed the conference as it moved on to Halifax after a week's discussion at Charlottetown and thence for oratorical festivities at St. John and Fredericton. These ambulatory proceedings issued in an agreement that a confederation of all British North America would be highly advantageous if it could be arranged on equitable terms and in a decision to meet at Quebec to discuss precise details. On October 10 the delegates from the provinces, including two representatives from Newfoundland, embarked at Quebec on the momentous discussions that laid the foundations for the new Dominion.

The essential outlines of the new scheme had already been drawn at Charlottetown. The starting point was a recognition that the union must be federal in structure. John Alexander Macdonald was strongly in favour of a legislative union that would extinguish the separate governments of the provinces, but this was beyond attainment. The Maritimes were unwilling to see their identity submerged, and they lacked the general municipal institutions that would be necessary to provide an effective system of local government under a unitary system. French Canada was an equally serious obstacle. Restive as they were under the existing union of the Canadas, the French were unlikely to accept a still wider union, which would accentuate their minority position. The price of their consent to any new arrangement was the creation of a predominantly French province in which their special rights would be guaranteed and their control of local affairs assured. "We had either," said George Brown in the subsequent debates, "to take a federal union or drop the negotiation.... There was but one choice open to us — federal union or nothing."

Having accepted this necessity, however, the delegates at Charlottetown were generally agreed on a strong central government, which should be vested with all the powers outside the list of strictly local topics to be left to the provinces. The governor of New Brunswick reported that, according to his information, it was contemplated that the powers of the local government "should be carefully restricted to certain local matters, to be specified and defined by

43

the Act establishing the confederation, whilst all general legislation should be dealt with by, and all undefined powers reside in, a central legislature, which should in fact be not only a federal assembly charged with the consideration of a few topics specially committed to its care, but the real legislature of the country, the local assemblies being allowed to sink to the position of mere municipalities."

There was little tendency at Quebec to depart from this fundamental basis. The conference met under the shadow of the terrible conflict that was being waged for the existence of the American union. To Canadians the Civil War seemed the disastrous outcome of the doctrine of states' rights and an object lesson that they took deeply to heart. Although the expressed desire was "to follow the model of the British constitution so far as our circumstances will permit," the federal nature of the proposed structure inevitably invited attention to the Constitution of the United States. But the tendency was less to copy its salient features than to avoid the defects that experience had so glaringly revealed. Its most significant expression was in the deliberate reversal of the American provision that restricted the powers of the federal government to those specifically granted and reserved all others to the states or the people. Both at Charlottetown and at Quebec there was general agreement on the desirability of vesting in the central government all residuary power outside the list of local subjects specifically assigned to the provinces; and this feature was further strengthened by the provision that gave the federal government a veto over provincial legislation.

The composition of the federal legislature gave rise to more serious controversy. There was no objection to a two-chamber system, and it was generally agreed that the lower house should be based on population, in spite of Prince Edward Island's objections to having only five members out of 194. But the upper house was the subject of heated arguments. The proposals outlined at Charlottetown envisaged the division of Canada into two provinces and amalgamation of the Maritimes into one and gave equal membership to each of these three units. Although it was soon clear that Maritime union was highly unlikely, the idea was retained of treating them as a single section and basing the upper house on sectional, rather than provincial equality. This roused considerable protest. There was no serious support for the suggestion that all provinces should have equal numbers, as had the states in the American Senate, but there was a strong demand that the Maritimes be given a larger representation. The presence of Newfoundland at Quebec provided the

basis for a modest compromise. The three Maritime provinces were still left with twenty-four members, the same number as Ontario and Quebec, but Newfoundland was to have an additional four if she entered the federation. It was a somewhat delusive concession, but it settled a question that almost threatened to wreck the conference. There remained the question of how the members of the upper house should be chosen, and this too was sharply debated. There was no real support for an elective basis, and Prince Edward Island was the chief advocate of appointment by the provinces. But there was some fear that the first appointments, if left to the federal government, might be on a partisan basis; and it was only after an agreement that the initial members should be nominated by the provincial governments from the existing councils, with due regard to the fair representation of all parties, that the general principle of life appointment by the federal government was conceded.

There was another hard battle over financial arrangements. A federal government that was charged with all the great functions outside of local affairs, and that was to assume the cost, not only of the administration and defense, but of an expensive program of railway construction, must necessarily have at its disposal the bulk of the revenue; and the need was increased by the decision that the provincial debts should be assumed by the central government. The provinces, left with little more than municipal functions and relieved of their debts, were expected to get along on an extremely frugal budget. Even so, it was a real question where they would find the money for education and roads and other local obligations. The federal government took over the customs duties, which provided one main source of revenue, and such publicly owned enterprises as railways and harbour works as could occasionally be regarded as paying assets. Yet it was reluctant to share its taxing power, and it was only after considerable opposition that the idea of federal subsidies to the provinces was accepted as an alternative.

The result was a somewhat complicated adjustment. The difference in provincial debts was equated by crediting each province with an amount roughly equivalent to $25 per head; and each was to pay or receive interest at 5 percent on any difference between this amount and the debt actually assumed by the central government. Their revenue from local license fees was to be supplemented by a federal grant. Taking the most economical estimate of future provincial expenses — that provided by Tupper of Nova Scotia — the conference worked out a system of grants-in-aid calculated on the basis of 80 cents per head. If the provinces still needed money, they were to raise it by direct taxation, and it was fully expected that the unpopularity of such a proceeding would act as an effective curb on any tendency toward extravagance on the part of provincial governments.

On October 27 the work of the conference was finished. It was embodied in seventy-two resolutions, which laid down in detail the proposals for the new scheme of government. In the first flush of enthusiasm there had been some talk of submitting the draft constitution to popular approval. But second thoughts brought doubts about the wisdom of this course and a decision to agree with Britain's preference for ratification by the provincial legislatures rather than by the electorate. Even this, as it turned out, was in most cases impossible to attain, and the returning delegates found themselves involved in a struggle that delayed the establishment of Canadian federation for nearly three more years.

Carrying Confederation

The motivating forces behind the movement for confederation showed themselves strongest in English-speaking Canada. The threat of political deadlock, accompanied as it was by the fear of economic stagnation, roused a widespread desire not merely to escape from present ills, but to open the way for future progress. The hope of westward expansion was particularly strong in rallying the support of both agrarian and business interests behind the proposals. This did not mean that opposition was absent. Although the Grits had approved the idea of federation in their convention of 1859, Brown and his followers thought chiefly of a purely Canadian federation accompanied by the annexation of the West. Brown looked on the inclusion of the Maritimes as more likely to be burdensome than advantageous, and he was particularly hostile to the Intercolonial Railway, which he viewed as another Grand Trunk scheme at the expense of the Canadian people. He had yielded to necessity when he realized that the inclusion of the Maritimes was needed in order to satisfy the French, who believed that it would redress the balance in their favour against Canada West, and that Maritime consent could be won by a promise to build the Intercolonial.

His surrender was attacked by radicals from both sections of Canada. "The confederation of all the British North American provinces," Dorion charged, "naturally suggested itself to the Grand Trunk officials as the surest means of bringing with it the construction of the Intercolonial Railway. Such

was the origin of this confederation scheme. The Grand Trunk people are at the bottom of it." There were also sharp attacks by the radicals on the conservative nature of the proposed structure; but Brown succeeded in winning the bulk of his followers to the support of the Quebec resolutions. With Galt assuring the English of Canada East that their minority rights would be protected within the new province of Quebec while their economic interests would be forwarded under the federal government, and with Macdonald's careful and persuasive exposition giving full satisfaction to the Conservatives, opposition in English Canada was confined to a small, though able, minority.

French Canada was much more divided. Quite apart from the *Rouges*, who disliked the whole idea of a broad federation, many Conservatives were gravely concerned over its effect on their racial and cultural prospects. French Canada was torn between fear of absorption into a united Canada with an English majority and fear of annexation to the United States if Canada continued weak and disunited. It was the task of the French leaders to minimize the first of these fears and to take full advantage of the second. Cartier and his associates stressed the protection that French institutions and culture would enjoy under the new provincial arrangements and insisted that American annexation was the inevitable alternative to confederation. The new scheme at last offered the means of reconciling racial diversity and national unity. To this view the clergy gave a somewhat guarded support, their desire to erect stronger bulwarks against the United States outweighing their reservations about the adequacy of the guarantees offered to French Canada.

Even so, the controversy was violent, and a number of French Conservatives went over to the opposition. The situation moved George Brown, during the debates in the assembly, to an eloquent appeal to the spirit of mutual generosity. He reminded his hearers:

> One hundred years have passed away since these provinces became by conquest part of the British Empire. Here sit today the descendants of the victors and vanquished in the fight of 1759, with all the differences of language, religion, civil law, and social habit nearly as distinctly marked as they were a century ago. Here we sit today seeking amicably to find a remedy for constitutional evils and injustice complained of — by the vanquished? No, sir, but complained of by the conquerors! Here sit the representatives of the British population claiming justice — only justice; and here sit representatives of the French population discussing in the French tongue whether we shall have it.

The debates in the Canadian assembly on the Quebec resolutions opened on February 3, 1865. In the early hours of March 11 the main motion was carried by a vote of 91 to 33. In contrast to the overwhelming majority of English members who supported the Quebec plan, the French were closely divided, with 27 in favour and 22 opposed. Nonetheless, Canada registered its approval in a decisive fashion and with a majority of votes from both sections. It was the only province that gave formal ratification to the confederation proposals. In none were they approved by popular vote, and in the Maritimes an opposition developed that threatened to wreck the whole project.

The situation revealed the relative weakness of unitary forces in the face of the deep-rooted localism of the lower provinces. The Quebec resolutions pledged the federal government to secure without delay the completion of the Intercolonial. Supporters of federation painted glowing pictures of increased trade between the provinces, of a great industrial expansion based on Maritime resources in coal and iron, of the ports of the Maritimes rivalling those of Britain as centres of world trade. But many of their hearers took a sceptical view of these prospects and were unconvinced that the benefits from the Intercolonial would outweigh the burdens and the loss of independence that the Quebec plan foreshadowed. The Maritimes had little interest in the acquisition of the West. They foresaw a costly program of transcontinental railway construction added to expenditures on communications and defense works in Canada, with a considerable part of the expense falling on the Maritime taxpayer. They envisaged the drift of their industries and other enterprises to the more populous region of the St. Lawrence and an imposition of the Canadian protective tariff on the Maritime consumer. It was easy to magnify what would be lost and to minimize prospective gains. The delegates, returning from Quebec full of satisfaction with their work, were met by angry charges that they had sold their constituents to Canada for 80 cents a head. "They gave the whole province away," asserted a Nova Scotia critic even after union had become a reality. "We had a well-working constitution; we made our own laws, raised our own revenues, and taxed ourselves. We owned railways, fisheries, and other public property, but they gave them all away for nothing. We can at any moment be taxed to any extent arbitrarily by an oligarchy in Canada."

This threat of taxation without recompense, coupled with the prospective curtailment of provincial authority, roused a storm of criticism. Both Prince Edward Island and Newfoundland rejected the Quebec proposals. In New Brunswick the premier, Samuel Leonard Tilley, felt forced by circumstances to risk an election on the issue. His party was overwhelmingly defeated, and under a new administration the New Brunswick Assembly passed a resolution asserting that "the consummation of the said scheme would prove politically, commercially and financially disastrous to the best interests of this province."

This was a serious defection, all the more so because of its effect on Nova Scotia. In that province the powerful influence of Joseph Howe had been thrown against confederation. Howe had on previous occasions expressed a somewhat vague approval of federation as an ultimate goal. He had been invited to form part of the delegation to Charlottetown; and though he alleged that his duties as imperial fisheries commissioner prevented his acceptance, he promised that he would be "very happy to cooperate in carrying out any measure upon which the conference shall agree." But it was his Conservative opponents under Dr. Charles Tupper who were responsible for the negotiations, and there is little doubt that this made it all the easier for Howe to convince himself with perfect sincerity that the scheme they had sponsored would be disastrous for Nova Scotia. He threw himself ardently into the campaign against federation, and became the leading spirit in the Anti-Confederation League that was formed to combat it. The violence of the opposition made it risky for Tupper to submit the resolutions to the legislature, let alone to the electorate; and without New Brunswick's adherence it would be almost physically impossible for Nova Scotia and Canada to join. Tupper marked time, reviving the proposal for Maritime union and delaying all further action until the situation was clarified.

The time had now come to invoke the overriding authority of the British government. At first Britain had been dubious about the desirability of Canadian union, which it was feared might result in a further weakening of the imperial tie. Maritime union was favoured as a necessary prelude, and the Colonial Office looked with disapproval on the intrusion of the Canadians at Charlottetown. With the progress of the negotiations, however, it began to dawn on Britain that a strong federation might go a long way to solving the problem of Canadian defense, particularly since it would also facilitate the building of the Intercolonial. Important British financial interests, fearing a decline in their Canadian securities, pressed the government in London to lend positive aid to the federation proposals. Thus when a Canadian delegation arrived in the autumn of 1865 to discuss the situation, it met with a favourable reception. A counter delegation from Nova Scotia under Howe found itself unable to persuade the British government that it should protect the province against being forced into union. Indeed, the imperial authorities now threw their influence on the side of confederation in none too subtle a fashion. The governor of Nova Scotia was replaced by a more energetic partisan of union. The governor of New Brunswick, who shared the earlier preference of the Colonial Office for Maritime union and had used his influence against the wider scheme, was ordered in no uncertain terms to give confederation his full support; and in pursuit of this new policy he succeeded in the spring of 1866 in maneuvering the anticonfederation administration out of office and clearing the way for a new election.

Already there were signs that opposition was weakening in New Brunswick. There had been a year in which to give fuller consideration to the Quebec proposals, and the advantages of union were underlined by the massing of a Fenian force just across the border and its threat of an irruption into the province. No means were spared to encourage the conversion of the electorate. The Fenian threat was played up heavily. Volunteers were called out to meet it and were kept under arms — and under pay — to maintain their patriotic fervour until the elections were over. Urgent appeals for election funds went to Canada, not without response.

The Grand Trunk Railway lent support in a distinctly practical way. From the inception of the movement for confederation the leading railway officials had been assiduous in their support, arranging excursions of press and politicians from one section to another, shepherding the delegations to London, mobilizing their financial connections in England to bring pressure on the British government. Tilley's appeal for "the needful" was generously answered, and he and his followers were returned with a handsome majority.

This success opened the way for the final stage of the negotiations. Once it was clear that New Brunswick was moving back into the fold, Tupper took steps to bring Nova Scotia into line. His task was made easier by a suggestion from one of the opponents of the Quebec resolutions that some arrangement should be sought on a more acceptable basis. Tupper succeeded in carrying a resolution that authorized the appointment of delegates to arrange with the British government for a scheme of union. A similar resolution was passed in New Brunswick; and in December 1866, delegates from the two Maritime provinces joined with those from Canada in a conference at the Westminster Palace Hotel in London.

The Quebec resolutions were the starting point for the new negotiations. Although they had received no approval in Nova Scotia and had been rejected in New Brunswick, their main provisions were accepted by the representatives of those provinces; and although they had been formally accepted in Canada, the Canadian delegates held themselves free to make such alterations as seemed necessary. The changes were not in fact extensive, though several of them were important. Subsidies to the provinces were increased by a provision for fixed grants in addition to the earlier provision of 80 cents a head. Construction of the Intercolonial was made more definitely mandatory. The Quebec clause on education, which safeguarded the separate schools of the religious minorities in Canada, was widened to apply to all provinces, and minorities were given the further right of appeal to the federal government if they felt unable to secure a redress of grievances from the provincial governments. Still other modifications were introduced at the instance of Britain when the London resolutions, sixty-nine in number, went through the process of being translated into a draft of the legislation. The power of pardon was taken from the lieutenant governors and concentrated in the hands of the governor general. To provide some measure of flexibility in case of a deadlock between the two houses of the legislature, power was given to add either three or six members to the Senate. Not least important, the title "Kingdom of Canada" which Macdonald strongly favoured was objected to on the ground that it might give offense to the United States, and the result was the dropping of a designation that would have expressed more effectively the aspirations behind the new union.

It now remained to give effect to the new constitution by securing its adoption as a statute of the imperial legislature. In the form of the British North America Act it was introduced into Parliament in March 1867, and passed with hardly more than formal attention. Anti-confederation delegates from Nova Scotia, who had kept up their unavailing battle to the end, remarked bitterly on the scanty attention that the measure attracted in the British House of Commons, compared to the eagerness with which members plunged into the debate on a new dog tax immediately afterward. On July 1, 1867, a proclamation brought the Act into force for the four provinces of Nova Scotia, New Brunswick, Ontario, and Quebec, and the Dominion of Canada entered into the first stage of its existence.

47

(d) Confederation and After: *Quebec Secession Reference*†

NOTE

The following are some of the Supreme Court's comments in *Quebec Secession Reference* on the birth and evolution of Confederation. The *Reference* itself is considered more generally in Chapter 12.

EXTRACT

[The COURT:]

[35] Confederation was an initiative of elected representatives of the people then living in the colonies scattered across part of what is now Canada. It was not initiated by Imperial fiat. In March 1864, a select committee of the Legislative Assembly of the Province of Canada, chaired by George Brown, began to explore prospects for constitutional reform. The committee's report, released in June 1864, recommended that a federal union encompassing Canada East and Canada West, and perhaps the other British North American colonies, be pursued. A group of Reformers from Canada West, led by Brown, joined with Étienne P. Taché and John A. Macdonald in a coalition government for the purpose of engaging in constitutional reform along the lines of the federal model proposed by the committee's report.

[36] An opening to pursue federal union soon arose. The leaders of the maritime colonies had planned to meet at Charlottetown in the fall to discuss the perennial topic of maritime union. The Province of Canada secured invitations to send a Canadian delegation. On September 1, 1864, 23 delegates (five from New Brunswick, five from Nova Scotia, five from Prince Edward Island, and eight from the Province of Canada) met in Charlottetown. After five days of discussion, the delegates reached agreement on a plan for federal union.

[37] The salient aspects of the agreement may be briefly outlined. There was to be a federal union featuring a bicameral central legislature. Representation in the Lower House was to be based on popula-

tion, whereas in the Upper House it was to be based on regional equality, the regions comprising Canada East, Canada West and the Maritimes. The significance of the adoption of a federal form of government cannot be exaggerated. Without it, neither the agreement of the delegates from Canada East nor that of the delegates from the maritime colonies could have been obtained.

[38] Several matters remained to be resolved, and so the Charlottetown delegates agreed to meet again at Quebec in October, and to invite Newfoundland to send a delegation to join them. The Quebec Conference began on October 10, 1864. Thirty-three delegates (two from Newfoundland, seven from New Brunswick, five from Nova Scotia, seven from Prince Edward Island, and twelve from the Province of Canada) met over a two and a half week period. Precise consideration of each aspect of the federal structure preoccupied the political agenda. The delegates approved 72 resolutions, addressing almost all of what subsequently made its way into the final text of the *Constitution Act, 1867*. These included guarantees to protect French language and culture, both directly (by making French an official language in Quebec and Canada as a whole) and indirectly (by allocating jurisdiction over education and "Property and Civil Rights in the Province" to the provinces). The protection of minorities was thus reaffirmed.

[39] Legally, there remained only the requirement to have the Quebec Resolutions put into proper form and passed by the Imperial Parliament in London. However, politically, it was thought that more was required. Indeed, Resolution 70 provided that "The Sanction of the Imperial and Local Parliaments shall be sought for the Union of the Provinces, on the principles adopted by the Conference." (Cited in J. Pope, ed., *Confederation: Being a Series of Hitherto Unpublished Documents Bearing on the British North America Act (1895)*, at p. 52 (emphasis added).)

[40] Confirmation of the Quebec Resolutions was achieved more smoothly in central Canada than in the Maritimes. In February and March 1865, the Quebec Resolutions were the subject of almost six weeks of sustained debate in both houses of

---

† *Reference Re Secession of Quebec*, [1998] 2 S.C.R. 217 at paras. 55–60.

the Canadian legislature. The Canadian Legislative Assembly approved the Quebec Resolutions in March 1865 with the support of a majority of members from both Canada East and Canada West. The governments of both Prince Edward Island and Newfoundland chose, in accordance with popular sentiment in both colonies, not to accede to the Quebec Resolutions. In New Brunswick, a general election was required before Premier Tilley's pro-Confederation party prevailed. In Nova Scotia, Premier Tupper ultimately obtained a resolution from the House of Assembly favouring Confederation.

[41] Sixteen delegates (five from New Brunswick, five from Nova Scotia, and six from the Province of Canada) met in London in December 1866 to finalize the plan for Confederation. To this end, they agreed to some slight modifications and additions to the Quebec Resolutions. Minor changes were made to the distribution of powers, provision was made for the appointment of extra senators in the event of a deadlock between the House of Commons and the Senate, and certain religious minorities were given the right to appeal to the federal government where their denominational school rights were adversely affected by provincial legislation. The *British North America Bill* was drafted after the London Conference with the assistance of the Colonial Office, and was introduced into the House of Lords in February 1867. The Act passed third reading in the House of Commons on March 8, received royal assent on March 29, and was proclaimed on July 1, 1867. The Dominion of Canada thus became a reality.

[42] There was an early attempt at secession. In the first Dominion election in September 1867, Premier Tupper's forces were decimated: members opposed to Confederation won 18 of Nova Scotia's 19 federal seats, and in the simultaneous provincial election, 36 of the 38 seats in the provincial legislature. Newly-elected Premier Joseph Howe led a delegation to the Imperial Parliament in London in an effort to undo the new constitutional arrangements, but it was too late. The Colonial Office rejected Premier Howe's plea to permit Nova Scotia to withdraw from Confederation. As the Colonial Secretary wrote in 1868:

> The neighbouring province of New Brunswick has entered into the union in reliance on having with it the sister province of Nova Scotia; and vast obligations, political and commercial, have already been contracted on the faith of a measure so long discussed and so solemnly adopted.... I trust that the Assembly and the people of Nova Scotia will not be surprised that the Queen's government feel that they would not

be warranted in advising the reversal of a great measure of state, attended by so many extensive consequences already in operation.... (Quoted in H. Wade MacLauchlan, "Accounting for Democracy and the Rule of Law in the Quebec Secession Reference" (1997), 76 Can. Bar Rev. 155, at p. 168.)

The interdependence characterized by "vast obligations, political and commercial", referred to by the Colonial Secretary in 1868, has, of course, multiplied immeasurably in the last 130 years.

[43] Federalism was a legal response to the underlying political and cultural realities that existed at Confederation and continue to exist today. At Confederation, political leaders told their respective communities that the Canadian union would be able to reconcile diversity with unity. It is pertinent, in the context of the present Reference, to mention the words of George-Étienne Cartier (cited in the *Parliamentary Debates on the subject of the Confederation* (1865), at p. 60):

> Now, when we [are] united together, if union [is] attained, we [shall] form a political nationality with which neither the national origin, nor the religion of any individual, [will] interfere. It was lamented by some that we had this diversity of races, and hopes were expressed that this distinctive feature would cease. The idea of unity of races [is] utopian — it [is] impossible. Distinctions of this kind [will] always exist. Dissimilarity, in fact, appear[s] to be the order of the physical world and of the moral world, as well as in the political world. But with regard to the objection based on this fact, to the effect that a great nation [can]not be formed because Lower Canada [is] in great part French and Catholic, and Upper Canada [is] British and Protestant, and the Lower Provinces [are] mixed, it [is] futile and worthless in the extreme.... In our own Federation we [will] have Catholic and Protestant, English, French, Irish and Scotch, and each by his efforts and his success [will] increase the prosperity and glory of the new Confederacy.... [W]e [are] of different races, not for the purpose of warring against each other, but in order to compete and emulate for the general welfare.

The federal-provincial division of powers was a legal recognition of the diversity that existed among the initial members of Confederation, and manifested a concern to accommodate that diversity within a single nation by granting significant powers to provincial governments. The *Constitution Act, 1867* was an act of nation-building. It was the first step in the transition from colonies separately dependent on the

Imperial Parliament for their governance to a unified and independent political state in which different peoples could resolve their disagreements and work together toward common goals and a common interest. Federalism was the political mechanism by which diversity could be reconciled with unity.

[44] A federal-provincial division of powers necessitated a written constitution which circumscribed the powers of the new Dominion and Provinces of Canada. Despite its federal structure, the new Dominion was to have "a Constitution similar in Principle to that of the United Kingdom" (*Constitution Act, 1867*, preamble). Allowing for the obvious differences between the governance of Canada and the United Kingdom, it was nevertheless thought important to thus emphasize the continuity of constitutional principles, including democratic institutions and the rule of law; and the continuity of the exercise of sovereign power transferred from Westminster to the federal and provincial capitals of Canada.

[45] After 1867, the Canadian federation continued to evolve both territorially and politically. New territories were admitted to the union and new provinces were formed. In 1870, Rupert's Land and the Northwest Territories were admitted and Manitoba was formed as a province. British Columbia was admitted in 1871, Prince Edward Island in 1873, and the Arctic Islands were added in 1880. In 1898, the Yukon Territory and in 1905, the provinces of Alberta and Saskatchewan were formed from the Northwest Territories. Newfoundland was admitted in 1949 by an amendment to the *Constitution Act, 1867.* The new territory of Nunavut was carved out of the Northwest Territories in 1993 with the partition to become effective in April 1999.

[46] Canada's evolution from colony to fully independent state was gradual. The Imperial Parliament's passage of the *Statute of Westminster*, 1931 (U.K.), 22 & 23 Geo. 5, c. 4, confirmed in law what had earlier been confirmed in fact by the *Balfour Declaration* of 1926, namely, that Canada was an independent country. Thereafter, Canadian law alone governed in Canada, except where Canada expressly consented to the continued application of Imperial legislation. Canada's independence from Britain was achieved through legal and political evolution with an adherence to the rule of law and stability. The proclamation of the *Constitution Act, 1982* removed the last vestige of British authority over the Canadian Constitution and re-affirmed Canada's commitment to the protection of its minority, aboriginal, equality, legal and language rights, and fundamental freedoms as set out in the *Canadian Charter of Rights and Freedoms.*

(e) The *Constitution Act, 1867*: Division of Powers†

An Act for the Union of Canada, Nova Scotia, and New Brunswick, and the Government thereof; and for Purposes connected therewith.

PREAMBLE

Whereas the Provinces of Canada, Nova Scotia, and New Brunswick have expressed their Desire to be federally united into One Dominion under the Crown of the United Kingdom of Great Britain and Ireland, with a Constitution similar in Principle to that of the United Kingdom:

And whereas such a Union would conduce to the Welfare of the Provinces and promote the Interests of the British Empire:

And whereas on the Establishment of the Union by Authority of Parliament it is expedient, not only that the Constitution of the Legislative Authority in the Dominion be provided for, but also that the Nature of the Executive Government therein be declared:

And whereas it is expedient that Provision be made for the eventual Admission into the Union of other Parts of British North America:

. . . .

---

† (U.K.) 30 & 31 Vict., c. 3. Enacted on 29 March 1867; proclaimed on 1 July 1867.

LEGISLATIVE AUTHORITY OF PARLIAMENT OF CANADA

91. It shall be lawful for the Queen, by and with the Advice and Consent of the Senate and House of Commons, to make Laws for the Peace, Order, and good Government of Canada, in relation to all Matters not coming within the Classes of Subjects by this Act assigned exclusively to the Legislatures of the Provinces; and for greater Certainty, but not so as to restrict the Generality of the foregoing Terms of this Section, it is hereby declared that (notwithstanding anything in this Act) the exclusive Legislative Authority of the Parliament of Canada extends to all Matters coming within the Classes of Subjects next hereinafter enumerated; that is to say, —

1. [NOTE: Repealed by the *Constitution Act, 1982,* Schedule, Item 1].
1A. The Public Debt and Property.
    [NOTE: Re-numbered 1A by the *Constitution Act, 1949*].
2. The Regulation of Trade and Commerce.
2A. Unemployment insurance.
    [NOTE: Added by the *Constitution Act, 1940*]
3. The raising of Money by any Mode or System of Taxation.
4. The borrowing of Money on the Public Credit.
5. Postal Service.
6. The Census and Statistics.
7. Militia, Military and Naval Service, and Defence.
8. The fixing of and providing for the Salaries and Allowances of Civil and other Officers of the Government of Canada.
9. Beacons, Buoys, Lighthouses, and Sable Island.
10. Navigation and Shipping.
11. Quarantine and the Establishment and Maintenance of Marine Hospitals.
12. Sea Coast and Inland Fisheries.
13. Ferries between a Province and any British or Foreign Country or between Two Provinces.
14. Currency and Coinage.
15. Banking, Incorporation of Banks, and the Issue of Paper Money.
16. Savings Banks.
17. Weights and Measures.
18. Bills of Exchange and Promissory Notes.
19. Interest.
20. Legal Tender.
21. Bankruptcy and Insolvency.
22. Patents of Invention and Discovery.
23. Copyrights.
24. Indians, and Lands reserved for the Indians.
25. Naturalization and Aliens.
26. Marriage and Divorce.
27. The Criminal Law, except the Constitution of Courts of Criminal Jurisdiction, but including the Procedure in Criminal Matters.
28. The Establishment, Maintenance, and Management of Penitentiaries.
29. Such Classes of Subjects as are expressly excepted in the Enumeration of the Classes of Subjects by this Act assigned exclusively to the Legislatures of the Provinces.

And any Matter coming within any of the Classes of Subjects enumerated in this Section shall not be deemed to come within the Class of Matters of a local or private Nature comprised in the Enumeration of the Classes of Subjects by this Act assigned exclusively to the Legislatures of the Provinces.

SUBJECTS OF EXCLUSIVE PROVINCIAL LEGISLATION

92. In each Province the Legislature may exclusively make Laws in relation to Matters coming within the Classes of Subjects next hereinafter enumerated; that is to say, —

1. [NOTE: Repealed by the *Constitution Act, 1982,* Schedule, Item 1]
2. Direct Taxation within the Province in order to the raising of a Revenue for Provincial Purposes.
3. The borrowing of Money on the sole Credit of the Province.
4. The Establishment and Tenure of Provincial Offices and the Appointment and Payment of Provincial Officers.
5. The Management and Sale of the Public Lands belonging to the Province and of the Timber and Wood thereon.
6. The Establishment, Maintenance, and Management of Public and Reformatory Prisons in and for the Province.
7. The Establishment, Maintenance, and Management of Hospitals, Asylums, Charities, and Eleemosynary Institutions in and for the Province, other than Marine Hospitals.
8. Municipal Institutions in the Province.
9. Shop, Saloon, Tavern, Auctioneer, and other Licences in order to the raising of a Revenue for Provincial, Local, or Municipal Purposes.
10. Local Works and Undertakings other than such as are of the following Classes: —

(a) Lines of Steam or other Ships, Railways, Canals, Telegraphs, and other Works and Undertakings connecting the Province with any other or others of the Provinces, or extending beyond the Limits of the Province:

(b) Lines of Steam Ships between the Province and any British or Foreign Country:

(c) Such Works as, although wholly situate within the Province, are before or after their Execution declared by the Parliament of Canada to be for the general Advantage of Canada or for the Advantage of Two or more of the Provinces.

11. The Incorporation of Companies with Provincial Objects.
12. The Solemnization of Marriage in the Province.
13. Property and Civil Rights in the Province.
14. The Administration of Justice in the Province, including the Constitution, Maintenance, and Organization of Provincial Courts, both of Civil and of Criminal Jurisdiction, and including Procedure in Civil Matters in those Courts.
15. The Imposition of Punishment by Fine, Penalty, or Imprisonment for enforcing any Law of the Province made in relation to any Matter coming within any of the Classes of Subjects enumerated in this Section.
16. Generally all Matters of a merely local or private Nature in the Province.

· · · ·

[Section 92A, added by s. 50 of the *Constitution Act, 1982*, amplifies provincial legislative jurisdiction over provincial non-renewable natural resources, forestry, and electrical energy. It enables them to control the export of these resources to other parts of Canada and to tax the resources directly or indirectly, regardless of how much is exported. However, this provincial legislation must not be inconsistent with valid federal legislation on interprovincial trade, and neither the export nor the tax legislation may discriminate against other parts of Canada.]

· · · ·

LEGISLATION RESPECTING EDUCATION

93. In and for each Province the Legislature may exclusively make Laws in relation to Education, subject and according to the following Provisions:—

(1) Nothing in any such Law shall prejudicially affect any Right or Privilege with respect to Denominational Schools which any Class of Persons have by Law in the Province at the Union:

(2) All the Powers, Privileges, and Duties at the Union by Law conferred and imposed in Upper Canada on the Separate Schools and School Trustees of the Queen's Roman Catholic Subjects shall be and the same are hereby extended to the Dissentient Schools of the Queen's Protestant and Roman Catholic Subjects in Quebec:

(3) Where in any Province a System of Separate or Dissentient Schools exists by Law at the Union or is thereafter established by the Legislature of the Province, an Appeal shall lie to the Governor General in Council from any Act or Decision of any Provincial Authority affecting any Right or Privilege of the Protestant or Roman Catholic Minority of the Queen's Subjects in relation to Education:

(4) In case any such Provincial Law as from Time to Time seems to the Governor General in Council requisite for the due Execution of the Provisions of this Section is not made, or in case any Decision of the Governor General in Council on any Appeal under this Section is not duly executed by the proper Provincial Authority in that Behalf, then and in every such Case, and as far only as the Circumstances of each Case require, the Parliament of Canada may make remedial Laws for the due Execution of the Provisions of this Section and of any Decision of the Governor General in Council under this Section.

[NOTE: Altered for Manitoba by s. 22 of the *Manitoba Act, 1870*, 33 Vict., c. 3 (Canada) (No. 8 *infra*) (confirmed by the *British North America Act, 1871*); for Alberta by s. 17 of the *Alberta Act*, 4–5 Edw. VII, c. 3 (Canada) (No. 19 *infra*); for Saskatchewan, by s. 17 of the *Saskatchewan Act*, 4–5 Edw. VII, c. 42 (Canada) (No. 20 *infra*); and for Newfoundland by Term 17 of the Terms of Union of Newfoundland with Canada, confirmed by the *British North America Act, 1949*, 12–13 Geo. VI, c. 22 (U.K.) (No. 30 *infra*).]

· · · ·

LEGISLATION RESPECTING OLD AGE PENSIONS AND SUPPLEMENTARY BENEFITS

94A. The Parliament of Canada may make laws in relation to old age pensions and supplementary benefits, including survivors' and disability benefits irrespective of age, but no such law shall affect the operation of any law present or future of a provincial legislature in relation to any such matter.

[NOTE: Substituted by the *British North America Act, 1964*, 12–13 Eliz. II, c. 73 (U.K.) (No. 37 *infra*) for s. 94A which was originally added by the *British North America Act, 1951*, 14–15 Geo. VI, c. 32 (U.K.) (No. 33 *infra*).]

CONCURRENT POWERS OF LEGISLATION RESPECTING AGRICULTURE, ETC.

95. In each Province the Legislature may make Laws in relation to Agriculture in the Province, and to Immigration into the Province; and it is hereby declared that the Parliament of Canada may from Time to Time make Laws in relation to Agriculture in all or any of the Provinces, and to Immigration into all or any of the Provinces; and any Law of the Legislature of a Province relative to Agriculture or to Immigration shall have effect in and for the Province as long and as far only as it is not repugnant to any Act of the Parliament of Canada.

APPOINTMENT OF JUDGES

96. The Governor General shall appoint the Judges of the Superior, District, and County Courts in each Province, except those of the Courts of Probate in Nova Scotia and New Brunswick.

. . . .

TENURE OF OFFICE OF JUDGES

99.(1) Subject to subsection (2) of this section, the judges of the superior courts shall hold office during good behaviour, but shall be removable by the Governor General on address of the Senate and House of Commons.

(2) A judge of a superior court, whether appointed before or after the coming into force of this section, shall cease to hold office upon attaining the age of seventy-five years, or upon the coming into force of this section if at that time he has already attained that age.

[NOTE: Section 99 is a new section enacted by the *British North America Act, 1960*, 9 Eliz. II, c. 2 (U.K.) (No. 36 *infra*).]

SALARIES, ETC., OF JUDGES

100. The Salaries, Allowances, and Pensions of the Judges of the Superior, District, and County Courts (except the Courts of Probate in Nova Scotia and New Brunswick), and of the Admiralty Courts in Cases where the Judges thereof are for the Time being paid by Salary, shall be fixed and provided by the Parliament of Canada.

GENERAL COURT OF APPEAL, ETC.

101. The Parliament of Canada may, notwithstanding anything in this Act, from Time to Time provide for the Constitution, Maintenance, and Organization of a General Court of Appeal for Canada, and for the Establishment of any additional Courts for the better Administration of the Laws of Canada.

. . . .

PROPERTY IN LANDS, MINES, ETC.

109. All Lands, Mines, Minerals, and Royalties belonging to the several Provinces of Canada, Nova Scotia, and New Brunswick at the Union, and all Sums then due or payable for such Lands, Mines, Minerals, or Royalties, shall belong to the several Provinces of Ontario, Quebec, Nova Scotia, and New Brunswick in which the same are situate or arise, subject to any Trusts existing in respect thereof, and to any Interest other than that of the Province in the same.

[NOTE: The Provinces of Manitoba, British Columbia, Alberta, and Saskatchewan were placed in the same position as the original provinces by the *British North America Act, 1930*, 21 Geo. V, c. 26 (U.K.), (No. 25 *infra*).

Newfoundland was also placed in the same position by the *British North America Act, 1949*, 12–13 Geo. VI, c. 22 (U.K.) (No. 30 *infra*).

With respect to Prince Edward Island, see the Schedule to the Order of Her Majesty in Council admitting Prince Edward Island into the Union (No. 12 *infra*).]

. . . .

CANADIAN MANUFACTURERS, ETC.

121. All Articles of the Growth, Produce, or Manufacture of any one of the Provinces shall, from and after the Union, be admitted free into each of the other Provinces.

. . . .

TREATY OBLIGATIONS

132. The Parliament and Government of Canada shall have all Powers necessary or proper for performing the Obligations of Canada or of any Province thereof, as Part of the British Empire, towards Foreign Countries, arising under Treaties between the Empire and such Foreign Countries.

. . . .

[NOTE: The Act as a whole can be found in Cheffins, at 155–216 (with all schedules); Hogg 2007, Appendix I (third and sixth schedules only, omits some sections of text); Reesor, Appendix A (no schedules).]

(f) Canadian Federalism, the Privy Council and the Supreme Court: Reflections on the Debate About Canadian Federalism[†]

Peter W. Hogg and Wade K. Wright

NOTE

Hogg and Wright suggest that academic commentary in Canada has been divided as to whether those who agreed to the *Constitution Act, 1867* intended a centralized or decentralized form of federal system. This kind of divergence of views is relevant to how one appraises the role of the Judicial Committee. If, for example, the Judicial Committee applied a decentralist approach to a highly centralist constitution, this might be grounds for criticism. Conversely, if it were accurately interpreting the decentralist intent of the framers, this might be grounds for praise. Beyond this, the framers' intent is at least one factor — among others — that is relevant to the meaning courts give to the *Constitution Act, 1867.*

In the McInnis extract earlier in this chapter, we saw that there were both centralist and decentralist pressures on the framers of Confederation before 1867. Military, trade, transportation, and diplomatic considerations pointed toward unification, and toward a relatively centralized form of union. On the other hand, there were strong cultural, historic, and administrative pressures that pushed against a centralized union.

Given this context, is it surprising that a federal form of union was chosen? As the Supreme Court of Canada observed in the *Quebec Secession Reference*, "[w]ithout it, neither the agreement of the delegates from Canada East nor that of the delegates from the maritime colonies would have been obtained." Similarly, it would not be surprising if there were both centralist and decentralist elements in the Confederation document itself.

This is what Hogg and Wright conclude. Indeed, they say that the *Constitution Act, 1867* was ambiguous about centralization or decentralization — "probably deliberately so" — in order to secure support from Confederation from a number of very diverse groups.

Do you agree? In their examples of centralist elements, do Hogg and Wright tend to neglect one of the most important of all, the federal paramountcy provision ("Notwithstanding anything in this Act") in s. 91? Is it significant whether ss. 91 and 92 contain one residual provision (the general Peace, Order and good Government power) or two (the POGG power plus s. 92(16))? Conversely, where Hogg and Wright look at decentralist elements, should they have stressed that in s. 109 and related provisions, the framers

---

[†] (2005) 38 U.B.C. L. Rev. 329 at 330–36, 338–47. [Notes omitted.] Reproduced with permission.

allocated the lion's share of ownership of natural resources to the provinces?

EXTRACT

Academic writing about the original intentions of the framers of the *Constitution Act*, 1867 can be divided, roughly, into two groups.[6] The first group, largely dominated by English-speaking academics from central Canada, suggests that the framers of the *Act* intended Canada to be a highly centralized federal system.[7] The second group, largely dominated by French-speaking academics from Quebec, suggests that the framers of the *Constitution Act*, 1867 intended Canada to be a loose confederacy of largely independent provinces.[8]

There are a number of explanations for these differences in opinion. The first is that much will hinge, as Mr. Justice Ian Binnie recently noted, on whom we regard as the framers of the Act.[9] If, for example, only Sir John A. Macdonald and the other English-Canadian federalists are regarded as the framers, the conclusion that will inevitably follow is that the framers intended Canada to be highly centralized.[10] On the other hand, if only the provincial politicians from Quebec and the Maritimes are regarded as the framers, the conclusion that will inevitably follow is that the framers intended Canada to be highly decentralized.

The second explanation is that the historical record is weak, making it difficult to determine, definitively, the intentions of any of the framers. There are no verbatim records of the discussions at the confederation conferences held at Charlottetown (1864), Quebec City (1864), and London, England (1866). Further, of the three uniting provinces (the united province of Canada, Nova Scotia and New Brunswick), the legislative assemblies of two of those provinces (Nova Scotia and New Brunswick) did not hold confederation debates. The Parliament of the United Kingdom debated the bill that was finally drafted in London, and that debate is recorded in Hansard. The result is that we have an incomplete historical record, consisting of only: the text of the 72 Quebec City resolutions; the text of the 69 London resolutions; the confederation debates in the legislative assembly of the united province of Canada (1865); and the confederation debates in the Parliament of the United Kingdom (1867).[11]

Not surprisingly, this led Alan Cairns to question whether "... the pursuit of the real meaning of the [*Constitution Act*, 1867] is ... a meaningless game, incapable of a decisive outcome."[12] Although there is

some force to that claim, in our view, there can be little doubt that the framers of the Act were divided, some intending Canada to be highly centralized, and others intending Canada to be a loose confederacy of largely independent provinces.[13]

The view that the framers were sharply divided on the appropriate degree of centralization or decentralization is more realistic than the competing theories that attribute an exclusively centralist or decentralist impulse to the framers. It accords with the historical context in which the *Constitution Act*, 1867[14] was drafted — the framers of the *Act* were required to accommodate two conflicting desiderata. On the one hand, English-Canadian politicians from central Canada, admiring the highly centralized form of government in the United Kingdom, and knowing that the principle of representation by population would give them control over the new Parliament of Canada, preferred a strong central government. This centralizing impulse was reinforced by the aftermath of the American Civil War, one cause of which was widely held to be the granting of excessive powers to the states by the United States Constitution. On the other hand, French-Canadian politicians were acutely aware that they would be a minority in the new Parliament of Canada, but also that they would control the Legislature of the new province of Quebec. Thus, they insisted that the provincial Legislature be vested with enough power to safeguard the French language and culture, the civil law, and the Roman Catholic religion of Quebec. Similarly fearful for their local traditions and institutions, and protective of their independence, the politicians from New Brunswick, Nova Scotia and Prince Edward Island also insisted that their legislatures be vested with enough power to regulate the daily life of the people, as they had been doing before confederation.

Considered against this historical backdrop, it is hardly surprising that those favouring a centralist interpretation of the *Constitution Act*, 1867 and those favouring a decentralist interpretation of the Act have been able to locate evidence to support their respective positions. G. P. de T. Glazebrook's suggestion that "... particular interpretations and points of view were rationalized by tailored versions of the constitution"[15] seems apposite. But, like Lysyk, we believe that these exclusively centralist or decentralist interpretations of the framers' intentions fail to acknowledge that "... the architects of our Constitution were far from unanimous in their stated objectives ... ".[16]

III. AS DRAFTED, DOES THE *CONSTITUTION ACT*, 1867 INDICATE THAT IT WAS INTENDED TO FORM THE FOUNDATION FOR A HIGHLY CENTRALIZED OR HIGHLY DECENTRALIZED FEDERAL SYSTEM?

As drafted, the *Constitution Act*, 1867[17] contains a number of features that indicate that it was intended to form the foundation for a highly centralized federal system. The first indication is that the *Act* subordinated the provinces to the federal government or the federal Parliament, in the following five respects: First, by section 90, the federal government was given the power to disallow (invalidate) provincial statutes. Second, by section 58, the federal government was given the power to appoint the Lieutenant Governor of each province (and, by section 92(1), the provinces were denied the power to alter that part of their constitutions). Third, by section 96, the federal government was given the power to appoint the judges of the superior, district and county courts of each province. Fourth, by section 93, the federal government was given the power to determine appeals from provincial decisions affecting minority education rights, and the federal Parliament was given the power to enforce a decision on appeal by the enactment of "remedial laws". Fifth, by sections 91(29) and 92(10)(c), the federal Parliament was given the unilateral power to bring local works within exclusive federal legislative jurisdiction by declaring them to be "for the general advantage of Canada".

The second indication that the *Constitution Act*, 1867 was intended to form the foundation for a highly centralized federal system is that the distribution of powers in the *Act* is, in the following three respects, more centralized than the distribution of powers in the United States' Constitution — the only useful[18] federal precedent available to the framers in 1867. First, in Canada, the federal Parliament was given the power to regulate "trade and commerce" without qualification, while in the United States, Congress was given the more limited power to regulate "commerce with foreign nations and among the several states and with the Indian tribes".[19] Second, in Canada, the list of specified federal heads of power included several topics left to the states in the United States' Constitution, including banking (section 91(15)), marriage and divorce (section 91(26)), the criminal law (section 91(27)), and penitentiaries (section 91(28)). Third, in Canada, the provincial Legislatures were given only enumerated powers to make laws, leaving the residue of power with the

federal Parliament,[20] while in the United States, residuary power had been left with the states.[21]

The final indication that the *Constitution Act*, 1867[22] was intended to form the foundation for a highly centralized federal system is that the distribution of power was structured to make the federal government fiscally dominant. By section 91(3), the federal government was given the power to levy indirect as well as direct taxes while, by section 92(2), the provinces were given only the authority to levy direct taxes. In 1867, the inability to levy indirect taxes placed serious fiscal restraints on the provinces, because at that time the indirect taxes of the customs and excise accounted for 80 percent of the revenues of the uniting colonies. The framers anticipated the shortfall between provincial revenues and provincial responsibilities, and the *Act* provided for federal grants to the provinces.

For a litany of commentators, these features of the *Constitution Act*, 1867 provide incontrovertible proof that the *Act* was intended to form the foundation for a highly centralized federal system.[23] There are, however, at least two major features of the *Act* that provide support for the opposite view, namely, that the *Act* was intended to form the foundation for a less centralized federal system.

The first such feature is the power, assigned to the provincial Legislatures by section 92(13), to make laws concerning "property and civil rights in the province." Prior to confederation, the phrase "property and civil rights" provided a compendious description of the entire body of private law that governs the relationship between subject and subject, including much of the law relating to property, the family, contracts and torts.[24] For some, including Lysyk, assignment of legislative authority over that broad class of subjects to the provinces is indicative of the intention to draft a document that, at the very least, granted extensive legislative powers to the provinces.[25]

To be sure, the historical definition of property and civil rights underwent some changes in its new context in section 92(13). The enumerated list of federal heads of legislative power in section 91 included a number of matters which would otherwise have come within property and civil rights in the province, for example, trade and commerce (section 91(2)), banking (section 91(15)), bills of exchange and promissory notes (section 91(18)), interest (section 19(19)), bankruptcy and insolvency (section 91(12)), patents of invention and discovery (section 91(22)), copyrights (section 91(23)), and marriage and divorce (section 91(28)). By vesting these matters in the federal Parliament exclusively, the *Act*[26] withdrew them from the rubric of property and civil rights. In addition, the opening language of section 91 (described below) presumably contemplated that certain matters that would have come within property and civil rights could attain such a national dimension as to come within federal competence.[27] But, even after making all required subtractions, the phrase "property and civil rights in the province" was still apt to cover most of the legal relationships between persons, leaving much of the law relating to property, the family, contracts and torts.

The second feature of the *Constitution Act, 1867* that arguably points in the direction of a less centralized federal system is the allocation of the residuary legislative power. The drafting of the residuary power is a triumph of ambiguity and uncertainty, and has remained a central concern of the courts since confederation.

According to the conventional reading of the *Act*, the residuary power was conferred exclusively on the federal Parliament by the introductory words of section 91. These words confer on Parliament the power "to make laws for the peace, order, and good government of Canada, in relation to all matters not coming within the classes of subjects by this Act assigned exclusively to the Legislatures of the provinces." According to this reading, of course, the assignment of the residuary power indicates a centralized model of federalism.

However, according to another (less conventional) reading of the *Constitution Act, 1867*,[28] it [contains] not one residuary power, but two complementary grants of power that distribute the residue between the federal Parliament *and* the provincial Legislatures.

.   .   .   .

[Hogg and Wright note that the federal residuary power to make laws for the Peace, Order, and good Government of Canada is accompanied by a provincial residuary power in s. 92(16). Following an earlier analysis in Kenneth M. Lysyk, "Constitutional Reform and the Introductory Clause of Section 91: Residual and Emergency Law-Making Authority" (1979) 57 Can. Bar Rev. 531 and Kenneth M. Lysyk, "Reshaping Canadian Federalism" (1979) 13 U.B.C. L. Rev. 1, they say that for an issue that does not come under the enumerated heads of power, the relevant question is "whether the matter is 'of a merely local or private nature', failing which it falls within federal jurisdiction." They conclude that this broad residual clause provides additional evidence of a decentralist intent. But if a

power is residual, its significance depends on the scope of the more specific categories it is supposed to complete. Hence, if the federal enumerated categories were extremely wide, they would leave little room for any residual power, federal or provincial.]

Of course, a good deal of water has flowed under the bridge since 1867, and these debates do not have much present practical significance. In practice, the provincial "residuary power" in section 92(16) has turned out to be relatively unimportant, because the wide scope of the "property and civil rights" power in section 92(13) has left little in the way of a residue of "merely local or private" matters. Indeed, at the hands of the Privy Council, the "property and civil rights" power became a kind of residuary power in its own right. Furthermore, a cluster of doctrine has now become embedded on the federal residuary power, authorizing laws to fill gaps, laws to deal with national emergencies, and laws to deal with matters of "national concern". But these outcomes are not inconsistent with the basic scheme elaborated by Lysyk — and of course he was well aware of the post-1867 developments. For our purposes, the important point is this: there is a plausible argument that the *Constitution Act, 1867*[38] includes not one, but two complementary residuary powers. This argument, in turn, strengthens the view that the *Act*, as drafted, was intended to form the foundation for a federal system that is less centralized than many English-Canadian commentators have supposed.

Our conclusion is that the *Constitution Act, 1867* includes conflicting signals as to the degree of centralization or decentralization stipulated by the federal scheme that the *Act* established. In our view, the framers deliberately tolerated these conflicting signals in the *Act* because they needed to accommodate conflicting goals — the desire for a strong central government (English-Canada) and the desire to protect local languages, cultures, and institutions (French-Canada and the Maritimes). The text is ambiguous, probably intentionally so.

The framers of the Constitution needed these conflicting signals in order to ensure approval of their handiwork by the British North American colonists, who were divided by language, religion, tradition, and location. In fact, the ambiguities helped the scheme to win immediate approval in both Canada West (Ontario) and Canada East (Quebec) and in two of the Maritime provinces (Nova Scotia and New Brunswick). Moreover, over the years the *Act*, without significant amendment, has proved capable of accommodating — in a federal union of ten provinces and three territories — most of the northern part of North America from the Atlantic to the Pacific Ocean. This expansion was one of the original goals of the *Act*, which made provision for other colonies to adhere to the scheme (and for territories to be created into provinces), and for railways to run across the continent. The difficulties of interpretation and finding a degree of centralization acceptable to all were left to be settled later, either by political practice (as in the case of the federal-provincial financial arrangements) or by the decisions of the courts (which at the time meant the Privy Council, which remained the final court of appeal for Canada until 1949).

[Hogg and Wright feel that the Judicial Committee's restrictive approach to federal powers such as Peace, Order and good Government and Trade and Commerce did derive in part from a provincial bias. However, they also note that the text of the *Constitution Act, 1867* is not unambiguously centralist, that not all economic and social considerations pointed toward centralism, and that the Judicial Committee's approach was consistent with the diversity of the country as a whole and the special situation in Quebec. They conclude (at page 347) that "although the Privy Council did favour the provinces, and perhaps more by accident rather than design, Canada was, on the whole, not badly served by the Privy Council." They go on to argue that in more recent times, the Supreme Court of Canada has provided a mild but not extreme corrective to the more excessive pro-provincial rulings of the Judicial Committee.]

4

The Judiciary

(a) Introduction

The question of the Judicial Committee's approach to the division of legislative powers involves not only Canadian federalism, but also an important branch of government, the judiciary. Before we consider the role of the judiciary in specific federalism and other constitutional cases, it is useful to look at this institution in more detail.

Our key concerns are: (i) What does the judiciary do? (ii) What is its constitutional framework, and how is it organized? (iii) How active a role should the judiciary play in regard to the Canadian federal system? This last concern is an aspect of the general question: how active a role should the judiciary play in Canadian public law?

(b) Aspects of the Judiciary[1]

FUNCTIONS[2]

The judiciary is the branch of government whose characteristic functions are to resolve disputes according to law and to interpret and develop the law. Note the word "characteristic" here. Each of the three branches of government has functions that overlap with those of the others. Judges, for example, often perform other tasks as well. Moreover, the Supreme Court of Canada has a wide discretion to decide which cases to hear, and establishes the law for all other courts. It engages in a significant amount of law-making as well as law-interpreting. Other courts make law too. All judges face policy choices and questions of value, and establish new norms, in the very process of selecting and applying formal rules.[3] The broader and more indeterminate the rules, the greater the room for policy, values, and law-making. In the constitutional field, courts sometimes find themselves working outside even the outer

bounds of law. See, for example, the *Constitutional Amendment Reference*[4] in Chapter 9 below. Consider what functions courts say they are performing — and are, in fact, performing — in the cases in this sourcebook.

FEATURES

Generally speaking, the judiciary is set up to provide:

- **F**air procedure and reconsideration;
- **A**uthoritative, enforceable, decisive results;
- **I**ndependent and impartial decision-making; and
- **R**ule-oriented decisions.

At the same time, these positive features involve a number of characteristic weaknesses. The judiciary tends to be:

- **S**low, formal, and expensive, with limited evidentiary scope;

- **L**egal reasoning limited by precedent and *ex post facto* problem-solving;
- **O**utside electoral controls; and
- **W**inner-loser oriented, with limited capacity for compromise.

Many of these strengths and weaknesses come as a "package deal". Procedural safeguards and appeals add to cost and formality. Decisive results allow less room for bargaining and compromise. Judicial independence militates against political accountability. Consistency through rules reduces the flexibility to plan for future contingencies. These constraints make it difficult to minimize the characteristic weaknesses of the judiciary without threatening its strengths at the same time. Nonetheless, these features can be useful in helping assess the ongoing question of how actively courts should exercise their functions. Once again, we should note the word "characteristic". Neither all the strengths nor the weaknesses are inevitably present in every situation.

BACKGROUND AND EARLY STRUCTURES

Pre-Confederation Canadian Courts[5]

Recall that the *Constitution Act, 1867*[6] provided for "a Constitution similar in principle to that of the United Kingdom." For the judiciary, this suggested that the principles of judicial independence[7] and impartiality,[8] the rule of law,[9] the system of precedent,[10] the division between inferior and superior courts,[11] and the hierarchy of appeals would be imported into Canada. Indeed, the local courts in the colonies immediately before Confederation had powers and functions roughly similar to those in Britain.[12] The courts at the top of the local hierarchies, the superior courts, were expressly given the general powers of the High Court in England. These local courts and powers were continued by s. 129 of the *Constitution Act, 1867*.[13]

Judicial Committee of the Privy Council[14]

Another institution that was also part of the court structures from early times was based outside Canada. Until the middle of the 20th century, the highest judicial body for this country was the Judicial Committee of the Privy Council, a tribunal that is not technically a court and is located in London, England. Although the Privy Council no longer hears Canadian cases and has only limited jurisdiction elsewhere, this was once the highest appellate tribunal for the world's largest empire.

The Judicial Committee is a committee of the British Privy Council that tenders legal advice to Her Majesty the Queen. Its members are normally drawn from the senior English judiciary, especially the Lords of Appeal in Ordinary (law lords) in the House of Lords. It generally sits in five-person boards. Although its decisions are technically only "advice", they are treated as binding law in the jurisdictions they affect. Although it is not technically governed by precedent, the Judicial Committee generally follows its own earlier decisions.[15] Before 1966, it did not permit dissenting reasons.

The Privy Council's role in advising the monarch on appeals from the colonies goes back many centuries. Originally based only on the royal prerogative, the Judicial Committee's appellate powers were stated in British statutes in 1833 and 1844.[16] In 1865, these powers were reinforced by the *Colonial Laws Validity Act*,[17] which made it clear that any colonial law that was inconsistent with a British statute was void.

When the *Constitution Act, 1867* was enacted, the Judicial Committee was already established as the highest appellate court for Canada. It had this role until appeals were abolished in 1949,[18] during the crucial formative years of Confederation. That is why many of the important constitutional decisions in the next few chapters were decisions of the Privy Council.

CONSTITUTIONAL FRAMEWORK

The following are some of the main provisions of the *Constitution Act, 1867* that relate to the Canadian judiciary today:[19]

> 92. In each Province the Legislature may exclusively make Laws in relation to Matters coming within the Classes of Subjects next herein-after enumerated; that is to say, —

> . . . .

> 14. The Administration of Justice in the Province, including the Constitution, Maintenance, and Organization of Provincial Courts, both of Civil and of Criminal Jurisdiction, and including Procedure in Civil Matters in those Courts.

. . . .

96. The Governor General shall appoint the Judges of the Superior, District, and County Courts in each Province, except those of the Courts of Probate in Nova Scotia and New Brunswick.

97. Until the laws relative to Property and Civil Rights in Ontario, Nova Scotia, and New Brunswick, and the Procedure of the Courts in those Provinces, are made uniform, the Judges of the Courts of those Provinces appointed by the Governor General shall be secured from the respective Bars of those Provinces.

98. The Judges of the Courts of Quebec shall be selected from the Bar of that Province.

99.(1) Subject to subsection (2) of this section, the judges of the superior courts shall hold office during good behaviour, but shall be removable by the Governor General on address of the Senate and House of Commons.

(2) A judge of a superior court, whether appointed before or after the coming into force of this section, shall cease to hold office upon attaining the age of seventy-five years, or upon the coming into force of this section if at that time he has already attained that age.

100. The Salaries, Allowances, and Pensions of the Judges of the Superior, District, and County Courts (except the Courts of Probate in Nova Scotia and New Brunswick), and of the Admiralty Courts in Cases where the Judges thereof are for the Time being paid by Salary, shall be fixed and provided by the Parliament of Canada.

101. The Parliament of Canada may, notwithstanding anything in this Act, from Time to Time provide for the Constitution, Maintenance, and Organization of a General Court of Appeal for Canada, and for the Establishment of any additional Courts for the better Administration of the Laws of Canada.

The general effect of these constitutional provisions is as follows. The *Constitution Act, 1867* gives the provincial legislatures power over the administration of justice within their boundaries.[20] This power includes the creation and administration of criminal and civil courts, and civil procedure. As a result, one can speak of 10 different "provincial" court structures, and three more in the territories.[21] However, Parliament has jurisdiction over the criminal procedure of these provincial and territorial courts.[22] As well, the federal government has the exclusive power to appoint, dismiss, and pay the salaries of judges of superior,[23] district, and county courts, including those in the provincial and territorial courts.[24] Beyond this, Parliament has power to create and maintain "a General Court of Appeal for Canada" and "any additional Courts for the better Administration of the Laws of Canada."[25] Acting under this power, Parliament created the Supreme Court of Canada[26] in 1875. It has also created the Federal Court and the Federal Court of Appeal,[27] the Court Martial Appeal Court,[28] and the Tax Court of Canada.[29]

The courts, which are subject to this framework, are part of a system that is hierarchical and, in many ways, unitary. Appeals (applications for reconsideration of a decision) from all parts of the system can lead — potentially — to a decision by the single final court of appeal for the entire country, the Supreme Court of Canada. For example, in Ontario, in some cases a decision of the Ontario Court of Justice can be appealed to the Divisional Court branch of the Ontario Superior Court of Justice. The latter's decision can then be appealed in some cases to the Ontario Court of Appeal, whose decision can be appealed in some cases (and if one's money lasts!) to the Supreme Court of Canada.

On the other hand, the division of constitutional responsibility imposed by the federal system has resulted, in effect, in four different categories of judiciary:

1. *The lower provincial judiciary*, who interpret federal and provincial laws, are administered by the province, and whose judges are appointed and paid by the province. Example: Provincial Court judges (formerly called magistrates in many jurisdictions).[30]
2. *The higher provincial judiciary*, who interpret federal and provincial laws, are administered by the province, and whose judges are appointed and paid by the federal government. Examples: the British Columbia Supreme Court (the trial level superior court for that province) and the British Columbia Court of Appeal (the appeal level superior court for that province).
3. *The federal judiciary*, who interpret federal laws only, are administered by the federal government, and whose judges are appointed and paid by the federal government. Main example: the Federal Court of Canada.

4. *The Supreme Court of Canada*, which interprets federal and provincial laws, is administered by the federal government, and whose judges are appointed and paid by the federal government.

THE SUPREME COURT OF CANADA[31]

Structure, Powers, and Composition

It is now over 50 years since the abolition of appeals to the Judicial Committee, which resulted in the Supreme Court of Canada becoming our highest appellate court. Although its enabling act is an ordinary statute, the Supreme Court has some indirect constitutional protection in the *Constitution Act, 1982*.[32] Section 41(d) of the latter Act provides that an amendment to the Constitution of Canada in relation to the composition of the Supreme Court of Canada can only be made where authorized by resolutions of the Senate and House of Commons, and of the legislative assemblies of all 10 provinces. Section 42(1) provides that other constitutional amendments in relation to the Supreme Court require resolutions of the Senate and House of Commons, and of the legislative assemblies of at least two-thirds of the provinces that have at least 50% of the combined provincial population.

The Supreme Court's power and importance derive from a number of factors. First, unlike that of the Supreme Court of the United States, the Supreme Court's appellate jurisdiction is not restricted to federal and constitutional issues — it is virtually unrestricted. The Court can hear appeals[33] involving federal and provincial law, civil and common law, and constitutional and non-constitutional matters.[34] It hears appeals from the Federal Court of Canada, the Court Martial Appeal Court, and the 13 provincial and territorial appellate courts. Second, since 1949 the Supreme Court has exercised a legal umpire role unique to federal states.[35] Third, since 1975, the Supreme Court has had an expanded discretion to select the cases it will decide.[36] Very little of its appellate jurisdiction is automatic; most is subject to its own control. Section 40(1) of the *Supreme Court Act* enables the Court to hear a case

> ... where ... the Supreme Court is of the opinion that any question involved therein is, by reason of its public importance or the importance of any issue of law or any issue of mixed law and fact ... one that ought to be decided by the Supreme Court or is, for any other rea-

son, of such a nature or significance as to warrant decision by it....[37]

Fourth, like the Judicial Committee but unlike most courts outside Canada, the Supreme Court has an advisory jurisdiction to hear cases referred to it for advice by the executive branch of government.[38] Matters can be referred to the Court on constitutional or other important legal issues by the federal Governor in Council.

Finally, since 1982, the Supreme Court has had a greatly expanded power to declare a legislation unconstitutional because of any violation of the *Canadian Charter of Rights and Freedoms* and other provisions of the *Constitution Act, 1982*. Clearly, the Court is a force to be reckoned with in Canadian public law.

Appointment, Salaries, Administration, and Removal

The Supreme Court has nine judges, three of whom must come from the Bar of Quebec. As well, by convention, three judges are normally appointed from Ontario, two from the four western provinces, and one from the Atlantic provinces. Also by convention, the Chief Justice usually alternates between a francophone and an anglophone. There are currently four women Supreme Court judges; before 1982 there were none.

Like all other judges, Supreme Court judges must be able to make decisions that are regarded as being as impartial as possible. To this end, the principle of judicial independence requires that judges and courts should be as independent as possible from others, especially Parliament and the executive branch.[39] On the other hand, our elected officials are accountable to the public regarding issues such as the general operation of the system of justice. Thus, issues such as the selection, tenure salaries, and dismissal of judges involve complex trade-offs between the needs of legislative accountability and judicial impartiality.

Who, then, controls the appointment, salaries, administration, and removal of Supreme Court judges?[40] Supreme Court judges are appointed by the Governor General on the advice of the federal Cabinet (usually on the recommendation of the Minister of Justice and the Prime Minister). There is a system of independent screening committees to examine candidates for other federal judicial positions,[41] but these bodies have no role in selecting Supreme Court judges. Nor is there a formal selection role for the provinces, despite the highest court's role as the ultimate legal umpire of federalism. The Meech Lake and Charlottetown Accords of 1990 and 1992 would have required the federal government to choose Supreme Court judges from candidates nominated from the relevant province, but these proposals vanished with the collapse of the accords.[42]

Under the pre-2004 appointment process, the federal justice minister selected candidates for a vacant position on the Supreme Court. The minister would consult privately with the Chief Justice of the Supreme Court, representatives or officials of the Canadian Bar Association, and the chief justice, attorney general, and law societies in the relevant province. The minister then discussed the candidates with the Prime Minister, who would recommend the successful individual to the federal Cabinet.[43] As the Supreme Court's profile and power have grown, so have concerns about the private, discretionary nature of this process.

As a temporary response to public criticism,[44] the federal government modified the selection process in 2004 when two vacancies appeared on the Court. After the traditional closed-door consultation, the Minister of Justice appeared before an ad hoc House of Commons Committee of MPs and legal and judicial representatives to answer questions about two Supreme Court nominees. Questions could not be addressed directly to the candidates, and the committee had no power to veto or even delay appointment. The hearing itself was rushed and superficial, with committee members being informed of the candidates' identity only days before the hearing. Clearly, more effective long-term reforms were needed.[45]

When a vacancy emerged in 2005, the temporary process changed again. In a first stage, the Minister of Justice would consult privately with the legal community and invite public input to identify five to eight names to be submitted to an advisory committee. In stage two, the advisory committee, comprising MPs from the major political parties, a retired judge, and nominees from the provincial Attorney General and bar association from the region concerned, would narrow this list to an unranked short list of three candidates. In stage three, the Prime Minister would select one candidate from this list. In the fourth stage, the Minister of Justice would explain the winning candidate's qualifications to the House of Commons Standing Committee on Justice, Human Rights, Public Safety and Emergency Preparedness.

However, before this process reached stage three, there was a change of government. Incoming Prime Minister Harper agreed to nominate a candidate from the short list, but announced a change to the fourth stage. Before the nomination was confirmed by Cabinet, the successful candidate[46] was required to answer questions in a televised hearing before a second committee comprising the Minister of Justice, MPs from the different parties, and a recognized academic constitutional expert. Committee members were not permitted to ask the candidate about decisions he had given in the past, controversial issues that might come before the Court in the future, and similar matters. The restraints seemed reasonable, and the hearing was relatively informative. On the other hand, as the committee had no power to veto, alter, or delay the Prime Minister's nomination, it was dealing with a fait accompli. This process is assessed in more detail later in this chapter.[47]

As seen in the *Provincial Judges Reference*, discussed later in this chapter,[48] the Canadian judiciary has gone to great lengths to protect judges' salaries from political interference. In response to that reference, the federal government established a Judicial Compensation and Benefits Commission to inquire at least every four years into the adequacy of the salaries and benefits of the federally appointed judiciary, including Supreme Court judges.[49] Government may reject the Commission's advice, but only if it provides rational reasons for doing so.[50] The judiciary itself makes the final decision as to whether reasons are rational. As a result, although judicial independence and impartiality are protected from undue salary pressures from the other branches of government, the mechanism for doing this raises the possibility of bias on the part of the judiciary!

As seen earlier, the Supreme Court of Canada is subject to the general administrative control of the federal government. However, while the general framework of the Supreme Court's operation, such as its budget and the normal requirement of three sessions per year, are set by the executive and legislative branches, the Court itself has control of administrative issues tied directly to its decision-making role, such as specific court sittings and the allocation of judges to specific decisions.

Another key aspect of judicial independence is security of tenure. Supreme Court judges hold office on good behaviour until age 75. Before retirement age, provincial superior court judges and Supreme Court judges cannot be removed except by the Governor General after a joint address of the Senate and House of Commons,[51] and there is comparable protection for Supreme Court judges.[52] As well as these original conditions, there must now be a prior judicial inquiry to determine if there is cause for dismissal, and an opportunity for the judge in question to be heard.[53] For federally appointed judges, the federal government created the Canadian Judicial Council in 1971 to conduct these inquiries. To date, the Council has recommended dismissal in only one case, involving a provincial superior court judge.[54] In two other cases, provincial superior court judges resigned before the end of the inquiry.[55] Since 1867, no Supreme Court of Canada judge — and indeed no other superior court judge in Canada — has been removed by the Governor General after a joint parliamentary address.[56]

Workload

Normally, a case is heard by either five, seven, or all nine Supreme Court judges. Decisions are often not unanimous, with sometimes two or more majority and dissenting judgments. The Supreme Court renders about 100 decisions per year, usually about six months to a year after the hearing. Constitutional cases, especially *Charter* cases, make up a large proportion of the Court's workload.

JUDICIAL ACTIVISM

We are now ready to ask a general question that underlies many of the cases and reforms referred to in this sourcebook — how active a role should the judiciary play in Canadian public law? In particular, how active a role should the courts play in regard to the Canadian federal system and other aspects of our constitutional law?[57]

There are different aspects to the question of judicial activism. Three are of special interest here:

(i) *intervention*: To what extent should a court assess the legality of government action, overturn, block or otherwise counter government action, or reverse a lower court's decision?

(ii) *innovation*: To what extent should a court change the existing case law?

(iii) *contextualism*: To what extent should a court consider matters beyond the strict letter or written text of the law — such as policy considerations of a social, economic, political, and pragmatic nature, and general principles?

Although some factors might suggest activism — or restraint — in all the three areas above, this need not be so.

Judicial activism can also be approached from a variety of general perspectives — philosophically, from the standpoint of the general goals of the state; institutionally, in regard to the structure, strengths and weaknesses of courts and related bodies; functionally, from the perspective of the subject matter in question and the prospects for addressing it elsewhere; and empirically, in terms of the track record of the courts themselves.

Because the general philosophical goals of the state are highly subjective concepts, we would probably look in vain here for absolute, universal, or conclusive answers to the question of judicial activism. As suggested in Chapter 1, there seem to be varying degrees of support in Canada for all major state goals, from protecting collective action, to promoting citizen control, securing private individual or group interests, and achieving equality. Moreover, while judicial activism can often be identified with the goal of protection of individual interests, it can affect other goals as well. For example, *Charter* victories for underrepresented groups may have the effect of broadening and enriching the general base for more traditional citizen control through the parliamentary system. Conversely, in some cases effort spent on active judicial solutions may divert attention and resources from action by elected representatives.

Institutional factors are a very useful part of any study of judicial activism. Relevant factors here are the general structural features of the courts, and the relationship of the courts to the other institutions involved in public law — the legislature and the executive. Some of these structural features were noted above. Note that Canadian courts are non-elected bodies — a feature that carries both advantages and disadvantages. What are the implications of other structural characteristics? What are the possible institutional alternatives to courts in different public law situations?

When considering judicial activism, it is also helpful to examine the functional context in which it is exercised. In public law cases, for example, three situations are common:

(i) division of powers disputes between the federal and provincial levels of government;

(ii) non-federalism constitutional issues, such as those arising under the *Charter*; and

(iii) non-constitutional controversies that generally occur in fields such as administrative law.

The effects of judicial involvement can vary with these contexts. In constitutional division of powers cases, for example, judicial invalidation of a federal statute will usually shift power to provincial legislatures, and *vice versa*. In *Charter* cases, on the other hand, a judicial invalidation does not shift power to another level of government, and may be difficult or impossible to reverse by ordinary statutory means. In sub-constitutional administrative law cases, the situation may be different again. Here a legislature may be able to reverse the effects of judicial intervention by an ordinary statute.

Should courts tread more cautiously where their decisions leave more indelible marks? Or does the fact of constitutional status suggest that an instrument should be interpreted more liberally?

Should division of powers cases be approached differently in this respect from other constitutional cases? For most of its tenure as ultimate constitutional arbiter for Canada, the Judicial Committee seemed to assume that the *Constitution Act, 1867* should be approached in much the same way as an ordinary statute, with emphasis on literal wording and grammatical construction. See, for example, Sir Montague Smith's close analysis of the words and relationship of ss. 91 and 92 in the *Citizens Insurance* case in Chapter 5. On one or two occasions, though, there were arguments for a more activist approach in constitutional cases, even from the Judicial Committee. See, for example, the *Edwards* case in the latter part of this chapter. Compare the approaches in *Citizens Insurance* and *Edwards* with that of the Supreme Court of Canada.

Another aspect of the context is the social or political situation in which an issue arises. In *Edwards*, the court noted that the role of women in public life in 20th-century Canada was far less restricted than it had been when the *Constitution Act, 1867* was enacted. *Quaere*, did social or political factors militate for or against judicial activism in division of powers cases? Would the answer be the same for the Supreme Court of Canada as for the Judicial Committee?

Finally, activism can and should be assessed by looking at the existing record of the courts themselves. We will be doing more of this in the remainder of this sourcebook.

Notes

1. See generally, Dyck, ch. 23; Hogg 2007, chs. 7 and 8; Ian Greene, *The Courts* (Vancouver: UBC Press, 2007); MacIvor, ch. 10; Monahan, ch. 2(D); Malcolmson, ch. 8; Bernard W. Funston & Eugene Meehan, *Canadian Constitutional Law in a Nutshell*, 3d ed. (Scarborough: Carswell, 2003) at 59–61; Statistics Canada, *Profile of Courts in Canada* (Ottawa: Statistics Canada, 1995); W.A. Bogart, *Courts and Country: The Limits of Litigation and the Social and Political Life of Canada* (Toronto: Oxford University Press, 1994); Reesor, at 109–25 and 251–59; Patrick McCormick & Ian Greene, *Judges and Judging: Inside the Canadian Judicial System* (Toronto: James Lorimer and Company, 1990); Peter H. Russell, *The Judiciary in Canada: The Third Branch of Government* (Toronto: McGraw-Hill Ryerson, 1987); Cheffins, ch. 8; James G. Snell & Frederick Vaughan, *The Supreme Court of Canada: History of the Institution* (Toronto: University of Toronto Press, 1985).

2. Bogart, *ibid.*, ch. 3; McCormick & Greene, *ibid.*, ch. 7; Russell, *ibid.*, ch. 1.

3. "... [I]n theory judges are supposed to be settling disputes according to pre-existing law, to be upholding rights and enforcing duties that exist under the law. But the fact remains that judges also shape and develop the law in the very process of settling disputes about it": Russell, *ibid.*, 13.

4. *Re Amendment of Constitution of Canada* (1981), 125 D.L.R. (3d) 1 (S.C.C.).

5. See generally W.R. Lederman, "The Independence of the Judiciary" (1956) 34 Can. Bar Rev. 769 and 1139.

6. 1867 (U.K.), 30 & 31 Vict., c. 3, preamble.

7. This is the principle that a court of law should be free of legislative, executive, or other outside interference, so that its decisions can be as impartial as possible in individual cases. The principle and that of judicial impartiality are guaranteed by s. 10 of the *Constitution Act, 1982*, which provides that "[e]veryone is entitled in full equality to a fair and public hearing by an independent and impartial tribunal, in the determination of his rights and obligations and of any criminal charge against him." Protections of judicial independence include security of tenure, and safeguards against arbitrary interference with judicial administration, pay, and conditions of employment. See generally *McEvoy v. New Brunswick (A.G.)* (1983), 143 D.L.R. (3d) 25 (S.C.C.); *Valente v. Canada* (1986), 24 D.L.R. (4th) 161 (S.C.C.); *R. v. Beauregard* (1986), 30 D.L.R. (4th) 481 (S.C.C.); *R. v. Genereux* (1992), 88 D.L.R. (4th) 110 (S.C.C.).

8. *Ibid.*

9. See the classic formulation in Albert V. Dicey, *An Introduction to the Study of the Law of the Constitution*, 10th ed. (London: Macmillan, 1965 [first ed., 1885; last revision by Dicey, 1915]) at 187–96. For some judicial references to this basic but protean ideal, see *Re Language Rights under Manitoba Act* (1985), 19 D.L.R. (4th) 1, 22–23 (S.C.C.); *MacMillan Bloedel Ltd. v. Simpson*, [1995] 4 S.C.R. 725 at 753.

10. Under this principle, courts are bound by decisions of courts in the same jurisdiction that are above them in the judicial hierarchy, and courts are expected normally to follow their own previous decisions. All lower courts are bound by decisions of the Supreme Court of Canada. See further, G.L. Gall, *The Canadian Legal System*, 4th ed. (Toronto: Carswell, 1995), ch. 10.

11. A "superior" court is one that has unlimited jurisdiction within its judicial boundaries and can make decisions that cannot be reviewed by other courts. A common law superior court is a provincial superior court that inherited the common law attributes of the High Court in Britain, by virtue of s. 129 of the *Constitution Act, 1867*. These attributes include the power to exercise judicial review over all "inferior" courts (including administrative bodies), within these boundaries, unless that power has been successfully excluded by statute.

12. Note, however, that colonial judges did not gain guarantees of security of tenure until about the time of the achievement of responsible government: see W.R. Lederman, "The Independence of the Judiciary" (1956) 34

Can. Bar Rev. 1139. British superior courts benefited much earlier from the *Act of Settlement* (U.K.) 1701, 12 & 13 Wm. III, c. 2, which contains the guarantee that:

> ... after the said limitations shall take effect as aforesaid judges commissions be made *quam diu se bene gesserint* and their salaries ascertained and established but upon the address of both Houses of Parliament it may be lawful to remove them.

13. "Except as otherwise provided by this Act, all Laws in force in Canada, Nova Scotia, or New Brunswick at the Union, and all Courts of Civil and Criminal Jurisdiction, and all legal Commissions, Powers, and Authorities, and all Officers, Judicial, Administrative, and Ministerial, existing therein at the Union, shall continue in Ontario, Quebec, Nova Scotia, and New Brunswick respectively, as if the Union had not been made; subject nevertheless (except with respect to such as are enacted by or exist under Acts of the Parliament of Great Britain or of the Parliament of the United Kingdom of Great Britain and Ireland) to be repealed, abolished, or altered by the Parliament of Canada, or by the Legislature of the respective Province, according to the Authority of the Parliament or of that Legislature under this Act": *Constitution Act, 1867* (U.K.), 30 & 31 Vict., c. 3, s. 129. [The restriction against altering laws enacted by or existing under British statutes was removed by the *Statute of Westminster*, 1931, 22 Geo. V, c. 4 (U.K.).]

14. See generally, Stanley de Smith and Rodney Brazier, *Constitutional and Administrative Law*, 8th ed. (London & New York: Penguin, 1998), ch. 8; P.A. Howell, *The Judicial Committee of the Privy Council, 1833-1876* (Cambridge, Eng.: Cambridge University Press, 1979); B. Hollander, *Colonial Justice; The Unique Achievement of the Privy Council's Committee of Judges* (London: Bowes, 1961); C.G. Pierson, *Canada and the Privy Council* (London: Stevens, 1960).

15. See, for example, *Ontario (A.G.) v. Canada Temperance Federation*, [1946] A.C. 193 (J.C.P.C.), discussed in Chapter 6, below.

16. *Act for the better Administration of Justice in His Majesty's Privy Council* ((1833) 3 & 4 Will. 4, c. 41 (U.K.) and the *Judicial Committee Act*.

17. 28 & 29 Vict., c. 63 (U.K.).

18. Appeals in civil as well as criminal matters were abolished as of December 23, 1949, but cases started earlier than that date could still be appealed to the Judicial Committee. Appeals in criminal matters had been abolished in 1933.

19. See also s. 129 of the *Constitution Act, 1867, supra* note 13; and ss. 41(d) and 42(d) of the *Constitution Act, 1982*, discussed in the section on "Supreme Court of Canada".

20. *Ibid.*, s. 91(14).

21. Note, however, that Parliament has supreme legislative power in relation to territorial court structures by virtue of the *Constitution Act, 1871* (U.K.), 34–35 Vict., c. 28, s. 4.

22. *Constitution Act, 1867*, s. 91(27).

23. *Supra* note 11.

24. *Constitution Act, 1867*, ss. 96, 99 and 100.

25. *Ibid.*, s. 101.

26. *Supreme Court and Exchequer Acts*, S.C. 1875, c. 11; now *Supreme Court Act*, R.S.C. 1985, c. S-6. For the history of the Supreme Court, see Snell & Vaughan, *supra* note 1.

27. *Federal Court Act*, R.S.C. 1985, c. F-7. (On June 2, 2003, the Federal Court and the Federal Court of Appeal replaced the Federal Court of Canada, which had two divisions, the Federal Court Trial Division and the Federal Court of Appeal. The Federal Court of Canada replaced the Exchequer Court in 1971.)

28. *National Defence Act*, R.S.C. 1985, c. N-5, ss. 234–45.

29. *Tax Court of Canada Act*, R.S.C. 1985, c. T-2.

30. There is a comparable division between the lower and upper territorial judiciary of the Yukon and the Northwest Territories. In Nunavut, however, the functions of both the lower and upper territorial courts are handled by the Nunavut Court of Justice, a body with the status of a superior court.

31. Katherine E. Swinton, *The Supreme Court and Canadian Federalism: The Laskin-Dickson Years* (Toronto: Carswell, 1990); Canadian Bar Association Committee on the Supreme Court of Canada, *Report of the Canadian Bar Association Committee on the Supreme Court of Canada* (Ottawa: Canadian Bar Association, 1987); Snell & Vaughan, *supra* note 1; Paul C. Weiler, *In the Last Resort: A Critical Study of the Supreme Court of Canada* (Toronto: Carswell, 1974).

32. Schedule B to the *Canada Act, 1982* (U.K.), 1982, c. 11.

33. One of the most important avenues of appeal is through the Court's discretion to grant leave to appeal for questions of public or legal importance. Appeals are also available, *inter alia*: (i) with leave, in criminal summary conviction cases (*Supreme Court Act*, s. 40(3)) and in criminal indictable offence cases where there has been no dissenting opinion on a question of law (*Criminal Code*, R.S.C. 1985, c. C-46, Part XXI); (ii) without leave, in criminal indictable offence cases, where there has been a dissenting opinion on a question of law (*Criminal Code*, Part XXI); (iii) without leave from the highest court of final resort in a province, in regard to a provincial reference (*Supreme Court Act*, s. 36); and (iv) with leave from the highest court of final resort in a province, in regard to a provincial reference (*Supreme Court Act*, s. 37).

34. None of these subjects is excluded from the Court's jurisdiction in s. 101 of the *Constitution Act, 1867*.

35. On the basis of this role, see Hogg 2007, ch. 5.5. As Hogg notes, however, courts may also declare legislation invalid in those unitary states that have adopted a rigid constitution: *ibid.* at 118.

36. See discussion in Russell, *supra* note 1 at 344–49.

37. *Supreme Court Act*, R.S.C. 1985, c. S-26, s. 40(1), discussed in Russell, *supra* note 1 at 344–49.

38. *Supreme Court Act*, R.S.C. 1985, c. S-6, s. 53. See J.L. Huffman & M. Saathoff, "Advisory Opinions and Canadian Constitutional Development: The Supreme Court's Reference Jurisdiction" (1990) 74 Minn. L. Rev. 1251; B.L. Strayer, *The Canadian Constitution and the Courts*, 3d ed. (Toronto: Butterworths, 1988), ch. 9; G. Rubin, "The Nature, Use and Effect of Reference Cases in Canadian Constitutional Law" in W.R. Lederman, *The Courts and the Canadian Constitution* (Toronto: McLelland & Stewart, 1964) 220–48. Provincial courts of appeal have a similar advisory jurisdiction on matters referred to them by provincial cabinets. Opinions on these matters can then be appealed to the Supreme Court of Canada.

39. See further, **Part (d)**, below.

40. See generally, Craig Forcese & Aaron Freeman, *The Laws of Government: The Legal Foundations of Canadian Democracy* (Toronto: Irwin Law, 2005), ch. 4(C), addressing Supreme Court appointments at ch. 4(C)(1)(b).

41. An independent Commissioner for Federal Judicial Affairs gives names of people interested in federal judicial positions to nominating committees in each province. The committees rank candidates for federal judicial positions, and their rankings are considered by the Minister of Justice when making appointments.

42. See Chapter 11, below.

43. See Derek Lee, M.P., Chair, Standing Committee on Human Rights, Public Safety, and Emergency Preparedness, Improving the Supreme Court of Canada Appointments Process at 1–4 <cmte.parl.gc.ca/Content/HOC/committee/373/just/reports/rp1350880/justrp01/justrp01-e.pdf>; and Forcese & Freeman, *supra* note 40.

44. See, for example, House of Commons Interim Ad Hoc Committee on the Appointment of Supreme Court

Judges, *Report*, 37th Parliament, 3rd Sess. (August 2004); Patrick J. Monahan & Peter W. Hogg, "We Need an Open Parliamentary Review of Court Appointments" *National Post* (24 April 2004) p. A19.

45. See the account and suggestions in Forcese & Freeman, *supra* note 40.

46. Justice Marshall Rothstein of the Federal Court of Appeal.

47. See **Part (f)**, below.

48. *Reference re Remuneration of Judges of the Provincial Court of Prince Edward Island*, [1997] 3 S.C.R. 3 in **Part (d)** below.

49. See s. 26.1 of the *Judges Act*, R.S.C. 1985, c. J-1; and Library of Parliament, Parliamentary Information and Research Branch, Nancy Holmes, *Bill C-37: Judges Act Amendments, Library of Parliament, 1999* <http://www.parl.gc.ca/common/Bills_ls.asp?Parl=36&Ses=1&ls=C37>.

50. *Provincial Court Judges' Assn. of New Brunswick v. New Brunswick (Minister of Justice)*, [2005] 2005 SCC 44. No. 47 at paras. 22–27; *Reference re Remuneration of Judges of the Provincial Court of Prince Edward Island*, [1997] 3 S.C.R. 3 at para. 182. Although these decisions were directed specifically at salaries of provincially appointed judges, their requirements would apply to salaries of federal judges as well.

51. See s. 99 of the *Constitution Act, 1867*, for superior provincial courts. It is not clear if the Supreme Court of Canada is a "superior court" within the meaning of ss. 96–100 of the *Constitution Act, 1867*: contrast the views of Hogg 2007, ch. 7.2(e) and Forcese & Freeman, *supra* note 40. In any event, the wording of s. 99 is replicated in substance by s. 9 of the *Supreme Court Act*, R.S.C. 1985, c. S-26. It says that before the retirement age of 75, Supreme Court judges "hold office during good behaviour, but are removable by the Governor General on address of the Senate and House of Commons."

52. As to whether the Supreme Court of Canada is a "superior court" within the meaning of ss. 96–100 of the *Constitution Act, 1867, cf.* Hogg 2007, ch. 7.2(e) and Forcese & Freeman, *supra* note 40. Section 71 of the *Judges Act*, R.S.C. 1985, c. J-1, provides that that statute does not affect "the power, right or duty of the House of Commons, the Senate or the Governor in Council in relation to the removal from office of a judge or any other person...".

53. An inquiry was first used in a 1966 case involving Justice Leo Landreville: Peter H. Russell, *The Judiciary in Canada: Third Branch of Government* (Toronto: McGraw-Hill Ryerson, 1987), ch. 7. Inquiries were required by legislation in 1971 with the creation of the Canadian Judicial Council. See *Re Therrien*, [2001] S.C.R. 3. at para. 39, saying that s. 11(d) of the *Charter* requires (i) that

removal must be for cause, and (ii) that cause must be determined at a judicial inquiry.

54. See the 1996 Bienvenue Inquiry: Canadian Judicial Council, *Report of the Bienvenue Inquiry Committee to the Canadian Judicial Council*, June 1996, published in (1998) 9 N.J.C.L. 1998, and the Council's *Report to the Minister of Justice*, reproduced as Appendix G in the Council's 1996–97 Annual Report. For other inquiries, see August 1990 *Report of the Nova Scotia Judges Inquiry Committee to the Canadian Judicial Council*; June 1996, *Report of the Bienvenue Inquiry Committee to the Canadian Judicial Council*; December 2002, *Report of the Flynn Inquiry Committee to the Canadian Judicial Council*, and *Council Report to the Minister of Justice*, March 2003; August 2003, *Report of the Boilard Inquiry Committee to the Canadian Judicial Council*, and *Council Report to the Minister of Justice*, December 2003; Inquiry Committee Regarding Mr. Justice Paul Cosgrove. All decisions and inquiries can be found at the Council's website: <http://www.cjc-ccm.gc.ca/>.

55. See April 1999, *Decision of Flahiff Inquiry Committee Re Preliminary Motions by Judge*; and February 1994, *Decision of the Gratton Inquiry Committee Re Constitutional Questions with Respect to the Jurisdiction of the Canadian Judicial Council and the Inquiry Committee*. The decisions can be found at the Council's website: <http://www.cjc-ccm.gc.ca/>.

56. Parliamentary removal proceedings have been started on four occasions, but in every case, proceedings have been dropped or dismissed or the judge in question has resigned before the introduction of a parliamentary resolution: see Hogg 2007, ch.7(1)(c); Peter H. Russell, *The Judiciary in Canada: Third Branch of Government* (Toronto: McGraw-Hill Ryerson, 1987), ch. 7.

57. For a small sample of some of the literature (which tends to focus on the *Charter*), see James B. Kelly, *Governing with the Charter: Legislative Intent and Judicial Activism and Framers' Intent* (Vancouver: UBC Press, 2005); William P. Marshall, Margit Cohn and Mordechai Kremnitzer, "Judicial Activism: A Multidimensional Model" (2005) 18 Can. J.L. & Juris. 333; Janet L. Hiebert, *Charter Conflicts: What is Parliament's Role?* (Montreal & Kingston: McGill-Queen's University Press, 2002); Ernest A. Young, "Judicial Activism and Conservative Politics" (2002) 73 U. Colo. L. Rev. 1139; Kent Roach, *The Supreme Court on Trial: Judicial Activism or Democratic Dialogue* (Toronto: Irwin Law, 2001); and Bradley C. Canon, "A Framework for the Analysis of Judicial Activism" in Stephen C. Halpern & Charles M. Lamb, eds., *Supreme Court Activism and Restraint* (Lexington, MA: Lexington Books, 1982) 385.

Edwards†

NOTE

Henrietta Muir Edwards, who had been active in the women's suffrage movement in the West, was recommended for an appointment to the Senate from Alberta. At issue was the appointment of any woman to the Senate. As well as Edwards, there were four other appellants: Nellie L. McClung and Louise C. McKinney, who had been members of the Alberta Legislative Assembly; Emily F. Murphy,

---

† *Edwards v. Canada (A.G.)* (the "Persons" case), [1930] 1 D.L.R. 98 at 99–103, 104–7, 109–13 (J.C.P.C.: 18 October 1929).

a police magistrate; and Irene Parlby, a member of the Alberta Legislative Assembly and its Executive Council.

On October 19, 1927, the Governor General in Council referred the following question to the Supreme Court of Canada:

> By s. 24 of the B.N.A. Act, 1867, it is provided that 'The Governor General shall from Time to Time, in the Queen's Name ... summon qualified Persons to the Senate; ...' The question at issue ... is whether the words 'qualified persons' in that section include a woman, and consequently whether women are eligible to be summoned to and become members of the Senate of Canada.

The Supreme Court held unanimously that the word "persons" did not include female persons, and that women were not eligible to be summoned to the Senate. This decision was appealed to the Judicial Committee of the Privy Council. The Judicial Committee set aside the decision of the Supreme Court and found that the word "persons" in s. 24 of the *Constitution Act, 1867* does include women. In this decision, Lord Sankey made his famous remarks about the constitution as a "living tree capable of growth and expansion...." He stressed the need to interpret constitutional language in light of changing social ideas and needs. Not until 1928 did women in Britain gain the right to vote on the same terms as men, after a long and difficult campaign. In Canada, women won the right to vote in federal elections in 1918. The "Persons" case was another important step towards women achieving full equality with men. That this step was achieved through a judgment of the JCPC may seem surprising.

EXTRACT

[LORD SANKEY for the Judicial Committee:]

Their Lordships are of opinion that the word "persons" in s. 24 does include women, and that women are eligible to be summoned to and become members of the Senate of Canada.

In coming to a determination as to the meaning of a particular word in a particular Act of Parliament it is permissible to consider two points, *viz.*: —

(i) The external evidence derived from extraneous circumstances such as previous legislation and decided cases.

(ii) The internal evidence derived from the Act itself.

As the counsel on both sides have made great researches and invited their Lordships to consider the legal position of women from the earliest times, in justice to their argument they propose to do so and accordingly turn to the first of the above points, *viz.*: —

(i) The external evidence derived from extraneous circumstances.

The exclusion of women from all public offices is a relic of days more barbarous than ours, but it must be remembered that the necessity of the times often forced on man customs which in later years were not necessary. Such exclusion is probably due to the fact that the deliberative assemblies of the early tribes were attended by men under arms, and women did not bear arms....

. . . .

Their Lordships now turn for a moment to the special history of the development of Canadian legislature as bearing upon the matter under discussion.

. . . .

No doubt in any code where women were expressly excluded from public office the problem would present no difficulty, but where instead of such exclusion those entitled to be summoned to or placed in public office are described under the word "person" different considerations arise.

The word is ambiguous and in its original meaning would undoubtedly embrace members of either sex. On the other hand, supposing in an Act of Parliament several centuries ago it had been enacted that any person should be entitled to be elected to a particular office it would have been understood that the word only referred to males, but the cause of this was not because the word "person" could not include females but because at Common Law a woman was incapable of serving a public office. The fact that no woman had served or has claimed to serve such an office is not of great weight when it is remembered that custom would have prevented the claim being made, or the point being contested.

Customs are apt to develop into traditions which are stronger than law and remain unchallenged long after the reason for them has disappeared.

The appeal to history therefore in this particular matter is not conclusive.

. . . .

[T]heir Lordships do not think it right to apply rigidly to Canada of to-day the decisions and the reasonings therefor which commended themselves, probably rightly, to those who had to apply the law in different circumstances, in different centuries to countries in different stages of development. Referring therefore to the judgment of the Chief Justice and those who agreed with him, their Lordships think that the appeal to Roman Law and to early English decisions is not of itself a secure foundation on which to build the interpretation of the B.N.A. Act, 1867.

Their Lordships fully appreciate the learned arguments set out in his judgment, but prefer, on this part of the case, to adopt the reasonings of Duff, J., who did not agree with the other members of the Court, for reasons which appear to their Lordships to be strong and cogent. As he says, [1928] 4 D.L.R., at p. 118: — "Nor am I convinced that the reasoning based upon the 'extraneous circumstances' we are asked to consider — the disabilities of women under the common law, and the law and practice of Parliament in respect of appointment to public place or office — establishes a rule interpretation for the B.N.A. Act, by which the construction of powers, legislative and executive, bestowed in general terms is controlled by a presumptive exclusion of women from participation in the working of the institutions set up by the Act."

Their Lordships now turn to the second point, namely:

(ii) the internal evidence derived from the Act itself.

Before discussing the various sections they think it necessary to refer to the circumstances which led up to the passing of the Act.

The communities included within the Britannic system embrace countries and peoples in every stage of social, political and economic development and undergoing a continuous process of evolution.

His Majesty the King in Council is the final Court of Appeal from all these communities and this Board must take great care therefore not to interpret legislation meant to apply to one community by a rigid adherence to the customs and traditions of another. Canada had its difficulties both at home and with the mother country, but soon discovered that union was strength. Delegates from the three Maritime Provinces met in Charlottetown on September 1, 1864, to discuss proposals for a Maritime Union. A delegation from the Coalition Government of that day proceeded to Charlottetown and placed before the Maritime delegates their schemes for a Union embracing the Canadian Provinces. As a result the Quebec conference assembled on October 10, continued in session till October 28, and framed a number of resolutions. These resolutions as revised by the delegates from the different provinces in London in 1866 were based upon a consideration of the rights of others and expressed in a compromise which will remain a lasting monument to the political genius of Canadian statesmen. Upon those resolutions the B.N.A. Act of 1867 was framed and passed by the Imperial legislature. The Quebec resolutions dealing with the Legislative Council, viz., Nos. 6–24, even if their Lordships are entitled to look at them, do not shed any light on the subject under discussion. They refer generally to the "members" of the Legislative Council.

The B.N.A. Act planted in Canada a living tree capable of growth and expansion within its natural limits. The object of the Act was to grant a Constitution to Canada.

"Like all written constitutions it has been subject to development through usage and convention:" (Canadian Constitutional Studies, Sir Robert Borden, 1922, p. 55).

Their Lordships do not conceive it to be the duty of this Board — it is certainly not their desire — to cut down the provisions of the Act by a narrow and technical construction, but rather to give it a large and liberal interpretation so that the Dominion to a great extent, but within certain fixed limits, may be mistress in her own house, as the provinces to a great extent, but within certain fixed limits, are mistresses in theirs.

"The Privy Council, indeed, has laid down that Courts of law must treat the provisions of this (British North America) Act by the same methods of construction and exposition which they apply to other statutes. But there are statutes and statutes; and the strict construction deemed proper in the case, for example, of a penal or taxing statute or one passed to regulate the affairs of an English parish, would be often subversive of parliament's real intent if applied to an Act passed to ensure the peace, order and good government of a British colony:" Clement's Canadian Constitution, 3rd ed., p. 347.

. . . .

It must be remembered, too, that their Lordships are not here considering the question of the legislative competence either of the Dominion or its provinces which arises under ss. 91 and 92 of the Act providing for the distribution of legislative powers and assigning to the Dominion and its provinces their respective spheres of Government.

Their Lordships are concerned with the interpretation of an Imperial Act, but an Imperial Act which creates a constitution for a new country. Nor are their Lordships deciding any question as to the rights of women but only a question as to their eligibility for a particular position. No one either male or female has a right to be summoned to the Senate. The real point at issue is whether the Governor-General has a right to summon women to the Senate.

. . . .

The word "person" as above mentioned may include members of both sexes, and to those who ask why the word should include females, the obvious answer is why should it not.

In these circumstances the burden is upon those who deny that the word includes women to make out their case.

. . . .

It will be observed that s. 21 provides that the Senate shall consist of 72 members who shall be styled senators. The word "member" is not in ordinary English confined to male persons. Section 24 provides that the Governor-General shall summon qualified persons to the Senate.

As already pointed out, "persons" is not confined to members of the male sex, but what effect does the adjective "qualified" before the word "persons" have.

In their Lordships' view it refers back to the previous section, which contains the qualifications of a Senator. Subsections (2) and (3) appear to have given difficulties to the Supreme Court. Subsection (2) provides that the qualification of a senator shall be that he shall be either a natural born subject of the Queen naturalized by an Act of Parliament of Great Britain or of one of the provincial legislatures before the Union or of the Parliament of Canada after the Union. The Chief Justice in dealing with this says that it does not include those who become subjects by marriage, a provision which one would have looked for had it been intended to include women as being eligible.

The attention of the Chief Justice, however, was not called to the Aliens Act, 1844 (Imp.), c. 66. s. 16 of which provides, "That any woman married

or who shall be married to a natural-born subject or person naturalized shall be deemed and taken to be herself naturalized, and have all the rights and privileges of a natural-born subject." The Chief Justice assumed that by Common Law a wife took her husband's nationality on marriage, but by virtue of that section any woman who marries a natural born or naturalized British subject was deemed and taken to be herself naturalized. Accordingly, s. 23(2) uses language apt to cover the case of those who become British subjects by marriage.

Their Lordships agree with Duff, J., when he says, [1928] 4 D.L.R., at p. 121, "I attach no importance ... to the use of the masculine personal pronoun in s. 23, and indeed, very little importance to the provision in s. 23 with regard to nationality" and refer to s. 1 of Interpretation Act, 1889 (Imp.), c. 63, which in s. 1(2) provides that words importing the masculine gender shall include females.

The reasoning of the Chief Justice would compel their Lordships to hold that the word "persons" as used in s. 11 relating to the constitution of the Privy Council for Canada was limited to "male persons" with the resultant anomaly that a woman might be elected a member of the House of Commons but could not even then be summoned by the Governor-General as a member of the Privy Council.

Section 23(3) provided that the qualification of a Senator shall be that he is legally and equitably seized of a freehold for his own use and benefit of lands and tenements of a certain value. This section gave some trouble to Duff, J., who says that subsection points to the exclusion of married women and would have been expressed in a different way if the presence of married women had been contemplated.

Their Lordships think that this difficulty is removed by a consideration of the rights of a woman under the Married Women's Property Acts. A married woman can possess the property qualification required by this subsection. Apart from statute a married woman could be equitably seized of freehold property for her own use only and by an Act respecting certain separate rights of property of Married Women, C.S.U.C. 1859, c. 73, s. 1, it was provided: —

"Every woman, who has married since the Fourth day of May, one thousand eight hundred and fifty-nine, or who marries after this Act takes effect, without any marriage contract or settlement, shall and may, notwithstanding her coverture, have, hold and enjoy all her real and personal property ... in as full and ample a manner as if she continued sole and unmarried...."

Their Lordships do not think it possible to interpret the word "persons" by speculating whether the framer of the B.N.A. Act purposely followed the system of Legislative Councils enacted in the Acts of 1791 and 1840 rather than that which prevailed in the Maritime Province for the model on which the Senate was to be formed, neither do they think that either of these subsections is sufficient to rebut the presumption that the word "persons" includes women. Looking at the sections which deal with the Senate as a whole (ss. 21–36) their Lordships are unable to say that there is anything in those sections themselves upon which the Court could come to a definite conclusion that women are to be excluded from the Senate.

So far with regard to the sections dealing especially with the Senate — are there any other sections in the Act which shed light upon the meaning of the word "persons?"

Their Lordships think that there are. For example, s. 41 refers to the qualifications and disqualifications of persons to be elected or to sit or vote as members of the House of Assembly or Legislative Assembly and by a proviso it is said that until the Parliament of Canada otherwise provides at any election for a member of the House of Commons for the District of Algoma in addition to persons qualified by the law of the Province of Canada to vote every male British subject aged 21 years or upwards being a householder shall have a vote. This section shows a distinction between "persons" and "males." If persons excluded females it would only have been necessary to say every person who is a British subject aged 21 years or upwards shall have a vote.

Again in s. 84 referring to Ontario and Quebec a similar proviso is found stating that every male British subject in contradistinction to "person" shall have a vote.

Again in s. 133 it is provided that either the English or the French language may be used by any person or in any pleadings in or issuing from any court of Canada established under this Act and in or from all of any of the courts of Quebec. The word "person" there must include females as it can hardly have been supposed that a man might use either the English or the French language but a woman might not.

If Parliament had intended to limit the word "persons" in s. 24 to male persons it would surely have manifested such intention by an express limita-

tion as it has done in ss. 41 and 84. The fact that certain qualifications are set out in s. 23 is not an argument in favour of further limiting the class, but is an argument to the contrary because it must be presumed that Parliament has set out in s. 23 all the qualifications deemed necessary for a Senator and it does not state that one of the qualifications is that he must be a member of the male sex.

. . . .

The history of these sections and their interpretation in Canada is not without interest and significance.

From Confederation to date both the Dominion Parliament and the provincial legislatures have interpreted the word "persons" in ss. 41 and 84 of the B.N.A. Act as including female persons and have legislated either for the inclusion or exclusion of women from the class of persons entitled to vote and to sit in the Parliament and legislature respectively, and this interpretation has never been questioned.

From Confederation up to 1916 women were excluded from the class of persons entitled to vote in both Federal and Provincial elections.

From 1916 to 1922 various Dominion and Provincial Acts were passed to admit women to the Franchise and to the right to sit as members in both Dominion and Provincial legislative bodies.

At the present time women are entitled to vote and to be candidates: —

1. At all Dominion elections on the same basis as men.
2. At all provincial elections save in the Province of Quebec.

From the date of the enactment of the Interpretation Acts in the Province of Canada, Nova Scotia and New Brunswick prior to Confederation and in the Dominion of Canada since Confederation and until the franchise was extended, women have been excluded by express enactment from the right to vote.

Neither is it without interest to record that when upon May 20, 1867, the Representation of the People Bill came before a committee of the House of Commons, John Stuart Mill moved an amendment to secure women's suffrage and the amendment proposed was to leave out the word "man" in order to insert the word "person" instead thereof. See 187 Hansard, 3rd series, col. 817.

A heavy burden lies on an appellant who seeks to set aside a unanimous judgment of the Supreme Court, and this Board will only set aside such a decision after convincing argument and anxious consideration, but having regard

1. To the object of the Act, *viz.*, to provide a constitution for Canada, a responsible and developing State;
2. That the word "person" is ambiguous and may include members of either sex;
3. That there are sections in the Act above referred to which show that in some cases the word "person" must include females;
4. That in some sections the words "male persons" is expressly used when it is desired to confine the matter in issue to males, and
5. To the provisions of the Interpretation Act;

their Lordships have come to the conclusion that the word "persons" in s. 24 includes members both of the male and female sex and that, therefore, the question propounded by the Governor-General must be answered in the affirmative and that women are eligible to be summoned to and become members of the Senate of Canada, and they will humbly advise His Majesty accordingly.

Appeal allowed.

(d) *Provincial Court Judges Reference*†

NOTE

What good is law that is not fairly applied? How fair is a decision that is not impartially made? Impartiality is vital to judicial decisions, and a key means of promoting judicial impartiality is the principle of the independence of the judiciary. Judicial independence requires that judges and courts be as independent as possible from others, especially from the executive and legislative branches of government.

In this reference, three provinces had imposed unilateral salary reductions on all provincially appointed bodies in the public sectors, including provincially appointed judges. Were there any judicial independence guarantees relevant to these actions? If so, what were they, and what did they require?

The main guarantees of judicial independence in constitutional texts are ss. 96 to 100 of the *Constitution Act, 1867*, and s. 11(d) of the *Canadian Charter of Rights and Freedoms*. The former include protections for the tenure of federally appointed superior court judges in provinces, and provide that their salaries shall be fixed by Parlia-

ment. Section 11(d) of the *Charter* says that "any person charged with an offence" has the right:

> ... to be presumed innocent until proven guilty according to law in a fair and public hearing by an independent and impartial tribunal.

The judges involved in this reference were provincially appointed judges of inferior courts (i.e., courts below the provincial Supreme Court or equivalent that lack inherent review powers), with criminal as well as civil jurisdiction. The Court found that s. 11(d) of the *Charter* was the relevant constitutional text.

Moreover, in *Valente v. The Queen*, [1985] 2 S.C.R. 673 the Supreme Court had identified the three main aspects of judicial independence as security of tenure, financial security, and administrative independence. In the present reference, the Court found that the relevant aspect of judicial independence was financial security.

If the Court had simply gone on from here to conclude whether or not there had been a breach of financial security, this would have been a less remarkable case. However, the majority noted that

---

† *Reference re Remuneration of Judges of the Provincial Court of Prince Edward Island*; *Reference re Independence and Impartiality of Judges of the Provincial Court of Prince Edward Island*; *R. v. Campbell*; *R. v. Ekmecic*; *R. v. Wickman*; *Manitoba Provincial Judges Assn. v. Manitoba (Minister of Justice)*, [1997] 3 S.C.R. 3.

the relevant textual guarantees of judicial independence did not specifically address the situation of provincially appointed courts in civil proceedings. Was their independence protected only by legally unenforceable political conventions? Or was it enforceable as a matter of constitutional law? If so, where did the requirement of independence get its legal status?

The majority's answers here, and the vigorous dissent by La Forest J., are striking. The majority concluded that the principle of judicial independence has constitutional legal status beyond the specific textual provisions of the *Constitution Act, 1867* and the *Charter*. What was the basis for this finding?

The majority went on to hold that the financial security aspect of the guarantee requires positive government action. Governments must create independent salary commissions. Government action that rejects the recommendations of these commissions must be justified. (This requirement was addressed in more detail in *Provincial Court Judges Association of New Brunswick v. New Brunswick (Minister of Justice)*, [2005] 2 S.C.R. 286.) If the courts find that the justification is unreasonable, the government action is unconstitutional and invalid.

These are strong sanctions for a vital principle. Arguably, judicial independence is too important to be left in the hands of politicians and administrators. Do you see any danger in leaving it in the hands of judges?

EXTRACT

[LAMER C.J. for himself, L'Heureux-Dubé, Sopinka, Gonthier, Cory and Iacobucci JJ.:]

[85] ... [T]here are serious limitations to the view that the express provisions of the Constitution comprise an exhaustive and definitive code for the protection of judicial independence. The first and most serious problem is that the range of courts whose independence is protected by the written provisions of the Constitution contains large gaps. Sections 96–100, for example, only protect the independence of judges of the superior, district, and county courts, and even then, not in a uniform or consistent manner....

. . . .

[87] The second problem with reading s. 11(d) of the *Charter* and ss. 96–100 of the *Constitution Act, 1867* as an exhaustive code of judicial independence

is that some of those provisions, by their terms, do not appear to speak to this objective....

. . . .

[94] In my opinion, the existence of many of the unwritten rules of the Canadian Constitution can be explained by reference to the preamble of the *Constitution Act, 1867*. The relevant paragraph states in full:

> Whereas the Provinces of Canada, Nova Scotia and New Brunswick have expressed their Desire to be federally united into One Dominion under the Crown of the United Kingdom of Great Britain and Ireland, with a Constitution similar in Principle to that of the United Kingdom:

. . . .

[95] ... [T]he preamble does have important legal effects. Under normal circumstances, preambles can be used to identify the purpose of a statute, and also as an aid to construing ambiguous statutory language.... The preamble to the *Constitution Act, 1867* certainly operates in this fashion. However, in my view, it goes even further. In the words of Rand J., the preamble articulates "the political theory which the Act embodies": *Switzman* v. *Elbling*, [1957] S.C.R. 285 at p. 306. It recognizes and affirms the basic principles which are the very source of the substantive provisions of the *Constitution Act, 1867*. As I have said above, those provisions merely elaborate those organizing principles in the institutional apparatus they create or contemplate. As such, the preamble is not only a key to construing the express provisions of the *Constitution Act, 1867*, but also invites the use of those organizing principles to fill out gaps in the express terms of the constitutional scheme. It is the means by which the underlying logic of the Act can be given the force of law.

[96] What are the organizing principles of the *Constitution Act, 1867*, as expressed in the preamble? The preamble speaks of the desire of the founding provinces "to be federally united into One Dominion", and thus, addresses the structure of the division of powers. Moreover, by its reference to "a Constitution similar in Principle to that of the United Kingdom", the preamble indicates that the legal and institutional structure of constitutional democracy in Canada should be similar to that of the legal regime out of which the Canadian Constitution emerged. To my mind, both of these aspects of the preamble explain many of the cases in which the Court has, through the normal process of constitutional inter-

pretation, stated some fundamental rules of Canadian constitutional law which are not found in the express terms of the *Constitution Act, 1867.*

[97] I turn first to the jurisprudence under the division of powers, to illustrate how the process of gap-filling has occurred and how it can be understood by reference to the preamble....

. . . .

[104] These examples — the doctrines of full faith and credit and paramountcy, the remedial innovation of suspended declarations of invalidity, the recognition of the constitutional status of the privileges of provincial legislatures, the vesting of the power to regulate political speech within federal jurisdiction, and the inferral [*sic*] of implied limits on legislative sovereignty with respect to political speech — illustrate the special legal effect of the preamble. The preamble identifies the organizing principles of the *Constitution Act, 1867*, and invites the courts to turn those principles into the premises of a constitutional argument that culminates in the filling of gaps in the express terms of the constitutional text.

[105] The same approach applies to the protection of judicial independence. In fact, this point was already decided in *Beauregard* v. *Canada*, [1986] 2 S.C.R. 56, and, unless and until it is reversed, we are governed by that decision today. In that case (at p. 72), a unanimous Court held that the preamble of the *Constitution Act, 1867*, and in particular, its reference to "a Constitution similar in Principle to that of the United Kingdom", was "textual recognition" of the principle of judicial independence. Although in that case, it fell to us to interpret s. 100 of the *Constitution Act, 1867*, the comments I have just reiterated were not limited by reference to that provision, and the courts which it protects.

[106] The historical origins of the protection of judicial independence in the United Kingdom, and thus in the Canadian Constitution, can be traced to the Act of Settlement of 1701. As we said in *Valente* v. *The Queen*, [1985] 2 S.C.R. 673 at p. 693, that Act was the "historical inspiration" for the judicature provisions of the *Constitution Act, 1867*. Admittedly, the Act only extends protection to judges of the English superior courts. However, our Constitution has evolved over time. In the same way that our understanding of rights and freedoms has grown, such that they have now been expressly entrenched through the enactment of the *Constitution Act, 1982*, so too has judicial independence grown into a princi-

ple that now extends to all courts, not just the superior courts of this country.

[107] I also support this conclusion on the basis of the presence of s. 11(d) of the *Charter*, an express provision which protects the independence of provincial court judges only when those courts exercise jurisdiction in relation to offences. As I said earlier, the express provisions of the Constitution should be understood as elaborations of the underlying, unwritten, and organizing principles found in the preamble to the *Constitution Act, 1867*. Even though s. 11(d) is found in the newer part of our Constitution, the *Charter*, it can be understood in this way, since the Constitution is to be read as a unified whole.... Section 11(d), far from indicating that judicial independence is constitutionally enshrined for provincial courts only when those courts exercise jurisdiction over offences, is proof of the existence of a general principle of judicial independence that applies to all courts no matter what kind of cases they hear.

[108] I reinforce this conclusion by reference to the central place that courts hold within the Canadian system of government.... As this Court has said before, there are three branches of government — the legislature, the executive, and the judiciary: *Fraser* v. *Public Service Staff Relations Board*, [1985] 2 S.C.R. 455 at p. 469; *R.* v. *Power*, [1994] 1 S.C.R. 601, at p. 620. Courts, in other words, are equally "definitional to the Canadian understanding of constitutionalism" (*Cooper* v. *Canada (Human Rights Commission)*), [1996] 3 S.C.R. 854 at para. 11) as are political institutions. It follows that the same constitutional imperative — the preservation of the basic structure — which led Beetz J. [in *OPSEU* v. *Ontario (Attorney General)*, [1987] 2 S.C.R. to limit the power of legislatures to affect the operation of political institutions, also extends protection to the judicial institutions of our constitutional system. By implication, the jurisdiction of the provinces over "courts", as that term is used in s. 92(14) of the *Constitution Act, 1867*, contains within it an implied limitation that the independence of those courts cannot be undermined.

[109] In conclusion, the express provisions of the *Constitution Act, 1867* and the *Charter* are not an exhaustive written code for the protection of judicial independence in Canada. Judicial independence is an unwritten norm, recognized and affirmed by the preamble to the *Constitution Act, 1867*. In fact, it is in that preamble, which serves as the grand entrance hall to the castle of the Constitution, that the true source of our commitment to this foundational prin-

ciple is located. However, since the parties and interveners have grounded their arguments in s. 11(d), I will resolve these appeals by reference to that provision.

. . . .

[111] The starting point for my discussion is *Valente*, where in a unanimous judgment this Court laid down the interpretive framework for s. 11(d)'s guarantee of judicial independence and impartiality. Le Dain J., speaking for the Court, began by drawing a distinction between impartiality and independence. Later cases have referred to this distinction as "a firm line": *R. v. Généreux*, [1992] 1 S.C.R. 259 at p. 283. Impartiality was defined as "a state of mind or attitude of the tribunal in relation to the issues and the parties in a particular case" (*Valente, supra*, at p. 685 (emphasis added)). It was tied to the traditional concern for the "absence of bias, actual or perceived". Independence, by contrast, focussed on the status of the court or tribunal. In particular, Le Dain J. emphasized that the independence protected by s. 11(d) flowed from "the traditional constitutional value of judicial independence", which he defined in terms of the relationship of the court or tribunal "to others, particularly the executive branch of government". As I expanded in *R. v. Lippé*, [1991] 2 S.C.R. 114, the independence protected by s. 11(d) is the independence of the judiciary from the other branches of government, and bodies which can exercise pressure on the judiciary through power conferred on them by the state.

. . . .

[114] After establishing these core propositions, Le Dain J. in *Valente* went on to discuss two sets of concepts; the three core characteristics of judicial independence, and what I term the two dimensions of judicial independence.

[115] The three core characteristics identified by Le Dain J. are security of tenure, financial security, and administrative independence. *Valente* laid down (at p. 697) two requirements for security of tenure for provincial court judges: those judges could only be removed for cause "related to the capacity to perform judicial functions", and after a "judicial inquiry at which the judge affected is given a full opportunity to be heard". Unlike the judicature provisions of the *Constitution Act, 1867*, which govern the removal of superior court judges, s. 11(d) of the *Charter* does not require an address by the legislature in order to dismiss a provincial court judge.

. . . .

[118] The three core characteristics of judicial independence — security of tenure, financial security, and administrative independence — should be contrasted with what I have termed the two dimensions of judicial independence. In *Valente*, Le Dain J. drew a distinction between two dimensions of judicial independence, the individual independence of a judge and the institutional or collective independence of the court or tribunal of which that judge is a member. In other words, while individual independence attaches to individual judges, institutional or collective independence attaches to the court or tribunal as an institutional entity. The two different dimensions of judicial independence are related in the following way (*Valente, supra*, at p. 687):

> The relationship between these two aspects of judicial independence is that an individual judge may enjoy the essential conditions of judicial independence but if the court or tribunal over which he or she presides is not independent of the other branches of government, in what is essential to its function, he or she cannot be said to be an independent tribunal.

. . . .

[166] Although provincial executives and legislatures, as the case may be, are constitutionally permitted to change or freeze judicial remuneration, those decisions have the potential to jeopardize judicial independence. The imperative of protecting the courts from political interference through economic manipulation is served by interposing an independent body — a judicial compensation commission — between the judiciary and the other branches of government. The constitutional function of this body is to depoliticize the process of determining changes or freezes to judicial remuneration. This objective would be achieved by setting that body the specific task of issuing a report on the salaries and benefits of judges to the executive and the legislature, responding to the particular proposals made by the government to increase, reduce, or freeze judges' salaries.

. . . .

[180] Furthermore, if after turning its mind to the report of the commission, the executive or the legislature, as applicable, chooses not to accept one or more of the recommendations in that report, it must be prepared to justify this decision, if necessary in a court of law. The reasons for this decision would be

found either in the report of the executive responding to the contents of the commission's report, or in the recitals to the resolution of the legislature on the matter. An unjustified decision could potentially lead to a finding of unconstitutionality....

. . . .

[182] I hasten to add that these comments should not be construed as endorsing or establishing a general duty to give reasons, either in the constitutional or in the administrative law context. Moreover, I wish to clarify that the standard of justification required under s. 11(d) is not the same as that required under s. 1 of the *Charter*. Section 1 imposes a very rigorous standard of justification. Not only does it require an important government objective, but it requires a proportionality between this objective and the means employed to pursue it. The party seeking to uphold the impugned state action must demonstrate a rational connection between the objective and the means chosen, that the means chosen are the least restrictive means or violate the right as little as reasonably possible, and that there is a proportionality between the effect of the measure and its objective so that the attainment of the legislative goal is not outweighed by the abridgment of the right.

[183] The standard of justification here, by contrast, is one of simple rationality. It requires that the government articulate a legitimate reason for why it has chosen to depart from the recommendation of the commission, and if applicable, why it has chosen to treat judges differently from other persons paid from the public purse. A reviewing court does not engage in a searching analysis of the relationship between ends and means, which is the hallmark of a s. 1 analysis. However, the absence of this analysis does not mean that the standard of justification is ineffectual. On the contrary, it has two aspects. First, it screens out decisions with respect to judicial remuneration which are based on purely political considerations, or which are enacted for discriminatory reasons. Changes to or freezes in remuneration can only be justified for reasons which relate to the public interest, broadly understood. Second, if judicial review is sought, a reviewing court must inquire into the reasonableness of the factual foundation of the claim made by the government, similar to the way that we have evaluated whether there was an economic emergency in Canada in our jurisprudence under the division of powers (*Reference re Anti-Inflation Act*, [1976] 2 S.C.R. 373).

[184] Although the test of justification — one of simple rationality — must be met by all measures which affect judicial remuneration and which depart from the recommendation of the salary commission, some will satisfy that test more easily than others, because they pose less of a danger of being used as a means of economic manipulation, and hence of political interference. Across-the-board measures which affect substantially every person who is paid from the public purse, in my opinion, are prima facie rational. For example, an across-the-board reduction in salaries that includes judges will typically be designed to effectuate the government's overall fiscal priorities, and hence will usually be aimed at furthering some sort of larger public interest. By contrast, a measure directed at judges alone may require a somewhat fuller explanation, precisely because it is directed at judges alone.

. . . .

[LA FOREST J., dissenting:]

[304] I take issue ... with the Chief Justice's view that the preamble to the *Constitution Act, 1867* is a source of constitutional limitations on the power of legislatures to interfere with judicial independence....

. . . .

[308] Even if it is accepted that judicial independence had become a "constitutional" principle in Britain by 1867, it is important to understand the precise meaning of that term in British law. Unlike Canada, Great Britain does not have a written constitution. Under accepted British legal theory, Parliament is supreme. By this I mean that there are no limitations upon its legislative competence. As Dicey explains, Parliament has "under the English constitution, the right to make or unmake any law whatever; and, further, that no person or body is recognised by the law of England as having a right to override or set aside the legislation of Parliament" (A. V. Dicey, *Introduction to the Study of the Law of the Constitution* (10th ed., 1959), at pp. 39–40)....

. . . .

[311] The idea that there were enforceable limits on the power of the British Parliament to interfere with the judiciary at the time of Confederation, then, is an historical fallacy. By expressing a desire to have a Constitution "similar in Principle to that of the United Kingdom", the framers of the *Constitution*

Act, 1867 did not give courts the power to strike down legislation violating the principle of judicial independence. The framers did, however, entrench the fundamental components of judicial independence set out in the Act of Settlement such that violations could be struck down by the courts. This was accomplished, however, by ss. 99–100 of the *Constitution Act, 1867*, not the preamble.

. . . .

[316] [The legitimacy of judicial review] is imperiled ... when courts attempt to limit the power of legislatures without recourse to express textual authority....

. . . .

[323] ...If one is to give constitutional protection to courts generally, one must be able to determine with some precision what the term "court" encompasses. It is clear both under the *Constitution Act, 1867* as well as under s. 11(d) of the *Charter* what courts are covered, those under the *Constitution Act, 1867* arising under historic events in British constitutional history, those in s. 11(d) for the compelling reasons already given, namely protection for persons accused of an offence. But what are we to make of a general protection for courts such as that proposed by the Chief Justice? The word "court" is a broad term and can encompass a wide variety of tribunals. In the province of Quebec, for example, the term is legislatively used in respect of any number of administrative tribunals. Are we to include only those inferior courts applying ordinary jurisdiction in civil matters, or should we include all sorts of administrative tribunals, some of which are of far greater importance than ordinary civil courts? And if we do, is a distinction to be drawn between different tribunals and on the basis of what principles is this to be done?

[324] These are some of the issues that have persuaded me that this Court should not precipitously, and without the benefit of argument of any real relevance to the case before us, venture forth on this uncharted sea. It is not as if the law as it stands is devoid of devices to ensure independent and impartial courts and tribunals. Quite the contrary, I would emphasize that the express protections for judicial independence set out in the Constitution are broad and powerful. They apply to all superior courts and other judges specified in s. 96 of the *Constitution Act, 1867* as well as to inferior (provincial) courts exercising criminal jurisdiction. Nothing presented in these appeals suggests that these guarantees are not sufficient to ensure the independence of the judiciary as a whole. The superior courts have significant appellate and supervisory jurisdiction over inferior courts. If the impartiality of decisions from inferior courts is threatened by a lack of independence, any ensuing injustice may be rectified by the superior courts.

(e) *Imperial Tobacco*†

NOTE

As more and more studies implicate tobacco as a major risk to human health, governments in Canada try to restrict its use. Parliament has prohibited the sale of tobacco products to minors, and has banned smoking on domestic commercial flights. Many provinces and municipalities restrict smoking in public places. Not surprisingly, the tobacco companies have fought back. When the federal government banned tobacco advertising in 1988,[1] the tobacco companies challenged the legislation. In 1995, they obtained a Supreme Court ruling that declared the ban an unjustified breach of freedom of expression.[2] In a second effort in 1997, the federal government banned lifestyle tobacco advertising, continued a prohibition on tobacco sales to minors, and assumed the power to regulate tobacco packaging.[3] Then it yielded to intensive lobbying by the tobacco companies, and agreed

---

† *British Columbia (A.G.) v. Imperial Tobacco Canada Ltd.*, [2005] 2 S.C.R. 273 at at paras. 44–69, 73, 76–78; aff'g (2004), 239 D.L.R. (4th) 412 (B.C.C.A.); rev'ing (2003), 227 D.L.R. (4th) 323 (B.C.S.C.).

to delay the ban on sponsorship advertising.[4] In 2001, the federal government enacted regulations requiring tobacco companies to print health warnings on their packages.[5] The companies responded with further court challenges.

In 1997, the province of *British Columbia* opened a new front in the tobacco war. It enacted a *Tobacco Damages Recovery Act*[6] that authorized the government to sue tobacco companies for public health costs resulting from tobacco-related illnesses. After the tobacco companies successfully challenged this legislation on jurisdictional grounds, the government redrafted the legislation,[7] and the tobacco companies challenged it again.

This time the companies had three main arguments. As before, they claimed that the statute was beyond provincial territorial jurisdiction to enact. Second, they said the statute violated the unwritten constitutional principle of the independence of the judiciary, by forcing courts to make irrational presumptions and by limiting their fact-finding role. Third, the companies said the law violated the unwritten constitutional principle of the rule of law, because it (i) was retroactive, (ii) was directed at only one part of society (the companies), (iii) imposed unfair advantages on government, and (iv) failed to ensure fair civil trials.

The Supreme Court rejected all the companies' arguments. The extract below focuses on the scope of the judicial independence and rule of law principles, and on the general nature of unwritten constitutional principles. What criteria are the Court looking at to determine (a) the content of a particular unwritten legal-constitutional principle, and (b) the circumstances in which such a principle may invalidate legislation? How does the Court's approach to unwritten constitutional principles here compare to its approach in the *Provincial Judges' Reference*? How does it compare with the comments in "Unwritten Constitutional Principles: What is Going On?" in Chapter 2?

Notes

1. *Tobacco Products Control Act*, S.C. 1988, c. 20.
2. *RJR-MacDonald Inc. v. Canada (A.G.)*, [1995] 3 S.C.R. 199.
3. *Tobacco Act*, S.C. 1997, c. 13.
4. See Bill C-42, *An Act to Amend the Tobacco Act*, assented to December 1998, phasing in the ban over a five-year period.
5. See Alan Rock, Minister of Health, *Announcement on New Tobacco Regulation Proposals* (19 January 2000), online: Health Canada <http://www.hc-sc.gc.ca/ahc-asc/minist/health-sante/speeches-discours/2000_01_19_e.html>.
6. S.B.C. 1997, c. 41.
7. *Tobacco Damages and Health Care Costs Recovery Act*, S.B.C. 2000, c. 30.

EXTRACT

[MAJOR J. for the Court:]

. . . .

B. JUDICIAL INDEPENDENCE

[44] Judicial independence is a "foundational principle" of the Constitution reflected in s. 11(d) of the Canadian Charter of Rights and Freedoms, and in both ss. 96–100 and the preamble to the Constitution Act.... It serves "to safeguard our constitutional order and to maintain public confidence in the administration of justice"....

[45] Judicial independence consists essentially in the freedom "to render decisions based solely on the requirements of the law and justice": *Mackin v. New Brunswick (Minister of Justice)*, [2002] 1 S.C.R. 405, 2002 SCC 13 (S.C.C.), at para. 37. It requires that the judiciary be left free to act without improper "interference from any other entity" (*Ell*, at para. 18) — i.e. that the executive and legislative branches of government not "impinge on the essential 'authority and function' ... of the court" (*MacKeigan v. Hickman*, [1989] 2 S.C.R. 796 (S.C.C.), at pp. 827–28).

. . . .

[46] Security of tenure, financial security and administrative independence are the three "core characteristics" or "essential conditions" of judicial independence: *Valente*, at pp. 694, 704 and 708, and *Reference re Remuneration of Judges of the Provincial Court of Prince Edward Island*, at para. 115. It is a precondition to judicial independence that they be maintained, and be seen by "a reasonable person who is fully informed of all the circumstances" to be maintained: *Mackin*, at paras. 38 and 40, and *Provincial Court Judges' Assn. (New Brunswick) v. New Brunswick (Minister of Justice)*, 2005 SCC 44 (S.C.C.), at para. 6.

[47] However, even where the essential conditions of judicial independence exist, and are reasonably seen to exist, judicial independence itself is not necessarily ensured. The critical question is whether the court is free, and reasonably seen to be free, to perform its adjudicative role without interference, including interference from the executive and legislative branches of government. See, for example, *Application under s. 83.28 of the Criminal Code (Re)*, at paras. 82–92.

[48] The appellants submit that the Act violates judicial independence, both in reality and appearance, because it contains rules of civil procedure that fundamentally interfere with the adjudicative role of the court hearing an action brought pursuant to the Act. They point to s. 3(2), which they say forces the court to make irrational presumptions, and to ss. 2(5)(a), (b) and (c), which they say subvert the court's ability to discover relevant facts. They say that these rules impinge on the court's fact-finding function, and virtually guarantee the government's success in an action brought pursuant to the Act.

[49] The rules in the Act with which the appellants take issue are not as unfair or illogical as the appellants submit. They appear to reflect legitimate policy concerns of the British Columbia legislature regarding the systemic advantages tobacco manufacturers enjoy when claims for tobacco-related harm are litigated through individualistic common law tort actions. That, however, is beside the point. The question is not whether the Act's rules are unfair or illogical, nor whether they differ from those governing common law tort actions, but whether they interfere with the courts' adjudicative role, and thus judicial independence.

[50] The primary role of the judiciary is to interpret and apply the law, whether procedural or substantive, to the cases brought before it. It is to hear and weigh, in accordance with the law, evidence that is relevant to the legal issues confronted by it, and to award to the parties before it the available remedies.

[51] The judiciary has some part in the development of the law that its role requires it to apply. Through, for example, its interpretation of legislation, review of administrative decisions and assessment of the constitutionality of legislation, it may develop the law significantly. It may also make incremental developments to its body of previous decisions — i.e. the common law — in order to bring the legal rules those decisions embody "into step with a changing society".... But the judiciary's role in developing the law is a relatively limited one. "[I]n a constitutional democracy such as ours it is the legislature and not the courts which has the major responsibility for law reform"....

[52] It follows that the judiciary's role is not, as the appellants seem to submit, to apply only the law of which it approves. Nor is it to decide cases with a view simply to what the judiciary (rather than the law) deems fair or pertinent. Nor is it to second-guess the law reform undertaken by legislators, whether that reform consists of a new cause of action or procedural rules to govern it. Within the boundaries of the Constitution, legislatures can set the law as they see fit. "The wisdom and value of legislative decisions are subject only to review by the electorate": *Wells v. Newfoundland*, [1999] 3 S.C.R. 199 (S.C.C.), at para. 59.

[53] In essence, the appellants' arguments misapprehend the nature and scope of the courts' adjudicative role protected from interference by the Constitution's guarantee of judicial independence. To accept their position on that adjudicative role would be to recognize a constitutional guarantee not of judicial independence, but of judicial governance.

[54] None of this is to say that legislation, being law, can never unconstitutionally interfere with courts' adjudicative role. But more is required than an allegation that the content of the legislation required to be applied by that adjudicative role is irrational or unfair, or prescribes rules different from those developed at common law. The legislation must interfere, or be reasonably seen to interfere, with the courts' adjudicative role, or with the essential conditions of judicial independence. As McLachlin C.J. stated in *Babcock* [*v. Canada (A.G.)*], at para. 57:

> It is well within the power of the legislature to enact laws, even laws which some would consider draconian, as long as it does not fundamentally alter or interfere with the relationship between the courts and the other branches of government.

[55] No such fundamental alteration or interference was brought about by the legislature's enactment of the Act. A court called upon to try an action brought pursuant to the Act retains at all times its adjudicative role and the ability to exercise that role without interference. It must independently determine the applicability of the Act to the government's claim, independently assess the evidence led to support and defend that claim, independently assign that evidence weight, and then independently determine whether its assessment of the evidence supports a finding of liability. The fact that the Act shifts certain onuses of proof or limits the compellability of information that the appellants assert is relevant does not in any way interfere, in either appearance or fact, with the court's adjudicative role or any of the essential conditions of judicial independence. Judicial independence can abide unconventional rules of civil procedure and evidence.

[56] The appellants' submission that the Act violates the independence of the judiciary and is therefore unconstitutional fails for the reasons stated above.

C. RULE OF LAW

[57] The rule of law is "a fundamental postulate of our constitutional structure" (*Roncarelli v. Duplessis*, [1959] S.C.R. 121 (S.C.C.), at p. 142) that lies "at the root of our system of government" (*Reference re Secession of Quebec*, [1998] 2 S.C.R. 217 (S.C.C.), at para. 70). It is expressly acknowledged by the preamble to the *Constitution Act, 1982*, and implicitly recognized in the preamble to the *Constitution Act, 1867*: see *Reference re Language Rights Under s. 23 of Manitoba Act*, 1870 & s. 133 of *Constitution Act, 1867*, [1985] 1 S.C.R. 721 (S.C.C.), at p. 750.

[58] This Court has described the rule of law as embracing three principles. The first recognizes that "the law is supreme over officials of the government as well as private individuals, and thereby preclusive of the influence of arbitrary power": *Reference re Manitoba Language Rights*, at p. 748. The second "requires the creation and maintenance of an actual order of positive laws which preserves and embodies the more general principle of normative order": *Reference re Manitoba Language Rights*, at p. 749. The third requires that "the relationship between the state and the individual ... be regulated by law": *Reference re Secession of Quebec*, at para. 71.

[59] So understood, it is difficult to conceive of how the rule of law could be used as a basis for invalidating legislation such as the Act based on its content. That is because none of the principles that the rule of law embraces speak directly to the terms of legislation. The first principle requires that legislation be applied to all those, including government officials, to whom it, by its terms, applies. The second principle means that legislation must exist. And the third principle, which overlaps somewhat with the first and second, requires that state officials' actions be legally founded. See R. Elliot, "References, Structural Argumentation and the Organizing Principles of Canada's Constitution" (2001), 80 Can. Bar Rev. 67, at pp. 114–15.

[60] This does not mean that the rule of law as described by this Court has no normative force. As McLachlin C.J. stated in *Babcock*, at para. 54, "unwritten constitutional principles", including the rule of law, "are capable of limiting government actions". See also *Reference re Secession of Quebec*, at para. 54. But the government action constrained by the rule of law as understood in *Reference re Manitoba Language Rights* and *Reference re Secession of Quebec* is, by definition, usually that of the executive and judicial branches. Actions of the legislative branch are constrained too, but only in the sense

that they must comply with legislated requirements as to manner and form (i.e. the procedures by which legislation is to be enacted, amended and repealed).

[61] Nonetheless, considerable debate surrounds the question of what additional principles, if any, the rule of law might embrace, and the extent to which they might mandate the invalidation of legislation based on its content. P. W. Hogg and C. F. Zwibel write in "The Rule of Law in the Supreme Court of Canada" (2005), 55 U.T.L.J. 715, at pp. 717–18:

> Many authors have tried to define the rule of law and explain its significance, or lack thereof. Their views spread across a wide spectrum.... T.R.S. Allan, for example, claims that laws that fail to respect the equality and human dignity of individuals are contrary to the rule of law. Luc Tremblay asserts that the rule of law includes the liberal principle, the democratic principle, the constitutional principle, and the federal principle. For Allan and Tremblay, the rule of law demands not merely that positive law be obeyed but that it embody a particular vision of social justice. Another strong version comes from David Beatty, who argues that the "ultimate rule of law" is a principle of "proportionality" to which all laws must conform on pain of invalidity (enforced by judicial review). In the middle of the spectrum are those who, like Joseph Raz, accept that the rule of law is an ideal of constitutional legality, involving open, stable, clear, and general rules, even-handed enforcement of those laws, the independence of the judiciary, and judicial review of administrative action. Raz acknowledges that conformity to the rule of law is often a matter of degree, and that breaches of the rule of law do not lead to invalidity.

See also W. J. Newman, "The Principles of the Rule of Law and Parliamentary Sovereignty in Constitutional Theory and Litigation" (2005), 16 N.J.C.L. 175, at pp. 177–80.

[62] This debate underlies Strayer J.A.'s apt observation in *Singh v. Canada (Attorney General)*, [2000] 3 F.C. 185 (C.A.), at para. 33, that "[a]dvocates tend to read into the principle of the rule of law anything which supports their particular view of what the law should be".

[63] The appellants' conceptions of the rule of law can fairly be said to fall at one extreme of the spectrum of possible conceptions and to support Strayer J.A.'s thesis. They submit that the rule of law requires that legislation (1) be prospective; (2) be general in character; (3) not confer special privileges on the government, except where necessary for effective governance; and (4) ensure a fair civil

trial. And they argue that the Act breaches each of these requirements, rendering it invalid.

[64] A brief review of this Court's jurisprudence will reveal that none of these requirements enjoy constitutional protection in Canada. But before embarking on that review, it should be said that acknowledging the constitutional force of anything resembling the appellants' conceptions of the rule of law would seriously undermine the legitimacy of judicial review of legislation for constitutionality. That is so for two separate but interrelated reasons.

[65] First, many of the requirements of the rule of law proposed by the appellants are simply broader versions of rights contained in the *Charter*. For example, the appellants' proposed fair trial requirement is essentially a broader version of s. 11(d) of the Charter, which provides that "[a]ny person charged with an offence has the right ... to ... a fair and public hearing". But the framers of the *Charter* enshrined that fair trial right only for those "charged with an offence". If the rule of law constitutionally required that all legislation provide for a fair trial, s. 11(d) and its relatively limited scope (not to mention its qualification by s. 1) would be largely irrelevant because everyone would have the unwritten, but constitutional, right to a "fair ... hearing". (Though, as explained in para. 76, infra, the Act provides for a fair trial in any event.) Thus, the appellants' conception of the unwritten constitutional principle of the rule of law would render many of our written constitutional rights redundant and, in doing so, undermine the delimitation of those rights chosen by our constitutional framers. That is specifically what this Court cautioned against in *Reference re Secession of Quebec*, at para. 53:

> Given the existence of these underlying constitutional principles, what use may the Court make of them? In [*Reference re Remuneration of Judges of the Provincial Court of Prince Edward Island*], at paras. 93 and 104, we cautioned that *the recognition of these constitutional principles ... could not be taken as an invitation to dispense with the written text of the Constitution. On the contrary, we confirmed that there are compelling reasons to insist upon the primacy of our written constitution.* A written constitution promotes legal certainty and predictability, and it provides a foundation and a touchstone for the exercise of constitutional judicial review. [Emphasis added.]

[66] Second, the appellants' arguments overlook the fact that several constitutional principles other than the rule of law that have been recognized by this Court — most notably democracy and constitutional-

ism — very strongly favour upholding the validity of legislation that conforms to the express terms of the Constitution (and to the requirements, such as judicial independence, that flow by necessary implication from those terms). Put differently, the appellants' arguments fail to recognize that in a constitutional democracy such as ours, protection from legislation that some might view as unjust or unfair properly lies not in the amorphous underlying principles of our Constitution, but in its text and the ballot box. See *Bacon v. Saskatchewan Crop Insurance Corp.* (1999), 180 Sask. R. 20 (Sask. C.A.), at para. 30, Elliot, at pp. 141–42, Hogg and Zwibel, at p. 718, and Newman, at p. 187.

[67] The rule of law is not an invitation to trivialize or supplant the Constitution's written terms. Nor is it a tool by which to avoid legislative initiatives of which one is not in favour. On the contrary, it requires that courts give effect to the Constitution's text, and apply, by whatever its terms, legislation that conforms to that text.

[68] A review of the cases showing that each of the appellants' proposed requirements of the rule of law has, as a matter of precedent and policy, no constitutional protection is conclusive of the appellants' rule of law arguments.

(1) Prospectivity in the Law

[69] Except for criminal law, the retrospectivity and retroactivity of which is limited by s. 11(g) of the Charter, there is no requirement of legislative prospectivity embodied in the rule of law or in any provision of our Constitution. Professor P. W. Hogg sets out the state of the law accurately (in *Constitutional Law of Canada* (loose-leaf ed.), vol. 1, at p. 48-29):

> Apart from s. 11(g), Canadian constitutional law contains no prohibition of retroactive (or *ex post facto* laws). There is a presumption of statutory interpretation that a statute should not be given retroactive effect, but, if the retroactive effect is clearly expressed, then there is no room for interpretation and the statute is effective according to its terms. Retroactive statutes are in fact common.

. . . . .

[73] Two decisions of this Court defeat the appellants' submission that the Constitution, through the rule of law, requires that legislation be general in character and devoid of special advantages for the government (except where necessary for effective

governance), as well as that it ensure a fair civil trial.

. . . .

[Major J. referred to *Air Canada v. British Columbia*, [1989] 1 S.C.R. 1161, where the Court upheld the constitutionality of a retroactive tax that benefited the Crown at the expense of a particular industry; and to *Authorson (Litigation Guardian of) v. Canada (A.G.)*, [2003] 2 S.C.R. 40, 2003 SCC 39 (S.C.C.), where the Court upheld the constitutionality of a law that deprived a particular group of vulnerable veterans of the ability to have any trial of their claims.]

. . . .

[76] Additionally, the appellants' conception of a "fair" civil trial seems in part to be of one governed by customary rules of civil procedure and evidence. As should be evident from the analysis concerning judicial independence, there is no constitutional right to have one's civil trial governed by such rules. Moreover, new rules are not necessarily unfair. Indeed, tobacco manufacturers sued pursuant to the Act will receive a fair civil trial, in the sense that the concept is traditionally understood: they are entitled to a public hearing, before an independent and impartial court, in which they may contest the claims of the plaintiff and adduce evidence in their defence. The court will determine their liability only following that hearing, based solely on its understanding of the law as applied to its findings of fact. The fact that defendants might regard that law (i.e. the Act) as unjust, or the procedural rules it prescribes as unprecedented, does not render their trial unfair.

[77] The Act does not implicate the rule of law in the sense that the Constitution comprehends that term. It follows that the Act is not unconstitutional by reason of interference with it.

V. CONCLUSION

[78] The Act is constitutionally valid. The appeals are dismissed, with costs to the respondents throughout. Each constitutional question is answered "no". The stay of proceedings granted by McLachlin C.J. on January 21, 2005 is vacated.

Appeals dismissed.

(f)   A New Era in the Selection of Supreme Court Judges[†]

Jacob Ziegel

NOTE

Although it is the executive branch — the first ministers and Cabinet — that formally appoints Canadian judges, most appointments follow recommendations from nominating committees comprising representatives of government, the bar, the judiciary, and the public. This approach widens the range of opinion that can inform the selection process, and provides a potential buffer between judicial appointments and partisan influences. However, as seen in *Aspects of the Judiciary* earlier in this chapter, the selection process for the most important court of all was until recently a closed-door affair, with consultation left to the discretion of the Prime Minister and federal Minister of Justice.

Since 2004, the selection process for the Supreme Court of Canada has been in a state of transition, taking a series of different approaches on an *ad hoc* basis. Why the indecision? And what are the interests and values that must be bal-

† Excerpt from "Commentary: A New Era in the Selection of Supreme Court Judges" (2006) 44 Osgoode Hall L.J. 547–55. Reproduced with permission.

Professor Ziegel is Professor of Law Emeritus and Senior Fellow at Massey College, University of Toronto.

anced in designing this process? In the extract below, Jacob Ziegel gives a qualified approval to the approach taken by the Harper government in early 2006. Do you agree with Ziegel's assessment?

EXTRACT

It was an adroit move on Prime Minister Stephen Harper's part to set up an ad [hoc] House of Commons committee to interview Justice Marshall Rothstein before confirmation of his appointment to the Supreme Court of Canada by the newly elected Conservative government. The selection procedure for appointments to the Supreme Court was not an issue during the federal election campaign; nevertheless, the Liberals and the Conservatives knew that an early decision would have to be made about Justice John Major's successor in the Supreme Court.

Justice Minister Irwin Cotler had paved the way in the summer of 2005 by establishing an advisory committee of nine members and asking the committee to cull a shortlist of three names from a list of eight potential candidates handed to them by the minister. The committee submitted its shortlist just before the election was called on 28 November 2005. After forming a government, Prime Minister Harper could have struck a new advisory committee to show that a new broom sweeps clean; he could also have introduced an entirely new selection procedure. Wisely, he decided there was insufficient time for a fresh start. According to newspaper reports, he accepted the shortlist prepared by the advisory committee established by Cotler, and selected as his first choice Justice Marshall Rothstein, a member of the Federal Court of Canada.

Harper's masterful stroke was the decision to ask an all-party committee of the House of Commons to publicly interview the candidate before the government confirmed his appointment. Previously, the Conservative members of the House of Commons Justice Committee had supported a system of parliamentary scrutiny of Supreme Court nominees, but this was premised on a different set of circumstances. It did not envisage a separate role for an advisory committee, which included a representative from each of the House of Commons' political parties, to compile a shortlist of candidates. Harper's decision to proceed with a public hearing gave him the best of both worlds. By convening a public hearing, he honoured his party's commitment to transparency and earned plaudits from the media. By selecting a candidate from the advisory committee's

shortlist he made sure that he was ideologically comfortable with the candidate and that the Liberals could not oppose the candidate since he was produced by a selection procedure they had themselves initiated. Justice Rothstein's well-known conservative legal philosophy nicely mirrored Harper's conception of the Supreme Court as an interpreter of the law and not as a social reformer. It did no harm either that the bar held Justice Rothstein in very high regard, not only for his competence and conscientiousness but also for his civility to counsel appearing before him.

Harper's announcement galvanized the Canadian media, who were familiar with the intensive grilling that nominees to the U.S. Supreme Court are subjected to in hearings before the U.S. Senate Judiciary Committee.[1] Knowing, too, how hostile Conservative members of the House of Commons were to activist judges, the media may have anticipated some lively exchanges before the ad hoc committee. They were also aware that Chief Justice Beverley McLachlin was on record as strongly opposing public hearings of nominees to the Supreme Court of Canada, as were former members of the Supreme Court, both the present and earlier presidents of the Canadian Bar Association, and other senior members of the bar. These critics warned repeatedly that public hearings would politicize the Supreme Court and compromise its independence.

Happily, these misgivings turned out to be unfounded. There were no verbal fireworks to feed the media's appetite for confrontations and no angry exchanges.[2] The Rothstein hearing was a model of decorum and sobriety. The rules of procedure were laid out carefully at the beginning, and there was no grandstanding or self-promotion by individual members of the committee. Few of the questions asked could be construed as likely to compromise Justice Rothstein's role as a future member of the Supreme Court, and he deftly turned aside those that might have done so without rancour or ill feeling. The judge was in fact the star of the hearing. He charmed the members of the committee and the large television audience with his informality, self-deprecating sense of humour, and willingness to explain his judicial philosophy in simple terms which were readily comprehensible even to non-lawyers. His performance showed that future candidates for appointment to the Supreme Court have nothing to fear from a public hearing and that the Court itself can only benefit from a better appreciation by Canadians of its role as the final adjudicator of Canada's public and private law values.

I. EARLIER HISTORY OF SUPREME COURT APPOINTMENTS

However, my sentiments may not satisfy the skeptics who are convinced that Canada has embarked on a course of action that can only harm the Supreme Court's independence and impeccable reputation. It is necessary therefore to recapitulate the sequence of events that led to the Rothstein hearing and to explain why the critics' concerns are ill founded.

Democratic countries in the Western hemisphere have adopted a variety of methods for selecting the members of their highest constitutional court or final appellate courts in civil and criminal appeals. Broadly speaking, these methods fall under one of the following heads: (1) appointment by the executive or constitutional head of government without recommendation from another agency (United Kingdom model before adoption of the *Constitutional Reform Act 2005*); (2) appointment by the executive or constitutional head of government based on nomination by another agency (United Kingdom model after adoption of *Constitutional Reform Act 2005*, South Africa, and Israel); (3) nomination by the executive and confirmation by the legislature (U.S. Supreme Court model); (4) election by legislative bodies or by popular vote (German model with respect to the Federal Constitutional Court and widely adopted U.S. state model with respect to election of members of state supreme courts).

Canada's system of appointments to the Supreme Court falls into the first category and is inherited from the United Kingdom. Just as important, appointments to the Supreme Court are not formally enshrined in the *Constitution Act, 1982* but are governed by an ordinary act of Parliament, the *Supreme Court Act*, which was first adopted [in] 1875.[3] The *Supreme Court Act* provides that appointments shall be made by the Governor-in-Council. By convention, this has been interpreted to mean that appointments are made on the recommendation of the incumbent prime minister. There is no formal requirement that the prime minister must consult anyone before making a recommendation, and the prime minister is free to ignore whatever advice is given. There is little doubt that the prime minister's untrammelled power of appointment and the partisanship with which it was exercised was an important factor — perhaps the key factor — in explaining the generally low esteem in which the Supreme Court was held prior to the abolition of appeals from Canadian courts to the Privy Council in London in 1949.[4]

The quality of appointments has undoubtedly improved greatly since then, and the Court has rightly been lauded for its stellar performance since 1982 in interpreting the *Canadian Charter of Rights and Freedoms*.[5] Nevertheless, it would be misleading to suggest that all the appointments in the post-*Charter* era have been of top quality and have not been diluted by the personal predilections and political biases of prime ministers and their advisors.

II. IMPACT OF THE CANADIAN CHAPTER

This lack of accountability and transparency in the appointment process to the nation's highest court was bad enough before 1982, but in the eyes of many observers, it became totally unacceptable in the post-*Charter* era. The Supreme Court had become one of the most powerful courts in the Western hemisphere — more powerful, for example, in the scope of its jurisdiction than the U.S. Supreme Court. The Canadian Supreme Court has the final say on all aspects of Canada's constitutional life and maintains its ultimate adjudicative role in the criminal law sphere as well as in matters of private law, whether of federal or provincial origin. Though Canadian politicians and legal commentators were slow to appreciate the fact, it is now abundantly clear that the open-ended norms of the *Charter* require members of the Supreme Court to make critical policy decisions on questions affecting the conduct of Canada's political, economic, and social affairs. This means that selecting members of the Supreme Court involves finding candidates with the right intellectual and personal qualities, and then considering their constitutional philosophies in relation to the broad spectrum of issues likely to come before the Court.

Efforts to broaden the selection procedure for appointments to the Supreme Court had long preceded the adoption of the Canadian *Charter* as part of the package of constitutional amendments considered in the 1960s and 1970s. None of them bore fruit, however, and the challenge was taken up again in the early 1980s by committees of the Canadian Bar Association (CBA) and the Canadian Association of Law Teachers (CALT). Their concern was more about the merit of judicial appointees than about greater political accountability. Both organizations issued important reports in 1986.[6] Both reports contained substantially similar recommendations for the establishment of advisory committees to advise the federal government on appointments to the provincial superior courts, the Federal Court of Canada, and the Supreme Court.

The Mulroney administration partially implemented the recommendations involving judicial appointments below the Supreme Court level. However, neither Mulroney in the 1980s nor Chrétien in the 1990s showed any interest in diluting their appointive powers with respect to the Supreme Court. Nevertheless, the pressures continued to mount. Newspaper commentators and editorialists were especially vociferous in articulating the case for a more transparent and accountable system of appointments to the Supreme Court.

III. THE MARTIN ERA INITIATIVES

Even before succeeding Jean Chrétien as prime minister in November 2003, Paul Martin publicly committed himself to curing the democratic deficit in the existing system of Supreme Court appointments, though he never made it clear how far he was willing to go. He invited the House of Commons Justice Committee in February 2004 to provide him expeditiously with the committee's own recommendations. Though the committee produced a slim report in record time in May of that year,[7] there was little consensus among the political parties about the desirable reforms. The Liberals, and seemingly the New Democrats, favoured some type of advisory committee but were opposed to public hearings for nominees. The Bloc Québécois favoured much stronger input from the provinces and a participatory role for the justice committee. The Conservative members emphasized the need for public hearings and parliamentary ratification.

Justice Minister Irwin Cotler and the Liberal members of the Justice Committee were hostile to any suggestion of public confirmation hearings. The minister confirmed his opposition when he unveiled the government's response to the committee's report in April 2005 and again during that same year.[8] Though the government accepted the appropriateness of some kind of an advisory committee, even here the minister was determined to ensure that the committee's mandate was carefully circumscribed. The committee, as appointed, had nine members: a nominee from each of the recognized political parties in the House of Commons, a retired judge, a nominee of the provincial attorneys general from one of whose jurisdictions the new member of the Supreme Court was to be appointed, a nominee of the provincial law societies of the same provinces, and two distinguished laypersons who were neither judges nor lawyers. Significantly, the committee was not left

free to compile its own list of potential candidates. Instead, the justice minister provided the committee with a list of eight candidates from which the committee was asked to select three for submission to the federal government. The minister's rationale for these restrictions was that the committee lacked the resources and the expertise to locate suitable candidates within a reasonable time frame. The committee was duly appointed with these terms of reference and presented the federal government with its list of three nominees shortly before the election was called on 28 November 2005.

IV. A UNIQUELY CANADIAN SOLUTION?

The question that now needs to be addressed is whether Harper, no doubt greatly to his own surprise, has found the perfect formula for combining the broad and long-standing public support for an advisory committee with the Conservative party's commitment to public hearings. We may not learn the answer until we know which government holds the reins of power when the next vacancy arises in the Supreme Court. This may not be until 2012, the mandatory retirement date of the oldest member of the current Supreme Court.

It is possible, of course, that an intervening administration will reject Harper's ingenious solution and adopt a new appointive system of its own or revert to the Liberals' penchant for an advisory committee sans public hearing. I doubt, however, that a future administration will want to invest the political capital necessary to reinvent this peculiarly Canadian wheel — a wheel not symmetrically circular, to be sure, but mobile nonetheless and capable of reaching its appointed destination. The critics will no doubt complain that the two-step process adopted by the Conservatives is a sham, as indeed would have been the Liberals' preferred one-step advisory committee procedure. The hybrid Harper approach, it will be argued, is a sham in two respects: first, because the powers of the advisory committee established by the Liberals were so circumscribed that they were more form than substance, and second, because of restrictions on the types of questions the parliamentary committee members were allowed to put to the nominee at the public hearing. Other critics may object that the belt and suspender approach adopted by Harper, while explicable in its particular context, should not be endorsed on a long-term basis because it is duplicative and wasteful. Canada, it will be argued, should embrace either one or the other approach to ensure high quality appointments to the Supreme Court, but not both.

I concede there is substance to these criticisms. But on balance, they do not undermine the case for combining the role of an advisory committee with the function of a public hearing. My reasons are outlined below.

As perceived in the earlier reports addressing the need for an advisory committee, the role of the committee was to ensure that the nominee was pre-eminently qualified, intellectually and otherwise, for membership of the Court and to avoid partisan appointments of less qualified candidates by the federal government. As a member of the CALT committee that reported in 1986, I can attest to the fact that the ideology of candidates for appointment to the Court did not figure prominently in the committee's deliberations. Perhaps somewhat naively, we assumed that if a candidate had the right intellectual and personal qualities, he or she would also make broadly acceptable policy decisions on the *Charter* and other sensitive branches of public law. Those were the early days when the Court's expansive normative options in interpreting *Charter* provisions were not as obvious as they are today. The advantages of the advisory committee model over the confirmation model [are] that it requires the committee to be proactive and not reactive, as is true of the confirmation model. A confirmation hearing can only approve or reject, and may lack the power to reject altogether if the executive holds majority representation on the committee. This disabling feature of the confirmation model is illustrated by the confirmation last year of Judge Samuel Alito, who was appointed to the U.S. Supreme Court despite strong opposition by the minority Democratic senators in the Senate.

V.   CHANGING POLITICAL ENVIRONMENT

Had the federal government accepted the CBA and CALT recommendations in the 1980s in favour of an advisory committee structure, the pressure for a confirmation process might never have arisen.[9] However, the Mulroney and Chrétien governments missed the opportunity, and the political environment has changed significantly since then. The Canadian public today is more conscious of the powers of the Supreme Court and much more suspicious of critical appointive decisions made behind closed doors. Marshall Rothstein's hearing has also confirmed that there is great public interest in the personalities of the members of the Supreme Court and a desire for better understanding of the Court's work. Hearings therefore serve an important educational func-

tion, for the members of the Court as well as for the members of the Justice Committee and the public at large. It may well be true that if the selection committee has done its work well, the nominee will sail through the hearing with flying colours. This does not mean that useful questions cannot be asked by the members of the Justice Committee. The Rothstein hearing was an innovation and one should not be too critical of the lack of sophistication in the committee members' questions.[10] There are many aspects of the Court's work that can be intelligently canvassed in nomination hearings without compromising the candidate's role as a future member of the Supreme Court, and members of the committee should be encouraged to ask them.[11]

Notes

1. The hearings involving Justice Samuel Alito's nomination to the U.S. Supreme Court in the fall of 2005 will have refreshed their memories about just how intrusive those hearings could be.

2. The whole hearing, which ran for some three hours, was televised live on the Cable Public Affairs Channel (CPAC) but, so far as I know, no official transcript has been made available for public distribution. Robert Blackwell, legal reporter for *The Globe and Mail*, kindly loaned me his videotape of about the first two hours of the hearing and I was able to persuade a former student, Carlin McGoogan (JD, University of Toronto 2005) to prepare what turned out to be a more than ample and very comprehensive summary.

3. See now R.S.C. 1985, c. S-26 am. *Supreme Court Act*. There is however an unresolved difference of opinion among constitutional scholars whether ss. 41(d) and 42 of the *Constitution Act, 1982* have entrenched all or part of the *Supreme Court Act*. For details see Jacob S. Ziegel, "Merit Selection and Democratization of Appointments to the Supreme Court of Canada" *IRPP Choices* 5:2 (June 1999) 3 at 18–19, online: Institute for Research on Public Policy <http://www.irpp.org./fastrack/index.htm> Given the importance of the questions, it is surprising that the uncertainty is still not resolved.

4. In Peter Russell's trenchant description, the Supreme Court before 1949 was "a thoroughly second rate institution and treated as such by the federal government." P.H. Russell, *The Judiciary in Canada: The Third Branch of Government* (Toronto: McGraw-Hill, 1987) at 387.

5. *Canadian Charter of Rights and Freedoms*, Part I of the *Constitution Act, 1982*, being Schedule B to the *Canada Act 1982* (U.K.), 1982, c. 11 [*Charter*].

6. For details see Jacob S. Ziegel, "Federal Judicial Appointments in Canada: The Time is Ripe for Change" (1987) 36 U.T.L.J. 1.

7. See Canada, The Standing Committee on Justice, Human Rights, Public Safety and Emergency Preparedness, *Improving the Supreme Court of Canada Appointments Process* (Ottawa: The Standing Committee on Justice, Human Rights, Public Safety and Emergency Preparedness, 2004) (Chair: Derek Lee), online:<http://cmte.parl.gc.ca/cmte/committee publication.aspx?com=8795&lang=1&sourceid=84157>.

8. See Department of Justice, News Release, Government of Canada Moves to Reform Supreme Court of Canada Appointments Process, (7 April 2005); Department of Justice, News Release, New Supreme Court of Canada Appointments Process Launched, (8 August 2005).

9. Neither the CBA nor the CALT reports recommended public confirmation hearings. The author was a member of the CALT committee.

10. This would be my response to the comment attributed to Justice Major that he thought some of the committee members' questions at the hearings were "inane."

11. To give some examples: (1) How realistic is it to expect every member of the Supreme Court to read conscientiously all the materials on each of the hundred or so cases in which leave to appeal is granted by the Supreme Court and if it is not realistic should the Court reduce the number of cases it is willing to hear? (2) Is the impression correct that the common law members of the Supreme Court do not involve themselves deeply in civil law appeals coming from Quebec but defer to the expertise of the civilian colleagues on the Court, and if it is correct, is this something we should worry about? (3) How significant is the role of law clerks in the preparation of Supreme Court judgments and should their role receive greater public recognition?

5

The Judicial Committee of the Privy Council and Early Federalism

(a) Introduction

THE JUDICIAL COMMITTEE AND EARLY FEDERALISM

For the first 80 years of Confederation, the highest judicial tribunal for Canada was not the Supreme Court of Canada. That court wasn't even created until 1875. It didn't become the highest tribunal for Canadian constitutional appeals until 1949. Instead, the highest tribunal was the Judicial Committee of the Privy Council, based in London, England.

Because of the long reign of the Judicial Committee as ultimate constitutional arbiter, its decisions are of interest historically. They are also of legal interest: the Judicial Committee played a role in the formative period of Canadian federalism, and many of its concepts are still law. Finally, as the first ultimate constitutional tribunal, the Judicial Committee provides us with a useful starting point for comparison and contrast with the present court of last resort, the Supreme Court of Canada.

In Chapter 3, we saw that while there were strong pressures for unity and centralism in the period before 1867, there were some significant regional and decentralist pressures too. The *British North America Act, 1867* reflected the ambivalence of this mandate for unity. It joined three colonies, but it opted for a federal system rather than a unitary structure. It created impressive-looking central powers and controls, but also added some potentially broad provincial powers. It did this in a document whose structure and wording were vague enough to convince most centralists and many provincialists that their interests were secured. The challenge of making sense of the *British North America Act, 1867* was postponed and transferred, ultimately, to the judiciary.[1]

In the final decades of the 19th century, when the Judicial Committee took up this challenge,

Canada was undergoing another period of significant change. Railway scandals, regional discontent with the Macdonald government's centralist National Policy, a depression in the mid-1970s, and the ongoing cultural concerns of francophone Canadians, all tended to undermine popular support for strong central government.[2] This was a time of upheaval and — after the 1870s — of growth.[3] Immigrants flowed into the country. Settlers, miners, and loggers moved westward, clearing vast areas of land. As the railways expanded, roads fanned out alongside them. As new villages and towns emerged, there was a growing demand for municipal, policing, educational, and social facilities. Forceful new provincial leaders, such as Oliver Mowat of Ontario, William Fielding of Nova Scotia, and Honoré Mercier of Quebec championed the cause of provincial rights, as did commentators such as Jeremiah Travis and J.J. Loranger.[4] Except for concerns such as railways and the war, the main burden of growth hit areas of apparent provincial responsibility, such as natural resources, municipal institutions, transportation, and education. In this environment, which tended to continue until the Depression,[5] there was pressure to construe provincial power generously to help provinces to cope. It is not surprising, then, that most of the Judicial Committee's earliest and most formative decisions on Canadian federalism seemed to point in a decentralist direction.

But in the 19th and early 20th century, courts were expected to focus on texts, not political contexts, and the text of the *British North America Act, 1867* presented three main interpretation challenges to the Judicial Committee. First, it was necessary to determine how to characterize the legislation that was being challenged on constitutional grounds. Should courts look for the main aspect or any aspect of a challenged statute? Could a statute have more than one main aspect? Second, it was necessary to decide on a relatively consistent analytical approach to interpreting ss. 91 and 92 of the *British North America Act*, the main sections to divide legislative power between the federal and provincial governments. Where should a court look first, in s. 91 or s. 92? In the event of apparent overlap between powers in different sections, how should it be resolved? In the event of apparent conflict between different powers, how should this be resolved? And what about the individual heads of power (jurisdiction) themselves — how should they be construed? Finally, there was a broader issue — could the Judicial Committee find an underlying theme to make sense of the division of powers as a whole, and to provide a rational basis for the answers to the questions above?

Many of these questions arise in regard to four heads of jurisdiction in ss. 91 and 92: Peace, Order and good Government, The Regulation of Trade and Commerce, Criminal Law, and Property and Civil Rights in the Province, and each of these posed special interpretation challenges of its own.

PEACE, ORDER, AND GOOD GOVERNMENT

Of all the grants of legislative power in the *Constitution Act, 1867*, few are more enigmatic than the federal power at the outset of s. 91, to make laws for the Peace, Order, and good Government (POGG). The *Constitution Act, 1867* no sooner confers this power than it goes on to limit it to "all matters not coming within" the heads of power in s. 92. This suggests that, whatever else its meaning is, POGG has a residual sense. In this sense, POGG catches all subject matter that is not, and never has been, in s. 92. Here, clearly, the scope to be given to POGG would depend on the width to be attributed to the heads of power in s. 92 and on the courts' willingness to characterize phenomena as distinct subject matters in their own right.

However, if a purely residual meaning had been desired, it would have been unnecessary to use the phrase "Peace, Order, and good Government" at all. The *Constitution Act, 1867* could simply have given the federal government the power to make laws in regard to all matters not covered by s. 92. Not only did Parliament specify a particular kind of law here, but it specified the broadest possible kind of law. The strictly residual interpretation would render this broad power redundant. Moreover, it would leave the Canadian constitution without a safety valve to permit strong action by the central government where required in the national interest. Hence, it is arguable that POGG also has a positive sense. In this sense, the POGG power catches all subject matter that relates to Peace, Order, and good Government, *regardless* of whether it would otherwise fall under s. 92.

But to give POGG a positive meaning is to let Parliament legislate in areas that may have been originally provincial in nature. Moreover, the phrase "Peace, Order, and good Government" has a literal meaning that is broad enough to extend to all the heads of power conferred on the provinces in s. 92. If the phrase were given its literal meaning, Canada could rapidly become a unitary rather than a federal state.

If POGG is given a positive meaning, other challenges arise. For example, how should this be reconciled with the residual wording following it? If the power were applicable to occasions of great national interest, this could involve broad policy and political considerations — matters on which judicial bodies generally defer to the elected representatives of the people. Deference in this area would be particularly prudent in an ultimate arbiter based in a foreign country, however colonially supreme. But if these same policy considerations related to the boundaries of the Canadian federal system, some judicial involvement would be necessary to keep the boundaries intact. How should these conflicting needs be met?

TRADE AND COMMERCE

If it stood alone in the *Constitution Act, 1867*, the federal power to legislate in relation to "[t]he Regulation of Trade and Commerce" would be very broad indeed. The words granting this power contain no restrictions. A comparable legislative power in the American constitution does contain restrictions, yet the United States Supreme Court has given it a wide interpretation.

Neither the broad language of s. 91 nor the American experience is surprising. The movement of goods is a dynamic process that could be seriously hindered by rigid geographical barriers. The desire to remove unnecessary boundaries to the free movement of goods and to encourage a form of national common market was a significant motivating factor behind Confederation and behind the American Constitution of 1787. In Canada, it was stipulated that provincial articles of trade must be "admitted free" (i.e., of tariffs) into other provinces.

One way to help ensure the freest possible movement of goods throughout the country is to entrust its control to the government for the country as a whole.

On the other hand, s. 91(2) does not stand in isolation. The provinces were given significant powers within their boundaries — over property and civil rights, publicly owned natural resources, direct taxation, and matters of a private or local nature. These would be stripped of much of their meaning by a literal interpretation of the federal trade and commerce power.

As a result, the task of interpreting s. 91(2) has required a particularly difficult balancing act. On the question of just where and how the balance should be struck, the Judicial Committee's approach was quite different from that which emerged later in the Supreme Court of Canada.

CRIMINAL LAW

The federal criminal power is another head of jurisdiction with significant growth potential. At its narrowest, the power might be limited to wrongs deemed to be so serious as to be obviously or inherently criminal in nature, such as murder. At the other extreme, the power might include everything that is accompanied by a criminal penalty. Clearly, while one extreme would deprive the power of much use, the other one could permit the federal government to legislate in most areas that would otherwise fall under s. 92. If some middle alternative was chosen, what criteria should be used?

PROPERTY AND CIVIL RIGHTS IN THE PROVINCE

For the most part, the provincial heads of jurisdiction lack the potential sweep of the federal powers considered above. Moreover, the general structure of the *British North America Act, 1867* imposed potential limits on provincial powers that do not have federal counterparts. For example, the paramountcy provision in s. 91 suggested that provincial powers must yield in the event of conflicts with matters within federal jurisdiction. Moreover,

the federal government was given power to refuse assent to provincial bills or to disallow provincial statutes.

Nevertheless, some provincial powers do have wide literal meanings. One of the widest[6] is s. 92(13), the power in relation to property and civil rights in the province. Conceivably, property could refer to anything capable of ownership, and civil rights could encompass legal status, all rights attaching to legal relationships between individuals.[7] Given its widest interpretation, property and civil rights could undermine many of the economic and financial powers assigned to Parliament.

But property and civil rights in s. 92(13) had a special meaning in earlier Canadian history. Soon after their conquest of New France in 1760, the British concluded that if they were to secure the loyalty of their new subjects, their laws and customs must be protected. Accordingly, the *Quebec Act* of 1774[8] provided that while criminal law would be British, Quebeckers' property and civil rights were to be determined by the "Laws and Customs of Canada". This document, which has been described as "virtually the Magna Carta of the French Canadians,"[9] was the formal basis of the policy of including French Canadians as part of Canada while recognizing their distinctive culture. The *Constitutional Act* of 1791 continued this policy by providing that the laws of Quebec would continue to apply to the new colonies of Upper and Lower Canada unless either of their legislatures should change them.[10] Confederation, arguably, was an attempt to pursue this policy through the vehicle of a federal structure "Property and Civil Rights in the Province" was not just a new jurisdictional grant, but the continuation of a historic safeguard. Did this consideration influence the Judicial Committee's interpretation of s. 92(13)?

KEY DECISIONS

With these questions in mind, we can now turn to some of the Judicial Committee's key decisions on the division of powers. The decisions considered in this chapter represent only a small fraction of the over 140 decisions of the Judicial Committee on the division of powers; for a full picture, many more would need to be considered. On the other hand, the decisions here helped shape a foundation for Canadian federalism, and — for better or for worse — much of this foundation remains in place today.

Notes

1. One of the members of the judiciary, Lord Haldane, speculated that "the form in which provisions in terms overlapping each other have been placed side by side shows that those who passed the *Confederation Act* intended to leave the working out and interpretation of these provisions to practice and to judicial decision": *John Deere Plow Company v. Wharton*, [1915] 1 A.C.3

2. See Edgar McInnis, *Canada: A Political and Social History*, 3d ed. (Toronto: Holt, Rhinehart and Winston, 1969), ch. 15.

3. See generally, John Weaver, *Crimes, Constables, and Courts: Order and Transgression in a Canadian City, 1816–1970* (Montreal & Kingston: McGill-Queen's University Press, 1995); J.M.S. Careless, *Frontier and Metropolis: Regions, Cities, and Identities in Canada Before 1914* (Toronto: University of Toronto Press, 1989); Robert Bothwell, Ian Drummond & John English, *Canada 1900–1945* (Toronto: University of Toronto Press, 1987).

4. See, for example, M.D. Behiels, "Loranger, Thomas-Jean-Jacques" in James H. Marsh, ed. in chief, *The Canadian Encyclopedia: Year 2000 Edition* (Toronto: McClelland & Stewart, 1999) at 1368; Christopher Armstrong, *The Politics of Federalism: Ontario's Relations with the Federal Government, 1867–1942* (Toronto: University of Toronto Press, 1981); Ramsey Cook, *Provincial Autonomy, Minority Rights, and the Compact Theory, 1867–1921* (Ottawa: Queen's Printer, 1969); J.C. Morrison, "Oliver Mowat and the Development of Provincial Rights in Ontario" in *Three History Theses* (Toronto: Ontario Department of Public Records and Archives).

5. After a pause in the decade before 1920, the battle for expanded provincial rights was taken up again by politicians such as Premier Howard Ferguson of Ontario and Louis-Alexandre Taschereau of Quebec: John Herd Thompson with Allen Seager, *Canada 1922–1939: Decades of Discord* (Toronto: McClelland & Stewart, 1985) at 133–35.

6. Another wide provincial power is s. 92(16), referring to "matters of a merely local or private nature in the province". However, this power contains the restrictive term "merely" and lacks the special historical antecedents of property and civil rights.

7. For example, contractual, tortious, possessory, proprietary, and fiduciary rights.

8. 14 George III, c. 83 (U. K.), s. 8.

9. Mason Wade, *The French Canadians*, Rev'd ed. (Toronto: MacMillan, 1968), vol. 1 at 63.

10. Stats. Upper Canada, 1992 (32 Geo. III), c. 1, s. 1.

(b) Key Early Decisions

(i) *Citizens Insurance*†

NOTE

William Parsons, an Orangeville hardware merchant, lost his hardware store in a spectacular blaze on August 3, 1877. Little did he know that this fire would lead to one of the leading decisions on the division of legislative powers under the *Constitution Act, 1867*. Mr. Parsons asked The Citizens Insurance Company for compensation, but they refused, saying he had failed to comply with a condition they had written into the fire insurance contract. Parsons replied that the condition was invalid because Citizens had failed to write it in the form required by the Ontario *Fire Insurance Policy Act*. Citizens responded that the statutory requirement was itself invalid because the *Constitution Act, 1867* gives jurisdiction over fire insurance policy contracts to Parliament, not the provincial legislatures. In the courts, Parsons argued that the Act was valid, while Citizens claimed it was not. At each level, Parsons won on the constitutional question.[1]

To answer this question, the members of the Judicial Committee had to decide just how courts should approach ss. 91 and 92 of the *Constitution Act, 1867*. Which should they consider first? How should prioritize the two sections? Then they had to give some content to two potentially important competing powers, the federal power in relation to "The Regulation of Trade and Commerce", and the provincial power in relation to "Property and Civil Rights in the Province". The first seemed sweeping in scope; the second was also wide, and resembled the wording of an historic early accommodation of French-English relations, the *Quebec Act* of 1774.[2] The Judicial Committee even had occasion to comment on a third major power, the federal power in relation to "Peace, Order, and good Government".

Notes

1. Although he won the constitutional battle, Parsons lost the war against Citizens. Citizens' condition required notification of any prior insurance on the property. Without informing Citizens, Parsons had already insured the store

---

† *Citizens Insurance Company v. Parsons* (1881–2), 7 A.C. 96 (J.C.P.C.).

with another company. He had clearly violated Citizens' condition, but since it was not in the form prescribed by the Ontario statute — and since the Ontario statute was constitutionally valid — Citizens' condition was invalid. Nevertheless, the Judicial Committee found that Parsons' conduct was prohibited by another part of the statute! (This wasn't the end of Parsons' insurance litigation. His claim against Citizens was heard at the same time as his claim against another company on another fire insurance policy he had bought, on the very same day as the fire!)

2. After Britain gained Quebec from France in the 1763 Treaty of Paris, King George III issued a Royal Proclamation on October 7 of that year. As well as reserving a large tract of land to the south of Quebec for the Hunting Grounds of Indians and attending to other matters of governance, the proclamation imposed English criminal and civil (non-criminal) laws on the people of Quebec. The English law provision was a source of great concern to francophone Quebekers, who had used the civil law legal system for over a century. The British government revoked its English law provision — in regard to non-criminal law in Quebec — in the *Quebec Act* of 1774. This was the "Act of 14 Geo. III, c. 83" referred to in the judgment of Sir Montague Smith below. Section 8 of the *Quebec Act* said that:

> And be it further enacted by the Authority aforesaid, That all his Majesty's Canadian Subjects within the Province of Quebec ... may also hold and enjoy their Property and Possessions, together with all Customs, and Usages relative thereto, and all other their Civil rights, in as large, ample, and beneficial Manner as if the said Proclamation [of 1763] ... had not been made, and as may consist with their Allegiance to his Majesty, and Subjection to the Crown and Parliament of Great Britain; and that in all Matters of Controversy, relative to Property and Civil Rights, Resort shall be had to the Laws of Canada, as the Rule for the Decision of the same; and all Causes that shall hereafter be instituted in any of the Courts of Justice, to be appointed within and for the said Province by his Majesty, his Heirs and Successors shall, with respect to such Property and Rights, be determined agreeably to the said Laws and Customs of Canada....

EXTRACT

[SIR MONTAGUE SMITH for the Judicial Committee:]

The scheme of this legislation, as expressed in the first branch of sect. 91, is to give to the dominion parliament authority to make laws for the good government of Canada in all matters not coming within the classes of subjects assigned exclusively to the provincial legislature. If the 91st section had stopped here, and if the classes of subjects enumerated in sect. 92 had been altogether distinct and different from those in sect. 91, no conflict of legislative authority would have arisen. The provincial legislatures would have had exclusive legislative power over the sixteen classes of subjects assigned to them, and the dominion parliament exclusive power over all

other matters relating to the good government of Canada. But it must have been foreseen that this sharp and definite distinction had not been and could not be attained, and that some of the classes of subjects assigned to the provincial legislature unavoidably ran into and were embraced by some of the enumerated classes of subjects in sect. 91; hence an endeavour appears to have been made to provide for cases of apparent conflict; and it would seem that with this object it was declared in the second branch of the 91st section, "for greater certainty, but not so as to restrict the generality of the foregoing terms of this section" that (notwithstanding anything in the Act) the exclusive legislative authority of the parliament of Canada should extend to all matters coming within the classes of subjects enumerated in that section. With the same object, apparently, the paragraph at the end of sect. 91 was introduced, though it may be observed that this paragraph applies in its grammatical construction only to No. 16 of sect. 92.

Notwithstanding this endeavour to give pre-eminence to the dominion parliament in cases of a conflict of powers, it is obvious that in some cases where this apparent conflict exists, the legislature could not have intended that the powers exclusively assigned to the provincial legislature should be absorbed in those given to the dominion parliament. Take as one instance the subject "marriage and divorce," contained in the enumeration of subjects in sect. 91; it is evident that solemnization of marriage would come within this general description; yet "solemnization of marriage in the province" is enumerated among the classes of subjects in sect. 92, and no one can doubt, notwithstanding the general language of sect. 91, that this subject is still within the exclusive authority of the legislatures of the provinces. So "the raising of money by any mode or system of taxation" is enumerated among the classes of subjects in sect. 91; but, though the description is sufficiently large and general to include "direct taxation within the province, in order to the raising of a revenue for provincial purposes," assigned to the provincial legislatures by sect. 92, it obviously could not have been intended that, in this instance also, the general power should override the particular one. With regard to certain classes of subjects, therefore, generally described in sect. 91, legislative power may reside as to some matters falling within the general description of these subjects in the legislatures of the provinces. In these cases it is the duty of the Courts, however difficult it may be, to ascertain in what degree, and to what extent, authority to deal with matters falling within these classes of subjects exists in each legislature, and to define in the particular case before them the limits of their respective powers. It could not have been the intention that a conflict should exist; and, in order to prevent such a result, the two sections must be read together, and the language of one interpreted, and, where necessary, modified, by that of the other. In this way it may, in most cases, be found possible to arrive at a reasonable and practical construction of the language of the sections, so as to reconcile the respective powers they contain, and give effect to all of them. In performing this difficult duty, it will be a wise course for those on whom it is thrown, to decide each case which arises as best they can, without entering more largely upon an interpretation of the statute than is necessary for the decision of the particular question in hand.

The first question to be decided is, whether the Act impeached in the present appeals falls within any of the classes of subjects enumerated in sect. 92, and assigned exclusively to the legislatures of the provinces; for if it does not, it can be of no validity, and no other question would then arise. It is only when an Act of the provincial legislature prima facie falls within one of these classes of subjects that the further questions arise, viz., whether, notwithstanding this is so, the subject of the Act does not also fall within one of the enumerated classes of subjects in sect. 91, and whether the power of the provincial legislature is or is not thereby overborne.

The main contention on the part of the respondent was that the Ontario Act in question had relation to matters coming within the class of subjects described in No. 13 of sect. 92, viz., "Property and civil rights in the province." The Act deals with policies of insurance entered into or in force in the province of Ontario for insuring property situate therein against fire, and prescribes certain conditions which are to form part of such contracts. These contracts, and the rights arising from them, it was argued, came legitimately within the class of subject, "Property and civil rights." The appellants, on the other hand, contended that civil rights meant only such rights as flowed from the law, and gave as an instance the status of persons. Their Lordships cannot think that the latter construction is the correct one. They find no sufficient reason in the language itself, nor in the other parts of the Act, for giving so narrow an interpretation to the words "civil rights." The words are sufficiently large to embrace, in their fair and ordinary meaning, rights arising from contract, and such rights are not included in express terms in any of the enumerated classes of subjects in sect. 91.

It becomes obvious, as soon as an attempt is made to construe the general terms in which the classes of subjects in sects. 91 and 92 are described, that both sections and the other parts of the Act must be looked at to ascertain whether language of a general nature must not by necessary implication or reasonable intendment be modified and limited. In looking at sect. 91, it will be found not only that there is no class including, generally, contracts and the rights arising from them, but that one class of contracts is mentioned and enumerated, viz., "18, bills of exchange and promissory notes," which it would have been unnecessary to specify if authority over all contracts and the rights arising from them had belonged to the dominion parliament.

The provision found in sect. 94 of the British North America Act, which is one of the sections relating to the distribution of legislative powers, was referred to by the learned counsel on both sides as throwing light upon the sense in which the words "property and civil rights" are used. By that section the parliament of Canada is empowered to make provision for the uniformity of any laws relative to "property and civil rights" in Ontario, Nova Scotia, and New Brunswick, and to the procedure of the Courts in these three provinces, if the provincial legislatures choose to adopt the provision so made. The province of Quebec is omitted from this section for the obvious reason that the law which governs property and civil rights in Quebec is in the main the French law as it existed at the time of the cession of Canada, and not the English law which prevails in the other provinces. The words "property and civil rights" are, obviously, used in the same sense in this section as in No. 13 of sect. 92, and there seems no reason for presuming that contracts and the rights arising from them were not intended to be included in this provision for uniformity. If, however, the narrow construction of the words "civil rights" contended for by the appellants were to prevail, the dominion parliament could, under its general power, legislate in regard to contracts in all and each of the provinces and as a consequence of this the province of Quebec, though now governed by its own Civil Code, founded on the French law, as regards contracts and their incidents, would be subject to have its law on that subject altered by the dominion legislature, and brought into uniformity with the English law prevailing in the other three provinces, notwithstanding that Quebec has been carefully left out of the uniformity section of the Act.

It is to be observed that the same words, "civil rights," are employed in the Act of 14 Geo. 3, c. 83, which made provision for the Government of the province of Quebec. Sect. 8 of that Act enacted that His Majesty's Canadian subjects within the province of Quebec should enjoy their property, usages, and other civil rights, as they had before done, and that in all matters of controversy relative to property and civil rights resort should be had to the laws of Canada, and be determined agreeably to the said laws. In this statute the words "property" and "civil rights" are plainly used in their largest sense; and there is no reason for holding that in the statute under discussion they are used in a different and narrower one.

The next question for consideration is whether, assuming the Ontario Act to relate to the subject of property and civil rights, its enactments and provisions come within any of the classes of subjects enumerated in sect. 91. The only one which the Appellants suggested as expressly including the subject of the Ontario Act is No. 2, "the regulation of trade and commerce."

A question was raised which led to much discussion in the Courts below and this bar, viz., whether the business of insuring buildings against fire was a trade. This business, when carried on for the sake of profit, may, no doubt, in some sense of the word, be called a trade. But contracts of indemnity made by insurers can scarcely be considered trading contracts, nor were insurers who made them held to be "traders" under the English bankruptcy laws; they have been made subject to those laws by special description. Whether the business of fire insurance properly falls within the description of a "trade" must, in their Lordships' view, depend upon the sense in which that word is used in the particular statute to be construed; but in the present case their Lordships do not find it necessary to rest their decision on the narrow ground that the business of insurance is not a trade.

The words "regulation of trade and commerce," in their unlimited sense are sufficiently wide, if uncontrolled by the context and other parts of the Act, to include every regulation of trade ranging from political arrangements in regard to trade with foreign governments, requiring the sanction of parliament, down to minute rules for regulating particular trades. But a consideration of the Act shows that the words were not used in this unlimited sense. In the first place the collocation of No. 2 with classes of subjects of national and general concern affords an indication that regulations relating to general trade and commerce were in the mind of the legislature, when conferring this power on the dominion parliament. If the words had been intended to have the full scope of which in their literal meaning they

are susceptible, the specific mention of several of the other classes of subjects enumerated in sect. 91 would have been unnecessary; as, 15, banking; 17, weights and measures; 18, bills of exchange and promissory notes; 19, interest; and even 21, bankruptcy and insolvency.

"Regulation of trade and commerce" may have been used in some such sense as the words "regulations of trade" in the Act of Union between England and Scotland (6 Anne, c. 11), and as these words have been used in Acts of State relating to trade and commerce. Article V of the Act of Union enacted that all the subjects of the United Kingdom should have "full freedom and intercourse of trade and navigation" to and from all places in the United Kingdom and the colonies; and Article VI enacted that all parts of the United Kingdom from and after the Union should be under the same "prohibitions, restrictions, and *regulations of trade*." Parliament has at various times since the Union passed laws affecting and regulating specific trades in one part of the United Kingdom only, without its being supposed that it thereby infringed the Articles of Union. Thus the Acts for regulating the sale of intoxicating liquors notoriously vary in the two kingdoms. So with regard to Acts relating to bankruptcy, and various other matters.

Construing therefore the words "regulation of trade and commerce" by the various aids to their interpretation above suggested, they would include political arrangements in regard to trade requiring the sanction of parliament, regulation of trade in matters of interprovincial concern, and it may be that they would include general regulation of trade affecting the whole dominion. Their Lordships abstain on the present occasion from any attempt to define the limits of the authority of the dominion parliament in this direction. It is enough for the decision of the present case to say that, in their view, its authority to legislate for the regulation of trade and commerce does not comprehend the power to regulate by legislation the contracts of a particular business or trade, such as the business of fire insurance in a single province, and therefore that its legislative authority does not in the present case conflict or compete with the power over property and civil rights assigned to the legislature of Ontario by No. 13 of sect. 92.

. . . .

[In the Supreme Court, Taschereau J. had said that if Parliament had no jurisdiction under the Trade and Commerce power to regulate the contracts of insurance companies, then it also lacked jurisdiction to incorporate such companies. Thus, since Citizens Insurance Company had been incorporated by Parliament, it was improperly incorporated. As a result, Parsons was suing a non-existent plaintiff! Sir Montague Smith rejected this argument. He said that the power to regulate the insurance contracts of companies is distinct from power to incorporate companies with non-provincial objects. Since the latter power was not provided for expressly in s. 92 (or in s. 91) of the *British North America Act, 1867*, Sir Montague Smith said

that it would fall under the Peace, Order and good Government power. This was the first Judicial Committee decision to attribute a residual sense or meaning to Peace, Order and good Government.]

. . . .

On the best consideration they have been able to give to the arguments addressed to them and to the judgments of the learned judges in Canada, their Lordships have come to the conclusion that the Act in question is valid.

(ii)   Russell [†]

NOTE

Charles Russell was another 19th-century merchant whose tangle with the law led to a major Judicial Committee decision. Russell was convicted of selling liquor contrary to the *Canada Temperance Act*, a federal temperance scheme whose prohibitions only applied in localities that adopted them. Russell challenged the Act by arguing that liquor prohibition fell under provincial rather than federal power. He lost in the New Brunswick Supreme Court, which followed an earlier Supreme Court of Canada decision that upheld the statute on the basis of the trade and commerce power. Although Russell appealed directly to the Judicial Committee, what was effectively being appealed was that earlier Supreme Court of Canada decision. Russell lost again in the Judicial Committee, but for different reasons.

Decided only a year after *Citizens Insurance*, *Russell* must have come as a surprise. In *Citizens Insurance*, the Judicial Committee had given trade and commerce very limited scope, and had suggested that Peace, Order and good Government (POGG) was confined to subject matter not expressly allocated to the provinces. Except perhaps for property and civil rights, *Citizens Insurance* had seemed to suggest that broad powers such as POGG would be narrowly construed. *Russell*, however, appeared to contemplate a broader, more flexible approach to POGG and, perhaps, to federal power as a whole.

When reading this case, note how the Judicial Committee members apply the same *general* approach to construing ss. 91 and 92 as set out in *Citizens Insurance*, with some interesting variations. Note how they say that where the subject matter of a statute can have more than one aspect, the task is to determine which aspect is dominant. In regard to POGG itself, are they departing from — or adding to — the notion that this power is confined to subject matter not expressly allocated to the provinces? Finally, note that while they did not reverse the decision of the Canadian court (a form of restraint that was typical of the Judicial Committee), they did refuse to commit themselves to relying on the trade and commerce power.

EXTRACT

[SIR MONTAGUE SMITH for the Judicial Committee:]

[Sir Montague Smith explained that the federal temperance legislation came into force for three years in a Canadian county or city whose electors had voted for the prohibition in a special poll.]

. . . .

The effect of the Act when brought into force in any county or town within the Dominion is, describing it generally, to prohibit the sale of intoxicating liquors, except in wholesale quantities, or for

---

[†] *Russell v. The Queen* (1881–82), 7 A.C. 829 (J.C.P.C.).

certain specified purposes, to regulate the traffic in the excepted cases, and to make sales of liquors in violation of the prohibition and regulations contained in the Act criminal offences, punishable by fine, and for the third or subsequent offence by imprisonment.

. . . .

The general scheme of the British North America Act with regard to the distribution of legislative powers, and the general scope and effect of sects. 91 and 92, and their relation to each other, were fully considered and commented on by this Board in the case of the *Citizens Insurance Company v. Parsons*. According to the principle of construction there pointed out, the first question to be determined is, whether the Act now in question falls within any of the classes of subjects enumerated in sect. 92, and assigned exclusively to the Legislatures of the Provinces. If it does, then the further question would arise, viz., whether the subject of the Act does not also fall within one of the enumerated classes of subjects in sect. 91, and so does not still belong to the Dominion Parliament. But if the Act does not fall within any of the classes of subjects in sect. 92, no further question will remain, for it cannot be contended, and indeed was not contended at their Lordships' bar, that, if the Act does not come within one of the classes of subjects assigned to the Provincial Legislatures, the Parliament of Canada had not, by its general power "to make laws for the peace, order, and good government of Canada," full legislative authority to pass it.

Three classes of subjects enumerated in sect. 92 were referred to, under each of which, it was contended by the appellant's counsel, the present legislation fell. These were:

9. Shop, saloon, tavern, auctioneer, and other licenses in order to the raising of a revenue for provincial, local, or municipal purposes.
13. Property and civil rights in the province.
16. Generally all matters of a merely local or private nature in the province.

With regard to the first of these classes, No. 9, it is to be observed that the power of granting licenses is not assigned to the Provincial Legislatures for the purpose of regulating trade, but "in order to the raising of a revenue for provincial, local, or municipal purposes."

The Act in question is not fiscal law; it is not a law for raising revenue; on the contrary, the effect of it may be to destroy or diminish revenue; indeed it was a main objection to the Act that in the city of Fredericton it did in point of fact diminish the sources of municipal revenue. It is evident, therefore, that the matter of the Act is not within the class of subject No. 9, and consequently that it could not have been passed by the Provincial Legislature by virtue of any authority conferred upon it by that subsection.

. . . .

[Sir Montague Smith said that provincial jurisdiction over the raising of revenue does not preclude Parliament from enacting laws that may affect provincial revenue.]

Next, their Lordships cannot think that the Temperance Act in question properly belongs to the class of subjects, "Property and Civil Rights." It has in its legal aspect an obvious and close similarity to laws which place restrictions on the sale or custody of poisonous drugs, or of dangerously explosive substances. These things, as well as intoxicating liquors, can, of course, be held as property, but a law placing restrictions on their sale, custody, or removal, on the ground that the free sale or use of them is dangerous to public safety, and making it a criminal offence punishable by fine or imprisonment to violate these restrictions, cannot properly be deemed a law in relation to property in the sense in which those words are used in the 92nd section. What Parliament is dealing with in legislation of this kind is not a matter in relation to property and its rights, but one relating to public order and safety. That is the primary matter dealt with, and though incidentally the free use of things in which men may have property is interfered with, that incidental interference does not alter the character of the law. Upon the same considerations, the Act in question cannot be regarded as legislation in relation to civil rights. In however large a sense these words are used, it could not have been intended to prevent the Parliament of Canada from declaring and enacting certain uses of property, and certain acts in relation to property, to be criminal and wrongful. Laws which make it a criminal offence for a man wilfully to set fire to his own house on the ground that such an act endangers the public safety, or to overwork his horse on the ground of cruelty to the animal, though affecting in some sense property and the right of a man to do as he pleases with his own, cannot properly be regarded as legislation in relation to property or to civil rights. Nor could a law which prohibited or restricted the sale or exposure of cattle having a contagious disease be so regarded. Laws of this nature designed for the promotion of public order, safety, or morals, and which subject those who contravene them to criminal procedure and punishment, belong to the subject of public wrongs rather than to that of civil rights. They are of a nature which falls within the general authority of Parliament to make laws for the order and good government of Canada, and have direct relation to criminal law, which is one of the enumerated classes of subjects assigned exclusively to the Parliament of Canada. It was said in the course of the judgment of this Board in the case of the *Citizens Insurance Company of Canada v. Parsons*, that the two sections (91 and 92) must be read together, and the language of one interpreted, and, where necessary, modified by that of the other. Few, if any, laws could be made by Parliament for the peace, order, and good government of Canada which did not in some incidental way affect property and civil rights; and it could not have been intended, when assuring to the provinces exclusive legislative authority on the subjects of property and civil rights, to exclude the Parliament from the exercise of this general power whenever any such incidental interference would result from it. The true nature and character of the legislation in the particular instance under discussion must always be determined, in order to ascertain the class of subject to which it really belongs. In the present case it appears to their Lordships, for the reasons already given, that the matter of the Act in question does not properly belong to the class of subjects "Property and Civil Rights" within the meaning of sub-sect. 13.

It was argued by Mr. Benjamin that if the Act related to criminal law, it was provincial criminal law, and he referred to sub-sect. 15 of sect. 92, viz., "The imposition of any punishment by fine, penalty, or imprisonment for enforcing any law of the province made in relation to any matter coming within any of the classes of subjects enumerated in this section." No doubt this argument would be well founded if the principal matter of the Act could be brought within any of these classes of subjects; but as far as they have yet gone, their Lordships fail to see that this has been done.

It was lastly contended that this Act fell within sub-sect. 16 of sect. 92, — "Generally all matters of a merely local or personal nature in the province."

. . . .

... The declared object of Parliament in passing the Act is that there should be uniform legislation in all the provinces respecting the traffic in intoxicating liquors, with a view to promote temperance in the Dominion. Parliament does not treat the promotion of temperance as desirable in one province more than in another, but as desirable everywhere throughout the Dominion. The Act as soon as it was passed became a law for the whole Dominion, and the enactments of the first part, relating to the machinery for bringing the second part into force, took effect and might be put in motion at once and everywhere within it. It is true that the prohibitory and penal parts of the Act are only to come into force in any county or city upon the adoption of a petition to that effect by a majority of electors, but this conditional application of these parts of the Act does not convert the Act itself into legislation in relation to a merely local matter. The objects and scope of the legislation are still general, viz., to promote temperance by means of a uniform law throughout the Dominion.

The manner of bringing the prohibitions and penalties of the Act into force, which Parliament has thought fit to adopt, does not alter its general and uniform character. Parliament deals with the subject as one of general concern to the Dominion, upon which uniformity of legislation is desirable, and the Parliament alone can so deal with it. There is no ground or pretence for saying that the evil or vice struck at by the Act in question is local or exists only in one province, and that Parliament, under colour of general legislation, is dealing with a provincial matter only. It is therefore unnecessary to discuss the considerations which a state of circumstances of this kind might present. The present legislation is clearly meant to apply a remedy to an evil which is assumed to exist throughout the Dominion, and the local option, as it is called, no more localises the subject and scope of the Act than a provision in an Act for the prevention of contagious diseases in cattle that a public officer should proclaim in what districts it should come in effect, would make the statute itself a mere local law for each of these districts. In statutes of this kind the legislation is general, and the provision for the special application of it to particular places does not alter its character.

Their Lordships having come to the conclusion that the Act in question does not fall within any of the classes of subjects assigned exclusively to the Provincial Legislatures, it becomes unnecessary to discuss the further question whether its provisions also fall within any of the classes of subjects enumerated in sect. 91. In abstaining from this discussion, they must not be understood as intimating any dissent from the opinion of the Chief Justice of the

97

Supreme Court of Canada and the other Judges, who held that the Act, as a general regulation of the traffic in intoxicating liquors throughout the Dominion, fell within the class of subject, "the regulation of trade and commerce," enumerated in that section, and was, on that ground, a valid exercise of the legislative power of the Parliament of Canada.

In the result, their Lordships will humbly recommend Her Majesty to affirm the judgment of the Supreme Court of Canada, and with costs.

(iii) Local Prohibition Reference†

NOTE

Which would prevail? The strict, constructionist approach in *Citizens Insurance* or the more flexible, pro-federal approach in *Russell*? An answer emerged in two parts. In 1883 in *Hodge v. The Queen*[1] and in the 1892 *Maritime Bank*[2] decision, Judicial Committee members articulated a general understanding of Canadian federalism under the *Constitution Act, 1867*. Then in *Local Prohibition* in 1896, they applied this idea to their interpretation of the individual powers in the Act, following *Citizens Insurance*. *Local Prohibition* confirmed that this policy would become the mainstream of Judicial Committee case law. *Russell* was destined to become a countercurrent — but one that never completely ended.

Hodge was another federal–provincial conflict over liquor control. Archibald Hodge, a Toronto tavern operator, was fined for violating a provincial licensing board regulation that prohibited weekend billiard playing in taverns. He argued that liquor licensing fell under the federal Peace, Order, and good Government (POGG) and trade and commerce powers. Moreover, he claimed that provincial legislatures are merely subordinate bodies, lacking the supremacy of Parliament itself. As a result, he said, Ontario could not validly delegate its lawmaking power to a board, so the board's regulation was invalid.[3] Addressing Hodge's first argument, Sir Barnes Peacock applied the "double aspect" doctrine from *Citizens Insurance*. Liquor control, he said, can have both a federal and a provincial aspect, and the provincial regulation was fully supported under the municipal, penalty, and local and private powers of s. 92. Since the *Canada Temperance Act* had not been adopted in Toronto, the provincial statute was valid. To Hodge's delegation argument, Sir Barnes replied that:

> [The provincial legislatures] are in no sense delegates of or acting under any mandate from the Imperial Parliament. When the *British North America Act* enacted that there should be a legislature for Ontario, and that its legislative assembly should have exclusive authority to make laws for the Province and for provincial purposes in relation to the matters enumerated in sect. 92, *it conferred powers not in any sense to be exercised by delegation from or as agents of the Imperial Parliament, but authority as plenary and as ample within the limits prescribed by sect. 92 as the Imperial Parliament, or the Parliament of the Dominion would have had under like circumstances....* [Emphasis added].[4]

This was the Judicial Committee's first articulation of the concept of coordinate federalism. Coordinate federalism is the idea that Canadian federalism requires a strict constitutional balance between two autonomous and relatively equal levels of government — one federal and the others provincial. The Judicial Committee repeated this view in the 1892 *Maritime Bank* decision.[5] Here it said that "[t]he Act places the constitutions of all provinces within the Dominion on the same level," with a federal government for matters of common interest and provincial "independence and autonomy" in provincial matters.

The Judicial Committee developed the idea of coordinate federalism further in the *Local Prohibition Reference*,[6] extracted below. The reference resulted from rivalry between two local option temperance schemes — one a later version of the federal statute upheld in *Russell*, and the other an Ontario statute. The federal government asked the Supreme Court if the provincial statute was valid.

---

† *Ontario (A.G.) v. Canada (A.G.): Local Prohibition Reference*, [1896] A.C. 348 (J.C.P.C.).

The Court said it was *ultra vires*. But the Judicial Committee disagreed. They held that although the federal statute was valid, so was the provincial statute, and that statute was only inoperative where its provisions conflicted in practice with the federal provisions.

After upholding the federal statute because of *Russell*, the Judicial Committee cautioned that normally POGG must be limited to only the most urgent, compelling circumstances. Any other interpretation, said Lord Watson, would "not only be contrary to the intendment of the Act, but would practically destroy the autonomy of the provinces." In other words, broad, open-ended powers such as POGG must be narrowly construed, because these have the most potential to upset the federal–provincial balance, and to subordinate one level — federal or provincial — to the other. The Judicial Committee had linked the strict *Citizens Insurance* approach for all open-ended powers, with the partial exception of property and civil rights,[7] to the notions of balance and autonomy stressed in *Hodge* and *Maritime Bank*.

Local Prohibition is significant in several other respects. Note the Judicial Committee's elaboration of the approach to ss. 91 and 92 pioneered in *Citizens Insurance*; the continued recognition of concurrent or "double aspect" powers, the tendency to uphold legislation wherever possible; and the negative treatment of trade and commerce. From here on, the dominant theme would be strict federal–provincial balance, strictly — often rigidly — enforced.

Notes

1. (1883–84), 9 A.C. 117.
2. *Liquidators of the Maritime Bank v. Receiver General of New Brunswick*, [1892] A.C. 437.
3. *Hodge* relied here on the *delegatus non delegare* rule of interpretation that prohibits subordinate bodies from delegating their law-making power to others, in the absence of express statutory authorization.
4. *Ibid.* at 132.
5. *Liquidators of the Maritime Bank v. Receiver General of New Brunswick*, [1892] A.C. 437, 442.
6. [1896] A.C. 348 (J.C.P.C.).
7. Why the special treatment for property and civil rights? As noted in the discussion of *Citizens Insurance* earlier in this chapter, Sir Montague Smith pointed out there the relation between this phrase and the historic guarantee to Quebeckers of their "property, usages, and other civil rights" in the *Quebec Act* of 1774. He said that in the earlier statute, the terms were "plainly used in their largest sense": *Citizens Insurance Company v. Parsons* (1881–82), 7 A.C. 96 at 111. On the other hand, even property and civil rights was subject to some limits: see, for example, *John Deere Plow Company v. Wharton*, [1915] 1 A.C. 330 at 340.

EXTRACT

[LORD WATSON for the Judicial Committee:]

The seventh question raises the issue, whether, in the circumstances which have just been detailed, the provincial legislature had authority to enact s. 18. In order to determine that issue, it becomes necessary to consider, in the first place, whether the Parliament of Canada had jurisdiction to enact the Canada Temperance Act; and, if so, to consider in the second place, whether, after that Act became the law of each province of the Dominion, there yet remained power with the Legislature of Ontario to enact the provisions of s. 18.

The authority of the Dominion Parliament to make laws for the suppression of liquor traffic in the province is maintained, in the first place, upon the ground that such legislation deals with matters affecting "the peace, order, and good government of Canada," within the meaning of the introductory and general enactments of s. 91 of the British North America Act; and, in the second place, upon the ground that it concerns "the regulation of trade and commerce," being No. 2 of the enumerated classes of subjects which are placed under the exclusive jurisdiction of the Federal Parliament by that section. These sources of jurisdiction are in themselves distinct, and are to be found in different enactments.

It was apparently contemplated by the framers of the Imperial Act of 1867 that the due exercise of the enumerated powers conferred upon the Parliament of Canada by s. 91 might, occasionally and incidentally, involve legislation upon matters which are prima facie committed exclusively to the provincial legislatures by s. 92. In order to provide against that contingency, the concluding part of s. 91 enacts that "any matter coming within any of the classes of subjects enumerated in this section shall not be deemed to come within the class of matters of a local or private nature comprised in the enumeration of the classes of subjects by this Act assigned exclusively to the legislature of the provinces." It was observed by this Board in *Citizens' Insurance Co. of Canada v. Parsons* that the paragraph just quoted "applies in its grammatical construction only to No. 16 of s. 92." The observation was not material to the question arising in that case, and it does not appear to their Lordships to be strictly accurate. It appears to them that the language of the exception in s. 91 was meant to include and correctly describes all the matters enumerated in the sixteen heads of s. 92, as being, from a provincial point of view, of a local or private nature. It also appears to their Lordships that the exception was not meant to derogate from the legislative authority given to provincial legislatures by those sixteen sub-sections, save to the extent of enabling the Parliament of Canada to deal with matters local or private in those cases where such legislation is necessarily incidental to the exercise of the powers conferred upon it by the enumerative heads of clause 91. That view was stated as illustrated by Sir Montague Smith in *Citizens' Insurance Co. of Canada v. Parsons* and *Cushing v. Dupuy*; and it has been recognized by this Board in *Tennant v. Union Bank of Canada* and in *Attorney-General of Ontario v. Attorney-General for the Dominion*.

The general authority given to the Canadian Parliament by the introductory enactments of s. 91 is "to make laws for the peace, order, and good government of Canada, in relation to all matters not coming within the classes of subjects by this Act assigned exclusively to the legislatures of the provinces"; and it is declared, but not so as to restrict the generality of these words, that the exclusive authority of the Canadian Parliament extends to all matters coming within the classes of subjects which are enumerated in the clause. There may, therefore, be matters not included in the enumeration, upon which the Parliament of Canada has power to legislate, because they concern the peace, order, and good government of the Dominion. But to those matters which are not specified among the enumerated subjects of legislation, the exception from s. 92, which is enacted by the concluding words of s. 91, has no application; and, in legislating with regard to such matters, the Dominion Parliament has no authority to encroach upon any class of subjects which is exclusively assigned to provincial legislatures by s. 92. These enactments appear to their Lordships to indicate that the exercise of legislative power by the Parliament of Canada, in regard to all matters not enumerated in s. 91, ought to be strictly confined to such matters as are unquestionably of Canadian interest and importance, and ought not to trench upon provincial legislation with respect to any of the classes of subjects enumerated in s. 92. To attach any other construction to the general power which, in supplement of its enumerated powers, is conferred upon the Parliament of Canada by s. 91, would, in their Lordships' opinion, not only be contrary to the intendment of the Act, but would practically destroy the autonomy of the provinces. If it were once conceded that the Parliament of Canada has authority to make laws applicable to the whole Dominion, in relation to matters which in each province are substantially of local or private interest,

upon the assumption that these matters also concern the peace, order, and good government of the Dominion, there is hardly a subject enumerated in s. 92 upon which it might not legislate, to the exclusion of the provincial legislatures.

In construing the introductory enactments of s. 91, with respect to matters other than those enumerated, which concern the peace, order, and good government of Canada, it must be kept in view that s. 94, which empowers the Parliament of Canada to make provision for the uniformity of the laws relative to property and civil rights in Ontario, Nova Scotia, and New Brunswick does not extend to the province of Quebec; and also that the Dominion legislation thereby authorized is expressly declared to be of no effect unless and until it has been adopted and enacted by the provincial legislature. These enactments would be idle and abortive, if it were held that the Parliament of Canada derives jurisdiction from the introductory provisions of s. 91, to deal with any matter which is in substance local or provincial, and does not truly affect the interest of the Dominion as a whole. Their Lordships do not doubt that some matters, in their origin local and provincial, might attain such dimensions as to affect the body politic of the Dominion, and to justify the Canadian Parliament in passing laws for their regulation or abolition in the interest of the Dominion. But great caution must be observed in distinguishing between that which is local and provincial, and therefore within the jurisdiction of the provincial legislatures, and that which has ceased to be merely local or provincial, and has become matter of national concern, in such sense as to bring it within the jurisdiction of the Parliament of Canada. An Act restricting the right to carry weapons of offence, or their sale to young persons, within the province would be within the authority of the provincial legislature. But traffic in arms, or the possession of them under such circumstances as to raise a suspicion that they were to be used for seditious purposes, or against a foreign State, are matters which, their Lordships conceive, might be competently dealt with by the Parliament of the Dominion.

The judgement of this Board in *Russell v. Reg.* has relieved their Lordships from the difficult duty of considering whether the Canada Temperance Act of 1886 relates to the peace, order, and good government of Canada, in such sense as to bring its provisions within the competency of the Canadian Parliament. In that case the controversy related to the validity of the Canada Temperance Act of 1878; and neither the Dominion nor the Provinces were represented in the argument. It arose between a private prosecutor and a person who had been convicted, at his instance, of violating the provisions of the Canadian Act within a district of New Brunswick, in which the prohibitory clauses of the Act had been adopted. But the provisions of the Act of 1878 were in all material respects the same with those which are now embodied in the Canada Temperance Act of 1886; and the reasons which were assigned for sustaining the validity of the earlier, are, in their Lordships' opinion, equally applicable to the later Act. It therefore appears to them that the decision in *Russell v. Reg.* must be accepted as an authority to the extent to which it goes, namely, that the restrictive provisions of the Act of 1886, when they have been duly brought into operation in any provincial area within the Dominion, must receive effect as valid enactments relating to the peace, order, and good government of Canada.

That point being settled by decision, it becomes necessary to consider whether the Parliament of Canada had authority to pass the Temperance Act of 1886 as being an Act for the "regulation of trade and commerce" within the meaning of No. 2 of s. 91. If it were so, the Parliament of Canada would, under the exception from s. 92 which has already been noticed, be at liberty to exercise its legislative authority, although in so doing it should interfere with the jurisdiction of the provinces. The scope and effect of No. 2 of s. 91 were discussed by this Board at some length in *Citizens' Insurance Co. v. Parsons*, where it was decided that, in the absence of legislation upon the subject by the Canadian Parliament, the Legislature of Ontario had authority to impose conditions, as being matters of civil right, upon the business of fire insurance, which was admitted to be a trade, so long as those conditions only affected provincial trade. Their Lordships do not find it necessary to reopen that discussion in the present case. The object of the Canada Temperance Act of 1886 is, not to regulate retail transactions between those who trade in liquor and their customers, but to abolish all such transactions within every provincial area in which its enactments have been adopted by a majority of the local electors. A power to regulate, naturally, if not necessarily, assumes, unless it is enlarged by the context, the conservation of the thing which is to be made the subject of regulation. In that view, their Lordships are unable to regard the prohibitive enactments of the Canadian statute of 1886 as regulations of trade and commerce. They see no reason to modify the opinion which was recently expressed on their behalf by Lord Davey in *Municipal Corporation of the City of Toronto v. Virgo* in these terms: "Their Lordships think there is marked

distinction to be drawn between the prohibition or prevention of a trade and the regulation or governance of it, and indeed a power to regulate and govern seems to imply the continued existence of that which is to be regulated or governed."

The authority of the Legislature of Ontario to enact s. 18 of 53 Vict. [c. 56] was asserted by the appellant on various grounds. The first of these, which was very strongly insisted on, was to the effect that the power given to each province by No. 8 of s. 92 to create municipal institutions in the province necessarily implies the right to endow these institutions with all the administrative functions which had been ordinarily possessed and exercised by them before the time of the Union. Their Lordships can find nothing to support that contention in the language of s. 92, No. 8, which, according to its natural meaning, simply gives provincial legislatures the right to create a legal body for the management of municipal affairs. Until confederation, the Legislature of each province as then constituted could, if it chose, and did in some cases, entrust to a municipality the execution of powers which now belong exclusively to the Parliament of Canada. Since its date a provincial Legislature cannot delegate any power which it does not possess; and the extent and nature of the functions which it can commit to a municipal body of its own creation must depend upon the legislative authority which it derives from the provisions of s. 92 other than No. 8.

Their Lordships are likewise of opinion that s. 92, No. 9, does not give provincial legislatures any right to make laws for the abolition of the liquor traffic. It assigns to them "shop, saloon, tavern, auctioneer and other licences, in order to the raising of a revenue for provincial, local or municipal purposes." It was held by this Board in *Hodge v. Reg.* to include the right to impose reasonable conditions upon the licences which are in the nature of regulation; but it cannot, with any show of reason, be construed as authorizing the abolition of the sources from which revenue is to be raised.

The only enactments of s. 92 which appear to their Lordships to have any relation to the authority of the provincial legislatures to make laws for the suppression of the liquor traffic are to be found in Nos. 13 and 16, which assign to their exclusive jurisdiction, (1) "property and civil rights in the province," and (2) "generally all matters of a merely local or private nature in the province." A law which prohibits retail transactions and restricts the consumption of liquor within the ambit of the province, and does not affect transactions in liquor between persons in the province and persons in other provinces or in foreign countries, concerns property in the province which would be the subject-matter of the transactions if they were not prohibited, and also the civil rights of persons in the province. It is not impossible that the vice of intemperance may prevail in particular localities within a province to such an extent as to constitute its cure by restricting or prohibiting the sale of liquor a matter of a merely local or private nature, and therefore falling *prima facie* within No. 16. In that state of matters, it is conceded that the Parliament of Canada could not imperatively enact a prohibitory law adapted and confined to the requirements of localities within the province where prohibition was urgently needed.

It is not necessary for the purposes of the present appeal to determine whether provincial legislation for the suppression of the liquor traffic, confined to matters which are provincial or local within the meaning of Nos. 13 and 16, is authorized by the one or by the other of these heads. It cannot, in their Lordships' opinion, be logically held to fall within both of them. In s. 92, No. 16 appears to them to have the same office which the general enactment with respect to matters concerning the peace, order, and good government of Canada, so far as supplementary of the enumerated subjects, fulfils in s. 91. It assigns to the provincial legislature all matters in a provincial sense local or private which have been omitted from the preceding enumeration, and, although its terms are wide enough to cover, they were obviously not meant to include, provincial legislation in relation to the classes of subjects already enumerated.

. . . .

The question must next be considered whether the provincial enactments of s. 18 to any, and if so to what, extent come into collision with the provisions of the Canadian Act of 1886. In so far as they do, provincial must yield to Dominion legislation, and must remain in abeyance unless and until the act of 1886 is repealed by the parliament which passed it.

. . . .

It thus appears that, in their local application within the province of Ontario, there would be considerable difference between the two laws; but it is obvious that their provisions could not be in force within the same district or province at one and the same time. In the opinion of their Lordships the question of conflict between their provisions which arises in this case does not depend upon their identity or non-identity, but upon a feature which is common to both. Neither statute is imperative, their prohibitions being of no force or effect until they have been voluntarily adopted and applied by the vote of a majority of the electors in a district or municipality....

. . . .

If the prohibitions of the *Canada Temperance Act* had been made imperative throughout the Dominion, their Lordships might have been constrained by previous authority to hold that the jurisdiction of the Legislature of Ontario to pass s. 18 or any similar law had been superseded. In that case no provincial prohibitions such as are sanctioned by s. 18 could have been enforced by a municipality without coming into conflict with the paramount law of Canada. For the same reason, provincial prohibitions in force within a particular district will necessarily become inoperative whenever the prohibitory clauses of the Act of 1886 have been adopted by that district. But their Lordships can discover no adequate grounds for holding that there exists repugnancy between the two laws in districts of the province of Ontario where the prohibitions of the Canadian Act are not and may never be in force. In a district which has by the votes of its electors rejected the second part of the Canadian Act, the option is abolished for three years from the date of the poll; and it hardly admits of doubt that there could be no repugnancy whilst the option given by the Canadian Act was suspended....

. . . .

Their Lordships, for these reasons, give a general answer to the seventh question in the affirmative. They are of opinion that the Ontario Legislature had jurisdiction to enact s. 18, subject to this necessary qualification, that its provisions are or will become inoperative in any district of the province which has already adopted, or may subsequently adopt, the second part of the *Canada Temperance Act* of 1886.

(c)   Haldane Era

The coordinate federalism of the late 19th century was enforced with increasing stringency, even rigidity, in the first three decades of the century that followed. For most of this time, the dominant Judicial Committee jurist was Richard Burton, Lord Haldane.[1] Lord Haldane believed strongly in the coordinate federalism concept.[2] He intensified the approach of enforcing it by construing wide legislative powers narrowly.

In fact, most of the widest-worded powers are federal powers such as Peace, Order, and good Government. Moreover, the broad provincial power over property and civil rights often seemed to escape the full impact of this restrictive approach. However, an early decision in this period indicated that even s. 92(13) must be subject to limits. In the 1914 *John Deere Plow* case, the federal government had incorporated a company whose objects went beyond provincial boundaries.[3] The company challenged a provincial law that barred it from carrying on business in the province concerned. Speaking for the Judicial Committee, Lord Haldane said:

> The expression "civil rights in the province" is a very wide one, extending, if interpreted literally, to much of the field of the other heads of s. 92, and also to much of the field of s. 91. But the expression cannot be so interpreted, and it must be regarded as excluding cases expressly dealt with elsewhere in the two sections, notwithstanding the generality of the words.[4]

Referring to *Citizens Insurance*, Lord Haldane said that the power to incorporate companies with non-provincial objects fell under the residual sense of POGG. He thought the power could also be supported by the general Dominion trade branch of the federal trade and commerce power. Accordingly, although provinces can regulate other aspects of federally incorporated companies, they cannot destroy the status and capacity of such companies to operate.

It soon became evident, though, that the widest federal powers would be subject to especially restrictive interpretation. For example, in the 1916 *Insurance Reference*, the Judicial Committee invalidated a federal law that regulated insurance transactions *other* than those confined exclusively to the insurance company's province of incorporation. Although the federal government argued that the legislation was mainly extra-provincial in nature, and that any interference with s. 92 powers was incidental, for Lord Haldane the fact that the legislation could regulate some insurance transactions wholly within a province — if not the province of incorporation — was enough to invalidate the entire scheme.[5]

In the 1922 *Board of Commerce Reference*, the Judicial Committee concluded that a federal anti-combines and anti-profiteering scheme[6] was an invalid interference with provincial jurisdiction. Referring to the *Local Prohibition Reference*, the federal government argued that the matter of trade combines and profiteering was so important that Parliament could address it under POGG, even though this could result in some incidental interference with provincial jurisdiction. Speaking for the Judicial Committee, Lord Haldane responded as follows:

> The first question to be answered is whether the Dominion Parliament could validly enact such a law. Their Lordships observe that the law is not one enacted to meet special conditions in wartime. It was passed in 1919, after peace had been declared, and it is not confined to any temporary purpose, but is to continue without limit in time, and to apply throughout Canada. No doubt the initial words of s. 91 of the British North America Act confer on the Parliament of Canada power to deal with subjects which concern the Dominion generally, provided that they are not withheld from the powers of that Parliament to legislate, by any of the express heads in s. 92, untrammelled by the enumeration of special heads in s. 91. It may well be that the subjects of undue combination and hoarding are matters in which the dominion has a great practical interest. In special circumstances, such as those of a great war, such an interest might conceivably become of such paramount and overriding importance as to amount to what lies outside the heads in s. 92, and is not covered by them. The decision in *Russell v. The Queen* appears to recognize this as constitutionally possible, even in time of peace; but it is quite another matter to say that under normal circumstances general Canadian policy can justify interference, on such a scale as the statutes in

controversy involve, with the property and civil rights of the inhabitants of the Provinces. It is to the Legislatures of the Provinces that the regulation and restriction of their civil rights have in general been exclusively confided, and as to these the Provincial Legislatures possess quasi-sovereign authority. It can, therefore, be only under necessity in highly exceptional circumstances, such as cannot be assumed to exist in the present case, that the liberty of the inhabitants of the Provinces may be restricted by the Parliament of Canada, and that the Dominion can intervene in the interests of Canada as a whole in questions such as the present one. For, normally, the subject-matter to be dealt with in the case would be one falling within s. 92. Nor do the words in s. 91, the "Regulation of trade and commerce," if taken by themselves, assist the present Dominion contention. It may well be, if the Parliament of Canada had, by reason of an altogether exceptional situation, capacity to interfere, that these words would apply so as to enable that Parliament to oust the exclusive character of the Provincial powers under s. 92.

...

It has already been observed that circumstances are conceivable, such as those of war or famine, when the peace, order and good Government of the Dominion might be imperilled under conditions so exceptional that they require legislation of a character in reality beyond anything provided for by the enumerated heads in either s. 92 or s. 91 itself. Such a case, if it were to arise would have to be considered closely before the conclusion could be properly reached that it was one which could not be treated as falling under any of the heads enumerated. Still, it is a conceivable case, and although great caution is required in referring to it, even in general terms, it ought not, in the view their Lordships take of the British North America Act, read as a whole, to be excluded from what is possible.

Board of Commerce is sometimes regarded as the origin of the "emergency" doctrine of POGG, but the foundations of the doctrine were laid in *Local Prohibition*. What *Board of Commerce* did was to supply some of the characteristics of the doctrine. In effect, it said that the federal government can legislate in relation to subject matter originally falling under s. 92 only in highly exceptional, grave, and temporary circumstances. The onus is on the federal government to prove the existence of these circumstances. The critical question here is, how serious must the circumstances be? By requiring something comparable to war or famine, the Judicial Committee was setting a high threshold. By refusing to consider postwar[7] legislation that addressed the practical *effects* of war, it was applying the threshold with extraordinary stringency.[8]

Counsel for the federal government relied as well on the general Dominion trade category of trade and commerce that had been referred to in *Citizens Insurance*. No, said Lord Haldane, trade and commerce is merely an ancillary power that can support federal legislation of this kind only where there is another federal power available to support it. This was a drastic proposition: at the very least, it deprived general Dominion trade — potentially the widest of the federal trade categories referred to in *Citizens Insurance* — of virtually any independent use. The federal government got no further with the criminal law power. Lord Haldane said that Parliament was attempting to legislate in regard to a subject within provincial jurisdiction and then to justify the interference on the ground that the legislation included a criminal-type penalty. This implied a power to invade provincial jurisdiction at will, simply by imposing a penalty and labelling it as criminal. Concerned about the need for a limit, Lord Haldane imposed a severe one. He said that the criminal law power applies only to subject matter, such as incest, that is inherently criminal. The federal government's last supporting ground was s. 101 of the *British North America Act, 1867*, the federal power to create additional courts for better administration of the laws of Canada. Lord Haldane said that this power could not be invoked to give the Parliament jurisdiction over subject matter not already within federal jurisdiction.

In contrast, the 1923 *Fort Francis* decision showed that the emergency doctrine could be used to uphold legislation. It also indicated that once an emergency has arisen, the courts shift the onus of proof onto those who oppose it to say that it has ended. Here a newspaper had sued a paper supplier for charging more than federal paper control legislation allowed. The key part of the legislation was enacted after the November 1918 armistice, but before the June 1919 Treaty of Versailles. When the supplier challenged the validity of the legislation, Lord Haldane said that it was addressed to wartime conditions, was enacted before the end of the war, and was temporary in duration. Accordingly it was valid emergency legislation.

Snider, in 1925, was the decision that established provincial predominance in the field of labour legislation. A Toronto electrical utility challenged the validity of federal legislation allowing a federal tribunal to investigate a local labour dispute in a province. Lord Haldane said that labour relations in the provinces is *prima facie* a matter of property and civil rights, and that there was no emergency here. He dismissed an argument based on *Russell* on the ground that in that case drunkenness must have been regarded in that case as a national emergency. For good measure, he suggested that Parliament might need independent support from other s. 91 powers in order to use the emergency power! Lord Haldane went on to dismiss arguments based on the criminal law and general trade and commerce powers for the reasons he had given in *Board of Commerce*.

The decisions in this period faced the challenging task of implementing the coordinate federalism concept by imposing meaningful limits on powers that could threaten the balance between federal and provincial jurisdiction. Most of the powers encountered in these cases — for example, POGG, the criminal law power, general Dominion trade and commerce, and the power to create additional courts — had been broadly written and were potentially open-ended. If coordinate federalism were to be enforced, these powers had to be reined in. Moreover, most of these powers were federal powers, which lacked the restrictions imposed by the Act on provincial powers. Meanwhile, outside the courts, immigration, settlement, and renewed regional unrest continued to increase pressures for greater provincial powers. There was a case for strict limits, then, but by the end of the 1920s, they were becoming too strict.

In the years immediately following Lord Haldane's death in 1928, there were some signs of change. After the defeat in the *Board of Commerce Reference*, the federal government had enacted new anti-combines legislation, removing most of the more regulatory provisions, and enforcing it by *Criminal Code* offences that required an indictment and trial. In the *Propriety Articles* decision of 1931, the Judicial Committee upheld the new legislation.[9] Lord Atkin disagreed with Lord Haldane's narrow approach to criminal law, with the suggestion that *Russell* must be explained as viewing gross intemperance as an emergency, and with the view that trade and commerce must be ancillary to other federal powers. Lord Atkin said there is only one test for the criminal quality of an act: "Is the act prohibited by criminal consequences?"

In *Re Aeronautics*,[10] Lord Sankey upheld the federal *Aeronautics Act*, mainly on the ground that it was supported by the s. 132 power of the federal government to implement treaties concluded by Canada as part of the British Empire. He said it was also supported by enumerated powers such as the postal service, defence, and non-local undertakings. Whatever was not covered under these heads, he added, did not fall under s. 92 and hence came under POGG. Then he said that the subject matter of aeronautics had attained such dimensions as to become a matter of national concern.[11] Was this merely a reference to the negative or residual sense of POGG applied in *Citizens Insurance*? Or was Lord Sankey suggesting that national importance or scale — not an emergency — might be sufficient to enable Parliament to legislate in regard to subjects originally assigned to the provinces? The answer was not clear, and Lord Sankey's summary of the earlier case law was ambiguous in this regard.[12]

Then, in *Re Radio*,[13] the Judicial Committee upheld the *Radio Telegraph Act*, partly on the basis of POGG.[14] What was surprising here was the breadth given to the negative sense of POGG. The Judicial Committee seemed to suggest that what was residual and new here was not radio, but the agreement on which the radio legislation was based — an international treaty concluded independently by Canada. If all that was needed to render a subject residual and under POGG was to conclude an independent international treaty, there would be virtually no limit to federal power. Apart from a brief reference to *Re Radio*, there was no mention at all of the earlier POGG jurisprudence.

The centralist comments in *Re Aeronautics* and *Re Radio* coincided with the onset of the most severe economic depression to hit Canada. As conditions continued to worsen, there were increasing calls for government action at the national level. On the other hand, many economic matters had been held to fall under provincial jurisdiction. In the event of a confrontation over division of powers, what would the Judicial Committee do?

Notes

1. Lord Haldane — who became Viscount Haldane in 1912 was appointed to the Judicial Committee in 1911 and continued to participate in its decisions until his death in 1928. He delivered most of the Judicial Committee's most significant division of powers decisions during this period, including *John Deere Plow Company v. Wharton*, [1915] 1 A.C. 330; *Canada (A.G.) v. Alberta (A.G.) (Insurance Reference)*, [1916] 1 A.C. 588; *Ontario (A.G.) v. Canada (A.G.)*, [1916] 1 A.C. 598; *Bonanza Creek Gold Mining Company v. The King*, [1916] 1 A.C. 566; *Great West Saddlery v. The King*, [1921] 2 A.C. 91; *In re the Board of Commerce Act 1919, and the Combines and Fair Prices Act, 1919*, [1922] 1 A.C. 191; *Fort Frances Pulp and Paper Co. v.*

Manitoba Free Press Go., [1923] A.C. 695; *Ontario (A.G.) v. Reciprocal Insurers*, [1924] A.C. 328; *Toronto Electric Commissioners v. Snider*, [1925] A.C. 396. One writer has criticized the work of this British Judge as "a sometimes bizarre amalgam of historical revisionism": John Saywell, *The Lawmakers: Judicial Power and the Shaping of Canadian Federalism* (Toronto: University of Toronto Press, 2002) at xix and ch. 7. What evidence does Saywell offer in support of this conclusion? Compare this view with those of others referred to in Saywell's chapter on Haldane, and with the general conclusions of Alan Cairns (in Postscript, in this chapter and of Peter Hogg and Wade Wright (in Chapter 3 and in Postscript of this chapter).

2. See, for example, Lord Haldane's description of the general scheme of the *British North America Act* in *In re the Initiative and Referendum Act*, [1919] A.C. 935 at 935.
3. *John Deere Plow Company v. Wharton*, [1915] 1 A.C.330.
4. *Ibid.* at 340.
5. This "taint" doctrine was not only arbitrary, but it later proved to be one-sided. In a 1938 case, when the Judicial Committee considered the validity of a *provincial* trade law, the fact that its main aspect was interprovincial was sufficient to ensure its invalidity: *Shannon v. Lower Mainland Dairy Products Board*, [1938] A.C. 708 at 719–20.
6. In 1919, as the First World War was ending, Parliament enacted legislation to prohibit excess profits, unfair trade combinations, and hoarding of scarce commodities. It imposed criminal penalties on violators, and created a Board of Commerce to enforce the prohibitions. The Board was empowered to state a case for the Supreme Court of Canada on questions of law or jurisdiction. After some controversy, it was decided that the Board should ask the Court if its enabling legislation was valid. Three judges said it was; three said it wasn't. The Supreme Court's "decision" was appealed to the Judicial Committee.
7. The legislation was enacted in July 1919 just one month after the June 1919 Treaty of Versailles that ended the war.

8. To support this proposition, Lord Haldane pointed to an earlier decision in legislation had been upheld on the basis of both general Dominion trade and another federal power.
9. Although the Judicial Committee said that some of the remedies in this case were not strictly linked to criminal penalties, it found that they could be supported under the federal taxation and patents powers.
10. [1932] A.C. 54.
11. Lord Sankey upheld the federal *Aeronautics Act*, partly on the ground that "aerial navigation has attained such dimensions so as to affect the body politic of the Dominion." Were they simply reviving the negative or residual sense of POGG applied in *Citizens Insurance*? Or were they suggesting that national importance or scale — not an emergency — might be sufficient to enable Parliament to legislate in regard to subjects originally assigned to the provinces?
12. At one point, Lord Sankey said the earlier case law prohibited statutes enacted under POGG from trenching on subjects enumerated in s. 92 "unless these matters have attained such dimensions as to affect the body politic of the Dominion": *Re Aeronautics*, [1932] A.C. 54 at 72. However, on the next page, he summarized his understanding of the law on POGG as follows: "It is obvious, therefore, that there may be cases of emergency where the Dominion is empowered to act for the whole."
13. [1932] A.C. 304.
14. The 1932 *Radio Reference* concerned federal legislation regulating radio, and enacted not pursuant to a British Empire Treaty, but pursuant to a treaty that Canada had signed as a wholly independent nation. Although the *British North America Act* gives Parliament power to implement British Empire treaties, it says nothing about treaties that Canada has concluded independently. Lord Dunedin said the legislation was valid, partly because radio was an undertaking between the provinces, and partly because an independent treaty-making power was not addressed in s. 92 or elsewhere in the *British North America Act*.

(d) *Employment and Social Insurance Act Reference*†

NOTE

From October 1929 to the late 1930s, Canada and the western world were hit by the Great Depression. The average yearly income dropped to below the poverty line, by 1933 almost a third of the labour force was out of work, and one-fifth of Canadians were dependent on government relief.[1] There were bankruptcies and protests, evictions and riots. The prairie provinces were especially hard hit, with locust plagues, drought, dust storms, crop failures, and famine.

Encouraged, no doubt, by the positive signals in *Re Radio* and *Re Aeronautics*, Conservative Prime Minister R.B. Bennett enacted eight wide-ranging "New Deal" statutes, modelled on Franklin Roosevelt's New Deal in the United States. The package included an unemployment insurance statute, three labour standards statutes, a natural products marketing statute, and others directed at

---

† *Canada (A.G.) v. Ontario (A.G.): Employment and Social Insurance Act Reference*,[1937] A.C. 355 (J.C.P.C.).

easing farmers' debt, curbing unfair prices, and regulating trade marks. However, R.B. Bennett's government was defeated before the statutes came into effect, and the new prime minister, Mackenzie King, referred them to the courts. In six separate reference decisions in 1937, the Judicial Committee declared five of the eight statutes invalid and one invalid in part.[2]

One of these decisions was the *Natural Products Marketing Act Reference*, involving a federal marketing scheme.[3] The Act was directed at products that went mainly outside the province of origin and at products that might be exported in part. Provincial governments had cooperated in designing the scheme, and were establishing complementary schemes at the local level. However, Lord Atkin held that the entire statute was invalid, because some of the products could remain in the province of origin. There was no comparison of the federal and provincial elements of the scheme to show how the former were predominant.[4] This cursory approach seemed to contrast with the approach that was taken when a *provincial* marketing scheme was involved. In the *Shannon* decision of 1938,[5] for example, the Judicial Committee addressed a challenge to a marketing scheme established by the government of B.C. Although products regulated by this scheme could come from outside B.C., the scheme applied only to transactions affecting these goods that occurred within the province of B.C. After carefully examining the structure and application of the scheme, Lord Atkin concluded that because the substance of the scheme fell within intraprovincial trade, the scheme as a whole was valid, and its validity was not affected by the incidental aspects beyond its authorized field.

In another New Deal reference, the Judicial Committee narrowed the scope of the residual sense of POGG. The *Labour Conventions Reference*[6] concerned legislation to regulate labour standards and hours of work. Although labour relations was generally considered to fall under property and civil rights, this legislation had been enacted pursuant to international treaties Canada had signed as an independent country. Relying on the 1931 *Radio Reference*, the federal government maintained that because independent treaty-making power is not addressed in the *British North America Act*, it falls under POGG. Lord Atkin said that the *Radio Reference* stood for no such principle. He said it should be interpreted as saying that radio — not treaty making — fell under the residual sense of POGG. In Lord Atkin's view, "... the

Dominion cannot, merely by making promises to foreign countries, clothe itself with legislative authority inconsistent with the constitution which gave it birth."[7] He cautioned that "[w]hile the ship of state now sails on larger ventures and into foreign waters she still retains the watertight compartments which are an essential part of her original structure."[8] Although Lord Atkin's reinterpretation of the *Radio Reference* is questionable,[9] his concern was hardly surprising. Treaty-making was the kind of instrumental, open-ended power that threatened the notion of balance that was so important in most Judicial Committee jurisprudence.

One of the most important of all the New Deal statutes was the *Employment and Social Insurance Act*, which purported to set up a national unemployment insurance scheme. A majority of the Supreme Court held it invalid, and the Judicial Committee agreed. Extracts from their decision, in the 1937 *Unemployment Insurance Reference*,[10] are provided below. What was the main provincial power relied on here? Why didn't the argument based on POGG succeed? Was not the depression an economic emergency? What other federal powers were relied on? Why were they unsuccessful? (Look especially at the federal "spending" power argument, that relied on ss. 91(1) and 91(3)). Three years later, in a rare display of unity, Canadian politicians agreed to a formal amendment to the *Constitution Act, 1867* to give the federal government power to implement an unemployment insurance scheme.

After the New Deal decisions, there were mounting concerns that this London-based tribunal had outlived its usefulness.[11] In the midst of a grave economic crisis, the Judicial Committee had blocked urgent government measures designed to alleviate suffering and to hasten recovery. At the same time, critics tended to overlook a number of considerations. For one thing, the Judicial Committee had not declared all of the New Deal statutes invalid. Most of the statutes that were invalidated by the Judicial Committee were also invalidated by the Supreme Court of Canada, or had failed to secure that court's majority support. Some of the Judicial Committee's rulings — such as the narrowing of POGG in *Labour Conventions* — made good sense from the perspective of maintaining a federal balance. Morever, protecting provincial power was still important to many Canadians, especially in Quebec. On the other hand, the peremptory rejection of a federal marketing scheme that had secured the support of all provinces, and the blunt refusal to view the Great Depression as a national crisis sufficient to trigger Peace, Order, and good Government, suggested that something should be done. Little more than a decade later, something was done: appeals to the Judicial Committee were brought to an end.[12]

Notes

1. See James Struthers, "Great Depression" in James H. Marsh, ed. in chief, *The Canadian Encyclopedia: Year 2000 Edition*, (Toronto: McClelland & Stewart, 1999) at 1012–13; Pierre Berton, *The Great Depression: 1929–1939* (Toronto: Penguin Books, 1991) at ix *et seq.*
2. The Judicial Committee held the three labour statutes and the unemployment insurance and marketing statutes to be invalid. It upheld the competition and farmers' credit statute. It held parts of the trade mark statute to be valid, and other parts to be invalid. Most of the Judicial Committee's New Deal decisions affirmed the relevant decisions of the Supreme Court of Canada.
   The six decisions were *Canada (A.G.) v. Ontario (A.G.) (Labour Conventions Reference)*, [1937] A.C. 326, aff'g [1936] S.C.R. 461; *Canada (A.G.) v. Ontario (A.G.) (Employment and Social Insurance Act Reference)*, [1937] A.C. 355, aff'g [1936] S.C.R. 427; *British Columbia (A.G.) v. Canada (A.G.) (Competition Reference)*, [1937] A.C. 368, aff'g [1936] S.C.R. 363; *British Columbia (A.G.) v. Canada (A.G.) (Natural Products Marketing Act Reference)*, [1937] A.C. 377, aff'g [1936] S.C.R. 398; *British Columbia (A.G.) v. Canada (A.G.) (Farmers' Creditors Reference)*, [1937] A.C. 391, aff'g [1936] S.C.R. 384 and *Ontario (A.G.) v. Canada (A.G.) (Trade Mark Reference)*, [1937] A.C. 405; varying [1936] S.C.R. 379. See further William McConnell, "The Judicial Review of Prime Minister Bennett's 'New Deal'" (1968) 6 Osgoode Hall L.J. 39.
3. *British Columbia (A.G.) v. Canada (A.G.) (Natural Products Marketing Act Reference)*, [1937] A.C. 377.
4. Lord Atkin did say that the *Natural Products Marketing Act* was "in pith and substance an encroachment upon the Provincial rights," and he seemed to regard the incursion on intraprovincal trade as significant. But he made no effort to show why a scheme that applied to products that are either mainly consumed outside the province of origin or are in part exported is mainly intraprovincial. However, Lord Atkin's position was strengthened by that of counsel for the federal government and B.C. In their formal written position they argued that the extraprovincial and international element were dominant. However, in oral argument, they abandoned this position and claimed that these elements were incidental and could be severed from the invalid intraprovincial portion!
5. *Shannon v. Lower Mainland Dairy Products Board* [1938] A.C. 708.
6. *Canada (A.G.) v. Ontario (A.G.)*, [1937] A.C. 326.
7. *Ibid.* at 352.
8. *Ibid.* at 354.
9. In the *Radio Reference*, Lord Dunedin supported the federal legislation on the basis (1) that treaty making by Canada (and not by Great Britain pursuant to s. 132) falls under POGG because it is "not mentioned explicitly in either s. 91 or s. 92" (*Radio Reference*, [1932] A.C. 312, and (2) that radio broadcasting extends beyond the limits of a province and therefore falls under federal jurisdiction pursuant to s. 92(10)(a) (*ibid.* at 316).
10. *Canada (A.G.) v. Ontario (A.G.) (Employment and Social Insurance Act Reference)* [1937] A.C. 355.
11. Many of the criticisms are referred to in the article by Alan Cairns, "The Judicial Committee and Its Critics" (1971) 4 Can. J. Pol. Sci. 301, reproduced in part below.

12. See S.C. 1949 (2nd Sess.) c. 37, s. 3, ending all appeals to the Judicial Committee that were not commenced before December 23, 1949. Appeals in criminal matters had been abolished in 1933.

EXTRACT

[LORD ATKIN for the Judicial Committee:]

The substance of the Act is contained in the sections constituting Part III. They set up a now familiar system of unemployment insurance under which persons engaged in employment as defined in the Act are insured against unemployment. The funds required for making the necessary payments are to be provided partly from money provided by Parliament, partly from contributions by employed persons, and partly from contributions by the employers of those persons. The two sets of contributions are to be paid by revenue stamps. Every employed person and every employer is to be liable to pay contributions in accordance with the provisions of the second schedule, the employer being liable to pay both contributions in the first instance, recovering the employed person's share by deduction from his wages, or, if necessary, in certain cases by action.

There can be no doubt that, *prima facie*, provisions as to insurance of this kind, especially where they affect the contract of employment, fall within the class of property and civil rights in the Province, and would be within the exclusive competence of the Provincial Legislature. It was sought, however, to justify the validity of Dominion legislation on grounds which their Lordships on consideration feel compelled to reject. Counsel did not seek to uphold the legislation on the ground of the treaty-making power. There was no treaty or labour convention which imposed any obligation upon Canada to pass this legislation, and the decision on this question in the reference of the three labour Acts does not apply. A strong appeal, however, was made on the ground of the special importance of unemployment insurance in Canada at the time of, and for some time previous to, the passing of the Act. On this point it becomes unnecessary to do more than to refer to the judgment of this Board in the reference on the three labour Acts, and to the judgment of the Chief Justice in the *Natural Products Marketing Act* which, on this matter, the Board have approved and adopted. It is sufficient to say that the present Act does not purport to deal with any special emergency. It founds itself in the preamble on general world-wide conditions referred to in the Treaty of Peace: it is an Act whose operation is intended to be permanent: and there is agreement between all the members of the Supreme Court that it could not be supported upon the suggested existence of any special emergency. Their Lordships find themselves unable to differ from this view.

It only remains to deal with the argument which found favour with the Chief Justice and Davis J., that the Legislation can be supported under the enumerated heads, 1 and 3 of s. 91 of the *British North America Act, 1867*: (1) The public debt and property, namely (3) The raising of money by any mode or system of taxation. Shortly stated, the argument is that the obligation imposed upon employers and persons employed is a mode of taxation: that the money so raised becomes public property, and that the Dominion have then complete legislative authority to direct that the money so raised, together with assistance from money raised by general taxation, shall be applied in forming an insurance fund and generally in accordance with the provisions of the Act.

That the Dominion may impose taxation for the purpose of creating a fund for special purposes, and may apply that fund for making contributions in the public interest to individuals, corporations or public authorities, could not as a general proposition be denied. Whether in such an Act as the present compulsion applied to an employed person to make a contribution to an insurance fund out of which he will receive benefit for a period proportionate to the number of his contributions is in fact taxation it is not necessary finally to decide. It might seem difficult to discern how it differs from a form of compulsory insurance, or what the difference is between a statutory obligation to pay insurance premiums to the State or to an insurance company. But assuming that the Dominion has collected by means of taxation a fund, it by no means follows that any legislation which disposes of it is necessarily within Dominion competence.

It may still be legislation affecting the classes of subjects enumerated in s. 92, and, if so, would be ultra vires. In other words, Dominion legislation, even though it deals with Dominion property, may yet be so framed as to invade civil rights within the Province, or encroach upon the classes of subjects which are reserved to Provincial competence. It is not necessary that it should be a colourable device, or a pretence. If on the true view of the legislation it is found that in reality in pith and substance the legislation invades civil rights within the province, or in respect of other classes of subjects otherwise encroaches upon the provincial field, the legislation

will be invalid. To hold otherwise would afford the Dominion an easy passage into the Provincial domain. In the present case, their Lordships agree with the majority of the Supreme Court in holding that in pith and substance this Act is an insurance Act affecting the civil rights of employers and employed in each Province, and as such is invalid. The other parts of the Act are so inextricably mixed up with the insurance provisions of [Part III] that it is impossible to sever them. It seems obvious, also, that in its truncated form, apart from [Part III], the Act would never have come into existence. It follows that the whole Act must be pronounced ultra vires, and in accordance with the view of the majority of the Supreme Court their Lordships will humbly advise His Majesty that this appeal be dismissed.

. . . .

[The Judicial Committee moved temporarily in a decentralist direction in the *Canada Temperance Federation Reference* 1946: *Ontario (A.G.) v. Canada Temperance Federation*, [1946] A.C. 193. In that reference, Lord Simon reaffirmed that Parliament has jurisdiction over prohibition of alcohol consumption under the positive sense of POGG. (This is the sense that permits Parliament to legislate in regard to matters that might otherwise be provincial in nature.) Lord Simon then suggested that POGG in this sense might extend beyond emergencies, to matters that have become of national concern. However, a year later, this initiative was either overlooked or ignored. In the *Japanese Canadians* case (*Co-operative Committee on Japanese Canadians v. Canada (A.G.)* [1947] A.C. 87), Lord Wright upheld federal *War Measures Act* provisions that permitted the deportation of Japanese Canadians. He did so on the basis of the emergency doctrine. There was no mention whatever of *Canada Temperance Federation*, and no indication that there could be a broader sense of POGG. Lord Simon did say that courts should be deferential to Parliament's conclusion regarding the existence and duration of an emergency. The onus should be on those who oppose the emergency to show that, as a matter of fact, it has not arisen or that it has ended. Later references affirmed that the positive sense of POGG should be limited to exceptional, emergency-type situations: see *C.P.R. v. British Columbia (A.G.)*, [1950] A.C. 122 at 140–41; *Canadian Federation of Agriculture v. Quebec (A.G.)*, [1951] A.C. 179 at 197–98].

(e) Pattern?

Was there any dominant pattern to the Judicial Committee's approach to the division of powers? Although there were numerous variations and departures, it is arguable that a general approach did evolve. Some of the salient features of this approach will be sketched in here. When you read the decisions of the Supreme Court of Canada in the later chapters, consider how much of this approach a) has been changed, and b) remains in place today.

CHARACTERIZATION

The Judicial Committee said that legislation should be characterized by looking for its main subject matter, that is, its "pith and substance".[1] To find this, the Judicial Committee tended to look for the purpose of the legislation, although its effects could also be relevant to determining its true nature.[2]

ALLOCATION

Once the main subject matter has been identified, the Judicial Committee said that a court should try allocate that subject matter to a particular head of classes of subject in s. 91 or 92. To do this, it tended to follow the general approach outlined in *Citizens Insurance*. The court should look first at the relevant heads of s. 92, to determine if the subject matter of the legislation falls *prima facie* (at first glance) under one of those heads. This, in turn, could require a look at the context of the relevant head to help determine its scope.[3] If the subject matter of the legislation does not fall under a s. 92 head, Parliament has jurisdiction over the subject matter by virtue of its residual power in POGG.

If, however, the subject matter *does* fall *prima facie* under a s. 92 head, it is necessary to look at POGG again to see if Parliament has jurisdiction over the subject matter by virtue of another sense of POGG. Where there are highly exceptional or urgent circumstances,[4] POGG gives Parliament power to legislate in regard to matters that would otherwise fall under provincial jurisdiction.

If there are no such circumstances, the next step is to see if the subject matter that falls *prima facie* under a s. 92 head also falls *prima facie* under an enumerated head of power in s. 91. If so, the subject matter should be allocated to the head of power it matches most closely.

If the subject matter could fall more or less equally under a s. 92 head and an enumerated s. 91 head (a "double aspect" subject matter),[5] the statute is valid if it is a federal statute. In the case of a provincial statute, courts should determine if the statute can operate without conflicting with another federal statute. If it can, the provincial statute is valid.

In the cases above, if the main subject matter of a statute is valid, the aspects that are necessarily incidental to or ancillary to that aspect[6] are also valid.[7]

CONFLICT

If a provincial statute cannot operate without conflicting with another federal statute, the provincial statute is inoperative to the extent of the conflict. The Judicial Committee tended to attribute this result to the paramountcy provision in s. 91.[8]

GENERAL SCHEME

According to the Judicial Committee, the general scheme of the *British North America Act, 1867* was to maintain coordinate federalism. This concept sees federalism as a structure for maintaining a strict balance between two relatively equal levels of government, each with supreme legislative jurisdiction in the areas allocated to it.[9]

ENFORCEMENT

To enforce this scheme, the Judicial Committee tended to construe narrowly virtually all grants of legislative powers with broad, "open-ended" wording.[10] The aim was to prevent one level of the federal system from using its own wide powers to undermine those of the other level, thereby upsetting the constitutional balance.[11]

SIGNIFICANCE

As most of the widely-worded powers are federal, this approach tended to produce decentralist results. Moreover, there was one exception to this approach. The Judicial Committee gave a wide — although not unlimited — construction to the provincial power in relation to s. 92(13), "Property and Civil Rights in the Province".[12] As a result, the "strict balance" policy tended to lean on the decentralist side.

If this was not an accidental result, was it intended as a counterweight to the federal government's weapons of reservation, disallowance, and paramountcy? Was it a recognition of the special foundation of s. 92(13) in the *Quebec Act* of 1774? Did it reflect the focus on provincial responsibilities and rights that gained momentum in the last decades of the 19th century and the early decades of the century that followed? Apart from a brief reference to the *Quebec Act* in *Citizens Insurance*,[13] the Judicial Committee did not say. It generally preferred to avoid discussing specific questions of policy, and to relate its reasons solely to the wording and scheme of the document immediately before it — the *British North America Act, 1867*.

Notes

1. See, for example, "primary matter" (*Russell v. The Queen* (1881–82), 7 A.C. 829 at 838); "true nature and character" (*Russell* at 839); "subject matter and subject matter" (*Hodge* at 131); "whole pith and substance" (*Union Colliery of British Columbia v. Bryden*, [1899] A.C. 580 at 587); "the pith and substance" and "the substance and not to the mere form" (*Saskatchewan (A.G.) v. Canada (A.G.)*, [1949] A.C. 110 at 124).
2. See, for example, *Social Insurance Reference* at 366–67 and *Alberta (A.G.) v. Canada (A.G.)*, [1939] A.C. 117 at 130. As indicated in both of these decisions, legislation will be held invalid if its expressed aim is "a colourable device, or a pretence" for what is in effect an invasion of the jurisdiction of another level of government.
3. For example, where two heads of power appear to overlap and one head is more specific than the other, where possible, courts carve the relevant subject matter of the more specific head (e.g., Solemnization of Marriage) from the more general head (e.g., Marriage and Divorce), leaving the remaining subject matter (e.g., all aspects of marriage other than solemnization of marriage, together with divorce) to the more general head: see *Citizens Insurance Company v. Parsons* (1881–2), 7 A.C. 96 at 108; *Great West Saddlery Co. v. The King*, [1921] 2 A.C. 91, 116.
4. The decision in *Russell* was not overruled, so it was unclear if there was an exception to this rule, allowing Parliament to invoke the positive sense of POGG in matters affecting public order, safety, and morals, in circumstances that were not exceptional or urgent.
5. As in *Hodge*. There Sir Barnes Peacock said at 130 that "subjects that in one aspect and for one purpose fall within sec. 92, may in another aspect and for another purpose fall within sec. 91," and upheld a provincial liquor licensing scheme even though a federal temperance scheme had been upheld in *Russell*. See also *Local Prohibition* in regard to temperance.
6. *Citizens Insurance* at 107–108; *Tennant v. Union Bank of Canada*, [1894] A.C. 31 at 45.
7. See *Attorney General of Ontario v. Attorney General of the Dominion*, [1896] A.C. 348 at 359, where Lord Watson attributed this effect to the "deeming clause" at the very end of s. 92 of the *British North America Act, 1867*. However, the validation of incidental aspects of a statute is also the result of basing validity on the statute's main subject matter. In *Workmen's Compensation Board v. C.P.R.*, [1920] A.C. 184 at 191–92, for example, Lord Haldane found that a provincial workers' compensation scheme related to direct taxation within the province, even though it could affect persons or property outside the province. Moreover, because it was "in substance a scheme for securing a civil right within the Province," the fact that it could affect some matters under federal jurisdiction did not affect its validity.
8. See, for example, *Local Prohibition Reference* at 369.
9. See, for example, *Hodge* at 132; *Liquidators of the Maritime Bank of Canada v. New Brunswick (Receiver General)*, [1892] A.C. 437 at 442–43; *Bank of Toronto v. Lambe* (1887), 12 App. Cas. 575 at 587.
10. For example, POGG, trade and commerce, and (usually) the criminal law power.
11. See, for example, the following statement by Lord Watson in *Local Prohibition* at 360–61: "If it were once conceded that the Parliament of Canada has authority to make laws applicable to the whole Dominion, in relation to matters which in each province are substantially of local or private interest, upon the assumption that these matters also concern the peace, order, and good government of the Dominion, there is hardly a subject enumerated in s. 92 upon which it might not legislate, to the exclusion of the provincial legislatures."
12. This tendency started in *Citizens Insurance*.
13. *Citizens Insurance* at 111.

(f)   Postscript

The role of the Judicial Committee in shaping Canadian federalism has been controversial, to say the least. For example, author John Saywell says that the Judicial Committee manipulated the text of the *Constitution Act, 1867*, twisted doctrine, and applied a pro-provincial bias that rendered the federal government almost impotent.[1] In contrast, G.P. Browne argued the Judicial Committee's general approach plausible, logical, and consistent with the jurisprudential assumptions of its time,[2] while former Prime Minister Trudeau suggested that the Judicial Committee's decisions had been a key factor in averting separatism.[3] Dozens of other commentators have taken up varied positions on the supposed decentralism, textual accuracy, bias, impartiality, judicial Imperialism, formalism, or responsiveness, of this tribunal.[4]

Two of the more nuanced commentaries are a 1971 article by Alan Cairns[5] and a 2005 article by Peter Hogg and Wade Wright.[6] Cairns said that both critics and supporters of the Judicial Committee were mistaken. Cairns said that although the *Constitution Act, 1867* may have been a very centralist document, the general provincial bias of the Judicial Committee was "remarkably appropriate" to the regional and provincial needs that became evident in Canada after the time of Confederation.[7] As for the Judicial Committee supporters, Cairns said that their stress on the impartiality of the tribunal was at odds with its provincial bias. In fact, he said, the Judicial Committee's supposed distance from local predispositions "simply meant relative ignorance, insensitivity, and misunderstanding of the Canadian scene."[8]

As we saw in the extract in Chapter 3, Hogg and Wright argue that the *Constitution Act, 1867* was not highly centralist but contained conflicting centralist and decentralist elements — an ambiguity that may have been intended to encourage support for Confederation from groups with very diverse interests. Like Saywell, Cairns, and many others, Hogg and Wright claim that the Judicial Committee had a pro-provincial bias. As evidence of this, they point to the narrow interpretation given to the wide federal powers in regard to Peace, Order, and good Government and trade and commerce, and the wide interpretation given to the provincial power in relation to property and civil rights.[9] They say that this resulted, in part, from "a preconceived notion about the proper form of a federal system, a notion that placed much emphasis on the protection and enhancement of the position of the provinces."[10] Nevertheless, they say that the Judicial Committee's work should be assessed in light of the fact that the *Constitution Act, 1867* was not uniformly centralist.[11] As well, they say that decentralization has helped to respond to (1) the need to encourage social innovation, (2) the need to keep government as close as possible to the people it affects, (3) the need to accommodate a jurisdiction in which French Canadians are an effective majority, and (4) the growth of the social service responsibilities of provinces since Confederation.[12] Hogg and Wright conclude that "although the Privy

Council did favour the provinces, in the end, and perhaps more by accident than design, Canada was, on the whole, not badly served by the Privy Council."[13]

Although these are both perceptive analyses, they are open to question in two respects, and invite further reflection in others. First, neither Cairns nor Hogg and Wright are able to explain the paradox that a tribunal that was guilty of "relative ignorance, insensitivity, and misunderstanding of the Canadian scene" (Cairns)[14] or that was "ill-informed about the country" (Hogg and Wright)[15] could have adopted an approach to federalism so apparently appropriate to Canadian needs. Second, if Hogg and Wright are right in stressing that the *Constitution Act, 1867* contained significant decentralist as well as centralist elements, are they also right in attributing the motivation of Judicial Committee members to pro-provincial bias?[16] Third, Cairns suggests that although the Judicial Committee's formalistic, text-based style was inappropriate for constitutional adjudication,[17] it was the best that could be expected in light of this tribunal's remote location and "the sterilities of the legal tradition it espoused."[18] But was there more to the choice of style than this? Finally, if the Judicial Committee's decisions were so apparently appropriate to Canadian conditions, why did Canadians bring them to an end?

In regard to the questions of misunderstanding and bias, assuming that the Judicial Committee's decisions did tend toward decentralism,[19] it might be argued that this was less a goal than a *consequence* of this tribunal's general policy of maintaining coordinate federalism — the requirement of a strict balance between two levels of government with autonomous powers.[20] Why might this be so?

Broad, open-ended powers threaten any effort to prevent one level of jurisdiction from overrunning the other. To maintain an overall balance of power in the federal system, then, it made sense to construe wide powers narrowly. As it happened, most of these wide powers were federal, so the main beneficiaries of this approach were the provinces. The narrow approach to wide powers provided a counterweight to the exclusive federal advantages of disallowance, reservation, and paramountcy.

The Judicial Committee relaxed its narrow construction approach in the case of one wide provincial power — property and civil rights. But there may have been more than simple provincial bias behind this special exception. As we have seen, property and civil rights was part of an historic constitutional guarantee from one founding cultural group to another.[21] That guarantee was considered vital to French Canadian culture in 1774 and 1791, and virtually the same guarantee was repeated in the constitutional settlement of 1867. But even this guarantee was not unlimited; it was balanced by a recognition of other kinds of law or power that were *not* considered essential to French Canadian culture.[22]

Of course, it is also likely that many Judicial Committee members were receptive to the strong regional and provincial trends that were sweeping Canada in the late 19th century and early 20th century. As Cairns' article suggests, the Judicial Committee's formative decisions were rendered when the pressures for Confederation had given way to a period of growing provincial strains and needs. But as suggested above, it is arguable that the dominant motivation behind the general approach of this tribunal was not provincial bias but maintenance of a federal–provincial balance.

This brings us to the third issue above. Was the Judicial Committee's style simply the consequence of a remote location and a sterile legal tradition? Beyond inferring a concept of coordinate federalism from the *Constitution Act, 1867*, the Judicial Committee was generally silent about the political factors that may have influenced its decisions.[23] Its style was text-based or "formalistic". Its characteristic techniques were interpretation presumptions, text-based comparisons, and logic.[24] Restraint about discussing specific domestic policy issues was matched by restraint about intervention. Overall, the Judicial Committee tended to uphold legislation. It upheld a higher portion of statutes in division of power cases before 1949 than the Supreme Court did in the next 40 years.[25] In more than 140 division of legislative powers decisions, the Judicial Committee upheld federal legislation in over 70% of cases in which it was challenged, and upheld provincial legislation in less than 60% of similar cases.[26]

There was some justification for this reticence and restraint. Although the much-criticized[27] formalistic style was short on transparency and could be heavy on semantics, members of the tribunal were poorly situated to engage actively in details of domestic politics or policy. For a London-based judicial tribunal, extensive policy discussion would likely have attracted major opposition far sooner than it did. Even for a domestic court, in the politically charged world of federal–provincial litigation, credibility depends heavily on perceived impartiality. This, in turn, is easier to maintain by appeals to texts than by extensive reliance on poli-

tics and policy. Similarly, mass judicial invalidation of democratically-enacted legislation raises a general credibility issue, and it raises a special credibility issue when the tribunal is British and the legislation is Canadian. Arguably, then, textualism was not merely the best that could be managed in the circumstances, but a defensible part of a broader policy, a general policy of restraint.

But appeals to the Judicial Committee were finally abolished in 1949[28] — why? Among critics, there is a tendency to blame in the rigidity of the Judicial Committee's dominant doctrines and the New Deal decisions of 1937.[29] Certainly, these decisions were widely regarded as too rigid to address the pressing needs of the time. Doctrines that were generally congruent with provincialist pressures needed adjustment when the climate changed. The Judicial Committee made this accommodation when it applied the emergency doctrine in response to the First World War, but it failed to adapt when Canada faced the greatest economic crisis since Confederation. With greater flexibility and a more forthright approach to earlier doctrine,[30] POGG might have been adapted to accommodate the depression, and the trade and commerce power might have been applied more equitably by a marketing scheme supported by the entire federation.[31] Moreover, these changes could have been accompanied by safeguards for coordinate federalism.[32] In a scheme based not on provincial bias but on federal–provincial balance, there was room for a correction in favour of the federal side.

But while greater flexibility might have reduced the problems of 1937, it would probably have not affected the long-term fate of the tribunal itself. Canada itself was continuing to change. In the new century, Canadian nationalism gradually started to shift from stressing Imperial ties to asserting more autonomy from Britain.[33] In 1919, for example, Prime Minister Borden fought successfully to secure separate Canadian representation at the peace conference and for Canadian membership in the League of Nations in its own right.[34] After several years of negotiations, the *Statute of Westminster* in 1931 recognized Canada's gained independence from Britain in virtually all respects except amendments to the *British North America Act*. By the mid-war period, the Supreme Court of Canada acquired a growing body of experience in constitutional issues.[35]

Criminal appeals to the Judicial Committee were abolished in 1933. It was probably only a matter of time before there would be an overwhelming call for an end to civil appeals as well. After delays caused by jurisdictional questions[36] and the onset of a second world war, civil appeals to the Judicial Committee were finally abolished as of December 23, 1949. These delays aside, what is remarkable, perhaps, is not that the rule of the Judicial Committee finally ended, but that it had lasted 82 years!

Notes

1. John Saywell, *The Lawmakers: Judicial Power and the Shaping of Canadian Federalism* (Toronto: University of Toronto Press, 2002) at xix–xx. Saywell is especially critical of Lord Watson, Lord Haldane, and Lord Akin: ibid. at xix and chs. 6, 7, and 9.
2. G.P. Browne, *The Judicial Committee and the British North America Act: An Analysis of the Interpretive Scheme for the Division of Legislative Powers* (Toronto: University of Toronto Press, 1967).
3. "... [I]f the law lords had not leaned in that direction [toward decentralism], Quebec separatism might not be a threat today: it might be an accomplished fact": Pierre E. Trudeau, *Federalism and the French Canadians* (Toronto: MacMillan, 1968) at 198.
4. For some other post-1965 commentaries, see John Saywell, *The Lawmakers: Judicial Power and the Shaping of Canadian Federalism* (Toronto: University of Toronto Press, 2002); David Schneiderman, "A.V. Dicey, Lord Watson and the Law of the Canadian Constitution in the Late Nineteenth Century" (1998) 16 Law and History Review 495; David Schneiderman, "Harold Laski, Viscount Haldane and the Law of the Canadian Constitution in the Early Twentieth Century" (1998) 48 U.T.L.J. 521; R.C.B. Risk, "The Scholars and the Constitution: P.O.G.G. and the Privy Council" (1996) Man. L.J. 496; Robert Vipond, *Liberty and Community: Canadian Federalism and the Failure of the Constitution* (Albany: State University of New York Press, 1991); Alan C. Cairns, "Comment on 'Critics of the Judicial Committee: The New Orthodoxy and an Alternative Explanation'" (1986) 19 Can. J. Pol. Sci. 521; Paul Romney, *Mr. Attorney, Attorney General of Ontario in Court, Cabinet, and Legislature, 1791–1899* (Toronto: Osgoode Society and University of Toronto Press, 1986); Peter H. Russell, "Comment on 'Critics of the Judicial Committee: The New Orthodoxy and an Alternative Explanation'" (1986) 19 Can. J. Pol. Sci. 495; Frederick Vaughan, "Critics of the Judicial Committee: The New Orthodoxy and an Alternative Explanation" (1986) 19 Can. J. Pol. Sci. 495; Frederick Vaughan, "Reply" (1986) 19 Can. J. Pol. Sci. 537; Kenneth M. Lysyk, "Constitutional Reform and the Introductory Clause of Section 91: Residual and Emergency Law-Making Authority" (1979) 57 Can. Bar Rev. 531; Kenneth M. Lysyk, "Reshaping Canadian Federalism" (1979) 13 U.B.C. L. Rev. 1; W.R. Lederman, "Comment" in Jacob S. Ziegel, ed., *Law and Social Change: Osgoode Hall Law School. Annual Lectures Series, 1971/72* (Toronto: Osgoode Hall Law School, York University, 1973); M. MacGuigan, "The Privy Council and the Supreme Court: A Jurisprudential Analysis" (1966) Alta. L. Rev. 419; Gerald P. Browne, *The Judicial Committee of the Privy Council* (Toronto: University of Toronto Press, 1967).
5. Alan C. Cairns, "The Judicial Committee and its Critics" (1971) 4 Can. J. Pol. Sci. 301.
6. Peter W. Hogg & Wade K. Wright, "Canadian Federalism, the Privy Council and the Supreme Court: Reflections on the Debate About Canadian Federalism" (2005) 38 U.B.C. L. Rev. 329, in Chapter 3.
7. *Ibid.* at 330, and see 319–27.
8. *Ibid.* at 328.
9. Hogg & Wright, *supra* note 6 at paras. 26–28.
10. Para. 29. See also paras. 25–28.
11. *Ibid.*, para. 31. Hogg and Wright argue at paras. 9 to 23 that the text of the *Constitution Act, 1867* contains significant decentralist features as well as significant centralist features.
12. *Ibid.*, paras. 32–41. At para. 40 Hogg and Wright cite provincial opposition to new federal policy initiatives as a justification for decentralization, but this could also be seen as a possible *consequence* of decentralization.
13. *Ibid.* para. 41.
14. Alan C. Cairns, "The Judicial Committee and its Critics" (1971) 4 Can. J. Pol. Sci. 301 at 328.
15. Hogg & Wright, *supra* note 6 at para. 37.
16. For Hogg and Wright, "[there is no doubt that the Privy Council favoured the provinces in federalism cases: para. 25. Hogg and Wright say that although the *Constitution Act, 1867* implied that the federal government was to be superior to the provinces, the Judicial Committee gave the provinces "coordinate status with the federal government." (*ibid.*). But the Judicial Committee's coordinate federalism approach did not reject superior federal powers such as disallowance. Instead, the doctrine's main aim was to ensure that the powers of both levels of government were equally entitled to protection against excessively broad interpretations of competing powers. Hogg and Wright's other main evidence of bias is the wide interpretation given by the Judicial Committee to property and civil rights. However, earlier in their article (at paras. 13 and 14) Hogg and Wright cite the property and civil rights power as a prime example of a decentralist aspect of the *Constitution Act, 1867*. They say that this provision was intended to confer extensive power. As elaborated below, there were cogent historical reasons for this. If this is so, it is difficult to see how judicial acknowledgement of this fact is evidence of bias!
17. Alan C. Cairns, "The Judicial Committee and its Critics" (1971) 4 Can. J. Pol. Sci. 301 at 327.
18. At 330, Cairns does say that given its London location, and "the sterilities of the legal tradition which it espoused, the decisions of the Privy Council were remarkably appropriate for the Canadian environment." Arguably, though, the text-based style was itself required by the lack of specific local knowledge and special vulnerability to domestic political criticism that resulted from the London location.
19. The degree to which this assumption is true depends, of course, on the extent to which the *Constitution Act, 1867* is seen as a decentralist document.
20. *Cf.* G.P. Browne, arguing that it is more plausible to attribute the decentralist tenor of the Judicial Committee's decisions to the logic of its interpretive scheme (i.e., its view that the enumerated heads of s. 91 are not merely illustrations of POGG, but have a constitutional position distinct from that of POGG) and to its unwillingness to engage in judicial legislation, than to a provincial bias": G.P. Browne, *The Judicial Committee and the British North America Act: An Analysis of the Interpretive Scheme for the Division of Legislative Powers* (Toronto: University of Toronto Press, 1967), ch. 12.
21. See, for example, the Introduction to this chapter.
22. Similarly, the Judicial Committee considered that even 92(13) of the *British North America Act* must be subject to some limits: see, for example, *Cushing v. Dupuy* (1879–80), 5 A.C. 409 at 415–16; *John Deere Plow Company v. Wharton*, [1915] 1 A.C. 330 at 340.
23. For an exception in a constitutional context that did not involve the division of legislative powers, see *Edwards v. Canada (A.G.)*, 1 D.L.R. 98 (J.C.P.C.) in Chapter 4.
24. *Cf.* G.P. Browne, arguing that the Judicial Committee tried to exercise restraint by way of minimizing "judicial legislation": G.P. Browne, *The Judicial Committee and the British North America Act: An Analysis of the Interpretive Scheme*

for the Division of Legislative Powers (Toronto: University of Toronto Press, 1967) at 7.

25. David W. Elliott, *Judicial Activism in Canadian Public Law*, 1988, unpublished survey of Judicial Committee and Supreme Court decisions, compiled with the assistance of Ms. Nancy Hansen and Ms. Kathy Nicholson and with support from the Social Sciences and Humanities Research Council.

26. *Ibid.*

27. By Cairns and others. In fact, the Judicial Committee was not alone in this respect. Most 19th- and early 20th-century judicial reasoning tends to involve much less policy discussion than its modern counterpart.

28. Criminal appeals were abolished in 1933 and civil appeals — appeals in all other matters — in 1949: see also *infra* note 36.

29. For example, John Saywell says that "[Lord Atkin's 1937] decisions had provoked a reaction in Canada that would lead to the abolition of appeals": John T. Saywell, *The Lawmakers: Judicial Power and the Shaping of Canadian Federalism* (Toronto: University of Toronto Press, 2002) at 228.

30. I.e., a practice of either clearly explaining or clearly over-ruling inconsistent earlier case law. Instead, for POGG, trade and commerce, and the criminal law power, the Judicial Committee tended to permit two contrary currents to flow — a restrictive dominant current and a broader countercurrent.

31. In the *Social Insurance Reference*, the depression could have been regarded as an emergency amounting to war or famine under POGG. Had it recognized an emergency here, the Judicial Committee could then follow *Fort Francis* in leaving the federal government a measure of discretion to determine the emergency's exact duration. Note that in one of its last decisions on the POGG power, the Judicial Committee was willing to extend the discretion in *Fort Francis* to the commencement as well as the duration of an emergency, saying that "very clear evidence that an emergency has not arisen, or that the emergency no longer exists" to justify intervention by the courts: *Co-operative Committee of Japanese Canadians v. Canada (A.G.)*, [1947] A.C. 87 at 101. What was needed in the *Natural Products Marketing Reference* was to apply the more grounded and balanced analysis the Judicial Committee took the following year when it considered the validity of a provincial marketing scheme in *Shannon*. In the *Labour Conventions Reference*, there was much to be said for its repudiation of the open-ended independent treaty approach to POGG that had been suggested in the earlier *Radio Reference*; the real problem, arguably,

was the unsuccessful attempt to distinguish the *Radio Reference*.

32. In the *Social Insurance Reference*, for example, the unemployment insurance scheme could have been validated for an interim period to coincide with the duration of the depression. Although the federal government would have discretion to determine when the depression had ended, its decision would be subject to review by the courts. In the *Natural Products Marketing Reference*, provincial interests could be safeguarded by requiring clear evidence that the interprovincial or international element was the dominant feature of the scheme.

33. A catalyst here may have been the opposition of many French Canadians to Canadian participation in overseas military commitments, whether through support for the British in the Boer War of 1899, or through conscription in the First World War: see Louis Balthazar, *Bilan du nationalisme au Québec* (Montreal: l'Hexagone, 1986); Casey Murrow, *Henri Bourassa and French-Canadian Nationalism: Opposition to Empire* (Montreal: Harvest House, 1968). See generally, Robert Craig Brown and Ramsay Cook, *Canada 1896–1921: A Nation Transformed*. (Toronto: McClelland & Stewart, 1974), chs. 9 and 13; Carl Berger, *The Sense of Power: Studies in the Ideas of Canadian Imperialism* (Toronto: University of Toronto Press, 1970).

34. *Ibid.*, 288–93. During the war itself, Borden had managed to secure separate Canadian representation in the deliberations on British and allied military policy: *ibid.* at 283–85.

35. For example, Supreme Court judges such as Lyman Duff were gaining recognition as constitutional experts: see R. Blake Brown, "The Supreme Court of Canada and Judicial Legitimacy: The Rise and Fall of Chief Justice Lyman Poore Duff" (2002) 47 McGill L.J. 559.

36. An early Canadian attempt to abolish criminal law appeals to the Judicial Committee was declared unconstitutional in *Nadan v. The King*, [1926] A.C. 482. In *British Coal Corporation v. The King*, [1935] A.C. 500, the Judicial Committee held that the obstacle to abolition of criminal law appeals (the *Colonial Laws Validity Act* of 1865, which said that colonial legislation repugnant to Imperial legislation was inoperative to the extent of the repugnancy) had been removed by the *Statute of Westminster* of 1931 (which repealed the *Colonial Laws Validity Act* except in regard to amendments to the *British North America Acts, 1867 to 1930*). Finally, in *Ontario (A.G.) v. Canada (A.G.)*, [1947] A.C. 127, the Judicial Committee affirmed that appeals could be abolished in all matters, both civil and criminal.

6 | Supreme Court of Canada: POGG, Trade and Commerce, and Criminal Law

(a) Introduction

Since it replaced the Judicial Committee as the highest constitutional tribunal, has the Supreme Court made a difference? As we will see in this chapter, POGG and trade and commerce are being re-shaped, and there are signs of change in areas such as criminal law.[1] The Supreme Court is edging away from the Judicial Committee's old concern with open-ended powers, from its emphasis on exclusive federal and provincial categories, and from its constant concern to safeguard provincial autonomy.

However, this is a trend, not a revolution. For all their concern for balance and exclusivity, the Judicial Committee did recognize the need for concurrent, shared, or related powers in several situations. In *Local Prohibition*,[2] for example, it held that temperance was an area of concurrent power, with paramountcy for Parliament. In *Hodge v. The Queen*,[3] it acknowledged that some subjects can have both a federal and a provincial aspect, permitting either level to legislate. Even the emergency doctrine recognized that two levels of government could occupy a single area in sequence, one normally, and the other exceptionally.

Moreover, it would be wrong to overemphasize the *importance* of this judicial trend. A comprehensive comparison of the Supreme Court's work with that of its predecessor would include other major federal[4] and provincial powers[5] as well. Beyond this, we must acknowledge Monahan, Covell, and Smith's point that many key functions of modern government, such as health care and the federal and provincial spending powers, are just not mentioned in the *Constitution Act, 1867*.[6] As a result, federal–provincial responsibilities in many of these areas are shaped not by courts but by agreements between federal and provincial executives.[7]

Still, where powers are explicit, courts can play a key role in shaping them.[8] Like the negotiation of executive agreements, this process is ongoing and incremental, in contrast with the more convulsive and sporadic process of formal amendment.

How actively *should* courts play this role? Clearly, if social needs don't remain static, neither should the law. Moreover, judicial activism in federalism review is arguably less "undemocratic" than it is in *Charter* control,[9] since it shifts power from one government level to another instead of blocking government action altogether.[10] On the other hand, some of the inheritance from the Judicial Committee may be worth preserving. While perhaps too extreme for our times, its emphasis on balance and avoidance of policy issues provides a useful caution about the essentials of a federal system and the limitations of courts.

Notes

1. See also Dyck, ch. 17 at 419–21; Hogg 2007, chs. 17 (POGG), 18 (Criminal Law), and 20 (Trade and Commerce); Monahan, chs. 8 (POGG), 9 (Trade and Commerce), and 10 (Criminal Law); Funston, ch. 4(3).
2. Chapter 5. See also *Ontario (A.G.) v. Canada (A.G.)*, [1894] A.C. 189, establishing concurrency over insolvency.
3. (1883–84), 9 A.C. 117. (This was the same decision that articulated their philosophy of coordinate federalism: see Note to *Local Prohibition Reference*, Chapter 5.)
4. For example, other key federal powers relate to *taxation* (see Hogg 2007, ch. 30; Funston, ch. 4(3)) and *transportation* (see Hogg 2007, ch. 22 [transportation and communication]; Monahan, ch. 10, section B).
5. For example, other key provincial powers relate to *direct taxation within the province* (see Hogg 2007, ch. 30); and *administration of justice in the province* (see Monahan, ch. 11, section D; Funston, at 113; Peter W. Hogg, *Constitutional Law of Canada*, 4th ed. (unabridged) (Scarborough, Ont.: Carswell, 1997), ch. 19).
6. Chapter 7. See also Monahan, ch. 7(E), noting that many modern problems cross-cut the original heads of power in

the *Constitution Act, 1867*. In the 1997 edition of his text, Monahan devoted a chapter to the environment, a topic that involves over a dozen different heads of federal and provincial constitutional powers.

7. See Chapter 8.
8. *Cf.* Patrick Monahan, *Politics and the Constitution: The Charter, Federalism and the Supreme Court of Canada*, 1987, ch. 10. Monahan argues that judicial federalism control has limited impact because governments can usually replace invalidated laws with less vulnerable alternatives. However, he concedes that federalism control can at least fix the initial bargaining position for intergovern-

mental negotiations: 240. See also Monahan, ch. 7(E). Monahan says that because the division of powers is open-ended and flexible, this obsolescence is not a serious problem. An alternative explanation might be that open-ended and flexible modern judicial interpretation of the division of powers has helped minimize the problem of obsolescence.

9. At least where the *Charter's* "notwithstanding" clause (s. 33) is legally or practically unavailable.
10. Patrick Monahan, *Politics and the Constitution*, *supra* note 8 at 6–7.

(b) *Anti-Inflation Act Reference*[†]

NOTE

Although it usually applied the emergency doctrine to the positive sense of POGG, and required specific, finite subject matter for the negative sense, the Judicial Committee never expressly repudiated the views in *Russell*, *Aeronautics*, *Radio*, and *Canada Temperance*. It left a divided inheritance on POGG, with these wider views paralleling the strict mainstream approach.

After 1949, when the Supreme Court of Canada became the highest constitutional arbiter, three ambiguous decisions generated more uncertainty. In *Johannesson v. West St. Paul*,[1] four of seven judges suggested that the fact that aeronautics had become a matter of national concern was enough to put it under POGG. In *Munro v. National Capital Commission*,[2] the Court held that development of a national capital region fell under POGG. They stressed the element of national concern, but also said the subject matter did not fall under the enumerated provincial categories. In the *Offshore Mineral Rights of British Columbia Reference*,[3] the Court invoked POGG because the subject matter did not fall under a head of provincial jurisdiction, but then added that "[t]he mineral resources of the lands underlying the territorial sea are of concern to Canada as a whole and go beyond local or provincial concerns or interests."[4] Clearly, some clarification was needed.

In December 1975, the federal government enacted an *Anti-Inflation Act* to combat an unprece-

dented combination of high unemployment and double-digit inflation. The Act set wage and price guidelines for the federal sector and for larger employers in the private sector, prescribed penalties, and created an administrative structure to enforce them. With provincial consent, the statute could include the provincial public sector. All provinces had agreed beforehand to participate, and all eventually brought their public sectors under the agreement. Ontario agreed to include its public sector, but used an order in council rather than a provincial statute to do so.

After several legal challenges, the federal government referred two questions to the Supreme Court of Canada in what became known as the *Anti-Inflation Reference*:[5]

(i) Was the *Anti-Inflation Act* constitutionally invalid?

(ii) If the *Anti-Inflation Act* was valid, was the agreement between the federal government and the government of Ontario effective to bind the Ontario public sector?

It is useful to look at the second question first, as the Court's answer to it was unanimous. How did they respond? How did their answer relate to the rule of law referred to in Chapter 2? Does it have anything to do with the notion of responsible government?

On the first question, the federal government claimed that Parliament could rely on POGG

[†] *Reference Re Anti-Inflation Act*, [1976] 2 S.C.R. 373.

because inflation was a matter of national concern, either falling outside the enumerated provincial categories or enabling Parliament to legislate in regard to subjects originally within these categories. In other words, they claimed support from either the negative or the positive sense of POGG. Only alternatively did they argue that the legislation could be supported by virtue of an emergency. Thus, before the Court could determine if the Act was *ultra vires*, they had to clarify the tests for POGG. They also had to decide how to appraise evidence of an emergency. Who should be required to prove or disprove the existence of an emergency? How much proof should be required? Must the Act specifically refer to an emergency or similar situation?

These are important questions, because the answers affect the balance of power both between federal and provincial legislatures and between legislatures and courts. How did the Court respond? Did the federal government win the war on issues of evidence and fact even while it lost the battle on law? Note that although Beetz J. dissented on the ultimate question of *vires*, his reasons are majority reasons on the test for POGG. What did he say about this? How successful was his attempt to reconcile the case law, to explain how "national concern" fits in, and to distinguish between the positive and negative senses of POGG? Was this the long-sought comprehensive case law synthesis that had eluded the Judicial Committee? Even if it was, it would soon be changed!

Notes

1. [1952] 1 S.C.R. 292.
2. [1966] S.C.R. 663.
3. [1967] S.C.R. 792.
4. *Ibid.* at 817.
5. *Reference Re Anti-Inflation Act*, [1976] 2 S.C.R. 373. For two helpful analyses, see James A. MacKenzie, "Three Comments on the A.I.B. Reference: The Anti-Inflation Act and Peace, Order and Good Government" (1977) Ottawa Law Rev. 169; and Peter H. Russell, "The *Anti-Inflation* Case: The Anatomy of a Constitutional Decision" (1977) 20 Cdn. Pub. Admin. 632.

EXTRACT

[LASKIN, C.J., for himself, Spence, Dickson and Judson JJ.:]

Since there was, in general, a concession by those opposing the legislation that it would be valid if it were what I may call crisis legislation, and since the proponents of the legislation urged this as an alternative ground on which its validity should be sustained, it appears to me to be the wise course to consider first whether the *Anti-Inflation Act* can be supported on that footing. If it is sustainable as crisis legislation, it becomes unnecessary to consider the broader ground advanced in its support, and this because, especially in constitutional cases, Courts should not, as a rule, go any farther than is necessary to determine the main issue before them.

The competing arguments on the question whether the Act is supportable as crisis legislation raised four main issues:

1. Did the *Anti-Inflation Act* itself belie the federal contention because of the form of the Act and, in particular, because of the exclusion of the provincial public sector from its imperative scope, notwithstanding that it is framed as a temporary measure albeit subject to extension of its operation?
2. Is the federal contention assisted by the preamble to the statute?
3. Does the extrinsic evidence put before the Court and other matters of which the Court can take judicial notice without extrinsic material to back it up, show that there was a rational basis for the Act as a crisis measure?
4. Is it a tenable argument that exceptional character could be lent to the legislation as rising beyond local or provincial concerns because Parliament could reasonably take the view that it was a necessary measure to fortify action in other related areas of admittedly federal authority, such as that of monetary policy?

I have referred to the first of these issues earlier in these reasons. It goes to the form of the *Anti-Inflation Act* and to the question whether the scope of the compulsory application of the *Anti-Inflation Act* may be taken to indicate that the Parliament of Canada did not act through any senses of crisis or urgency in enacting it. I note that the federal public service, a very large public service, is governed by the Act and the Guidelines, that private employers of five hundred or more persons are subject to the Act and Guidelines, that the construction industry is particularly dealt with by making those who employ twenty or more persons in that industry subject to the Act and Guidelines and that the Act and Guidelines apply also to persons in various professions, including architects, accountants, dentists, engineers, lawyers, doctors and management consultants. Again, the Act provides for bringing within the Act and Guidelines businesses, irrespective of numbers employed, which are declared by Order in Council to be of strategic importance to the containment and reduction of inflation in Canada. Having regard to the enormous administrative problems which the programme entails, the coverage is comprehensive indeed in its immediately obligatory provisions. What is left out of compulsory coverage is the provincial public sector, including the municipal public sector, but provision is made for bringing this area into the programme under the Guidelines by agreements under s. 4(3) or s. 4(4) or s. 5.

I do not regard the provisions respecting the provincial public sector as an indicator that the Government and Parliament of Canada were not seized with urgency or manifested a lack of any sense of crisis in the establishment of the programme. Provincial governmental concern about rising inflation and concurrent unemployment was a matter of public record prior to the inauguration of the programme, and this Court was provided with copies of agreements that eight of the ten Provinces had made with the federal Government for the application therein of the federal Guidelines. Only British Columbia and Saskatchewan had not entered into agreements. With private industry and private services bound to the extent that they are, and with the federal public service also bound, I see it as a reasonable policy from the standpoint of administration to allow the Provinces to contract into the programme in respect of the provincial public sector under their own administration if this was their preference rather than by simply accepting, as they could, the federal administration. Since the "contracting in" is envisaged on the basis of the federal Guidelines the national character of the programme is underlined.

. . . .

The Attorney-General of Canada relied upon the preamble to the *Anti-Inflation Act* both in respect of his primary argument and in respect of his alternative argument. He emphasized the words therein "that the containment and reduction of inflation has become a matter of *serious* national concern" and as well the following words that "to accomplish such containment and reduction of inflation it is *necessary* to restrain profit margins, prices, dividends and compensation" (the italicized words were especially emphasized). I do not regard it as telling against the Attorney-General's alternative position that the very word "emergency" was not used. Forceful language would not carry the day for the Attorney-General of Canada if the circumstances attending its use did not support the constitutional significance sought to be drawn from it. Of course, the absence of any preamble would weaken the assertion of crisis conditions, and I have already drawn attention to the fact that no preamble suggesting a critical economic situation, indeed no preamble at all was included in the legislation challenged in the *Board of Commerce* case.

The preamble in the present case is sufficiently indicative that Parliament was introducing a far-reaching programme prompted by what in its view was a serious national condition. The validity of the *Anti-Inflation Act* does not, however, stand or fall on that preamble, but the preamble does provide a base for assessing the gravity of the circumstances which called forth the legislation.

This brings me to the third of the four issues above-mentioned, namely, the relevancy and weight of the extrinsic evidence and the assistance to be derived from judicial notice. When, as in this case, an issue is raised that exceptional circumstances underlie resort to a legislative power which may properly be invoked in such circumstances, the Court may be asked to consider extrinsic material bearing on the circumstances alleged, both in support of and in denial of the lawful exercise of legislative authority. In considering such material and assessing its weight, the Court does not look at it in terms of whether it provides proof of the exceptional circumstances as a matter of fact. The matter concerns social and economic policy and hence governmental and legislative judgement. It may be that the existence of exceptional circumstances is so notorious as to enable the Court, of its own motion, to take judicial notice of them without reliance on extrinsic material to inform it. Where this is not so evident, the extrinsic material need go only so far as to persuade the Court that there is a rational basis for the legislation which it is attributing to the head of power invoked in this case in support of its validity.

. . . .

... What the Consumer Price Index shows, and Professor Lipsey himself relies on its figures, is that for the first time in many years Canada had a double digit inflation rate for successive years, *i.e.*, in 1974 and 1975, the index rising 10.9 per cent in 1974 above its reading for 1973 and being 10.8 per cent higher in 1975 than it was in 1974. Some monthly drops slightly below double digit rises do not materially affect the relevance of the annual figures.

There have been inflationary periods before in our history but, again referring to Professor Lipsey's study, "the problem of the coexistence of high unemployment and high inflation rates was not, however, encountered before the late 1960s." These

119

twin conditions continued to the time that the Government and Parliament acted in establishing its prices and incomes policy under the *Anti-Inflation Act* and Guidelines, and were the prime reason for the policy.

. . . .

In my opinion, this Court would be unjustified in concluding, on the submissions in this case and on all the material put before it, that the Parliament of Canada did not have a rational basis for regarding the *Anti-Inflation Act* as a measure which, in its judgment, was temporarily necessary to meet a situation of economic crisis imperilling the well-being of the people of Canada as a whole and requiring Parliament's stern intervention in the interests of the country as a whole. That there may have been other periods of crisis in which no similar action was taken is beside the point.

The rationality of the judgment so exercised is, in my view, supported by a consideration of the fourth of the issues which I enumerated above. The fact that there had been rising inflation at the time federal action was taken, that inflation is regarded as a monetary phenomenon and that monetary policy is admittedly within exclusive federal jurisdiction persuades me that the Parliament of Canada was entitled, in the circumstances then prevailing and to which I have already referred, to act as it did from the springboard of its jurisdiction over monetary policy and, I venture to add, with additional support from its power in relation to the regulation of trade and commerce. The Government White Paper refers to a prices and incomes policy as one element in a four-pronged programme of which the first engages its fiscal and monetary authority; and although the White Paper states that the Government rejects the use of severe monetary and fiscal restraints to stop inflation because of the alleged heavy immediate cost in unemployment and foregone output, it could seek to blend policies in those areas with a prices and incomes policy under the circumstances revealed by the extrinsic material.

Since no argument was addressed to the trade and commerce power I content myself with observing only that it provides the Parliament of Canada with a foothold in respect of "the general regulation of trade affecting the whole dominion," to use the words of the *Privy Council in Citizens Ins. Co. of Canada v. Parsons* (1881), 7 App. Cas. 96 at p. 113....

. . . .

For all the foregoing reasons, I would hold that the *Anti-Inflation Act* is valid legislation for the peace, order and good government of Canada and does not, in the circumstances under which it was enacted and having regard to its temporary character, invade provincial legislative jurisdiction. It is open to this Court to say, at some future time, as it in effect said in the *Margarine* case, [1949] 1 D.L.R. 433, [1949] S.C.R. 1; affirmed [1950] 4 D.L.R. 689, [1951] A.C. 179, that a statutory provision valid in its application under circumstances envisaged at the time of its enactment can no longer have a constitutional application to different circumstances under which it would, equally, not have been sustained had they existed at the time of its enactment.

[LASKIN C.J. for the Court:]

The second question referred to this court relates to the construction of s. 4(3) of the *Anti-Inflation Act* and to whether the intergovernmental agreement between Canada and Ontario, for the application of the Act and the Guidelines to the provincial public sector, was consummated in a manner that would make it effective in Ontario pursuant to s. 4(3)....

. . . .

The contention of the Attorney-General of Ontario that the Crown in right of Ontario, represented by the Lieutenant-Governor, has a common law power and capacity to enter into agreements if there are no statutory restrictions does not answer the question of authority to effect changes in Ontario law through such agreements. The issue here is not prerogative power alone or the authority to exercise a prerogative power when given by Order in Council so as to place responsibility for it upon the Ministers present at the meeting of the Executive Council. Nor does the issue engage any concern with responsible Government and the political answerability of the Ministers to the Legislative Assembly. Rather what is at issue is the right of the Crown, although duly protected by an order in Council, to bind its subjects in the Province to laws not enacted by the Legislature nor made applicable to such subjects by adoption under authorizing legislation. There is no principle in this country, as there is not in Great Britain, that the Crown may legislate by proclamation or Order in Council to bind citizens where it so acts without the support of a statute of the Legislature: see Dicey, *Law of the Constitution*, 10th ed. (1959), pp. 50–54.

. . . .

[RITCHIE J. for himself, Martland and Pigeon JJ.:]

I have had the privilege of reading the reasons for judgment of the Chief Justice and his comprehensive review of the authorities satisfies me that the answer to the question of whether or not the *Anti-Inflation Act*, 1974–1975 (Can.), c. 75, hereinafter referred to as the "Act," is *ultra vires* the Parliament of Canada, must depend upon whether or not the legislation was enacted to combat a national economic emergency. I use the phrase "national emergency" in the sense in which I take it to have been used by Lord Wright in *Co-operative Committee on Japanese Canadians et al. v. A.G. Can. et al.*, [1947] 1 D.L.R. 577, [1947] A.C. 87 (hereinafter referred to as the *Japanese Canadian* case), and accepted by this Court in *Reference re Wartime Leasehold Regulations*, [1950] 2 D.L.R. 1, [1950] S.C.R. 124. In those cases the "emergency" was occasioned by war and the aftermath of war, but I see nothing to exclude the application of the principles there enunciated from a situation created by highly exceptional economic conditions prevailing in times of peace.

In my opinion such conditions exist where there can be said to be an urgent and critical situation adversely affecting all Canadians and being of such proportions as to transcend the authority vested in the Legislatures of the Provinces and thus presenting an emergency which can only be effectively dealt with by Parliament in the exercise of the powers conferred upon it by s. 91 of the *British North America Act, 1867* "to make laws for the peace, order and good government of Canada." The authority of Parliament in this regard is, in my opinion, limited to dealing with critical conditions and the necessity to which they give rise and must perforce be confined to legislation of a temporary character.

I do not consider that the validity of the Act rests upon the constitutional doctrine exemplified in earlier decisions of the Privy Council, to all of which the Chief Justice has made reference, and generally known as the "national dimension" or "national concern" doctrine. It is not difficult to envisage many different circumstances which could give rise to national concern, but at least since the *Japanese Canadians* case, I take it to be established that unless such concern is made manifest by circumstances amounting to a national emergency, Parliament is not endowed under the cloak of the "peace, order and good government" clause with the authority to legislate in relation to matters reserved to the Provinces under s. 92 of the *British North America Act, 1867*. In this regard I am in full agreement with the reasons for judgment prepared for delivery by

my brother Beetz which I have had the advantage of reading, and I have little to add to what he has said.

I should also say, however, that I cannot find that the authority of Parliament to pass legislation such as the present Act stems from any of the enumerated classes of subjects referred to in s. 91. The source of the federal power in relation to the *Anti-Inflation Act* must, in my opinion, be found in the "peace, order and good government" clause, and the aura of federal authority to which that clause relates can in my view only be extended so as to invade the provincial area when the legislation is directed to coping with a genuine emergency in the sense to which I have made reference.

In order to determine whether the legislation here in question was enacted to combat such an emergency, it is necessary to examine the legislation itself, but in so doing I think it not only permissible but essential to give consideration to the material which Parliament had before it at the time when the statute was enacted for the purpose of disclosing the circumstances which prompted its enactment. The most concrete source of this information is, in my opinion, the White Paper tabled in the House by the Minister of Finance and made a part of the case which was submitted on behalf of the Attorney-General of Canada.

The preamble to the *Anti-Inflation Act* is quoted in full in the reasons for judgment of the Chief Justice and it is unnecessary for me to repeat it. It is enough to say that it manifests a recognition of the fact "that inflation in Canada at current levels is contrary to the interest of all Canadians" and that it has become a matter of such serious national concern as to make it necessary to enact this legislation. Neither the terms of the preamble nor any provisions of the Act specifically declare the existence of a national emergency, nor is there anything in the Act which could of itself be characterized as a proclamation that such a situation exists, but when the language of the preamble is read as I have suggested in conjunction with the White Paper, it does not appear to me that it was necessary for Parliament to use any particular form of words in order to disclose its belief that an emergency existed. The "Introduction" and "Conclusion" of the White Paper appear to me to be descriptive of the conditions with which Parliament purported to cope in enacting the legislation. The "Introduction" contains the following statement:

> Canada is in the grip of serious inflation.
> If this inflation continues or gets worse there is a grave danger that economic recovery

121

will be stifled, unemployment increased and the nation subjected to mounting stresses and strains.

It has thus become absolutely essential to undertake a concerted national effort to bring inflation under control.

There are no simple or easy remedies for quickly resolving this critical problem. The inflationary process in Canada is so deeply entrenched that it can be brought under control only by a broad and comprehensive program of action on a national scale.

The "Conclusion" contains the following passage:

As a first essential, it is imperative that we take determined action as a nation to halt and reverse the spiral of costs and prices that jeopardizes the whole fabric of our economy and of our society.

When the words "serious national concern" are read against the background of these excerpts from the White Paper it becomes apparent that they were employed by Parliament in recognition of the existence of a national emergency.

The provisions of the Act quite clearly reveal the decision of Parliament that exceptional measures were considered to be required to combat this emergency and it has not been seriously suggested that these provisions were colourably enacted for any other purpose.

I am accordingly satisfied that the record discloses that in enacting the *Anti-Inflation Act* the Parliament of Canada was motivated by a sense of urgent necessity created by highly exceptional circumstances and that a judgement declaring the Act to be *ultra vires* could only be justified by reliance on very clear evidence that an emergency had not arisen when the statute was enacted. In this regard I reiterate what was said by Lord Wright in the *Japanese Canadians* case, *supra*, at pp. 585–6 D.L.R., pp. 101–2 A.C., in the following passage:

Again, if it be clear that an emergency has not arisen, or no longer exists, there can be no justification for the exercise or continued exercise of the exceptional powers. The rule of law as to the distribution of powers between the Parliaments of the Dominion and the Parliaments of the Provinces comes into play. But very clear evidence that an emergency has not arisen or that the emergency no longer exists, is required to justify the judiciary, even though the question is one of *ultra vires*, in overruling the decision of the Parliament of the Dominion that exceptional measures were required or were still required.

To this may be added as a corollary that it is not pertinent to the judiciary to consider the wisdom or the propriety of the particular policy which is embodied in the emergency legislation.

In my opinion, the evidence presented to the Court by those opposed to the validity of the legislation did not meet the requirements set by Lord Wright and I am unable to say that the exceptional measures contained in the Act were not required.

It is for these reasons I am in agreement with the Chief Justice that the first question posed by this Reference should be answered in the negative.

As to the second question posed by the Reference, I am in complete agreement with the reasons for judgment of the Chief Justice.

. . . .

[BEETZ J., dissenting, for himself and De Grandpré J.:]

The *Anti-Inflation Act* authorizes the imposition of guidelines for the restraint of prices, profit margins, dividends and compensation in those sectors of the economy which it specifies and which may be described as the federal public sector, the federal private sector and the provincial private sector. With provincial consent, the guidelines can be extended, in whole or in part, to the provincial public sector. It is conceded that the Parliament of Canada has legislative competence to enact such legislation with respect to both the public and private federal sectors and to regulate prices, profit margins, dividends and compensation for commodities and services supplied by the federal Government and its agencies or by private institutions or undertakings coming within exclusive federal jurisdiction such as banks, railways, bus lines and other transportation undertakings extending beyond the limits of a Province, navigation and shipping undertakings and the like.

However, the *Anti-Inflation Act* is not confined to the federal public and private sectors. It extends compellingly to a substantial part of the provincial private sector, which is the most important one in quantitative terms and which comprises, for instance manufacturers of commodities such as automobiles and clothes, department stores and other large retailers, hotels, insurance companies, trust companies, all large suppliers of services, [and] professionals such as doctors, dentists and lawyers.

The control and regulation of local trade and of commodity pricing and of profit margins in the provincial sectors have consistently been held to lie, short of a national emergency, within exclusive provincial jurisdiction....

. . . .

[Beetz J. turned to the federal government's first submission, that inflation had become a matter of serious national concern, and that this, as well as an emergency, could support the use of POGG.]

Such are the constitutional imports of the first submission in terms of the so-called subject-matter of inflation.

Its effects on the principles which underlie the distribution of other powers between Parliament and the Legislatures are even more far-reaching assuming there would be much left of the distribution of powers if Parliament has exclusive authority in relation to the "containment and reduction of inflation."

If the first submission is correct, then it could also be said that the promotion of economic growth or the limits to growth or the protecting of the environment have become global problems and now constitute subject-matters of national concern going beyond local provincial concern or interest and coming within the exclusive legislative authority of Parliament. It could equally be argued that older subjects such as the business of insurance or labour relations, which are not specifically listed in the enumeration of federal and provincial powers and have been held substantially to come within provincial jurisdiction have outgrown provincial authority whenever the business of insurance or labour [has] become national in scope. It is not difficult to speculate as to where this line of reasoning would lead: a fundamental feature of the Constitution, its federal nature, the distribution of powers between Parliament and the provincial Legislatures, would disappear not gradually but rapidly.

I cannot be persuaded that the first submission expresses the state of the law. It goes against the persistent trend of the authorities. It is founded upon an erroneous characterization of the *Anti-Inflation Act*. As for the cases relied upon by counsel to support the submission, they are quite distinguishable and they do not, in my view, stand for what they are said to stand.

. . . .

I have no reason to doubt that the *Anti-Inflation Act* is part of a more general programme aimed at inflation and which may include fiscal and monetary measures and Government expenditure policies. I am prepared to accept that inflation was the occasion or the reason for its enactment. But I do not agree that inflation is the subject-matter of the Act. In order to characterize an enactment, one must look at its operation, at its effect and at the scale of its effects rather than at its ultimate purpose where the purpose is practically all-embracing. If for instance Parliament is to enact a tax law or a monetary law as a part of an anti-inflation programme no one will think that such laws have ceased to be a tax law or a monetary law and that they have become subsumed into their ultimate purpose so that they should rather be characterized as "anti-inflation laws," an expression which, in terms of actual content, is not meaningful. They plainly remain and continue to be called a tax law or a monetary law, although they have been enacted by reason of an inflationary situation. When the Bank of Canada changes its rate of interest, it must obviously take inflation into account; even if inflation is the main reason for such a measure, this measure will still be characterized by everyone as a central banking measure relating to interest. The same would also be said of a measure relating to the issue of currency; although it may have been dictated by inflationary trends, it remains a measure relating to currency, coinage or the issue of paper money. Similarly, the *Anti-Inflation Act* is, as its preamble states, clearly a law relating to the control of profit margins, prices, dividends and compensation, that is, with respect to the provincial private sector, a law relating to the regulation of local trade, to contract and to property and civil rights in the Provinces, enacted as part of a programme to combat inflation. Property and civil rights in the Provinces are, for the greater part, the pith and substance or the subject-matter of the *Anti-Inflation Act*. According to the Constitution, Parliament may fight inflation with the powers put at its disposal by the specific heads enumerated in s. 91 or by such powers as are outside of s. 92. But it cannot, apart from a declaration of national emergency or from a constitutional amendment, fight inflation with powers exclusively reserved to the Provinces, such as the power to make laws in relation to property and civil rights. This is what Parliament has in fact attempted to do in enacting the *Anti-Inflation Act*.

The authorities relied upon by Counsel for Canada and Ontario in support of the first submission are connected with the constitutional doctrine that became known as the national concern doctrine or national dimension doctrine....

. . . .

In my view, the incorporation of companies for objects other than provincial, the regulation and control of aeronautics and of radio, the development, conservation and improvement of the National Capital Region are clear instances of distinct subject-matters which do not fall within any of the enumerated heads of s. 92 and which, by nature, are of national concern.

I fail to see how the authorities which so decide lend support to the first submission. They had the effect of adding by judicial process new matters or new classes of matters to the federal list of powers. However, this was done only in cases where a new matter was not an aggregate but had a degree of unity that made it indivisible, an identity which made it distinct from provincial matters and a sufficient consistence to retain the bounds of form. The scale upon which these new matters enabled Parliament to touch on provincial matters had also to be taken into consideration before they were recognized as federal matters: if an enumerated federal power designated in broad terms such as the trade and commerce power had to be construed so as not to embrace and smother provincial powers (*Parson's* case) and destroy the equilibrium of the Constitution, the Courts must be all the more careful not to add hitherto unnamed powers of a diffuse nature to the list of federal powers.

The "containment and reduction of inflation" does not pass muster as a new subject matter. It is an aggregate of several subjects some of which form a substantial part of provincial jurisdiction. It is totally lacking in specificity. It is so pervasive that it knows no bounds. Its recognition as a federal head of power would render most provincial powers nugatory.

I should add that inflation is a very ancient phenomenon, several thousand years old, as old probably as the history of currency. The Fathers of Confederation were quite aware of it.

It was argued that other heads of power enumerated in s. 91 of the Constitution and which relate for example to the regulation of trade and commerce, to currency and coinage, to banking, incorporation of banks and the issue of paper money may be indicative of the breadth of Parliament's jurisdiction in economic matters. They do not enable Parliament to legislate otherwise than in relation to their objects and it was not argued that the *Anti-Inflation Act* was in relation to their objects. The Act does not derive any assistance from those powers any

more than the legislation found invalid in the *Board of Commerce* case.

For those reasons, the first submission fails.

[Beetz J. continued with the federal government's second submission.]

The second submission made in support of the validity of the *Anti-Inflation Act* is that the inflationary situation was in October of 1975, and still is such as to constitute a national emergency of the same significance as war, pestilence or insurrection and that there is in Parliament an implied power to deal with the emergency for the safety of Canada as a whole; that such situation of exceptional necessity justified the enactment of the impugned legislation. The following cases, amongst others, were relied upon: *Fort Frances Pulp & Paper Co. v. Manitoba Free Press Co.*, [1923] 3 D.L.R. 629, [1923] A.C. 695, 25 O.W.N. 60; *Co-operative Committee on Japanese Canadians et al. v. A.G. Can. et al.*, [1947] 1 D.L.R. 577, [1947] A.C. 87; *Reference re Wartime Leasehold Regulations*, [1950] 2 D.L.R. 1, [1950] S.C.R. 124.

Before I deal with this second submission I should state at the outset that I am prepared to assume the validity of the following propositions:

- the power of Parliament under the national emergency doctrine is not confined to war situations or to situations of transition from war to peace; an emergency of the nature contemplated by the doctrine may arise in peace time;
- inflation may constitute such an emergency;
- Parliament may validly exercise its national emergency powers before an emergency actually occurs; a state of apprehended emergency or crisis suffices to justify Parliament in taking preventive measures including measures to contain and reduce inflation where inflation amounts to [a] state of apprehended crisis.

. . . .

I disagree with the proposition that the national concern or national dimension doctrine and the emergency doctrine amount to the same. Even if it could be said that "where an emergency exists it is the emergency which gives the matter its dimension of national concern or interest" (Le Dain, *op. cit.* p. 291) the emergency does not give the matter the same dimensions as the national concern doctrine applied for instance in the *Aeronautics* case, in the *Johannesson* case or in the *Munro* case.

The national concern doctrine illustrated by these cases applies in practice as if certain heads such as aeronautics or the development and conservation of the national capital were added to the categories of subject-matters enumerated in s. 91 of the Constitution when it is found by the courts that, in substance, a class of subjects not enumerated in either s. 91 or s. 92 lies outside the first fifteen heads enumerated in s. 92 and is not of a merely local or private nature. Whenever the national concern theory is applied, the effect is permanent although it is limited by the identity of the subject newly recognized to be of national dimensions. By contrast, the power of Parliament to make laws in a great crisis knows no limits other than those which are dictated by the nature of the crisis. But one of those limits is the temporary nature of the crisis.

. . . .

Perhaps it does not matter very much whether one chooses to characterize legislation enacted under the emergency power as legislation relating to the emergency or whether one prefers to consider it as legislation relating to the particular subject-matter which it happens to regulate. But if one looks at the practical effects of the exercise of the emergency power, one must conclude that it operates so as to give to Parliament for all purposes necessary to deal with the emergency, concurrent and paramount jurisdiction over matters which would normally fall within exclusive provincial jurisdiction. To that extent, the exercise of that power amounts to a temporary *pro tanto* amendment of a federal Constitution by the unilateral action of Parliament. The legitimacy of that power is derived from the Constitution: when the security and the continuation of the Constitution and of the nation are at stake, the kind of power commensurate with the situation "is only to be found in that part of the constitution which establishes power in the state as a whole" (Viscount Haldane in the *Fort Frances* case, p. 634 D.L.R., p. 704 A.C.).

The extraordinary nature and the constitutional features of the emergency power of Parliament dictate the manner and form in which it should be invoked and exercised. It should not be an ordinary manner and form. At the very least, it cannot be a manner and form which admits of the slightest degree of ambiguity to be resolved by interpretation. In cases where the existence of an emergency may be a matter of controversy, it is imperative that Parliament should not have recourse to its emergency power except in the most explicit terms indicating that it is acting on the basis of that power....

. . . .

The *Anti-Inflation Act* fails in my opinion to pass the test of explicitness required to signal that it has been enacted pursuant to the national emergency power of Parliament.

The preamble has been much relied upon:

WHEREAS the Parliament of Canada recognizes that inflation in Canada at current levels is contrary to the interests of all Canadians and that the containment and reduction of inflation has become a matter of serious national concern;

AND WHEREAS to accomplish such containment and reduction of inflation it is necessary to restrain profit margins, prices, dividends and compensation;

The words "a matter of serious national concern" have been emphasized.

I remain unimpressed.

The death penalty is a matter of national concern. So is abortion. So is the killing or maiming of innumerable people by impaired drivers. So is the traffic in narcotics and drugs. One can conceive of several drastic measures, all coming within the ordinary jurisdiction of the Parliament of Canada, and which could be preceded by a preamble reciting that a given situation had become a matter of serious national concern. I fail to see how the adding of the word "serious" can convey the meaning that Parliament has decided to embark upon an exercise of its extraordinary emergency power. The *Canada Water Act*, 1969–70 (Can.), c. 52 [now R.S.C. 1970, c. 5 (1st Supp.)], on the constitutionality of which, again, I refrain from expressing any view, contains a preamble where it is stated that pollution of the water resources of Canada has become "a matter of urgent national concern." Is the *Canada Water Act* an emergency measure in the constitutional sense? It does not seem to present itself as such. How is a matter of serious national concern to be distinguished from a matter of urgent national concern? I cannot read the preamble of the *Anti-Inflation Act* as indicating that the act was passed to deal with a national emergency in the constitutional sense.

Counsel for Canada has also insisted upon the temporary nature of the *Anti-Inflation Act*. I note that the duration of the Act could, under s. 46 [since am. 1974–75–76, c. 98, s. 11], be extended by Order in Council with the approval of both Houses of Parliament, although I am not inclined to attach undue importance to this point. None the less, while it would be essential to the validity of a measure enacted under the national emergency power of Parliament that it be not permanent, still the temporary character of an Act is hardly indicative and in no way conclusive that it constitutes a measure passed to deal with a national emergency: Parliament can and often does enact temporary measures relating to matters coming within its normal jurisdiction.

I have dealt with the arguments based on the preamble and the limited duration (s. 46) of the *Anti-Inflation Act*.

There is nothing in the rest of the Act and in the Guidelines to show that they have been passed to deal with a national emergency. There is much, on the other hand, within the Act and the Guidelines, in terms of actual or potential exemptions which is inconsistent with the nature of a global war launched on inflation considered as a great emergency. It would not be within our province to judge the efficacy and wisdom of the legislation if it were truly enacted to deal with an extraordinary crisis but its lack of comprehensiveness may be indicative of its ordinary character.

· · · ·

The *Anti-Inflation Act* is in my opinion *ultra vires* of Parliament in so far at least as it applies to the provincial private sector; but severability having not been pleaded by counsel for Canada, I would declare the Act *ultra vires* of Parliament in whole.

The second constitutional question is predicated upon the validity of the *Anti-Inflation Act*. Since, however, this is a constitutional reference I believe I should state my opinion with respect to the second question as if I held the view that the *Anti-Inflation Act* is *intra vires*. I agree with the Chief Justice's disposition of the second question.

In the result, I would answer the two questions referred to this Court as follows:

Question 1: Yes. The *Anti-Inflation Act* is *ultra vires* of the Parliament of Canada in whole.

Question 2: No. The agreement is not effective to render the *Anti-Inflation Act* binding on and the Guidelines made thereunder applicable to the provincial public sector in Ontario as defined in the agreement.

(c) *Crown Zellerbach*†

NOTE

Environmental protection is an issue of great current interest. Depending on the precise subject matter and circumstances, it may lie under either federal or provincial jurisdiction.

The *Crown Zellerbach* case involved a wide-ranging federal statute intended to control marine pollution. Section 4(1) of the *Ocean Dumping Control Act* prohibited dumping of substances at sea. The section was not expressly limited to dumping causing harm to marine life, to other specific parts of the environment, or to humans. Another part of the Act defined "sea" to include Canadian internal waters.

Crown Zellerbach, a large lumber company, was charged with dumping wood waste (into Beaver Cove, off the coast of Vancouver Island), contrary to the *Ocean Dumping Control Act*. The company defended itself by arguing that the provision was *ultra vires* Parliament.

The lower courts agreed with the company that the provision fell within provincial jurisdiction. They held that Beaver Cove was within the province of British Columbia, and the British Columbia Court of Appeal said the provision involved provincial powers over "Management of Public Lands belonging to the Province"; property and civil rights; and local or private matters within the province.

The federal government relied in part on its jurisdiction over "sea coast and inland fisheries", but s. 4(1) made no reference to fisheries, and there was no evidence in this case that the dumping had harmed marine life. They also referred to the federal power over criminal law, but there was nothing to limit the section to dangers to human health. Other specific federal heads, such as navigation and shipping, beacons, buoys, and

---

† *R. v. Crown Zellerbach Canada Ltd.* (1988), 49 D.L.R. (4th) 161 at 175–204 (S.C.C.).

lighthouses, and interprovincial and international ferries, were of little direct help. The crucial question, then, was whether the federal marine pollution control legislation could be supported on the basis of the general power in relation to Peace, Order, and good Government.

In the *Anti-Inflation Act Reference*, a majority of the Supreme Court of Canada had held that only in an emergency situation could Parliament invoke POGG to legislate in regard to subject matter already under provincial jurisdiction. Where the situation fell short of an emergency, POGG could only support federal legislation if its subject matter was (i) distinct, (ii) of national concern, and (iii) new in the sense that it did not already fall under any of the enumerated heads of s. 92.

Since the *Anti-Inflation Reference*, a handful of Supreme Court decisions had contained *dicta* that POGG might support some matters of national concern even if they were not "new" in the sense specified in the reference. Should this new route be taken, and with it a more wide-ranging, open-ended approach to federal power and to the judiciary's own role in patrolling this part of the division of powers? Or should POGG be restricted to the more traditional boundaries of the *Anti-Inflation Reference*? This was a key legal question facing the court in *Crown Zellerbach*.

In his majority judgment in *Crown Zellerbach*, Le Dain J. appeared to say that while the emergency doctrine supports laws that are exceptional and temporary, even in regard to subject matter originally falling under s. 92, the national concern doctrine supports federal laws that have a distinctive (clearly of national rather than provincial concern) and indivisible (not an aggregate) subject matter, and are not federally unintrusive (do not represent a major intrusion on provincial power). Le Dain J. said that distinctness and indivisibility and can be assessed both conceptually and functionally. Functionally, it may be helpful to determine if the subject matter has extraprovincial aspects that cannot be addressed, or addressed effectively, by provinces acting on their own. If the requirements of distinctiveness, indivisibility, and unobtrusiveness are met, then the legislation can be supported under the national concern doctrine, (a) whether or not the subject matter originally fell under s. 92, (b) on a permanent basis, and (c) to the exclusion of any provincial jurisdiction over the same subject matter.

Arguably, the majority decision in *Crown Zellerbach* gave the national concern doctrine two related but different branches. The first is a strictly residual branch. This is the traditional negative sense that Beetz J. associated with the national concern doctrine in the *Anti-Inflation Reference*. Under this branch, the subject matter must be a conceptually distinctive and indivisible concern that has never fallen under s. 92 of the *Constitution Act, 1867*. As such a law is outside s. 92, there is no need to apply a functional test for distinctiveness and indivisibility. For similar reasons, a law of this kind would automatically meet the requirement that it must not intrude on the fundamental distribution of legislative powers. Under the positive branch of national concern, Parliament can legislate in regard to matter that would have ordinarily fallen under s. 92, but meets the distinctiveness and indivisibility criteria (measured by conceptual and, if necessary, functional tests) and the unobtrusiveness criteria referred to above.

However, the interpretation above is necessarily speculative, and the *Crown Zellerbach* restatement of POGG raises many questions. What constitutes provincial inability? Mere inaction? Financial inability? Unwillingness? Inability of several provinces to secure agreement? What level of proof of provincial inability is required? What scale of impact would be "reconcilable with the fundamental distribution of legislative power"? What, exactly, is meant by "the effect on extra-provincial interests of a provincial failure to deal effectively with the control or regulation of the intraprovincial aspects of the matter"?

Note

1. Although singleness and indivisibility are sometimes referred to separately, Le Dain J.'s reasons as a whole suggest that he considered singleness as a synonym for indivisibility.

EXTRACT

[LE DAIN J. (Dickson C.J.C., McIntyre and Wilson JJ. concurring):]

I agree with Schmidt Prov. Ct. J. and the British Columbia Court of Appeal that federal legislative jurisdiction with respect to sea coast and inland fisheries is not sufficient by itself to support the constitutional validity of s. 4(1) of the Act because that section, viewed in the context of the Act as a whole, fails to meet the test laid down in *Fowler* and *Northwest Falling*. While the effect on fisheries of marine pollution caused by the dumping of waste is clearly one of the concerns of the Act it is not the only effect of such pollution with which the Act is concerned. A basis for federal legislative jurisdiction to control marine pollution generally in provincial waters cannot be found in any of the specified heads of federal jurisdiction in s. 91 of the *Constitution Act, 1867,* whether taken individually or collectively.

IV

It is necessary then to consider the national dimensions or national concern doctrine (as it is now generally referred to) of the federal peace, order and good government power as a possible basis for the constitutional validity of s. 4(1) of the Act, as applied to the control of dumping in provincial marine waters.

The national concern doctrine was suggested by Lord Watson in the *Local Prohibition* case (*A.G. Ont. v. A.G. Can.,* [1896] A.C. 348) and given its modern formulation by Viscount Simon in *A.G. Ont. v. Canada Temperance Federation* (1946), 85 C.C.C. 225, [1946] 2 D.L.R. 1, [1946] A.C. 193. In *Local Prohibition,* Lord Watson said at p. 361:

> Their Lordships do not doubt that some matters, in their origin local and provincial, might attain such dimensions as to affect the body politic of the Dominion, and to justify the Canadian Parliament in passing laws for their regulation or abolition in the interest of the Dominion. But great caution must be observed in distinguishing between that which is local or provincial and therefore within the jurisdiction of the provincial legislatures, and that which has ceased to be merely local or provincial, and has become matter of national concern, in such sense as to bring it within the jurisdiction of the Parliament of Canada.

In *Canada Temperance Federation,* Viscount Simon said at pp. 230–1 C.C.C., pp. 5–6 D.L.R., pp. 205–6 A.C.:

> In their Lordships' opinion, the true test must be found in the real subject-matter of the legislation: if it is such that it goes beyond local or provincial concern or interests and must from its inherent nature be the concern of the Dominion as a whole....

.   .   .   .

The national concern doctrine, as enunciated in *Canada Temperance Federation,* was referred to with approval by a majority of this court in *Johannesson* as supporting exclusive federal legislative jurisdiction with respect to the whole field of aeronautics. In *Munro,* where the *National Capital Act* was upheld on the basis of the federal peace, order and good government power, Cartwright J., delivering the unanimous judgment of the court said that the national concern doctrine had been adopted by this court in *Johannesson* and that the development of the National Capital Region was "a single matter of national concern."

The national concern doctrine was the subject of important commentary in this court in the *Anti-Inflation Act* reference. A majority of the court (Laskin C.J.C., and Martland, Judson, Ritchie, Spence, Pigeon and Dickson JJ.) upheld the Act on the basis of the emergency doctrine of the federal peace, order and good government power as legislation required to meet a "crisis" (the word used by Laskin C.J.C.) or "national emergency" (the words used by Ritchie J.). In the course of a comprehensive review of the judicial decisions with respect to the federal peace, order and good government power, Laskin C.J.C., with whom Judson, Spence and Dickson JJ. concurred, referred, with implicit approval, to the dictum of Viscount Simon in *Canada Temperance Federation,* but indicated that if he found, as he did, that the Act was valid on the basis of the emergency doctrine, as "crisis" legislation, he did not intend to express an opinion as to its possible validity on the basis of the national concern doctrine, on which the Attorney-General of Canada had principally relied. He said at p. 493 D.L.R., p. 419 S.C.R.:

> If it is sustainable as crisis legislation, it becomes unnecessary to consider the broader ground advanced in its support, and this because, especially in constitutional cases, Courts should not, as a rule, go any further than is necessary to determine the main issue before them.

He indicated, however, that he did not think it wise to attempt to define the scope of the federal peace, order and good government power in such precise or fixed terms as to make it incapable of application to changing or unforeseen circumstances. There is, moreover, a hint that he was disposed to seek a unified theory of the peace, order and good government power and that he regarded the emergency doctrine as a particular application of the national concern doctrine. Referring to the use of the word "emergency" in *Fort Frances Pulp & Power Co. Ltd. v. Manitoba Free Press Co. Ltd.,* [1923] 3 D.L.R. 629, [1923] A.C. 695, 25 O.W.N. 60, he said at p. 483 D.L.R., p. 407 S.C.R.: "Here then was a particular application of what Lord Watson said in the *Local Prohibition* case...."

Ritchie J., with whom Martland and Pigeon JJ. concurred, held that the validity of the Act could rest only on the emergency doctrine of the peace, order and good government power and that the national concern doctrine, in the absence of national emergency, could not give Parliament jurisdiction with respect to matters which would otherwise fall within provincial legislative jurisdiction. He said that he was in agreement with what was said by Beetz J. with reference to the national concern doctrine. Beetz J., with whom de Grandpré J. concurred, was obliged to consider the contention based on the national concern doctrine because he was of the view that the validity of the *Anti-Inflation Act* could not be supported on the basis of national emergency. He held that the national concern doctrine applied, in the absence of national emergency, to single, indivisible matters which did not fall within any of the specified heads of provincial or federal legislative jurisdiction. He held that the containment and reduction of inflation did not meet the test of singleness or indivisibility. Referring to aeronautics, radio and the development of the National Capital Region as distinct matters of national concern, he said at p. 524 D.L.R., p. 458 S.C.R.:

> I fail to see how the authorities which so decide lend support to the first submission. They had the effect of adding by judicial process new matters or new classes of matters to the federal list of powers. However, this was done only in cases where a new matter was not an aggregate but had a degree of unity that made it indivisible, an identity which made it distinct from provincial matters and a sufficient consistence to retain the bounds of form. The scale upon which these new matters enabled Parliament to touch on provincial matters had also to be taken into consideration before they were recognized as federal matters: if an enumerated federal power designated in broad terms such as the trade and commerce power had to be construed so as not to embrace and smother provincial powers (*Parson's* case) and destroy the equilibrium of the Constitution, the Courts must be all the more careful not to add hitherto unnamed powers of a diffuse nature to the list of federal powers.
>
> The "containment and reduction of inflation" does not pass muster as a new subject matter. It is an aggregate of several subjects some of which form a substantial part of provincial jurisdiction. It is totally lacking in specificity. It is so pervasive that it knows no bounds. Its recognition as a federal head of power would render most provincial powers nugatory.
>
> I should add that inflation is a very ancient phenomenon, several thousands years old, as old

probably as the history of currency. The Fathers of Confederation were quite aware of it.

In *Hauser* a majority of the court (Martland, Ritchie, Pigeon and Beetz JJ.) held that the constitutional validity of the *Narcotic Control Act* rested on the peace, order and good government power of Parliament rather than on its jurisdiction with respect to criminal law. Pigeon J., who delivered the judgment of the majority said that the principal consideration in support of this view was that the abuse of narcotic drugs, with which the Act dealt, was a new problem which did not exist at the time of Confederation, and that since it did not come within matters of a merely local or private nature in the province it fell within the "general residual power" in the same manner as aeronautics and radio.

In *Labatt Breweries*, in which a majority of the full court held that certain provisions of the *Food and Drugs Act* and regulations thereunder were *ultra vires*, Estey J., with whom Martland, Dickson and Beetz JJ. concurred, had occasion to consider the peace, order and good government power as a possible basis of validity. He summed up the doctrine with respect to that basis of federal legislative jurisdiction as falling into three categories: (a) the cases "basing the federal competence on the existence of a national emergency"; (b) the cases in which "federal competence arose because the subject matter did not exist at the time of Confederation and clearly cannot be put into the class of matters of a merely local or private nature," of which aeronautics and radio were cited as examples; and (c) the cases in which "the subject matter 'goes beyond local or provincial concern or interest and must, from its inherent nature, be the concern of the Dominion as a whole'," citing *Canada Temperance Federation*. Thus Estey J. saw the national concern doctrine enunciated in *Canada Temperance Federation* as covering the case, not of a new subject-matter which did not exist at Confederation, but of one that may have begun as a matter of a local or provincial concern but had become one of national concern. He referred to that category as "a matter of national concern transcending the local authorities' power to meet and solve it by legislation," and quoted in support of this statement of the test a passage from Professor Hogg's *Constitutional Law of Canada* (1977), p. 261, in which it was said that "the most important element of national dimension or national concern is a need for one national law which cannot realistically be satisfied by cooperative provincial action because the failure of one province to cooperate would carry with it grave consequences for the residents of other provinces."

In *Schneider*, in which the court unanimously held that the *Heroin Treatment Act* of British Columbia was *intra vires*, Dickson J. (as he then was), with whom Martland, Ritchie, Beetz, McIntyre, Chouinard and Lamer JJ. concurred, indicated, with particular reference to the national concern doctrine and what has come to be known as the "provincial inability" test, why he was of the view that the treatment of heroin dependency, as distinct from the traffic in narcotic drugs, was not a matter falling within the federal peace, order and good government power. He referred to the problem of heroin dependency as follows at pp. 466–7 C.C.C., pp. 434–5 D.L.R., pp. 131–2 S.C.R.:

> It is largely a local or provincial problem and not one which has become a matter of national concern, so as to bring it within the jurisdiction of the Parliament of Canada under the residuary power contained in the opening words of the *B.N.A. Act, 1867* (now *Constitution Act, 1867*).
>
> There is no material before the court leading one to conclude that the problem of heroin dependency as distinguished from illegal trade in drugs is a matter of national interest and dimension transcending the power of each province to meet and solve its own way. It is not a problem which "is beyond the power of the provinces to deal with" (Professor Gibson (1976–77), 7 Man. L.J. 15 at p. 33). Failure by one province to provide treatment facilities will not endanger the interests of another province. The subject is not one which "has attained such dimension as to affect the body politic of the Dominion" *Re Aerial Navigation; A.G. Can. v. A.G. Ont. et al.*, [1932] 1 D.L.R. 58 at p. 70, [1931] 3 W.W.R. 625, [1932] A.C. 54 at p. 77), *sub nom. Re Regulation and Control of Aeronautics in Canada*. It is not something that "goes beyond local or provincial concern or interests and must from its inherent nature be the concern of the Dominion as a whole (as, for example, in the *Aeronautics Case* ... and the *Radio Case*)" *per* Viscount Simon in *A.G. Ont. et al. v. Canada Temperance Foundation et al.* (1946), 85 C.C.C. 225 at p. 230. [1946] 2 D.L.R. 1 at p. 5, [1946] A.C. 193 at p. 205; see also *Johannesson et al. v. Rural Municipality of West St. Paul et al.*, [1951] 4 D.L.R. 609. [1952] 1 S.C.R. 292, 69 C.R.T.C. 105; *Re C.F.R.B. Ltd. and A.G. Can. et al.*, (1973), 14 C.C.C. (2d) 345, 38 D.L.R. (3d) 335, [1973] 3 O.R. 819. Nor can it be said, on the record, that heroin addiction has reached a state of emergency as will ground federal competence under residual power.
>
> I do not think the subject of narcotics is so global and indivisible that the legislative domain cannot be divided, illegal trade in narcotics com-

ing within the jurisdiction of the Parliament of Canada and the treatment of addicts under provincial jurisdiction.

In *Wetmore*, where the issue was whether the federal Attorney-General was entitled to conduct the prosecution of charges for violation of the *Food and Drugs Act*, Dickson J., dissenting considered whether the applicable provisions of the *Food and Drugs Act* had their constitutional foundation in the federal criminal law power, or as was held in *Hauser* with respect to the *Narcotic Control Act*, in the peace, order and good government power. In rejecting the latter basis of jurisdiction, he referred to what was said concerning the national concern doctrine of the peace, order and good government power in the *Anti-Inflation Act* reference, *Labatt* and *Hauser* as follows at p. 516 C.C.C., p. 586 D.L.R., pp. 294–5 S.C.R.:

> In *Re Anti-Inflation Act* (1968), 68 D.L.R. (3d) 452, [1976] 2 S.C.R. 373, Beetz J., whose judgment on this point commanded majority support, reviewed the extensive jurisprudence on the subject and concluded that the peace, order and good government power should be confined to justifying (i) temporary legislation dealing with a national emergency (p. 525 D.L.R., p. 459 S.C.R.) and (ii) legislation dealing with "distinct subject matters which do not fall within any of the enumerated heads of s. 92 and which, by nature, are of national concern" (p. 524 D.L.R., p. 457 S.C.R.). In the *Labatt case, supra*, at pp. 465–6 C.C.C., p. 627 D.L.R., pp. 944–5 S.C.R., Estey J. divided this second heading into (i) areas in which the federal competence arises because the subject-matter did not exist at the time of Confederation and cannot be classified as of a merely local and private nature, and (ii) areas where the subject-matter "'goes beyond local or provincial interests and must from its inherent nature be the concern of the Dominion as a whole'." This last category is the one enunciated by Viscount Simon L.C. in *A.G. Ont. v. Canada Temperance Federation* (1946), 85 C.C.C. 225 at p. 230, [1942] 2 D.L.R. 1 at p. 5, [1946] A.C. 193 at p. 205. The one preceding it formed the basis of the majority decision in *Hauser* that the *Narcotic Control Act*, R.S.C. 1970, c. N–1, came under the peace, order and good government power as dealing with a "genuinely new problem which did not exist at the time of Confederation."

Applying these principles to the subject-matter of the *Food and Drugs Act*, Dickson J. noted that there was no question of emergency or of a new matter that did not exist at Confederation and rejected the national concern doctrine of the peace, order and good government as a basis for the constitutional validity of the provisions in question for the following reasons at pp. 517–8 C.C.C., p. 587 D.L.R., p. 296 S.C.R.:

> Finally, it cannot be maintained that ss. 8(a), 9(1) and 26 address a subject that goes beyond local or provincial interest and must from its intrinsic nature be the concern of the Dominion as a whole, as that concept has been interpreted in the cases. Their subject-matter would clearly not satisfy the requirements cited by Beetz J. in the *Anti-Inflation Reference, supra,* nor would it come within the criteria proposed by Hogg, *Constitutional Law of Canada* (1977), p. 261, in a passage cited by Estey J. in *Labatt, supra,* at p. 466 C.C.C., p. 627 D.L.R., p. 945 S.C.R.:
>
> > "These cases suggest that the most important element of national dimension or national concern is a need for one national law which cannot realistically be satisfied by cooperative provincial action because the failure of one province to co-operate would carry with it grave consequences for the residents of other provinces. A subject-matter of legislation which has this characteristic has the necessary national dimension of concern to justify invocation of the p.o.g.g. power."
>
> The same factors that prevent ss. 8(a) and 9(1) from qualifying as "general regulation of trade affecting the whole Dominion" also stand in the way of characterizing them as legislation in relation to peace, order and good government under the *Canada Temperance* test. Aside from their purported application throughout Canada and from certain financial and logistical difficulties in enacting comparable provincial legislation, there is nothing inherently "national" in these sections. And as is demonstrated by a line of cases stretching from *Re Insurance Act (Can.) 1910,* (1913), 15 D.L.R. 251, 48 S.C.R. 260, 5 W.W.R. 488; affirmed 26 D.L.R. 288, 10 W.W.R. 405, [1916] 1 A.C. 588, to the *Labatt* case, *supra,* neither of these criteria separately or together is sufficient to validate a federal enactment under the peace, order and good government power.

From this survey of the opinion expressed in this court concerning the national concern doctrine of the federal peace, order and good government power I draw the following conclusions as to what now appears to be firmly established:

1. The national concern doctrine is separate and distinct from the national emergency doctrine of the peace, order and good government power, which is chiefly distinguishable by the fact that it provides a constitutional basis for what is necessarily legislation of a temporary nature.

2. The national concern doctrine applies to both new matters which did not exist at Confederation and to matters which, although originally matters of a local or private nature in a province, have since, in the absence of national emergency, become matters of national concern.

3. For a matter to qualify as a matter of national concern in either sense it must have a singleness, distinctiveness and indivisibility that clearly distinguishes it from matters of provincial concern and a scale of impact on provincial jurisdiction that is reconcilable with the fundamental distribution of legislative power under the Constitution.

4. In determining whether a matter has attained the required degree of singleness, distinctiveness and indivisibility that clearly distinguishes it from matters of provincial concern it is relevant to consider what would be the effect on extra-provincial interests of a provincial failure to deal effectively with the control or regulation of the intraprovincial aspects of the matter.

This last factor, generally referred to as the "provincial inability" test and noted with apparent approval in this court in *Labatt, Schneider* and *Wetmore,* was suggested, as Professor Hogg acknowledges, by Professor Gibson in his article, "Measuring 'National Dimensions'," (1976) 7 Man.L.J. 15, as the most satisfactory rationale of the cases in which the national concern doctrine of the peace, order and good government power has been applied as a basis of federal jurisdiction. As expounded by Professor Gibson, the test would appear to involve a limited or qualified application of federal jurisdiction. As put by Professor Gibson at p. 345:

> By this approach, a national dimension would exist whenever a significant aspect for a problem is beyond provincial reach because it falls within the jurisdiction of another province or of the federal Parliament. It is important to emphasize however that the *entire* problem would not fall within federal competence in such circumstances. Only that aspect of the problem that is beyond provincial control would do so. Since the "P.O. & G.G." clause bestows only residual powers, the existence of a national dimension justifies no more federal legislation than is necessary to fill the gap in provincial powers. For example, federal jurisdiction to legislate for pollution of interprovincial waterways or to control "pollution

price-wars" would (in the absence of other independent sources of federal competence) extend only to measures to reduce the risk that citizens of one province would be harmed by the non cooperation of another province or provinces.

To similar effect, he said in his conclusion at p. 36:

Having regard to the residual nature of the power, it is the writer's thesis that "national dimensions" are possessed by only those aspects of legislative problems which are beyond the ability of the provincial legislatures to deal because they involve either federal competence or that of another province. Where it would be possible to deal fully with the problem by co-operative action of two or more legislatures, the "national dimension" concerns only the risk of non-co-operation, and justifies only federal legislation addressed to that risk.

This would appear to contemplate a concurrent or overlapping federal jurisdiction which, I must observe, is in conflict with what was emphasized by Beetz J. in the *Anti-Inflation Act* reference — that where a matter falls within the national concern doctrine of the peace, order and good government power, as distinct from the emergency doctrine, Parliament has an exclusive jurisdiction of a plenary nature to legislate in relation to that matter, including its intraprovincial aspects.

As expressed by Professor Hogg in the first and second editions of his *Constitutional Law of Canada*, the "provincial inability" test would appear to be adopted simply as a reason for finding that a particular matter is one of national concern falling within the peace, order and good government power: that provincial failure to deal effectively with the intraprovincial aspects of the matter could have an adverse effect on extra-provincial interests. In this sense, the "provincial inability" test is one of the indicia for determining whether a matter has that character of singleness or indivisibility required to bring it within the national concern doctrine. It is because of the interrelatedness of the interprovincial and extra-provincial aspects of the matter that it requires a single or uniform legislative treatment. The "provincial inability" test must not, however, go so far as to provide a rationale for the general notion, hitherto rejected in the cases, that there must be a plenary jurisdiction in one order of government or the other to deal with any legislative problem. In the context of the national concern doctrine of the peace, order and good government power, its utility lies, in my opinion, in assisting in the determination whether a matter has the requisite single-

ness or indivisibility from a functional as well as a conceptual point of view.

. . . .

V

Marine pollution, because of its predominantly extra-provincial as well as international character and implications, is clearly a matter of concern to Canada as a whole. The question is whether the control of pollution by the dumping of substances in marine waters, including provincial marine waters, is a single, indivisible matter, distinct from the control of pollution by the dumping of substances in other provincial waters. The *Ocean Dumping Control Act* reflects a distinction between the pollution of salt water and the pollution of fresh water. The question, as I conceive it, is whether that distinction is sufficient to make the control of marine pollution by the dumping of substances a single, indivisible matter falling within the national concern doctrine of the peace, order and good government power.

Marine pollution by the dumping of substances is clearly treated by the Convention of the Prevention of Marine Pollution by Dumping of Wastes and other Matter as a distinct and separate form of water pollution having its own characteristics and scientific considerations. This impression is reinforced by the United Nations Report of the Joint Group of Experts on the Scientific Aspects of Marine Pollution, Reports and Studies No. 15, *The Review of The Health of the Oceans* (UNESCO 1982) (hereinafter referred to as the "United Nations Report"), which forms part of the materials placed before the court in the argument. It is to be noted, however, that, unlike the *Ocean Dumping Control Act*, the Convention does not require regulation of pollution by the dumping of waste in the internal marine waters of a state. Article III, para. 3, of the Convention defines the "sea" as "all marine waters other than the internal waters of the States." The internal marine waters of a state are those which are landward of the baseline of the territorial sea, which is determined in accordance with the rules laid down in the United Nations Convention on the Law of the Sea, 1982. The limitation of the undertaking in the Convention, presumably for reasons of state policy, to the control of dumping in the territorial sea and the open sea cannot, in my opinion, obscure the obviously close relationship, which is emphasized in the United Nations Report, between pollution in coastal waters, including the internal marine waters of a state, and pollution in the territorial sea. Moreover, there is much force, in my opinion, in the appellant's contention that the difficulty of ascertaining by visual observation the boundary between the territorial sea and the internal marine waters of a state creates an unacceptable degree of uncertainty for the application of regulatory and penal provisions. This, and not simply the possibility or likelihood of the movement of pollutants across that line, is what constitutes the essential indivisibility of the matter of marine pollution by the dumping of substances.

There remains the question whether the pollution of marine waters by the dumping of substances is sufficiently distinguishable from the pollution of fresh waters by such dumping to meet the requirement of singleness or indivisibility. In many cases the pollution of fresh waters will have a pollutant effect in the marine waters into which they flow, and this is noted by the United Nations Report, but that report, as I have suggested, emphasizes that marine pollution, because of the differences in the composition and action of marine waters and fresh waters, has its own characteristics and scientific considerations that distinguish it from fresh water pollution. Moreover, the distinction between salt water and fresh water as limiting the application of the *Ocean Dumping Control Act* meets the consideration emphasized by a majority of this court in the *Anti-Inflation Act* reference — that in order for a matter to qualify as one of national concern falling within the federal peace, order and good government power it must have ascertainable and reasonable limits, in so far as its impact on provincial jurisdiction is concerned.

For these reasons I am of the opinion that s. 4(1) of the *Ocean Dumping Control Act* is constitutionally valid as enacted in relation to a matter falling within the national concern doctrine of the peace, order and good government power of the Parliament of Canada, and, in particular, that it is constitutional in its application to the dumping of waste in the waters of Beaver Cove. I would accordingly allow the appeal, set aside the judgments of the Court of Appeal and Schmidt Prov. Ct. J. and refer the matter back to the Provincial Court judge. The constitutional question should be answered as follows:

> Is Section 4(1) of the *Ocean Dumping Control Act*, S.C. 1974–75–76, c. 55, *ultra vires* of the Parliament of Canada, and, in particular, is it *ultra vires* of the Parliament of Canada in its application to the dumping of waste in the waters of Beaver Cove, an area within the Province of British Columbia?

> Answer: No.

. . . .

[LA FOREST J., dissenting (Beetz and Lamer JJ., concurring with La Forest J.):]

Why Parliament should have chosen to enact a prohibition in such broad terms is a matter upon which one is left to speculate. It may be that, in view of the lack of knowledge about the effects of various substances deposited in water, it may be necessary to monitor all such deposits. We have no evidence on the extent to which it is necessary to monitor all deposits into the sea to develop an effective regime for the prevention of ocean pollution. A system of monitoring that was necessarily incidental to an effective legislative scheme for the control of ocean pollution could constitutionally be justified. But here not only was no material advanced to establish the need for such a system, the Act goes much further and prohibits the deposit of any substance in the sea, including provincial internal waters. If such a provision were held valid, why would a federal provision prohibiting the emission of any substance in any quantity into the air, except as permitted by federal authorities, not be constitutionally justifiable as a measure for the control of ocean pollution, it now being known that deposits from the air are a serious source of ocean pollution? ...

. . . .

... on a more traditional approach to the underlying issues Parliament has very wide powers to deal with ocean pollution, whether within or outside the limits of the province, but ... even if one stretches this traditional approach to its limits, the impugned provision cannot constitutionally be justified. It requires a quantum leap to find constitutional justification for the provision, one, it seems to me, that would create considerable stress on Canadian federalism as it has developed over the years. What he argues for, we saw, is that the dumping of any substances in the sea beginning, apparently, from the coasts of the provinces and the mouths of provincial rivers falls exclusively within the legislative jurisdiction of Parliament as being a matter of national concern or dimension even though the seabed is within the province and whether or not the substance is noxious or potentially so.

Le Dain J. has in the course of his judgment discussed the cases relating to the development of the "national concern or dimension" aspect of the peace, order and good government clause, and I find it unnecessary to review that development in any detail. It is sufficient for my purpose to say that this development has since the 1930's particularly been resorted to from time to time to bring into the ambit of federal power a number of matters, such as radio (*Re Regulation & Control of Radio Communication*, [1932] 2 D.L.R. 81, [1932] A.C. 304, 39 C.R. 49, [1932] 1 W.W.R. 563), aeronautics (*Johannesson v. Rural Municipality of West St. Paul*, [1951] 4 D.L.R. 609, [1952] 1 S.C.R. 292, 69 C.R.T.C. 105), and the national capital region (*Munro v. National Capital Com'n* (1966), 57 D.L.R. (2d) 753, [1966] S.C.R. 663), that are clearly of national importance. They do not fit comfortably within provincial power. Both in their workings and in their practical implications they have predominantly national dimensions. Many of these subjects are new and are obviously of extra-provincial concern. They are thus appropriate for assignment to the general federal legislative power. They are often related to matters intimately tied to federal jurisdiction. Radio (which is relevant to the power to regulate interprovincial undertakings) is an example. The closely contested issue of narcotics control (*cf. R. v. Hauser* (1979), 46 C.C.C. (2d) 481, 98 D.L.R. (3d) 193, [1979] 1 S.C.R. 984, and *Schneider v. The Queen* (1982), 68 C.C.C. (2d) 449, 139 D.L.R. (3d) 417, [1982] 2 S.C.R. 112, *per* Laskin C.J.C.) is intimately related to criminal law and international trade.

The need to make such characterizations from time to time is readily apparent. From this necessary function, however, it is easy but, I say it with respect, fallacious to go further, and, taking a number of quite separate areas of activity, some under accepted constitutional values within federal, and some within provincial legislative capacity, consider them to be a single indivisible matter of national interest and concern lying outside the specific heads of power assigned under the Constitution. By conceptualizing broad social, economic and political issues in that way, one can effectively invent new heads of federal power under the national dimensions doctrine, thereby incidentally removing them from provincial jurisdiction or at least abridging the provinces' freedom of operation. This, as I see it, is the implication of the statement made by my colleague, then Professor Le Dain, in his article, "Sir Lyman Duff and the Constitution," 12 *Osgoode Hall L.J.* 261 (1974). He states, at p. 293:

> As reflected in the *Munro* case, the issue with respect to the general power, where reliance cannot be placed on the notion of emergency, is to determine what are to be considered to be single, indivisible matters of national interest and concern lying outside the specific heads of

jurisdiction in sections 91 and 92. It is possible to invent such matters by applying new names to old legislative purposes. There is an increasing tendency to sum up a wide variety of legislative purposes in single, comprehensive designations. Control of inflation, environmental protection, and preservation of the national identity or independence are examples.

Professor Le Dain was there merely posing the problem; he did not attempt to answer it. It seems to me, however, that some of the examples he gives, notably the control of inflation and environmental protection, are all-pervasive, and if accepted as items falling within the general power of Parliament, would radically alter the division of legislative power in Canada. The attempt to include them in the federal general power seems to me to involve fighting on another plane the war that was lost on the economic plane in the Canadian new deal cases.

. . . .

All physical activities have some environmental impact. Possible legislative responses to such activities cover a large number of the enumerated legislative powers, federal and provincial. To allocate the broad subject-matter of environmental control to the federal government under its general power would effectively gut provincial legislative jurisdiction. As I mentioned before, environment protection, of course, encompasses far more than environmental pollution, which is what we are principally concerned with here. To take an example from the present context, woodwaste in some circumstances undoubtedly pollutes the environment, but the very depletion of forests itself affects the ecological balance and, as such, constitutes an environmental problem. But environmental pollution alone is itself all-pervasive. It is a byproduct of everything we do. In man's relationship with his environment, waste is unavoidable. The problem is thus not new....

. . . .

It is true, of course, that we are not invited to create a general environmental pollution power but one restricted to ocean pollution. But it seems to me that the same considerations apply. I shall, however, attempt to look at it in terms of the qualities or attributes that are said to mark the subjects that have been held to fall within the peace, order and good government clause as being matters of national concern. Such a subject, it has been said, must be marked by a singleness, distinctiveness and indivisibility that clearly distinguishes it from matters of provincial concern. In my view, ocean pollution fails to meet this test for a variety of reasons. In addition to those applicable to environmental pollution generally, the following specific difficulties may be noted. First of all, marine waters are not wholly bounded by the coast; in many areas, they extend upstream into rivers for many miles. The application of the Act appears to be restricted to waters beyond the mouths of rivers (and so intrude less on provincial powers), but this is not entirely clear, and if it is so restricted, it is not clear whether this distinction is based on convenience or constitutional imperative. Apart from this, the line between salt and fresh water cannot be demarcated clearly; it is different at different depths of water, changes with the season and shifts constantly; see *U.N. Report, supra*, p. 12. In any event, it is not so much the waters, whether fresh or salt, with which we are concerned, but their pollution. And the pollution of marine water is contributed to by the vast amounts of effluents that are poured or seep into fresh waters everywhere (*ibid.*, p. 13). There is a constant intermixture of waters; fresh waters flow into the sea and marine waters penetrate deeply inland at high tide only to return to the sea laden with pollutants collected during their incursion inland. Nor is the pollution of the ocean confined to pollution emanating from substances deposited in water. In important respects, the pollution of the sea results from emissions into the air, which are then transported over many miles and deposited into the sea: see *U.N. Report*, p. 15; *I.J.C. Report*, p. 22. I cannot, therefore, see ocean pollution as a sufficiently discrete subject upon which to found the kind of legislative power sought here....

. . . .

This leads me to another factor considered in identifying a subject as falling within the general federal power as a matter of national domain: its impact on provincial legislative power. Here, it must be remembered that in its supposed application within the province the provision virtually prevents a province from dealing with certain of its own public property without federal consent. A wide variety of activities along the coast or in the adjoining sea involves the deposit of some substances in the sea. In fact, where large cities like Vancouver are situated by the sea, this has substantial relevance to recreational, industrial and municipal [concerns] of all kinds. As a matter of fact, the most polluted areas of the sea adjoin the coast; see *U.N. Report*, pp. 3–4. Among the major causes of this are various types

of construction, such as hotels and harbours, the development of mineral resources and recreational activities (*ibid.*, p. 3). These are matters of immediate concern to the province. They necessarily affect activities over which the provinces have exercised some kind of jurisdiction over the years. Whether or not the "newness" of the subject is a necessary criterion for inventing new areas of jurisdiction under the peace, order and good government clause, it is certainly a relevant consideration if it means removing from the provinces areas of jurisdiction which they previously exercised. As I mentioned, pollution, including coastal pollution, is no new phenomenon, and neither are many of the kinds of activities that result in pollution.

A further relevant matter, it is said, is the effect on extra-provincial interests of a provincial failure to deal effectively with the control of intraprovincial aspects of the matter. I have some difficulty following all the implications of this, but taking it at face value, we are dealing here with a situation where, as we saw earlier, Parliament has extensive powers to deal with conditions that lead to ocean pollution wherever they occur. The difficulty with the impugned provision is that it seeks to deal with activities that cannot be demonstrated either to pollute or to have a reasonable potential of polluting the ocean. The prohibition applies to an inert substance regarding which there is no proof that it either moves or pollutes. The prohibition in fact would apply to the moving of rock from one area of provincial property to another. I cannot accept that the federal Parliament has such wide legislative power over local matters having local import taking place on provincially owned property. The prohibition in essence constitutes an impermissible attempt to control activities on property held to be provincial in *Reference re Ownership of Bed of Strait of Georgia, supra*. It may well be that the *motive* for enacting the provision is to prevent ocean pollution, but as Beetz J. underlines in *Reference re Anti-Inflation Act, supra*, Parliament cannot do this by attempting to regulate a local industry, although it can, of course, regulate the activities of such an industry that fall within federal power, whether such activities are expressly encompassed within a specific head of power, *e.g.*, navigation, or affect areas of federal concern, *e.g.*, health under the criminal law power, or cause pollution to those parts of the sea under federal jurisdiction. But here the provision simply overreaches. In its terms, it encompasses activities — depositing innocuous substances into provincial waters by local undertakings on provincial lands —

135

that fall within the exclusive legislative jurisdiction of the province.

. . . .

(d)   *General Motors*†

NOTE

The Supreme Court of Canada has been breathing life back into the trade and commerce power. Since the 1950s, it has abandoned the taint doctrine in clashes between interprovincial and intraprovincial trade, and now looks for the dominant aspect regardless of whether federal or provincial laws are challenged.[1]

Although this is a more even-handed approach, it does little to simplify the task of identifying categories of trade. Commercial transactions are fluid and often geographically dispersed. Production may be in one province; distribution and consumption in another. Different statutes will emphasize different transaction stages. It may be hard to determine if a transaction is influenced more by a regulatory scheme or by external factors such as world prices. If distribution and consumption count heavily in determining the focus of a scheme, the intraprovincial trade category will be rare in low-population producer provinces. Some of these problems were illustrated in *Canadian Industrial Gas & Oil Ltd. v. Saskatchewan* (the *CIGOL*) case, where the Supreme Court struck down a provincial attempt to levy tax and royalties on Saskatchewan oil.[2]

Beyond these labelling difficulties is the challenge of balancing a broadly-worded federal power over a fluid and dispersed activity against significant provincial interests. Property and civil rights and natural resources have an economic component that is considered vital by provinces. Indeed, provincial concern over decisions such as *CIGOL*[3] led to a 1982 amendment to the *Constitution Act,*

DISPOSITION

I would dismiss the appeal with costs and reply to the constitutional question in the affirmative.

Appeal Allowed.

1867 that clarified provincial control over natural resources.

But the fluidity and dispersal of commercial transactions can make them extremely difficult to regulate effectively within the boundaries of a single province. Conversely, uncoordinated regional regulation can generate excessive trade barriers at the national level. What may be needed is a generous construction of provincial "trade" powers, subject to federal paramountcy for trade matters going beyond provincial boundaries. This general approach was followed in the 1982 amendment to the *Constitution Act, 1867*. Section 92A gives provinces explicit power to control and tax their natural resources, but the power is subject to federal paramountcy.

The Supreme Court may be developing a rather similar approach for the long-dormant federal power over general Dominion trade. Of the four categories of trade identified in *Citizens Insurance*, this one has the most growth potential. It lacks the geographical constraints of the other categories; its limits are undefined. It is the kind of potentially open-ended power that most threatened the Judicial Committee's philosophy of coordinate federalism. It is hardly surprising, then, that general Dominion trade fared poorly in their hands — targeted by Lord Haldane's ancillary doctrine and successfully invoked only twice.

In the *General Motors* case,[4] general Dominion trade (re-christened "general trade and commerce") has made a dramatic comeback. The Supreme Court seems to be saying that while provinces can play an active role in regulating trade, federal legislation should be permitted to prevail under carefully prescribed conditions where the

---

† *General Motors of Canada Limited v. City National Leasing*, [1990] 1 S.C.R. 641 at 655–63, 671–72 (S.C.C.).

only effective means of trade regulation is at the national level. What are these conditions? Will the new approach reduce the need to draw fine distinctions between interprovincial and intraprovincial trade? Is the Supreme Court moving toward a position of *de facto* federal paramountcy in national economic areas and relative provincial autonomy in others?

In *General Motors* an automobile leasing company argued that the financial preference General Motors was giving to the leasing company's competitors was contrary to the federal *Combines Investigation Act*. The company tried to sue General Motors under a section of the act permitting civil actions. When General Motors challenged the validity of the Act, the leasing company relied on *Canada (A.G.) v. Canadian National Transportation Ltd.*, [1983] 2 S.C.R. 206. Here, in a separate concurring decision, Dickson C.J. had said (at 278) that:

> Given the free flow of trade across provincial boundaries guaranteed by s. 121 of the *Constitution Act, 1867*, Canada is, for economic purposes, a single huge market place. If competition is to be regulated at all, it must be regulated federally.

In the earlier case, Dickson C.J. had enumerated five criteria for determining whether the general trade and commerce power could be invoked. In *General Motors*, Dickson C.J. now spoke for a unanimous Court. He stressed again the importance of the economic unity of Canada and the need for effective central regulation, and reaffirmed the five criteria. In the end, the section of the *Combines Investigation Act* on which the leasing company had relied was declared valid, under the general trade and commerce power.

Notes

1. An important step was the Supreme Court's refusal of leave to appeal from the Manitoba Court of Appeal's decision in *R. v. Klassen* (1959), 20 D.L.R. (2d) 406.
2. (1977), 80 D.L.R. (3d) 449 (S.C.C.). The oil company successfully challenged the Saskatchewan tax and royalty statute. Virtually all the oil was exported for consumers outside Saskatchewan. There was a controversy as to whether the prices paid by these consumers were set by the scheme or by the world market. A majority of the Court found that they were set by the scheme, which was thus "aimed" at interprovincial trade.
3. And *Central Canada Potash v. Saskatchewan*, [1979] 1 S.C.R. 42.
4. *General Motors of Canada Limited v. City National Leasing*, [1990] 1 S.C.R. 641.

EXTRACT

[DICKSON C.J. found that the section in question did encroach on provincial power, and that the *Combines Investigation Act* contained a regulatory scheme. He continued]:

In *Canadian National Transportation, supra*, I had occasion to trace the history of s. 91(2) in the courts. It would be otiose to repeat that discussion here. For the purposes of this appeal it is sufficient to summarize the general principles that, in my view, have emerged from judicial consideration of s. 91(2) and which are relevant to the present appeal.

The leading case of *Citizens' Insurance Company of Canada* v. *Parsons* (1881), 7 App. Cas. 96, sets out the most frequently quoted statement of the scope of s. 91(2). Speaking for the Privy Council, Sir Montague Smith noted at p. 112 that if the words trade and commerce were given their ordinary meaning, s. 91(2) conceivably granted very wide-ranging powers to the federal government:

> The words "regulation of trade and commerce," in their unlimited sense are sufficiently wide, if uncontrolled by the context and other parts of the Act, to include every regulation of trade ranging from political arrangements in regard to trade with foreign governments, requiring the sanction of parliament, down to minute rules for regulating particular trades.

To limit the breadth of a literal interpretation of s. 91(2), Sir Montague Smith settled upon the following construction, at p. 113:

> Construing therefore the words "regulation of trade and commerce" by the various aids to their interpretation above suggested, they would include political arrangements in regard to trade requiring the sanction of parliament, regulation in matters of inter-provincial concern, and it may be that they would include general regulation of trade affecting the whole dominion.

Sir Montague Smith continued, on the same page:

> Having taken this view of the present case, it becomes unnecessary to consider the question how far the general power to make regulations of trade and commerce, when competently exercised by the dominion parliament, might legally modify or affect property and civil rights in the provinces, or the legislative power of the provincial legislatures in relation to those subjects....

In *Canadian National Transportation, supra*, at p. 258, I suggested that *Parsons* had established three important propositions with regard to the federal trade and commerce power:

> ... (i) it does not correspond to the literal meaning of the words "regulation of trade and commerce"; (ii) it includes not only arrangements with regard to international and interprovincial trade but "it may be that ... (it) would include general regulation of trade affecting the whole dominion"; (iii) it does not extend to regulating the contracts of a particular business or trade.

Since *Parsons*, the jurisprudence on s. 91(2) has largely been an elaboration on the boundaries of the two aspects or "branches" of federal power: (1) the power over international and interprovincial trade and commerce; and (2) the power over general trade and commerce affecting Canada as a whole. The first branch has been the subject of considerable constitutional challenge and judicial scrutiny. The second branch, in contrast, has remained largely unexplored, *terra incognita*. In this appeal, however, it is under this second branch of s. 91(2) that CNL and the Attorney General of Canada seek to uphold s. 31.1.

So far as I can gather, legislation has been upheld under the second branch by a final appellate court on only two occasions. In 1937 the Privy Council upheld a federal scheme creating a national trade mark to be used in conjunction with federally established commodity standards under the general trade and commerce power: *Attorney-General for Ontario v. Attorney-General of Canada (Canada Standards Trade Mark)*, [1937] A.C. 405. (But compare: *Dominion Stores Ltd. v. The Queen*, [1980] 1 S.C.R. 844, where this Court struck down federal products standards legislation.) The second occasion was in *John Deere Plow Co. v. Wharton*, [1915] A.C. 330, where the Privy Council located the regulation of federally incorporated companies within the general branch of s. 91(2), although they also upheld the legislation under the "peace, order and good government" power.

Aside from these two cases, at least until of late, the general trade and commerce power met with consistent rejection by the courts. Professor Hogg in the second edition of his work *Constitutional Law of Canada* (1985), at pp. 447–48, notes that the courts refused to accept it as the basis for regulation of the insurance industry in the *Attorney-General for Canada v. Attorney-General for Alberta (Insurance Reference)*, [1916] 1 A.C. 588; prices and profits in *In re the Board of Commerce Act, 1919, and the Combines and Fair Prices Act, 1919* (the *Board of Commerce* case), [1922] 1 A.C. 191; labour rela-

tions in *Toronto Electric Commissioners v. Snider*, [1925] A.C. 396; marketing in *The King v. Eastern Terminal Elevator Co.*, [1925] S.C.R. 434, and *Attorney-General for British Columbia v. Attorney-General for Canada (Natural Products Marketing Reference)*, [1937] A.C. 377; and the prohibition of margarine in *Canadian Federation of Agriculture v. Attorney-General for Quebec (The Margarine Reference)*, [1951] A.C. 179.

The treatment of the general trade and commerce power in the cases just mentioned was no doubt strongly influenced by earlier Privy Council decisions on s. 91(2) and in particular what Anglin C.J. referred to in *The King v. Eastern Terminal Elevator Co.*, *supra*, at p. 441, as "...their Lordships' emphatic and reiterated allocation of 'the regulation of trade and commerce' to ... [a] subordinate and wholly auxiliary function...." As Professor McDonald observed in his article "Constitutional Aspects of Canadian Anti-Combines Law Enforcement" (1969), 47 *Can. Bar Rev.* 161, at p. 189:

> The British North America Act was framed with a greater interest in central control than motivated the constitutional fathers to the south. Reaction in the founding provinces to the consequences of decentralized control in the United States has been well documented. The broad and unqualified language of section 91(2) reflected the basic interest that strength from economic unity replace the floundering provincial economies. Yet, as the American courts broadened their commerce clause until it meant essentially what the Fathers of Confederation had sought for Canada, so have the Privy Council and the Canadian courts reacted against the hopes of the framers of their constitution and have decentralized commercial control.
>
> At least until relatively recently the history of interpretation of the trade and commerce power has almost uniformly reinforced the federal paralysis which resulted from a series of Privy Council decisions in the years 1881–1896. The predominant view was that section 91(2) did not in any way go to either general commerce, contracts, particular trades or occupations, or commodities so far as those things might be intraprovincial. The test for the local nature of a transaction was abstractly legal, divorced from commercial effect.

Since 1949 and the abolition of appeals to the Privy Council, the trade and commerce power has, I think it fair to say, enjoyed an enhanced importance in such cases as *Murphy v. Canadian Pacific Railway Co.*, [1958] S.C.R. 626, upholding the validity of the federal *Canadian Wheat Board Act; The Queen v.*

Klassen (1959), 20 D.L.R. (2d) 406 (Man. C.A.), upholding the application of the *Canadian Wheat Board Act* to intraprovincial transactions; and *Caloil Inc. v. Attorney General of Canada*, [1971] S.C.R. 543, upholding a federal scheme regulating the movement of imported gasoline. See also *Reference respecting the Agricultural Products Marketing Act*, [1978] 2 S.C.R. 1198.

In examining cases which have considered s. 91(2), it is evident that courts have been sensitive to the need to reconcile the general trade and commerce power of the federal government with the provincial power over property and civil rights. Balancing has not been easy. Following the initial articulation of the scope of the general trade and commerce power in *Parsons, supra*, the Privy Council briefly adopted what might be regarded as an overly inclusive interpretation of the power in *John Deere Plow Co. v. Wharton, supra*, before retreating to an overly restrictive stance to its interpretation in the *Board of Commerce, supra*, case. In *Wharton*, Viscount Haldane, at p. 340, speaking of federally-incorporated companies, sketched in broad terms the federal power to regulate trade and commerce under the second branch of *Parsons*:

> ... if it be established that the Dominion Parliament can create such companies, then it becomes *a question of general interest throughout the Dominion* in what fashion they should be permitted to trade. [Emphasis added.]

In contrast, in the *Board of Commerce* case, the Privy Council rejected the trade and commerce power (without distinguishing between the two branches) as the basis for anti-combines legislation, holding that the trade and commerce power had no independent content and could only be invoked as ancillary to other federal powers. This view of the trade and commerce power was rejected some nine years later by the Privy Council in *Proprietary Articles Trade Association, supra*, in the passage quoted earlier.

With respect, in my view, neither the position articulated in *Wharton* nor that advanced in the *Board of Commerce* case correctly assesses the balance to be struck between ss. 91(2) and 92(13). *Wharton* is clearly overly expansive, sweeping all general economic issues into the grasp of s. 91(2). On the other hand, the residual interpretation articulated in the *Board of Commerce* case fails to breathe life into the trade and commerce power and fails to recognize that provincial powers are a [subtraction] from the federal powers. The true balance between property and civil rights and the regulation of trade and commerce must lie somewhere between an all pervasive interpretation of s. 91(2) and an interpretation that renders the general trade and commerce power to all intents vapid and meaningless.

This Court took the first step towards delineating more specific principles of validity for legislation enacted under the general trade and commerce power in *Vapor Canada, supra*. In that case, s. 7(e) of the *Trade Marks Act*, R.S.C. 1970, c. T–10, was challenged as *ultra vires* Parliament. Section 7 prohibited certain commercial practices, including the making of false and misleading statements to discredit a competitor, passing off goods or services, and making use of false descriptions likely to mislead the public, under the general heading of unfair competition. The impugned subsection was a general catch-all provision, unrelated to the rest of the statute, which prohibited a person from doing "any other act" or adopting "any other business practice contrary to honest industrial or commercial usage in Canada." The respondent, Vapor Canada Ltd., supported by the Attorney General of Canada, argued that s. 7(e) could be sustained as legislation regulating general trade and commerce under s. 91(2).

The Court struck down the provision as *ultra vires*. Chief Justice Laskin, speaking for five members of the Court, proposed three hallmarks of validity for legislation under the second branch of the trade and commerce power. First, the impugned legislation must be part of a general regulatory scheme. Second, the scheme must be monitored by the continuing oversight of a regulatory agency. Third, the legislation must be concerned with trade as a whole rather than with a particular industry. Each of these requirements is evidence of a concern that federal authority under the second branch of the trade and commerce power does not encroach on provincial jurisdiction. By limiting the means which federal legislators may employ to that of a regulatory scheme overseen by a regulatory agency, and by limiting the object of federal legislation to trade as a whole, these requirements attempt to maintain a delicate balance between federal and provincial power. On the basis of these criteria, Laskin C.J. then rejected the general trade and commerce power as the constitutional foundation for s. 7(e).

Three members of the Court affirmed the *Vapor Canada* criteria in *Canadian National Transportation*. At issue in *Canadian National Transportation* was the authority of the Attorney General of Canada to conduct prosecutions under the *Combines Investigation Act*. Four members of the Court held that provincial authority over the administration of justice in s. 92(14) of the *Constitution Act, 1867*, did not preclude the federal government from conducting prosecutions of criminal offences. I was of the view that s. 92(14) did preclude the federal government from prosecuting criminal offences — unless the offences could be upheld under a head of power other than s. 91(27). I then took the further position, in which Beetz and Lamer JJ. agreed in substance, that the section could be sustained as legislation relating to the general trade and commerce power and thus the federal government was competent to prosecute a violation of s. 32(1) of the *Combines Investigation Act*.

In reaching the conclusion that s. 32(1)(c) of the *Combines Investigation Act* was within the scope of the general trade and commerce power, and writing for the minority of the Court, I adopted Laskin C.J.'s three criteria in *Vapor Canada, supra*, but added two factors that I considered *indicia* of the valid exercise of the general trade and commerce power: (i) the legislation should be of a nature that the provinces jointly or severally would be constitutionally incapable of enacting; and (ii) the failure to include one or more provinces or localities in a legislative scheme would jeopardize the successful operation of the scheme in other parts of the country. These two requirements, like Laskin C.J.'s three criteria, serve to ensure that federal legislation does not upset the balance of power between federal and provincial governments. In total, the five factors provide a preliminary check-list of characteristics, the presence of which in legislation is an indication of validity under the trade and commerce power. These *indicia* do not, however, represent an exhaustive list of traits that will tend to characterize general trade and commerce legislation. Nor is the presence or absence of any of these five criteria necessarily determinative. As noted in *Canadian National Transportation, supra*, at p. 268:

> The above does not purport to be an exhaustive list, nor is the presence of any or all of these *indicia* necessarily decisive. The proper approach to the characterization is still the one suggested in *Parsons*, a careful case by case assessment. Nevertheless, the presence of such factors does at least make it far more probable that what is being addressed in a federal enactment is genuinely a national economic concern and not just a collection of local ones.

On any occasion where the general trade and commerce power is advanced as a ground of constitutional validity, a careful case by case analysis remains appropriate. The five factors articulated in *Canadian National Transportation* merely represent a principled

way to begin the difficult task of distinguishing between matters relating to trade and commerce and those of a more local nature.

. . . .

The steps in the analysis may be summarized as follows: First, the court must determine whether the impugned provision can be viewed as intruding on provincial powers, and if so to what extent (if it does not intrude, then the only possible issue is the validity of the act). Second, the court must establish whether the act (or a severable part of it) is valid; in cases under the second branch of s. 91(2) this will normally involve finding the presence of a regulatory scheme and then ascertaining whether that scheme meets the requirements articulated in *Vapor Canada, supra*, and in *Canadian National Transportation, supra*. If the scheme is not valid, that is the end of the inquiry. If the scheme of regulation is declared valid, the court must then determine whether the impugned provision is sufficiently integrated with the scheme that it can be upheld by virtue of that relationship. This requires considering the seriousness of the encroachment on provincial powers, in order to decide on the proper standard for such a relationship. If the provision passes this integration test, it is *intra vires* Parliament as an exercise of the general trade and commerce power. If the provision is not sufficiently integrated into the scheme of regulation, it cannot be sustained under the second branch of s. 91(2). I note that in certain cases it may be possible to dispense with some of the aforementioned steps if a clear answer to one of them will be dispositive of the issue. For example, if the provision in question has no relation to the regulatory scheme then the question of its validity may be quickly answered on that ground alone. The approach taken in a number of past cases is more easily understood if this possibility is recognized.

. . . .

I am also of the view that the *Combines Investigation Act* meets the remaining three *indicia* of *Canadian National Transportation*. These criteria share a common theme: all three are indications that the scheme of regulation is national in scope and that local regulation would be inadequate. The Act is quite clearly concerned with the regulation of trade in general, rather than with the regulation of a particular industry or commodity. Ryan J., in upholding the validity of s. 37.1 of the Act, in *Miracle Mart, supra*, described the Act in terms I agree with. At page 259 he said:

... s. 37.1 is part of, as I previously indicated, a complete regulatory scheme aimed at eliminating commercial practices which are contrary to healthy competition *across the country*, and not in a specific place, in a specific business or industry. [Emphasis in original.]

This generality of application distinguishes the Act from the legislation which was found *ultra vires* in *Labatt Breweries of Canada Ltd. v. Attorney General of Canada*, [1980] 1 S.C.R. 914. In that case the legislation regulated a single trade or industry. As I noted earlier, the purpose of the Act is to ensure the existence of a healthy level of competition in the Canadian economy. The deleterious effects of anti-competitive practices transcend provincial boundaries. Competition is not an issue of purely local concern but one of crucial importance for the national economy.

Various factors underlie the need for national regulation of competition in the economy. Professors Hogg and Grover, in "The Constitutionality of the Competition Bill" (1976), 1 *Can. Bus. L.J.* 197, at pp. 199–200 (an abridged version of a paper written for the federal government's Department of Consumer and Corporate Affairs) provide a useful discussion of the diverse economic, geographical, and political factors which make it essential that competition be regulated on the federal level:

> It is surely obvious that major regulation of the Canadian economy has to be national. Goods and services, and the cash or credit which purchases them, flow freely from one part of the country to another without regard for provincial boundaries. Indeed, a basic concept of the federation is that it must be an economic union....

. . . .

> With respect to businesses which are confined to Canada, with few exceptions, any individual or corporation, including a provincially incorporated corporation, has the capacity to "walk across" provincial boundaries in order to buy or sell, lend or borrow, hire or fire. In the absence of artificial impediments, therefore, the market for goods and services is competitive on a national basis, and provincial legislation cannot be an effective regulator.

. . . .

It is evident from this discussion that competition cannot be effectively regulated unless it is regulated nationally. As I have said, in my view combines legislation fulfills the three *indicia* of national scope as described in *Canadian National Transportation*: it

is legislation "aimed at the economy as a single integrated national unit rather than as a collection of separate local enterprises," it is legislation "that the provinces jointly or severally would be constitutionally incapable of passing" and "failure to include one or more provinces or localities would jeopardize successful operation" of the legislation "in other parts of the country."

The above arguments also answer the claim of the Attorney General of Quebec that the regulation of competition does not fall within federal jurisdiction in its intraprovincial dimension and thus the Act should be read down so that s. 31.1 only applies to interprovincial trade. Quebec relies on two points to support its position. First, in the *Interim Report on Competition Policy* of the Canadian Economic Council, the Report which the federal government relies on to show that competition is exclusively federal, there is a passage at p. 108 that recognizes that the provinces have an important role to play in local competition laws:

> We would like to make it emphatically clear that in recommending such a test we intend no implication whatever that the federal government should seek exclusive occupancy of the field of competition policy under civil law, or that only the federal government is competent to manage competition policy in Canada. On the contrary, while it is clear that a considerable proportion of Canadian economic activity crosses provincial and international boundaries, and would be impossible to subject effectively to any provincial competition policy, we believe that the provinces could play a most useful role in respect of other lines of activity under their existing constitutional powers....

. . . .

The second point is that provincial law, both *Civil Code* and common law, already provides some remedies for unfair competition, as in the *Quebec Ready Mix* case where the suit was brought under art. 1053 of the *Civil Code*, as well as s. 31.1 of the *Combines Investigation Act*. Quebec points out that in the United States, forty-three states have adopted competition acts to combat local restraints on trade, in co-ordination with the federal government.

The arguments made above offer a response to these points. They make it clear that not only is the Act meant to cover intraprovincial trade, but that it must do so if it is to be effective. Because regulation of competition is so clearly of national interest and because competition cannot be successfully regulated by federal legislation which is restricted to interprovincial trade, the Quebec argument must fail. I also note that, contrary to the view of Marceau J. in the Trial Division of the Federal Court in *Quebec Ready Mix, supra,* at p. 208, [...] the presence of an already existing action in Quebec law does not argue for invalidating federal legislation. I would repeat what I said at p. 175 of *Multiple Access, supra,* (which words were also quoted by MacGuigan J. in the Court of Appeal's judgment in *Attorney General of Canada v. Québec Ready Mix, supra,* at p. 78): "The validity of the federal legislation must be determined without heed to the ... [provincial] legislation."

On the other hand, competition is not a single matter, any more than inflation or pollution. The provinces[,] too, may deal with competition in the exercise of their legislative powers in such fields as consumer protection, labour relations, marketing and the like. The point is, however, that Parliament also has the constitutional power to regulate intraprovincial aspects of competition.

In sum, the *Combines Investigation Act* is a complex scheme of competition regulation aimed at improving the economic welfare of the nation as a whole. It operates under a regulatory agency. It is designed to control an aspect of the economy that must be regulated nationally if it is to be successfully regulated at all. As Linden J. of the Ontario High Court of Justice said, when discussing the Act in *R. v. Hoffman-La Roche, supra,* at p. 191:

> It is part of a legislative scheme aimed at deterring a wide range of unfair competitive practices that affect trade and commerce generally across Canada, and is not limited to a single industry, commodity or area. The conduct being prohibited is generally of national and of international scope. The presence or absence of healthy competition may affect the welfare of the economy of the entire nation. It is, therefore, within the

sphere of the federal Parliament to seek to regulate such competition in the interest of all Canadians.

I am therefore of the view that the *Combines Investigation Act* as a whole is *intra vires* Parliament as legislation in relation to general trade and commerce and I would reiterate the conclusion I reached in *Canadian National Transportation, supra,* at p. 278:

> A scheme aimed at the regulation of competition is in my view an example of the *genre* of legislation that could not practically or constitutionally be enacted by a provincial government. Given the free flow of trade across provincial borders guaranteed by s. 121 of the *Constitution Act, 1867* Canada is, for economic purposes, a single huge marketplace. If competition is to be regulated at all it must be regulated federally. This fact leads to the syllogism cited by Hogg and Grover, *The Constitutionality of the Competition Bill* (1977), 1 *Can Bus. L.J.* 197, at p. 200:
>
> > ... regulation of the competitive sector of the economy can be effectively accomplished only by federal action. If there is no federal power to enact a competition policy, then Canada cannot have a competition policy. The consequence of a denial of federal constitutional power is therefore, in practical effect, a gap in the distribution of legislative powers.

· · · ·

[Finally, Dickson C.J. found that the section challenged was sufficiently integrated with the regulatory scheme in the *Combines Investigation Act* and that it could be upheld under the general trade and commerce power.]

(e) *Morgentaler*[†]

NOTE

In 1988, the Supreme Court upheld a challenge by abortion activist Dr. Henry Morgentaler and declared that the provisions of the *Criminal Code* that prohibited abortion in Canada were contrary to the *Canadian Charter of Human Rights and Freedoms*. Efforts at enacting federal replacement

---

[†] *R. v. Morgentaler*, [1993] 3 S.C.R. 463, aff'g. (1991), 104 N.S.R. (2d) 361 (N.S.C.A.), which aff'd. (1990), 99 N.S.R. (2d) 293, 270 A.P.R. 293 (N.S.S.C.), acquitting the respondent of violating the *Medical Services Act* on the ground that the legislation was *ultra vires* the province.

legislation were unsuccessful, so Canada was left without criminal law restrictions on abortion. However, when Dr. Morgentaler attempted to establish an abortion clinic in Halifax, the Nova Scotia government enacted the *Medical Services Act* and an accompanying regulation prohibiting abortions outside hospitals and denying health insurance coverage for abortions performed in violation of the Act.

Did this provincial legislation interfere with the federal criminal law power in s. 91(27) of the *Constitution Act, 1982*, or could it be supported under provincial powers over hospitals, health, the medical profession, and the practice of medicine, by virtue of heads (7) (hospitals), (13) (property and civil rights), and (16) (local or private matters) of s. 92?

As well as illustrating the division of jurisdiction in the two important fields of criminal law and health, the decision provides a useful summary of some of the main interpretation techniques employed by the Court in division of powers issues. Do you agree that the process "is not and never can be an exact science"? For another good illustration of division of powers interpretation techniques, see *Ward v. A.G. (Canada)*, [2002] 1 S.C.R. 569 at paras. 16–22 and 41–44.

Compare this decision with *Siemens v. Manitoba (A.G.)*, [2003] S.C.R. 6. Why the different results?

EXTRACT

[SOPINKA J. for the Court:]

. . . .

... The only issues are whether the legislation is within the competence of the province under s. 92 of the *Constitution Act, 1867*, or whether it is in relation to the criminal law and thus within the exclusive competence of Parliament under s. 91(27).

. . . .

CLASSIFICATION OF LAWS

"What's the 'matter'?"

Classification of a law for purposes of federalism involves first identifying the "matter" of the law and then assigning it to one of the "classes of subjects" in respect to which the federal and provincial governments have legislative authority under ss. 91 and 92 of the *Constitution Act, 1867*. This process of classification is "an interlocking one, in which the *British North America Act* and the challenged legisla-

tion react on one another and fix each other's meaning" ... Courts apply considerations of policy along with legal principle; the task requires "a nice balance of legal skill, respect for established rules, and plain common sense. It is not and never can be an exact science." ...

. . . .

A law's "matter" is its leading feature or true character, often described as its pith and substance.... There is no single test for a law's pith and substance. The approach must be flexible and a technical, formalistic approach is to be avoided.... While both the purpose and effect of the law are relevant considerations in the process of characterization ... it is often the case that the legislation's dominant purpose or aim is the key to constitutional validity....

. . . .

Purpose and Effect

"Legal Effect" or Strict Legal Operation

Evidence of the "effect" of legislation can be relevant in two ways: to establish "legal effect" and to establish "practical effect." The analysis of pith and substance necessarily starts with looking at the legislation itself, in order to determine its legal effect. "Legal effect" or "strict legal operation" refers to how the legislation as a whole affects the rights and liabilities of those subject to its terms, and is determined from the terms of the legislation itself.... Legal effect is often a good indicator of the purpose of the legislation ... but is relevant in constitutional characterization even when it is not fully intended or appreciated by the enacting body.

The analysis of pith and substance is not, however, restricted to the four corners of the legislation (see, e.g., *Reference re Anti-Inflation Act*, [1976] 2 S.C.R. 373, at pp. 388–89). Thus the court "will look beyond the direct legal effects to inquire into the social or economic purposes which the statute was enacted to achieve," its background and the circumstances surrounding its enactment ... and, in appropriate cases, will consider evidence of the second form of "effect," the actual or predicted practical effect of the legislation in operation.... The ultimate long-term, practical effect of the legislation will in some cases be irrelevant....

The Use of Extrinsic Materials

In determining the background, context and purpose of challenged legislation, the court is entitled to refer to extrinsic evidence of various kinds provided it is relevant and not inherently unreliable.... This clearly includes related legislation (such as, in this case, the March regulations and the former s. 251 of the *Criminal Code*), and evidence of the "mischief" at which the legislation is directed.... It also includes legislative history, in the sense of the events that occurred during drafting and enactment; as Ritchie J., concurring in *Reference re Anti-Inflation Act, supra,* wrote at p. 437, it is "not only permissible but essential" to consider the material the legislature had before it when the statute was enacted.

... Provided that the court remains mindful of the limited reliability and weight of Hansard evidence, it should be admitted as relevant to both the background and the purpose of legislation. Indeed, its admissibility in constitutional cases to aid in determining the background and purpose of legislation now appears well established....

I would therefore hold ... that the excerpts from Hansard were properly admitted by the trial judge in this case. In a nutshell, this evidence demonstrates that members of all parties in the House understood the central feature of the proposed law to be prohibition of Dr. Morgentaler's proposed clinic on the basis of a common and almost unanimous opposition to abortion clinics *per se*....

Practical Effect

In the present case the Attorney General of Nova Scotia submits that the evidence shows that the future administration of the Act will not result in a restriction on abortion services; the respondent submits the opposite. This raises the question of the relevance of evidence of practical effect. I have noted that the legal effect of the terms of legislation is always relevant. Barring material amendments, it does not change over time. The practical effect of legislation, on the other hand, has a less secure status in constitutional analysis. Practical effect consists of the actual or predicted results of the legislation's operation and administration (see, e.g., *Saumur, supra*). Courts are often asked to adjudicate the constitutionality of legislation which is not yet in force or which, as here, has only been in force a short time. In such cases any prediction of future practical effect is necessarily short-term, since the court is not equipped to predict accurately the future consequential impact of legislation.

... The difficulty with practical effect is that whereas in one context practical effect may reveal the true purpose of the legislation..., in another context it may be incidental and entirely irrelevant even though it is drastic...; and in yet another context pro-

vincial and federal enactments with the same practical impact may both stand if the matter to which they relate has two "aspects" of roughly equivalent importance, one within federal and the other within provincial competence (*Hodge* v. *The Queen* (1883), 9 App. Cas. 117 (P.C.), at p. 130; *Bell Canada* v. *Quebec* (*Commission de la santé et de la sécurité du travail*), [1988] 1 S.C.R. 749).

In the majority of cases the only relevance of practical effect is to demonstrate an *ultra vires* purpose by revealing a serious impact upon a matter outside the enacting body's legislative authority and thus either contradicting an appearance of *intra vires* or confirming an impression of *ultra vires*.... It was in light of the difficult status of practical effect ... that Wilson J., concurring in *R.* v. *Big M Drug Mart Ltd.*, [1985] 1 S.C.R. 295, held that legislative purpose is the focal point in distribution of powers analysis.... [Wilson J. concluded at p. 358, that]:

> Only when the effects of the legislation so directly impinge on some other subject matter as to reflect some alternative or ulterior purpose do the effects themselves take on analytic significance.

If, however, pith and substance can be determined without reference to evidence of practical effect, the absence of evidence that the legislation has a practical effect in line with this characterization will not displace the conclusion as to the legislation's invalidity. In such a case, "evidence as to the likely effect of legislation would not add anything useful to the task of characterization, but would merely bear on the wisdom or efficacy of the statute. In those cases the evidence is not relevant" (Hogg, *supra*, at pp. 15–16). See also *Reference re Anti-Inflation Act, supra*, at pp. 424–25. Such evidence will not change the legislation's "matter," and only goes to the effectiveness of the statute to fulfil its object. The court is not concerned with the wisdom of a statute, and the government surely cannot justify legislation already determined to be *ultra vires* by arguing that it will not realize its aim or objective. Moreover, as I have said, legislation is often considered before experience has shown its actual impact, and prediction of future impact is necessarily short-term. I would adapt what La Forest J. said in another context (*R.* v. *Edwards Books and Art Ltd.*, *supra*, at p. 803) to this situation: "[i]t is undesirable that an Act be found constitutional today and unconstitutional tomorrow" simply because of the absence of conclusive evidence as to future impact or the possibility of a change in practical effect.

Scope of the Applicable Heads of Power

The issue we face in the present case is whether Nova Scotia has, by the present legislation, regulated the place for delivery of a medical service with a view to controlling the quality and nature of its health care delivery system, or has attempted to prohibit the performance of abortions outside hospitals with a view to suppressing or punishing what it perceives to be the socially undesirable conduct of abortion. The former would place the legislation within provincial competence; the latter would make it criminal law.

The Criminal Law

Section 91(27) of the *Constitution Act, 1867* gives the federal Parliament exclusive legislative jurisdiction over criminal law in the widest sense of the term.... In *Proprietary Articles Trade Association* v. *Canada (A.G.)*, [1931] A.C. 310 (P.C.), at p. 324, the Judicial Committee took this to include any act prohibited with penal consequences, but this interpretation was too generous and the missing ingredient was supplied by Rand J. in his classic formulation of the scope of the tests for criminal law in the *Reference re Validity of Section 5(a) of the Dairy Industry Act*, [1949] S.C.R. 1 (the *Margarine Reference*), at pp. 49–50:

> ... we can properly look for some evil or injurious or undesirable effect upon the public against which the law is directed. That effect may be in relation to social, economic or political interests; and the legislature has had in mind to suppress the evil or to safeguard the interest threatened.
>
> ...
>
> Is the prohibition then enacted with a view to a public purpose which can support it as being in relation to criminal law? Public peace, order, security, health, morality: these are the ordinary though not exclusive ends served by that law....

The presence or absence of a criminal public purpose or object is thus pivotal: see *Lord's Day Alliance of Canada* v. *Attorney General of British Columbia*, [1959] S.C.R. 497, at pp. 508–9; *Goodyear Tire and Rubber Co. of Canada* v. *The Queen*, [1956] S.C.R. 303, at p. 313; and *Boggs* v. *The Queen*, [1981] 1 S.C.R. 49....

Provincial Health Jurisdiction

The provinces have general legislative jurisdiction over hospitals by virtue of s. 92(7) of the *Constitution Act, 1867*, and over the medical profession and the practice of medicine by virtue of ss. 92(13) and (16). Section 92(16) also gives them general jurisdiction over health matters within the province: *Schneider* v. *The Queen*, [1982] 2 S.C.R. 112, at p. 137. The *Schneider* case gives an indication of the watershed between valid health legislation and criminal law. In that case, *British Columbia's Heroin Treatment Act* was held to be *intra vires* because its object was not to punish narcotics addicts, but to treat their addiction and ensure their safety and security. Narcotic addiction was targeted not as a public evil but as a "physiological condition necessitating both medical and social intervention" (at p. 138). Accordingly, if the central concern of the present legislation were medical treatment of unwanted pregnancies and the safety and security of the pregnant woman, not the restriction of abortion services with a view to safeguarding the public interest or interdicting a public harm, the legislation would arguably be valid health law enacted pursuant to the province's general health jurisdiction.

In addition, there is no dispute that the heads of s. 92 invoked by the appellant confer on the provinces jurisdiction over health care in the province generally, including matters of cost and efficiency, the nature of the health care delivery system, and privatization of the provision of medical services.

The Regulation of Abortion

In the U.K. and Canada, the prohibition of abortion with penal consequences has long been considered a subject for the criminal law....

. . . .

In [*R.* v. *Morgentaler*, [1988] 1 S.C.R. 30 (1988)], this Court unanimously reaffirmed the holding [in *Morgentaler* v. *The Queen*, [1976] 1 S.C.R. 616] that s. 251 was valid criminal law for purposes of the distribution of powers. Beetz J. (with whom Estey J. concurred), at pp. 82 and 122–3, and Wilson J., at p. 181, held that while s. 251 had as an ancillary objective the protection of the life or health of pregnant women, its principal objective was the protection of the state interest in the foetus. (I would note that although in this case the objective of the legislation was also discussed in the context of the Charter, a statute's "objective" for Charter purposes necessarily reflects its "purpose" for distribution of powers purposes: *R.* v. *Big M Drug Mart Ltd.*, *supra*, at pp. 353, 361–62.) Beetz J. held, at pp. 128–29, that this made it a valid exercise of the criminal law power. On the other hand, Dickson C.J. (Lamer J., as he then was, concurring), at p. 75, and McIntyre J. (dissenting, La Forest J. concurring), at pp. 135

and 156, held that the objective of the section was to balance the interests of the foetus and the pregnant woman. McIntyre J. held, at p. 156, that this objective made the section a valid exercise of the criminal law power. Dickson C.J. and Wilson J. did not give reasons for finding the section *intra vires*.

The two *Morgentaler* decisions focus attention on the purpose or concern of abortion legislation to determine if it is truly criminal law: is the performance or procurement of abortion prohibited as socially undesirable conduct; is protecting the state interest in the foetus or balancing the interests of the foetus against those of women seeking abortions a primary objective of the legislation; is the protection of the woman's health only an ancillary concern; and are other provincial concerns such as the establishment of hospitals or the regulation of the medical profession or the practice thereof merely incidental?

It is not necessary for the purposes of this appeal to attempt to delineate the scope of provincial jurisdiction to regulate the performance of abortions. Suffice it to say that any provincial jurisdiction to regulate the delivery of abortion services must be solidly anchored in one of the provincial heads of power which give the provinces jurisdiction to legislate in relation to such matters as health, hospitals, the practice of medicine and health care policy.

. . . .

CONCLUSION

Pith and Substance

This legislation deals, by its terms, with a subject historically considered to be part of the criminal law — the prohibition of the performance of abortions with penal consequences. It is thus suspect on its face. Its legal effect partially reproduces that of the now defunct s. 251 of the *Criminal Code*, in so far as both precluded the establishment and operation of free-standing abortion clinics. Its legislative history, the course of events leading up to the Act's passage and the making of N.S. Reg. 152/89, the Hansard excerpts and the absence of evidence that privatization and the cost and quality of health care services were anything more than incidental concerns, lead to the conclusion that the *Medical Services Act* and the *Medical Services Designation Regulation* were aimed primarily at suppressing the perceived public harm or evil of abortion clinics. The legislation meets the tests set out in the *Margarine Reference*, *supra* and of *Morgentaler* (1975) and (1988), *supra*.

The primary objective of the legislation was to prohibit abortions outside hospitals as socially undesirable conduct, and any concern with the safety and security of pregnant women or with health care policy, hospitals or the regulation of the medical profession was merely ancillary. This legislation involves the regulation of the place where an abortion may be obtained, not from the viewpoint of health care policy, but from the viewpoint of public wrongs or crimes....

Paraphrasing what Lamer J. said in *Starr* v. *Houlden*, *supra*, at p. 1405: I find unpersuasive the argument that this legislation is solidly anchored in s. 92(7), (13) or (16) of the *Constitution Act, 1867*. There is nothing on the surface of the legislation or in the background facts leading up to its enactment to convince me that it is designed to protect the integrity of Nova Scotia's health care system by preventing the emergence of a two-tiered system of delivery, to ensure the delivery of high quality health care, or to rationalize the delivery of medical services so as to avoid duplication and reduce public health care costs. Any such objectives are clearly incidental to the central feature of the legislation, which is the prohibition of abortions outside hospitals as socially undesirable conduct subject to punishment.

Practical Effect

This legislation will certainly restrict abortion in the sense that it makes abortions unavailable in any place other than hospitals. But will it lead to a practical restriction of access to abortion in Nova Scotia? Will the present hospital system be able and willing to accommodate all the women who desire to terminate a pregnancy, given among other things that the hospital in which 83% of all abortions are performed has lost half of its medical staff willing to perform the procedure? These are questions that the trial judge did not answer, and on which the parties are resolutely divided. Women may not wish to have an abortion in a hospital for any number of legitimate reasons. Clearly restrictions as to place can have the effect of restricting abortions in practice, and indeed it was the operation of s. 251 of the *Criminal Code* in restricting abortions to certain hospitals that contributed largely to its demise. One of the reasons that the former s. 251 of the *Criminal Code* was struck down in *Morgentaler* (1988), *supra*, was that the in-hospital requirement in that section led to unacceptable delays, undue stress and trauma, and a severe practical restriction of access to abortion services. Several years of experience under s. 251 showed that the combined decisions and actions of individual anti-abortion hospital boards could render access to legal abortion non-existent in large areas of the country. Something similar may occur in Nova Scotia but that is something we have no way of predicting. One of the effects of the legislation is consolidation of abortions in the hands of the provincial government, largely in one provincially-controlled institution. This renders free access to abortion vulnerable to administrative erosion.

Having applied the ordinary tests as to the matter of the present legislation, I am able to conclude that the legislation was an *ultra vires* invasion of the field of criminal law. I am able to reach this conclusion without predicting the ultimate practical effect of this legislation, and it is consequently unnecessary to adjudicate the intractable dispute between the parties as to whether this legislation will, in fact, restrict access to abortion in Nova Scotia.... In view of my conclusion as to the pith and substance of the legislation, I am not concerned with whether the legislation is effective and such evidence can no more be used to validate *ultra vires* legislation than to invalidate *intra vires* legislation, as was held in *Reference re Anti-Inflation Act, supra*.

(f) *Firearms Reference*†

NOTE

The federal *Firearms Act* of 1995 amended the *Criminal Code* to require all firearms holders to obtain licences and register their guns. Victims' and police associations and many others were delighted. Sport hunters, gun clubs, Aboriginal groups, and many others in rural and northern communities were extremely upset. The Alberta government referred the Act to its Court of Appeal. It argued that the Act invaded provincial power over property and civil rights, and was *ultra vires* the federal criminal law power. Unanimously, the Supreme Court of Canada upheld the decision of the majority of the Alberta Court of Appeal that the legislation was valid under the criminal law power.

Such a result was not surprising. The criminal law power is one of the strongest sources of federal legislative jurisdiction today. This was not always so. In *Board of Commerce*, [1921] A.C. 199, Lord Haldane suggested that s. 91(27) was limited to "inherently" criminal subject matter: 198–99. A decade later, though, the Judicial Committee veered to the other side. It suggested that the s. 91(27) power includes any act that is prohibited with penal consequences: *Proprietary Articles Association v. Canada (A.G.)*, [1931] A.C. 310, 324.

The Supreme Court has travelled — cautiously — on the expansive side of these two extremes. In 1949, the Court said that the criminal law power requires (i) a prohibition, (ii) a penalty, and (iii) a criminal purpose such as public peace, order, security, health, and morality: *Reference re section 5(1) of the Dairy Federation the Dairy Industry Act (the Margarine Reference)*, [1949] 1 S.C.R. 1., 50. Later, the Court emphasized the broader requirements that the purpose be "legitimate" and "public": *RJR-Macdonald Inc. v. Canada (A.G.)*, [1995] 3 S.C.R. 199, paras. 28, 32, and 56; *R. v. Hydro-Québec*, [1997] 3 S.C.R. 213, paras. 121 and 132. The *Firearms Reference* continued this liberal approach.

The Court did warn that "[a]lthough the criminal law power is broad, it is not unlimited": *Firearms Reference*, para. 30. It followed up on this caution in *Ward v. Canada (A.G.)*, [2002] S.C.R. 569. In *Ward*, the federal government relied on its criminal law power as well as its fisheries power to support a regulation banning the sale of baby seals. The Court rejected the criminal law argument, holding that the relevant legislative history failed to disclose a concern based on public peace, order, security, health, or morality: paras. 51–56.

Despite these notes of restraint, though, the s. 91(27) power has grown dramatically since the days of Lord Haldane. In fact, the *Firearms* statement should perhaps be rephrased. Although the criminal law power is not unlimited, it is broad!

After the *Firearms Reference* and news of huge gun registry cost overruns, some provincial gov-

---

† *Reference re Firearms Act (Can.)*, [2000] 1 S.C.R. 783.

ernments said they would refuse to prosecute for federal firearms registry violations. Would this be constitutionally possible?

EXTRACT

[THE COURT:]

[24] ... [T]he effects of the law suggest that its essence is the promotion of public safety through the reduction of the misuse of firearms, and negate the proposition that Parliament was in fact attempting to achieve a different goal such as the total regulation of firearms production, trade, and ownership. We therefore conclude that, viewed from its purpose and effects, the *Firearms Act* is in "pith and substance" directed to public safety.

[25] Having assessed the pith and substance or matter of the law, the second step is to determine whether that matter comes within the jurisdiction of the enacting legislature. We must examine the heads of power under ss. 91 and 92 of the *Constitution Act, 1867* and determine what the matter is "in relation to". In this case, the question is whether the law falls under federal jurisdiction over criminal law or its peace, order and good government power; or under provincial jurisdiction over property and civil rights. The presumption of constitutionality means that Alberta, as the party challenging the legislation, is required to show that the Act does not fall within the jurisdiction of Parliament....

. . . .

[27] As a general rule, legislation may be classified as criminal law if it possesses three prerequisites: a valid criminal law purpose backed by a prohibition and a penalty: *RJR-MacDonald Inc.* v. *Canada (Attorney General)*, [1995] 3 S.C.R. 199; *R.* v. *Hydro-Québec*, [1997] 3 S.C.R. 213; and *Reference re Validity of Section 5(a) of the Dairy Industry Act*, [1949] S.C.R. 1 (the *"Margarine Reference"*)....

. . . .

[28] ... Criminal law, as this Court has stated in numerous cases, constitutes a broad area of federal jurisdiction.... The criminal law stands on its own as federal jurisdiction. Although it often overlaps with provincial jurisdiction over property and civil rights, it is not "carved out" from provincial jurisdiction....

[29] Not only is the criminal law a "stand-alone" jurisdiction, it also finds its expression in a broad range of legislation. The *Criminal Code* is the quintessential federal enactment under its criminal jurisdiction, but it is not the only one. The *Food and Drugs Act*, the *Hazardous Products Act*, the *Lord's Day Act*, and the *Tobacco Products Control Act* have all been held to be valid exercises of the criminal law power.... Thus the fact that some of the provisions of the *Firearms Act* are not contained within the *Criminal Code* has no significance for the purposes of constitutional classification.

[30] Although the criminal law power is broad, it is not unlimited....

[31] Within this context, we return to the three criteria that a law must satisfy in order to be classified as criminal. The first step is to consider whether the law has a valid criminal law purpose. Rand J. listed some examples of valid purposes in the *Margarine Reference* at p. 50: "Public peace, order, security, health, morality: these are the ordinary though not exclusive ends served by [criminal] law". Earlier, we concluded that the gun control law in pith and substance is directed at public safety. This brings it clearly within the criminal law purposes of protecting public peace, order, security and health.

[32] In determining whether the purpose of a law constitutes a valid criminal law purpose, courts look at whether laws of this type have traditionally been held to be criminal law.... Courts have repeatedly held that gun control comes within the criminal law sphere....

[33] Gun control has traditionally been considered valid criminal law because guns are dangerous and pose a risk to public safety....

[34] The finding of a valid criminal law purpose does not end the inquiry, however. In order to be classified as a valid criminal law, that purpose must be connected to a prohibition backed by a penalty. The 1995 gun control law satisfies these requirements. Section 112 of the *Firearms Act* prohibits the possession of a firearm without a registration certificate. Section 91 of the *Criminal Code* (as amended by s. 139 of the *Firearms Act*) prohibits the possession of a firearm without a licence and a registration certificate. These prohibitions are backed by penalties....

[35] It thus appears that the 1995 gun control law possesses all three criteria required for a criminal law. However, Alberta and the provinces raised a

number of objections to this classification which must be considered.

[The Court rejected Alberta's argument that the statute was "regulatory" rather than criminal. The Court noted that the offences were not defined by an administrative body, and that the prohibitions and penalties were concerned with public safety, not a purpose such as revenue generation. In response to the argument that the criminal law power required an outright prohibition, the Court said Parliament is entitled to use indirect means to further public safety.]

. . . .

[49] The argument that the 1995 gun control law upsets the balance of Confederation may be seen as an argument that, viewed in terms of its effects, the law does not in pith and substance relate to public safety under the federal criminal law power but rather to the provincial power over property and civil rights.... [T]he question is whether the "provincial" effects are incidental, in which case they are constitutionally irrelevant, or whether they are so substantial that they show that the law is mainly, or "in pith and substance", the regulation of property and civil rights.

[50] In our view, Alberta and the provinces have not established that the effects of the law on provincial matters are more than incidental. First, the mere fact that guns are property does not suffice to show that a gun control law is in pith and substance a provincial matter....

[51] Second, the Act does not significantly hinder the ability of the provinces to regulate the property and civil rights aspects of guns. Most provinces already have regulations dealing with hunting, discharge within municipal boundaries, and other aspects of firearm use, and these are legitimate subjects of provincial regulation.... The Act does not affect these laws.

[52] Third, the most important jurisdictional effect of this law is its elimination of the ability of the provinces to not have any regulations on the ownership of ordinary firearms. The provinces argue that it is in their power to choose whether or not to have such a law. By taking over the field, the federal government has deprived the provinces of that choice. Assuming (without deciding) that the provincial legislatures would have the jurisdiction to enact a law in relation to the property aspects of ordinary firearms,

this does not prevent Parliament from addressing the safety aspects of ordinary firearms. The double aspect doctrine permits both levels of government to legislate in one jurisdictional field for two different purposes....

[53] Fourth, as discussed above, this law does not precipitate the federal government's entry into a new field. Gun control has been the subject of federal law since Confederation. This law does not allow the federal government to significantly expand its jurisdictional powers to the detriment of the provinces. There is no colourable intrusion into provincial jurisdiction, either in the sense that Parliament has an improper motive or that it is taking over provincial powers under the guise of the criminal law....

[54] Yet another argument is that the ownership of guns is not criminal law because it is not immoral to own an ordinary firearm. There are two difficulties with this argument. The first is that while the ownership of ordinary firearms is not in itself regarded by most Canadians as immoral, the problems associated with the misuse of firearms are firmly grounded in morality. Firearms may be misused to take human life and to assist in other immoral acts, like theft and terrorism. Preventing such misuse can be seen as an attempt to curb immoral acts. Viewed thus, gun control is directed at a moral evil.

[55] The second difficulty with the argument is that the criminal law is not confined to prohibiting immoral acts: see *Proprietary Articles Trade Association* v. *Attorney-General for Canada*, [1931] A.C. 310 (P.C.). While most criminal conduct is also regarded as immoral, Parliament can use the criminal law to prohibit activities which have little relation to public morality. For instance, the criminal law has been used to prohibit certain restrictions on market competition: see Attorney-General for British Columbia v. Attorney-General for Canada, supra. Therefore, even if gun control did not involve morality, it could still fall under the federal criminal law power.

[56] We recognize the concerns of northern, rural and aboriginal Canadians who fear that this law does not address their particular needs. They argue that it discriminates against them and violates treaty rights, and express concerns about their ability to access the scheme, which may be administered from a great distance. These apprehensions are genuine, but they do not go to the question before us — Parliament's jurisdiction to enact this law. Whether a law could have been designed better or whether the federal government should have engaged in more consultation before enacting the law has no bearing

on the division of powers analysis applied by this Court. If the law violates a treaty or a provision of the Charter, those affected can bring their claims to Parliament or the courts in a separate case. The reference questions, and hence this judgment, are restricted to the issue of the division of powers.

[57] We also appreciate the concern of those who oppose this Act on the basis that it may not be effective or it may be too expensive. Criminals will not register their guns, Alberta argued. The only real effect of the law, it is suggested, is to burden law-abiding farmers and hunters with red tape. These concerns were properly directed to and considered by Parliament; they cannot affect the Court's decision. The efficacy of a law, or lack thereof, is not relevant to Parliament's ability to enact it under the division of powers analysis. Furthermore, the federal government points out that it is not only career criminals who are capable of misusing guns. Domestic violence often involves people who have no prior criminal record. Crimes are committed by first-time offenders. Finally, accidents and suicides occur in the homes of law-abiding people, and guns are stolen from their homes. By requiring everyone to register their guns, Parliament seeks to reduce misuse by everyone and curtail the ability of criminals to acquire firearms. Where criminals have acquired guns and used them in the commission of offences, the registration system seeks to make those guns more traceable. The cost of the program, another criticism of the law, is equally irrelevant to our constitutional analysis.

[58] We conclude that the impugned sections of the *Firearms Act* contain prohibitions and penalties in support of a valid criminal law purpose. The legislation is in relation to criminal law pursuant to s. 91(27) of the Constitution Act, 1867 and hence intra vires Parliament. It is not regulatory legislation and it does not take the federal government so far into provincial territory that the balance of federalism is threatened or the jurisdictional powers of the provinces are unduly impaired.

[59] Having determined that the legislation constitutes a valid exercise of Parliament's jurisdiction over criminal law, it is unnecessary to consider whether the legislation can also be justified as an exercise of its peace, order and good government power.

[60] We would dismiss the appeal. The licensing and registration provisions in the Firearms Act do not constitute an infringement of the jurisdiction of the Legislature of Alberta with respect to the regulation of property and civil rights pursuant to s. 92(13) of the *Constitution Act, 1867*. The Act is a valid exercise of Parliament's jurisdiction over criminal law pursuant to s. 91(27).

7   Overlap and Cooperative Federalism

(a)   Introduction

Despite their vital role, the formal division of legislative powers and its interpretation by the courts are only one part of the story of Canadian federalism. Another part, equally important, is the network of administrative and financial arrangements that links the various governments of the country. Here, the lead branch of government is not the judiciary, but the executive.

There are several reasons for the significance of this second aspect of federalism. First, although ss. 91 and 92 of the *Constitution Act, 1867* purport to confer "exclusive" legislative powers, both the wording and the structure of these sections made strict exclusivity unlikely from the start.[1] Although the Judicial Committee tried to assign distinct areas of responsibility to different levels of government,[2] it was prepared in many situations to recognize overlap.[3] Usually, it aimed less for the "watertight compartments" referred to in 1937,[4] and more for balanced compartments. Overlap, then, was a reality from the beginning, and where there is overlap, there is a need for coordination between the administrations of the governments concerned.

Second, as Monahan, Covello, and Smith point out in this chapter, many of the subjects of government that are important today — such as health care and the environment — were considered less so by the framers of Confederation, and are not recognized separately in the original division of powers. In almost all cases, the wording of ss. 91 and 92 cross-cuts these subjects, so that both levels of government are responsible for most of them.[5] Again, jurisdictional overlap requires administrative coordination.

Third, there has been a change in the character of the political dispute-resolution process between the provinces and the federal government.

The 1867 arrangement contemplated a "top-down" political process, which gave the federal government the power to control provincial bills and policies through its power to appoint and instruct the provincial lieutenant governor, to reserve provincial bills for its assent, and to disallow provincial statutes. As provinces have gained a position of greater equality with the federal government, and the old techniques of instructions, reservation, and disallowance have fallen into disuse, there has been a need for federal–provincial agreements to coordinate federal and provincial policies and to prevent or resolve conflict.[6]

Finally, Canadian federalism is a union of partners with significant inequalities of size and wealth. With its control over all forms of taxation power federal government has traditionally had access to greater financial resources than all or most of the provinces. As well as this "vertical" imbalance, there has been an historic imbalance between provinces that are rich in natural resources and manufacturing bases, and those that are not. If federalism is to be more than a trading pact, it is important to redress the worst of these imbalances.[7] Originally, the dominant approach to equalization was the device of federal subsidies. Although this is still the case, the administration of the modern grants is quite different, taking the form of interjurisdictional agreements.

These agreements are negotiated and administered by the elected executives and bureaucrats of the governments concerned. As a result, many important fields of modern government, from interjurisdictional fiscal relations to health care administration and other aspects of the welfare state, are dominated by the executive branch. Court decisions, so prominent in helping shape the formal division of powers, have played a secondary role here. Could this situation be changing? On this question, see the *Chaoulli* decision at the end of this chapter.

Notes

1. See Chapters 3 and 5.
2. For example, by subtracting the more specific powers from those that were more general: see Chapter 5.
3. For example, through its concurrency and double aspect doctrines, and in specific areas such as taxation. In *Atlantic Smoke Shops v. Conlon*, [1943] A.C. 550, holding that a sales tax is a "direct" tax, available to provincial governments as well as the federal government.

4. "Watertight compartments" was the well-known phrase used by Lord Wright in *Canada (A.G.) v. Ontario (A.G.)*, [1937] A.C. 326 at 354.
5. Note that 20th-century amendments to the *Constitution Act, 1867* have provided expressly for concurrency in regard to pensions (s. 94A: 1951), supplementary benefits (s. 94A: 1964), and taxation of certain forms of non-renewable natural resources (s. 92A, 1982). In 1867, there was express concurrency only in regard to agriculture and immigration: s. 95.
6. Similarly, as the territorial governments have become more independent of the federal government, there has been an increasing need for consensual rather than unilateral arrangements with them.
7. Again, the need to redress imbalances applies to the situation of the territories as well as to that of the provinces.

(b) From Watertight Compartments to Shared Responsibility†

Patrick Monahan, Lynda Covello and Nicola Smith

NOTE

As suggested above, the powers in ss. 91 and 92 of the *Constitution Act, 1867* were never entirely exclusive.[1] However, Monahan, Covello, and Smith are quite right to stress that in modern Canadian federalism, overlap and functional concurrency have become the norm.[2] Shared responsibilities are even more pronounced today than in 1867 or in the Judicial Committee years. What, according to these authors, are the main causes of this phenomenon? What, in their view, are its main implications? Can you think of others?

Notes

1. See *Overlap and Cooperative Federalism*, above.
2. In a few areas, such as pensions and certain forms of natural resources taxation, concurrency is required expressly: *ibid.*

EXTRACT

The original conception of the division of powers in Canada was premised on the idea that each level of government would exercise exclusive jurisdiction over a series of "watertight compartments." It is well known that this description no longer applies

to Canadian federalism. Instead, overlapping of jurisdiction and functional concurrency have become the norm. In most important areas of public policy, both levels of government are active and have a range of policy instruments at their disposal.[15]

There are a variety of reasons for this, but one of the most important is the fact that the categories in the *Constitution Act, 1867* omit reference to many of the most important functions of modern government. While the 1867 *Act* sets out an extensive list of powers for each level of government, these lists were drafted at a time when the conception and role of government was much more limited. Thus, the lists of powers in the 1867 *Act* do not mirror the complexity or the expanse of the contemporary roles of government. The categories in sections 91 and 92 simply do not mention, explicitly, many of the most significant aspects of contemporary government in Canada.

An illustration of this can be found by comparing the lists of powers set out in the Allaire Report with those set out in the 1867 *Act*. The Allaire Report sets out a list of twenty-two powers which, it states, should be under the full sovereignty of the province of Quebec. Significantly, over two-thirds of these powers are not mentioned at all in the 1867 *Act*. The other sixteen powers, including the environ-

---

† Excerpt from Patrick Monahan, Lynda Covello and Nicola Smith, *A New Division of Powers for Canada*, Study No. 8, Final Report of the York University Constitutional Reform Project (Toronto: York University Centre for Public Law and Public Policy, 1992) at 9–12. Reproduced with permission. See also Patrick Monahan, *Constitutional Law*, 3d ed. (Scarborough: Carswell, 2006) at 247–51.

ment, regional development, research and development, culture, health, social affairs, and housing are not referred to explicitly in either section 91 or section 92 of the 1867 *Act*. They are, instead, categories which reflect our contemporary understanding of what government does, categories which simply have no counterpart in the 1867 *Act*.

In this sense, the phrase "division of powers" is somewhat misleading; the 1867 *Act*, in fact, does not formally and explicitly divide many of the most important functions of modern government. Provincial Ministries of Health, for example, consume by far the largest proportion of all provincial tax dollars. Yet, the division of powers set out in the *Constitution Act, 1867* makes no explicit reference to legislative responsibility for health care. This has permitted a high degree of flexibility in the evolution of the division of powers; as new areas of government responsibility emerge, the absence of a specific allocation of responsibility in the field will typically permit intervention by either level of government.

Thus, the fact that the categories in the 1867 Act do not mention many of the important contemporary aspects of public policy has permitted a high degree of functional concurrency. In this sense, it is simply wrong for governments in Canada to complain that they lack "jurisdiction." With relatively few exceptions (these exceptions involve judicially-imposed limitations on federal regulation over the economy),[16] "jurisdiction" as such is not a problem under the Canadian constitution. Either level of government has sufficient constitutional authority to intervene in virtually any policy area that is deemed to be of significance in the 1990s. The suggestion that the division of powers needs to be comprehensively rewritten in order to "transfer jurisdiction," either to the provinces or to the federal government, is simply unfounded. Indeed, it is precisely because of the flexibility inherent in the current division of powers that the country is able to operate under a set of categories drafted one hundred and twenty-five years ago. As new social, political or economic problems have arisen, both levels of government have been able to adapt and respond to these new challenges. This is one of the great virtues of the 1867 *Act*, and a key explanation for its political durability.

To further illustrate the plasticity of the 1867 division of powers, consider again the list of twenty-two exclusive provincial powers identified in the Allaire Report. While only six of these categories are even mentioned in the *Constitution Act, 1867*, the provinces are *de facto* active in twenty-one of the twenty-two fields of jurisdiction. In fact, the only area that is not now under provincial authority

— unemployment insurance — would be subject to exclusive provincial jurisdiction but for a constitutional amendment in 1940. Unemployment insurance was not mentioned in the 1867 *Act*, but the Privy Council determined in the 1930s that it fell within provincial responsibility for "property and civil rights." The federal government, likewise, is also active in virtually all of the twenty-two policy areas identified in the Allaire Report as appropriate for exclusive provincial jurisdiction. In most of these areas (including culture, housing, education, recreation and sports, health, tourism, regional development, and the environment) federal involvement is based on the exercise of the spending power. The federal ability to directly regulate many of these areas has been hampered by a very narrow judicial interpretation of the federal authority over trade and commerce.[17]

An emerging critique of this structure is that such a permissive system is inefficient — it leads to too much overlapping of jurisdiction, too much government, and is too costly to the taxpayer. This appears to be the underlying critique mounted by the Allaire Report. The Report argues that the Canadian federal system is too expensive and that costs could be reduced by constitutionally limiting the role of the federal government. The Report would reduce the field of overlapping jurisdiction and restore some form of compartmentalization to the formal division of powers, largely by eliminating any federal presence in a wide range of policy areas.[18]

Is the case for reducing overlap and duplication a plausible one? In the Introduction to this paper, we suggested that any attempt to restore watertight compartments would be unwise and unworkable.

Notes

15. For a general discussion which makes these points, see G. Stevenson, "The Division of Powers in Canada: Evolution and Structure," and J. Whyte, "Constitutional Aspects of Economic Development Policy," in R. Simeon, ed., *The Division of Powers and Public Policy* (Toronto: University of Toronto Press, 1985).

16. It should be noted that the most recent judicial interpretations of the federal authority over trade and [commerce] and over matters of "national concern" have given a broader role to Parliament. For an extended analysis, see R. Howse, *Economic Union Social Justice and Constitutional Reform: Towards a High But Level Playing Field* (North York: York University Centre For Public Law and Public Policy, 1992).

17. See, however, the comments of Howse, ibid., who argues that recent judicial interpretations have opened the door for more extensive direct federal regulation.

18. As an aside, it is significant that the Allaire approach would not increase the jurisdiction of the provinces to any great degree since the provinces are already active in most of the areas that the Allaire approach would reserve to them.

153

[See also Monahan, at 251, stressing the interrelated nature of modern problems, and arguing that reform efforts should be directed at managing concurrent powers more efficiently, not at trying to redraft categorical boundaries.]

(c)   Federal–Provincial Financial Arrangements[1]

For a full understanding of the operation of Canada's federal system, we have to look beyond the division of legislative powers to a complex network of federal–provincial agreements negotiated within the executive branch of government. Although these agreements have some support in the division of legislative powers and other constitutional provisions, their dominant element is not law, but compact.

TAX COLLECTION AGREEMENTS

While the provinces have jurisdiction over direct taxation and licences,[2] the federal government has jurisdiction over direct and indirect taxation.[3] Because of this overlap, taxation by one level of government affects taxation by another. In order to coordinate tax collection, the federal and provincial governments have since 1941 entered into five-year taxation agreements. The federal government collects taxes for both itself and the provinces, and then returns the provincial share to each province.[4] The key exceptions to this arrangement are Quebec, which collects its own personal income tax and provincial corporate tax, and Quebec, Ontario and Alberta, which collect their own provincial corporate tax.

INTERGOVERNMENTAL TRANSFERS

Although the *Constitution Act, 1867* gave provincial governments responsibilities in social areas such as health, welfare, and education, and control over direct taxation, it gave the federal government greater power to raise money.[5] As matters of social concern became more important, the provinces found themselves increasingly dependent on federal help. The result has been a movement of money from the federal government to the provinces, regulated largely by means of federal–provincial agreements.

For its part, the federal government has asserted a general "spending power" to allocate its revenue whenever it deems this fit.[6] Although the spending power is not defined in the Constitution of Canada, it has a number of possible supports, such as the Crown's prerogative power to dispose of public revenues; s. 91(1A) of the *Constitution Act, 1867*, relating to "The Public Debt and Property"; s. 91(3), the taxation power; s. 102, authorizing a Consolidated Revenue Fund; and s. 106, the power to appropriate federal funds. The courts have said little about the spending power, although they have suggested that it should not amount to "regulation" of matters within provincial jurisdiction.[7]

Predictably, although provinces need money, they object to federal conditions, especially when these affect subject matter otherwise within provincial jurisdiction. Provinces have often argued that conditional federal spending in provincial areas is a *de facto* invasion of provincial authority. Yet they have little choice but to accept the restrictions if they want the money. A limit to the federal spending power was one of the five main demands of the Quebec Liberal party during the 1980s.[8] It would have been incorporated into both the Meech Lake[9] and Charlottetown[10] accords. On the other hand, intergovernmental transfers utilizing the spending power have been central to the growth of the Canadian welfare state and crucial in reducing regional inequality.

INTERGOVERNMENTAL TRANSFER AGREEMENTS

Social programs based on federal grants generally take the form of conditional or unconditional grants to the provinces. A conditional grant is one that is provided to a province on the condition that it comply with specific requirements. An unconditional grant lacks such requirements. In the past, conditional grants were often in the form of shared-cost arrangements in which the federal government agreed to pay a proportion of program costs on the condition that provincial government also pay a stipulated proportion. However, conditions may take many other forms, including legislative requirements.

Unconditional grants are generally in the form of block-funding arrangements or "block grants". In a block grant, the federal transfer is typically a dollar-per-capita amount multiplied by the provincial population. If there are no special administrative or legislative requirements, the block grant can be classed as unconditional.

The most important social programs involved post-secondary education (1952), hospital insurance (1957), the Canada Assistance Plan (1961), and medical insurance (1968, later combined with hospital insurance). After 1977, post-secondary education and health insurance were changed from a conditional grant and shared-cost basis to a block funding basis. They were treated as components of an "Established Programs Financing" (EPF) arrangement, comprising a combination of cash and tax-points transfers.[11] In 1984, Parliament enacted the *Canada Health Act*, returning health insurance to conditional grant status by prohibiting — among other things — transfers for services subject to extra billing or user fees.[12] The sums involved were huge: by 1993–94, for example, health insurance, post-secondary education, and Canada Assistance Plan payments amounted to about $28 billion, and equalization, another $8 billion, for an adjusted total of about $36.2 billion.[13]

In the last part of the 20th century, however, two trends emerged. First, federal influence over the intergovernmental transfer agreements began to decline. Second, in the mid-1990s, amid concern about rising deficits and accumulating debt, the federal government started to cut back on the size of the transfers. The shift in emphasis from cash payments to tax-point transfers in 1977 reduced federal leverage to withhold money in order to enforce compliance with its conditions and expectations. In 1996–1997, the post-secondary education and heath insurance programs in the EPF and the shared-cost Canada Assistance Program were combined into a single block grant, the Canada Health and Social Transfer (CHST).[14] Although the *Canada Health Act* conditions were kept, the former Canada Assistance Program requirements were reduced to a single bar against minimum residency requirements. Moreover, the CHST was significantly smaller than its predecessors,[15] further reducing the federal government's leverage to enforce the standards that remained.

By 1999–2000, the CHST was approximately $28 billion, and equalization was another $9 billion.[16] Although this was more than in the early 1990s, provinces complained that it fell short of provincial expenses, especially for health care. Meanwhile, the Auditor General of Canada criticized the federal transfer system for lack of transparency and accountability.[17]

The 2003 Romanow Report on health care reform recommended an increase in federal health transfer payments of $15 billion over three years.[18] After the Report, the federal government agreed to provide an additional $16 billion over five years for provincial and territorial health costs.[19] As well, starting on April 1, 2004, the CHST was split into a Canada Health Transfer (CHT) and a Canada Social Transfer (CST),[20] and the first ministers signed a "10-Year Plan to Strengthen Health Care".[21] Under the plan, the provinces agreed to establish benchmarks for wait times, and the federal government agreed to provide $41 billion to the provinces and territories for health care over a 10-year period. For 2006–2007, federal cash funding for the CHT and wait times assistance was to reach $21.3 billion; by 2013–14 it was to reach $30.5 billion.[22] Meanwhile, the cash portion of the CST was to come to $9.5 million.[23] Despite the scale of these amounts, it seemed likely that the customary federal–provincial financial tensions would continue.

EQUALIZATION

One attribute of a federal system is its capacity to improve the living conditions of residents in its poorer units. Some provinces have far less fiscal capacity — that is, fewer resources available for funding social services — than others. This situation is sometimes referred to as horizontal fiscal imbalance. To address this situation, s. 36 of the *Constitution Act, 1982* commits Canadian governments to the principle of equalization.[24] The principle is implemented through equalization payments, a system of unconditional federal grants to provinces to help ensure "reasonably comparable levels of public services at reasonably comparable levels of taxation."[25] The amounts are significant: for 2007–2008, under the 2007 budget formula discussed below, federal equalization payments were expected to come to $12.7 billion.[26]

Equalization was formally instituted in 1957, building on a 1940 Rowell-Sirois Commission recommendation that provinces should be entitled to financial assistance on the basis of relative fiscal need.[27] The basic idea is to help poorer provinces bring their revenue up to an agreed national standard of fiscal capacity.[28] The higher this standard, the higher the overall level of equalization, and *vice versa*.[29] From 1986 to the early 21st century, the target standard was the average per capita revenue of Ontario, Quebec, British Columbia, Manitoba, and Saskatchewan. Provinces below that standard received payments; those above it did not.

The formula for equalization contributions is subject to renegotiating in five-year agreements. Unlike previous arrangements, the 2004–2005 "New Framework" formula was subjected to a fixed floor and ceiling. Although equalization payments would not fall below a specified level and would rise at regular intervals, there would be an upper limit on the total amount of redistribution possible. As well, the principle of redistribution based on relative fiscal capacity was qualified in 2005 by the offshore accords with Nova Scotia[30] and Newfoundland and Labrador.[31] For a specific period, the accords allowed these provinces to keep all their offshore natural resources without any reduction in their levels of equalization.

As a result of the 2004–2005 changes, the original principle of basing allocations on comparative fiscal capacity was diluted. The new upper limit on total funds provided greater stability for federal budgeting, but it meant that more money for one province was financed by less for another. Moreover, under the offshore accords, some provinces were being treated differently from others. Meanwhile, the federal government continued its policy of "associated equalization", adjusting the cash portions of CHT and CST to compensate for the fact that their tax point portions generated less revenue in some provinces than others.[32] As result of all these arrangements, although Ontario taxpayers contributed more than 40% of equalization revenues, Ontario ended up with a lower per capita fiscal capacity than the poorest recipient province, Newfoundland and Labrador.[33] Predictably, there were calls for reform.

In 2006, for example, a Council of the Federation advisory panel recommended that equalization should be based on the fiscal capacity of all 10 provinces, and that the revenue pool should include all natural resource revenue.[34] Later that year, a federally-appointed panel headed by former Alberta government minister Al O'Brien agreed that all 10 provinces should be included in the fiscal capacity calculation, but recommended that only 50% of provincial revenues should be included in the revenue pool, and that a cap should be

applied to ensure that equalization should not result in a receiving province with a greater fiscal capacity than that of the lowest non-receiving province.[35]

The spring 2007 federal budget ended the New Framework system and implemented many of the O'Brien panel proposals. As the panel had recommended, the budget based payments to poorer provinces on the average fiscal capacity of all 10 provinces, and included 50% of their revenues from natural resources.[36] Associated equalization was removed from the CHT and CST,[37] and regular equalization payments were capped to prevent equalization recipients from gaining greater fiscal capacities than donor provinces.[38] The budget gave Newfoundland and Labrador and Nova Scotia the choice of continuing under the old equalization program for the duration of their offshore accords, or opting into the new program sooner.[39] The arrangement pleased neither these provinces nor Saskatchewan, and the equalization debates continued.[40]

Despite their complex and technical framework, the debates about equalization are central to Canadian federalism. Because of big differences in natural resources, population bases, and manufacturing potential, the Canadian provinces have never been economic equals. Under s. 109 of the *Constitution Act, 1867*, the framers of Confederation gave most of the ownership of natural resources to the provinces.[41] Because of the growing value of resources such as oil, this ownership provides great new wealth for provinces such as Alberta, and potential prosperity for provinces such as Newfoundland and Labrador and Nova Scotia.[42] Historically, many of the new resource-rich regions have lacked the manufacturing and population base of central Canada, and have felt neglected by central Canadian policy makers.[43] Not surprisingly, resource-rich present donors[44] will want to keep what they regard as theirs. For its part, a donor province without significant natural resources[45] will not want resource revenues to be included in equalization calculations if they are not also deducted from equalization payments. On the other hand, resource revenue differences are a major source of the inequality that equalization is intended to address, and some provinces[46] lack either resource or non-resource revenues. Donors today may become recipients in future. Arguably, then, provincial resource ownership and equalization are both key Canadian concerns — and so are the challenges of balancing between them.

Notes

1. See generally Dyck, ch. 18; Hogg 2007, ch. 6; Peter W. Hogg, *Constitutional Law of Canada*, 4th ed. (unabridged) (Scarborough, Ont.: Carswell, 1997), ch. 6; Robert J. Jackson & Doreen Jackson, *Canadian Government in Transition: Disruption and Continuity* (Scarborough, Ont.: Prentice-Hall, 1996) at 85–94; W.I. Gillespie, *Tax, Borrow and Spend: Financing Federal Spending in Canada* (Ottawa: Carleton University Press, 1991); J.-D. Fréchette, Library of Parliament, *Federal–Provincial Fiscal Arrangements* (Ottawa: Library of Parliament, 1990); K. Banting, *The Welfare State and Canadian Federalism*, 2d ed. (Montreal & Kingston: McGill-Queen's University Press, 1987); M. Krasnik, ed., *Fiscal Federalism*, vol. 65, Royal Commission on the Economic Union and Development Prospects for Canada (Toronto: University of Toronto Press, 1985); K. Norrice *et al.*, *Federalism and Economic Union in Canada*, vol. 59, Royal Commission on the Economic Union and Development Prospects for Canada (Toronto: University of Toronto Press, 1985); Privy Council Office, *Report of the Royal Commission on the Economic Union and Development Prospects for Canada* (Macdonald Commission) (Ottawa: Supply and Services Canada, 1985), vol. 3, ch. 22; House of Commons Task Force on Federal–Provincial Fiscal Arrangements, *Fiscal Federalism in Canada* (Ottawa: Supply and Services Canada, 1981); *Federal Transfers to Provinces and Territories*, online: Department of Finance <http://www.fin.gc.ca/FEDPROV/eqpe.html>.

2. Sections 92(2) and 92(9) of the *Constitution Act, 1867*, respectively. The provinces were also given the ownership of most public property (and resulting royalty potential) within their boundaries: s. 109.

3. *Ibid.*, s. 91(3). For the distinction between direct and indirect taxation, see Hogg, *Constitutional Law of Canada*, 4th ed. (unabridged), *supra* note 1, ch. 30.2.

4. To facilitate this process, provincial tax rates are expressed as a proportion of federal tax or tax bases: see Hogg 2007, ch. 6.4.

5. That is, the unrestricted taxation power in s. 91(3). For the main provincial sources of revenue, see *supra* note 2.

6. See, for example, Hogg 2007, ch. 6.8; and Macdonald Commission, *supra* note 1 at 243–44.

7. See the comment in *Re Canada Assistance Plan*, [1991] 1 S.C.R. 525 at 567, cited in Hogg 2007, in ch. 6.8(a), where the Court said that the mere withholding of money the federal government had previously spent within provincial jurisdiction did *not* amount to regulation.

8. Speech by G. Rémillard, Quebec Minister of Justice, "Nothing Less than Quebec's Dignity is at Stake in Future Constitutional Discussions" Mont Gabriel, Quebec (9 May 1986) at 7.

9. (Proposed) *Constitution Amendment, 1987*, part 7.

10. *Draft Legal Text*, 9 October 1992, Part IV.

11. Under the tax-point transfers, the federal government agrees to lower its levels of taxation by a specified amount, enabling provinces to raise theirs correspondingly. Unlike continuing cash transfers, which can be withheld to enforce compliance with the terms of an agreement, a tax-point transfer is a one-time arrangement.

12. *Canada Health Act*, R.S.C. 1985, c. 6, ss. 7–13; and *Extra-billing and User Charge Regulations* (SOR/86-259). See further *The Constitution and Health Care* and *Chaoulli* in this chapter.

13. 1999 Federal Budget tables, reproduced in Rand Dyck, *Canadian Politics: Critical Approaches*, 3d ed. (Scarborough, Ont.: Thomson Nelson, 2000) at 414–15.

14. See Dyck, *supra* note 1, ch. 17, text at Table 17.3; and Jackson & Jackson, *supra* note 1 at 91–92.

15. The new CHST constituted a significant reduction in federal payments: Dyck, *ibid.*

16. *Supra* note 13.

17. Canada, 2002 *Status Report of Auditor General: Federal Support of Health Care Delivery* (Ottawa: Office of Auditor General of Canada, 2002), ch. 3; and Canada, *1999 Report of the Auditor General of Canada: Federal Support of Health Care Delivery* (Ottawa: Office of Auditor General of Canada, November 1999), ch. 29.

18. Canada, *Final Report of the Commission on the Future of Health Care in Canada* (Ottawa: Communications Group, November 28, 2002) (Roy Romanow Report).

19. *Federal Transfers to Provinces and Territories*, online: Department of Finance <http://www.fin.gc.ca/FEDPROV/eqpe.html> (accessed February 2003). The sum of $5.2 billion included $1.0 billion for the Health Reform Fund, mentioned below, $2.5 billion for miscellaneous programs, such as official languages and youth justice, and $1.7 billion for territorial formula financing.

20. *Ibid.*

21. *First Minister's Meeting on the Future of Health Care 2004, A 10-year Plan to Strengthen Health Care* (16 September 2004), online: Health Canada <http://www.hc-sc.gc.ca/hcs-sss/delivery-prestation/fptcollab/2004-fmm-rpm/index_e.html>

22. *2007 Budget Plan*, Chart A4.7, online: Department of Finance Canada <http://www.budget.gc.ca/2007/bp/bpa4e.html#health>.

23. *Ibid.*, "Social Transfer", online: Department of Finance Canada <http://www.budget.gc.ca/2007/bp/bpc4e.html#social>.

24. Section 36(2).

25. *Ibid.* A somewhat similar system, the Territorial Formula Financing program, applies to the northern territories: see Expert Panel on Equalization and Territorial Formula Financing, "Territorial Formula Financing: A Brief History" in *Achieving a National Purpose: Putting Equalization Back on Track* (26 May 2006) at Annex 3 <http://www.eqtff-pfft.ca/english/tfftreasury/annex3-1.asp>. For the latest version of the TFF program, see *The Budget Plan 2007: Aspire to a Stronger, Safer, Better Canada* (19 March 2007), online: Department of Finance Canada <http://www.budget.gc.ca/2007/pdf/bp2007e.pdf> at 117–19.

26. *Equalization Program*, online: Department of Finance Canada <http://www.fin.gc.ca/FEDPROV/eqpe.html>. As noted earlier, for 2003–2004, equalization payments were projected to come to more than $10.5 billion; for 2005–2006, they were to exceed $11 billion: Expert Panel on Equalization and Territorial Formula Financing, *Achieving a National Purpose: Putting Equalization Back on Track* (26 May 2006) <http://www.eqtff-pfft.ca/ereports/EQ_Report_e.pdf>, at 8.

27. *Achieving a National Purpose, ibid.* at 20.

28. Hogg 2007, *supra* note 1, part 6.6.

29. From 1957 to 1967, the standard was based on the average per capita fiscal capacity of the two wealthiest provinces; from 1967 to 1973, it was lowered to the average per capita fiscal capacity of all 10 provinces; from 1967 to 1973 this formula continued, but with some high-yielding non-renewable natural resources excluded from the calculation; and from 1973 to 2004 all resources were included, but the standard was based on the average per capita fiscal capacity of five provinces, excluding oil-rich Alberta.

30. On January 28, 2005.

31. On February 14, 2005.

32. See Council of the Federation, Advisory Council on Fiscal Imbalance, *Reconciling the Irreconcilable: Addressing Canada's Fiscal Imbalance* (31 March 2006), at 72–79 <http://www.councilofthefederation.ca/pdfs/Report_Fiscalim_Mar3106.pdf>. The Council also recommended that the cash portion of the CHT and SCT should be tied directly to the size of the recipient populations, an approach urged by Ontario. This approach, and a similar recommendation in the O'Brien Report (*infra* note 34 at 47), were adopted in the 2007 budget: *infra* note 35.

33. E.g., Thomas J. Courchene, *Vertical and Horizontal Fiscal Imbalances: An Ontario Perspective, Background Notes for*

157

a *Presentation to the Standing Committee on Finance House of Commons* (4 May 2005), online: Institute for Research on Public Policy <http://www.irpp. org/miscpubs/archive/tjc_050504.pdf>; Keith Leslie, "Using equalization to fix so-called fiscal gap unfair to Ontario: McGuinty" *Canadian Press* (10 May 2006), online: Canada.com <http://www.canada.com/topics/news/national/story.html?id=763cc2b3-3dce-4ec4-871a-1b37f5ce4351&k=49784&p=1>; Marie Bountrogianni, Fairness: Delivering Results for the People of Ontario: Speaking Notes for Minister Bountrogianni to the Senate Committee on National Finance, Government of Ontario, online: Fairness.ca <http://www.fairness.ca/english/milestones/nov21_06.asp>.

34. Council of the Federation, *supra* 32, at 87. This recommendation contrasted with the election promise of the new Conservative government to exclude non-renewable natural resource revenue from equalization formulas: see "Fiscal Imbalance", in Conservative Party of Canada, *Federal Election Platform 2006: Stand Up for Canada* <http://www.conservative.ca/media/20060113-Platform.pdf>.

35. Expert Panel on Equalization and Territorial Formula Financing, *Achieving a National Purpose: Putting Equalization Back on Track* (26 May 2006), at 12–13 <http://www.eqtff-pfft.ca/epreports/EQ_Report_e.pdf>.

36. *The Budget Plan 2007: Aspire to a Stronger, Safer, Better Canada* (19 March 2007) at 113, online: Department of Finance Canada <http://www.budget.gc.ca/2007/pdf/bp2007e.pdf>.

37. Associated equalization had adjusted the cash portion of the CHT and CST to compensate for inequalities between provinces in the revenue potential of the tax point portion of these payments: Council of the Federation, *supra* note 32. As sought by Ontario and as recommended by the Council of the Federation and the O'Brien panel, the cash portion of the CHT and the CST was to be paid on a strict per capita basis: *Budget Plan, ibid.* at 359.

38. *Ibid.* at 341–42.

39. *Ibid.* at 115 and 347.

40. Although the old formula that was offered to Newfoundland and Labrador and Nova Scotia kept the offshore accords, without any cap on equalization payments, the payments themselves looked as if they would be smaller than the payments under the new formula. The Atlantic provinces argued that their offshore accords were supposed to apply to whatever equalization formula was in place at a given time, and should therefore apply to the new formula as well. Saskatchewan was also unhappy with the equalization cap, and considered suing the federal government for interference with the equitable principles underlying equalization and with provincial ownership of natural resources: Gloria Galloway, "Saskatchewan threatens to take Ottawa to court" *The Globe and Mail* (14 June 2007) at A1 and A4. Meanwhile, the Premier of Ontario warned against any side deals that would require Ontario residents to contribute to equalization payments to any provinces with fiscal capacities greater than that of Ontario: Gloria Galloway and Oliver Moore, "Ontario talks tough on equalization" *The Globe and Mail* (15 June 2007) at A9.

41. See Chapter 3 above and Gerard V. La Forest, *Natural Resources and Public Property under the Canadian Constitution* (Toronto: University of Toronto Press, 1969), ch. 2 Although this ownership was originally denied to the prairie provinces, they finally gained it in 1930: *ibid.*, ch. 3.

42. Canada has the second largest oil reserves in the world, and many of these are contained in the oil sands of northern Alberta: In Depth, "Alberta's Oilsands" *CBC News* (updated 6 March 2007), online: cbc.ca <http://www.cbc.ca/news/background/oil/alberta_oilsands.html>. There are also significant petroleum reserves in other regions, such as the maritime area adjacent to Newfoundland and Labrador: CBC News, In Depth, *ibid.* (updated 3 June 2006), online: cbc.ca <http://www.cbc.ca/money/story/2006/06/02/newfoundland-oil.html>.

43. See, for example, *Roger Gibbins and Loleen Berdahl, Western Visions, Western Futures: Perspectives on the West in Canada* (Peterborough, Ont.: Broadview Press, 2003), ch. 2; Roger Gibbins, "Western Alienation" in R. Douglas Francis and Howard Palmer, eds., *The Prairie West: Historical Readings* (Edmonton: Pica Pica Press, 1985) at 585–610 and T.D. Regehr, "Western Canada and the Burden of National Transportation Policies" in David Jay Bercuson, ed., *Canada and the Burden of Unity* (Toronto: Macmillan: 1977) at 115–41. In the Maritimes — where recent offshore oil (Newfoundland and Labrador and Nova Scotia) and nickel (Newfoundland and Labrador) discoveries could transform provincial economies, regional economic discontent goes as far back as Confederation: see E.R. Forbes and D.A. Muise, eds., *The Atlantic Provinces in Confederation* (Toronto: University of Toronto Press 1993).

44. Such as Alberta.

45. I.e., Ontario, whose natural resources do not constitute a major proportion of its total revenue.

46. Such as Newfoundland and Labrador.

(d) *Social Union* Agreement[†]

NOTE

For a long time, provincial governments have sought some control over the direction of joint social programs that are funded wholly or mainly by the federal government. They were especially upset at the unilateral federal cutbacks to the Canada Health and Social Transfer that were made after 1995. They also wanted an end to future federal transfers to individuals. For its part, the federal government was concerned about provincial violations of the rules or intent of federally funded pro-

† *A Framework to Improve the Social Union for Canadians: An Agreement between the Government of Canada and the Governments of the Provinces and Territories*, 4 February 1999.

grams, and it insisted on its right to continue making transfers to individuals.

In February 1999, all first ministers except one agreed on a modest set of principles that addressed some of the parties' concerns. Its core was a general commitment by all governments to consult before making unilateral changes that substantially affected other governments. For a number of reasons, including a concern that the agreement recognized the federal spending power, the Quebec government refused to sign.

EXTRACT

The following agreement is based upon a mutual respect between orders of government and a willingness to work more closely together to meet the needs of Canadians.

1. Principles

Canada's social union should reflect and give expression to the fundamental values of Canadians — equality, respect for diversity, fairness, individual dignity and responsibility, and mutual aid and our responsibilities for one another.

Within their respective constitutional jurisdictions and powers, governments commit to the following principles:

All Canadians are equal

- Treat all Canadians with fairness and equity
- Promote equality of opportunity for all Canadians
- Respect the equality, rights and dignity of all Canadian women and men and their diverse needs

Meeting the needs of Canadians

- Ensure access for all Canadians, wherever they live or move in Canada, to essential social programs and services of reasonably comparable quality
- Provide appropriate assistance to those in need
- Respect the principles of medicare: comprehensiveness, universality, portability, public administration and accessibility
- Promote the full and active participation of all Canadians in Canada's social and economic life
- Work in partnership with individuals, families, communities, voluntary organizations, business and labour, and ensure appropriate opportunities for Canadians to have meaningful input into social policies and programs

Sustaining social programs and services

- Ensure adequate, affordable, stable and sustainable funding for social programs

Aboriginal peoples of Canada

- For greater certainty, nothing in this agreement abrogates or derogates from any Aboriginal, treaty or other rights of Aboriginal peoples including self-government

2. Mobility within Canada

All governments believe that the freedom of movement of Canadians to pursue opportunities anywhere in Canada is an essential element of Canadian citizenship.

Governments will ensure that no new barriers to mobility are created in new social policy initiatives.

Governments will eliminate, within three years, any residency-based policies or practices which constrain access to post-secondary education, training, health and social services and social assistance unless they can be demonstrated to be reasonable and consistent with the principles of the Social Union Framework.

Accordingly, sector Ministers will submit annual reports to the Ministerial Council identifying residency-based barriers to access and providing action plans to eliminate them.

Governments are also committed to ensure, by July 1, 2001, full compliance with the mobility provisions of the Agreement on Internal Trade by all entities subject to those provisions, including the requirements for mutual recognition of occupational qualifications and for eliminating residency requirements for access to employment opportunities.

3. Informing Canadians — Public Accountability and Transparency

Canada's Social Union can be strengthened by enhancing each government's transparency and accountability to its constituents. Each government therefore agrees to:

Achieving and Measuring Results

- Monitor and measure outcomes of its social programs and report regularly to its constituents on the performance of these programs
- Share information and best practices to support the development of outcome measures, and work with other governments to develop, over time,

159

comparable indicators to measure progress on agreed objectives
- Publicly recognize and explain the respective roles and contributions of governments
- Use funds transferred from another order of government for the purposes agreed and pass on increases to its residents
- Use third parties, as appropriate, to assist in assessing progress on social priorities

Involvement of Canadians

- Ensure effective mechanisms for Canadians to participate in developing social priorities and reviewing outcomes

Ensuring fair and transparent practices

- Make eligibility criteria and service commitments for social programs publicly available
- Have in place appropriate mechanisms for citizens to appeal unfair administrative practices and bring complaints about access and service
- Report publicly on citizen's appeals and complaints, ensuring that confidentiality requirements are met

4. Working in partnership for Canadians

Joint Planning and Collaboration

The Ministerial Council has demonstrated the benefits of joint planning and mutual help through which governments share knowledge and learn from each other.

Governments therefore agree to

- Undertake joint planning to share information on social trends, problems and priorities and to work together to identify priorities for collaborative action
- Collaborate on implementation of joint priorities when this would result in more effective and efficient service to Canadians, including as appropriate joint development of objectives and principles, clarification of roles and responsibilities, and flexible implementation to respect diverse needs and circumstances, complement existing measures and avoid duplication

Reciprocal Notice and Consultation

The actions of one government or order of government often have significant effects on other governments. In a manner consistent with the principles of our system of parliamentary government and the budget-making process, governments therefore agree to:

- Give one another advance notice prior to implementation of a major change in a social policy or program which will likely substantially affect another government
- Offer to consult prior to implementing new social policies and programs that are likely to substantially affect other governments or the social union more generally. Governments participating in these consultations will have the opportunity to identify potential duplication and to propose alternative approaches to achieve flexible and effective implementation

Equitable Treatment

For any new Canada-wide social initiatives, arrangements made with one province/territory will be made available to all provinces/territories in a manner consistent with their diverse circumstances.

Aboriginal Peoples

Governments will work with the Aboriginal peoples of Canada to find practical solutions to address their pressing needs.

5. The federal spending power — Improving social programs for Canadians

Social transfers to provinces and territories

The use of the federal spending power under the Constitution has been essential to the development of Canada's social union. An important use of the spending power by the Government of Canada has been to transfer money to the provincial and territorial governments. These transfers support the delivery of social programs and services by provinces and territories in order to promote equality of opportunity and mobility for all Canadians and to pursue Canada-wide objectives.

Conditional social transfers have enabled governments to introduce new and innovative social programs, such as Medicare, and to ensure that they are available to all Canadians. When the federal government uses such conditional transfers, whether cost-shared or block-funded, it should proceed in a cooperative manner that is respectful of the provincial and territorial governments and their priorities.

Funding predictability

The Government of Canada will consult with provincial and territorial governments at least one year prior to renewal or significant funding changes in existing social transfers to provinces/territories, unless otherwise agreed, and will build due notice provisions into any new social transfers to provincial/territorial governments.

New Canada-wide initiatives supported by transfers to Provinces and Territories

With respect to any new Canada-wide initiatives in health care, post-secondary education, social assistance and social services that are funded through intergovernmental transfers, whether block-funded or cost-shared, the Government of Canada will:

- Work collaboratively with all provincial and territorial governments to identify Canada-wide priorities and objectives
- Not introduce such new initiatives without the agreement of a majority of provincial governments

Each provincial and territorial government will determine the detailed program design and mix best suited to its own needs and circumstances to meet the agreed objectives.

A provincial/territorial government which, because of its existing programming, does not require the total transfer to fulfil the agreed objectives would be able to reinvest any funds not required for those objectives in the same or a related priority area.

The Government of Canada and the provincial/territorial governments will agree on an accountability framework for such new social initiatives and investments.

All provincial and territorial governments that meet or commit to meet the agreed Canada-wide objectives and agree to respect the accountability framework will receive their share of available funding.

Direct federal spending

Another use of the federal spending power is making transfers to individuals and to organizations in order to promote equality of opportunity, mobility, and other Canada-wide objectives.

When the federal government introduces new Canada-wide initiatives funded through direct transfers to individuals or organizations for health care, post-secondary education, social assistance and social services, it will, prior to implementation, give at least three months' notice and offer to consult. Governments participating in these consultations will have the opportunity to identify potential duplication and

to propose alternative approaches to achieve flexible and effective implementation.

6. Dispute Avoidance and Resolution

Governments are committed to working collaboratively to avoid and resolve intergovernmental disputes. Respecting existing legislative provisions, mechanisms to avoid and resolve disputes should:

- Be simple, timely, efficient, effective and transparent
- Allow maximum flexibility for governments to resolve disputes in a non-adversarial way
- Ensure that sectors design processes appropriate to their needs
- Provide for appropriate use of third parties for expert assistance and advice while ensuring democratic accountability by elected officials

Dispute avoidance and resolution will apply to commitments on mobility, intergovernmental transfers, interpretation of the Canada Health Act principles, and, as appropriate, on any new joint initiative.

Sector Ministers should be guided by the following process, as appropriate:

DISPUTE AVOIDANCE

- Governments are committed to working together and avoiding disputes through information-sharing, joint planning, collaboration, advance notice and early consultation, and flexibility in implementation

SECTOR NEGOTIATIONS

- Sector negotiations to resolve disputes will be based on joint fact-finding
- A written joint fact-finding report will be submitted to governments involved, who will have the opportunity to comment on the report before its completion
- Governments involved may seek assistance of a third party for fact-finding, advice, or mediation
- At the request of either party in a dispute, fact-finding or mediation reports will be made public

REVIEW PROVISIONS

- Any government can require a review of a decision or action one year after it enters into effect or when changing circumstances justify

Each government involved in a dispute may consult and seek advice from third parties, including interested or knowledgeable persons or groups, at all stages of the process.

Governments will report publicly on an annual basis on the nature of intergovernmental disputes and their resolution.

Role of the Ministerial Council

The Ministerial Council will support sector Ministers by collecting information on effective ways of implementing the agreement and avoiding disputes and receiving reports from jurisdictions on progress on commitments under the Social Union Framework Agreement.

7. Review of the Social Union Framework Agreement

By the end of the third year of the Framework Agreement, governments will jointly undertake a full review of the Agreement and its implementation and make appropriate adjustments to the Framework as required. This review will ensure significant opportunities for input and [feedback] from Canadians and all interested parties, including social policy experts, private sector and voluntary organizations.

(e)   The Constitution and Health Care†

Howard Leeson

NOTE

The Canadian health care system is arguably as distinctive a national symbol as hockey or the maple leaf. The 2002 Romanow Commission captured the nature and the status of this system when it said that:

> Canadians consider equal and timely access to medically necessary health care services on the basis of need as a right of citizenship, not a privilege of status or wealth.[1]

Yet, as everyone knows, this symbol is under siege. Overcrowded waiting emergency rooms, long wait times, de-listed medical procedures, c-difficile outbreaks in hospitals, family doctor and nursing shortages, and escalating costs, are only some of the more obvious symptoms. As seen at the beginning of this chapter, Canadian health care concerns have been an ongoing concern in federal–provincial relations, where provinces have demanded more money and flexibility, while federal governments have struggled to balance their own budgetary needs on one hand, and their commit-

ment to maintain the *Canada Health Act*,[2] on the other.

Underlying these questions of value, money, and politics are some very complex constitutional issues. In the following extract, can you see what Leeson identifies as the main constitutional foundations for (a) provincial and (b) federal involvement in the Canadian health care system? Do you agree with the supporters or the critics of federal constitutional involvement in this area? Do the criticisms of the federal spending power in this area apply to the federal criminal law power? Compare the discussion here with the Supreme Court's comments on legislative jurisdiction and health care in the *Chaoulli* decision[3] later in this chapter. What level or levels of government will need to act to address the concerns in that decision?

Notes

1. The five basic principles of the *Act* are public administration: s. 8; comprehensiveness: s. 9; universality: s. 10; portability: s. 11; and accessibility: s. 12: *Canada Health Act*, R.S.C. 1985, c. C-6. See further, Library of Parliament Parliamentary Research Branch, *The Canada Health Act:*

---

† Royal Commission on the Future of Health Care in *Canada, Constitutional Jurisdiction Over Health and Health Care Services in Canada*, Discussion Paper No. 12 by Howard Leeson, August 2002, Catalogue No. CP32-79/12-2002E-IN; ISBN 0-662-32782-9 <http://dsp-psd.pwgsc.gc.ca/Collection/CP32-79-12-2002E.pdf>, at 3, 5–16, 18, 20, and 24–25. [Notes omitted.] Reproduced with permission of Dr. Howard Leeson.

Overview and Options, by Odette Madore (Ottawa: Library of Parliament, May 21, 2004).

2. Canada, *Commission on the Future of Health Care in Canada. Building on Values: The Future of Health Care in Canada: Final Report* (Ottawa: The Commission, 2002) at xvi.

3. *Chaoulli v. Quebec (A.G.)*, [2005] 1 S.C.R. 791.

EXTRACT

I. HEALTH CARE AND THE CONSTITUTION

Any examination of constitutional powers with regard to health care in Canada must be based upon the recognition of several important considerations. First, "health care" is not a head of power in the Canadian Constitution in the same way that banking, buoys, or Sable Island is. The common perception is that health care is a matter of provincial jurisdiction. Such a statement is at best misleading. As Peter Hogg, one of Canada's preeminent constitutional experts[,] says:

> Health is not a single matter assigned by the Canadian constitution exclusively to one level of government. Like inflation, and the environment, health is an 'amorphous topic' which is distributed to the federal parliament or the provincial legislatures depending on the purpose and effect of the particular health measure at issue. (Hogg 1998, 445)

Why then is there a perception that the provinces have exclusive jurisdiction in this important social area? Part of the misunderstanding arises from the fact that section 92(7) assigns exclusive provincial control over hospitals and psychiatric institutions. Insofar as health care was concerned in 1867, it was thought of in terms of disease and hospitals....

[Leeson says that the other reasons for the misunderstanding are also historical. He says that judicial interpretation by the Judicial Committee expanded the scope of provincial powers that are closely related to health, education, and other social concerns. Although these fields were not considered to be important state responsibilities in 1867, the public demanded government intervention now in the 20th century, especially after the depression of the 1930s. But despite the high jurisdictional profile of the provinces, it was the federal government that had the greater financial resources. As a result, the financial government intervened financially more than jurisdictionally. As a result, the growth of health and other social programs in Canada has involved both the provinces and the federal government. Leeson says that the federal government's role is not just financial, as it retains broad legislative powers with potential application to health care, especially in the post-Judicial Committee era.]

. . . .

With this background we can now turn to the explicit heads of constitutional power involved in health care.

Provincial Powers

92(7) — The Establishment, Maintenance, and Management of Hospitals, Asylums, Charities, and Eleemosynary Institutions In and For the Province, Other Than Marine Hospitals.

This section constitutes one of the central sources of provincial jurisdiction in the area of health care. By natural implication, the regulation of personnel, and functions associated with these institutions broadens the ambit of jurisdiction. Originally these institutions were under the control of private and religious groups. The fact that most are now owned by the government makes their control a matter of government proprietorship also. It should be noted that there are major exceptions to the above. The first is marine hospitals, which are explicitly mentioned in 91(11)[,] and hospitals and care in federal territories and defense establishments.

92(10) — Local Works and Undertakings...

This section could be used to bolster provincial control since most hospitals are not parts of interprovincial enterprises. However, many health care delivery organizations, such as nursing homes, are now both private and national in scope, and might be susceptible to federal regulation through competition legislation, or by virtue of the fact that they are economic enterprises that are covered by treaties such as NAFTA.

92(13) — Property and Civil Rights in the Province

This section, aside from the fact that it has received wide ambit in judicial interpretation, is the basis by which the provinces regulate labour relations and the professions involved in the health care field.

92(16) — Generally All Matters of a Merely Local or Private Nature in the Province

This section is similar to Section 92(10) but involves private matters as well. This would bolster the provincial power to regulate religious health care delivery agencies.

93 — In and for each province the Legislature may exclusively make laws in relation to education...

This section allows the provinces to regulate the education and training of all health care delivery personnel. It also allows them, in conjunction with section 92(13), to establish self-regulating professions and registration procedures in the field.

95 — In each Province the legislature may make laws in relation to... immigration....

This is a concurrent power with the federal government and provincial laws may not be "repugnant" to federal laws. Immigration has been important in some provinces attempting to cope with a lack of domestic health care personnel by bringing immigrants into the province.

These are the major provincial constitutional powers over health care. They are supplemented by the general power over provincial public lands and assets, as well as the provincial taxation power.

Federal Powers

Section 91 —

The most important powers in this section have been the enumerated heads, which we will examine below. It is worth noting, however, that the residual or general power remains. Despite the fact that it was restricted by judicial interpretation in the period up to 1930, some think it possible that it could be important in the future. Indeed, the Supreme Court has several times indicated that it remains a possible potent source of federal power.[2] The most often cited examples of "national concern" usually involve health matters.

> There are however, cases where uniformity of law throughout the country is not merely desirable but essential, in the sense that the problem 'is beyond the power of the provinces to deal with.' ... The often-cited case of an epidemic of pestilence is a good example. The failure by one province to take preventative measures would probably lead to the spreading of disease into those provinces, which had taken preventative measures. (Hogg 1998, 415)

The recent events after September 11, 2001, and the attacks in the United States, have led the national government to look at health measures designed to combat the release of deadly diseases such as smallpox. As well the federal government has acted to stockpile needed drugs to cope with something like the mailing of envelopes with deadly anthrax bacterial spores in them. No one would dispute that these are health measures, but they are generated from security and national defense concerns.

91(2) — The Regulation of Trade and Commerce

This head of power was thought in 1867 to be one of the most important. Given the economic expectations associated with Confederation, and the anticipated role of the federal government in this area, it was a reasonable expectation. However, judicial review of this section in relation to section 92(13) led to the diminution of the federal power over trade and commerce. There is too little time in this paper to fully explore the constitutional changes and debates involved in this matter. However, one aspect is crucial, the regulation of international trade and commerce. How is this related to health care and the delivery of health care services? For the most part it relates to the production and trade in health care related goods and services. Most of the products relevant to the delivery of health care[,] such as machines, drugs, tools, and construction of facilities, are produced in the private sector. Quite often they are imported from another country. They are treated no differently than other products that are produced or traded. As well, many of the services related to health care delivery, such as training programs, are also undertaken by the private sector, often with manuals or procedures developed in other countries and sold in Canada. In short, the economic aspect of health care is both international and subject to regulation by the federal government.

This is especially true when it comes to comprehensive international agreements. In agreements like NAFTA general regulations about trade and trade practices are put in place, even though the implementation of those regulations may trench on an area of provincial jurisdiction. Thus obligations in the field of health care may result from general trade agreements, despite the fact that health care delivery is largely a provincial responsibility.[3] We will explore this more fully later in this paper.

91(9) — Beacons, Buoys, Lighthouses and Sable Island

Since the federal government was given exclusive jurisdiction over Sable Island, all health care related matters on the island come under federal jurisdiction.

91(11) — Quarantine and the Establishment and Maintenance of Marine Hospitals

The federal government has exclusive jurisdiction over marine hospitals in Canada. As well, it has the health-related power of quarantine.

91(22) — Patents of Invention and Discovery

This power has had a major impact on health care in Canada. Patents allow the individual or corporation to claim the exclusive right to manufacture and profit from "inventions." This is particularly important with regard to drugs that are now used extensively in the prevention and treatment of illness. The cost of these drugs has risen dramatically in the last two decades, in part because Canada, along with other governments in the developed world, has extended the time of patent protection. In Canada it was lengthened from 7 years to 21 years. The effect of this has been to preclude generic manufacturers from providing cheaper copies of the patented products, usually until after their effectiveness has been superceded by newer patented drugs.

91(24) — Indians and Land Reserved for Indians

Initially this power included all health matters for "Indian" people (excluding Metis in most cases). This is now not the case. The matter of health care and the delivery of health care services for "Indians" is a matter of ongoing negotiation between federal, provincial, and First Nations governments. First Nations generally want to deliver their own services wherever possible. However, they believe that the federal government is responsible for the cost of this care under treaty obligation. For its part, the federal government has now restricted its fiscal role to First Nations people on reserves. Provincial governments have now unwillingly assumed the cost of health care for all Aboriginal peoples off reserves.[4]

91(27) — The Criminal law...

The criminal law power is intimately associated with matters of health care. By using its power to declare something a crime the federal government has the power to restrict or expand many health activities. Current examples that illustrate this are:

the criminalization or decriminalization of such procedures as abortion, cloning, genetic research on embryos, and sperm banks. As well the use of certain foods and drugs can be made illegal or restricted. For example, marijuana can be used for medicinal as well as recreational purposes. By classifying it as illegal, the use of this substance for health purposes is restricted.

92(10c) — The Power to Declare Works...

Federal power in this area results from its declaration of a "work." As a result, such as in the uranium area, the federal government becomes responsible for labour relations, work safety, and health issues, all of which would normally be under provincial jurisdiction. Thus, if the political will were present, any hospital or group of hospitals could be declared to be a work for the general advantage of Canada by Parliament.

Federal Territories

The territories of Yukon, Northwest Territories, and Nunuvat are all ultimately under federal jurisdiction, since their own jurisdiction is delegated from Parliament. Although the three jurisdictions have various legislative bodies and treaty arrangements that govern the delivery of health care services, ultimately constitutional power in these areas is with the federal government.

International Treaties

It is possible for the federal government to intrude on or frustrate provincial jurisdiction through the power to sign international treaties. In other federal countries, this power is virtually unchecked.[5] In Canada the situation is somewhat more complex. The constitutional power to implement treaties originally resided in Section 132 of the *Constitution Act*. It allowed the federal parliament to implement treaties signed on behalf of the empire.[6] However, in a landmark decision rendered in 1937, the Judicial Committee of the Privy Council declared this section to be exhausted as a result of the fact that treaties had ceased to be treaties of the empire. It rejected the idea that the federal parliament would automatically have the right under Section 91 to intrude on areas of provincial jurisdiction to implement the provisions of international treaties. This has left Canada with a "bifurcated treaty power." Simply put, if the federal government signs a treaty in an area of provincial jurisdiction, it means that the provincial legislature must implement the provisions of the treaty in its area of jurisdiction. It may or may not do so. Since 1937, the Supreme Court of Canada has "nibbled" around the edges of this decision, but never reversed it.[7] This has meant that economic treaties such as the FTA and NAFTA, which obviously have implications for health care, have yet to be tested. It could be that the Supreme Court may find that the power exercised over international trade by the federal government can incidentally trench on the provincial power over the delivery of health care. This would be especially relevant in the matter of private sector hospitals, etc.

The above is not an exhaustive list of specific powers, or the discussion about them. However, it does touch on most of the relevant major heads of power. Of equal interest for this paper are areas that are either ambiguous or that overlap.

Unassigned or Ambiguous Jurisdiction

As with any constitutional document, powers assigned to governments at one time often become redundant or inapplicable in another time. This has been especially true in Canada in the last century as the political and social roles of the federal and provincial governments have changed dramatically. Sometimes these ambiguities have been directly remedied through judicial decision or constitutional amendment....

... In some cases both federal and provincial legislatures have legitimate and pressing concerns. ... The type, extent, and time of the matter all affect the exercise of jurisdiction. Finally, the matter of politics also enters into the equation. It may be politically desirable for one order or the other to be seen to be doing something about a particular issue or problem at any given time....

Of greater concern perhaps, are matters that require federal and provincial governments to coordinate their areas of jurisdiction to deal with a particular issue. For example, in the matter of inflation the primary powers are federal, but the exercise of provincial jurisdiction with regard to spending and borrowing is very important. In a modern interconnected and complex society it is almost impossible to have watertight jurisdictional compartments. This is certainly the case with regard to health care and the delivery of health care services. Even without the exercise of the spending power by the federal government, which will be discussed below, health care is an area where constitutional coordination is required. Thus, while it is useful to know the specific areas of jurisdiction, such knowledge alone gives you no sense of the actual exercise of power by the two

orders of government. Other matters, as discussed below, become equally important.

II   HEALTH AND THE FEDERAL SPENDING POWER

. . . .

The term "spending power" requires some definition in order to ensure that we deal with it in a precise manner. There are many ways that a government can use its power to "spend." The first and most obvious use of the federal spending power involves the expenditure of monies on projects and services within the federal jurisdiction. These can include direct payments to individuals or corporations for goods or services. As well, the federal government expends monies on various programs that are within the federal jurisdiction. This includes the expense of the public service in managing these programs.

The federal government also makes direct payments to individuals for a variety of purposes. There is nothing to restrict the federal government in these payments. The only question may revolve about the purpose involved, or the qualifications to receive the payment. The purpose may be something that is offered or regulated by the provinces. For example, there is nothing to prevent the federal government from giving cash bursaries to students attending educational institutions, or from providing research grants to university faculty engaged in research at a provincial university.

The federal government may also use its taxing power as part of the spending power. We have all heard of the term "tax expenditures." This usually means revenue forgone by not exercising or transferring certain taxes, in Canada, most often to the provinces. These are considered as real expenditures and their transfer is often referred to by federal ministers when talking about their "share" of the cost of programs like Medicare.

Another way to use the spending power is to transfer monies to other governments in Canada. In the case of the federal government, this application has a long and honourable history. Many of the crucial arrangements and debates in 1867 involved the level of Dominion payments to the new provinces, division of property, and assumption of debts. Several parts of the original *British North America Act* refer specifically to such arrangements.[10] This has continued to be the case, and has often been the subject of federal–provincial conferences. ...

166

. . . .

Whatever the motivation, the outcome was that over 100 shared cost programs were established after WWII, the best known of which were in the health care field. The constitutionality of this use of the spending power has caused considerable debate.

Generally arguments against federal involvement in shared cost programs involve two matters. The first is that by its use of the spending power the federal government skews provincial priorities. By offering federal dollars for certain programs in the area of provincial jurisdiction it ensures that others, not funded by the federal government, will be relegated to a lower priority. Insofar as the area of health care is concerned, this was an initial argument when the federal government first attempted to induce the provinces to establish a national Medicare system. No province now seriously argues against a Medicare system, but there is considerable debate about the lack of adequate federal financing, and consequently its role in determining the shape and priorities of the system.

The centre of debate in the last two decades, however, has concerned the use of the federal spending power in order to "enforce" certain health care goals outlined in the *Canada Health Act* (CHA). These "principles" are public administration, comprehensiveness, universality, portability, and accessibility. If a provincial system does not meet these criteria it is liable to lose some or all of the federal funding designated for health care delivery.

There are, therefore, two important questions involved. Is it constitutional for the federal government to use its spending power in the area of health care? Second, is it constitutional for the federal government to impose conditions upon provinces like those in the CHA?

While there are still many who argue against a positive answer to the first question, the majority of scholars support the kind of interpretation outlined by Peter Hogg.

It seems to me that the better view of the law is that the federal parliament may spend or lend its funds to any government or institution or individual it chooses, for any purpose it chooses; and that it may attach to any grant or loan any conditions it chooses, including conditions it could not directly legislate. There is a distinction in my view, between compulsory regulation, which can obviously only be accomplished by legislation enacted within the limits of legislative power, and spending or loaning or contracting, which either imposes no obligations on the recipient (as in the case of family allowances) or obligations which are voluntarily assumed....
(Peter Hogg, [*Constitutional Law of Canada* (Scarborough, ON: Carswell, 1998) at] 157)

He supports this view in two ways. First he refers to Parliament's power under sections 91(3), the power to levy taxes, and 91(1A) to legislate in regard to public property, and 106, the right to appropriate federal funds. Second, he refers to the judgement of the Supreme Court in *Re Canada Assistance Plan*, [[1991] 2 S.C.R. 525, where Sopinka J. said that Parliament can withhold money it had previously granted to the provinces in a cost-sharing plan without "regulating" matters outside provincial authority: (Hogg 1998, 158)]....

Hogg is supported in his view by many other scholars. In particular Martha Jackson, writing in the *Health Law Journal*, outlines exhaustively the arguments and cases supporting the legitimacy of the federal government's role in health care. For example, she reviews the criminal law power involving environmental cases [and concludes that decisions such as *RJR-MacDonald v. Canada (Attorney-General)*, [1995] 3 S.C.R. 199 and *R. v. Hydro-Québec*, [1997] 3 S.C.R. 213 have significantly expanded potential federal power in regard to health care: Martha Jackman, "Constitutional Jurisdiction over Health in Canada," (2000) 8 Health Law Journal 95, text at notes 55 and 56)].

If Hogg and Jackman are categorical in this matter, some others are not. In an excellent article on this issue, Dale Gibson [says that courts would likely restrict a wide interpretation of the federal spending power if it appeared to threaten the balance between federal and provincial powers, and that the theoretical foundation of the spending power is itself open to some question: (Dale Gibson, "The *Canada Health Act* and the Constitution," (1996) 4 Health Law Journal1 at 7)].

Gibson ... concentrates in particular on legal justifications that rely on Section 91(1A), Public Debt and Property. He reviews the argument used by most in favour of this broad power, which concludes that monies raised by the federal government are really property, and that the federal government is allowed to dispose of its property in any way that it desires. In the case of the *Canada Health Act*, therefore, it is really an act about federal property, and not health care.

He goes on to argue that this approach has two "Achilles heels." First, there is doubt as to the ability of the federal authority to raise money for provincial purposes, and second, there is a legal requirement that legislation authorizing spending be in "pith and substance" really about the disposal of federal property and not some other purpose. The second is potentially most telling. In examining the *Canada Health Act*, no reasonable person would conclude that it is only about the distribution of federal property. Several parts of the Act make specific reference to health objectives and requirements. However, the Act could still survive if it was deemed to have a dual aspect. Again, Gibson notes that such a conclusion is by no means guaranteed. In particular, he cites the Supreme Court decision on the *Canada Assistance Plan*. (Gibson 1996, 10) He concludes by saying:

> In light of this uncertainty, those who support federal health care initiatives under the *Canada Health Act* and other uses of the federal 'spending power' would be well advised, as a safeguard against the possibility that the 'property' rationale will eventually succumb to siege, to explore alternative rationales. (Gibson 1996, 16)

In the remainder of his paper Gibson provides a cogent and well-argued case that acts like the *Canada Health Act* can be justified under Section 91, the Peace Order and Good Government clause (POGG). In particular, he stresses that "national dimension" aspect of several judicial decisions involving POGG.

> While the applicability of the POGG power to federal legislation relating to health has never been determined conclusively, the Supreme Court of Canada has suggested that the power has a role to play in that field, [*Margarine Reference*, 1985] and in 1993 the Quebec [Court] of Appeal held that federal legislation restricting tobacco advertising could be justified by POGG. (Gibson 1996, 17 and 18)

Gibson's arguments are compelling, if not conclusive, especially as they relate to some elements of the CHA such as portability, one of the five principles in the Act.

Gibson wrote his article before the negotiation and agreement of the nine provinces and the federal government to the *Social Union Framework Agreement* (SUFA). This agreement obligates all governments to respect the principles in the CHA. It is possible that this agreement could bolster the legal case that the requirements of the CHA are justiciable.[13]

We are left, therefore, with the uneasy feeling that the present constitutional justifications of the *Canada Health Act* are assailable, while other justifi-cations, such as those proposed by Gibson, are not yet accepted.

Recent initiatives by the government of Alberta in response to the provincial study on the health care system headed up by former Deputy Prime Minister Don Mazankowski may serve as the catalyst for some judicial activity in this regard. The provincial government appears poised to privatize parts of the hospital system, and to de-list some services. It is possible that this could be construed as a violation of the principles of the CHA. Preliminary reaction by the federal government is cautious, with no indication that the federal government might penalize the province of Alberta for these proposed actions. This approach is not shared by many in the province itself, or by some of the opposition parties in Parliament. The lack of federal response raises a corollary question, however. Should the federal Cabinet not act to penalize the province of Alberta, is that the end of the matter? The answer by at least one scholar is that this is not the case. He argues in a lengthy article that the courts could be asked to force the federal government to enforce the legislation, to penalize the province. In particular, this action could be taken by individuals seeking to enforce the principle of the Act. Should such a court decision be forthcoming, the federal government would be forced to act or change the legislation. (Choudhry 1996, 462–509)

In the final analysis, at least in the near future, the constitutional status of the CHA may not be of great consequence. All governments have shown a distinct lack of appetite for a judicial challenge to its requirements. This is true even of the PQ government in Quebec. However, the continuing reduction of the federal fiscal role in health care may yet prove to be the catalyst for legal action. The outcome of that action would not, as Gibson has indicated, be a foregone conclusion.

III   THE *CHARTER* OF RIGHTS AND FREEDOMS AND HEALTH CARE JURISDICTION

. . . .

... We can conclude by saying that it is likely that the *Charter* will be used to ensure equality of access in the area of health care in the future. Indeed, it may even be used to guarantee the system itself.

The Interrelationship of Definitions of Health and Constitutional Jurisdiction

. . . .

Definitions of Health

As noted earlier in the paper, conceptions of what constitutes health and health care services have changed dramatically since the time of confederation. Indeed they have changed more dramatically in the last three decades than at any time in between. We now conceive of "health" in broader social terms, indicating that we understand that disease and its implications arise in a more holistic sense from everyday life and being. Many of the recent commissions studying health in the past two years have taken pains to point this out.

> High tech medicine and emergency room dramas may get all of the media attention, but a quiet revolution has been taking place at the other end of the health system that is just as important. The evidence from around the world is clear. When it comes to improving health, high tech care takes a back seat to primary health services. The 'miracles of modern medicine' are not limited to drugs and surgery. Research on heart disease and diabetes, for example, demonstrates that years can be added to people's lives by healthy lifestyles, early intervention, monitoring and health management — simple everyday health measures. (Fyke 2001, 9)

The Commission goes further to say that the "health effects of poverty and inequality are becoming more evident, particularly in the case of aboriginal people." (Fyke 2001, 12)

Lifestyles, poverty, inequality, drugs, high tech equipment, and the equity goals of accessibility, and comprehensiveness, all make for a complex multi-faceted system that does not fit neatly into the constitutional categories of 1867. It is clear, however, that as the definitions of health change and expand, they bring with them new ideas on what to do, and in many cases, how to do it more efficiently. Thus promotion of health prevention measures is justified not only on the grounds that it will keep people healthier, but that it will do it cheaper. The old maxim "an ounce of prevention is worth a pound of cure" is at the heart of much of the reform of Medicare and health care in general in Canada. Yet, despite cost savings, there is still the need to deal with rapidly expanding and costly health care measures in the existing system, while investing in new approaches that will ultimately save money. In other words,

we need to invest now, to save later. The first part of this equation is what has caused so much consternation in the past 10 years. It is obvious that how you define health, health care services, and even medical necessity all have profound implications for federal provincial relations. If, as suggested in the Mazankowski Report in Alberta, certain medical services are removed from the list of covered services, it will undoubtedly cause at least discussion with the federal government, if not confrontation. But will it affect constitutional jurisdiction, the subject of this paper? The answer is probably that it could, although this answer is hardly satisfactory. The most obvious way that this could happen would be through a court challenge involving the *Canada Health Act*, or even a *Charter* challenge, as discussed earlier in this paper. If such a challenge were successful, it could alter the jurisdiction of the provinces or the federal government. The more likely outcome, however, is that such definitional changes will alter federal provincial discussion and agreement.

. . . .

IV   GENERAL CONCLUSIONS

This study set out to answer four questions. They were:

- What are the constitutional bases for the federal and provincial roles in the provision of health care in Canada?
- What is the constitutional basis for the exercise of the federal spending power as it relates to health?
- Does the *Charter of Rights and Freedoms* affect the distribution of jurisdiction with respect to health care and the delivery of health care?
- Insofar as Canadian health policy increasingly involves broader definitions of "health" each year, how might the interrelationship of broader parameters and overlapping jurisdictions affect health care policy and the discharge of responsibilities for the delivery of health care in the future? In particular, how do various jurisdictional responsibilities for economic matters affect health policy?

The answer to the first question has raised some interesting issues. Actual heads of jurisdiction have changed little since the original *BNA Act* was adopted. However, judicial interpretation of some of those provisions has altered their ambit significantly. During the same period, both orders of government have increased their overall involvement in general

169

social matters, including health care. As a result, although provincial governments have a firm jurisdictional basis for the delivery of health care services, the increasing overlap and expanding scope of services means that the federal government has become a major player in the area.

Given the recent history of constitutional amendment in Canada there is little likelihood of amendments that would either clarify the current heads of power, or add new jurisdiction to the federal or provincial governments. It may be that the courts might reinterpret some existing powers in an effort to remedy a specific problem, but they would be loath to cast a broad net into such a sea of overlapping jurisdiction. As a result, we can anticipate that changes will occur, if at all, by way of practice or agreement.

The answer to our second question has also provided some interesting insights. As noted above, the common conception is that health care is a matter of provincial jurisdiction. We have demonstrated that the actual situation is more complex than that simple understanding. The second common conception is that the federal government is on firm ground using its spending power in the area of health care. Put differently, most agree that health is a matter of provincial jurisdiction, but also agree that the federal government can make transfer payments to provinces for health care purposes and attach conditions to those transfers, even if they appear to invade provincial jurisdiction. Provinces agree to this only because they want to keep federal funding.

Although most constitutional experts agree that the federal government can dispose of its property in any way it sees fit, some, like Dale Gibson, think that this power may be on shaky ground.

Since the *Canada Health Act* is the main instrument of federal involvement, it is interesting that Gibson thinks that this Act may be assailable if it is defended solely as an exercise in the disposition of property. He believes that it can be defended under POGG on the "national aspect" dimension. He may

or may not be right, but it would be far better if the two orders of government could jointly agree on the principles involved and enshrine it in an agreement that carried with it a mutually agreeable dispute settlement mechanism. Unfortunately, this is unlikely to happen without some agreement on long-term funding.

Question three dealt with the impact of the *Charter* on jurisdiction in the area of health care. Specifically, does the *Charter* affect the distribution of jurisdiction with respect to health care in Canada? We interpreted this to mean can the *Charter* be used to alter jurisdiction in health care. In a formal sense the answer is no. However, the potential to influence or enhance the exercise of jurisdiction is another matter. It is conceivable that the *Charter*, primarily through Section 6, Mobility Rights, and Section 15, Equality rights, might influence the role of the federal government. The kind of arguments made by Gibson that portability, for example, might be justified under POGG, could certainly be applied to Sections 6 and 15 as well.

Finally, question four asked us to speculate on broadening definitions of health and how that might relate to the economic powers of the federal government. These were broad questions that were only partially addressed in this paper. We concluded that economic powers would play an increasingly important role in health care because of globalization, economic powers like the power over patents, possible privatization, and finally, the important fiscal role that the federal government maintains in the funding of health care.

It is unlikely that there will be formal constitutional change in the area of health care. It is also probable that the courts will tread carefully in this area as well. If there is change needed in the exercise of jurisdiction, it will have to be brought about by political agreement, enshrined in some form of semi-permanent contract or arrangement. However, as one famous baseball person noted, making predictions is difficult, especially about the future.

(f) *Chaoulli*†

NOTE

The historical and constitutional underpinnings of Canada's public health care system are both complex and unsettled. Factors such as divided provincial and federal powers, unequal financial resources, changing social needs, and evolving social needs and legal trends, all generate tension in the system. They give the system a "pushmi-pullyu" character, with both federal and centralist features. One commentator describes Canadian health care as "a system of 10 provincial and three territorial health insurance plans, bound together by certain norms" (see A. Maioni, "Health Care in the New Millennium" in H. Bakvis and G. Skogstad, *Canadian Federalism: Performance, Effectiveness, and Legitimacy* (Don Mills, Ont.: Oxford University Press, 2002) at 88). These factors above also make the health care system highly fluid, the product of ongoing financial deals struck at federal and provincial bargaining tables.

Complicating the tensions over power and money are different views about the relative importance of equity and efficiency, about the role of the state, and about the nature of health itself. On one hand, there appears to be strong public support for the *Canada Health Act*'s basic goals of comprehensiveness, universality, and equality of access. On the other hand, the system is beset by line-ups for emergency services and operations, by spiralling costs, and by threats from provinces such as Alberta to allow more private alternatives for those who can afford them. Many of these tensions came to a head in the *Chaoulli* case.

The case involved a Quebec medical patient, Mr. George Zéliotis, who had to wait a year for hip surgery, and a Quebec doctor, Jacques Chaoulli, who wanted to be able to offer private medical services. The two men challenged the constitutionality of a Quebec law that prohibited its residents from buying private insurance for health care services that were available in the public system. The province had enacted this requirement in support of the goals of the *Canada Health Act*. It requires federally funded health services to be accessible and universal, publically administered, and comprehensive and portable.

One of the arguments of Mr. Zéliotis and Dr. Chaoulli was that the provincial law went beyond provincial jurisdiction because it interfered with federal power over criminal law. On this issue, the Supreme Court upheld the provincial power to impose the prohibition, and provided some helpful judicial commentary on federal–provincial powers in this highly complex field of shared jurisdictional responsibility. Deschamps J.'s comments on this issue were endorsed by a majority of the Court, and are included below.

Note, though, that it was a *Charter* challenge, not a federalism challenge, that carried the day for Mr. Zéliotis and Dr. Chaoulli. Among other things, they had argued that the provincial law violated an individual's rights to personal security in the Quebec *Charter of human rights and freedoms*, because delays in the public system, combined with the prohibition on private insurance, could threaten a person's life or security. A majority of the Supreme Court agreed that the prohibition on private health insurance could constitute an unjustified breach of the *Quebec Charter*. Moreover, three judges held that there could be a violation of s. 7 of the *Canadian Charter* as well.

What effect would this decision have on Canadian health care? Would it force governments to drastically cut waiting times? Or would it hasten the drift to private care alternatives? Was this the beginning of a new era of judicial activism in areas previously left mainly in the hands of the executive branch? For these questions, the answers remained to be seen. In another respect, though, *Chaoulli* was less ambiguous — it was another clear sign that *Charter* control is eclipsing federalism control in Canadian constitutional law.

EXTRACT

[DESCHAMPS J.:]

. . . .

---

† *Chaoulli v. Quebec (A.G.)*, [2005] 1 S.C.R. 791, rev'g. [2002] R.J.Q. 1205, [2002] Q.J. No. 759 (QL) and [2002] Q.J. No. 763 (QL), aff'g. a decision of Piché J., [2000] R.J.Q. 786, [2000] Q.J. No. 479 (QL).

I. LEGISLATIVE CONTEXT

[16] Although the federal government has express jurisdiction over certain matters relating to health, such as quarantine, and the establishment and maintenance of marine hospitals (s. 91(11) of the *Constitution Act, 1867*), it is in practice that it imposes its views on the provincial governments in the health care sphere by means of its spending power: *Eldridge v. British Columbia (Attorney General)*, autumn [1997] 3 S.C.R. 624, at para. 25; *YMHA Jewish Community Centre of Winnipeg Inc. v. Brown*, [1989] 1 S.C.R. 1532, at p. 1548; see also: P. W. Hogg, *Constitutional Law of Canada* (loose-leaf ed.), vol. 1, at p. 6-15; A. Lajoie, "L'impact des Accords du Lac Meech sur le pouvoir de dépenser", in *L'adhésion du Québec à l'Accord du Lac Meech* (1988), 163, at pp. 164 *et seq.* In order to receive federal funds, a provincial plan must conform to the principles set out in the *Canada Health Act*, R.S.C. 1985, c. C-6: it must be administered publicly, it must be comprehensive and universal, it must provide for portability from one province to another and it must be accessible to everyone. These broad principles have become the hallmarks of Canadian identity. Any measure that might be perceived as compromising them has a polarizing effect on public opinion. The debate about the effectiveness of public health care has become an emotional one. The Romanow Report stated that the *Canada Health Act* has achieved an iconic status that makes it untouchable by politicians (*Building on Values: The Future of Health Care in Canada: Final Report* (2002) (Romanow Report), at p. 60). The tone adopted by my colleagues Binnie and LeBel JJ. is indicative of this type of emotional reaction. It leads them to characterize the debate as pitting rich against poor when the case is really about determining whether a specific measure is justified under either the *Quebec Charter* or the *Canadian Charter*. I believe that it is essential to take a step back and consider these various reactions objectively. The *Canada Health Act* does not prohibit private health care services, nor does it provide benchmarks for the length of waiting times that might be regarded as consistent with the principles it lays down, and in particular with the principle of real accessibility.

[17] In reality, a large proportion of health care is delivered by the private sector. First, there are health care services in respect of which the private sector acts, in a sense, as a subcontractor and is paid by the state. There are also many services that are not delivered by the state, such as home care or care provided by professionals other than physicians. In 2001, private sector services not paid for by the state accounted for nearly 30 percent of total health care spending (Canadian Institute for Health Information, *National Health Expenditure Trends, 1975–2003* (2003), at p. 16, Figure 13, "Public and Private Shares of Total Health Expenditure, by Use of Funds, Canada, 2001"). In the case of private sector services that are not covered by the public plan, Quebeckers may take out private insurance without the spectre of the two-tier system being evoked. The *Canada Health Act* is therefore only a general framework that leaves considerable latitude to the provinces. In analysing the justification for the prohibition, I will have occasion to briefly review some of the provisions of Canada's provincial plans. The range of measures shows that there are many ways to deal with the public sector/private sector dynamic without resorting to a ban.

[18] The basis for provincial jurisdiction over health care is more clear. The *Constitution Act, 1867* provides that the provinces have jurisdiction over matters of a local or private nature (s. 92(16)), property and civil rights (s. 92(13)), and the establishment of hospitals, asylums, charities and eleemosynary institutions (s. 92(7)). In Quebec, health care services are delivered pursuant to the *Act respecting health services and social services*, R.S.Q., c. S-4.2 ("*AHSSS*"). The *AHSSS* regulates the institutions where health care services are delivered and sets out the principles that guide the delivery of such services in Quebec. For example, under s. 5 *AHSSS*, Quebeckers are "entitled to receive, with continuity and in a personalized and safe manner, health services and social services which are scientifically, humanly and socially appropriate".

[19] The other two main legislative instruments that govern the health care system in Quebec are the *HOIA* and the *HEIA*. The *HOIA* establishes access to hospital services in Quebec; it also regulates hospitals. The purpose of the *HEIA* is to ensure that Quebeckers have access to certain medical services that they need for health reasons.

[20] Before discussing the effect of waiting times on human rights, I will address the question of whether the province has the power to impose a prohibition on private insurance.

II. VALIDITY OF THE PROHIBITION IN RELATION TO PROVINCIAL JURISDICTION

[21] The appellant Chaoulli argues that the prohibition is a criminal law matter. In his submission, it

was adopted because the provincial government of the time wished to impose an egalitarian system and to eliminate the opportunity for profit in the provision of health care services. He contends that the operation of a health care service for profit was regarded at that time as socially undesirable.

[22] If the Court is to accept this argument, it must find, first, that the effect of the prohibition on private insurance is to exclude the private sector and, second, that the main purpose of excluding the private sector, as distinct from the overall purpose of the *HOIA* and the *HEIA*, is to avert criminal conduct.

[23] The Superior Court judge found that the purpose of the prohibition is to ensure that health care is available [TRANSLATION] "by significantly limiting access to, and the profitability of, the private system in Quebec" (p. 812). I will review later in these reasons the evidence accepted by the Superior Court judge in finding that the prohibition is useful having regard to the intended purpose, and so for the moment I reserve comment on this point. It is sufficient, at the stage of identification of the intended purpose, to determine whether ensuring access to health care services by limiting access to the private system is a valid objective for the provincial govern-

ment. On this point, and based on the division of powers analysis in the preceding section, it is indisputable that the provincial government has jurisdiction over health care and can put mechanisms in place to ensure that all Quebeckers have access to health care.

[24] It is difficult to see the argument that the provision of parallel private sector services was perceived as being socially undesirable as an independent objective, unconnected with the social policy pursued by the government in the area of health care. The appellants were alone in contending that the purpose of the prohibition was to eliminate morally reprehensible conduct. The Attorney General of Quebec argued that the prohibition resulted from a desire to pool the financial resources available for health care. This explanation coincides with the objective identified by the Superior Court judge, which is not, strictly speaking, a criminal law objective. Rather, it is a social objective that the provincial legislature may pursue in accordance with the powers conferred on it by s. 92 of the *Constitution Act, 1867*. In my opinion, the argument that the provincial government has trenched on the federal criminal law power cannot succeed.

(g)   The Kyoto Protocol and the Constitution[†]

Philip Barton

NOTE

The federal government signed the Kyoto Protocol to the United Nations Framework Convention on Climate Change [(1998) 37 Int. Leg. Mat. 32 in 1998. It ratified the Protocol in 2002. The Protocol

requires a reduction in greenhouse gas (GHG) emissions to 6% below 1990 levels by 2012. GHG emissions are a major source of pollution and a major cause of global warming.

Signing and ratifying international treaties is a matter fully within the jurisdiction of the fed-

---

† Excerpt from "Economic Instruments and the Kyoto Protocol: Can Parliament Implement Emissions Trading Without Provincial Co-operation?" (2002) 40 Alta. L. Rev. 417 at 428–31, 437–40, 442–45. [Notes omitted.] Reproduced with permission of Alberta Law Review.

See also Andrew Coyne, "Kyoto Hypocrisy: A Bipartisan Cause," *National Post* (27 April 2007), online: <http://www.andrewcoyne.com/columns/2007/04/kyoto-hypocrisy-bipartisan-cause.php>; Bill C-30, *Canada's Clean Air and Climate Change Act*, first reading, 19 October 2006; David Suzuki Foundation, *Canada's Record on Climate Change* (circa 2005), online: <http://www.davidsuzuki.org/files/climate/cop/Canadas_Record.pdf>; Nigel D. Bankes and Alastair R. Lucas, *Kyoto, Constitutional Law and Alberta's Proposals* (2004) 42 Alberta L. Rev. 355; Jamie Benidickson, *Environmental Law*, 2d ed. (Toronto: Irwin Law, 2002), chs. 2 and 4; Steven Bernstein & Christopher Gore, *Policy Implications of the Kyoto Protocol for Canada*, (2001) 2 ISUMA: Canadian Journal of Policy Research, online: <http://www.isuma.net/v02n04/index_e.shtml>; and James T. Bryce, "Controlling the Temperature: An Analysis of the Kyoto Protocol" (1999) 62 Sask. Law Rev. 379.

eral government. However, international treaties do not become law in Canada until they are implemented by the level of government that has jurisdiction over their subject matter. Sections 92, 92A(1), 92(13), and 109 of the *Constitution Act, 1867* give the Canadian provinces extensive responsibilities over natural resources and other environment-related matters. As a result, it would have been helpful if the federal government had secured provincial agreement to the signing or the ratification of the Protocol.

But prior provincial agreement was not secured, and provinces such as Alberta were alarmed. Alberta and Ontario account for more than half the GHG emissions in Canada. Moreover, GHG emissions are produced mainly from fossil-burning fuels such as petroleum, and government royalties and corporate profits in Alberta could be significantly affected by an emissions reduction program. The Alberta government said that the Protocol could unleash sweeping federal intervention in the provincial domain. The possibility of a constitutional challenge loomed in the background.

The constitutional situation could well be affected by the mechanisms adopted by the federal government to implement the Protocol. Under the Liberal government, implementation centred mainly on techniques such as voluntary agreements and financial incentives. When it left office in early 2006, the government was falling far short of its Protocol objectives. The federal Conservative government said the Kyoto goals were unrealistic, and proposed a "Clean Air Act" involving tax incentives and general long-term objectives. After a storm of public criticism, the government amended its environmental proposals and extended them to regulation of industrial pollutants. However, it continued to rely heavily on voluntary agreements and incentives, and still claimed it would not try to achieve the full Kyoto targets. On the other hand, these targets are supported by all the federal opposition parties, and the broad objective of emissions reductions has general support.

Apart from voluntary agreements and simple financial incentives, what are the main options for moving fully or part way down the Kyoto road? Two possible alternatives are a GHG emissions trading program and a simple GHG taxation scheme. Under a trading program, potential polluters would be assigned pollution ceilings. If they reduced their pollution levels below their ceiling, they could sell their unused pollution amounts to others. In this extract, Philip Barton reviews two earlier discussions of the powers that might support federal trading or taxing implementation legislation, and considers the relative strengths and weaknesses of the constitutional alternatives. What is your view?

EXTRACT

Can the federal government rely on the national concern doctrine of the POGG power to justify a GHG-emissions trading program? Two environmental lawyers disagree on this issue. Rolfe [C. Rolfe, Turning Down the Heat: Emissions Trading and Canadian Implementation of the Kyoto Protocol (Vancouver: West Coast Environmental Law Research Foundation, 1998)] believes there is a "strong likelihood that the courts would uphold direct federal regulation as a matter of national concern, but the exact limits of this federal power are uncertain." Castrilli [J.F. Castrilli, "Legal Authority for Emissions Trading in Canada," The Legislative Authority to Implement a Domestic Emissions Trading System (Ottawa: National Round Table on the Environment and the Economy, 1999) App. 1] believes that the courts would be greatly reluctant to justify federal legislation on the "national concern doctrine given the potential impact on provincial authority in the same area." Rather than POGG, Castrilli is of the opinion that, for trading, the trade and commerce power is most appropriate for federal constitutional authority. This enumerated head of power is analyzed in Part III.

Rolfe has two main arguments for his opinion: that greenhouse gas regulations possess the requisite singleness, distinctiveness and indivisibility; and that the Kyoto Protocol is analogous to the Convention on the Prevention of Marine Pollution by Dumping of Wastes and other Matter. Even though the sources of GHG emissions are numerous, Rolfe believes that, in the case law, they are "treated as a distinct topic within environmental protection distinct from local air pollution, toxic pollution and regional air pollution."

There are number of reasons supporting Rolfe's first argument:

(1) climate change is a new environmental issue;
(2) GHG substances possess certainty;
(3) ascertainable and reasonable limits on new federal powers can reconcile the intrusion into previously provincial jurisdiction;
(4) GHGs have the singleness, distinctiveness and indivisibility that require uniform national regulation;

(5) provincial failure to regulate GHGs [has] extra-provincial and international implications.

However, his second argument is unsubstantiated by *Crown Zellerbach*. The majority in *Crown Zellerbach* only recognized the international convention from the perspective of the provincial inability test. The majority was much more concerned with the singleness, distinctiveness and indivisibility aspect; they were cognizant of the principle from the *Labour Conventions* case that the existence of an international treaty does not affect the constitutionality of domestic legislation.

The international concern over GHG-induced climate change is a new environmental issue separate from other air-pollution issues such as acid rain, smog and mercury emissions. There is little uncertainty with "greenhouse gases." The Kyoto Protocol specifies four natural chemicals and two groups of man-made chemicals: carbon dioxide, methane, nitrous oxide, sulphur [hexafluoride] and hydrofluorocarbons and perfluorocarbons. Environment Canada has been monitoring the national emissions of these chemicals since 1990. As a result, "GHGs" don't suffer from the same uncertainty as the "toxic substances" that nearly caused the *CEPA* to be held *ultra vires* Parliament.

As demonstrated in the dissents in *Crown Zellerbach* and *Hydro-Québec*, it is important that "ascertainable and reasonable" limits be established that allow reconciliation of new federal powers with the constitutional division of powers. Since the environment is a shared federal–provincial responsibility, GHG control must not overwhelm provincial environmental protection authority. GHG control by emissions trading could be approached by setting a cap by province, by region or by economic sector. However, a provincial allocation may be unworkable because of a heavy burden on Alberta and Ontario (these two provinces alone represent 31 percent and 28 percent, respectively, of national emissions in 1999). Also, a provincial cap with federal instructions to do whatever is necessary to reduce emissions is a circular argument that comes back to the provincial inability test. In other words, if the provinces are capable of reducing GHGs then why is POGG being invoked? As a result, a cap declared on each economic sector (such as a certain reduction for the oil and gas industry, another for the pulp and paper industry, another for agriculture, etc.) may be more palatable and would, furthermore, recognize that some provinces may resist implementing GHG reductions.

Emissions trading in a sector-by-sector approach assists in the argument that federal intrusion has ascertainable and reasonable limits. A cap is set, yet direct intrusion into any specific facilities in any given province is prevented. This could go a long way to reconciling POGG with the "property and civil rights" powers of the provinces. The resulting certainty from the allocation of reductions by sector, likely to be a source of intense federal–provincial and/or federal–industry negotiations, would allay concerns that federal powers would overwhelm the provincial power over industries within their jurisdiction. Therefore, a strong argument can be made for a federal trading system on a sector-by-sector approach.

A further argument assisting the national concern doctrine is that GHGs have the singleness, distinctiveness and indivisibility that requires uniform national management. For emissions trading to function, participation must be mandatory amongst competing businesses. Participation is most likely to be consistent under a federal system. If it were regulated provincially, and provinces were not consistent, businesses in one province may be forced to implement expensive measures while competitors in an adjacent province would not be subjected to similar measures. In fact, this situation would create an incentive for businesses to relocate to so-called "pollution havens" that require less strict GHG measures — a wholly unsatisfactory situation. Preventing these competitiveness issues by using a national management process would be important for emissions trading, for ensuring confidence in the carbon commodity, and to prevent some businesses from being penalized for being located in GHG-proactive provinces.

. . . .

Arguments opposing the national concern doctrine for GHG regulation would likely begin with s. 92A of the Constitution. GHG control is arguably direct legislation that would restrict the development of Alberta's fossil-fuel resources and thus conflict with s. 92A(1). This provision of the Constitution grants provincial governments the exclusive authority over the "exploration ... development, conservation and management of non-renewable natural resources." However, the counter-argument to any province asserting s. 92A(1) is that non-renewable natural resources, that is, fossil-fuel resources, are no longer simply a provincial matter. Because of climate change, these resources have been elevated to the status of national concerns. The federal gov-

175

ernment could argue that the intent of provincial powers under the Constitution is only for jurisdiction over local or provincial matters. Evidence of this intent is demonstrated by s. 92(10), where provinces have authority over transportation or communication related to "local works and undertakings" unless they are extra-provincial or international. Further evidence can be found in the residuary clause, s. 92(16): "generally all matters of a merely local or private nature in the province."

An additional argument opposing the national concern doctrine would bring attention to the sheer number of potential sources of emissions. Environment Canada divides the inventory of national emissions into seven main groups — electricity and petroleum industries; transportation; industry; residential, commercial and institutional sector; agriculture; land-use change and forestry; and waste. These main groups are then further divided into numerous subcategories. Provincial governments will likely argue that federal regulation of GHGs would involve regulating every industrial, commercial, institutional and private activity which occurs in each of the provinces. This argument can be rebutted by heeding the previous discussion on ascertainable and reasonable limits. Trading only sets mandatory targets — it does not specify the measures to be taken to reach those targets. By these tenets, federal regulations can be carefully designed with clear boundaries that minimize intrusion into local or provincial matters, such as land-use planning or transportation, while still realizing GHG reductions.

In summary, the POGG power presents a strong possibility for federal legislative authority to implement a GHG-trading system. As long as legislation is carefully designed with balanced federalism and "ascertainable" limits in mind, there is a good possibility that the national concern doctrine of POGG could provide the constitutional basis for instituting mandatory emission targets.

.   .   .   .

Can the federal government rely on the criminal law power to implement a national emissions trading regime? As an example, Parliament could pass legislation which relies on the criminal sanction to prohibit emissions above a certain level (thereby establishing a "cap"), while allowing trading to occur between the organizations subject to the cap. This trading could be within a single economic sector or between different sectors that are each subject to their own respective criminally sanctioned caps.

Castrilli believes that it would be difficult for the federal government to justify a GHG trading system:

> Given the elaborate administrative characteristics of an effective emissions trading regime and the likely need to trade emissions of "non-toxic substances," it would be very difficult to justify such a program under the traditionally narrow ambit of the criminal law power; that is, a prohibition and penalty type regime.

Rolfe is not as pessimistic as Castrilli, though he states "using the criminal law power to support a complex system of regulation through systems such as emission trading would involve an unprecedented extension of what is considered criminal law." While not specifically examining emissions trading, Dean Hogg is of the opinion, after reviewing *Hydro-Québec*, that "the federal Parliament probably does have the legal power to enact ... legislation that would force emissions targets down to the Kyoto target." [P.W. Hogg, "Kyoto and Canada: A Legal Perspective" (1998) 1:3 Alberta Views 7–8.]

Recognizing the three prerequisites to criminal law (a criminal purpose, a prohibition and a penalty), unco-operative provincial governments would likely challenge such legislation using the following arguments:

(1) that Parliament must completely prohibit GHG emissions for such prohibitions to be criminal law — merely [setting] caps is regulatory;
(2) that GHG emissions have always been lawful, so Parliament can't criminalize them now;
(3) that an emissions trading system will be complex and so must be regulatory;
(4) that emissions trading systems will probably need exemptions and ministerial discretion to accommodate the difficulties of certain sectors; and
(5) that the "environment" is a shared federal–provincial responsibility, so the federal government cannot make an aspect of environmental protection its exclusive jurisdiction.

Similar arguments to these were addressed and ultimately rejected in *RJR-MacDonald*, *Hydro-Québec* and the *Firearms Reference*. The fact that GHG emissions have been completely unrestricted in the past will not preclude Parliament from creating new criminal law. Remember that criminal law is not "frozen as of some particular time." Furthermore, a strong analogy can be made between the new criminal sanction on tobacco advertising and new criminal sanctions on GHG emissions. In *RJR-MacDonald*, La Forest J. observed that unrestricted tobacco advertising and consumption preceded the scientific understanding of the hazards of tobacco. Now that considerable evidence of the hazards of tobacco exists, Parliament can respond with new legislation. In a similar manner, the previous absence of any restrictions on GHG emissions, which began long before the greenhouse effect was understood, cannot now be a defence to the policy response to the risks of climate change....

The important legal principle from *Hydro-Québec* was that environmental protection could be included along with the traditional criminal law purposes of maintaining public peace, order, security, health and morality. Obviously, this raises the possibility that the GHG aspect of environmental protection could also be valid criminal law in a similar manner to the "toxic substances" aspect.

The argument that, in order for Parliament to enact criminal law there must be a complete prohibition, can also be rejected based on the jurisprudence on this issue. Indirect prohibitions occurred in both the *Prostitution Reference* and *RJR-MacDonald*. The effectiveness of challenged legislation is not at issue — only the constitutionality is....

. . . .

Even if legislation for an emissions trading system is complex and requires exemptions and ministerial discretion, it can still be valid criminal law. As previously discussed, both the *Food and Drugs Act* and the *CEPA* are complex, yet both were upheld as criminal law. Ministerial discretion existed in the *CEPA* for deeming substances as "toxic," and the Chief Firearms Officer defined in the Firearms Act has discretion to refuse to licence a firearm. Also previously addressed was the recognition of the existence of exemptions in criminal law.

Provincial governments challenging federal legislation may also argue that because the environment is a shared federal–provincial responsibility, using the criminal law power would create an exclusive federal component, thereby infringing on the shared nature. This argument neglects the fact that while "health" is a shared federal–provincial responsibility, health was the basis for banning tobacco advertising. In fact, the federal government relied upon the health purpose of criminal law in order to acquire legislative authority in this area. *Hydro-Québec* stands as a further example of Parliament successfully carving an exclusive federal component out of another shared

responsibility — that of the "toxic substances" portion of environmental protection.

In summary, the criminal law power could be relied upon as the constitutional basis for a GHG-trading program. While this basis is uncertain because of the many similar characteristics it would have with a regulatory system, the argument may still be made and is supported by the jurisprudence in this area.

. . . .

Rolfe observes that the federal trade and commerce power has never been upheld in the context of environmental protection, and he is not optimistic as to its application for emissions trading. In fact, the four-justice dissent in *Hydro-Québec* actually considered and rejected an argument by an intervenor that the *CEPA* could be justified based on trade and commerce. They rejected the argument on the basis that "it is clear that the 'pith and substance' of the impugned legislation does not concern trade and commerce." Rather, the pith and substance was one of environmental protection.

In contrast, Castrilli believes that the trade and commerce power is "the most appropriate constitutional authority for federal emissions trading law." He believes that both components of the federal trade and commerce power could be relied upon for legislative authority. The relevant jurisprudence for the two areas of the federal trade and commerce power, and Castrilli's reasoning, [are] examined below.

. . . .

[As with] competition legislation, Castrilli believes that federal emissions trading legislation could also rely on the "general" trade and commerce power for jurisdiction. To the necessary pith-and-substance analysis, Castrilli makes two strong arguments why the dissent in *Hydro-Québec* was incorrect:

> First, pollution does have an important economic dimension in its impact on trade and commerce. There is little incentive for company A to clean up in one province if company B in another province can continue to pollute and thereby obtain an economic advantage over company A.... Second ..., [e]missions trading adopts an economic or market approach to environmental pollution by turning, for example, a pollution/ emission reduction credit/allowance into an article of trade; that is, a commodity that has economic value to industry.

177

The first assertion can also be restated as the "pollution haven" argument first discussed in Part II, above: if province A forces its industries to implement costly pollution measures, some of these industries may elect to move to province B where similar measures do not exist. Thus environmental pollution is at the mercy of the fluid nature of trade and commerce (thereby necessitating a national regime).

To complete the general trade and commerce argument, Castrilli believes that federal trading legislation could also meet each of the five criteria from *General Motors*:

> First, it would require a general regulatory scheme to implement what would appear to be elaborate components characteristically necessary for emission trades. Second, the regulatory scheme would require continuing oversight and monitoring by the regulatory agency. Third, emissions trading legislation would be concerned with trading in general, albeit trading of emission reduction credits or allowances for certain pollutants, rather than in respect of a particular industry. Fourth, the legislation would be of such a nature that the provinces jointly or severally would be constitutionally incapable of enacting such legislation. Fifth, the failure to include one or more provinces or localities in an emissions trading regime would jeopardize the successful operation of emissions trading in other parts of the country. ...

However, there are a number of weaknesses in these arguments. While GHG-emission trading can have implications in the area of trade and commerce, that does not change the fact that the dominant purpose of trading is one of environmental protection. Reducing GHG emissions is a response to the concern of global climate change — thus GHG control is an environmental protection initiative. As reviewed in Part 2 above, the environment is a shared federal–provincial responsibility; if the dominant purpose of trading is one of environmental protection, the result is all the inherent constitutional difficulties associated with that subject matter.

The second assertion — that trading is a market-based approach — also faces a similar dominant-purpose argument. In spite of the fact that policy-makers have elected to use an economic instrument to control GHG emissions, the dominant purpose is still one of environmental protection. The commercial relationship with trading is only incidental to the main purpose of environmental protection.

The final weakness with the "pollution haven" argument is evident when one recognizes that Canadian industry only accounts for about one-third of national emissions (the bulk of the remaining emissions are from transportation, residential and commercial buildings and agriculture).... If trading was justified under trade and commerce (because of the possibilities of pollution havens), then trading could only be justified for the industrial sector. This is because transportation and buildings are not subject to the same competitiveness pressures as industry. As a result, trading would not be applicable to municipal operations, government buildings, agriculture, and so on. In conclusion, even though it is possible for trading to satisfy the five-part test from *General Motors*, it would probably be rejected by the prerequisite pith-and-substance analysis.

V. TAXATION

Assuming provincial opposition, if Parliament is of the opinion that the constitutional authority for emissions trading is vulnerable to challenge, this complicated policy measure may not be pursued. In this situation, the alternative economic instrument of taxing emissions would conceivably gain significance as a possible strategy for reducing national GHGs. This final section of this article examines the federal taxing power.

Section 91(3) of the Constitution confers on Parliament the power to make laws in relation to "the raising of Money by any Mode or System of Taxation." This taxing power is "expressed in the broadest of terms." Both Rolfe and Hogg agree that this provides the federal government with the authority to impose a carbon tax or energy tax on gasoline or other fossil fuels. The taxation of non-energy GHG emissions is also possible. The only limitation which Hogg perceives on this federal power is that which Alberta successfully argued in Reference re Proposed Federal Tax on Exported Natural Gas, "that federal taxes could not apply to natural gas that the province had extracted from its own Crown lands. This limitation does not help private producers." ... In summary, Parliament's ability to implement a carbon or energy tax to tax GHG emissions is not subject to the same uncertainty as the authority for establishing a trading regime. As a result, taxation may grow in importance as an alternative economic instrument.

VI. CONCLUSION

Nearly five years after Canada signed the Kyoto Protocol, our federal government is still struggling with treaty ratification and domestic implementation. During this time a significant research effort has investigated GHG emissions trading as a policy measure for realizing cost-effective reductions. However, the recent provincial opposition to the binding emissions targets of the treaty may obstruct the adoption of a trading regime. Without the benefit of provincial co-operation, Parliament would have to rely solely on the federal powers of the Constitution to implement emissions trading. This article has explored three powers which could provide federal jurisdiction: the POGG power, the criminal law power, and, the trade and commerce power. As a result of the lack of clear legislative authority for trading, and public statements by Alberta's provincial government that they will challenge federal GHG initiatives, this article has also analyzed the federal jurisdiction for taxation. Taxing emissions is an alternative economic instrument that is not subject to the same constitutional uncertainty as trading.

The two federal enumerated powers investigated in this article, the criminal law power and the trade and commerce power, are possibilities for providing jurisdiction for trading. However, both present a number of difficulties which may not be overcome in the context of a constitutional challenge. The characteristics a trading program would have in common with a regulatory system may cause a rejection of the assertion that trading is valid criminal law. Reliance on the trade and commerce power for federal jurisdiction over trading will likely fail because trading is in pith and substance environmental protection. Despite the "pollution haven" argument, the dominant purpose of emissions trading is environmental protection and the environment is a shared federal–provincial responsibility.

The residuary federal POGG power increases in importance because of the difficulties with the enumerated powers. As long as legislation is carefully designed with balanced federalism and ascertainable limits in mind, there is a good possibility that the national concern doctrine of the POGG power could provide the constitutional basis for implementing trading. It will be important from the perspective of the constitutionality of trading legislation that trading only sets the emissions cap. Trading does not dictate the specific measures to be undertaken.

The federal taxing power could provide an alternative to emissions trading. Through this power Parliament could establish a carbon or energy tax. The possibility of taxing non-energy GHG emissions also expands the taxation's applicability away from simply the energy or carbon context. Taxation is a broad federal power and does not suffer from the same jurisdictional uncertainty as trading. While there is clear legislative authority for taxation, trading does have the advantage of focusing private or public-sector effort on the lowest-cost reduction initiatives. If emissions taxation is used as an alternative, this advantage will be lost.

8   The Legislative and Executive Branches

(a)   Introduction

As we saw in Chapter 1, there are three branches of government — the legislative branch, the executive branch, and the judicial branch. All are affected by the federal system, which divides the country into 13 governments, each with its own legislature, executive, and judiciary.[1]

We have already examined the judiciary, and its important role in patrolling the division of legislative powers under the *Constitution Act, 1867*.[2] Here we will look more closely at the legislative and executive branches, and at the coordination of executive power.

Canada's legislative and executive branches are much less separate from each other than their equivalents in countries such as the United States.[3] Our principle of responsible government requires that the leaders of the governing party who control the executive are also elected members of the legislature, and are accountable to it. Moreover, the formal head of the executive branch, the Queen or her federal or provincial representative, is a necessary part of the legislature for the purpose of assenting to bills.

THE LEGISLATURE

Despite these vital links, the normal functions of the legislative and executive branches are distinct. The legislature is the branch of government whose characteristic functions are to represent the electorate, formally enact laws, and monitor the executive. At the federal level, the legislature, called Parliament,[4] is bicameral. Because it is the elected house, the House of Commons[5] is by far the more important. Legally, the powers of the Senate are almost equal to these of the House of Commons,[6] and the Senate must assent to all bills. However, Senators are appointed, not elected, and so lack the legitimacy that comes from a popular mandate. Because of this mandate, it is to the House of Commons, not the Senate, that the executive branch is accountable through the principle of responsible government.

The third component of Parliament is the Queen, who is normally represented by the Governor General.[7] Although the Governor General virtually always acts on the advice of the Prime Minister and cabinet, the Governor General's signature is necessary before a bill passed by both houses can become law. Unlike Parliament, the provincial legislatures are unicameral bodies.[8] The Lieutenant Governor, who is the Queen's representative in the province, is a constituent part of the provincial legislature and must assent to all bills passed by the legislative assembly.

Because of its electoral base, the legislative branch lies at the core of our democratic system. Citizens elect representatives who have a formal role in enacting laws and holding the government of the day responsible for its actions. Because the government is accountable to elected members of the legislature, it is also accountable to you and me, the voters.

Yet the legislative branch suffers from a lack of prestige and power. People seem to view elected politicians with distrust.[9] Legislatures seem to be overshadowed by other bodies, such as the media and the judiciary. At times, even politicians bypass parliamentary processes.[10] Voter turnout has been hitting new lows.[11] Why?

Only a few possible causes will be noted here. First, the legislative branch is at a relative disadvantage because of the great size and power of the executive branch. The legislature does have monitoring tools, such as the debate on the speech from the Throne, the budget and estimates debates, Question period, House committee scrutiny of bills, and general opposition and backbencher criticism. But these tools are often blunted by tight party discipline, limited opposition resources, and restrictive House of Commons rules.[12] Second, the legislative branch has been weakened by a general shift in focus to other forums, such as federal–provincial–territorial negotiations, the courts, and the media. Third, for a variety of reasons, women and members of minority groups continue to be underrepresented in Canadian legislatures.[13] Fourth, the federal upper chamber, the Senate, is unelected, unequal, expensive, and — in the view of some — unnecessary.[14] Fifth, the present first-past-the-post (or "winner take all") electoral system can distort electors' choices, minimize representation by minority parties, and exaggerate regional differences throughout the country.[15]

On the other hand, there have been some signs of change. In November 2002, the House of Commons voted to elect committee chairs by secret ballot, weakening the Prime Minister's influence and strengthening that of committee members. In the same month, the House agreed to permit votes on all private members' bills. In 2003, the federal government introduced election campaign reforms to extend disclosure requirements and to limit corporate donations. The following year, it created an independent Ethics Commissioner. Following the sponsorship scandal and the Gomery reports of 2005 and 2006,[16] the federal government enacted the 2006 *Federal Accountability Act*.[17] Among other things, this massive enactment provided indirect support for Parliament's monitoring role by creating several new parliamentary "watchdog" bodies such as the Commissioner of Lobbying.[18] In 2007, the federal government amended the *Elections Act* to provide that — subject to earlier dissolutions — future federal elections would take place on fixed dates.[19] Another proposal sought to provide Alberta and British Columbia with enough Commons seats to correspond with their share of the total Canadian population,[20] but failed to give the same treatment to Ontario.[21] Not surprisingly, it was opposed by that province.[22]

There were also renewed attempts at Senate reform. This was not easy, as the Senate is well insulated from major change. Earlier efforts, such as the "Triple-E" proposal in the Charlottetown Accord, had gone down to defeat.[23] Most constitutional change affecting the Senate requires provincial consent.[24] Enhanced Senate powers could threaten the legislative plans of the federal govern-

ment, and an elected Senate might undermine the accountability of the executive branch to the House of Commons. And the Senate itself has legal power to block legislative change. In 2006 the federal government introduced a bill to limit the term of Senators to eight years,[25] but the opposition-dominated Senate refused to approve it until the Supreme Court had ruled in its constitutionality. Another bill would have required the federal government to appoint Senators following consultative elections in the relevant provinces.[26] The term-limit bill and the consultation bill were opposed by some provinces — some arguing that they should have been consulted first![27] By mid-2007, both initiatives had stalled in the Senate.

Meanwhile, as we will see in the "Electoral Reform?" item in this chapter, several provinces have been considering the possibility of major changes to the voting system itself. In a 2003 decision,[28] the Supreme Court held that a 50-candidate minimum requirement for federal political party status infringed the *Charter* right to vote and run for election, as it deprived citizens of a right to a genuine opportunity to participate in the electoral system. Could the Court make a similar pronouncement about the first-past-the post system? Or about underrepresentation of provinces, women, minorities, and others in Canadian legislative bodies? Should it?

THE EXECUTIVE

The executive branch contains the driving force of Canadian government. The executive really has two different sets of heads, a formal set who are largely (but not wholly) ceremonial, and an informal set who control the policy and actions of government. At the top of the formal set is the Queen,[29] who is represented in almost all Canadian and federal matters by the Governor General. For provincial matters, she is represented by the Lieutenant Governor of the relevant province. In each territory the formal executive is headed by a Commissioner.

In the informal set are the Prime Minister (of Canada) and the premiers (of the provinces and territories), referred to collectively as the first ministers. Except in the Northwest Territories and Nunavut, these are elected politicians who head the political party that commands the support of the elected part of the legislature. Together with his or her cabinet, the first minister has the task of directing the affairs of the executive branch (including the public service and the other parts of the administrative process) and of the government in general.

Power to carry out this task is facilitated by the principle of responsible government, which requires that normally the formal head of government must act on the advice of the first minister. At the same time, responsible government holds the first minister and cabinet accountable to the electorate for carrying out this task properly. Normally, they must maintain the confidence of the electorate — and of a plurality of the elected part of the legislature — or either resign or ask for a dissolution of Parliament to permit a new election.[30] In the Northwest Territories and Nunavut, the premiers and their cabinets are elected by the legislative members at large. Those who are not elected cabinet become the opposition parties. As those who are in opposition outnumber the premiers and their cabinets, the latter must govern by consensus.[31]

COORDINATION OF EXECUTIVE POWER

Like legislative power, the power exercised by the executive is constrained by the federal system. In the *1916 Bonanza Creek* decision,[32] the Judicial Committee formulated the base rule that:

> ... subject to certain express provisions in [the *Constitution Act, 1867*] and to the supreme authority of the Sovereign, who delegates to the Governor-General and through his instrumentality to the Lieutenant Governors the exercise of the prerogative on terms defined in their commissions, the distribution under the new grant of executive authority in substance follows the new grant of legislative powers [that are conferred in the *Constitution Act, 1867*].

As well, provisions such as s. 109 of the *Constitution Act, 1867* give the ownership of most public land and resources within provincial boundaries to the provincial level of government.[33]

Although executive power is limited by the federal system's boundaries, federal and provincial executives play a key role in coordinating its day-to-day operation. This coordinating role is especially important in the economic sphere, as examined briefly below in the note on *Federal–Provincial Financial Arrangements*.

The courts have defined the federal boundaries of executive power, but the relationship between the formal and informal executives, and the role of executives in coordinating the federal system have been governed more by administrative practice and political conventions than by litigation and judicial decisions. The judiciary reaches most, but not all, aspects of the Canadian state.

Notes

1. As well as the federal government and the 10 governments, there are three territorial governments that are modelled on the provinces.
2. Chapters 4, 5, and 6 above.
3. On the separation of powers in Canada, see Forcese, ch. 2(C). For the American situation, see M.J.C. Vile, *Constitutionalism and the Separation of Powers* (Oxford: Clarendon Press, 1967); and W.B. Gwyn, *The Meaning of the Separation of Powers: An Analysis of the Doctrine from Its Origin to the Adoption of the United States Constitution*, Tulane Studies in Political Science, vol. 9 (New Orleans: Tulane University, 1965). *Cf.* Philip Resnick, "Montesquieu Revisited, or the Mixed Constitution and the Separation of Powers in Canada" (March 1987) 20 Can. J. Pol. Sci., arguing that the framers of Confederation in Canada borrowed the French philosopher Montesquieu's idea of a "mixed constitution" that combines democratic institutions with those that are more monarchical and aristocratic, and did not use Montesquieu's concept of the separation of powers.
4. See s. 17 of the *Constitution Act, 1867*, creating a Parliament of Canada, comprising the Queen, the Senate, and the House of Commons.
5. See generally, Hogg 2007, part 9.4(b).
6. The Senate cannot introduce bills that impose taxes or delay for more than 180 days constitutional amendments that have been passed by the House of Commons: ss. 53 and 54 of the *Constitution Act, 1867* and s. 47 of *Constitution Act, 1982*, respectively. Otherwise, the legal powers of the Senate are virtually identical to those of the House of Commons. Thus, bills must be approved by the Senate as well as the House of Commons before they can become law, after the signature of the Governor General. See generally, Hogg 2007, part 9.4(c); Serge Joyal, *Protecting Canadian Democracy: The Senate You Never Knew* (Montreal & Kingston: McGill-Queen's University Press, 2003); and David E. Smith, *The Canadian Senate in Bicameral Perspective* (Toronto: University of Toronto Press, 2003). On the other hand, except when the Senate and the House are controlled by different parties, the Senate rarely vetoes bills passed by the House: Parliament of Canada, *About Parliament: A Legislative and Historical Overview of the Senate of Canada* (revised May 2001) <http://www.parl.gc.ca/information/about/process/senate/legisfocus/legislative-e.htm>.
7. Under letters patent, the British monarch has provided that the powers and authorities of the Crown in respect to Canada can be exercised by the Governor General. For the current letters patent, see Letters Patent Constituting the Office of Governor General for Canada, effective October 1, 1947, in Maurice Ollivier, ed., *British North America Acts and Selected Statutes, 1867–1962* (Ottawa: Queen's Printer, 1962), at 653.
8. Manitoba, Prince Edward Island, New Brunswick, Nova Scotia and Quebec originally had upper legislative chambers. The last remaining provincial upper house, the Legislative Council of Quebec, was abolished in 1968.
9. Canadian Press, "Canadians trust judges, but not politicians" *CTV News* (20 March 2006), online: ctv.ca <http://www.ctv.ca/servlet/ArticleNews/story/CTVNews/20060319/profession_jobs060319/20060319?hub=Canada>.
10. In 2003, for example, the Ontario provincial government presented its spring budget from a car parts assembly plant instead of the legislative chamber: Editorial, "The choice in Ontario's election" *The Globe and Mail* (27 September 2003), online: globeandmail.com <http://www.theglobeandmail.com/series/election2k3/news/analysis6.html>. The newspaper editorial said that this action "showed contempt for the traditions of parliamentary democracy" and went on to endorse the opposition party in the forthcoming election.

11. See, for example, Elections Canada, *Past Elections Voter Turnout at Federal Elections and Referendums, 1867–2006* <http://www.elections.ca/content.asp?section=pas&document=turnout&lang=e&textonly=false>. Recent provincial voter turnouts have also been at or near record lows: e.g., the 2004 Alberta election, the 2006 Nova Scotia election, and the 2007 Quebec and Manitoba elections.

12. See, for example, Dyck, chs. 16 and 23; MacIvor, ch. 5; and Ronald Landes, *The Canadian Polity: A Comparative Introduction*, 6th ed. (Scarborough, Ont.: Prentice Hall Canada, 2002) at 160–62 and 166–76.

13. In 2006, for example, women — who comprise roughly half the Canadian population had 20.8% of the seats in the House of Commons and 35% of the seats in the Senate: Julie Cool, Political and Social Affairs Division, Library of Parliament, *Women in Parliament* (20 February 2006), PRB 05-62E, online: Parliament of Canada <http://www.parl.gc.ca/information/library/PRBpubs/prb0562-e.htm#awomentxt> Table 1, and text at note 5. The Library of Parliament study says that the representation of women on municipal councils (21.7%) and in provincial/territorial legislatures (20.6%) is similar to that at the federal level: *ibid.* text at notes 6 and 7. For underrepresentation of minority groups, see for example, Brooke Thomas, *Malapportionment of Canadian Minorities*, Paper prepared for presentation at the 2006 Annual Meeting of the Canadian Political Science Association, York University, June 1–3 2006, online: Canadian Political Science Association <http://www.cpsa-acsp.ca/papers-2006/Thomas.pdf>.

14. Why, it can be asked, should 105 appointees selected by the Prime Minister (and appointed by the Governor General) be able to veto legislation approved by 308 democratically elected politicians? If this veto is rarely used, why have a second legislative chamber? Although Senate committees have produced valuable investigative reports, such as the 2002 Kirby report on Canada's health care system, this kind of work can also be performed by their counterparts in the House of Commons. The Senate was intended to give equal representation to the regions, without direct correspondence to population, but the addition and growth of the western provinces has produced some anomalous results. The present allocation is Ontario: 24 seats, Quebec: 24 seats, Nova Scotia: 10 seats, New Brunswick: 10 seats, Prince Edward Island: 4 seats; each western province: 6 seats, and each territory: 1 seat. British Columbia, with 6 seats, now has a population that is four times as great as Nova Scotia, with 10 seats. In 2007, the basic salary for each of the 105 Senators was $125,800: Parliament of Canada, *Indemnities, Salaries, and Allowances: Senators* <http://www2.parl.gc.ca/Parlinfo/Lists/Salaries.aspx?Section=b571082f-7b2d-4d6a-b30a-b6025a9cbb98>.

15. See "Electoral Reform?" item in this chapter.

16. See "Comment on Gomery Reports" in this chapter.

17. *Federal Accountability Act*, S.C. 2006, c. 9.

18. *Ibid.*, s. 81. The Act also created a Parliamentary Budget Officer, a Director of Public Prosecutions, and a Procurement Auditor, and a new Conflict of Interest and Ethics Commissioner.

19. "Subject to subsection (1) [preserving the power of the Governor General to dissolve Parliament at the Governor General's discretion], each general election must be held on the third Monday of October in the fourth calendar year following polling day for the last general election, with the first general election after this section comes into force being held on Monday, October 19, 2009": *An Act to amend the Canada Elections Act*, S.C. 2007, c. 10, s. 1, adding s. 56.1(2) to the *Canada Elections Act*, R.S.C. 1985, c. E-4.
    Currently, three provinces have fixed election dates: British Columbia (since 2001), Newfoundland and Labrador(since 2004), and Ontario (since 2005).

20. Bill C-56, *Constitution Act, 2007* (Democratic representation), first reading, 11 May 2007. Subject to some qualifications, such as a requirement that a province's Commons seats should not fall below its allocation of Senate seats, the *Constitution Act, 1867*, requires provincial representation in the House of Commons to be in proportion to population. This, in turn, is to be determined on the basis of each decennial census. Subject to these qualifications, provinces with a higher ratio of population to total seats are entitled to additional seats to bring their ratio to the average, while provinces with a lower ratio have their number of seats decreased. However, at the time of the last readjustment in the *Constitution Act, 1985* (Representation), 33-34-35 Eliz. II, c. 8 (Canada) [Assented to 4th March 1986], the number of total seats for purposes of the calculation was fixed at 279: Reesor, at 179–81. As a result, for faster growing provinces such as Alberta and British Columbia, the number of additional seats failed to keep pace with population growth. Bill C-56 was intended to redress that imbalance. See Government of Canada, Privy Council Office, *Canada's New Government Moves to Restore the Principle of Representation by Population* (Ottawa, May 11, 2007), Canada News Centre online: news.gc.ca <http://news.gc.ca/web/view/en/index.jsp?articleid=302359>.

21. After 2011, Ontario would have 116 seats or about 35% of the House of Commons under the formula, but by then that province would have approximately 39% of the total Canadian population: Brian Lahgi, "Ontario ponders legal action, sources say" *The Globe and Mail* (24 May 2007) A6. *Constitution Act, 2007* (Democratic representation).

22. *Ibid.*

23. See further, Chapter 11 below.

24. See the *Constitution Act, 1982*, s. 41(b) requiring unanimity for an amendment affecting a guarantee of House of Commons representation that is linked to representation in the Senate; s.41(e) (requiring unanimity for an amendment to the Part V amending procedure (in which the Senate plays a role); s. 41(b) "the powers of the Senate and the method of selecting Senators"; and 41(c) "the number of members by which a province is entitled to be represented in the Senate and the residence qualifications of Senators."

25. Bill S-4: *An Act to amend the Constitution Act, 1867* (Senate tenure), 17 November 2006, first reading 30 May 2006.

26. Bill C-43, *Senate Appointment Consultations Act*, first reading 13 December 2006. *Cf.* Prime Minister Mulroney's 1987 Meech Lake Accord promise to appoint Senators from lists of provincial nominees, and his appointment of Mr. Stan Walters as Senator from Alberta in 1990, after Mr. Walters had been nominated in provincially conducted elections: see Dyck, "Senate Reform", ch. 24; and Patrick Malcolmson, "Reflections on Canada's First Senate 'Election'" (1991) 14 Canadian Parliamentary Review <http://www.parl.gc.ca/Infoparl/english/issue.htm?param=138&art=906>.

27. Joan Bryden, Canadian Press, "Ontario, Quebec demand voice on Senate reform" *thestar.com* (1 June 2007), online: thestar.com <http://www.thestar.com/News/article/220603>. New Brunswick and Quebec argued that the term-limit proposal required provincial consent; Quebec argued that the consultation bill also required provincial consent; and Ontario argued that these initiatives *should* have provincial consent, whether or not it is constitutionally required. Is it constitutionally required? See *supra* note 24.

28. *Figueroa v. Canada (A.G.)*, [2003] 1 S.C.R. 912.

29. Section 9 of the *Constitution Act, 1867* provides that "[t]he Executive Government and Authority of and over Canada is hereby declared to continue and be vested in the Queen."

30. This has been called "the most important rule of our parliamentary system": Andrew Heard, *Canadian Constitutional Conventions: The Marriage of Law and Politics* (Toronto: University of Toronto Press, 1991) at 68. Heard notes, though, that this conventional rule is "seldom invoked": *ibid.*
31. See Legislative Assembly of the Northwest Territories, *Consensus Government* <http://www.assembly.gov.nt.ca/visitorinfo/factsheets/index.html>; Legislative Assembly of Nunuvat, *Frequently Asked Questions: What is the Role of the Premier; How is the Executive Council (Cabinet) Selected?* <http://www.assembly.nu.ca/english/about/faq.pdf>.
32. *Bonanza Creek Gold Mining Co. v. The King*, [1916] 1 A.C. 1916 at 581. This accompanies the base rule in the *Hodge* and *Maritime Bank* decisions that "With [the limits set by s. 92 of the *Constitution Act, 1867*], the local [provincial] legislature is supreme, and has the same authority as the Imperial Parliament, or the Parliament of the Dominion": *Hodge v. The Queen*, [1883–84] 9 App. Cas. 117 at and *Liquidators of the Maritime Bank of Canada v. Receiver General of New Brunswick*, [1892] A.C. 437 at 442.
33. See the discussion of s. 109 in *St. Catherines Milling and Lumber Co. v. The Queen*, [1889] 14 A.C. 46 at 57–58. In the three northern territories, public land is owned by the federal government, but that government has transferred varying degrees of control over the land and capacity to benefit from royalties, to the territorial governments.

(b)   House of Commons Procedure and Practice†

Robert Marleau and Camille Montpetit

NOTE

At the heart of parliamentary democracy in Canada is Parliament itself, and its counterparts, the provincial and territorial legislatures. The excerpts below highlight some important features of Parliament and Parliament's legislative process. The function and procedure of the provincial and territorial legislatures are very similar, except that they are all unicameral (one-house) institutions.

When you read about the legislative process, keep in mind that proposed bills undergo an extensive planning, drafting, and scrutiny process before they are introduced in the House of Commons, Senate, or provincial or territorial legislative assembly. This vital early process occurs within the executive branch — not the legislative branch — of government. For the pre-parliamentary legislative process at the federal level, see the Privy Council Office publication: *Guide to Making Federal Acts and Regulations.*[1]

Note

1. Government of Canada, Privy Council Office, *Guide to Making Federal Acts and Regulations*, 2d ed., 2003 <http://www.pco-bcp.gc.ca/default.asp?Language=E&Page=Publications&doc=legislation/lmgtoc_e.htm>.

EXTRACT

1.   PARLIAMENTARY INSTITUTIONS

. . . .

The Canadian System of Government

Canada is a parliamentary democracy: its system of government holds that the law is the supreme authority. The *Constitution Act, 1867*, which forms the basis of Canada's written constitution, provides that there shall be one Parliament for Canada, consisting of three distinct elements: the Crown, the Senate and the House of Commons. However, as a federal state, responsibility for lawmaking in Canada is shared among one federal, ten provincial and three territorial governments.

The power to enact laws is vested in a legislature composed of individuals selected to represent the Canadian people. Hence, it is a "representative" system of government. The federal legislature is bicameral: it has two deliberative "houses" or "chambers" — an upper house, the Senate, and a lower house, the House of Commons.[9] The Senate is composed of individuals appointed by the Governor General to represent Canada's provinces and territories.

† Source: Tiré de Robert Marleau and Camille Montpetit. © 2000. *House of Commons Procedure and Practice*, les Édition de la Chenlière Éducation at 3–4; 307–308; 621–27; 697–98. [Notes omitted.] Reproduced with permission. (Subject to updates in Standing Orders on the Parliament <http://www.parl.gc.ca/MarleauMontpetit/DocumentViewer.aspx?Sec=ch16&Seq=6&Lang=E>.)

Members of the House of Commons are elected by Canadians who are eligible to vote.[10] The successful candidates are those who receive the highest number of votes cast among the candidates in their electoral district in this single-member, simple-plurality system.

Canada is also a constitutional monarchy, in that its executive authority is vested formally in the Queen through the Constitution.[11] Every act of government is carried out in the name of the Crown, but the authority for those acts flows from the Canadian people.[12] The executive function belongs to the Governor in Council, which is, practically speaking, the Governor General acting with, and on the advice of, the Prime Minister and the Cabinet.[13]

Political parties play a critical role in the Canadian parliamentary system.[14] Parties are organizations, bound together by a common ideology, or other ties, which seek political power in order to implement their policies. In a democratic system, the competition for power takes place in the context of an election.

Finally, by virtue of the Preamble to the *Constitution Act, 1867*, which states that Canada is to have "[a] Constitution similar in Principle to that of the United Kingdom", Canada's parliamentary system derives from the British, or "Westminster", tradition. The Canadian system of parliamentary government has the following essential features:

- Parliament consists of the Crown and an upper and lower legislative Chamber;
- Legislative power is vested in "Parliament"; to become law, legislation must be assented to by each of Parliament's three constituent parts (i.e., the Crown, the Senate and the House of Commons);
- Members of the House of Commons are individually elected to represent their constituents within a single electoral district; elections are based on a single-member constituency, first-past-the-post or simple-plurality system (i.e., the candidate receiving more votes than any other candidate in that district is elected);
- Most Members of Parliament belong to and support a particular political party;[15]
- The leader of the party having the support of the majority of the Members of the House of Commons is asked by the Governor General to form a government and becomes the Prime Minister;
- The party, or parties, opposed to the government is called the opposition (the largest of these parties is referred to as the "official" opposition);

- The executive powers of government (the powers to execute or implement government policies and programs) are formally vested in the Crown, but effectively exercised by the Prime Minister and Cabinet, whose membership is drawn principally from Members of the House belonging to the governing party;
- The Prime Minister and Cabinet are responsible to, or must answer to, the House of Commons as a body for their actions; and
- The Prime Minister and Cabinet must enjoy the confidence of the House of Commons to remain in office. Confidence, in effect, means the support of a majority of the House.

. . . .

8. THE PARLIAMENTARY CYCLE

. . . .

The life cycle of a Parliament is regulated by constitutional provisions as well as Standing Orders. The most fundamental of these are the Constitution Acts, 1867 to 1982, which provide first, that only the Crown may "summon and call together the House of Commons";[1] second, that subject to a dissolution, five years is the maximum lifespan of the House between general elections;[2] and third, that "there be a sitting of Parliament at least once every twelve months".[3]

At the same time, the financial requirements of the government render a meeting of Parliament every year a practical necessity for the annual granting of Supply by Parliament for a fiscal year (April 1 of one year to March 31 of the following year).[4] As such, the date selected for the opening of each new Parliament following a general election and of each new session within a Parliament, can and does vary — within constitutional limitations — according to the political and financial priorities of the government.

Against this backdrop, the Standing Orders of the House provide for a pre-determined annual calendar of sittings, known as the parliamentary calendar, which applies only when the House is in session.[5] In this way, within each session, the days on which the House is likely to meet are known long in advance, thus allowing for a more orderly planning of House business.

. . . .

16. THE LEGISLATIVE PROCESS

. . . .

Structure of Bills

A bill is composed of a number of elements, some of which, such as the title, are essential or fundamental, while others, such as the preamble, are optional. The following is a description of the various elements of a bill.

Number

When a bill is introduced in the House, it is assigned a number to facilitate filing and reference.[103] Government bills are numbered consecutively from C-2 to C-200,[104] while private members' bills are numbered consecutively from C-201 to C-1000. Although private bills are rarely introduced in the House, they are numbered beginning at C-1001. In order to differentiate between bills that are introduced in the two Houses of Parliament, the number assigned to bills introduced in the Senate begins with an "S" rather than a "C". Senate bills are numbered consecutively beginning at S-1, whether they are government bills, private Members' bills or private bills, and are not renumbered or reprinted when they are sent to the Commons.

Title

The title is an essential element of a bill. A bill may have two titles: a full or long title and a short title.[105] The long title appears both on the bill's cover page, under the number assigned to the bill, and at the top of the first page of the document. It sets out the purpose of the bill, in general terms, and must accurately reflect its content. The short title is used mainly for citation purposes, and does not necessarily cover all aspects of the bill.[106] The first clause of the bill normally sets out the short title (except in the case of bills amending other Acts, which do not have a short title).

Preamble

Sometimes a bill has a preamble, which sets out the purposes of the bill and the reasons for introducing it.[107] The preamble appears between the long title and the enacting clause.

Enacting Clause

The enacting clause is an essential part of the bill. It states the authority under which it is enacted, and consists of a brief paragraph following the long title and preceding the provisions of the bill: "Her Majesty, by and with the advice and consent of the Senate and House of Commons of Canada, enacts as follows:". Where there is a preamble, the enacting clause follows it.[108]

Clause

A clause is a fundamental element of a bill. It may be divided into subclauses, and then into paragraphs and even subparagraphs.[109] A bill may be comprised of parts, divisions and subdivisions, but not necessarily; however, the numbering of the clauses is continuous from beginning to end. A clause should contain a single idea, which is most often expressed in a single sentence. A number of related ideas will be set out in subclauses within a single clause.[110]

. . . .

Explanatory Notes

When the purpose of a bill is to amend an existing Act, the drafters will insert notes to explain the amendments made by the bill. Among other things, these notes provide the original text of the provisions affected by the bill. They are considered not to be part of the bill, and they disappear from subsequent reprints of the bill.[115]

Summary

The summary is a general description of the bill. It consists of "a clear, factual, non-partisan summary of the purpose of the bill and its main provisions".[116] The purpose of the summary is to improve the explanatory material that is available to understand better the contents of the bill. The summary is not part of the contents but appears separately at the beginning of the bill. Once the bill has been passed, it will also appear on a page preceding the resulting Act.[117]

Marginal Notes

Marginal notes consist of short explanations that appear in the margin of the bill. They do not form part of the bill, and appear only as readers' aids or for information purposes.[118]

. . . .

Headings

To make the reader's job easier, legislative drafters insert headings throughout the text. However, those headings are not considered to be part of the bill and therefore cannot be amended.[119]

Table of Contents

As an aid to readers, legislative drafters sometimes add a table of contents at the beginning or end of a bill. It is not, however, considered to be part of the bill.

Royal Recommendation

Bills that involve the expenditure of public funds must have a Royal Recommendation.[120] The recommendation is made by the Governor General. Generally, it is communicated to the House before a bill is introduced, and it must be published in the Notice Paper and printed in or annexed to the bill.[121] The Royal Recommendation is not part of the bill but appears separately at the beginning of the bill.[122] After the bill is given first reading, the text of the Royal Recommendation is printed in the Journals. The Royal Recommendation may only be obtained by the government.

Stages in the Legislative Process

A bill is carried forward through all the stages of the legislative process "by a long chain of standardized motions" which must be adopted by the House before the bill becomes law.[123] It is these motions, and not the bill, that are the subject of the decisions and debates of the House. These stages "constitute a simple and logical process in which each stage transcends the one immediately before it, so that although the basic motions — that the bill be read a first (second or third) time — ostensibly are the same, and seem repetitious, they have very different meanings".[124] Moreover, the House does not commit itself conclusively in favour of a bill until the final stage, when it takes a decision to let the bill pass from the House or not.[125]

The Standing Orders of the House require that every bill receive three readings, on different days, before being passed.[126] The practice of giving every bill three separate readings derives from an ancient parliamentary practice which originated in the United Kingdom.[127] At that time, when the technology was not yet available to reproduce large numbers of copies at low cost, bills were introduced in handwritten form, one copy at a time. In order for Members to know what the content of the bill was, the clerk read the document to them; the idea of "reading" the bill was taken literally.[128]

Today, a bill is no longer read aloud, but the formality of holding a reading is still preserved. When the Speaker declares that the motion for first reading has passed, a clerk at the Table rises and announces "First reading of this bill", thus signifying that the order of the House has been obeyed. That scenario is repeated when the House has ordered a second and then a third reading of the bill.

A certification of reading must be affixed to every bill immediately after each of the three readings is adopted. The Clerk of the House is responsible for certifying each reading, and entering the date it passed at the foot of the bill.[129] A bill remains in the custody of the Clerk throughout all the stages of consideration. No substantive alteration to the bill is permitted without the express authority of the House or a committee, in the form of an amendment. The original bills, certified by the Clerk, form part of the records of the House.[130]

All bills must go through the same stages of the legislative process, but they do not necessarily follow the same route. Since the House adopted new rules to make the legislative process more flexible,[131] three avenues now exist for the adoption of legislation (see Figure 16.1):

- After appropriate notice, a Minister or a private Member may introduce a bill, which will be given first reading immediately. The bill is then debated generally at the second reading stage. It is then sent to a committee for clause-by-clause study.
- A Minister or a private Member may propose a motion that a committee be instructed to prepare a bill. A bill will be presented by the committee and carried through the second reading stage without debate or amendment.
- A Minister may move that a bill be referred to a committee for study before second reading.

Regardless of the avenue that the House decides to take, the bill will then have to be carried through report stage, be read a third time and be sent to the Senate for passage before receiving Royal Assent. At the start of a new session, a public bill may, if it is the same bill as was introduced in the preceding session, be reinstated at the stage it had reached at the time of prorogation. This procedure may be effected either by passing a motion to that effect[132] or, in the case of a private Member's bill, by invoking the provision of a new Standing Order adopted in 1998.[133]

On urgent or extraordinary occasions, if the House so decides, a bill may be given two or three readings on the same day, or advanced two or more stages in one day.[134] This provision of the Standing Orders refers only to the reading stages.[135] It is up to the House itself, and not the Chair, to determine whether the matter is urgent.[136]

The following are the stages that a bill must go through when it is introduced in the House of Commons:

- Notice of motion for leave to introduce and place on the Order Paper;
- Preparation of a bill by a committee (where applicable);
- Introduction and first reading;
- Reference to a committee before second reading (where applicable);
- Second reading and reference to a committee;
- Consideration in committee;
- Report stage;
- Third reading (and passage);
- Consideration and passage by the Senate;
- Passage of Senate amendments by the Commons (where applicable);
- Royal Assent;
- Coming into force.

A bill that is introduced in the Senate must go through essentially the same stages, except that it is considered first in the Senate and then in the House of Commons.[137] Most bills may be introduced in either House, with the exception of bills which involve spending or relate to taxation, which must be introduced in the House of Commons.

. . . .

18. FINANCIAL PROCEDURES

. . . .

The development of parliamentary procedure is closely bound up with the evolution of the financial relationship between Parliament and the Crown. As the Executive power,[1] the Crown is responsible for managing all the revenue of the state, including all payments for the public service.[2] The Crown, on the advice of its Ministers, makes the financial requirements of the government known to the House of Commons which, in return, authorizes the necessary "aids" (taxes) and "supplies" (grants of money). No tax may be imposed, or money spent, without the consent of Parliament.

The direct control of national finance has been referred to as the "great task of modern parliamentary government".[3] That control is exercised at two levels. First, Parliament must assent to all legislative measures which implement public policy and the House of Commons authorizes both the amounts and objects or destination of all public expenditures. Second, through its review of the annual departmental performance reports, the Public Accounts and the reports of the Auditor General, the House ascertains that no expenditure was made other than those it had authorized.[4]

The practices and procedures which govern how Parliament deals with the nation's finances are set out principally in the *Constitution Act, 1867*,[5] the *Financial Administration Act*,[6] unwritten conventions, and the rules of the House of Commons and the Senate.

(c)   The Canadian Legislature†

Ronald G. Landes

By the time the Canadian Confederation was established in 1867, the role of the legislature had been well developed, with the basic principles of parliamentary supremacy and parliamentary privilege accepted as fundamental. However, in contrast to the British pattern, the adoption of federalism and the resulting use of the courts to settle jurisdictional disputes between the two levels of government limited

† Excerpts from *The Canadian Polity: A Comparative Introduction*, 6th ed. (Scarborough: Prentice Hall Canada, 2002) at 160–62, 166–76 (illustrations and boxed inserts omitted). Reproduced with permission by Pearson Education Canada Inc.

See also Dyck, ch. 20 (policy-making process) and ch. 21 (executive); MacIvor, ch. 5 (legislature) and ch. 6 (executive); Monahan, ch. 3(E); Malcolmson, ch. 7; Funston, ch. 4(2) (federal legislative branch), ch. 4(4) (federal executive branch), and ch. 5(3) (provincial executive branch); Peter W. Hogg, *Constitutional Law of Canada*, 4th ed. [unabridged] (Scarborough: Carswell, 1997), ch. 6 (financial arrangements), ch. 9 (responsible government), ch. 10 (the Crown); Reesor, at 157–92 (federal legislative power) and 196–204 (provincial executive and legislative power); and Cheffins, ch. 7. For a comparative study, see Richard Bauman & Tsvi Kahana, eds., *The Least Examined Branch: the Role of Legislatures in the Constitutional State* (New York: Cambridge University Press, 2006).

the supremacy of the Canadian Parliament. The federal and provincial legislatures were supreme, but only within their own areas of competence. From the beginning, Canadian federalism has made parliamentary sovereignty something of an illusion.

Likewise, the notion of the legislature making the laws has been a mirage. While in the early years of Confederation governments had their legislation rejected in Parliament (Forsey, 1974: 123–138), defeating a piece of legislation is reactive, and not the same thing as writing legislation. Moreover, it is often forgotten that the so-called golden age of legislatures occurred at a time of extremely limited government: governments passed little legislation in few substantive areas in the late 19th century.

The expansion of government in the 20th century is the fundamental reason why executives have become the key actors in the political process. Power between institutions, as with individuals, is relative: executives and legislatures both gained power in the 20th century, but executives did so at a much faster rate. Canadian legislatures currently deal with more topics in a greater number of areas in more detail than ever before; in that sense, legislators in the modern era have little in common with their 19th century counterparts. Moreover, although the national legislature in Canada is bicameral, the two parts have never been equal. The House of Commons has always been pre-eminent and has become more so in recent decades: from a broad historical perspective, rarely does the Canadian Senate awake from its institutional slumber to take an active, if fleeting, role in the political process.

THE HOUSE OF COMMONS

The institutional and physical structure of the House of Commons influences the way it performs its various political functions. After the 1991 census and redistribution of parliamentary seats based on it (implemented in January 1997), the size of the House of Commons was increased to 301 seats from its previous number of 295. [In 2003, the total size was increased again to 308.] Ontario gained four seats and British Columbia two, with further increases projected after each decennial census. Seats are allocated among the geographical units (provinces) primarily on the basis of population: the largest province, Ontario, has 103 seats, while the smallest province, Prince Edward Island, has 4.

Criteria other than population are also included in the seat allocation process (Sections 51 and 51A of the 1867 Constitution Act, as amended). For example, no province can have fewer seats in the House than members in the Senate, which means that the small provinces are overrepresented in the Commons. In order to protect the French-Canadian minority, Quebec is basically assigned a given number of seats and the other provincial seat allocations are then computed from that starting point. Thus, the membership structure of the House is territorially based around the provincial units, with population the main basis in assigning provincial seat totals.

The physical structure of the Commons is divided between government and opposition members, with the Speaker of the House presiding over both. The government sits on the Speaker's right and the opposition on his or her left, a seating arrangement with perhaps Biblical connotations. However, in Prince Edward Island and Newfoundland the seating arrangement is reversed, due apparently to the historical anomaly that the heater in the legislature was positioned on the opposite side. Perhaps this fact is indicative of the opposition's legislative power.

Each member is assigned a particular seat, with government and opposition members facing each other across the centre aisle, symbolic of the antagonistic and adversarial relationship between them. The prime minister and cabinet occupy the first two rows in the centre on the government side, with the official opposition leader and his or her shadow cabinet facing them. The shadow cabinet is *the official opposition's "proposed cabinet" if they were to win power, with its structure paralleling that of the government's cabinet.* Those *MPs not in the cabinet or shadow cabinet* fill in the remaining rows on each side of the aisle; hence, they are called backbenchers. If more than two parties are in opposition, the minor parties sit on the opposition benches farthest removed from the Speaker, with any independents on the far side of them.

The Speaker of the House

The most important position in the House of Commons is that of the Speaker. The Speaker was, until 1986, nominated by the prime minister but elected by the House; since then, the House of Commons has been directly electing the Speaker. As the presiding officer it is the Speaker's job to ensure the smooth and fair functioning of the lower House. In so doing, he or she recognizes those members who wish to participate in the debate, attempts to be impartial in the business of the House, and rules on disputed questions of procedure.

Decisions of the Speaker should be nonpartisan and fair to all participants: if they are not seen as impartial, then the ability of the legislature to carry out its political tasks becomes seriously impaired. The Speaker is expected to be bilingual; by tradition, the choice of Speaker alternates between members with English or French as their mother tongue. A deputy Speaker, whose primary task is to replace the Speaker when the Speaker is unable to carry out the job, is selected as well. For example, in May of 1993, when Commons Speaker John Fraser suffered a mild heart attack, he was replaced by Deputy Speaker Andrée Champagne. The deputy Speaker needs to be bilingual, although his or her mother tongue is usually opposite to that of the Speaker.

The importance of the Speaker's role can be seen in the kinds of decisions he or she is called upon to make. For example, the Speaker decides who is recognized to talk, and if the Speaker chooses not "to see" a member, that member is excluded from the debate. Failure to get Speaker John Bosley to recognize him led Tory MP Jack Shields to complain in 1986 that the only way to get on national television was to "moon the Speaker." The Speaker likewise rules on whether a member has exceeded the time limit for discussion and whether a member's parliamentary privileges have been violated, and he or she resolves disputes about parliamentary procedure, ranging from motions of adjournment to those of closure to acceptable amendments. In March of 2001, for example, the Deputy Speaker Bob Kilger rejected a joint opposition party motion for an emergency parliamentary debate concerning Prime Minister Jean Chrétien's business dealings in his Saint-Maurice riding. In a majority government situation, the Speaker must pay particular attention to ensure that the government does not trample on the rights of the opposition or of Parliament as a whole (Newman, 1973: 88).

. . . .

Committee Structure

. . . .

There are numerous kinds of legislative committees. The two most important types are the striking or selection committee and the standing committees. The striking committee is *the committee which decides on the membership of all the other committees in the legislature.* It meets in the first few days of a session and is composed of party representatives. In practice the striking committee accepts the committee assignments decided on by the parties themselves, rather than getting into the contentious practice of assigning individual members to specific

committees. Each party caucus, in consultation with its party and House leaders, decides which of its members will sit on which committees. The party whips then take these committee assignments to the striking committee, which approves them. Such a process avoids the possibility that the government party could use its majority to assign the least able opposition members to the most important committees, thereby undercutting the effectiveness of the opposition in the legislature.

The second and most important committee type is the standing committee, that is, *those committees which give clause-by-clause consideration to each piece of legislation between its second and third readings.* It is at the standing committee stage where much of the real work of the legislature occurs, in that detailed consideration, sometimes including witnesses both for and against the legislation, is given.

The structure of the standing committees is roughly parallel to that of the executive departments, with each committee considering the legislation related to one or more departments. During the Mulroney years, for example, while the executive had a Department of Veterans Affairs and a Department of National Defence, the Commons had a single standing committee called National Defence and Veterans Affairs, which oversaw the legislation for both departments. Membership on each standing committee, given recent rule changes, is now set at a minimum of 10 and a maximum of 15; cabinet members are not assigned to them but a cabinet minister's parliamentary secretary may be; and the committees have the legal power to call witnesses, with testimony given under oath. Each committee selects a chair and vice-chair to preside over its meetings.

The composition of the standing committees, as well as of all other types, is party-based. The basic principle is that a party's strength in the full House is reflected within each committee. For example, if a party has 60 percent of the seats in the Commons, it will gain approximately 60 percent of the positions on each committee. Since the committees select their own chair and vice-chair, these positions are typically allocated to the governing party as well. Based on custom only, the Public Accounts Committee, which oversees government expenditures, is chaired by an opposition member. Not even that small token of influence has been granted the opposition in some provinces: in Nova Scotia, for example, during the 1970s, the Liberal Minister of Finance was also chair of the Public Accounts Committee, which produced a fairly blatant conflict of interest between his executive and legislative roles.

The party-basis of the standing committees means that party discipline ensures executive-dominance of the legislative process. In a majority government situation, the standing committees will often refuse to investigate matters that might be embarrassing to their own party. At the federal level, for example, former prime minister Pierre Trudeau always refused to allow his top aides, in particular Michael Pitfield, to testify before parliamentary committees. Only once in his career, on November 4, 1980, did Trudeau condescendingly appear before a Commons committee. A similar pattern of committee control was evident during the Chrétien years. In May of 2000, the Liberal chair of the House of Commons committee stopped the meeting that was hearing testimony from Human Resources Minister Jane Stewart regarding alleged financial problems in her department when the questions became hostile. In October of 2000, just days before a federal election was called, Liberal members did not show up at the committee meeting to hear the Auditor General's report regarding the Human Resources Development Canada (HRDC) scandal.

In a majority situation, the standing committees, given this party base, are not in a position to change government legislation against the wishes of the government. Even if they do revise a bill, such alterations can be reversed when the bill reappears at third reading before the full House. If a committee does object to a government bill, recalcitrant government committee members can always be removed and replaced. Moreover, committee assignments can be used to enforce party discipline. For example, Newfoundland MP George Baker "resigned" as chair of the committee looking into management problems in the fishery after the committee issued a highly critical report of its own government in September of 1998. Likewise, Ontario MP Albina Guarnieri was transferred from her position as chair of the Human Resources Committee after publicly criticizing Justice Minister Anne McLellan.

In a minority government, the influence of the committees is temporarily enhanced if the opposition parties can overcome their differences and work together to amend the government's legislation. For example, in 1973, the Conservative and New Democratic parties combined at the committee stage to amend the minority Liberal government's wiretap legislation. The opposition parties inserted a notice provision in the bill requiring the government to inform people that they had been under surveillance if, after 90 days, no wrongdoing had been discovered. When the bill came back to the full House, the government tried to have the notice amend-ment deleted, but was unsuccessful. However, even in a minority government situation, the opposition parties usually do not co-operate, since they are usually more opposed to each other than to the government of the day. Minority governments create the potential for increased standing committee influence in the legislative process, but they certainly do not guarantee it.

The Passage of Legislation

Having considered the institutional structure and context of the House, we can now proceed to a discussion of how legislation is passed. The rites of passage that turn a bill into a law are extremely complex: it may take a neophyte MP several sessions before even the basic intricacies are mastered. The fundamentals, however, centre around three topics: first, the different types of bills; second, the stages of legislation; and third, legislative procedures such as closure and question period.

Any member of Parliament can introduce legislation, but the kind of legislation proposed and its chance of passage varies depending on whether it is a government bill or a private member's bill. A government bill is *one that is part of the ruling party's legislative program, is introduced by a minister, and is backed by the full weight of the government party caucus.* Government bills are given priority and are usually passed, especially under majority governments.

Private members' bills are *those bills introduced by an MP that do not have government support.* They are most often introduced by opposition members, but may be introduced by a government backbencher as well. Private members' bills are given little time for consideration in the Commons, have been traditionally dealt with in the order in which they were introduced (which means that many are not even debated), and are almost never passed. A rare exception occurred in September of 1996 when, despite clear objections from key cabinet members, Liberal backbenchers managed to pass a private member's bill that outlawed the practice of negative billing used by cable companies. However, before the bill was completely through the legislative process in the House, it died on the order paper when the House was dissolved for the 1997 election. In 1998, all five parties in the Commons agreed to strengthen the possibility of passing private members' bills, with one result being the passage again of a private member's bill in 1999 to ban the practice of negative billing.

The most common use of private members' bills is to influence public opinion, with the intent of changing future government policy. Reform proposals have often appeared first as private members' bills, only to be co-opted as government bills in later Parliaments, as public support and acceptance of the individual ideas become apparent.

Although specific details may vary from one type of bill to the next, all legislation goes through six stages: first reading; second reading; committee stage; third reading; consideration by the other House; and royal assent. Even this six-stage process greatly simplifies the actual passage of a bill by Parliament. In most cases, first reading, third reading, and royal assent are mere formalities; the crucial steps are the second reading and committee stages.

At first reading, the bill is introduced into the legislature by indicating the title of the bill and perhaps giving a very brief statement about the bill's subject matter. The legislation at this point is not open to amendment or debate, although in extremely rare cases it may be rejected. For example, in an almost unprecedented move, the Conservatives in the Ontario legislature denied a member the right to introduce a bill at first reading in May 1981.

The initial debate on a bill takes place at second reading, which is known as "approval in principle." The bill cannot be amended, but must be accepted or rejected in total. Second reading usually involves the major debate on a bill, for once it has been "approved in principle" it becomes difficult, although not impossible, to defeat it at a later stage.

In contrast to steps one and two, the committee stage does not usually involve the full House, but only a part of it. In most instances, a bill is sent to one of the standing committees for detailed, clause-by-clause review. It is at this step that the bill can be amended for the first time, in addition to being debated. Witnesses, both pro and con, may be called to testify, and the process may take a number of weeks.

Once the committee is finished with a bill, it is sent back to the full House for third reading. It is possible for the committee to have made changes in the legislation, but the full House has the right to accept or reject such revisions when it receives the bill back from the committee. If approval in principle has been given to a bill at second reading, plus a detailed look at its contents has been made during the committee stage, then there is little work to be accomplished at third reading. Usually, by this time, it is a foregone conclusion that the bill will pass, although the opposition parties may debate a controversial bill at some length at third reading. Government defeats, however, can happen at this stage, as with the rejection of a tax bill that provoked

the Constitutional Crisis of 1968. [Editor's Note: From time to time, especially where the Senate and House of Commons are dominated by different parties, there may be confrontations between the two. Usually the Senate eventually backs down, but in extreme cases the government in power may have to call an election or consider appointing up to eight additional senators pursuant to s. 26 of the *Constitution Act, 1867* (used once, in 1990), in order to get its legislation passed. See Table 23.3, "The 15 Most Controversial Senate Votes" and accompanying discussion in Dyck, ch. 23.]

Once the bill is passed by one of the Houses of the legislature, the same basic steps are repeated by the other House of Canada's bicameral legislature. Although either House may initially consider any bill — except for money bills, which have to originate in the Commons — the usual practice is for government legislation to be presented first to the Commons and then to the Senate. Although the Senate may traditionally make minor changes in a piece of legislation, for all intents and purposes its approval has been, in most eras, perfunctory. However, in a bicameral legislature, the bill as passed by both Houses must be identical, so that if the Senate amends legislation coming from the Commons, the revisions must be sent back to the lower House for its approval.

The sixth and final stage concerns approval by the formal executive through the royal assent procedure, which takes place in the Senate chamber. Royal assent has never been refused to a federal piece of legislation, and the bill usually becomes the law of the land as soon as royal assent has been granted. In some instances, a section of the bill or the entire bill itself may not become operative until it is proclaimed. For example, NAFTA (the North American Free Trade Agreement) was passed by the Conservative government of Brian Mulroney in 1993, but it was not proclaimed by the new Liberal government of Jean Chrétien until December 30 — to go into effect on January 1, 1994.

Given this process for the passage of legislation, it should not be surprising to discover that legislative approval is often a long-drawn-out affair consuming many weeks, months, or even years. If the opposition parties make full use of their rights to talk and debate, as well as to propose amendments, then the government may be delayed, but not defeated, in obtaining legislative enactment of its policy proposals. For example, in September of 2000, the Bloc Québécois, in an attempt to stop the Liberal government's revisions to the Young Offenders Act, proposed a record [3,133] amendments to the bill. In order to prevent future use of this tactic, the Liberal government, using closure, changed the rules of the House in February of 2001 to allow the Speaker to reject motions or amendments that are deemed to be "frivolous" or "vexatious."

Each step of the legislative process normally occurs on a different day, with several days required between some steps, as between the committee stage and third reading. If the opposition desires it, the legislative process can become very time-consuming. However, if the parties in the House are in agreement, a piece of legislation can literally breeze through. In June of 1998, the House of Commons voted itself a $13,000 pay increase after two hours of debate. However, the record for speedy action appears to be held by the provincial legislature in Newfoundland, which voted itself a 7 percent pay raise, without debate, in just 41 seconds in December 1998. There is nothing like self-interest to make short work of the legislative obstacle course.

Such consensus in the legislature is rare, however; typically, the parties confront each other over almost every piece of legislation. If the government has a majority mandate, there is usually no way that the opposition parties can stop the ruling party's legislative program from becoming law. If the opposition parties utilize their delaying tactics and if the government is adamant about the need for a particular measure, then the government can always force it through the legislature by invoking closure, or by using a somewhat less powerful version of closure known as "time allocation." For example, in April of 1997, in an attempt to stop the Ontario Conservative government from merging the various Toronto municipalities into one large mega-city, the opposition in the provincial legislature proposed over [11,000] amendments to the bill. As expected, the government moved to limit the debate. Closure is *the cutting off of debate by the government*, and it is a powerful tool for ensuring the passage of government legislation.

Historically, closure has been only occasionally used in the Canadian House, although the frequency of its usage has increased in recent years. For example, the Mulroney government, in February of 1990, moved closure to end the debate at the second reading of its controversial legislation to implement the Goods and Services Tax (GST). In its first six years of government, the Mulroney Tories utilized closure 27 times. In contrast, since it was first adopted, closure was used only 19 times from 1913 to 1984. Every major piece of legislation adopted by the Mulroney government between 1984 and 1990, except for the Meech Lake Accord, was passed with the use of closure or time allocation. In 1991, changes in the procedures of the House of Commons that make the use of closure easier were adopted by invoking closure! Between 1993 and 2001 the Chrétien governments invoked closure an unprecedented 70 times.

At the provincial level, closure has been more rarely used than at the federal level. For example, the use of closure in the Manitoba legislature in January 1984 was the first time it had been used since 1929. However, in British Columbia in the fall of 1983, the Social Credit government, in forcing its restraint package through the legislature, invoked closure extensively (20 times between September 19 and October 13, 1983). Previous to this brutal use of majority power, closure had only been invoked once (in 1957) in British Columbia's entire history (*The Globe and Mail*, October 14, 1983). The first use of closure in the history of Saskatchewan did not occur until August 1989.

The threat of closure is often sufficient to bring the opposition into line, unless the opposition is attempting to force the government to use closure, so it can then claim that the government is "abusing Parliament." Closure, combined with party discipline, ensures the passage of the government's legislation, especially in a majority context. Using closure, it would take approximately 10 sitting days of Parliament for any bill to become law. Thus, if a majority government is not successful in enacting a bill, it is for the quite simple reason that it does not really want it passed (e.g., the failure of freedom of information legislation throughout the late 1970s and early 1980s).

With this process of legislative approval, it is apparent that much of the work of the legislature involves disputes about procedure rather than about content or subject matter. The reason for a procedural emphasis is quite clear: with a government that has a majority mandate, the substance of legislation cannot be altered without that government's concurrence. Hence, if the opposition wants to delay a bill, it will try to tie it up in a series of procedural disputes and points of privilege. While such tactics may not defeat a government, they may embarrass it, as in December 1974, when the NDP pointed out to the Speaker that a quorum of MPs was not present to vote on a 47 percent increase in their own salaries.

In minority government situation[s], the opposition may be more successful, for the government may agree to substantive changes rather than risk defeat in the House. However, minority governments have rarely feared legislative rejection: several examples, such as Trudeau's defeat in 1974 or Clark's defeat in December 1979, probably indicate that the executive wanted to be brought down in each case so as to force an election. It would be hard to demonstrate in either situation that the legislature was exercising effective control over the executive.

Although the government is rarely defeated in the legislature, it is, nonetheless, kept from doing everything its little heart desires. Probably the best check against government pigheadedness, incompetence, or downright malfeasance is the oral question period in the Commons. Oral question period is *the process by which members of the legislature can ask the government questions that the government is required to respond to.* When the House is in session, the opposition members, or once in a while a brave government backbencher, can challenge the government over its past, present, or projected behaviour, for 45 minutes a day. Since the government ministers do not know what the questions will be, the opposition attempts to embarrass them over policy, patronage, or corruption.

While the opposition cannot force ministers to answer, their failure to do so, or their seeming unwillingness to do so, influences their own and their party's image among the electors. It is quickly apparent whether a minister has control over, or an understanding of, his or her department. Yet ministers with political savvy can answer a question without really being specific, thereby frustrating the opposition. Another possibility is to take the particular question "on notice," that is, to say that one does not have the answer on hand, but will, of course, search diligently for it and report back. On highly controversial matters, a court case may have started or a royal commission may have been appointed to look into the matter. In these situations, the minister refuses to answer the questions on the grounds that he or she does not want to prejudice the court case now underway, or refuses to respond since a royal commission is investigating the problem. In the late 1970s, anyone appointed to the position of solicitor general had to learn two things: first, the oath of office; and second, a statement indicating an inability to answer any questions about RCMP activities and wrongdoings because the McDonald Royal Commission was currently investigating the matter.

Such techniques of avoidance have done much to undercut the effectiveness of the question period, but it remains one of the few ways the legislature, and particularly the opposition, can bring the government to task. The fact that the question period is significant in its impact is demonstrated by the lengths to which governments sometimes go to try to

undercut it. One technique of undermining the question period is evident in the practice of not allowing past ministers to answer questions, even if they are still members of the House. A new minister can feign ignorance of past events, and the former minister, sitting only a few feet away, is not forced to respond.

The most serious attack on question period occurred between 1968 and 1972, after former prime minister Trudeau's first election victory. Arguing that it was inefficient to have all ministers present every single day (an outside observer might assume that it was part of their job), Trudeau introduced the infamous roster system, whereby *only a given number of ministers would be present (say one-half) on any specific day.* Amazingly, a number of ministers who were to have been absent from question period would appear on the floor once the routine business of the House began. The roster system was rightly attacked by the press and opposition parties as a blatant attempt to muzzle question period. After the Liberals won only a minority government in 1972, the roster system was dropped at the insistence of the opposition members. Although it has not been formally reintroduced, many governments unofficially follow it: a common complaint of federal and provincial opposition members is the poor turnout of government ministers during question period.

An interesting development with respect to question period occurred in New Brunswick after the Liberals won all 58 seats in the 1987 provincial election. For three years there was no question period in the New Brunswick Legislature. However, in an unprecedented move in 1991, Premier Frank McKenna allowed the opposition parties to sit in the press gallery and to ask questions of the government as though they were elected opposition members. Fortunately, this unusual parliamentary invention was not needed for long: in the 1991 provincial election, the opposition parties gained 12 seats and, thus, question period returned to its more traditional format.

Functions of the House of Commons

It should be clear from our discussion of both the structure and procedure in the House of Commons that its role is heavily influenced by the nature of the executive-legislative relationship. In the Canadian parliamentary system, the fusion of executive and legislative power, based on party cohesion and cabinet direction, has meant that the notion of parliamentary supremacy is a myth. Parliament does not write the legislation, revise it to any great extent, or defeat the government's program. Control of the legislature by the executive has, however, produced a system wherein the government of the day has the capacity, if not always the will, to act decisively. Given such a pattern, these questions might rightfully be asked: Why is the concept of parliamentary supremacy maintained? If Parliament does not in any real sense make the laws, what functions does the legislature perform?

The principle of parliamentary sovereignty is retained because it is useful for the legislature in carrying out its two most important remaining and interdependent political functions of legitimation and representation. In approving executive decisions, the legislature legitimates the exercise of influence and power by the prime minister and cabinet; that is, it makes the government's actions acceptable to the public. Because it is a representative institution, the House of Commons can continue to serve as a repository of public authority, even if that authority is effectively exercised by the political executive. People may not like increases in their taxes, but if approved by Parliament, then they will most likely accept them. In many respects, Parliament is based on both traditional and legal-rational bases of authority. If the traditional basis is not sufficient, then the fact that the proper procedure has been followed can be used to justify obedience.

A good example of the legitimation function of the legislature can be seen with respect to a government's budget. Probably no piece of legislation is more fundamental than a budget, for it sets the priorities of the polity. The typical and traditional procedure in a budget's preparation, which is done in secret, is for the Minister of Finance, in consultation with the prime minister and perhaps several other cabinet ministers, to set the broad outlines of policy, which are then specified in detail by the bureaucracy. The budget is written and printed before the full cabinet sees it or before the government party caucus is informed of its content. It is then presented by the Minister of Finance in the Commons and becomes the subject of a special debate. Following the 1993 election, the new finance minister, Paul Martin, opened up the budgetary process, which included "public consultations" before the budget was finalized. However, clear government control of the budget process remains in place.

However, while the budget debate rarely changes the content of the document, it gives the opposition a chance to air public grievances about the decisions already taken. Such a procedure allows the legislature to legitimate decisions that have already been taken by the political executive. If any further evidence

of this point is required, then the implementation of wage-and-price controls in the mid-1970s would provide it. Although Pierre Trudeau went on national television in early October 1975 to announce the immediate imposition of wage-and-price controls, the bill authorizing such a move was not passed by Parliament until several months later. The extent to which Parliament can effectively legitimate such actions is based in part on the public's perception of it as a representative institution.

The House of Commons is representative in the obvious sense that the people, through the election process, select its members. However, the representative function usually comprises more than simply the process of selection, including in most cases the implication that once the members are chosen they will make known the concerns of their constituents and reflect the socio-economic attributes of the electorate. With respect to the latter point, it is clear that Canadian legislators have never been a mirror image of the general public. Lawyers have traditionally dominated the membership in the House (about 30 percent are now lawyers), but they currently rank third behind MPs with business or educational backgrounds. [In the summer of 2007, most MPs had been (in order): business men and women, lawyers, "consultants", teachers, managers, administrators, professors, and farmers.] In 1988, 39 out of 295 MPs were women, with that number increasing to 60 (out of 301) after the 1997 election and to 62 (out of 301) in the 2000 election. [By the summer of 2007, this proportion had got slightly worse: 63 of the 305 MPs were women.] However, minority women (i.e., other than French or English) and other social and ethnic groups are still poorly represented in Parliament (Black, 2000).

Legislators attempt to represent their constituents by their activities in the House, including the debates, committee hearings, and question period. Through such mechanisms, individual MPs, particularly opposition members, make their constituents' views known and publicize government wrongdoing or incompetence in handling the affairs of the nation. In that sense, then, the "essential day-to-day business of the Canadian House of Commons is not decision-making but representation" (Hockin, 1973: 361).

Although the current legislative functions of representation and legitimation are not as grand as the principle of parliamentary sovereignty, they are important tasks. The House of Commons has adapted to changing circumstances and thereby has maintained a significant place for itself in the political system. In the process, some of the initial patterns of Canadian politics have been altered, such as the lack of party unity in the Commons. Moreover, parliamentary privilege, which emerged historically in the battles between the king and Parliament, is now used to buttress the representational tasks of the legislators, guaranteeing their right to question the government, as well as to raise issues of concern to their constituents. The 20th century witnessed changes in the structure of the House (e.g., number of members and number of provinces) and in its procedures (e.g., closure, standing committees). Such changes reflect the evolution of the House of Commons from a law-making institution (if it ever truly was) to one concerned with the remaining functions of representation and legitimation.

In adapting to its changing functions and environment, the House of Commons has often been seen as a focal point for political reform. Opposition parties favour reform, while governments typically become reluctant to consider major changes, especially after they have been in office for any length of time. As a result, reform is typically high on the political agenda when there has been a turnover in the governing party.

THE CANADIAN SENATE

Unfortunately for Senate admirers (one assumes there are a few, at least, outside of current, former, or prospective aspirants), the upper House of Canada's legislature has neither performed as expected nor adapted to the changing circumstances of the 21st century. As a result the Senate, although never the equal of the House of Commons, has witnessed a steady erosion of its legislative role. For example, one study of the Canadian Parliament uses the "terms parliament and House of Commons interchangeably," because of the minimal legislative power retained by the Senate (Kornberg and Mishler, 1976: 17–18). Technically, however, Parliament includes the Senate, the House of Commons, and the formal executive. While the imminent demise of the Senate is not apparent, neither is its permanent rejuvenation, even given its temporary resurgence around a limited number of issues, such as the GST, in recent years....

(d)   Electoral Reform?

How likely is electoral reform?[1] At present, Canadian federal, provincial, and territorial jurisdictions use the first-past-the-post (FPTP), or single-member plurality electoral system. This system is simple to use, facilitates representation by local constituencies, and reduces the likelihood of unstable minority governments.[2] On the other hand, the FPTP system can generate large discrepancies between seats won and the popular vote, can minimize representation by women and non-regional minorities, and tends to exaggerate regional electoral differences.[3]

The FPTP system has produced some dramatic distortions, leaving some voters with the feeling that their votes don't count. In the 1987 New Brunswick election, for example, the Liberals won 60% of the popular vote but gained 100% of the seats. In Saskatchewan in 1986, in British Columbia in 1996, and in Quebec in 1998, parties that placed second in overall votes won a majority of the seats. In the 1997 House of Commons elec-

tion, the Quebec-based Bloc Québécois had about half the popular vote of the Conservatives, but won more than twice as many seats.[4] In the 2006 federal election, the Bloc Québécois, gained 51 seats with less than 11% of the popular vote, while the New Democratic Party, with more than 17% of the popular vote, won only 29 seats.[5]

Distortions such as this can work against high voter turnout, national unity, general faith in democratic solutions. Outside Canada, very few countries still use pure FPTP systems.[6] Most Western democracies use some kind of proportional representation.[7] One of the most common forms is the party list (PL) system, in which preferential votes are cast in multi-member constituencies, and each party receives the number of seats that corresponds to its share of the popular vote.[8] The single transferrable vote (STV) system also involves preferential votes that are cast in multi-member constituencies. However, after identifying the top preference in each constituency, this system then aggregates second, third, and lower preferences until all available constituency seats have been filled.[9] Under the alternative vote (AV) system, preferential votes are cast in single member constituencies. If no candidate gains at least 50% of the first choices, second and lower choices are aggregated to determine which candidate has plurality support.[10] Another approach is the mixed member proportional system (MMP), in which some candidates are chosen on an FPTP basis, and the remainder are chosen on a proportional basis, usually from a party list. Although the MMP system involves two different categories of representative, it combines FPTP strengths, such as strong local constituency representation, with the greater representativeness of the proportional system.[11]

Despite widespread criticism of the present system, there has been little concrete change so far in this country. There has been some movement in the provinces, but with no concrete results. One of the highest profile initiatives took place in British Columbia. The provincial government appointed a 160-member Citizens Assembly on Electoral Reform, evenly balanced by gender and containing two representatives from each of B.C.'s electoral districts, and two Aboriginal representatives. After a year of public consultation and research, the Assembly recommended an STV voting system. At a public referendum on May 17, 1985, their recommendation was defeated. It was approved in 77 of B.C.'s 79 constituencies, and gained 57% support overall, but the referendum rules required majority support in 60% of the ridings, and 60% support overall. In light of the narrow margin of defeat, the government promised to hold another referendum on STV in November 2008.

Later that year, proportional representation suffered a bigger setback in Prince Edward Island. Following an introductory study, the eight-person Commission on Prince Edward Island's Electoral Future recommended a mixed member proportional system that combined FPTP and party list procedures.[12] For the plebiscite, the provincial government imposed the same rigorous levels of support as in British Columbia, and announced them a month before the vote. The P.E.I. government refused a request by the Commission to extend its consultation and education time, denied public funding to the yes and no campaigns, failed to circulate a voter's list, and opened only 20% of the polling stations normally used for elections. The public was given only a month before the plebiscite to consider the Commission's final rec-

ommendation. At the plebiscite on November 28, 2005, 63% of those who voted chose to keep the existing FPTP system. In the circumstances, perhaps not too surprising a result!

Mixed member systems adding a party list to a core of FPTP seats have also been recommended in New Brunswick, Quebec, and Ontario,[13] and have yet to be voted on. It is unclear, then, if proportional representation is around the corner in Canada, or if it will remain part of "that untravell'd world, whose margin ever fades For ever and forever when [we] move"[14] when reforms are attempted. Pessimists can point to the fact that governments in power have a vested interest in preserving the system that helped bring them to power. Optimists can point to the fact that public interest in electoral reform is growing; they can hope their governments are listening.

Notes

1. On electoral systems and reform generally, see generally *ACE: The Electoral Knowledge Network* <http://ace.at.org/epic-en/es/Epic_view/ES05>; MacIvor, ch. 4: Scott Reid, M.P., "The Road to Electoral Reform" (2005) 28 Canadian Parliamentary Review 4; John Ibbitson, "A balanced act for voters" *The Globe and Mail* (7 June 2003), A19; Law Commission of Canada, *Renewing Canadian Democracy* (Ottawa: Law Commission of Canada, 2002); online: <http://ww.lcc.gc.ca/en/themes/gr/er/discussion_paper/toc.asp>; Policy Options, Arend Lijphart, *Patterns of Democracy: Government Forms and Performance in Thirty-Six Countries* (New Haven: Yale University Press, 1999); Henry Milner, ed. *Making Every Vote Count: Reassessing Canada's Electoral System* (Peterborough, Ont.: Broadview Press, 1999); and William Irvine, *Does Canada Need a New Electoral System?* (Kingston: Institute of Intergovernmental Relations, 1979).

2. See, for example, ACE *supra* note 1, *Advantage and Disadvantages of FPTP Systems*, online: <http://aceproject.org/ace-en/topics/es/esd/esd01/esd01a/esd01a01>.

3. *Ibid.*

4. Andrew Heard, Simon Fraser University, *Elections: Electoral Reform* <http://www.sfu.ca/~aheard/elections/index.htm>.

5. Canada Votes 2006, "Analysis and Commentary: Election Day Analysis" *CBC News* (23 January 2006), online: cbc.ca <http://www.cbc.ca/canadavotes/analysiscommentary/elexblog060123.html>.

6. Examples are the United Kingdom (the House of Commons, but not the Scottish, Welsh, and Northern Ireland assemblies), the United States, and countries such as India, Nigeria, Trinidad and Tobago, and Barbados.

7. The discussion here summarizes some of the main forms of proportional representation. For a more detailed discussion, addressing other proportional representation models such as the FPTP system, see Ontario Citizens Assembly Secretariat, *From Votes to Seats: Four Families of Electoral Systems* (Toronto: Ontario Citizen's Assembly, circa 2006), online: <http://www.citizensassembly.gov.on.ca/assets/From%20Votes%20to%20Seats.pdf>.

8. See summaries in ACE *supra* note 1, *List PR* <http://ace.at.org/ace-en/topics/es/esd/esd02/esd02c/default>; ACE *supra* note 1, *Advantages and Disadvantages of List PR* <http://ace.at.org/ace-en/topics/es/esd/esd02/esd02c/esd02c01>. List PR is the most common electoral sys-

tem, used in one form or another by about 70 countries, including nearly all the members of the European Union.

9. See summaries in ACE *supra* note 1, *The Single Transferrable Vote* <http://aceproject.org/ace-en/topics/es/esd/esd 02/esd02d> and ACE *supra* note 1, *Advantages and Disadvantages of STV* <http://aceproject.org/ace-en/topics/es/ esd/esd02/esd02d/esd02d01>. ACE *supra* note 1, *List PR* <http://ace.at.org/ace-en/topics/es/esd/esd02/esd02c/default>; ACE *supra* note 1, *Advantages and Disadvantages of List PR* <http://ace.at.org/ace-en/topics/es/esd/esd02/esd02c/ esd02c01>.

10. See summaries in ACE *supra* note 1, *The Alternative Vote* <http://ace.at.org/ace-en/topics/es/esd/esd01/esd01d> and ACE *supra* note 1, *Advantages and Disadvantages of AV* <http://aceproject.org/ace-en/topics/es/esd/esd01/esd01d/ esd01d01>. The alternative vote system is used in Australia.

11. See summaries in ACE *supra* note 1, *Mixed Member Proportional* <http://www.aceproject.org/ace-en/topics/es/esd/ esd03/esd03a> and ACE *supra* note 1, *Advantages and Disadvantages of MMP* <http://aceproject.org/ace-en/ topics/es/esd/esd03/esd03a/esd03a01>. The MMP system is used in countries such as New Zealand, Germany, Hungary, and Mexico, and in Scotland and Wales.

12. See Jeannie Lea, "The Prince Edward Island Plebiscite on Electoral Reform" (2006) 29:1 Canadian Parliamentary Review, online: <http://www.parl.gc.ca/Infoparl/english/ issue.htm?param=173&art=1176>; John Andrew Cousins, "Electoral Reform for Prince Edward Island" (2002–2003) 25:4 Canadian Parliamentary Review, online: <http://www. parl.gc.ca/Infoparl/english/issue.htm?param=85&art=277>.

13. On May 15, 2007, the randomly-selected, 104-member Ontario Citizens' Assembly on Electoral Reform recommended a mixed member proportional system of voting for Ontario, combining 90 FPTP seats with 29 seats selected on a party list basis, with the relevant political party selecting a ranked list of candidates. Each voter would have two votes — one for the voter's preferred local candidate, and one for the voter's preferred party. The parties' share of the 29 party list seats would correspond to their share of the party votes. A referendum on the recommendation was set for October 10, 2007, the provincial election day. To be accepted, the new system would require at least 60% of voter support, and be approved by a majority of voters in at least 60% of electoral districts.

14. Alfred Lord Tennyson, *Ulysses*, in Jerome H. Buckley, ed., *Poems of Tennyson* (Boston, MA: Houghton Mifflin, 1958), 66.

(e) Executive Authority[†]

R.I. Cheffins and P.A. Johnson

The events of 1982 did not change the fact that Canada remains a monarchy with its traditional form of cabinet government. As previously indicated, the changes in the Constitution Act, 1867 were minimal, and certainly no changes were made with respect to the formal role of the Crown and its representatives. Section 9 of that Act provides that "the Executive Government and Authority of and over Canada, is hereby declared to continue and be vested in the Queen." This means that government is carried on in the name of the monarch and all of the traditional rules relating to the monarchy are still in existence. The Constitution Act, 1982 contained one reference to the office of the monarch, the governor general and the lieutenant governors of the provinces: it provided in section 41 that no change could be made in these offices without a resolution authorized by the Senate, the House of Commons and

the legislative assembly of each province. Thus the likelihood of Canada moving from a monarchical to a republican form of government in the immediate future is extremely remote. Furthermore, since the decision in *Re the Initiative and Referendum Act*[,][1] the word "office" also includes the powers relating to the office, any attempt to change the major legal powers of these office holders would need the unanimous consent required by the section 41 amending process.

One of the most perplexing features of the Canadian constitutional system is the subtle line distinguishing the formal executive, the monarch and her representatives, from the purely informal executive, the cabinet, to which the law makes relatively little reference. An exhaustive search through all of the documents defined in section 52 of the Constitution Act, 1982 as being included in the "Consti-

---

† Reproduced from *The Revised Canadian Constitution: Politics as Law* (Toronto: McGraw-Hill Ryerson, 1986) at 77–90 by permission of the authors.

See also MacIvor, ch. 6; Malcolmson, ch. 3 (responsible government) and ch. 7 (the Crown and its servants); Funston, ch. 4(4) (federal executive), and ch. 5(3) (provincial executive); Hogg 2007, ch. 9 (responsible government and executive) and ch. 10 (The Crown); Reesor, at 152–57 (federal), 192–96 (provincial), and 259–70 (revenues, debts, assets, taxation).

tution of Canada" reveals no reference to either the office of prime minister [or the] cabinet. [See, however, *Constitution Act, 1982*, ss. 35.1 and 49.] Nevertheless, in our constitutional and political system, power has shifted inexorably in the direction of first the cabinet and, increasingly in recent years, the first minister, whether at the federal or provincial level. It is our view that one of the unfortunate consequences of constitutional review in 1982 was the failure to examine and reform the excessively executive-dominated parliamentary system. The chances of any substantial revision of the cabinet and the parliamentary model of government now practised in Canada [are] unlikely.

Perhaps, however, the model is particularly suitable to a country which leading students of sociology and political culture such as Seymour Lipset and Gad Horowitz[2] regard as deferential and geared to an interventionist statist model of society. The Tory touch as defined by Horowitz means that Canada has adopted from Great Britain a system involving a high degree of state intervention in all aspects of human life. Our executive-dominated system thus blends very satisfactorily with a sense of deferential hierarchy with which Canadians feel both familiar and comfortable. As Van Loon and Whittington point out,[3] lobbyists in Canada spend very little time talking to M.P.s and M.L.A.s, but instead try to convince the bureaucracy, recognizing its substantial impact on decisions made by the cabinet. It is because of this executive dominance that the provincial premiers have become the only viable alternative, other than the courts, to the incredible power vested in the office of the Prime Minister of Canada.

The Crown

Executive government in Canada can be viewed from two perspectives, the formal executive and the political executive. They are of course closely interlinked but the formal executive is much more defined by legal rules than is the political executive. As indicated earlier, the head of the formal executive is the queen of Canada, who is at the time of writing Queen Elizabeth II. She is represented in Canada by the governor general at the federal level and by the lieutenant governors at the provincial level. Her powers derive from two sources, namely the prerogative powers of the Crown, that is, the residue of traditional authority which the monarch has had over the years, and a few provisions of the Constitution Act 1867.

It is the prerogative powers of the Crown which are, in many respects, the most important of the powers vested in the monarch. These prerogative powers are referred to in the Letters Patent of 1947 which, along with its precursors, is the document which delegated to the governor general the prerogative powers of the Crown. In fact, the creation of the office of governor general was done by Letters Patent and is accordingly a prerogative action of the monarch. As we shall see, the governor general, like the monarch, derives powers from two sources: prerogative powers delegated from the monarch and a series of designated powers in the Constitution Act, 1867. Undoubtedly the two most important statutory powers mentioned in the Constitution Act, 1867 relating to the monarch are, as already indicated, section 9 which vests executive authority in her person and section 17 which provides that "there will be One Parliament for Canada consisting of the Queen, an Upper House styled the Senate and a House of Commons." As we shall see, these powers are exercised on her behalf by the governor general.

The Office of Governor General

No exhaustive analysis of the role of the Crown and its representatives in Canada will be made here as this has already been done in several other books on the Canadian government and constitution.[4] The office of governor general was not created by the Constitution Act, 1867, but instead was created by the prerogative powers of the monarch. The prerogative powers vested in the monarch are those residual powers, recognized by the common law, which have not been taken away by statute. These powers of course find their antecedents in early times and have only continued through the sufferance of parliament. Parliament in the United Kingdom, if it wishes, can remove prerogative powers of the Crown, or it can put them into statutory form; thus the continued existence of the power depends upon the whim of parliament. Nevertheless, despite a continual whittling away of the prerogative powers of the Crown by parliament, a substantial number of these powers still exist and are of considerable importance in the Constitution of Canada.

In an earlier era all governors of British colonies were appointed by prerogative authority of the Crown as direct representatives of the monarch in the overseas milieu in which they served. It is to this historical origin, therefore, that the office of governor general owes its existence. Though the office is not created by statute, many of the most important powers vested in the governor general are in fact specifically elucidated in the Constitution Act, 1867. We can thus say that the office of governor general is created by the royal prerogative and has a combination of legal powers derived from two sources, namely through delegation by the monarch and in addition through specific provisions of Canada's fundamental constitutional document, the Constitution Act, 1867.

There have been a series of letters patent issued by the monarch relating to the office of governor general and allocating monarchical authority to the governor general to be exercised in Canada on behalf of the monarch. The most recent of these letters patent were those issued in October 1947, which provided that "there shall be a Governor General and Commander-in-Chief in and over Canada, and appointments to the Office of Governor General and Commander-in-Chief in and over Canada shall be made by Commission under Our Great Seal of Canada." The unique feature of the Letters Patent of 1947 was that for the first time in Canadian history the letters patent delegated all of the monarch's prerogative powers with respect to Canada. This authority was expressed in these words, "We do hereby authorize and empower our Governor General, with the advice of Our Privy Council for Canada or any members thereof or individually, as the case requires, to exercise all powers and authorities lawfully belonging to Us in respect of Canada...." The Letters Patent then go on to outline by specific example the authority vested in the governor general through this delegation of authority from the monarch, including the power to appoint a number of important Canadian officials.

The most significant of the prerogative powers assigned to the governor general is of course the power to ask someone to undertake the position of prime minister of Canada and accordingly to form a government in the monarch's name. This prerogative power also includes the authority to appoint ministers of the Crown as recommended by the prime minister. The letters patent go on to provide that the governor general is authorized "to remove from his office, or to suspend from the exercise of the same, any person exercising any office within Canada under or by virtue of any Commission or Warrant granted, or which may be granted, by Us in Our name or under Our Authority." This would, of course, allow the governor general to legally remove either the prime minister or cabinet ministers from office. This has never happened in the history of Canada at the federal level but it is an important weapon in the hands of the prime minister in the face of a recalcitrant minister who is not prepared to

resign. The prime minister would be entitled to go to the governor general and recommend, as his first minister, that the minister in question be removed from office.

It is clear that, in legal theory although highly unlikely in practice, the governor general could dismiss the prime minister if he or she thought fit. This happened in Australia in 1975 when a deadlock between the Liberal-dominated upper house and the Labour-dominated lower house produced a stalemate over the budget introduced by the labour government. Sir John Kerr, the governor general, took it upon himself to first dismiss the prime minister, order the dissolution of the House, thereby precipitating a general election, and to call upon the leader of the opposition to form a government. These dramatic actions by Kerr, who, it should be noted, was an appointee of the Crown on the advice of the Labour government, are unique in the history of the [major dominions] forming part of the former British Empire and colonies. They of course precipitated a good deal of critical comment in Australia as well as street demonstrations. Nevertheless, John Fraser, the newly appointed prime minister, was maintained in office by the general election which followed the actions of Kerr.[5]

The primary function of the Crown and its representatives is to make certain that there is always a first minister in office assigned the responsibility of advising the Crown on the conduct of government in the country. In addition to this important prerogative power is the authority to prorogue and dissolve parliament and thus precipitate a general election. It should be remembered that this important power of dissolution, in all but the most unusual circumstances, is exercised on the advice of the first minister. One of the two incidents in which a governor general refused to act on the advice of a first minister centred around the refusal, by Lord Byng, to grant a dissolution of the House of Commons to the then Prime Minister Mackenzie King. There were very solid constitutional traditions which justified the action by Lord Byng. There had been a recent general election and in addition there was, within the House of Commons, an alternate government capable of carrying the responsibility of office. The situation was a rather unusual one in that the election of October 29, 1925, resulted in a House composed of 101 Liberals, 116 Conservatives and 24 Progressives, plus assorted Independents. Prime Minister King chose to remain in office despite having fewer seats than the opposition Conservative party. When faced with a vote of non-confidence based on a serious custom scandal, Mr. King went to the governor general and asked for dissolution of the House. Lord Byng, acting on the aforementioned principles, refused to grant him dissolution and called on Opposition Leader Arthur Meighen to form a government. This government was only briefly in office, being defeated by one vote when a member of the opposition broke his pair with a member of the government.

This extraordinary turn of events led to another general election won by Mackenzie King, although again he did not obtain a majority in the House of Commons. He was able, through the support of the smaller parties, including the Progressives, United Farmers, Labourites and Independents, to carry on a stable government until his defeat in the general election of 1930. The leading scholar on the Crown in Canada has written a major book justifying the position of Lord Byng. Readers further interested in this subject should see the work, by Dr. Eugene Forsey: *The Royal Power of Dissolution of Parliament in the British Commonwealth.*[6]

The prerogative powers of the Crown also allow the governor general on behalf of Her Majesty to enter into treaties on behalf of Canada, to declare war and peace, and to name ambassadors to other countries. Naturally these legal powers are only carried out on the advice of the prime minister. In the case of a declaration of war it would be virtually unthinkable for the prime minister to render this advice to the governor general without debate in the House of Commons and a resolution approving the prime minister's action. Historically, the summoning of the House of Commons was a prerogative act of the Crown, but in Canada it is provided for by section 38 of the Constitution Act, 1867.

There are also a number of other very important legal powers vested in the governor general through the Constitution Act, 1867. For example, section 11 provides that the Queen's Privy Council for Canada is "chosen and summoned by the Governor General and sworn in as Privy Councillors, and Members thereof may be from Time to Time removed by the Governor General." Every cabinet minister is sworn in as a member of the Privy Council, though it should be noted that it is quite possible for persons to be summoned to the Privy Council without being members of the cabinet. The governor general will, however, only select persons to serve as members of the Privy Council on the advice of the prime minister. For example, it is quite common for the leader of the opposition, even though he has never been a member of cabinet, to be sworn in as a member of the Privy Council and thus be entitled to the use of the term "Honourable." The chief jus-

tice of Canada is also a member of the Queen's Privy Council for Canada. When parliament delegates powers in reality to the cabinet this is always done using the legal form of the governor in council. This simply means that selected members of the cabinet sign the order in council in their capacities as members of the Privy Council and then the approval of the governor general is obtained. Almost all major pieces of legislation contain some form of delegation. Probably the most frequent recipient of delegated authority is the governor in council.

As has already been noted, one of the crucial sections of the Constitution Act, 1867 is section 17, which provides that the Parliament of Canada shall consist of the Queen, the Senate and the House of Commons. This, in effect, means that no bill can be turned into law until it has been approved by votes in the House of Commons and the Senate and then given Royal Assent. Since the governor general is the queen's representative, Royal Assent is given on behalf of Her Majesty by the governor general. It is theoretically possible for the governor general to refuse assent but this is most unlikely. No governor general has ever refused assent to a bill after its passage through the Senate and House of Commons.

Another very significant legal power of the governor general is outlined in section 24 of the Constitution Act, 1867, which provides that the governor general, acting in the queen's name, will "summon qualified Persons to the Senate...." These appointments are only made by the governor general on the advice of the prime minister. An interesting provision of the Act is section 26, which allows the governor general, if the Queen thinks fit, to appoint four or eight extra members to the Senate. This was obviously intended as a deadlock breaking mechanism in case the upper house refused to pass a bill sent to it by the House of Commons. [Before 1990, when Prime Minister Mulroney used this section to appoint eight new Senators to secure Senate support for the GST bill, section 26 had] never been used because the general pattern of the Canadian Senate has been for one party to be overwhelmingly represented in the upper house at the expense of all other parties and independents.

Another interesting provision with respect to the power of the governor general is that provided by section 34, that he or she shall appoint the speaker of the Senate and, if necessary, remove the speaker. The speaker of the House of Commons, at least in theory, is elected by the members of that chamber, but the oligarchic position of the Senate is reflected not only in the method of appointment of its members but also in the selection of its spokesman. It almost goes without saying that the governor general will only select a speaker of the Senate upon the advice of the prime minister.

An often-neglected provision of the Constitution Act, 1867 which has very important consequences is section 54. Summarized in its briefest form, it provides that no measure can be introduced into the House of Commons dealing with the raising or expenditure of public funds without a "... Message of the Governor General in the Session in which such Vote, Resolution, Address, or bill is proposed." The significance of this particular provision is that Canadian tradition dictates that the governor general will give a message in relation to financial measures only to a member of the cabinet. This has the effect of prohibiting government back benchers and members of the opposition from introducing any measures, including private members' bills, which deal with fiscal matters. It does not take a great deal of acumen to realize that the scope provided for ordinary members to take legislative initiative is thus very limited. This provision is another reason for the executive dominance in the Canadian political and constitutional system.

Section 55 provides that where a bill has passed the two houses of the Canadian parliament, the governor general shall give Royal Assent in the queen's name or that assent can be withheld or the bill reserved for the pleasure of Her Majesty. As already indicated, the governor general has never, since 1867, refused Royal Assent and an Imperial Conference[7] recognized that the governor general's power of reservation would never be used. Under extremely unusual circumstances, it might perhaps be defensible to refuse assent, but certainly it would never be justifiable to utilize the technique of reservation.

Other than the aforementioned Byng crisis, there has been only one other occasion in which a Canadian governor general has refused to act on the advice of the prime minister. This occurred in 1896 with the defeat of the Conservative government of Dr. Charles Tupper. After the defeat the prime minister recommended to the governor general, Lord Aberdeen, that he appoint a number of prominent Conservatives to the judiciary and to the Senate. The governor general took the position that although the prime minister was technically still in office, he had been repudiated by the electorate and it was inappropriate for him to find jobs for party supporters before the swearing in of the Laurier government. Unlike the furor which raged with respect to the King-Byng crisis, the actions of the governor general

in this instance seemed, to most observers, appropriate and within the spirit of constitutional democracy.

The Office of Lieutenant Governor

The provincial equivalent of the office of governor general is the position of lieutenant governor. The lieutenant governor fulfils within his provincial context the same role and function as does the governor general within the federal context. The office of lieutenant governor, unlike that of governor general, is created by the Constitution Act, 1867. Section 58 provides that there shall be a lieutenant governor in each province, "appointed by the Governor General in Council by Instrument under the Great Seal of Canada." Section 59 provides that he or she holds office at the pleasure of the governor general, and can only be removed during his five-year appointment for some specifically defined cause. On a few occasions the lieutenant governor's five-year term has been extended by an additional one or two years. Section 60 provides that the salary of the lieutenant governor is designated and provided for by the Canadian parliament. Readers will undoubtedly recognize the close linkage, at least in law, between the office of lieutenant governor and the federal government. This close relationship certainly substantiates the position taken by Professor John Saywell in his book *The Office of Lieutenant Governor*,[8] that originally the lieutenant governor was more a federal officer than a representative of the monarch. In fact, it was envisaged that the lieutenant governor would represent federal interests within the provincial context and assure that provincial policies were not altogether out of line with those of the federal government. The function of a lieutenant governor as a federal officer probably made sense at a time when the provinces were far-flung and all forms of transportation and communication were difficult.

The legal role of the lieutenant governor was clarified with the decision of the Judicial Committee of the Privy Council in the case of *The Liquidators of the Maritime Bank of Canada v. The Receiver General of New Brunswick*.[9] The court had to decide the question of whether the lieutenant governor was the representative of the sovereign in such a way that all the privileges, powers and immunities of the Crown passed to the lieutenant governor of the province. The court held that the lieutenant governor was the representative of the Crown and that the prerogative rights of the Crown, insofar as they related to the province, passed to the holder of that office. This meant that, like the governor general, the lieutenant governor possessed all the prerogative powers of the monarch, such as the summoning and dismissal of a premier or cabinet minister and the dissolution of the legislature, in addition to those statutory powers set out in the Constitution Act, 1867.

It is sometimes forgotten that the prerogative includes special rules which apply only to the Crown and the Crown's representatives. For example, in the *Maritime Bank* case the Province of New Brunswick had deposited money in the Maritime Bank of Canada, which found itself in serious difficulty and had to wind up its financial affairs. The question arose as to whether the province enjoyed the traditional priorities of the Crown such that it could have its claims satisfied prior to other depositors and simple contract creditors of the bank. The province would only have a prior claim if it enjoyed the privileges of the royal prerogative. The court held that the lieutenant governor was, in fact, the representative of the Crown and enjoyed all the rights and privileges of a representative of the monarch. Thus, in this case, the province of New Brunswick was able to stand first in line when creditors had to be satisfied out of the limited assets of the bank.

This decision handed down in 1892 begins the redefinition of the office of lieutenant governor from that of federal officer to representative of the monarch. In the first fifty years after Confederation, lieutenant governors were involved in a good deal of political controversy largely because of the uncertainty over their role. For example, lieutenant governors have reserved seventy bills for the pleasure of the governor in council, thirteen of which ultimately received Royal Assent in the form of a federal order in council. Forty-two of these reservations took place in the first twenty-one years after Confederation and only one has been reserved since 1937.[10]

Everyone was astonished when Lieutenant Governor Bastedo of Saskatchewan in April of 1961 indicated that he was reserving for the pleasure of the governor in council a bill passed by the Legislative Assembly of Saskatchewan. The federal government indicated its surprise that the lieutenant governor would take this action without consultation with the prime minister, and through federal order in council gave speedy Royal Assent as provided for by section 57 of the Constitution Act, 1867.[11]

It should be noted that section 90 of the Constitution Act, 1867 makes sections 53, 54, 55, 56 and 57 applicable to the provinces. Thus, since the lieutenant governor is a component part of the legislature of each province, he is legally entitled[,] when presented with a bill passed by the legislative assem-

bly, to give or refuse Royal Assent or to reserve the bill for the pleasure of the Queen's Privy Council for Canada. As already indicated, lieutenant governors have reserved seventy bills for the pleasure of the governor in council, but it should also be noted that there have been twenty-eight refusals of assent. In twenty-seven of these cases assent was withheld on the advice of, or at least with the approval of, the provincial cabinet. There has been only one instance where a lieutenant governor unilaterally withheld assent to a bill passed by the legislative assembly of a province, namely Prince Edward Island.[12] There have been five occasions on which lieutenant governors have dismissed premiers, and three occasions on which lieutenant governors have refused requests by the premier of the day for a dissolution of the legislative assembly.[13]

It must be stressed that the generally turbulent times of lieutenant governors are certainly over. It would be extraordinary today for a lieutenant governor to refuse assent, a dissolution of the legislature or any other prerogative of the Crown without the advice of his or her first minister. It is now safe to say that the lieutenant governor plays within the provincial political structure the same role that the governor general fulfils within the federal political structure. Both are representatives of the monarch and both are assigned the traditional responsibilities of representing the Crown in their own constitutional bailiwick. Their first and most important responsibility is to make certain that the Crown is advised, that is to say, that someone is given a commission to form a government.

It is in the selection of a first minister that the governor general or lieutenant governor might have some discretion, depending upon the circumstances. For example, if a first minister should die in office then it is the responsibility of the Crown's representative to ask someone to form a government. Usually this does not present a problem, because if a political party has won the majority of seats in a general election then obviously their leader is asked to become prime minister or premier. If a prime minister should resign after the political party which is in power has had a convention and selected a new leader, then obviously the governor general or lieutenant governor will select the choice of the party. An element of discretion enters the picture, however, when a prime minister or premier dies in office. It then becomes the duty of the Crown's representative to ask a member of the ruling party to form a government. The queen's representative is entitled to consult with anyone that he or she wishes and, in fact, should consult as widely as possible. Ultimately, however, the choice of selecting a successor devolves upon the governor general or lieutenant governor. Should the new first minister not be chosen as party leader then, of course, he or she would have to resign to make way for the new leader of the majority party.[14]

The role of the Crown was vividly illustrated in Great Britain in 1956 when Sir Anthony Eden resigned as prime minister and Her Majesty Queen Elizabeth II was faced with the task of choosing between Mr. Harold Macmillan and Mr. R.A.B. Butler. After consultation with leading Conservatives, she called upon Mr. Macmillan to form a government.

The foregoing indicates the immense legal powers of the governor general and lieutenant governors, but as has been continually reiterated these powers, except in the most exceptional circumstances, are exercised on the advice of the appropriate first minister. This logically brings us to an analysis of the role, structure and function of a cabinet in the Canadian political system, and in particular points to the very special role of the first minister of that cabinet.

The First Minister and the Cabinet

The engine room of the Canadian governmental system at both the federal and provincial levels is the cabinet. Readers will remember that there had developed before 1867 the concept of responsible government. This is still undoubtedly the most important principle of Canada's constitutional structure. There are carefully defined conventions of the Constitution which determine who is called upon to form a government. Normally the leader of the party with the largest number of seats in the House of Commons is given by the governor general the queen's commission to form a government. It is then the responsibility of this person to submit to the governor general a list of ministers, to which the governor general will give his approval. Thus, legally, the first minister and cabinet are appointed by the governor general acting under the prerogative authority of the Crown. Those persons who can be designated as the first minister and ministers of the Crown are, of course, determined by convention.

This collective group of ministers and first minister is known as the cabinet, and remains as the cabinet only so long as a first minister is in office. In the event that a prime minister or premier should die, cabinet ministers remain ministers but a cabinet is no longer in existence. It is for this reason that the Crown's representative has a discretion as to whom he or she can call upon to form a government. This, in essence, is because only the first minister can give constitutional advice which is binding on the representative of the Crown. This is why it is so important that the representative of the Crown discharge the task of asking someone to form a government as quickly as possible after the resignation or death of a prime minister or premier. There is no lawful requirement that a prime minister or premier must have a seat in either the Senate or the House of Commons. However, it would be considered improper for a first minister not to seek a seat as soon as possible. An example of this, of course, was the governor general asking Mr. John Turner to form a government, even though he was not at the time a member of the House of Commons.

It should be noted that nowhere in the entrenched documents of the Canadian Constitution is there any mention of the office of prime minister or that collectivity known as the cabinet. In their judgment in the case of *Reference Re Amendment of the Constitution of Canada*,[15] the majority of the judges suggested that the phrase in the preamble to the Constitution Act, 1867, "with a Constitution similar in Principle to that of the United Kingdom," might well involve a recognition of the principle of responsible government. Though that phrase has been given other interpretations by the courts, such as the concept of parliamentary supremacy or the recognition of civil liberties, the judges are probably correct in identifying the ideas of responsible government as being at the heart of what was intended by that phrase.

Other than the foregoing, there is no specific mention in any of our legal documents of the responsibility of the office of prime minister, premier or cabinet. However these offices do not go unrecognized in other statutory provisions governing salaries and the residence of the prime minister at the federal level. The latter, though important, do not define in any way the nature and structure of the office of the first minister and his cabinet. Similarly, at the provincial level, most provinces have statutes called the Executive Council Act or, in the case of British Columbia, the Constitution Act, which refer to the executive council of the province and, in some cases, to the premier.

All of this legislation, however, at both federal and provincial levels, totally ignores the real authority and functioning of the cabinet in the Canadian constitutional context. Certainly under Prime Minister Trudeau, the cabinet seemed to become less important than under a number of other regimes, in that the ministers seemed to have less latitude and scope for individual initiative. It has been suggested that in recent years more and more authority has been vested in various standing committees of the cabinet. As Van Loon and Whittington suggest in their book on the Canadian political system, more and more decisions are being made at the committee stage of cabinet, rather than by the cabinet meeting to collectively determine solutions. All of the committee decisions must be funnelled through cabinet, but the outcomes are in essence determined by the appropriate committee.[16]

The development of a committee system has in turn strengthened the role of the bureaucracy in determining the force of policy in Canada. Each of these committees has assigned to it full-time civil servants who are members of the Privy Council Office. It is the function of these civil servants to brief and guide members of the committee in their deliberations. The size of the Privy Council Office grew dramatically during the regime of Prime Minister Trudeau. Alongside the Privy Council Office is the Prime Minister's Office which, as Van Loon and Whittington indicate, grew to include over [one hundred] members by the latter years of the Trudeau administration. The result of these factors has been to dramatically increase the power of the prime minister at the expense of individual ministers and of parliament itself. The sheer number of cabinet ministers has lessened their individual importance.

This is not to say, however, that the office of prime minister was not traditionally a very powerful one, since a Privy Council minute, P.C. 3374, issued by the cabinet on October 25, 1935, stated that

> the following recommendations are the special prerogative of the prime minister: dissolution and Convocation of Parliament: Appointment of — Privy Councillors; cabinet Ministers; lieutenant governors (including leave of absence to same); Provincial Administrators; Speaker of the Senate; Chief Justices of All Courts; Senators; Sub-Committees of Council; Treasury Board; ...[17]

This minute alone would be sufficient to give the reader some indication of the stranglehold which the prime minister has on power in the context of the federal government. This means, in effect, that especially by using the powers of the governor general, the prime minister has effective control of the appointment of all of the Senate, the speaker of the Senate, the appointment of cabinet ministers and their removal, the summoning, prorogation and dissolution of parliament, the selection of a speaker for the House of Commons, control of the appointment of deputy ministers, appointment of members of boards and commissions and effective control of the appointment of judges of all the federal courts and of all provincially created courts, starting with those of the county court right through to the court of appeal of each province. A brief refinement should probably be made with respect to the appointment of members of the judiciary, as the fundamental responsibility for making recommendations other than those of chief justices rests with the minister of justice. Nevertheless, one can be fairly certain that if the prime minister strongly objected to a recommendation of the minister of justice, the likelihood of that appointment being made is extremely small.

Considering further the powers of the cabinet, it must be remembered that the cabinet dictates the functioning of the legislative process. As already indicated, the cabinet determines when parliament sits and the order of business before the House. Its members control the budget and, by virtue of section 54 of the Constitution Act, 1867, no money bill is ever introduced in the House of Commons without a message from the governor general. Convention dictates that no message is ever provided by the governor general except to a minister of the Crown on the advice of the cabinet.

Notes

1. [1919] A.C. 935 (P.C.).
2. "Conservatism, Liberalism, and Socialism in Canada: An Interpretation" (1966), 32 Can. J. Econ. Poli. Sci., 143.
3. Richard J. Van Loon and Michael S. Whittington, *The Canadian Political System*. Toronto: McGraw-Hill Ryerson, 3d ed., 1981.
4. See R.I. Cheffins and R.N. Tucker, *The Constitutional Process in Canada*. Toronto: McGraw-Hill Ryerson, 2d ed., 1976, chapter 4; R. MacGregor Dawson, *The Government of Canada*. Toronto: University of Toronto Press, 5th ed., revised by Norman Ward, 1970; J.R. Mallory, *The Structure of Canadian Government*. Toronto: Gage, rev. ed., 1984, chapter 2.
5. For an exposition of the position of Sir John Kerr see John Kerr, *Matters for Judgment: An Autobiography*. New York: St. Martin's Press, 1979.
6. Toronto: Oxford University Press, 1943. For a brief synthesis of this crisis see Cheffins and Tucker, supra, note 4, pp. 83–84; Forsey, "Was the Governor General's Refusal Constitutional?" *Politics: Canada*. Toronto: McGraw-Hill Ryerson, 5th ed., Paul W. Fox, ed., 1982, p. 431. A further analysis of this incident can be found in Roger Graham, ed., *The King-Byng Affair, 1926; A Question of Responsible Government*. Toronto: Copp Clark, 1967.
7. Held in 1887.
8. Toronto: University of Toronto Press, 1957.
9. [1892] A.C. 437 (P.C.).
10. G.V. La Forest, *Disallowance and Reservation of Provincial Legislation*. Ottawa: Department of Justice, 1955.
11. For a more detailed account of this incident, see Mallory. "The Lieutenant-Governor's Discretionary Powers: The Reservation of Bill 56" (1961), 27 Can. J. Econ. Poli. Sci., 518.
12. This event took place in 1945 in connection with a measure designed to liberalize the liquor law of the province. See further Saywell, supra, note 8, p. 222.
13. For further details with respect to the office of lieutenant governor see Saywell, "The Lieutenant-Governors,"

The Provincial Political Systems. Toronto: Methuen, David J. Bellamy, Jon H. Pammett and Donald C. Rowat, eds., 1976, p. 297.

14. Professor J. Mallory describes the rather unusual course of events which followed the deaths of Premiers Duplessis and Sauve in Quebec, whereby all the members of the Union Nationale caucus signed a petition to the lieutenant governor indicating who they wanted to succeed the deceased

premier: see Mallory, "The Royal Prerogative in Canada: The Selection of Successors to Mr. Duplessis and Mr. Sauve" (1960), 26 Can. J. Econ. Poli. Sci., 314.

15. [1981] 1 S.C.R. 753.

16. Van Loon and Whittington, *supra*, note 3, at p. 493.

17. This minute can be found in Heeney, "Functions of the Prime Minister," *Politics: Canada*. Toronto: McGraw-Hill, 3d ed., Paul W. Fox, ed., 1970, p. 347.

(f) Gomery Reports†

NOTE

The Gomery Inquiry into the 1990s federal sponsorship scandal provided Canadians with a fascinating look at the upper reaches of the executive branch of government, where senior appointed members of the administrative process interface with Cabinet ministers and their assistants. The ill-conceived, badly managed sponsorship program raised specific concerns about control of the administrative process and more wide-ranging concerns about the operation concepts of democracy, responsible government and ministerial responsibility. Instead of promoting national unity, the program stirred public anger, and helped bring down a government.

(i) The Theory

Among other things, democracy means rule by the people, or government accountable to the people.[1] In the British parliamentary system, a key tool of democracy is responsible government, which makes the Cabinet accountable to the elected members of the House of Commons.[2] For government as a whole, this principle requires a general culture of openness. Members of the House of Commons can't hold government to account, and members of the public can't make informed electoral choices, unless they know what is happening. For particular departments, responsible government has an individual aspect: ministe-

rial responsibility. Individual ministers are expected to provide general policy direction to their deputy ministers, who offer advice, and then implement and monitor this policy through directions to their subordinates and ongoing supervision. This process requires a hierarchical chain of command, to ensure that ultimate power and general responsibility are in the hands of the ministers and, through them, the Cabinet.

These accountability conditions may come under strain in situations that involve high-stakes political issues, large sums of money, propaganda, pressure for secrecy, and efforts to bypass established processes for ministerial responsibility. Unfortunately, the sponsorship program managed to combine all five of these ingredients. Morever, as Justice Gomery was to find, it suggested that there was a misconception about the needs of responsible government at the very highest political level in the country.

(ii) The Program

The sponsorship program started as an effort to promote national unity through advertising. As the commentary below suggests, things went downhill from there. The program was a case of management gone wrong, lacking clear objectives, bypassing normal departmental supervision, violating established contracting procedures, wast-

† Commission of Inquiry into the Sponsorship Program and Advertising Activities (Justice John H. Gomery, Chair), *Who is Responsible?: Fact Finding Report* (Ottawa: Public Works and Government Services Canada, 1 November 2005), online:ttp://epe.lac-bac.gc.ca/100/206/301/pco-bcp/commissions/sponsorship-ef/06-02-10/www.gomery.ca/en/phase1report/default.htm>; and *Restoring Accountability: Recommendations* (Phase 2 Report) (Ottawa: Public Works and Government Services Canada, February 2006), online: <http://epe.lac-bac.gc.ca/100/206/301/pco-bcp/commissions/sponsorship-ef/06-02-10/www.gomery.ca/en/phase2report/default.htm>.

ing millions of dollars of public money, and, in at least one case, subsidizing fraud.

(iii) The media and Ms. Fraser

In September 1999, *Globe and Mail* reporter Daniel Leblanc filed the first of several access to information requests about the program, which would lead to newspaper revelations in the following years about questionable spending and possible fraud. In August 2000, an internal departmental audit found that CCSB was providing inadequate supervision of advertising contracts. Early in 2002, the minister in charge was appointed Ambassador to Denmark. The new minister found that an advertising agency called Groupaction had received more than one million dollars for producing two brief and nearly identical reports. He ordered an audit. In May 2002, the Auditor General, Ms. Sheila Fraser, said the federal government had failed to follow proper procedures in its Groupaction contracts.[3] Amid growing public criticism, the government asked the RCMP to investigate the firm's actions, and announced new advertising policies. On December 13, 2004, in one of his first acts as Prime Minister, Paul Martin cancelled the sponsorship program.

On February 10, 2004, the Auditor General tabled her November 2003 report on the sponsorship scandal was tabled in the House of Commons.[4] Ms. Fraser found that senior federal government officials had failed to follow the *Financial Administration Act* and Treasury Board rules for tendering and monitoring contracts, and that the government had spent hundreds of millions of dollars on advertising, with little in return.

(iv) The inquiry

Clearly, more action was needed. On February 19, 2004, the federal Cabinet appointed Justice John Gomery from the Superior Court of Quebec to head a commission of inquiry into the sponsorship scandal.[5] Justice Gomery was empowered to investigate the problems indicated by the Auditor General and to recommend measures to prevent mismanagement of federal sponsorship and advertising programs in future.[6] In the last half of 2004, the Gomery inquiry held public hearings in Ottawa on the nature and administration of the sponsorship program; in the first half of 2005, it held public hearings in Montreal on where the sponsorship funds actually went and on who was involved in spending them. The testimony suggested a plethora of wrongs, from abuses of responsible government to "kickbacks" in the form of illegal contributions to the federal Liberal party. The public hearings were closely followed, and confidence in the federal government and ruling Liberal party plummeted.

The inquiry itself attracted controversy. In December 2005 media interviews, Justice Gomery was quoted as describing the management of the sponsorship program as "catastrophically bad" and referring to a key witness as a "charming scamp".[7] Later, Justice Gomery said he was disappointed to have heard evidence that a Prime Minister (former Prime Minister Jean Chrétien) would allow his name to be used on autographed golf balls, describing the practice as "small-town cheap".[8] The Commissioner said that he was coming to the same conclusion about mismanagement as had the Auditor General.

Mr. Chrétien's lawyers argued that these remarks indicated a reasonable apprehension of bias, and asked that the Commissioner resign. Justice Gomery refused. He conceded that some of his media comments were "ill-advised and inappropriate", but he said he had not prejudged the results and would come to no final conclusions until all the evidence had been considered.[9] Mr. Chrétien's lawyers started, halted, recommenced, and then ended bias proceedings in the Federal Court of Canada. The episode raised interesting questions about the nature of public inquiries and about the extent to which their commissioners should be held to the strict impartiality standards of judges in ordinary courts: see, for example, the *Beno v. Canada* decision.[10] When Mr. Chrétien finally testified before the Commission, he ended theatrically by producing golf balls that had been autographed by other well-known people from small towns.

(v) The reports[11]

On April 21, 2005, to try to shore up his minority government, Prime Minister Martin promised to call an election within 30 days of the release of the final Gomery report. The inquiry issued two reports: a report of factual findings in November 2005, and a report of recommendations in March 2006. Before the last report was issued, the Liberal federal government was defeated. A major plank in the platform of the incoming Conservatives was "accountability".

In its Phase 1 Report, the Commission found that the normal processes of responsible government had broken down.[12] Administrators had been permitted to operate free of the usual bureaucratic, regulatory, and political controls. Some politicians had interfered directly in administration, while others had failed to ensure that their policy initiatives were properly implemented.[13]

More specifically, Justice Gomery found that PWGSC Minister Alphonso Gagliano was directly involved in the initiatives that led to the diverting of public funds for partisan purposes. The judge found that although there was no evidence that Mr. Chrétien and his chief of staff were directly involved in the kickback scheme. However, Mr. Pelletier had authorized the activities that led to the scheme, and Mr. Chrétien was at fault for failing to supervise the policy initiative adequately. The other ministers, including former finance minister Paul Martin, were exonerated as they had not been informed of the initiatives authorized by Mr. Pelletier.

Some of Justice Gomery's comments on responsible government and his main recommendations are summarized in the extracts below. As can be seen, many of the recommendations were aimed at boosting the independence of the public service from improper political interference. For example, they sought to make deputies answerable in their own right before the Public Accounts Committee, and to give them greater security of tenure. Some of these ideas were criticized for trying to draw too rigid a boundary between the overlapping realms of the political and administrative concerns; others, for undermining the exclusive responsibility of elected ministers to Parliament.[14] What do you think about this?

When the Harper Conservative government implemented its own reforms in the 2006 *Federal Accountability Act*,[15] it took an approach quite different from Justice Gomery's, as will be seen below. Which approach do you prefer, and why?

Notes

1. *Cf. Reference re Secession of Quebec*, [1998] 2 S.C.R. 217 at paras. 61–69. Although the Supreme Court was at pains here to describe what democracy is *not*, and to stress that it coexists with other principles, the Court did refer there to "representative government" and the "consent of the governed".

2. For the Gomery Commission's discussions of the concepts of responsible government, ministerial responsibility, accountability, and answerability, see Commission of Inquiry into the Sponsorship Program and Advertising Activities, "Structure, Responsibility and Lines of Accountability in the Federal Government: Roles, Responsibilities, and Accountability of Ministers and Public Servants" (from *Who is Responsible? Fact Finding Report*, part 3.1, and "Summary" at 15–21), in the extract below. Accountability

can be used in a general sense, to mean any obligation to another in regard to the exercise of a particular administrative mandate, or in the more specific sense referred to in this extract from the Gomery Commission — a duty to inform or explain, to avoid problems or to take corrective action to redress problems, and a corresponding liability to sanctions in the event of failure to fulfill this duty. In this note, the sense used will depend on the context in which the term is used.

3. Office of the Auditor General, *Report to the Minister of Public Works and Government Services on Three Contracts Awarded to Groupaction* (Ottawa: Office of the Auditor General, May 8, 2002).

4. Office of the Auditor General of Canada, *Report of the Auditor General to the House of Commons: Government-Wide Audit of Sponsorship, Advertising, and Public Opinion Research* (Ottawa: Minister of Public Works and Government Services Canada, November 2003), Ch. 3 — *The Sponsorship Program*; In Depth, "Auditor General's Report 2004" *CBC News* (11 February 2004), online: cbc.ca <http://www.cbc.ca/news/background/auditorgeneral/report2004.html>. The Auditor General concluded that Parliament had not been properly informed of the sponsorship program's objectives, the program had a weak control environment, there was a lack of transparent decision-making, the sources of the funding were hidden to the Crown agencies concerned, and government had obtained questionable value for its money.

5. Order in Council P.C. 2004-110, promulgated on February 19, 2004 pursuant to Part I of the *Inquiries Act*.

6. See Commission of Inquiry into the Sponsorship Program and Advertising Activities, *Terms of Reference* <http://www.gomery.ca/en/termsofreference/>.

7. In Depth, "Sponsorship Scandal: Timeline" *CBC News* (5 April 2007), online: cbc.ca <http://www.cbc.ca/news/background/groupaction/timeline.htm>.

8. "Gomery refuses to step down" *CBC News* (1 February 2005), online: cbc.ca <http://www.cbc.ca/story/canada/national/2005/02/01/sponsorship050201.html>.

9. *Who is Responsible? Phase 1 Report: Fact Finding Report*, Appendix G: "Ruling on Motion for Recusal" (February 2005), online: <http://www.cbc.ca/news/background/groupaction/report/FF_Eng_app_rulings.pdf>.

10. *Beno v. Canada (Commissioner and Chairperson, Commission of Inquiry into the Deployment of Canadian Forces to Somalia)*, [1997] 2 F.C. 527 (C.A.).

11. For a general discussion, see David Sugarman and Ian Greene, "Review Essay: Commission of Inquiry into the Sponsorship Program and Advertising Activities, Phase 1 Report and Phase 2 Report" (2006) 49 Can. Public Admin. 220–32

12. "Major Findings" (from *Who is Responsible? Phase 1 Report, 2005: Summary*, at 5–9.

13. *Ibid.* at 9.

14. See, for example, February 7 letter to *The Globe and Mail* by Mr. Arthur Kroeger, former Deputy Minister, and reply by Professor C.E.S. Franks, discussed in Norman Spector, "Waging a civil battle over Gomery" *The Globe and Mail* (20 February 2006) A15; *Prominent Canadians urge Prime Minister to reject Gomery recommendations increasing the powers of unelected officials at the expense of elected politicians*: open letter to Prime Minister Harper, online: University of Regina <http://www.uregina.ca/gspp/documents/publications/kroegerLetter.pdf>; "Harper Rejects Key Gomery Proposals" *CBC News* (21 December 2006), online: cbc.ca <http://www.cbc.ca/canada/story/2006/12/21/harper-gomery.html>.

15. *Federal Accountability Act*, S.C. 2006, c-2 (An Act providing for conflict of interest rules, restrictions on election financing and measures respecting administrative transparency, oversight and accountability).

EXTRACT

Structure, Responsibility and Lines of Accountability in the Federal Government: Roles, Responsibilities, and Accountability of Ministers and Public Servants[†]

[Part 3.1 of the *Fact Finding Report* described responsible government as the collective and individual accountability of Ministers of the Crown to Parliament for the conduct of government. The excerpt below from the *Summary Report* continues this discussion in regard to ministerial responsibility.]

In brief, **Ministers** are responsible for the departments over which they have overall direction and management. They are accountable to Parliament for how their ministerial responsibilities have been carried out. The Minister must take corrective action should problems occur, correct any problems that have been identified, and accept the consequences if the problem is attributable to the Minister's own actions or inaction.

Answerability refers to a duty to inform and explain to Parliament what has occurred in a government department. Ministers are answerable to Parliament for the department under their jurisdiction, even if the questions refer to the administration under a previous Minister. Accordingly, answerability is narrower in scope than accountability.

The Prime Minister has special responsibilities in the areas of national unity, national security, and intergovernmental and international affairs. The Right Honourable Jean Chrétien testified that Canadian unity had been his number one priority. There are no established limits to restrict the involvement of the Prime Minister and his senior staff in whatever issue they decide to take over and manage. The Prime Minister's accountability for the government as a whole is heightened by such direct involvement, but in principle individual Ministers retain primary responsibility and accountability for what is done within their portfolios.

The Prime Minister has political staff headed by the Chief of Staff, who generally works more closely than anyone else with the Prime Minister. At least that was the case when Jean Pelletier was Prime Minister Chrétien's Chief of Staff, which covers the period under review by this Commission. Mr. Pelletier was among a select group of advisors and the Prime Minister's closest collaborator.

The **Privy Council Office** (PCO) is responsible for providing the Prime Minister with non-partisan and non-political advice on government policy and operations. The PCO is headed by the Clerk of the Privy Council, who also acts as Secretary to the Cabinet and is the head of the public service. In effect, the Clerk of the Privy Council is the Prime Minister's Deputy Minister, meeting daily with the PM and the Chief of Staff. Jocelyne Bourgon became Clerk on March 28, 1994, until she was succeeded by Mel Cappe on January 18, 1999.

Ministerial responsibility has to do with the relationship between a Minister and the public servants working in the department of which the Minister has charge. Law, tradition or convention dictate that the Minister has sole authority for the management and direction of a department. However, the principle of Cabinet solidarity requires that the Minister seek the approval of or inform other members of the Cabinet regarding policies and decisions that may have relevance to other portfolios and the conduct of government as a whole. In addition, the Minister has an obligation to report to Parliament, which can discharge this obligation only if it is kept informed of the commitment and disbursement of public monies by individual Ministers and their departments.

The size of modern government places a constraint on the attribution of ministerial responsibility. Most commentators say that it is not fair today to hold a Minister responsible for errors or maladministration attributable to departmental officials if the Minister was not aware of them. The exception occurs if it can be determined that the Minister failed to ensure that appropriate systems were in place to manage the risks that led to those errors or mismanagement.

It is incumbent upon a Minister, according to law and the relevant government policies, to work with the public service to assure the proper implementation of government policy delivered through the program or activity under the Minister's charge. Some witnesses, and the submissions made by certain participants, take the position that individual Ministers and Cabinet are limited to formulating policy, and that their administrative officials, directed by the Deputy Minister, are responsible for implementing the policy. Thus, if errors occur in the implementa-

---

† Source: *Who is Responsible? Phase 1 Report*: "Summary", pages 15–21, November 2005. Reproduced courtesy of The Privy Council Office and Dr. Robert S. Remis, with the permission of the Minister of Public Works and Government Services, 2007.

tion of policy of which the Minister is unaware, he or she bears no responsibility other than the obligation to take the appropriate corrective measures. According to this view, the Minister is entitled to assume that the public servants charged with the implementation and administration of the policy decisions made by the government will act honestly and competently and will, of their own volition, adopt appropriate practices and procedures in so doing.

Mr. Pelletier testifies that Prime Minister Chrétien, on taking office in 1993, met with all Deputy Ministers and expressed the view that they would be entirely responsible for government administration, and that the politicians would be responsible only for policy decisions. Mr. Pelletier acknowledged that subordinate officials might obtain advice from the Prime Minister's Office (PMO) about a program, such as the Sponsorship Program, while still retaining full responsibility for any administrative decisions, even those following suggestions made by persons such as Mr. Pelletier himself. Mr. Pelletier does not consider this to be political interference in administrative matters.

Ministerial responsibility for a department is to be distinguished from the Minister's responsibility for the **political staff** (also known as **"exempt staff"**) in his or her office. The Minister chooses to employ staff members (they are "exempt" from the general authority of the Public Service Commission, including the appointment process) and works with them closely. A Minister is *personally* responsible for the actions of his or her political staff. Therefore, if a staff member becomes involved in the department's program administration, the Minister is directly and personally responsible for all consequences.

I believe that the proposition that Ministers and their political staff have no responsibility for the proper implementation and administration of government programs and policies is an inadequate and incomplete expression of the principle of ministerial responsibility. The Minister should take steps, in consultation with the Deputy Minister, to see that trained personnel are available to administer any new initiatives and to establish proper procedures and oversight mechanisms. The Minister should give sufficient directions to the Deputy Minister so that the latter will be able to properly supervise the actions of the subordinate personnel. Willful ignorance of administrative inadequacies will not absolve a Minister from responsibility for failures within the department.

The **Deputy Minister** is the principal source of support for a Minister in fulfilling his or her collective and individual responsibilities and, in particular,

ensuring sound advice on policy development and implementation, effective departmental management, and the fulfilment of authorities that have been assigned to the Deputy Minister or his officials. The role of a Deputy Minister is to be in charge of program management and departmental administration, but also to be sensitive to the political side. The Minister may exercise some discretion in what is delegated to the Deputy Minister. If there is a disagreement between a Minister and a Deputy Minister, the Minister may contact the Prime Minister, and the Deputy Minister may contact the Clerk of the Privy Council, and the problem would be worked out between them.

Ms. Bourgon agreed that a Deputy Minister would be obliged, in the context of program or project management, to ensure that the appropriate structure, policies, personnel and risk management scheme were in place; that the program or project was within the authority of the department; and that managers had clear delegated authority and information management systems so the Deputy Minister could receive feedback.

The **Treasury Board**, supported by the **Treasury Board Secretariat**, functions as a management board overseeing all federal government operations. Its jurisdiction includes general administrative policy, the organization of the public service, financial management and personnel management. Treasury Board establishes standards through its policies, but it cannot oversee Deputy Ministers' compliance with every transaction. The Treasury Board exercises its oversight role most actively through its review of submissions for spending initiatives. The principal expenditure controls are found in legislation, especially sections 32, 33 and 34 of the *Financial Administration Act*. In brief, section 32 ensures that funds are available to pay for any goods or services contracted; section 33 deals with requisitions for payment; and section 34 ensures that no payment for goods or services requisitioned by the government shall be made unless there is a certification on record that the goods or services have been supplied in accordance with the government contract which authorized the expenditure. These provisions are supplemented by legally binding Treasury Board regulations and nonbinding guidelines and policies which public servants must follow.

The **Minister of Finance** establishes the fiscal framework within which overall government spending takes place. Once that framework is set, departments are responsible for the management of the expenditures allocated to them, with general oversight by Treasury Board. The Department of Finance and its

Minister have no oversight role for other departments' expenditures, other than setting the financial context via the fiscal framework. The Minister can spend money only after Parliament has approved the spending, and it is primarily the role of that department to ensure proper management and compliance with legislation.

Definition of a "Program"

The Attorney General of Canada argued before the Commission that no Sponsorship Program existed until September 1, 2001, when Communication Canada established formal guidelines, criteria and procedures to govern the administration of sponsorships.

The *Financial Administration Act* and other legislation create responsibilities and obligations where funds are paid out in the context of a program. For example, section 32 of the *FAA* imposes upon a person "charged with the administration of a program" the duty to "establish procedures and maintain records respecting the control of financial commitments." The word "program" appears in other sections of the *FAA*, but it is defined nowhere.

Despite some contrary points of view, I have concluded that the series of projects and initiatives launched by the Government of Canada in 1996 unquestionably constituted a "program." Sponsorship initiatives were a series of projects or activities planned and undertaken to accomplish the objective of enhancing the visibility of the federal presence and promoting its programs and services. As such, they fit precisely into the dictionary definitions of "program." The fact that the program was not formally structured and had not been specifically approved by Cabinet, Treasury Board and the Privy Council Office did not make it less of a program.

. . . .

Major Findings[†]
[In this part of the report, the Commission made 13 major findings. Among other things, it found that there had been political involvement in administering the program, inadequate oversight at senior public service levels of contracting procedures, secrecy in the contracting process, fear by public servants of criticizing violations of estab-

lished procedures, extreme overcharging by private contractors, vague or inadequate spending guidelines, deliberate action to avoid established legislative and policy requirements, illegal contributions to a political party and channelling of public money for fundraising, and "the refusal of Ministers, senior officials in the Prime Minister's Office and public servants to acknowledge their responsibility for the problems of mismanagement that occurred": p. 9.]

"Rebalancing the Relationship Between Parliament and Government"[‡]

In my first Report, I was able to establish that there had been partisan political involvement in the administration of the Sponsorship Program; insufficient oversight by senior public servants; deliberate actions taken to avoid compliance with federal legislation and policies; a culture of entitlement among political officials and public servants involved with Sponsorship initiatives; and the refusal of Ministers, senior officials in the Prime Minister's Office and public servants to acknowledge any responsibility for the mismanagement that had occurred. I asked why it is that we have a system of responsible government, yet no one is prepared to accept responsibility for the abuses committed in the administration of the Sponsorship initiatives. No one has provided an answer.

The Sponsorship initiatives alarmed many Canadians. How is it, they asked, that politicians and public servants are able to violate the public trust in such a flagrant manner? How could the Sponsorship Program be abused for so long without either Parliament or, in particular, the Government, with its central agencies and oversight bodies, not putting an end to it? As I observed in the Introduction to this Report, I have become convinced that we need to rebalance the relationship between Parliament and the Government in order to attain better accountability within government.

The Government of Canada is the country's largest organization, employing 450,000 individuals, spending about $200 billion a year, and managing over 350 million transactions every year. It is impossible for anyone to assure Canadians that their federal government will, in future, be error free or even scandal free. Given the size and the variety of its

---

† Source: *Who is Responsible? Phase 1 Report*: "Summary", pages 5–7, 9. November 2005. Reproduced courtesy of The Privy Council Office and Dr. Robert S. Remis, with the permission of the Minister of Public Works and Government Services, 2007.

‡ Source: *Restoring Accountability: Recommendations, Phase 2 Report*, Ch. 11, pages. 196–204, February 2006. Reproduced courtesy of The Privy Council Office and Dr. Robert S. Remis, with the permission of the Minister of Public Works and Government Services, 2007.

activities, such a goal could not be realized, even if we were to impose an elaborate menu of red tape, many centrally prescribed administrative rules, and several newly created oversight bodies. There will always be unscrupulous individuals in any public organization who will find a way to draw improper benefits from its activities.

Canadians are fortunate in that the great majority of the people who serve in Parliament and in the public service hold very high ethical standards. We must not forget that only a handful of government officials failed to live up to those standards in the Sponsorship Program.

What is particularly disturbing is that the mismanagement went on for so long without being stopped.

The recommendations that are found throughout this Report and repeated below have one central purpose: to rebalance the relationship between Parliament and Government and to assign clearer accountability to both politicians and public servants. The recommendations are directed to Parliament, to the Prime Minister and his or her office, to Ministers and their exempt staff, and to public servants.

Rebalancing the relationship between Parliament and the Government would enable the House of Commons to hold the Government, individual Ministers and their departments to account and to review more effectively the Government's proposed spending plans. In assigning accountability more clearly, there is greater likelihood that officials at all levels will assume their responsibilities more fully and, in so doing, reduce the risk of mismanagement and scandals. Canadians will also be able to identify more readily who is responsible and for what.

I recognize that reports and their recommendations, particularly when they seek to make changes that are not necessarily welcome to an administration that is accustomed to established practices, tend to be pushed to the side. Governments have developed a well-honed capacity to batten down the hatches in the hope that "this too shall pass." For this reason, I am recommending, in my final recommendation, a reasonable time period for the government to respond to all 18 of my previous recommendations.

Recommendation 1 To redress the imbalance between the resources available to the Government and those available to parliamentary committees and their members, the Government should substantially increase funding for parliamentary committees. (See page 61 [of Phase 2 Report])

Recommendation 2 The Government should adopt legislation to entrench into law a Public Service Charter. (See page 67)

Recommendation 3 To enable the Public Accounts Committee to perform its responsibilities more effectively, the Government should increase its funding substantially to provide the Committee with its own research personnel, legal and administrative staff, and experts as needed. (See page 80)

Recommendation 4 In order to clear up the confusion over the respective responsibilities and accountabilities of Ministers and public servants, the Government should modify its policies and publications to explicitly acknowledge and declare that Deputy Ministers and senior public servants who have statutory responsibility are accountable in their own right for their statutory and delegated responsibilities before the Public Accounts Committee. (See page 100)

Recommendation 5 The Government should establish a formal process by which a Minister is able to overrule a Deputy Minister's objection to a proposed course of action in an area of jurisdiction over which the Deputy Minister possesses statutory or delegated powers. The decision of the Minister should be recorded in correspondence to be transmitted by the Deputy Minister concerned to the Comptroller General in the Treasury Board Secretariat, and be available there for examination by the Office of the Auditor General. (See page 105)

Recommendation 6 The Government should adopt as a policy that Deputy Ministers and senior public servants are appointed to their positions for a minimum of three years, with the expectation that a standard appointment would normally have a duration of at least five years. In cases where it is deemed necessary to derogate from this policy, the Government should be required to explain publicly the reason for such a derogation. The Government should take the steps to apply the same policy to Assistant Deputy Ministers. (See page 109)

Recommendation 7 The members of the Public Accounts Committee should be appointed with the expectation that they will serve on the Committee for the duration of a Parliament. (See page 118)

Recommendation 8 The Public Accounts Committee should ensure that Deputy Ministers, other heads of agencies and senior officials are the witnesses called to testify before it. As a general principle, Ministers should not be witnesses before the Committee. (See page 119)

Recommendation 9 Special reserves should be managed by a central agency experienced in administrative procedures, such as the Treasury Board or the Department of Finance. The Government should be required at least once a year to table a report in the House of Commons on the status of each reserve, the criteria employed in funding decisions and the use of the funds. (See page 132)

Recommendation 10 The Government should remove the provision in the law and in its policies that enables exempt staff members to be appointed to a position in the public service without competition after having served in a Minister's office for three years. (See page 138)

Recommendation 11 The Government should prepare and adopt a Code of Conduct for Exempt Staff that includes provisions stating that exempt staff have no authority to give direction to public servants and that Ministers are fully responsible and accountable for the actions of exempt staff. On confirmation of their hiring, all exempt staff should be required to attend a training program to learn the most important aspects of public administration. (See page 139)

Recommendation 12 The Government of Canada should adopt an open and competitive process for the selection of Deputy Ministers, similar to the model used in Alberta. (See page 151)

Recommendation 13 The functions and titles of the Clerk of the Privy Council should be redefined, by legislation if necessary. The title of this official should be "Secretary to the Cabinet," and his or her main role should be to represent the public service to the Prime Minister and the Cabinet. The designations "Clerk of the Privy Council" and "Deputy Minister to the Prime Minister" should be abolished. The Privy Council Office should be renamed the "Cabinet Secretariat." The Secretary of the Treasury Board should assume the title and function of "Head of the Public Service." (See page 152)

Recommendation 14 The Government of Canada should amend its current definition of "advertising" to conform to accepted advertising industry standards, and the new definition should be promulgated in the Government of Canada Communications Policy and related documents. (See page 161)

Recommendation 15 The Registrar of Lobbyists should report directly to Parliament on matters concerning the application and enforcement of the *Lobbyists Registration Act*, and the Office of the Registrar of Lobbyists should be provided with sufficient resources to enable it to publicize and enforce the requirements of the Act, including investigation and prosecution by its own personnel. The limitation period for investigation and prosecution should be increased from two to five years from the time the Registrar becomes aware of an infringement. (See page 174)

Recommendation 16 The Government should adopt legislation requiring public servants to document decisions and recommendations, and making it an offence to fail to do so or to destroy documentation recording government decisions, or the advice and deliberations leading up to decisions. (See page 181)

Recommendation 17 The Financial Administration Act should be amended to add a new section stipulating that deliberate violation of section 34 of the Act by an employee of the federal government is grounds for dismissal without compensation. (See page 188)

Recommendation 18 The Chief Executive Officer of a Crown Corporation should be appointed, evaluated from time to time, and, if deemed advisable, dismissed by the Board of Directors of that corporation. Initial appointments to the Board of Directors of a Crown Corporation should be made by the Government on the basis of merit. Thereafter, the remaining directors should be responsible for filling any vacancies on a corporation's board. (See page190)

[In addition to these recommendations, the Commission wishes to establish a reasonable timeframe for their consideration and implementation.]

Recommendation 19 Within 24 months of receiving this Report, the Government should table before Parliament a report detailing how it has dealt with each of the Commission's recommendations.

[The Harper Conservatives' response to the sponsorship scandal and the Gomery recommendations was to implement their own set of reforms, whose centrepiece was the *Federal Accountability Act*, S.C. 2006, c-2 (royal assent, 12 December 2006). Although this massive statute addressed several of the Gomery recommendations, it also tackled many other subjects, such as conflicts of interest and the tenure of directors of Crown corporations.

Moreover, there were significant differences in the general approach of the Gomery Commission and the *Accountability Act* to responsible government. For example, the 2006 legislation rejected the general idea that deputy ministers should be more independent of ministers, keeping the former as wholly discretionary appointees, answerable to Parliament solely on behalf of their ministers.

As well, while the Gomery recommendations stressed direct executive answerability to parliamentary committees, the 2006 legislation focused on a different kind of accountability: supervision of the executive by a host of new Cabinet-appointed officers of Parliament. These included a Conflict of Interest and Ethics Commissioner, a Commissioner of Lobbying, a Parliamentary Budget Officer, a Director of Public Prosecutions, and a Procurement Auditor. Which approach do you consider more effective?

There were also contrasting approaches to access to information. Although it provided for rewards for whistleblowers and extended access requirements to some Crown corporations and other bodies, the *2006* legislation created new exemptions to the *Access to Information Act*. Compare its access provisions with the access recommendations in the 2002 Report of the Information Commissioner: John M. Reid, Information Commissioner of Canada, *Response to the Report of the Access to Information Review Task Force A Special Report to Parliament* (October 2002), online: Office of the Information Commissioner of Canada <http://www.infocom.gc.ca/media/default-e.asp>. Is there a risk that the new accountability regime could be undermined by inadequate guarantees of transparency?

Finally, note that Justice Gomery said that "only a handful" of government officials had been directly involved in the sponsorship scandal: see *Phase 2 Report*, February 2006, Chapter XI, p. 198. Indeed, as of the summer of 2007, only five individuals, including former bureaucrat Mr. Charles Guité and four former private sector advertising executives, had been found guilty of sponsorship-related fraud: Jonathon Montpetit, "Five-year prison term sought for LaFleur" *The Globe and Mail* (2 June 2007), A8. Is there any danger that an array of watchdogs, regulations, and whistleblowers could impose accountability at the expense of two other qualities important in public service — efficiency and trust?]

IV

Constitution Act, 1982
and After

9 | Origins and Structure of the *Constitution Act, 1982*

(a) Introduction

The spring of 1982 marked a revolution in Canadian constitutional law. In the *Canada Act 1982*, Britain gave up the right to make changes to the formal part of our constitution. The formal part was significantly enlarged, and renamed the "Constitution of Canada". The *Canada Act 1982*'s important schedule, the *Constitution Act, 1982*, included a new *Canadian Charter of Rights and Freedoms*; a recognition of Aboriginal and treaty rights and the principle of equalization; a new set of all-Canadian amending procedures; and a constitutional supremacy clause. Even the old *British North America Act, 1867* was renamed the *Constitution Act, 1867*, and

was amended to give provinces increased control over aspects of natural resources.

Beyond doubt, this was the single biggest change to the Canadian constitution since Confederation. Yet it lacked the formal agreement of all provincial governments. Ironically, in light of the background of these changes, the dissenting government was the government of Quebec.

In this chapter, we will look at two questions:

1. How did the changes of 1982 come about?
2. What are the main elements of the *Constitution Act, 1982*?

(b) Road to Reform

FOUR HISTORIC PROBLEMS

By the early 1980s, Confederation and Canada had managed to survive for a century. By that time, many other nations and constitutions had come and gone. On the other hand, four historic Canadian problems loomed unresolved:

1. securing the place of French-speaking Canadians in Canada;
2. addressing the grievances and claims of Canadian Aboriginal peoples;
3. accommodating the concerns of people in the regions outside central Canada; and
4. patriating the written portion of the Canadian constitution and agreeing on an amending formula for it.

FRENCH CANADIAN CONCERNS

From early times, French-speaking Canadians have been concerned to protect their distinct way of life against threats and perceived threats from their increasingly numerous anglophone neighbours. For example, prior to the 1837 Lower Canada Rebellion, the Ninety-Two Resolutions included the grievance that key appointed positions in the colony were monopolized by people of British origin.[1] In the Province of Canada, francophone leaders like Lafontaine were upset with many aspects of the 1840 *Union Act*, including its restrictions on the use of French.[2] Confederation had less than overwhelming support from French-speaking politicians in Canada; they supported it by a majority of 27

216

to 22.[3] In the late 19th century, Quebec premier Honoré Mercier won support by championing Quebec nationalism and provincial autonomy.[4] In the 1890s and 1912, restrictions on educational rights of Roman Catholics and francophones outside Quebec generated national controversies.[5] During both world wars, strong francophone opposition to conscription contrasted with the strong support by most English-speaking Canadians.[6] In Quebec, French-speaking concerns took on new significance in the "Quiet Revolution" of the 1960s.[7] During this important period, among Quebec francophones the long-standing dominance of the Roman Catholic church gave way to the government of the province of Quebec.[8] A series of nationalist measures, including legislation to protect the use of French, culminated in the election of the separatist Parti Québécois in 1976. There was a pressing need for some kind of response from the federal government.

ABORIGINAL CONCERNS

Aboriginal peoples lived in northern North America as long as 12,000 years ago,[9] many thousands of years before the appearance of the first European explorers, traders, and settlers. What happened since was described by a Dene witness before the Berger northern pipeline inquiry in 1976:

> White people came as visitors to our land. Suddenly they claim it as their land. They claim we have no right to call it Indian land, land that we have occupied and used for thousands of years.
>
> Is this the great system of justice, which your nation is so proud of?[10]

Land was taken without compensation, or without fair compensation. Traditional laws and cultures were overridden or replaced. Many Aboriginal peoples were confined to small, isolated reserves. The *Indian Act* legislated artificial legal distinctions, created a top-down administrative régime, and enforced a sexually discriminatory status system. From 1883 until the 1960s, many Aboriginal children were placed in native residential schools that often involved physical or sexual abuse.[11] Before 1951, traditional customs such as the potlatch and the sun dance were banned.[12] Until 1960, most status Indians could not vote in federal elections.[13] By the 1980s, many Aboriginal people still faced poverty and illness, at the bottom of Canada's economic ladder.[14] As with the concerns of

French-speaking Canadians, some kind of government response was needed.

REGIONAL CONCERNS

Historically, outlying provinces and territories have tended to complain that Confederation is weighted in favour of central Canada, especially Ontario. Most regions lie at some distance from cities such as Toronto and Montreal. Most have focused on resource interest development, whose pricing and transportation needs can clash with the manufacturing and consumer interests of central Canada. Without the high population base of central Canada, the regions have lacked its political influence in the federal electoral system.

At a distance from the Province of Canada, with interests of their own, the Atlantic provinces were less than overjoyed at the prospect of Confederation. The pro-Confederation New Brunswick premier suffered a temporary defeat that was remedied only by external forces.[15] In Nova Scotia, where maritime interests and ties with New England were as strong as any links to Canada, the first post-Confederation government adopted a resolution in favour of secession.[16] Prince Edward Island waited until financial problems helped force it to join in 1873,[17] and Newfoundland did not decide to join Confederation until 1949.[18] The creation of Manitoba and the pre-history of Saskatchewan were marked by armed Métis and Indian rebellions, directed at least in part against central Canadian control.[19] Until 1930, the prairie provinces complained that they had not been given the same ownership and control of natural resources that had been given to the original confederating provinces.[20] Other regional grievances involved tariffs that favoured manufacturing interests in central Canada, and transportation and banking policies that appeared to discriminate against outlying areas.[21]

In the 1970s, rising world prices for natural resources such as oil and potash gave increased leverage to outlying resource-producing regions, especially in western Canada, and generated more conflict with the federal government. The federal government moved to keep Canadian petroleum prices below world levels, a policy that oil and natural producers saw as biased in favour of central Canada.[22] Meanwhile, residents of the two northern territories sought more control over their affairs. Again, there was pressure for some form of federal response.

THE PATRIATION-AMENDMENT TANGLE[23]

Of the four issues above, the patriation-amendment problem was the most technical. Before 1982, several kinds of constitutional amendments could be made by neither the federal nor the provincial level of government. For example, the *Constitution Act, 1867* prohibited Parliament from making amendments to the Constitution of Canada that affected provincial interests (s. 91(1)), but the Act specified no alternative amending procedure. By default, the only body competent to make such amendments was the legislature that had enacted the *Constitution Act, 1867*: the Parliament of the United Kingdom.

In making these amendments, the British Parliament had developed and followed a constitutional convention by which it would act only if an amendment had been requested by both houses of Parliament in Canada, transmitted by the Governor General. However, where the amendment affected provincial interests, it was unclear as to how much provincial support, if any, was needed before the British Parliament should act.

As Canada grew more independent in the 20th century, the requirement of obtaining an act of the Parliament of the old parent country seemed more and more like a colonial relic. Many thought it would be more appropriate if the Canadian constitution could be patriated, with full amending power in Canadian hands. But patriation required agreement in Canada on an all-Canadian amending formula and, for many decades, this agreement lay beyond reach.

It was because of this lack of internal consensus, not British intransigence, that s. 7(1) of the 1931 *Statute of Westminster* was enacted. Section 7(1) excluded amendments to the *Constitution Act, 1867* from the commitment that future British statutes would not apply to the dominions except at their request and with their consent. Before 1981, there were numerous attempts at securing federal–provincial agreement on a formal amending formula. All efforts ended in failure. Not only were the parties' interests too divergent, but the stakes were too high. Control over the making and blocking of constitutional change is in many ways the ultimate constitutional control.

In this situation, only an extraordinary initiative seemed capable of breaking the stalemate. That initiative came from the federal government, in the fall of 1980, and it was linked to at least one of the three other historic problems described above.

THE PACKAGE AND THE OPPOSITION[24]

To encourage a "no" vote in the May 1980 Quebec referendum on sovereignty-association, Prime Minister Trudeau promised major constitutional renewal to Confederation. A majority of Quebekers did vote "no", and federal–provincial constitutional talks began immediately. But the parties disagreed over the topics and the format, and there were deep divisions about the desired constitutional shape of the country. Many provinces had special goals of their own, there was a general distrust of the federal government, and Quebec was still headed by a separatist government. Amid dramatic television confrontations in September, the talks broke down.

After the collapse of the talks, on October 2, 1980, Prime Minister Trudeau introduced the government's constitutional reform resolution into the House of Commons. He said he would pursue it with or without provincial support. The "Trudeau package" included (i) an entrenched *Charter of Rights*, including official language guarantees and basic individual rights and freedoms; (ii) an all-Canadian amending procedure that gave an individual veto to Ontario and Quebec and combined vetoes to the other provinces, and included an alternative referendum amending process; (iii) a patriation provision stipulating that no future British law would have force as the law of Canada.

The general philosophy behind the package seemed quite clear.[25] The federal government was offering French-speaking people an alternative to Quebec nationalism as a response to their concerns: pan-Canadian language rights. To balance this offer, English-speaking Canadians would be guaranteed equivalent language rights within the province of Quebec. And to balance the special group rights of both English and French minorities, the federal government was offering Canadians as a whole guaranteed individual rights and freedoms in a patriated constitution. A vital aspect of the package was its emphasis on rights: on legal rights and on constitutional rights. The emphasis was very much on the first and the fourth of the four historical concerns described above. Aboriginal concerns were given little attention in the first draft of the package; regional concerns, almost no attention at all.

The package was referred to a parliamentary committee, where the proposed *Charter* proved popular. Most groups appearing before the committee wanted the *Charter* and related rights expanded. The parliamentary committee recommended (a) extending the *Charter of Rights* guarantees; (b) including an Aboriginal rights provision; and (c) granting slightly more power to the provinces over natural resources. These recommendations were included in later versions of the package.

Seven and, eventually, eight of the 10 provinces opposed the Trudeau package. They argued that much of the *Charter* would interfere with provincial rights. They opposed the amendment formula, which most thought was unfairly weighted in favour of central Canada. Most of all, they disputed the federal claim to be able to proceed unilaterally with a resolution that could result in drastic changes to the constitution.

Notes

1. Mason Wade, *The French Canadians: 1760–1967*, Rev'd ed., vol. 1 (Toronto: MacMillan, 1968) at 143. Although the Rebellion had important non-ethnic aspects, there was substantial mistrust between the two main groups in Lower Canada during this period. Referring to this in 1839, Lord Durham said, "I expected to find a contest between a government and people; instead I found two nations warring in the bosom of a single state...": Lord Durham, "British North America Report to the Queen's Most Excellent Majesty (1839)" in Gerald M. Craig, *Lord Durham's Report* (Toronto: McClelland & Stewart, 1963) at 23.

2. Wade, *Ibid.* at 230 *et seq.*

3. Edgar McInnis, *Canada: A Political and Social History*, 4th ed. (Toronto: Holt, Rinehart and Winston of Canada, 1982) at 351.

4. Wade, *supra* note 2 at 417–22.

5. P.E. Crunican, "Manitoba Schools Question" in James H. Marsh, ed., *The Canadian Encyclopedia*, Year 2000 ed. (Toronto: McClelland & Stewart, 1999) at 1426; and M. Barber, "Ontario Schools Question" in Marsh, *ibid.* at 1721.

6. J.L. Granatstein, "Conscription", *ibid.* at 544.

7. Edward McWhinney, *Quebec and the Constitution, 1960–1978* (Toronto: University of Toronto Press, 1979).

8. Ramsay Cook, *Canada, Quebec and the Political Uses of Nationalism*, 2d ed. (Toronto: McClelland & Stewart, 1995) at 88–97; McWhinney, *ibid.*

9. Marsh, *supra* note 5 at 1885, 1886. See also Olive P. Dickason, *Canada's First Nations: A History of Founding Peoples from Earliest Times*, 3d ed. (Toronto: Oxford University Press, 2002), ch. 1; T.D. Dillehay, *The Settlement of the Americas: A New Prehistory* (New York: Basic Books, 2000); R. McGhee, *Ancient People of the Arctic* (Vancouver: UBC Press, 1996); B.M. Fagan, *The Great Journey: The Peopling of Ancient America* (London: Thames and Hudson, 1987), ch. 5; and D.M. Hopkins *et al.*, eds., *Palaeontology of Beringia* (New York: Academic Press, 1982).

10. P. Blake, "A Dene's Views on the Pipeline (A Presentation to the Berger Commission), CASNP Bulletin, March 1976, at 25.

11. See James R. Miller, *Shingwauk's Vision: A History of Native Residential Schools* (Toronto: University of Toronto Press, 1996); Royal Commission on Aboriginal Peoples, *Report of the Royal Commission on Aboriginal Peoples* (Ottawa: Canada Communication Group, 1996), vol. 1, ch. 10.

12. Dickason, *supra* note 9, ch. 19.

13. J.C. Courtney, "Franchise" in Marsh, *supra* note 5 at 907, 908. It was not until 1969 that status Indians were able to vote without restriction in provincial elections in Quebec.

14. The situation in the 1960s was sadly similar to the following 2005 account:

    > Many of Canada's Aboriginal people grapple with extreme poverty, continuous unemployment, high infant mortality, and high rates of suicide, illness, and disease. Traditional land has been dug up, ploughed under, and paved over for mines, farms, roads, shopping centres, and golf courses. Cultures that used to thrive on hunting, fishing, and trapping are weakened as acid rain, dams, logging, and pollution undermine the resource base on the lands that remain.... [T]elevision signals to remote fishing and trapping communities are beaming in soap operas, urban talk shows, and cigarette ads: David W. Elliott, *Law and Aboriginal Peoples in Canada*, 5th ed. (Concord, Ont.: Captus Press, 2005) at 4.

    See further, Royal Commission on Aboriginal Peoples, *Report of the Royal Commission on Aboriginal Peoples* (Ottawa: Canada Communication Group, 1996), vol. 2, ch. 5, s. 1.2, at 800–801: high levels of dependence on social assistance; *ibid.* at 802–803: poverty; *ibid.* at 802–803: high unemployment; *ibid.*, vol. 3, ch. 3, s. 1.1, at 120–21: low life expectancy; *ibid.* at 137–42: high levels of infectious diseases; *ibid.* at 175–98 and ch. 4: and poor living conditions and housing; and *ibid.*, vol. 3, ch. 3, s. 1.2, at 108. See also *ibid.* at 153–65 regarding "disturbingly high" rates of injury, violence, and self-destructive behaviour.

15. McInnis, *supra* note 3 at 352–53.

16. Garth Stevenson, *Ex Uno Plures: Federal–Provincial Relations in Canada, 1867–1896* (Montreal & Kingston: McGill-Queen's University Press, 1993) at 109–11.

17. H.T. Holman, "Prince Edward Island" in Marsh, *supra* note 5 at 1895, 1900.

18. W.F. Summers, "Newfoundland and Labrador" in Marsh, *supra* note 5 at 1629, 1635.

19. McInnis, *supra* note 3 at 362–68, 394–400.

20. Gerald V. La Forest, *Natural Resources and Public Property under the Canadian Constitution* (Toronto: University of Toronto Press, 1969) at 35.

21. See generally, Dyck, ch. 3.

22. MacIvor, at 87.

23. See also Dyck, ch. 17; Hogg 2007, ch. 4, part 4.1; Monahan, ch. 5; James R. Hurley, *Amending Canada's Constitution: History, Processes, Problems and Prospects* (Ottawa: Supply and Services Canada, 1996), chs. 2 and 3; Reesor, ch. 6; Milne, chs. 1–5; Cheffins, at 6–9, 57–65.

24. See generally Dyck, ch. 17; MacIvor, ch. 9; Peter H. Russell, *Constitutional Odyssey: Can Canadians Become a Sovereign People?*, 3d ed. (Toronto: University of Toronto Press, 2004), ch. 8; Milne, ch. 3; Roy Romanow, John Whyte & Howard Leeson, *Canada — Notwithstanding: The Making of the Constitution, 1976–1982* (Toronto: Carswell/Methuen, 1984), chs. 3–5.

25. *Cf.* the interpretations in A.C. Cairns, "Reflections on the Political Purposes of the Charter: The First Decade" in A.C. Cairns, *Reconfigurations: Canadian Citizenship and Constitutional Change* (Toronto: McClelland & Stewart, 1995), ch. 8, at 197–99; Hon. R. McMurtry, "Historical Considerations in Relation to the Constitution" (1999) 18:3 Advocates' Soc. J.

(c)   Re Amendment of Constitution of Canada†

NOTE

The provinces who opposed the federal action referred it to the courts. In February 1981, the Manitoba Court of Appeal decided in favour of the federal package by a majority of 3–2.[1] In March a unanimous Newfoundland Court of Appeal decided against it.[2] In April, the Quebec Court of Appeal decided in favour of it by a majority of 4–1.[3]

By April 1981, it was clear from the Kershaw Report[4] in Britain and from the provincial victory in the Newfoundland Court of Appeal[5] that there were serious constitutional concerns with the federal government's way of proceeding. At the same time, filibustering by the federal opposition party was holding up progress in the House of Commons. The two main federal parties struck a deal: the federal government would refer the questions addressed by the lower courts to the Supreme Court of Canada, and the Supreme Court's answer would determine whether the package would go ahead. Never before in Canadian constitutional history had more depended on a single decision of the Supreme Court of Canada.

In its decision,[6] rendered on September 28, 1981, the Court addressed three main questions (as well as a specific question involving the province of Newfoundland):

(i) Would the proposed *Canada Act*, if validly enacted, affect provincial powers?

(ii) Was the proposed procedure (a resolution of the two federal houses of Parliament supported by only two of the provinces) valid as a matter of constitutional law? and

(iii) Was the proposed procedure valid as a matter of constitutional convention?

Unanimously, the Supreme Court said the proposed *Canada Act* would affect provincial powers, although they found it unnecessary to specify how. A seven-judge majority[7] — including four who were in the majority on the conventionality issue[8] — held that the proposed procedure was legally constitutional. The remaining two[9] — the remainder of the six-judge majority on the conventionality issue — held that it was not legally constitutional. On the other hand, a six-judge majority[10] held that the proposed procedure was conventionally unconstitutional; the remaining three[11] held that it was not.

The legality issue in this case illustrates the dependence of the answers to a broad constitutional issue on the precise framing of the question. To the seven-judge majority on this issue, the key question was whether there were any legal limits to the power of a house of Parliament to initiate the proposed amendment. Not surprisingly, they found no such limit. To the two-judge minority on this issue, the key question was whether there was any legal power authorizing the two houses to initiate the proposed amendment. Not surprisingly, they found no such power.

One of the provincial contentions respecting the legality issue was that a constitutional convention could "crystallize" into law and had, indeed, done so. The majority denied that such crystallization was possible, and the minority failed to address the issue. This is rather puzzling: if the common law cannot under any circumstances gradually absorb and recognize conventions and other forms of custom and precedent, how, one might ask, can it grow and adjust to changing social conditions?

The hardest-fought legality issue was whether the exclusive legislative jurisdiction conferred on the provinces in the *Constitution Act, 1867*, entitled them to legal protection against unilateral federal changes to this jurisdiction by way of the amendment powers. The seven-judge majority said it did not. They said that to the extent that this argument rested on the "compact" theory of Confederation, it rested on a theory that was discredited and, in any event, non-legal. To the extent that it was based on the Preamble to the *Constitution Act, 1867*, it had no legal force because the Preamble carries no weight in law. They added that the distribution of powers in the *Constitution Act, 1867* is an internal arrangement only, not affecting Canada's relations with other countries.[12]

---

† *Reference Re Amendment of Constitution of Canada* (1981), 125 D.L.R. (3d) 1 at 22, 29–30, 32–33, 49, 78–79, 82–87, 93–94, 103, 106, 122 (S.C.C.).

The two-judge minority said the exclusive provincial legislative jurisdiction in the *Constitution Act, 1867* did give them legal protection against unilateral federal change through the amending process. Otherwise, they said, the federal government would be doing indirectly through the resolution procedure what it could not do directly through legislation. The minority felt that this position was reinforced by the Preamble to the *Constitution Act, 1867*, which stated the provinces' desire to be "federally united".

Like the legality issue, the conventionality issue illustrates how judicial answers can depend heavily on the precise nature of the questions asked. To the majority, the question was whether a certain amount of provincial consent was required by convention. The minority, on the other hand, asked themselves a more demanding question: was *unanimous* provincial consent required by convention?

The reasons in the conventions issue constituted the Court's first sustained discussion about the nature of these important elements of the unwritten part of our constitution. Both the majority and the minority agreed that constitutional conventions cannot be enforced by courts.[13] Although this was technically correct in the sense that a positive form of judicial relief would not issue for breach of a convention, the Court's reference was itself arguably an example of indirect "enforcement" of a convention of provincial consent. By formally declaring that the federal government's proposed action was conventionally if not legally unconstitutional, was not the Supreme Court giving at least some weight to the convention? What is this if not a form of enforcement? Did not this finding play a role in persuading the federal government to return once more to the bargaining table?

Although the three-judge minority said conventions are less important in federal than unitary states,[14] the majority considered them a valid and, in some cases, fundamental part of our constitution.[15] This affirmation may prove significant in the years ahead, when our remaining conventions are in danger of being overshadowed by the explicit written precepts of the *Charter*.

The majority formulated a three-part test for determining the existence of constitutional conventions: (i) Are they supported by the precedents?; (ii) Are they considered binding by those to whom they relate?; and (iii) Is there a good reason for them?

The different answers to the precedent issue again illustrate how judges' responses can vary sharply with the precise question asked. The majority asked themselves whether provincial consent had been secured for the five amendments changing provincial legislative powers,[16] and had little difficulty in finding that it had. The minority, however, asked themselves whether provincial consent had been secured for all previous constitutional amendments.[17] Not surprisingly, they found no strong trend of securing provincial consent.

As to whether the political actors regarded themselves as bound by a convention of provincial consent, the majority focused on a 1965 policy paper by the federal Justice Minister that arguably supported this proposition, whereas the minority found no consistent support in the other evidence they considered. The third part of the majority's test, whether there was a good reason for the convention, was not addressed by the minority. To the majority, the good reason was the preservation of the federal system.

Then the majority indicated in general terms how much provincial consent was required, as a matter of constitutional convention, for the proposed amendment. In their view, "at least a substantial measure of provincial consent"[18] was required, and the support of only two of the 10 provinces did not meet this test.

This was an important finding. On one hand, it opened the door to potential future litigation in which the Court might have to be more precise about what it meant by "a substantial measure" and, in so doing, "legislate" an amending formula itself. At the same time, the finding raised questions about the inherent veto power that had been traditionally claimed by the province of Quebec on major amendments affecting it.

On the other hand, the finding made the possibility of a federal–provincial constitutional agreement much more likely than when it had been assumed — at least by the eight dissident provinces — that unanimous provincial consent would be necessary. Under their old "rules", a more unyielding province could be as recalcitrant as it wished, knowing that its support was necessary. Under the "substantial measure" rule, a province taking an extreme position could find itself isolated. Similarly, there must have been some who wondered if any federal–provincial compromise would be endorsed by the government of Quebec, which was still committed ultimately to sovereignty-association.

The government of Quebec was indeed isolated in the accord that was finally reached in November 1981. Was an accord without Quebec better than no accord at all? Reasonable Canadians may well disagree on the answer to this question.

In some respects, the *Constitutional Amendment Reference* was a backward-looking decision. It clarified key aspects of the amending process under the old *Constitution Act, 1867*, one year before this process was to be replaced by the new procedures of the *Constitution Act, 1982*. In one important respect, though, the reference was a sign of the future. At the centre of a highly charged political confrontation, the Court was called upon to decide issues with the widest possible policy implications, to show mediation and even diplomatic skills, and — to some extent — to "legislate" a rule where none had clearly existed before. Under the *Constitution Act, 1982*, the Court now faces these challenges on a routine basis.

NOTES

1. *Re Amendment of the Constitution of Canada (No. 1)*, [1981] 2 W.W.R. 193 (Man. C.A.).
2. *Re Amendment of the Constitution of Canada (No. 2)* (1981), 29 Nfld. & P.E.I.R. 503 (Nfld.C.A.).
3. *Re Amendment of the Constitution of Canada (No. 3)* (1981), 120 D.L.R. (3d) 385 (Q.C.A.).
4. United Kingdom, House of Commons, *First Report from the Foreign Affairs Committee, Session 1980–81, British North America Acts: the Role of Parliament*, Vols. 1 and 2, 21 January 1981.
5. *Supra* note 2, decided 31 March 1981.
6. *Reference Re Amendment of the Constitution of Canada (Nos. 1, 2, 3)* (1981), 125 D.L.R. (3d) 1 (S.C.C.).
7. Laskin C.J. and Dickson, Beetz, Estey, McIntyre, Chouinard and Lamer J.
8. Dickson, Beetz, Chouinard and Lamer JJ.
9. Martland and Ritchie JJ., dissenting on this issue.
10. Martland, Ritchie, Dickson, Beetz, Chouinard and Lamer J.
11. Laskin C.J. and Estey and McIntyre JJ., dissenting on this issue.
12. On this point, contrast the Judicial Committee's approach in the *Labour Conventions Reference*, [1937] A.C. 326.
13. *Ibid.* at 84 (majority: conventions); 111 (minority: conventions).
14. *Ibid.* at 110.
15. *Ibid.* at 83.
16. *Ibid.* at 93.
17. *Ibid.* at 116–18.
18. *Ibid.* at 103.

EXTRACT

Legality

[Reasons of majority on legality (LASKIN C.J.C., DICKSON, BEETZ, ESTEY, McINTYRE, CHOUINARD and LAMER JJ.):]

The proposition was advanced on behalf of the Attorney-General of Manitoba that a convention may crystallize into law and that the requirement of provincial consent to the kind of Resolution that we have here, although in origin political, has become a rule of law. (No firm position was taken on whether the consent must be that of the Governments or that of the Legislatures.)

In our view, this is not so. No instance of an explicit recognition of a convention as having matured into a rule of law was produced. The very nature of a convention, as political in inception and as depending on a consistent course of political recognition by those for whose benefit and to whose detriment (if any) the convention developed over a considerable period of time is inconsistent with its legal enforcement.

The attempted assimilation of the growth of a convention to the growth of the common law is misconceived. The latter is the product of judicial effort, based on justiciable issues which have attained legal formulation and are subject to modification and even reversal by the Courts which gave them birth when acting within their role in the State in obedience to statutes or constitutional directives. No such parental role is played by the Courts with respect to conventions.

. . . .

Turning now to the authority or power of the two federal Houses to proceed by Resolution to forward the address and appended draft statutes to Her Majesty the Queen for enactment by the Parliament of the United Kingdom. There is no limit anywhere in law, either in Canada or in the United Kingdom (having regard to s. 18 of the *British North America Act, 1867*, as enacted by 1875 (U.K.), c. 38, s. 1, which ties the privileges, immunities and powers of the federal Houses to those of the British House of Commons) to the power of the Houses to pass resolutions. Under s. 18 aforesaid, the federal Parliament may by statute define those privileges, immunities and powers, so long as they do not exceed those held and enjoyed by the British House of Commons at the time of the passing of the federal statute.

. . . .

[The majority said the exclusive legislative jurisdiction conferred on the provinces by the *Constitution Act, 1867* was an internal arrangement only, and was irrelevant to Canada's relations with other countries.]

The stark legal question is whether this Court can enact by what would be judicial legislation a formula of unanimity to initiate the amending process which would be binding not only in Canada but also on the Parliament of the United Kingdom with which amending authority would still remain. It would be anomalous indeed, overshadowing the anomaly of a Constitution which contains no provision for its amendment, for this Court to say retroactively that in law we have had an amending formula all along, even if we have not hitherto known it; or, to say, that we have had in law one amending formula, say from 1867 to 1931, and a second amending formula that has emerged after 1931. No one can gainsay the desirability of federal-provincial accord of acceptable compromise. That does not, however, go to legality. As Sir William Jowitt said, and quoted earlier, we must operate the old machinery perhaps one more time.

. . . .

[Reasons of dissenting judges on legality (MARTLAND and RITCHIE JJ.):]

The *B.N.A. Act* created a federal union. It was of the very essence of the federal nature of the Constitution that the Parliament of Canada and the provincial Legislatures should have distinct and separate legislative powers. The nature of the legislative powers of the Provinces under s. 92 and the status of the provincial Legislatures was declared by the Privy Council in the *Hodge* case, *supra*, and in the *Maritime Bank* case, *supra*. We repeat the statement of Lord Watson in the latter case at pp. 441–2:

> The object of the Act was neither to weld the provinces into one, nor to subordinate provincial governments to a central authority, but to create a federal government in which they should all be represented, entrusted with the exclusive administration of affairs in which they had a common interest, each province retaining its independence and autonomy.

The continuation of that basic division of legislative powers was recognized in s-s. 7(3) of the *Statute of Westminster, 1931*. The Parliament of Canada has no power to trespass on the area of legislative powers given to the provincial Legislatures. Section 7 of the statute was intended to safeguard provincial legislative powers from possible encroachment by the federal Parliament as a result of the powers being conferred upon the Parliament of Canada by the statute.

The fact that the status of Canada became recognized as a sovereign State did not alter its federal nature. It is a sovereign State, but its Government is federal in character with a clear division of legislative powers. The Resolution at issue in these appeals could only be an effective expression of Canadian sovereignty if it had the support of both levels of government.

The two Houses of the Canadian Parliament claim the power unilaterally to effect an amendment to the *B.N.A. Act* which they desire, including the curtailment of provincial legislative powers. This strikes at the basis of the whole federal system. It asserts a right by one part of the Canadian governmental system to curtail, without agreement, the powers of the other part.

There is no statutory basis for the exercise of such a power. On the contrary, the powers of the Senate and the House of Commons, given to them by para. 4(a) of the *Senate and House of Commons Act*, excluded the power to do anything inconsistent with the *B.N.A. Act*. The exercise of such a power has no support in constitutional convention. The constitutional convention is entirely to the contrary. We see no other basis for the recognition of the existence of such a power. This being so, it is the proper function of this Court, in its role of protecting and preserving the Canadian Constitution, to declare that no such power exists. We are, therefore, of the opinion that the Canadian Constitution does not empower the Senate and the House of Commons to cause the Canadian Constitution to be amended in respect of provincial legislative powers without the consent of the Provinces.

. . . .

Convention

[Reasons of majority on convention (MARTLAND, RITCHIE, DICKSON, BEETZ, CHOUINARD, and LAMER JJ.):]

Those parts of the Constitution of Canada which are composed of statutory rules and common law rules are generically referred to as the law of the Constitution. In cases of doubt or dispute, it is the function of the Courts to declare what the law is and since the law is sometimes breached, it is generally the function of the Courts to ascertain whether it has in fact been breached in specific instances and, if so, to apply such sanctions as are contemplated by the law, whether they be punitive sanctions or civil sanctions such as a declaration of nullity. Thus, when a federal or a provincial statute is found by the Courts to be in excess of the legislative competence

223

of the Legislature which has enacted it, it is declared null and void and the Courts refuse to give effect to it. In this sense it can be said that the law of the Constitution is administered or enforced by the Courts.

But many Canadians would perhaps be surprised to learn that important parts of the Constitution of Canada, with which they are the most familiar because they are directly involved when they exercise their right to vote at federal and provincial elections, are nowhere to be found in the law of the Constitution. For instance it is a fundamental requirement of the Constitution that if the Opposition obtains the majority at the polls, the Government must tender its resignation forthwith. But fundamental as it is, this requirement of the Constitution does not form part of the law of the Constitution.

It is also a constitutional requirement that the person who is appointed Prime Minister or Premier by the Crown and who is the effective head of the Government should have the support of the elected branch of the Legislature; in practice this means in most cases the leader of the political party which has won a majority of seats at a general election. Other ministers are appointed by the Crown on the advice of the Prime Minister or Premier when he forms or reshuffles his cabinet. Ministers must continuously have the confidence of the elected branch of the Legislature, individually and collectively. Should they lose it, they must either resign or ask the Crown for a dissolution of the Legislature and the holding of a general election. Most of the powers of the Crown under the prerogative are exercised only upon the advice of the Prime Minister or the Cabinet which means that they are effectively exercised by the latter, together with the innumerable statutory powers delegated to the Crown in council.

Yet none of these essential rules of the Constitution can be said to be a law of the Constitution. It was apparently Dicey who, in the first edition of his *Law of the Constitution*, in 1885, called them "the conventions of the constitution" (W.S. Holdsworth, "The Conventions of the Eighteenth Century Constitution," 17 Iowa Law Rev. 161 (1932)), an expression which quickly became current. What Dicey described under these terms are the principles and rules of responsible government, several of which are stated above and which regulate the relations between the Crown, the Prime Minister, the Cabinet and the two Houses of Parliament. These rules developed in Great Britain by way of custom and precedent during the nineteenth century and were exported to such British colonies as were granted self-government.

. . . .

Within the British Empire, powers of government were vested in different bodies which provided a fertile ground for the growth of new constitutional conventions unknown to Dicey whereby self-governing colonies acquired equal and independent status within the Commonwealth. Many of these culminated in the *Statute of Westminster*, 1931, 22 Geo. V, c. 4 (U.K.).

A federal constitution provides for the distribution of powers between various Legislatures and Governments and may also constitute a fertile ground for the growth of constitutional conventions between those Legislatures and Governments. It is conceivable for instance that usage and practice might give birth to conventions in Canada relating to the holding of federal-provincial conferences, the appointment of Lieutenant-Governors, the reservation and disallowance of provincial legislation. It was to this possibility that Duff C.J.C. alluded when he referred to "constitutional usage or constitutional practice" in *Reference re Power of Disallowance and Power of Reservation*, [1938] 2 D.L.R. 8 at p. 13, [1938] S.C.R. 71 at p. 78. He had previously called them "recognized constitutional conventions" in *Wilson v. E. & N.R. Co.* (1921), 61 D.L.R. 1 at p. 6, [1922] 1 A.C. 202 at p. 210, [1921] 3 W.W.R. 817.

The main purpose of constitutional conventions is to ensure that the legal framework of the Constitution will be operated in accordance with the prevailing constitutional values or principles of the period. For example, the constitutional value which is the pivot of the conventions stated above and relating to responsible government is the democratic principle: the powers of the State must be exercised in accordance with the wishes of the electorate; and the constitutional value or principle which anchors the conventions regulating the relationship between the members of the Commonwealth is the independence of the former British colonies.

Being based on custom and precedent, constitutional conventions are usually unwritten rules. Some of them, however, may be reduced to writing and expressed in the proceedings and documents of Imperial conferences, or in the preamble of statutes such as the *Statute of Westminster, 1931*, or in the proceedings and documents of federal-provincial conferences. They are often referred to and recognized in statements made by members of governments.

The conventional rules of the Constitution present one striking peculiarity. In contradistinction to the laws of the Constitution, they are not enforced by the Courts. One reason for this situation is that, unlike common law rules, conventions are not judge-made rules. They are not based on judicial precedents but on precedents established by the institutions of government themselves. Nor are they in the nature of statutory commands which it is the function and duty of the Courts to obey and enforce. Furthermore, to enforce them would mean to administer some formal sanction when they are breached. But the legal system from which they are distinct does not contemplate formal sanctions for their breach.

Perhaps the main reason why conventional rules cannot be enforced by the Courts is that they are generally in conflict with the legal rules which they postulate and the Courts are bound to enforce the legal rules. The conflict is not of a type which would entail the commission of any illegality. It results from the fact that legal rules create wide powers, discretions and rights which conventions prescribe should be exercised only in a certain limited manner, if at all.

Some examples will illustrate this point. As a matter of law, the Queen, or the Governor General or the Lieutenant-Governor could refuse assent to every bill passed by both Houses of Parliament or by a Legislative Assembly as the case may be. But by convention they cannot of their own motion refuse to assent to any such bill on any ground, for instance because they disapprove of the policy of the bill. We have here a conflict between a legal rule which creates a complete discretion and a conventional rule which completely neutralizes it. But conventions, like laws, are sometimes violated. And if this particular convention were violated and assent were improperly withheld, the Courts would be bound to enforce the law, not the convention. They would refuse to recognize the validity of a vetoed bill. This is what happened in *Gallant v. The King*, [1949] 2 D.L.R. 425, 93 C.C.C. 237, 23 M.P.R. 48 (see also for a comment on the situation by K.M. Martin in 24 Can. Bar Rev. 434 (1946)), a case in keeping with the classic case of *Stockdale v. Hansard* (1839), 9 Ad. & E. 1, 112 E.R. 1112, where the English Court of Queen's Bench held that only the Queen and both Houses of Parliament could make or unmake laws. The Lieutenant-Governor who had withheld assent in *Gallant* apparently did so towards the end of his term of office. Had it been otherwise, it is not inconceivable that his withholding of assent might have produced a political crisis leading to his removal from office which shows that if the remedy for a breach of a convention does not lie with the Courts, still the breach is not necessarily without a remedy. The remedy lies with some other institutions

of Government; furthermore, it is not a formal remedy and it may be administered with less certainty or regularity than it would be by a Court.

Another example of the conflict between law and convention is provided by a fundamental convention already stated above: if after a general election where the Opposition obtained the majority at the polls the Government refused to resign and clung to office, it would thereby commit a fundamental breach of conventions, one so serious indeed that it could be regarded as tantamount to a *coup d'état*. The remedy in this case would lie with the Governor General or the Lieutenant-Governor as the case might be who would be justified in dismissing the Ministry and in calling on the Opposition to form the Government. But should the Crown be slow in taking this course, there is nothing the Courts could do about it except at the risk of creating a state of legal discontinuity, that is a form of revolution....

This conflict between convention and law which prevents the Courts from enforcing conventions also prevents conventions from crystallizing into laws, unless it be by statutory adoption.

It is because the sanctions of convention rest with institutions of government other than Courts, such as the Governor General or the Lieutenant-Governor, or the Houses of Parliament, or with public opinion and ultimately, with the electorate that it is generally said that they are political.

We respectfully adopt the definition of a convention given by the learned Chief Justice of Manitoba, Freedman C.J.M., in the Manitoba Reference at pp. 13–4:

> What is a constitutional convention? There is a fairly lengthy literature on the subject. Although there may be shades of difference among the constitutional lawyers, political scientists and Judges who have contributed to that literature, the essential features of a convention may be set forth with some degree of confidence. Thus there is general agreement that a convention occupies a position somewhere in between a usage or custom on the one hand and a constitutional law on the other. There is general agreement that if one sought to fix that position with greater precision he would place convention nearer to law than to usage or custom. There is also general agreement that "a convention is a rule which is regarded as obligatory by the officials to whom it applies." Hogg, *Constitutional Law of Canada* (1977), p. 9. There is, if not general agreement, at least weighty authority, that the sanction for breach of a convention will be political rather than legal.

It should be borne in mind, however, that, while they are not laws, some conventions may be more important than some laws. Their importance depends on that of the value or principle which they are meant to safeguard. Also they form an integral part of the Constitution and of the constitutional system. They come within the meaning of the word "Constitution" in the preamble of the *British North America Act, 1867*:

> Whereas the Provinces of Canada, Nova Scotia, and New Brunswick have expressed their Desire to be federally united...with a Constitution similar in principle to that of the United Kingdom:

That is why it is perfectly appropriate to say that to violate a convention is to do something which is unconstitutional although it entails no direct legal consequence. But the words "constitutional" and "unconstitutional" may also be used in a strict legal sense, for instance with respect to a statute which is found *ultra vires* or unconstitutional. The foregoing may perhaps be summarized in an equation: constitutional conventions plus constitutional law equal the total Constitution of the country.

. . . .

Of these twenty-two amendments or groups of amendments, five directly affected federal-provincial relationships in the sense of changing provincial legislative powers: they are the amendment of 1930, the *Statute of Westminster, 1931*, and the amendments of 1940, 1951 and 1964.

Under the agreements confirmed by the 1930 amendment, the western Provinces were granted ownership and administrative control of their natural resources so as to place these Provinces in the same position vis-à-vis natural resources as the original confederating colonies. The western Provinces, however, received these natural resources subject to some limits on their power to make laws relating to hunting and fishing rights of Indians. Furthermore, the agreements did provide a very substantial object for the provincial power to make laws relating to "The Management and Sale of Public Lands belonging to the Province and of the Timber and Wood thereon" under s. 92(5) of the *B.N.A. Act*. The long title reads as follows [1930, 20–21 Geo. V, c. 26 (U.K.)]:

> An Act to confirm and give effect to certain agreements entered into between the Government of the Dominion of Canada and the Government of the Provinces of Manitoba, British Columbia, Alberta and Saskatchewan respectively

The preamble of the Act recites that "each of the said agreements has been duly approved by the Parliament of Canada and by the Legislature of the Province to which it relates." The other Provinces lost no power, right or privilege in consequence. In any event, the proposed transfer of natural resources to the western Provinces had been discussed at the 1927 Dominion-Provincial Conference and had met with general approval: Paul Gérin-Lajoie, *Constitutional Amendment in Canada* (1950, University of Toronto Press), pp. 91–2.

All the Provinces agreed to the passing of the *Statute of Westminster, 1931*. It changed legislative powers: Parliament and the Legislatures were given the authority, within their powers, to repeal any United Kingdom statute that formed part of the law of Canada; Parliament was also given the power to make laws having extra-territorial effect.

The 1940 amendment is of special interest in that it transferred an exclusive legislative power from the provincial Legislatures to the Parliament of Canada.

In 1938, the Speech from the Throne stated:

> The co-operation of the provinces has been sought with a view to an amendment of the *British North America Act*, which would empower the parliament of Canada to enact forthwith a national scheme of unemployment insurance. My ministers hope the proposal may meet with early approval, in order that unemployment insurance legislation may be enacted during the present session of parliament. (Commons Debates, 1938, p. 2.)

In November, 1937, the Government of Canada had communicated with the Provinces and asked for their views in principle. A draft amendment was later circulated. By March, 1938, five of the nine Provinces had approved the draft amendment. Ontario had agreed in principle, but Alberta, New Brunswick and Quebec had declined to join in. The proposed amendment was not proceeded with until June, 1940, when Prime Minister King announced to the House of Commons that all nine Provinces had assented to the proposed amendment. (Paul Gérin-Lajoie (*op. cit.*) p. 106.)

The 1951 and 1964 amendments changed the legislative powers: areas of exclusive provincial competence became areas of concurrent legislative competence. They were agreed upon by all the Provinces.

These five amendments are the only ones which can be viewed as positive precedents whereby federal-provincial relationships were directly affected in the sense of changing legislative powers.

Every one of these five amendments was agreed upon by each Province whose legislative authority was affected.

In negative terms, no amendment changing provincial legislative powers has been made since Confederation when agreement of a Province whose legislative powers would have been changed was withheld.

There are no exceptions.

. . . .

It would not be appropriate for the Court to devise in the abstract a specific formula which would indicate in positive terms what measure of provincial agreement is required for the convention to be complied with. Conventions by their nature develop in the political field and it will be for the political actors, not this Court, to determine the degree of provincial consent required.

It is sufficient for the Court to decide that at least a substantial measure of provincial consent is required and to decide further whether the situation before the Court meets with this requirement. The situation is one where Ontario and New Brunswick agree with the proposed amendments whereas the eight other Provinces oppose it. By no conceivable standard could this situation be thought to pass muster. It clearly does not disclose a sufficient measure of provincial agreement. Nothing more should be said about this.

. . . .

Furthermore, as was stated in the fourth general principle of the White Paper, the requirement of provincial consent did not emerge as early as other principles, but it has gained increasing recognition and acceptance since 1907 and particularly since 1930. This is clearly demonstrated by the proceedings of the Dominion-Provincial Conference of 1931.

Then followed the positive precedents of 1940, 1951 and 1964 as well as the abortive ones of 1951,

1960 and 1964, all discussed above. By 1965, the rule had become recognized as a binding constitutional one formulated in the fourth general principle of the White Paper already quoted reading in part as follows:

> *The fourth general principle* is that the Canadian Parliament will not request an amendment directly affecting federal-provincial relationships without prior consultation and agreement with the provinces.

The purpose of this conventional rule is to protect the federal character of the Canadian Constitution and prevent the anomaly that the House of Commons and Senate could obtain by simple resolutions what they could not validly accomplish by statute.

It was contended by counsel for Canada, Ontario and New Brunswick that the proposed amendments would not offend the federal principle and that, if they became law, Canada would remain a federation. The federal principle would even be reinforced, it was said, since the Provinces would as a matter of law be given an important role in the amending formula.

It is true that Canada would remain a federation if the proposed amendments became law. But it would be a different federation made different at the instance of a majority in the Houses of the federal Parliament acting alone. It is this process itself which offends the federal principle.

. . . .

[Reasons of dissenting judges on convention (LASKIN C.J.C., ESTEY and McINTYRE JJ.):]

After examining the amendments made since Confederation, and after observing that out of the twenty-two amendments listed above only in the case of four was unanimous provincial consent sought or obtained and, even after according special weight to those amendments relied on by the Provinces, we cannot agree that history justifies a conclusion that the convention contended for by the Provinces has emerged.

(d)   General Structure of 1982 Package

How is the constitutional package of 1982 structured? The key to the package is the *Canada Act 1982*,[1] a very short statute enacted by the British Parliament on March 29, 1982, and proclaimed in force on that day. The *Canada Act 1982* formally patriated the formal part of the Constitution of Canada. It provides that no British statute enacted after the *Constitution Act, 1982*[2] is proclaimed in force shall extend to Canada as part of its law. The imperial amending tie, long retained at the request of Canadians, was severed at last.

The *Canada Act 1982* contains two important schedules that are each more than two-dozen times its length: Schedule A contains the French version of the *Constitution Act, 1982*; and Schedule B contains the English version.[3] Both versions were proclaimed in force on April 17, 1982 (except for s. 15, the equality guarantee, which came into effect three years later, and except for a minority language educational right guarantee that has yet to come into effect).

Two key elements of the political bargain that led to these changes were the *Charter* and the amending procedures. For its part, the federal government retained its proposed charter with its language rights intact. The provinces, on the other hand, secured a basic amending formula with a provincial support requirement and opting-out provision similar to the one proposed in a provincial Accord of April 1981.

The *Charter* comprises the first 34 sections of the *Constitution Act, 1982*. It has three main components: (i) several provisions that describe its scope, (ii) a statement of rights and freedoms, and (iii) a guarantee and justification provision.

The most important scope provision is s. 32. It says that the *Charter* applies to the federal and provincial governments and to all matters within their legislative jurisdiction. Another is s. 33, which enables legislatures to declare that a statute or a portion of it shall operate notwithstanding the *Charter*'s fundamental freedoms, legal rights, and/ or equality rights. Note also s. 25, regarding rights or freedoms of the Aboriginal peoples of Canada; s. 26, regarding rights and freedoms outside the *Charter*; s. 27, regarding Canada's multicultural heritage; and s. 29, regarding constitutional rights or privileges guaranteed in respect of denominational, separate, or dissentient schools.

The second main component, and the core of the *Charter*, is its statement of nine individual classes of rights and freedoms: (i) fundamental freedoms (s. 2); (ii) democratic rights (ss. 3–5); (iii) mobility rights (s. 6); (iv) legal rights (ss. 7–14); (v) equality rights (s. 15); (vi) male and female equality rights (s. 28); (vii) official language rights (ss. 16–22); (viii) minority language educational rights (s. 23); and (ix) enforcement rights (s. 24).

The third main *Charter* component is s. 1. It guarantees the *Charter* rights and freedoms, "subject only to such reasonable limits prescribed by law as can be demonstrably justified in a free and democratic society."

We can only note briefly here the complex amending procedures in the *Constitution Act, 1982*. Although Part V of the *Charter* is entitled "Procedure for Amending Constitution of Canada", Canada now has not one but four distinct and different formal amending procedures, dealing with what might be called "national", "fully-entrenched", "regional", and "internal" subject matter.

The "national" or "50% plus 2/3" formula can be found in ss. 38–40 and s. 42 of the *Constitution Act, 1982*; the "unanimity" formula in s. 41; the "regional" formula in s. 43; and the "internal" formula in ss. 44 and 45.

Finally, note the provisions relating to Aboriginal peoples (especially s. 35); s. 36 on equalization and regional disparities; ss. 50 and 51, which amended the *Constitution Act, 1867* to give the provinces more power over taxation and control over their natural resources; and s. 52, which defines the "Constitution of Canada" and gives it supremacy over other law.

Notes

1. (U.K.), 1982, c. 11.
2. *Constitution Act, 1982*, being Schedule B of the *Canada Act 1982* (U.K.), 1982, c.11.
3. *Supra* note 2.

(e) *Canada Act, 1982*†

An Act to give effect to a request by the Senate and House of Commons of Canada

Whereas Canada has requested and consented to the enactment of an Act of the Parliament of the United Kingdom to give effect to the provisions hereinafter set forth and the Senate and the House of Commons of Canada in Parliament assembled have submitted an address to Her Majesty requesting that Her Majesty may graciously be pleased to cause a Bill to be laid before the Parliament of the United Kingdom for that purpose.

Be it therefore enacted by the Queen's Most Excellent Majesty, by and with the advice and consent of the Lords Spiritual and Temporal, and Commons, in this present Parliament assembled, and by the authority of the same as follows:

CONSTITUTION ACT, 1982 ENACTED

1. The *Constitution Act, 1982* set out in Schedule B to this Act is hereby enacted for and shall have the force of law in Canada and shall come into force as provided in that Act.

TERMINATION OF POWER TO LEGISLATE FOR CANADA

2. No Act of the Parliament of the United Kingdom passed after the *Constitution Act, 1982* comes into force shall extend to Canada as part of its law.

FRENCH VERSION

3. So far as it is not contained in Schedule B, the French version of this Act is set out in Schedule A to this Act and has the same authority in Canada as the English version thereof.

SHORT TITLE

4. This Act may be cited as the *Canada Act, 1982*.

(f) *Constitution Act, 1982*‡

PART I: CANADIAN CHARTER OF RIGHTS AND FREEDOMS

[Am. by *Constitution Amendment Proclamation, 1983*, SI/84-102; *Constitution Amendment, 1993 (New Brunswick)*, SI/93-54.]

Whereas Canada is founded upon principles that recognize the supremacy of God and the rule of law:

GUARANTEE OF RIGHTS AND FREEDOMS

Rights and freedoms in Canada

1. The *Canadian Charter of Rights and Freedoms* guarantees the rights and freedoms set out in it subject only to such reasonable limits prescribed by law as can be demonstrably justified in a free and democratic society.

FUNDAMENTAL FREEDOMS

2. Everyone has the following fundamental freedoms:

---

† *Canada Act* (U.K.) 1982, c. 11.

‡ *Constitution Act, 1982*, being Schedule B to the *Canada Act, 1982* (U.K.), 1982, c. 11, ss. 1–50, 52–60.

These extracts omit repealed provisions; Part VI adding a new section 92A to the *Constitution Act, 1867* and adding a new Sixth Schedule to that Act; and the Schedule to the *Constitution Act, 1982*. Complete versions can be found in Hogg 2007, Appendix III (Appendix I for Part VI); and Reesor, Appendix B. For general assessments of the *Constitution Act, 1982*, see Cheffins, chs. 10 and 11 (an early view); Hogg 2007, ch. 33, parts 33.2, 33.3, and 33.4; Milne, ch. 6; Reesor, at 85–86 (federalism) and 410–15 (role of courts); and the relevant section of the Bibliography.

(a) freedom of conscience and religion;

(b) freedom of thought, belief, opinion and expression, including freedom of the press and other media of communication;

(c) freedom of peaceful assembly; and

(d) freedom of association.

DEMOCRATIC RIGHTS

Democratic rights of citizens

3. Every citizen of Canada has the right to vote in an election of members of the House of Commons or of a legislative assembly and to be qualified for membership therein.

Maximum duration of legislative bodies

4.(1) No House of Commons and no legislative assembly shall continue for longer than five years from the date fixed for the return of the writs at a general election of its members.

Continuation in special circumstances

(2) In time of real or apprehended war, invasion or insurrection, a House of Commons may be continued by Parliament and a legislative assembly may be continued by the legislature beyond five years if such continuation is not opposed by the votes of more than one-third of the members of the House of Commons or the legislative assembly, as the case may be.

Annual sitting of legislative bodies

5. There shall be a sitting of Parliament and of each legislature at least once every twelve months.

MOBILITY RIGHTS

Mobility of citizens

6.(1) Every citizen of Canada has the right to enter, remain in and leave Canada.

Rights to move and gain livelihood

(2) Every citizen of Canada and every person who has the status of a permanent resident of Canada has the right

(a) to move to and take up residence in any province; and

(b) to pursue the gaining of a livelihood in any province.

Limitation

(3) The rights specified in subsection (2) are subject to

(a) any laws or practices of general application in force in a province other than those that discriminate among persons primarily on the basis of province of present or previous residence; and

(b) any laws providing for reasonable residency requirements as a qualification for the receipt of publicly provided social services.

Affirmative action programs

(4) Subsections (2) and (3) do not preclude any law, program or activity that has as its object the amelioration in a province of conditions of individuals in that province who are socially or economically disadvantaged if the rate of employment in that province is below the rate of employment in Canada.

LEGAL RIGHTS

Life, liberty and security of person

7. Everyone has the right to life, liberty and security of the person and the right not to be deprived thereof except in accordance with the principles of fundamental justice.

Search or seizure

8. Everyone has the right to be secure against unreasonable search or seizure.

Detention or imprisonment

9. Everyone has the right not to be arbitrarily detained or imprisoned.

Arrest or detention

10. Everyone has the right on arrest or detention

(a) to be informed promptly of the reasons therefor;

(b) to retain and instruct counsel without delay and to be informed of that right; and

(c) to have the validity of the detention determined by way of habeas corpus and to be released if the detention is not lawful.

Proceedings in criminal and penal matters

11. Any person charged with an offence has the right

(a) to be informed without unreasonable delay of the specific offence;

(b) to be tried within a reasonable time;

(c) not to be compelled to be a witness in proceedings against that person in respect of the offence;

(d) to be presumed innocent until proven guilty according to law in a fair and public hearing by an independent and impartial tribunal;

(e) not to be denied reasonable bail without just cause;

(f) except in the case of an offence under military law tried before a military tribunal, to the benefit of trial by jury where the maximum punishment for the offence is imprisonment for five years or a more severe punishment;

(g) not to be found guilty on account of any act or omission unless, at the time of the act or omission, it constituted an offence under Canadian or international law or was criminal according to the general principles of law recognized by the community of nations;

(h) if finally acquitted of the offence, not to be tried for it again and, if finally found guilty and punished for the offence, not to be tried or punished for it again; and

(i) if found guilty of the offence and if the punishment for the offence has been varied between the time of commission and the time of sentencing, to the benefit of the lesser punishment.

Treatment or punishment

12. Everyone has the right not to be subjected to any cruel and unusual treatment or punishment.

Self-crimination

13. A witness who testifies in any proceedings has the right not to have any incriminating evidence so given used to incriminate that witness in any other proceedings, except in a prosecution for perjury or for the giving of contradictory evidence.

Interpreter

14. A party or witness in any proceedings who does not understand or speak the language in which the proceedings are conducted or who is deaf has the right to the assistance of an interpreter.

EQUALITY RIGHTS

Equality before and under law and equal protection and benefit of law

15.(1) Every individual is equal before and under the law and has the right to the equal protection and equal benefit of the law without discrimination and, in particular, without discrimination based on race, national or ethnic origin, colour, religion, sex, age or mental or physical disability.

Affirmative action programs

(2) Subsection (1) does not preclude any law, program or activity that has as its object the amelioration of conditions of disadvantaged individuals or groups including those that are disadvantaged because of race, national or ethnic origin, colour, religion, sex, age or mental or physical disability.

OFFICIAL LANGUAGES OF CANADA

Official languages of Canada

16.(1) English and French are the official languages of Canada and have equality of status and equal rights and privileges as to their use in all institutions of the Parliament and government of Canada.

Official languages of New Brunswick

(2) English and French are the official languages of New Brunswick and have equality of status and equal rights and privileges as to their use in all institutions of the legislature and government of New Brunswick.

Advancement of status and use

(3) Nothing in this Charter limits the authority of Parliament or a legislature to advance the equality of status or use of English and French.

English and French linguistic communities in New Brunswick

16.1(1) The English linguistic community and the French linguistic community in New Brunswick have equality of status and equal rights and privileges, including the right to distinct educational institutions and such distinct cultural institutions as are necessary for the preservation and promotion of those communities.

Role of the legislature and government of New Brunswick

(2) The role of the legislature and government of New Brunswick to preserve and promote the status, rights and privileges referred to in subsection (1) is affirmed. En. by Constitution Amendment, 1993 (New Brunswick), SI/93-54, Canada Gazette Part II, April 7, 1993, effective March 12, 1993.

Proceedings of Parliament

17.(1) Everyone has the right to use English or French in any debates and other proceedings of Parliament.

Proceedings of New Brunswick legislature

(2) Everyone has the right to use English or French in any debates and other proceedings of the legislature of New Brunswick.

Parliamentary statutes and records

18.(1) The statutes, records and journals of Parliament shall be printed and published in English and French and both language versions are equally authoritative.

New Brunswick statutes and records

(2) The statutes, records and journals of the legislature of New Brunswick shall be printed and published in English and French and both language versions are equally authoritative.

Proceedings in courts established by Parliament

19.(1) Either English or French may be used by any person in, or in any pleading in or process issuing from, any court established by Parliament.

Proceedings in New Brunswick courts

(2) Either English or French may be used by any person in, or in any pleading in or process issuing from, any court of New Brunswick.

Communications by public with federal institutions

20.(1) Any member of the public in Canada has the right to communicate with, and to receive available services from, any head or central office of an institution of the Parliament or government of Canada in English or French, and has the same right with respect to any other office of any such institution where

(a) there is a significant demand for communications with and services from that office in such language; or

(b) due to the nature of the office, it is reasonable that communications with and services from that office be available in both English and French.

Communications by public with New Brunswick institutions

(2) Any member of the public in New Brunswick has the right to communicate with, and to receive available services from, any office of an institution of the legislature or government of New Brunswick in English or French.

Continuation of existing constitutional provisions

21. Nothing in sections 16 to 20 abrogates or derogates from any right, privilege or obligation with respect to the English and French languages, or either of them, that exists or is continued by virtue of any other provision of the Constitution of Canada.

Rights and privileges preserved

22. Nothing in sections 16 to 20 abrogates or derogates from any legal or customary right or privilege acquired or enjoyed either before or after the coming into force of this Charter with respect to any language that is not English or French.

MINORITY LANGUAGE EDUCATIONAL RIGHTS

Language of instruction

23.(1) Citizens of Canada

(a) whose first language learned and still understood is that of the English or French linguistic minority population of the province in which they reside, or

(b) who have received their primary school instruction in Canada in English or French and reside in a province where the language in which they received that instruction is the language of the English or French linguistic minority population of the province,

have the right to have their children receive primary and secondary school instruction in that language in that province.

Continuity of language instruction

(2) Citizens of Canada of whom any child has received or is receiving primary or secondary school instruction in English or French in Canada, have the right to have all their children receive primary and secondary school instruction in the same language.

Application where numbers warrant

(3) The right of citizens of Canada under subsections (1) and (2) to have their children receive primary and secondary school instruction in the lan-

guage of the English or French linguistic minority population of a province

(a) applies wherever in the province the number of children of citizens who have such a right is sufficient to warrant the provision to them out of public funds of minority language instruction; and

(b) includes, where the number of those children so warrants, the right to have them receive that instruction in minority language educational facilities provided out of public funds.

Enforcement of guaranteed rights and freedoms

24.(1) Anyone whose rights or freedoms, as guaranteed by this Charter, have been infringed or denied may apply to a court of competent jurisdiction to obtain such remedy as the court considers appropriate and just in the circumstances.

Exclusion of evidence bringing administration of justice into disrepute

(2) Where, in proceedings under subsection (1), a court concludes that evidence was obtained in a manner that infringed or denied any rights or freedoms guaranteed by this Charter, the evidence shall be excluded if it is established that, having regard to all the circumstances, the admission of it in the proceedings would bring the administration of justice into disrepute.

GENERAL

Aboriginal rights and freedoms not affected by Charter

25. The guarantee in this Charter of certain rights and freedoms shall not be construed so as to abrogate or derogate from any aboriginal, treaty or other rights or freedoms that pertain to the aboriginal peoples of Canada including

(a) any rights or freedoms that have been recognized by the Royal Proclamation of October 7, 1763; and

(b) any rights or freedoms that now exist by way of land claims agreements or may be so acquired.

[am. by *Constitution Amendment Proclamation, 1983*, proclaimed in force June 21, 1984, SI/84-102. See *Canada Gazette*.]

Other rights and freedoms not affected by Charter

26. The guarantee in this Charter of certain rights and freedoms shall not be construed as denying the existence of any other rights or freedoms that exist in Canada.

Multicultural heritage

27. This Charter shall be interpreted in a manner consistent with the preservation and enhancement of the multicultural heritage of Canadians.

Rights guaranteed equally to both sexes

28. Notwithstanding anything in this Charter, the rights and freedoms referred to in it are guaranteed equally to male and female persons.

Rights respecting certain schools preserved

29. Nothing in this Charter abrogates or derogates from any rights or privileges guaranteed by or under the Constitution of Canada in respect of denominational, separate or dissentient schools.

Application to territories and territorial authorities

30. A reference in this Charter to a province or to the legislative assembly or legislature of a province shall be deemed to include a reference to the Yukon Territory and the Northwest Territories, or to the appropriate legislative authority thereof, as the case may be.

Legislative powers not extended

31. Nothing in this Charter extends the legislative powers of any body or authority.

APPLICATION OF CHARTER

Application of Charter

32.(1) This Charter applies

(a) to the Parliament and government of Canada in respect of all matters within the authority of Parliament including all matters relating to the Yukon Territory and Northwest Territories; and

(b) to the legislature and government of each province in respect of all matters within the authority of the legislature of each province.

Exception

(2) Notwithstanding subsection (1), section 15 shall not have effect until three years after this section comes into force.

[Note: this section came into force on April 17, 1982.]

Exception where express declaration

33.(1) Parliament or the legislature of a province may expressly declare in an Act of Parliament or of the legislature, as the case may be, that the Act or a provision thereof shall operate notwithstanding a provision included in section 2 or sections 7 to 15 of this Charter.

Operation of exception

(2) An Act or a provision of an Act in respect of which a declaration made under this section is in effect shall have such operation as it would have but for the provision of this Charter referred to in the declaration.

Five year limitation

(3) A declaration made under subsection (1) shall cease to have effect five years after it comes into force or on such earlier date as may be specified in the declaration.

Re-enactment

(4) Parliament or a legislature of a province may re-enact a declaration made under subsection (1).

Five year limitation

(5) Subsection (3) applies in respect of a re-enactment made under subsection (4).

CITATION

34. This Part may be cited as the *Canadian Charter of Rights and Freedoms.*

PART II: RIGHTS OF THE ABORIGINAL PEOPLES OF CANADA

Recognition of existing aboriginal and treaty rights

35.(1) The existing aboriginal and treaty rights of the aboriginal peoples of Canada are hereby recognized and affirmed.

Definition of "aboriginal peoples of Canada"

(2) In this Act, "aboriginal peoples of Canada" includes the Indian, Inuit and Metis peoples of Canada.

Land claims agreements

(3) For greater certainty, in subsection (1) "treaty rights" includes rights that now exist by way of land claims agreements or may be so acquired.

Aboriginal and treaty rights are guaranteed equally to both sexes

(4) Notwithstanding any other provision of this Act, the aboriginal and treaty rights referred to in subsection (1) are guaranteed equally to male and female persons.

[Note: Subsections 35(3) and (4) were added by the *Constitution Amendment Proclamation, 1983*, SI/84-102.]

Commitment to participation in constitutional conference

35.1 The government of Canada and the provincial governments are committed to the principle that, before any amendment is made to Class 24 of section 91 of the *"Constitution Act, 1867,"* to section 25 of this Act or to this Part,

(a) a constitutional conference that includes in its agenda an item relating to the proposed amendment, composed of the Prime Minister of Canada and the first ministers of the provinces, will be convened by the Prime Minister of Canada; and

(b) the Prime Minister of Canada will invite representatives of the aboriginal peoples of Canada to participate in the discussions on that item.

[Note: Section 35.1 was added by the *Constitution Amendment Proclamation, 1983*, SI/84-102.]

PART III: EQUALIZATION AND REGIONAL DISPARITIES

Commitment to promote equal opportunities

36.(1) Without altering the legislative authority of Parliament or of the provincial legislatures, or the rights of any of them with respect to the exercise of their legislative authority, Parliament and the legislatures, together with the government of Canada and the provincial governments, are committed to

(a) promoting equal opportunities for the well-being of Canadians;

(b) furthering economic development to reduce disparity in opportunities; and

(c) providing essential public services of reasonable quality to all Canadians.

(2) Parliament and the government of Canada are committed to the principle of making equalization payments to ensure that provincial governments have sufficient revenues to provide reasonably comparable levels of public services at reasonably comparable levels of taxation.

PART IV: CONSTITUTIONAL CONFERENCE

37. [repealed effective April 17, 1983]

PART IV.1: CONSTITUTIONAL CONFERENCES

37.1 [repealed effective April 18, 1987]

PART V: PROCEDURE FOR AMENDING CONSTITUTION OF CANADA

General procedure for amending Constitution of Canada

38.(1) An amendment to the Constitution of Canada may be made by proclamation issued by the Governor General under the Great Seal of Canada where so authorized by
(a) resolutions of the Senate and House of Commons; and
(b) resolutions of the legislative assemblies of at least two-thirds of the provinces that have, in the aggregate, according to the then latest general census, at least fifty per cent of the population of all the provinces.

Majority of members

(2) An amendment made under subsection (1) that derogates from the legislative powers, the proprietary rights or any other rights or privileges of the legislature or government of a province shall require a resolution supported by a majority of the members of each of the Senate, the House of Commons and the legislative assemblies required under subsection (1).

Expression of dissent

(3) An amendment referred to in subsection (2) shall not have effect in a province the legislative assembly of which has expressed its dissent thereto by resolution supported by a majority of its members prior to the issue of the proclamation to which the amendment relates unless that legislative assembly, subsequently, by resolution supported by a majority of its members, revokes its dissent and authorizes the amendment.

Revocation of dissent

(4) A resolution of dissent made for the purposes of subsection (3) may be revoked at any time before or after the issue of the proclamation to which it relates.

Restriction on proclamation

39.(1) A proclamation shall not be issued under subsection 38(1) before the expiration of one year from the adoption of the resolution initiating the amendment procedure thereunder, unless the legislative assembly of each province has previously adopted a resolution of assent or dissent.

(2) A proclamation shall not be issued under subsection 38(1) after the expiration of three years from the adoption of the resolution initiating the amendment procedure thereunder.

Compensation

40. Where an amendment is made under subsection 38(1) that transfers provincial legislative powers relating to education or other cultural matters from provincial legislatures to Parliament, Canada shall provide reasonable compensation to any province to which the amendment does not apply.

Amendment by unanimous consent

41. An amendment to the Constitution of Canada in relation to the following matters may be made by proclamation issued by the Governor General under the Great Seal of Canada only where authorized by resolutions of the Senate and House of Commons and of the legislative assembly of each province:
(a) the office of the Queen, the Governor General and the Lieutenant Governor of a province;
(b) the right of a province to a number of members in the House of Commons not less than the number of Senators by which the province is entitled to be represented at the time this Part comes into force;
(c) subject to section 43, the use of the English or the French language;
(d) the composition of the Supreme Court of Canada; and
(e) an amendment to this Part.

Amendment by general procedure

42.(1) An amendment to the Constitution of Canada in relation to the following matters may be made only in accordance with subsection 38(1):
(a) the principle of proportionate representation of the provinces in the House of Commons prescribed by the Constitution of Canada;
(b) the powers of the Senate and the method of selecting Senators;
(c) the number of members by which a province is entitled to be represented in the Senate and the residence qualifications of Senators;

(d) subject to paragraph 41(d), the Supreme Court of Canada;

(e) the extension of existing provinces into the territories; and

(f) notwithstanding any other law or practice, the establishment of new provinces.

Exception

(2) Subsections 38(2) to (4) do not apply in respect of amendments in relation to matters referred to in subsection (1).

Amendment of provisions relating to some but not all provinces

43. An amendment to the Constitution of Canada in relation to any provision that applies to one or more, but not all, provinces, including

(a) any alteration to boundaries between provinces, and

(b) any amendment to any provision that relates to the use of the English or the French language within a province,

may be made by proclamation issued by the Governor General under the Great Seal of Canada only where so authorized by resolutions of the Senate and House of Commons and of the legislative assembly of each province to which the amendment applies.

Amendments by Parliament

44. Subject to sections 41 and 42, Parliament may exclusively make laws amending the Constitution of Canada in relation to the executive government of Canada or the Senate and House of Commons.

Amendments by provincial legislatures

45. Subject to section 41, the legislature of each province may exclusively make laws amending the constitution of the province.

Initiation of amendment procedures

46.(1) The procedures for amendment under sections 38, 41, 42 and 43 may be initiated either by the Senate or the House of Commons or by the legislative assembly of a province.

Revocation of authorization

(2) A resolution of assent for the purposes of this Part may be revoked at any time before the issue of a proclamation authorized by it.

Amendment without Senate resolution

47.(1) An amendment to the Constitution of Canada made by proclamation under section 38, 41, 42 or 43 may be made without a resolution of the Senate authorizing the issue of the proclamation if, within one hundred and eighty days after the adoption by the House of Commons of a resolution authorizing its issue, the Senate has not adopted such a resolution and if, at any time after the expiration of that period, the House of Commons again adopts the resolution.

Computation of period

(2) Any period when Parliament is prorogued or dissolved shall not be counted in computing the one hundred and eighty day period referred to in subsection (1).

Advice to issue proclamation

48. The Queen's Privy Council for Canada shall advise the Governor General to issue a proclamation under this Part forthwith on the adoption of the resolutions required for an amendment made by proclamation under this Part.

Constitutional conference

49. A constitutional conference composed of the Prime Minister of Canada and the first ministers of the provinces shall be convened by the Prime Minister of Canada within fifteen years after this Part comes into force to review the provisions of this Part.

PART VI: AMENDMENT TO THE CONSTITUTION ACT, 1867

Amendment to Constitution Act, 1867

50. The *Constitution Act, 1867* (formerly named the *British North America Act, 1867*) is amended by adding thereto, immediately after section 92 thereof, the following heading and section:

. . . .

Laws respecting non-renewable natural resources, forestry resources and electrical energy

[The content of this Part is summarized in Chapter 3 in *The Constitution Act, 1867, Division of Powers*].

. . . .

PART VII: GENERAL

Primacy of Constitution of Canada

52.(1) The Constitution of Canada is the supreme law of Canada, and any law that is inconsistent with the provisions of the Constitution is, to the extent of the inconsistency, of no force or effect.

Constitution of Canada

(2) The Constitution of Canada includes

(a) the *Canada Act 1982*, including this Act;

(b) the Acts and orders referred to in the schedule; and

(c) any amendment to any Act or order referred to in paragraph (a) or (b).

Amendments to Constitution of Canada

(3) Amendments to the Constitution of Canada shall be made only in accordance with the authority contained in the Constitution of Canada.

Repeals and new names

53.(1) The enactments referred to in Column I of the schedule are hereby repealed or amended to the extent indicated in Column II thereof and, unless repealed, shall continue as law in Canada under the names set out in Column III thereof.

Consequential amendments

(2) Every enactment, except the *Canada Act 1982*, that refers to an enactment referred to in the schedule by the name in Column I thereof is hereby amended by substituting for that name the corresponding name in Column III thereof, and any *British North America Act* not referred to in the schedule may be cited as the *Constitution Act* followed by the year and number, if any, of its enactment.

Repeal and consequential amendments

54. Part IV is repealed on the day that is one year after this Part comes into force and this section may be repealed and this Act renumbered, consequentially upon the repeal of Part IV and this section, by proclamation issued by the Governor General under the Great Seal of Canada.

French version of Constitution of Canada

55. A French version of the portions of the Constitution of Canada referred to in the schedule shall be prepared by the Minister of Justice of Canada as expeditiously as possible and, when any portion thereof sufficient to warrant action being taken has been so prepared, it shall be put forward for enactment by proclamation issued by the Governor General under the Great Seal of Canada pursuant to the procedure then applicable to an amendment of the same provisions of the Constitution of Canada.

English and French versions of certain constitutional texts

56. Where any portion of the Constitution of Canada has been or is enacted in English and French or where a French version of any portion of the Constitution is enacted pursuant to section 55, the English and French versions of that portion of the Constitution are equally authoritative.

English and French versions of this Act

57. The English and French versions of this Act are equally authoritative.

Commencement

58. Subject to section 59, this Act shall come into force on a day to be fixed by proclamation issued by the Queen or the Governor General under the Great Seal of Canada.

Commencement of paragraph 23(1)(a) in respect of Quebec

59.(1) Paragraph 23(1)(a) shall come into force in respect of Quebec on a day to be fixed by proclamation issued by the Queen or the Governor General under the Great Seal of Canada.

Authorization of Quebec

(2) A proclamation under subsection (1) shall be issued only where authorized by the legislative assembly or government of Quebec.

Repeal of this section

(3) This section may be repealed on the day paragraph 23(1)(a) comes into force in respect of Quebec and this Act amended and renumbered, consequentially upon the repeal of this section, by proclamation issued by the Queen or the Governor General under the Great Seal of Canada.

Short title and citations

60. This Act may be cited as the *Constitution Act, 1982*, and the *Constitution Acts* 1867 to 1975 (No. 2) and this Act may be cited together as the *Constitution Acts, 1867 to 1982*.

(g) A New World†

Alan C. Cairns

NOTE

The constitutional package of 1982 raises myriad questions. For example:

1. How does the *Constitution Act, 1982* affect
    (a) our traditional system of parliamentary democracy?
    (b) minority rights?
    (c) the conventions and principles that still lie outside the formal part of our constitution?
    (d) the balance between public and private power?
    (e) non-governmental abuse of power?
    (f) the federal system?

2. How does the *Constitution Act, 1982* affect the dynamics of constitutional change?

3. How is the *Constitution Act, 1982* affecting administrative law, criminal law, and the law relating to civil liberties?

4. What is the significance of the *Constitution Act, 1982* for the Canadian judiciary?

5. How does the *Constitution Act, 1982* affect *non*-legal means of resolving social problems?

These questions go well beyond technical matters of structure, wording, and legal interpretation. In the following extracts, Alan Cairns considers a key sociological consequence of the 1982 changes. Look for other, broader, implications in the chapters that follow.

EXTRACT

The constitutional world we have lost was simplicity itself compared with the constitutional world we have gained. One of its organizing rubrics, federalism, was the vehicle between our federal and provincial selves, both as governments and as peoples, as well as how the two historic founding French and English peoples should relate to each other. A second rubric, responsible government and parliamentary suprem-

acy, provided us with a focus for organizing our thoughts on the appropriate relationship between executive leadership and representative democracy. A third organizing rubric, now departed but a significant if admittedly diminishing presence until only a few years ago, was how we were to manage or modify the coexistence our Canadian selves and our inherited constitutional links to the mother country.

By and large, all three of these foci for constitutional introspection were elitist and governmental. Governments played a leading role in the great battles over federalism in our country. They fought each other in court, bargained with each other in executive federalism, and commissioned the great official inquiries, such as the Rowell-Sirois and Trembly Reports, that sought to impart new senses of direction to our federalist future. Responsible parliamentary government raised crucial constitutional questions, but they all presupposed the centrality of relations among the institutions at the top of our political pyramid — cabinet, Commons, Senate, and representative of the Crown, or their provincial counterparts. The colony-to-nation focus, to simplify only slightly, addressed the page at which imperial functions performed by British constitutional actors should be devolved to governments in Canada, or in the case of the Judicial Committee, to the Supreme Court.

What was strikingly absent from this constitutional world? Gender, the status of Aboriginal peoples as a constitutional concern, the relationship between the two founding peoples and the "others", and indeed virtually all the other minoritiarians [such as ethnic Canadians and those who are minorities within provincial, territorial, and national boundaries]. Finally, and directly related to the preceding of course, there was no Charter or Bill of Rights that explicitly incorporated the citizenry into the constitutional order. Thus, the constitutional law that preceded the Charter rarely addressed "relationships between governments and citizens ... because the Constitution Act, 1867 was virtually silent about those relationships."

---

† From "Constitutional Minoritarianism in Canada," in D.E. Williams and A. Cairns, ed., *Reconfigurations: Canadian Citizenship and Constitutional Change* (Toronto: University of Toronto Press, 1995) 119 at 138–40. [Notes omitted.] Copyright © 1995. Reproduced by permission of the author and Oxford University Press Canada.

The constitutional world we have lost had many virtues.... On the other hand... [the debate about the role of the Judicial Committee deflected attention from questions about the appropriate role, composition, and status of an autonomous Canadian Supreme Court; and the continuing British role in amending the Canadian constitution prevented us from considering where sovereignty should reside in Canada once the British tie was ended]. More generally, the very British absence of a Charter until 1982 not only deprived us of a rich constitutional language organized around "rights", but, in conjunction with the absence of a revolutionary tradition, left us with only a very thinly developed conception of citizenship. These characteristics of the constitutional world we have lost ill-prepared us for the new constitutional world that we gained by the 1982 Constitution Act providing us with a Charter and purely domestic amending formula.

Success in manoeuvring through the new constitutional world will not come easily. The cultural support base of the constitutional order has been irreversibly modified. The constitutional hegemony of the concept of founding peoples restricted to the British and French is in retreat, encroached on [on] one side by Aboriginal peoples who claim real founding status and from the other side by a rapidly growing multicultural, multiracial population that resists linking status to the length of one's Canadian ancestral line.

... In our new constitutional world, majorities will be less easy to create and to maintain; elites will have to be more sensitive to the suspicious minorities that have come out of the recesses of our society; in brief, we will have to pay more attention to the citizen base of the constitutional order.

10 Specific Aspects of the *Constitution Act, 1982*

(a) Introduction

This chapter will look at three especially important components of the *Constitution Act, 1982*: the *Canadian Charter of Rights and Freedoms*; the provisions regarding Aboriginal peoples, as amended in June 1984; and the formal amending procedures. The text of the *Charter* comprises Part I, the first 34 sections, of the *Constitution Act, 1982*. The Aboriginal provisions are in s. 25 (a non-derogation provision located in the *Charter*), and in Part II of the *Constitution Act, 1982*. The amending provisions are in Part V of the *Constitution Act, 1982*

(Parts IV and IV.1, now repealed, related to Aboriginal constitutional conferences that have now been held).

Part III of the *Constitution Act, 1982* on equalization is addressed in Chapter 8, and aspects of Part VII, the general part, are addressed in Chapters 2 and 9. Part VI, the amendment to s. 92 of the *Constitution Act, 1982* to give the provinces greater control over their non-renewable resources, is summarized in Chapter 3.

(b) *Canadian Charter of Rights and Freedoms*†

The *Canadian Charter of Rights and Freedoms* was introduced briefly in Chapter 9. The case law on the *Charter* is considered at length in a companion volume, *Introduction to Public Law: Readings on the State, the Administrative Process, and Basic*

Values.[1] Hence, this section will be limited to some comments on leading provisions of the *Charter* and its general impact.

As seen in Chapter 9, the *Charter* has three main components. The first addresses the general

† See generally, Dyck, ch. 19; Hogg 2007, chs. 33–54; MacIvor, ch. 10; Monhahan, ch. 13; G.-A. Beaudoin & E. Mendes, *The Canadian Charter of Rights and Freedoms*, 4th ed. (Markham, Ont: LexisNexis Butterworths, 2005); Brooks, part 5; P.H. Russell, *Constitutional Odyssey: Can Canadians Become a Sovereign People?* 3d ed. (Toronto: University of Toronto Press, 2004), ch. 8; Funston, ch. 9; C.P. Manfredi, *Judicial Power and the Charter: Canada and the Paradox of Liberal Constitutionalism*, 2d ed. (Don Mills, Ont.: Oxford University Press, 2001); K. Roach, The Supreme Court on Trial: Judicial Activism or Democratic Dialogue (Toronto: Irwin Law, 2001); R. Knopff and F.L. Morton, *The Charter Revolution and the Court Party* (Peterborough, Ont.: Broadview Press, 2000); Alan C. Cairns, *Reconfigurations: Canadian Citizenship and Constitutional Change* (Toronto: McClelland & Stewart, 1995); A. Hutchinson, *Waiting for Coraf: A Critique of Law and Rights* (Toronto: University of Toronto Press, 1995); W.A. Bogart, *Courts and Country: The Limits of Litigation and the Social and Political Life of Canada* (Toronto: Oxford University Press, 1994), ch. 9; P. Bryden *et al.*, eds., *Protecting Rights and Freedoms* (Toronto: University of Toronto Press, 1994); R. Knopff and F.L. Morton, *Charter Politics* (Scarborough: Nelson, 1992); Reesor, ch. 8; Milne, ch. 5; D. Beatty, *Talking Heads and the Supremes* (Agincourt, Ont.: Carswell, 1990); I. Greene, *The Charter of Rights* (Toronto: James Lorimer and Company, 1989); M. Mandel, *The Charter of Rights and the Legalization of Politics in Canada*, rev'd. ed. (Toronto: Thompson Educational Publishing, 1989); R. Romanow et al., *Canada...Notwithstanding* (Agincourt, Ont.: Carswell, 1984), ch. 8.

scope of the *Charter*. The second sets out nine individual classes of rights and freedoms. The third is a guarantee and justification provision, which enables the guaranteed rights or freedoms to be restricted in certain individual situations.

Logically, the first question is whether the *Charter* applies at all to a given kind of subject matter. Section 32 of the *Charter* applies it to the federal and provincial governments in regard to all matters within their jurisdiction, including matters relating to the territories. There was an early controversy as to whether this provision limited the *Charter* to "government", or whether the *Charter* applies to all private activity as well. Although courts have held that the *Charter* is limited to government,[2] they have interpreted "government" to include not only the legislative and executive branches,[3] but also statutory regulation of private activity,[4] proceedings initiated for public purposes by courts,[5] and actions of non-government bodies that carry out specific government policies.[6]

The general scope of the *Charter* can also be affected by s. 33, the override or notwithstanding clause. Section 33 is the result of the compromise agreement of November 5, 1981 between premiers determined to restrict the *Charter* guarantees and a federal government determined to keep them. The provision permits legislatures to override the guarantees in ss. 2 and 7 to 15 for five-year renewable periods, provided that they do so explicitly. In contrast, the language guarantees, the heart of the original Trudeau package, are among those that cannot be overridden.

The override has been used in only three provinces. The first occasion was in Quebec. As part of their protest against the *Constitution Act, 1982*, the Parti Québécois government applied the override to all their legislation until 1987, and to some of it until 1989. Then, in 1986, the Saskatchewan government applied the override clause to the fundamental freedoms in order to protect public service back-to-work legislation, not long before the Supreme Court held the legislation to be valid apart from the override.[7] Quebec used the override again in December 1988. Four days after the Supreme Court struck down the French-only signs and firm names provisions in Quebec's Bill 101,[8] the provincial government invoked the override against the freedom of expression guarantee. This was done to protect new Quebec legislation designed to maintain French-only commercial signs and firm names outdoors while permitting multilingual signs and names inside shop premises. The override has been used in Quebec on about a

dozen other occasions, attracting much less attention than the blanket override of the early 1980s and the 1988 language signs override.[9]

So far, the only other province to use the override is Alberta. In 2000, the Alberta government used the override to protect legislation that limited marital status to opposite-sex couples.[10] In light of the rarity of these examples, it may be that outside Quebec s. 33 is yielding to a general convention of non-use.

Once it is established that the subject matter is within the general scope of the *Charter*, the next question is whether one or more of the individual rights or freedoms have been breached. First are four sets of fundamental freedoms, including freedom of thought, expression, and association. Of these, the most litigated has been freedom of expression. Here, as with most *Charter* rights, the most difficult questions are not about "core" forms of the freedom, such as freedom of political speech, but about more tenuous forms, such as commercial signs and advertising,[11] pornography,[12] and alleged hate propaganda.[13] The courts have tended to construe freedom of expression broadly.[14] Most of these cases are determined mainly on the basis of the justification provision in s. 1.[15] Paradoxically, despite their name, the fundamental freedoms are subject to the override in s. 33.

The democratic rights in ss. 3 to 5 guarantee the right to vote, and limit federal and provincial legislatures to a normal duration of five years. The right to vote has helped to end franchise restrictions for judges and mental patients, and to end most of them for prisoners. The democratic rights cannot be overridden.

Section 7 has involved the most litigation of any single *Charter* provision. It guarantees the right not to be deprived of life, liberty, and security of the person, except in accordance with fundamental justice. When the *Constitution Act, 1982* was being drafted, it was generally thought that fundamental justice would be limited to procedural natural justice. However, courts have construed the provision much more broadly, to include the fundamental tenets of the justice system,[16] and one of these tenets is a broadly drawn notion of "arbitrariness".[17] So far, "life, liberty, and security of the person" has been applied mainly to physical[18] or physiological[19] deprivations. This has given s. 7 an important role in criminal law and refugee proceedings, and in other matters such as abortion. If s. 7 were extended to include economic deprivations, it could cover much of the field of administrative law.

The more specific legal rights in ss. 8 to 14 have also had a significant effect on criminal law. These rights include a protection against unreasonable search and seizure,[20] the right not to be arbitrarily imprisoned or detained,[21] the right to trial within a reasonable time,[22] and the right to trial before an independent and impartial tribunal.[23] Like s. 7, these provisions are subject to the override.

The equality guarantees in s. 15 are an important part of the *Charter*. They have been construed broadly to include "adverse effect" discrimination, which can result even from a racially neutral statute.[24] Section 15 has produced some important decisions involving sexual orientation,[25] disabilities,[26] social benefits,[27] and the family.[28] Note, however, that economic inequality is not included among the examples of prohibited categories of discrimination in s. 15. Unlike the special gender equality guarantee in s. 28, s. 15 is subject to the s. 33 override.

The other *Charter* rights to be noted here are the language guarantees.[29] Sections 16 to 23 reflect the Trudeau government's philosophy of attempting to counter the desire for special francophone rights in Quebec with a broader constitutional guarantee of official language minority rights across Canada as a whole.

Sections 16 to 22 give English and French equal status in the legislative and other governmental institutions of the federal government and New Brunswick. Section 23(1)(a) says that parents whose mother tongue is the official minority language of the province in which they reside have the right to have their children educated in that language in the province.[30] However, this right does not apply in Quebec, where it is not to come into effect until the Quebec government or legislative assembly so decides.[31] Section 23(1)(b) says that parents who were educated in a primary school in Canada in the official minority language of the province in which they reside have the right to have their children educated in that language in the province. Section 23(1)(c) extends language instruction rights to siblings. Section 23(2) extends the right to minority language instruction, and to language educational facilities, where the number of the children "so warrants".[32]

Also relevant to language rights are s. 2, guaranteeing freedom of expression, ss. 26 and 27, safeguarding "other rights and freedoms" and "the multicultural heritage of Canadians", respectively, and ss. 55 to 58 regarding the official languages and the Constitution of Canada.

The *Charter* language guarantees should be read in conjunction with s. 133 of the *Constitution Act, 1867*. It guarantees the right to use English or French in Parliament, in the Quebec legislature, and before federally created courts and those in Quebec, and requires that federal and Quebec statutes be published in both languages. Similar guarantees are included in s. 23 of the *Manitoba Act* of 1870.[33]

Meanwhile, provincial governments in Quebec passed a series of laws designed to help ensure the survival of the French language in that province. Confrontation with the *Charter*'s language and related guarantees was inevitable. In 1977, the Parti Québécois enacted the *Charter of the French Language*.[34] Many of this Charter's French language safeguards, including its provisions limiting entry into English language schools,[35] its language restrictions in legislative proceedings,[36] and its limits on the use of languages other than French on commercial signs and firm names,[37] have been declared unconstitutional. As seen above, when the Supreme Court invalidated Quebec Bill 101's commercial signs and firm names provisions,[38] the Quebec government invoked the override provision to protect its language restrictions.[39]

The third key component of the *Charter* is s. 1, the reasonable justification provision. Unlike s. 33, this restriction applies to virtually all *Charter* guarantees (except perhaps the gender equality guarantee, which applies "[n]otwithstanding anything in this Charter"). Courts have given the literal wording of s. 1 a special interpretation, known as the "*Oakes*" test, after the decision in which it was formulated.[40] As restated in a later case,[41] the test says:

A limitation to a constitutional guarantee will be sustained once two conditions are met. First, the objective of the legislation must be pressing and substantial. Second, the means chosen to attain this legislative end must be reasonable and demonstrably justifiable in a free and democratic society. In order to satisfy the second requirement, three criteria must be satisfied: (1) the rights violation must be rationally connected to the aim of the legislation; (2) the impugned provision must minimally impair the Charter guarantee; and (3) there must be a proportionality between the effect of the measure and its objective so that the attainment of the legislative goal is not outweighed by the abridgement of the right. In all S. 1 cases the burden of proof is with the government to show on a balance of probabilities that the violation is justifiable.

Compare this test with the actual wording of s. 1. Could there be a more dramatic illustration of the power of judicial interpretation?

It is too soon to offer any definitive conclusions about the general impact of the *Charter*. The document could evolve as much in its second two decades as its first. Instead, nine general propositions will be offered here. Which, in your view, is the most (and the least) arguable?

1. Together with the amending formula, the *Charter* lies at the heart of the constitutional changes of 1982.

2. From the outset, the *Charter* was one of the most popular (for many) and controversial (for some) elements of the 1982 package.

3. The *Charter* is part of a general "rights revolution" that has characterized much of the world from the latter half of the 19th century.

4. The *Charter* is also part of a growing general emphasis on constitutionalism.

5. Although the scope of the *Charter* is technically limited to "government", its influence in recent decades has gone far beyond government in a narrow sense.

6. The Supreme Court of Canada has construed the *Charter* quite actively, with significant effects on social issues, such as rights of accused people, abortion, freedom of speech, and equality.

7. The *Charter* contains both individual and group rights, and some rights (such as equality) with features of both.

8. Some very significant issues, such as economic inequalities, are untouched or barely touched by the *Charter*.

9. The *Charter* has significantly expanded and changed the role of Canadian courts in relation to elected politicians and society as a whole.

Notes

1. David W. Elliott, ed., *Introduction to Public Law: Readings on the State, the Administrative Process, and Basic Values*, 6th ed. (Concord, Ont.: Captus Press, 2007).
2. *RWDSU v. Dolphin Delivery*, [1986] 2 S.C.R. 573 at 598–600.
3. *Ibid.*
4. *Vriend v. Alberta*, [1998] 1 S.C.R. 493 at para. 65.
5. *B.C. Government Employees' Union v. British Columbia*, [1988] 2 S.C.R. 214 at 244.
6. *Eldridge v. British Columbia (A.G.)*, [1997] 3 S.C.R. 624 at paras. 41–43.
7. *Saskatchewan v. Retail, Wholesale and Department Store Union*, [1987] 1 S.C.R. 424.
8. In *Ford v. Quebec*, [1988] 2 S.C.R. 712.
9. See generally, Hogg 2007, section 36.2; T. Kahana, "The Notwithstanding Mechanism and Public Discussions: Lessons from the Ignored Practice of Section 33" (2001) 43 Can. J. of Public Admin. 255; L. Weinrib, "Learning to Live with the Override'" (1990) 35 McGill L.J. 541.
10. *Marriage Amendment Act*, S.A. 2000, c. 3, s. 5.
11. For example, *Ford v. Quebec (A.G.)*, [1988] 2 S.C.R. 712; *Irwin Toy Ltd. v. Quebec (A.G.)*, [1989] 1 S.C.R. 927.
12. For example, *R. v. Butler*, [1992] 1 S.C.R. 452.
13. For example, *R. v. Keegstra*, [1990] 3 S.C.R. 697; *R. v. Zundel*, [1990] 2 S.C.R. 202.
14. Expression is essentially defined as activity attempting to convey meaning: *Irwin Toy Ltd. v. Quebec (A.G.)*, [1989] 1 S.C.R. 927 at 968.
15. As in *Thomson Newspapers Co. v. Canada (A.G.)*, [1998] 1 S.C.R. 877.
16. *Re section 94(2) of Motor Vehicle Act, R.S.B.C. 1979*, [1985] 2 S.C.R. 486.
17. See, for example, *Rodriguez v. British Columbia (A.G.)*, [1993] 3 S.C.R. 519 at 594–95; *R. v. Malmo-Levine*, [2003] 3 S.C.R. 571 at para. 135; and *Chaoulli v. Quebec (A.G.)*, [2005] 1 S.C.R. 791 at paras. 130–31 and (a narrower approach) paras. 233–34.
18. For example, *Singh v. Minister of Employment and Immigration*, [1985] 1 S.C.R 517.
19. See *R. v. Morgentaler (No. 2)*, [1988] 1 S.C.R. 30.
20. For example, *R. v. Edwards*, [1996] 1 S.C.R. 128; *R. v. Feeney*, [1997] 2 S.C.R. 13.
21. See *R. v. Latimer*, [1997] 1 S.C.R. 217.
22. *R. v. Askov*, [1990] 2 S.C.R. 1199.
23. *Valente v. The Queen*, [1985] 2 S.C.R. 673.
24. See *Symes v. Canada*, [1993] 4 S.C.R. 645 (although the majority found that discrimination had not been proved here).
25. *Vriend v. Alberta*, [1998] 1 S.C.R. 489.
26. *Eldridge v. British Columbia*, [1997] 3 S.C.R. 624.
27. *Law v. Minister of Employment and Immigration*, [1999] 1 S.C.R. 497; *Eldridge*, *ibid.*
28. *Miron v. Trudel*, [1995] 2 S.C.R. 418.
29. For commentary on the *Charter* and other constitutional language guarantees, see Dyke, ch. 5; Hogg 2007, ch. 53; André Tremblay, "Les Droits Linguistiques (articles 16 à 22)" in Gérald-A. Beaudoin & Errol Mendes, *The Canadian Charter of Rights and Freedoms*, 4th ed. (Markham, Ont.: LexisNexis Butterworths, 2005), chs. 15 and 16; P. Foucher, *Les droits scolaires des minorités linguistiques*, in Beaudoin & Mendes, *ibid.*, ch. 16; C.M. MacMillan, *The Practice of Language Rights in Canada* (Toronto: University of Toronto Press, 1998); Reesor, at 274–79 and 358–67.
30. See *Re Public Schools Act (Man.)*, [1993] 1 S.C.R. 839.
31. See *Constitution Act, 1982*, s. 59.
32. See *Mahe v. Alberta*, [1990] 1 S.C.R. 342; *Arsenault-Cameron v. P.E.I.*, [1999] 3 S.C.R. 851.
33. R.S.C. 1985, Appendix II, No. 8. See *A.G. Manitoba v. Forest*, [1979] 2 S.C.R. 1032, holding a 19th-century attempt by the province to repeal this provision to be unconstitutional. See also s. 110 of the *North-West Territories Act*.
34. S.Q. 1977, c. 5.
35. See *Quebec (A.G.) v. Quebec Protestant School Boards*, [1984] 2 S.C.R. 66.
36. See *A.G. v. Blaikie*, [1979] 2 S.C.R. 1016.
37. See *Ford v. Quebec*, [1988] 2 S.C.R. 712.
38. Under the freedom of expression provision of the *Canadian Charter of Rights and Freedoms* and the Quebec *Charter of Rights and Freedoms*: *Ford v. Quebec*, [1988] 2 S.C.R. 712.
39. *Ibid.*, as discussed above in regard to s. 33 of the *Charter*.
40. *R. v. Oakes*, [1986] 1 S.C.R. 103.
41. *Egan v. Canada*, [1995] 2 S.C.R. 513 at para. 182.

(c)   Aboriginal Provisions†

The year 1982 was a turning point for the law relating to Canadian Aboriginal peoples. Rights with uncertain status in common law[1] were enshrined in the written part of the Canadian constitution. Two years later, these rights were refined and enlarged. As a result of the changes of 1982 and 1984, Aboriginal-government relations and Aboriginal/non-Aboriginal relations were given a much more legal framework. What had been mainly a political responsibility was now shared with courts. Before looking at the provisions themselves, it is useful to see how they came about.

As seen in Chapter 9, in the early 1980s the federal government sought to dissuade French-speaking Canadians in Quebec from supporting separatism by offering them special guaranteed rights in a revised constitution, and to balance this with guaranteed rights for English-speaking minorities and guaranteed individual rights for Canadians generally. Against this background, Aboriginal Canadians sought constitutional protection for their own group rights.

In the spring of 1980, the federal government proposed a draft constitutional preamble that would include a provision to "enshrine the rights of our native peoples." However, the proposed constitutional package released in October 1980 contained only a negative non-derogation provision. It said *Charter* guarantees would not deny the existence of "any rights or freedoms that pertain to the native peoples of Canada."[2] There was a strong reaction from Aboriginal groups. When the constitutional package was considered by the Special Joint Committee of the Senate and the House of Commons on the Constitution of Canada, 17 of the 104 groups who appeared before the Committee were groups representing Aboriginal people.[3] Nearly all Aboriginal groups sought a constitutional provision to entrench Aboriginal and treaty rights against federal and provincial legislation. Some sought recognition of sovereignty and Aboriginal governmental powers.[4]

On January 30, 1981, representatives of the three national Aboriginal organizations and political parties agreed to include a new provision as follows:

1. The aboriginal and treaty rights of the Aboriginal peoples of Canada are hereby recognized and affirmed.
2. In this Act, "aboriginal peoples of Canada" includes the Indian, Inuit, and Métis peoples of Canada.

When the parliamentary committee reported on February 23, it supported (i) the non-derogation clause, (ii) a guaranteed constitutional conference for the "identification and definition" of the rights of Aboriginal peoples, and (iii) the provision recognizing and affirming Aboriginal and treaty rights. On April 23, 1981, the House of Commons formally approved the revised package.[5] Meanwhile, the National Indian Brotherhood and the Native Council of Canada withdrew their support for the constitutional proposals, calling for an Aboriginal right to veto future constitutional amendments that affected them.

In the Constitutional Accord reached between the federal government and nine provinces on November 5, 1981, the non-derogation and constitutional conference provisions were retained, but the recognition and affirmation provision was missing. Apparently some of the governments were concerned about the potential implications of this provision for government jurisdiction and expenditures, and for third-party interests.[6] After a strong lobbying campaign by Aboriginal groups and media and other supporters, the governments agreed on November 23 to reinstate the Aboriginal and treaty rights recognition and affirmation, but to preface it with the word "existing".

---

† This discussion is adapted from D.W. Elliott, *Law and Aboriginal Peoples in Canada*, 5th ed. (Concord, Ont.: Captus Press, 2005), chs. 7 and 12. See also D. Milne, *The Canadian Constitution* (Toronto: James Lorimer and Company, 1991); D.W. Elliott, *The Legal Status of Aboriginal and Treaty Rights in Section 35(1) of the Constitution Act, 1982* (Ottawa: Canadian Bar Association, 1990) at 19–30; B. Schwartz, *First Principles, Second Thoughts; Aboriginal Peoples, Constitutional Reform and Canadian Statecraft* (Kingston: Institute of Intergovernmental Relations, 1985); R. Romanow, J. Whyte, H. Leeson, *Canada...Notwithstanding: The Making of the Constitution, 1976–1982* (Toronto: Carswell/Methuen, 1984); N.K. Zlotkin, *Unfinished Business: Aboriginal Peoples and the Constitutional Conference* (Kingston: Institute of Intergovernmental Relations, 1983); E. McWhinney, *Canada and the Constitution: 1979–1982* (Toronto: University of Toronto Press, 1982); R. Sheppard and M. Valpy, *The National Deal: The Fight for a Canadian Constitution* (Toronto: Fleet Books, 1982).

The Assembly of First Nations and several other Aboriginal groups launched a court action in England against the package, claiming that it would interfere with treaty obligations still owed by the Imperial Crown. On January 23, 1982, the English Court of Appeal rejected this argument, saying that as Canada became independent, the Imperial Crown's treaty obligations had been transferred to Canada.[7]

Meanwhile the *Constitution Act, 1982*, including the Aboriginal[8] provisions, came into effect on April 17, 1982.[9] Section 25 of the Act is based on the non-derogation provision from the original October 1980 proposal. It provides that the *Charter* guarantee of rights and freedoms should not be construed as derogating from rights relating to Aboriginal peoples. Section 35 recognizes and affirms the existing Aboriginal and treaty rights of the Aboriginal peoples of Canada (s. 35(1)), and says these people include the Indian, Métis, and Inuit people of Canada (s. 35(2)). Section 37,[10] now repealed, provided for an Aboriginal constitutional conference within a year of April 17, 1982.

The Aboriginal constitutional conference was held on 15 and 16 in March 1983. It resulted in the *Constitution Amendment Proclamation, 1983*, proclaimed in force on June 21, 1984.[11] This added s. 35(3), which said that for greater certainty "treaty rights" in s. 35(1) includes present and future land claims agreement rights; s. 35(4), which guaranteed gender equality with respect to s. 35(1) rights; s. 35.1, which committed governments to consult with Aboriginal peoples before amending constitutional provisions that directly affected them; and s. 37.1,[12] now repealed, which committed governments to hold two additional Aboriginal conferences, the last to be held by April 17, 1987.

The most important of the constitutional Aboriginal provisions is s. 35, which recognizes and affirms existing Aboriginal and treaty rights. Because s. 35 is outside the *Charter*, it lacks both the "guarantee" and the "limits" provided in s. 1 of the *Charter*. For several years, it was unclear whether s. 35 *guarantees* Aboriginal and treaty rights against conflicting legislation and other government action, or whether it has some other effect, such as raising a strong presumption in favour of the rights. In its 1990 decision in *Sparrow*,[13] the Supreme Court said that all Aboriginal and treaty rights that have not been lawfully ended before April 17, 1982 (the date of the proclamation of the *Constitution Act, 1982*) are guaranteed against all government action, unless government can provide a reasonable justification for infringing them. The

result, then, was somewhat similar to placing the rights in the *Charter*.

It took the Court longer to try to say just what Aboriginal rights are, and even today their exact contours are uncertain. Generally, Aboriginal rights might be described as activities based on practices that were integral to distinctive Aboriginal cultures before the coming or sovereignty of the Europeans.[14] These include Aboriginal title, a special form of Aboriginal right that involves exclusive occupancy of land.[15]

Section 35(1) also guarantees treaty rights. Treaties are solemn agreements between the Crown and groups of Aboriginal people. Treaties covered roughly half of the country in the early 1920s, when the traditional treaty process came to an end. Because of s. 35(4), though, treaty rights include land claims agreement rights. Accordingly, as Aboriginal peoples agree to have their Aboriginal rights defined in land claims agreements, these agreements normally acquire constitutional status and protection. Approximately 20 dozen land claims agreements have been concluded since 1975, One example is the British Columbia *Nisga'a Final Agreement* of 2000.[16] On the other hand, there are more than 50 Aboriginal land claims still unresolved in British Columbia alone.

The construction of s. 35 and the other Aboriginal provisions is more than a complex task of legal interpretation. Courts must balance long-standing grievances of the first peoples of this country with public interests and the third party interests of over 30 million "newcomers". They must also balance their own role in this field with that of elected politicians.

Notes

1. Aboriginal rights had been given some qualified recognition in *Calder v. British Columbia (A.G.)*, [1973] S.C.R. 313, but the Court was split on most of the substantive issues. Before 1982, one of the leading cases on treaty rights was *R. v. Sikyea* (1964), 43 D.L.R. (2d) 150 (B.C.C.A.), aff'd. in (1965), 50 D.L.R. (2d) 80 (S.C.C.), giving the rights limited content and subordinating them to federal legislation.
2. Mr. Jean Chrétien, then Minister of Justice, later explained that the government did not propose a simple positive affirmation of rights because of concerns that this could result in other rights inadvertently being left out of the affirmation: Minutes of Proceedings and Evidence of the Special Joint Committee of the Senate and of the House of Commons on the Constitution of Canada, First Session of the Thirty-second Parliament, 1980–81, vol. 3, at 33.
3. David W. Elliott, *The Legal Status of Aboriginal and Treaty Rights in Section 35(1) of the Constitution Act, 1982* (Ottawa: Canadian Bar Association, 1990) at 21.
4. *Ibid.*
5. The Senate approved it on April 24, 1981.

6. *Ibid.* at 24–25.
7. *The Queen v. Secretary of State for Foreign and Commonwealth Affairs*, [1982] 2 All E.R. 118 (C.A.U.K.).
8. Note: although the text of s. 35 and of the other provisions of the *Constitution Act, 1982* use the form "aboriginal" (i.e., with a lower case "a"), the form "Aboriginal" is becoming more common in ordinary usage.
9. Except for the equality guarantee in s. 15 of the *Charter* and the operation of a language guarantee in Quebec.
10. Also Part IV of the *Constitution Act, 1982*.

11. 1983, R.S.C. 1985, Appendix II No. 46.
12. Part IV.1 of the *Constitution Act, 1982*.
13. *R. v. Sparrow*, [1990] S.C.R. 1075.
14. See generally, *R. v. Van der Peet*, [1996] 2 S.C.R. 507.
15. The leading decision on Aboriginal title is *Delgamuukw v. British Columbia*, [1997] 3 S.C.R. 1010 (Supreme Court of Canada: December 11, 1997).
16. *Final Agreement*, 4 August 1998. See also the *Nisga'a Final Agreement Act*, S.C. 2000, c. 7, implementing the Agreement.

(d)   Amending Procedures[†]

1.   FORMAL PROCEDURES

As noted in Chapter 9, Part V, the *Constitution Act, 1982* contains four different formal procedures for amending the Constitution of Canada. These are: a "national" formula (ss. 38, 39, 40, and 42); a "unanimity" formula (s. 41); a "regional" formula (s. 43); and an "internal" formula (ss. 44 and 45).

In its simplest form, the national formula requires authorizing resolutions of the Senate and the House of Commons, and of at least two-thirds of the legislative assemblies of provinces comprising at least 50% of the combined provincial population (the "2/3 + 50%" requirement), followed by a proclamation of the Governor General. If the Senate fails to adopt an authorizing resolution within 180 days of the House of Commons resolution, the House of Commons can act alone. To do this, it must adopt its authorizing resolution a second time. This bypass provision also applies to other formulas that require a Senate resolution.

The national formula is the only formal process that is subject to a time limit. The Governor General cannot issue a proclamation before a year has expired from the time of the first authorizing resolution (federal or provincial), and he or she cannot issue a proclamation after three years from the time of this initiating resolution. The expiry of a three-year time limit was a major reason for the collapse of the *Meech Lake Accord* on June 23, 1990.

The national formula has both a designated and a general role. It applies to all subjects listed in s. 42 of the *Constitution Act, 1982*, including the principle of the proportionate representation of provinces in the House of Commons, the powers of the Senate, the Supreme Court of Canada (except in regard to its composition), and the creation of new provinces. However, the opening words of s. 38 say that the national formula may be used for "[a]n amendment to the Constitution of Canada." This suggests that this formula also applies to amendments to the Constitution of Canada in regard to subject matter that lacks a designated amending formula.[1]

Two special variations of the national formula stipulate additional requirements. For national formula amendments that derogate from provincial powers, the national formula requires authorizing resolutions by absolute majorities. For these amendments, if within three years of the initiating resolution an absolute majority of a provincial legislative assembly opposes the proposed amendment, it will not have effect in that province. However, the legislative assembly can change its mind and "opt in" to the amendment at any time.

For national formula amendments that transfer provincial legislative powers regarding education or other cultural matters to Parliament, the federal government must provide reasonable compensation to any province that has opted out of the amendment. This provision was offered as a concession to Quebec in the months following the November 5, 1981 accord between the federal government and the nine other provinces.[2] The unsuccessful Meech Lake and Charlottetown accords would have extended this provision to include reasonable compensation for a province opting out of *any* provision transferring legislative powers to

---

† See J.R. Hurley, *Amending Canada's Constitution: History, Processes, Problems and Prospects* (Ottawa: Supply and Services Canada, 1996), chs. 4 and 7. See also Hogg 2007, ch. 4; Monahan, ch. 6; Funston, ch. 10; Reesor, at 389–409; Cheffins, ch. 5.

the federal government. However, even without this extension, the wide sweep of the notion of "cultural matters", the awkwardness of formal patchwork changes and the cost of providing compensation should all work to discourage centralist formal amendments in a large number of areas.

The unanimity formula requires authorizing resolutions of the Senate and House of Commons, and of the legislative assemblies of all provinces, followed by a proclamation of the Governor General. This formula applies to the subjects listed in s. 41 of the *Constitution Act, 1982*: the office of the Queen, the Governor General, and the Lieutenant Governor, the right of a province to at least as many MPs as it has Senators, the use of the English and French language affecting all provinces, the composition of the Supreme Court, and the amendment of Part V of the *Constitution Act, 1982*. Unanimity is the most rigorous of all the amending formulae, and to date the formula has never been used.[3] Lack of unanimity was a major reason for the collapse of the *Meech Lake Accord* in 1990.

The regional formula applies to subjects affecting one or more but not all the provinces, including changes to boundaries or to the use of the English and French language within the provinces concerned. As seen below, this formula has been used relatively frequently.

At the federal level, the internal federal formula gives Parliament exclusive jurisdiction to make laws amending the Constitution of Canada in regard to the executive government of Canada or the Senate and House of Commons, except where another formula is required. For the provinces, the internal formula gives the legislature of each province exclusive jurisdiction to make laws amending the constitution of that province, except where s. 41 requires otherwise.

2. FEDERAL EXTENDED VETO

The procedures above give the federal government (acting through the Senate and House of Commons) a veto over all proposed amendments except amendments to provincial constitutions under the internal provincial formula. They also give each province (acting through its legislative assembly) a veto over the amendments involving matters subject to the unanimity formula.

In response to earlier demands by Quebec for a general veto, Parliament enacted the *Constitutional Amendments Act* in 1996.[4] Although this is an "ordinary" federal statute, it can have a direct impact on the formal amending process because

federal consent is constitutionally required for all but the internal provincial formula. In substance, the *Constitutional Amendments Act* commits the federal government to use its veto on behalf of certain individual provinces or groupings of provinces, in regard to all areas that are presently under the national formula and are not subject to its opting out procedure. The effect is to extend an effective veto to Ontario, Quebec, and British Columbia; to any Prairie province or provinces whose combined population is at least 50% of that of all Prairie provinces (at present, this gives an individual veto to Alberta); and to any Atlantic province or provinces whose combined population is at least 50% of that of all Atlantic provinces.[5] The *Constitutional Amendments Act* will help ensure that beyond the level of the internal and regional formulae, formal amendments will be rare.

3. JUDICIAL SUPPLEMENTS TO FORMAL PROCEDURES

In the *Quebec Secession Reference*,[6] the Supreme Court of Canada added an additional set of legal-constitutional requirements for amending the Constitution. First, if a clear majority of the people of a province responds positively in a referendum to a clearly worded question about secession, then the federal government and other provinces are obliged to enter into good faith negotiations with that province on the issue of secession.[7] Conversely, no province can secede legally under Canadian domestic law without having first entered good faith negotiations on secession.[8] It may be that similar good faith negotiations will be constitutionally required for all proposed constitutional changes.[9] Good faith negotiations are presumably an addition to, rather than a substitute for, the use of the amendment procedures in Part V of the *Constitution Act, 1982*. However, in the case of secession, this point has yet to be clearly resolved.[10]

4. CONVENTIONAL SUPPLEMENTS TO FORMAL AMENDMENTS

It may be that a successful constitutional amendment of general concern to Canadians now requires, as a matter of constitutional convention, a referendum or some equivalent form of general public involvement. The widespread criticism of the lack of public consultation in the Meech Lake Accord process, and the massive consultation and the referendums involved in the Charlottetown Accord process, point in this direction.[11] Two provinces require referendums to be held prior to constitutional changes, and there have been important constitutional referendums recently in Quebec[12] and Newfoundland.[13]

5. FORMAL AMENDMENTS SINCE 1982

Since 1982 there have been 10 formal amendments to the Constitution of Canada under the designation "Constitution Act", "Constitution Amendment", or "Constitution Amendment Proclamation". As well, there are an indeterminate number of statutes which may constitute formal amendments in substance.[14] As noted above, the unanimity formula has never been successfully invoked. Some elements of the Meech Lake Accord required unanimity, other elements imposed a time limit of three years, and all elements were considered to be part of a single package. By the three-year deadline, Manitoba and Newfoundland had not given their assent, and the Accord died. Elements of the 1992 Charlottetown Accord would also have required unanimity, but this accord was abandoned after being defeated in referendum votes.

There has only been one successful amendment under the national formula, the *Constitution Amendment Proclamation, 1983*. This amendment had the support of all provinces except Quebec, and came into force on June 21, 1984. It provided protections for Aboriginal land claims agreements; guaranteed gender equality in regard to Aboriginal and treaty rights; required consultation with Aboriginal peoples prior to constitutional amendments relating to provisions directly affecting Aboriginal peoples; and provided for at least two conferences on Aboriginal rights, to be held before mid-1987.[15]

Seven of the formal amendments since 1982 have involved the regional formula. The *Constitution Amendment Proclamation, 1993 (New Brunswick)* gave French and English equal status in that province, while the Constitution Amendment Proclamation, 1993 (Prince Edward Island) provided that a fixed-link bridge could replace the constitutional steamship service to P.E.I. Three amendments[16] made successive changes to the constitutional situation of denominational schools in Newfoundland. The first of these extended denominational school rights to Pentecostal Church schools. The second gave the provincial legislature power to create non-

denominational schools, and the third gave the provincial legislature unrestricted power over all schools, with the exception of a right to religious observance when requested by parents. The *Constitution Amendment, 1997 (Quebec)* enabled that province to replace its denominational school boards with boards organized on a linguistic basis. Interestingly, this amendment was negotiated with a provincial government that does not recognize the legitimacy of the *Constitution Act, 1982*. The *Constitution Amendment 2001 (Newfoundland and Labrador)* changed the name Newfoundland to Newfoundland and Labrador.

There have been two formal uses of the internal formula at the federal level. One amendment[17] enabled Parliament to make future changes to provincial representation in the House of Commons, according to a number of prescribed conditions. The *Constitution Act, 1999 (Nunavut)* increased the size of the Senate to 105 members, and provided for representation for the territory of Nunavut in that body and in the House of Commons. Although it is not designated as a formal constitutional amendment, legislation that may have this status is the *Nunavut Act*.[18] It brought Canada's third territory into existence on April 1, 1999.

What is the constitutional effect of a land claims agreement implementation statute that confers paramount Aboriginal self-government powers in provinces?[19] Is it a formal amendment? Or is it an exercise of power already authorized in s. 35(1) of the *Constitution Act, 1982*? If it is a constitutional amendment,[20] which amending formula should apply?

Notes

1. Whether the national formula is the *only* formula that can be used in these cases, or whether amendments can only be made by specific formula, has not been decided by the courts. The answer will depend partly on the meaning to be given to s. 52(3) of the *Constitution Act, 1982*.
2. See Milne, at 180–81.
3. Prior to the *Constitution Act, 1982*, when there was no textual procedure to govern most formal amendments, unanimous consent was last secured in 1964. This was for the *Constitution Act, 1964*, in regard to benefits supplementary to old age pensions.
4. S.C. 1996, c. C-1: see Chapter 10.
5. No single Atlantic province meets this requirement at present.
6. [1998] 2 S.C.R. 217: see Chapters 2, 3 and 12.
7. *Ibid.* at para. 88.
8. *Ibid.* at para. 104.
9. The Court indicated that the obligation to negotiate was based both on the fact that secession would require "an amendment to the Constitution" (para. 84) and on the requirements of the principles of federalism, democracy, the rule of law and constitutionalism, and protection of minority rights (para. 151). All proposed constitutional

changes meet the first criterion, and many would involve at least some of these principles.

10. The Court said that "we refrain from pronouncing on the applicability of any particular constitutional procedure to effect secession unless and until sufficiently clear facts exist to squarely raise an issue for judicial determination."

11. *Cf.* similar suggestions in Patrick Boyer, *Direct Democracy in Canada: The History and Future of Referendums* (Toronto: Dundurn Press, 1992) at 254.

12. In 1980 and 1995, on sovereignty-association or secession.

13. In 1995 and 1997, on denominational schools.

14. As seen, the internal amending formula permits some formal amendments by way of ordinary federal or provincial statutes, and not all of these may be designated as "Constitution Amendments". See, for example, *Nunavut Act,* *S.C. 1993,* in which Parliament established the new territory of Nunavut and provided for its government.

15. See further *Aboriginal Provisions* in this chapter and *Aboriginal Changes* in Chapter 11(b).

16. The *Constitution Amendment Proclamation, 1987 (Newfoundland)*, the *Constitution Amendment Proclamation, 1997 (Newfoundland)*, and the *Constitution Amendment Proclamation, 1998 (Newfoundland)*.

17. The *Constitution Act, 1985 (Representation)*.

18. S.C. 1993, c. 28.

19. For example, the *Nisga'a Final Agreement Act*, S.C. 2000, c. 7.

20. See, however, *Campbell v. British Columbia (A.G.)* (2000), 189 D.L.R. (4th) 333 (B.C.S.C.), implying that s. 35 provides for the definition of existing s. 35 rights, not the creation of new ones.

(e) *Constitutional Amendments Act*[†]

Her Majesty, by and with the consent and of the Senate and House of Commons of Canada, enacts as follows:

(1) No Minister of the Crown shall propose a motion for a resolution to authorize an amendment to the Constitution of Canada, other than an amendment in respect of which the legislative assembly of a province may exercise a veto under section 41 or 43 of the *Constitution Act, 1982* or may express its dissent under subsection 38(3) of that Act, unless the amendment has first been consented to by a majority of the provinces that includes

(a) Ontario;

(b) Quebec;

(c) British Columbia;

(d) two or more of the Atlantic provinces that have, according to the then latest general census, combined populations of at least fifty per cent of the population of all the Atlantic provinces; and

(e) two or more of the Prairie provinces that have, according to the then latest general census, combined populations of at least fifty per cent of the population of all the Western provinces.

(2) In this section,

"Atlantic provinces" means the provinces of Nova Scotia, New Brunswick, Prince Edward Island and Newfoundland;

"Prairie provinces" means the provinces of Manitoba, Saskatchewan and Alberta.

† *An Act Respecting Constitutional Amendments*, S.C. 1996, c. C-1 (Bill C-110). (Bill C-110 was passed by the House of Commons on 13 December 1995, and by the Senate on 2 February 1996.)

11

Formal and Informal
Constitutional Changes

(a) Introduction

As noted in Chapter 9, the 1982 package was a mixed success. The *Constitution Act, 1982* and its parent *Canada Act 1982* patriated the Canadian constitution in 1982, and provided a major addition to its formal part. On the other hand, the package failed to gain the support of a key player, the government of Quebec. Other groups, such as Canadian Aboriginal peoples, were also critical. Moreover, the *Constitution Act, 1982* was incomplete. For example, it required at least two more Aboriginal constitutional conferences to define the rights of Aboriginal peoples.

Not surprisingly, the ink was barely dry on the 1982 package when politicians made several dramatic efforts at further large-scale, formal constitutional change. One effort produced an amendment under the national amending formula to extend Aboriginal protections. Then it lost momentum in three failed constitutional conferences on Aboriginal self-government.

Another effort gained unanimous federal and provincial support at Meech Lake in 1987, but it collapsed at midnight on June 23, 1990. A third effort also won unanimous governmental support, at Charlottetown in August 1992, but was voted down in a national referendum two months later.

What were the dynamics and key elements of these major efforts at formal constitutional change? What drove these efforts? Which succeeded? Which failed? Why? What, if anything, can be learned from the mistakes?

Meanwhile, in the 1980s and beyond, the federal government continued its efforts at informal constitutional changes — constitutional and related changes outside the formal amending process. Individually, at least, these changes seemed less spectacular; on the other hand, they risked less. When studying these developments, consider if formal and informal changes each have characteristic features, strengths, and weaknesses. If they do, where should each be used?

(b) Aboriginal Changes†

As seen in Chapter 10, the *Constitution Act, 1982* was amended in 1984 to protect land claims agreement rights, to guarantee gender equality in regard to Aboriginal and treaty rights, to require consultation prior to constitutional amendments affecting Aboriginal constitutional provisions, and to provide for at least two more Aboriginal constitutional conferences.[1] This was to be the first and

---

† This discussion is adapted from D.W. Elliott, *Law and Aboriginal Peoples in Canada*, 5th ed. (Concord, Ont.: Captus Press, 2005), chs. 7 and 12.

(so far) the only amendment to the *Constitution Act, 1982* under the national amending formula. It secured the support of all provinces except Quebec, which was boycotting all amendments to the *Constitution Act, 1982*. It was proclaimed in force in June 1994.

Many Aboriginal groups were still unhappy with the *Constitution Act, 1982* and the 1984 amendment. They wanted an entrenched right of Aboriginal self-government. Three additional constitutional conferences were held — in 1984, 1985, and 1987. All focused on Aboriginal self-government. These were followed by the 1987–1990, Meech Lake Accord whose only Aboriginal provision would have been a non-derogation clause, and by the Charlottetown Accord, in which Aboriginal self-government was a major theme. All of these constitutional amendment initiatives ended in failure.[2] At the 1984 conference, a federal proposal for negotiated delegated self-government was rejected by the four national Aboriginal associations.[3] At the 1985 conference the federal government proposed a "contingent rights" approach that would entrench a general concept of self-government, with specific content to depend on negotiations. This was opposed by the Assembly of First Nations and by three provinces. At the 1987 conference the federal government proposed a similar approach, but with a more specific entrenched right of self-government. This, too, was unsuccessful. Most Aboriginal groups wanted immediate entrenchment of a constitutional right of Aboriginal self-government, with details to be negotiated later. In contrast, most governments wanted to negotiate agreements on the nature of Aboriginal self-government first, before entrenching it in the Constitution.[4]

As seen in the next section, at the end of April 1987, little more than a month after the last Aboriginal conference, the first ministers secured unanimous agreement at Meech Lake on major constitutional amendments to secure Quebec's support for the *Constitution Act, 1982*.[5] Quebec would get special constitutional guarantees, but the self-government guarantees were being denied to the Aboriginal peoples. The early version of the Meech Lake Accord made no mention of Aboriginal peoples. The later Langevin version provided only a non-derogation provision to protect rights of Aboriginal peoples from the new distinct society clause.

Aboriginal people were strongly opposed to the Accord.[6] Mr. Elijah Harper, a Manitoba Aboriginal MLA, played a crucial role in toppling it. The Accord required unanimous support from Parliament and the provincial legislative assemblies by midnight Saturday, June 23, 1990. On the Friday before the deadline, Mr. Harper withheld the unanimous consent needed to permit the Manitoba legislature to continue its debate and move to a vote. Debate on the Accord ended in Manitoba, ending any chance of unanimous support by the following evening.[7]

When the next wave of constitutional change swept the country, the reformers tried to ensure that Aboriginal concerns would be addressed this time. The 1992 Charlottetown Accord,[8] considered in the next section, contained many Aboriginal guarantees. The centrepiece was an entrenched inherent right of self-government. This was to be implemented by negotiation if possible, but after a delay of five years it could be defined by the courts.[9]

The Charlottetown Accord was rejected on October 22, 1992. Some Aboriginal peoples felt that decades of planning, lobbying, and negotiating had been suddenly and catastrophically overturned.[10] For others, the end of the Accord removed a serious threat to the treaties.[11] Some had been concerned about the impact of the Aboriginal self-government provisions on the individual rights of Aboriginal women.[12] Others were relieved to see the end of a document that failed to deal with them as equal sovereign nations.[13] Still others shared the general concern that once again Canadian governments had failed to consult adequately with the people.

Although large-scale formal change had failed, there were a number of Aboriginal changes on other fronts. Starting in 1990, a series of court decisions enhanced the protections given to s. 35(1) Aboriginal and treaty rights.[14] Moreover, in the last two and a half decades of the century, more than a dozen land claims agreements were signed with individual groups of Aboriginal peoples. Most of the provisions of these agreements enjoyed constitutional protection under s. 35(1) of the *Constitution Act, 1982*.

One land claims agreement, the *Nunavut Final Agreement* of 1993, was accompanied by a special political accord. This resulted in the creation of a third northern territory, Nunavut, on April 1, 1999.[15] Because the Inuit people comprise the vast majority of the new territory's population, the result is a public form of Aboriginal self-government.

On the other hand, the opportunities for creating new territories are limited, many other Aboriginal peoples lacked land claims agreements, and all agreements faced massive implementation challenges. Meanwhile, poor housing, malnutrition, disease, unemployment, high suicide rates, and poverty were still serious problems in many Aboriginal communities. Perhaps something more than macro constitutional amendments, legal documents, and court orders was needed.

Notes

1. *Constitution Amendment Proclamation, 1983*, proclaimed in force on June 21, 1984; in 1983, R.S.C. 1985, Appendix II No. 46.
2. For Meech Lake and Charlottetown generally, see the next section in this chapter. See also Peter H. Russell, *Constitutional Odyssey: Can Canadians Become a Sovereign People?* (Toronto: University of Toronto Press, 1993), ch. 11; *Report*, vol. 1, ch. 7, s. 1, at 202–17.
3. The Assembly of First Nations, representing status Indians under the *Indian Act*, the Native Council of Canada (now the Congress of Aboriginal Peoples), representing non-status and off-reserve Indians, the Inuit Tapirisat of Canada, representing Inuit people, and the Métis National Council, representing Métis people.
4. See generally, D. Sanders, "An Uncertain Path: The Aboriginal Constitutional Conferences" in Joseph M. Weiler & Robin M. Elliot, eds., *Litigating the Values of a Nation: the Canadian Charter of Rights and Freedoms* (Toronto: Carswell, 1986) at 63.
5. On the Meech Lake Accord, see Milne, chs. 6 and 7; Patrick J. Monahan, *Meech Lake: The Inside Story* (Toronto: University of Toronto Press, 1991); Michael Behiels, ed., *The Meech Lake Primer: Conflicting Views of the 1987 Constitutional Accord* (Ottawa: University of Ottawa Press, 1989); P.W. Hogg, *Meech Lake Accord Annotated* (Toronto: Carswell, 1988); Katherine E. Swinton & Carol J. Rogerson, eds., *Competing Constitutional Visions: The Meech Lake Accord* (Toronto: Carswell, 1988).
6. See, for example, the trenchant criticisms summarized in T. Hall, "What are We? Chopped Liver? Aboriginal Affairs in the Constitutional Politics of Canada in the 1980s" in Behiels, *ibid.* at 423–56.
7. Monahan, *supra* note 5, ch. 8.
8. See generally, Alan C. Cairns, "The Charlottetown Accord: Multinational Canada v. Federalism" in Curtis Cook, ed., *Constitutional Predicament: Canada after the Referendum of 1992* (Montreal & Kingston: McGill-Queen's University Press, 1994) at 25; Robert M. Campbell & Leslie A. Pal, "The Rise and Fall of the Charlottetown Accord" in *The Real Worlds of Canadian Politics*, 3d ed. (Peterborough, Ont.: Broadview Press, 1994), ch. 3; Kenneth McRoberts & Patrick J. Monahan, eds., *The Charlottetown Accord, the Referendum, and the Future of Canada* (Toronto: University of Toronto Press, 1993).
9. Draft Final Agreement, proposed ss. 35.1 to 35.5 of *Constitution Act, 1982*. Other key provisions included recognition of Aboriginal people and their governments in the Accord's "Canada clause": *ibid.*, proposed s. 2 of *Constitution Act, 1867*; guaranteed representation in the new elected Senate: *ibid.*, proposed s. 21(1)(c) of *Constitution*

Act, 1867; dispensation for Aboriginal governments from the *Charter's* right to vote and qualify as a member of a legislative assembly: *ibid.*, proposed amendment to s. 3 of *Constitution Act, 1982*; inclusion of Aboriginal governments in the *Charter's* application and "override" provisions: *ibid.*, proposed s. 33.1 of *Constitution Act, 1982*; a right to initiate processes to clarify, implement, or rectify treaties: *ibid.*, proposed s. 35.6 of *Constitution Act, 1982*; an Aboriginal gender equality guarantee: *ibid.*, proposed s. 35.7 of *Constitution Act, 1982*; a guarantee of at least four more Aboriginal constitutional conferences, to be held by the year 2002: *ibid.*, proposed s. 35.9 of *Constitution Act, 1982*: the right to prior consultation at a constitutional conference: *ibid.*, proposed s. 35.8 of *Constitution Act, 1982*: and a veto (*ibid.*, proposed s. 45.1 of *Constitution Act, 1982*) in regard to proposed constitutional amendments directly referring to Aboriginal peoples or their governments; a clarification that s. 91(24) of the *Constitution Act, 1867* includes all the Aboriginal people of Canada: *ibid.*, proposed s. 91A of *Constitution Act, 1867*; constitutional protection for Alberta Métis lands and their governing body: *ibid.*, proposed s. 24 of *Alberta Act*; and provision for the negotiation of constitutional accords between the federal, Ontario, and western provincial governments and Métis people: Charlottetown Accord: Consensus Report on the Constitution (the political agreement), 28 August 1982, s. 56. As well, there were numerous non-derogation provisions to ensure that Aboriginal peoples, their governments, and their rights would not be prejudiced by other provisions in the Accord: Draft Final Agreement, proposed ss. 2(2), 2(4) and 127 of *Constitution Act, 1867*, and s. 35.6(6) of *Constitution Act, 1982*. Other provisions, such as changes to the rules for the creation of new provinces, would have affected Aboriginal peoples indirectly: Proposed s. 2 of *Constitution Act, 1871*.
10. For example, the national leadership of the four main Aboriginal associations — the Assembly of First Nations, the Native Council of Canada (now the Congress of Aboriginal Peoples), the Inuit Tapirisat of Canada, and the Métis National Council — all of which supported the Accord. Although the main national leadership of the Assembly of First Nations played an especially forceful role in the negotiations leading to the Accord, referendum polling stations indicated that 60% of those voting on Indian reserves opposed the Accord: Russell, *supra* note 1 at 195, referring to a *Globe and Mail* article of October 28, 1992.
11. This was especially true of some prairie Indian groups.
12. For example, the Native Women's Association of Canada. The Association was concerned not only that Aboriginal self-government might prejudice equality rights of Aboriginal women, but also that Aboriginal women were insufficiently represented in the constitutional process.
13. A concern, for example, of numerous Mohawk people in Ontario and Quebec.
14. For example, *R. v. Sparrow*, [1990] 1 S.C.R. 1075; *R. v. Marshall*, [1999] 3 S.C.R. 456; *R. v. Van der Peet*, [1996] 2 S.C.R. 507; *Delgamuukw v. British Columbia*, [1997] 3 S.C.R. 1010; and *R. v. Marshall*, [1999] 3. S.C.R. 533 (motion for rehearing and stay).
15. See *Nunavut Act*, S.C. 1993, c. 28.

(c)   Journey of Disappointment

QUEBEC LIBERAL GOVERNMENT'S CONSTITUTIONAL CONDITIONS

The Quebec government had not signed the November 5, 1981 Accord that resulted in the *Canada Act 1982* and the *Constitution Act, 1982*. In May 1986, the (Liberal) Quebec provincial government set out five conditions that would have to be met before it would sign:

(i) recognition of Quebec as a distinct society;
(ii) either a constitutional veto for Quebec or the right to opt out of amendments, with full compensation;
(iii) a limit on the federal spending power;
(iv) Quebec's right to participate in selecting Supreme Court judges; and
(v) greater Quebec powers over immigration.

MEECH LAKE ACCORD

To respond to these concerns and to secure Quebec's signature, Prime Minister Mulroney set in motion a round of low-profile federal–provincial meetings in 1986–87. These culminated in two rounds of closed-door first ministers' negotiations. The first, an 11-hour meeting at Willson House, Meech Lake, on April 30, 1987, produced an agreed statement of principles that became known as the Meech Lake Accord. The second round, a 19-hour meeting at the Langevin Block in Ottawa, on June 2 and 3, 1987, resulted in agreement on the legal text of the constitutional amendment to implement aspects of the Accord.

The Meech Lake Accord was a package of three documents: (i) the statement of principles (which, among other things, committed the federal government, on an interim basis, to making Senate appointments from lists of nominees from the relevant provinces); (ii) agreed wording for a motion for a resolution to introduce a constitutional amendment; and (iii) a proposed 17-section constitutional amendment called the *Constitution Amendment, 1987*.

The Accord would have required

(i) recognition of Quebec as a "distinct society" within Canada;

(ii) recognition of the English and French-speaking minorities in Quebec and the rest of Canada, respectively;
(iii) unanimity for proposed amendments presently expressed under the "national" amending formula as well as those under the present "unanimity" formula;
(iv) a provincial right to opt out, with compensation, of proposed amendments transferring provincial powers to Parliament under what was left of the national formula;
(v) a right to compensation for a province opting out of future shared-cost programs in areas of exclusive legislative jurisdiction, provided that the province's own programs are consistent with "the national objectives";
(vi) provincial participation in Senate and Supreme Court of Canada appointments;
(vii) annual first ministers' constitutional and economic conferences; and
(viii) negotiation of expanded provincial powers over immigration.

It seemed that the Prime Minister had hit upon a winning formula. His general strategy was to give the powers sought by Quebec to all the provinces. If the federal government was willing to give, how could the provinces refuse to receive? However, there were problems. For example, not all parts of the Accord did treat Quebec and the other provinces alike.[1] Notably, the Accord added both a distinct society recognition and a linguistic duality recognition, and then treated the first somewhat differently from the second. The relevant provisions required the Constitution of Canada to be interpreted consistently with:

(a) the recognition that the existence of French-speaking Canadians, centred in Quebec but also present elsewhere in Canada, and English-speaking Canadians, concentrated outside Quebec but also present in Quebec, constitutes a fundamental characteristic of Canada; and
(b) the recognition that Quebec constitutes within Canada a distinct society.[2]

In these provisions, while Canadian legislatures were given the role of preserving linguistic duality

253

in Canada, the legislature *and government* of Quebec were given the role of both preserving *and promoting* the distinct society.[3] What was the effect of these provisions? Although the answer was not clear, for many groups outside Quebec, it was not good.

MEECH LAKE ACCORD: CRITICISM AND FATE

After the agreements of April and June 1987, concerns started to surface about the distinct society provisions and other aspects of the Accord. Quebec Anglophones worried that the distinct society provisions were weighted toward Quebec francophones. Outside Quebec, there were concerns about the impact of the provisions on provincial equality. Women and minority groups said the distinct society provision would weaken the *Charter*. Mr. Trudeau said the Accord would weaken the federal government. Aboriginal groups were concerned that their self-government demands were ignored. People outside Quebec felt the Accord gave Quebec too much power; inside Quebec, some worried that it gave too little. Many disliked the "closed-door" environment in which the Accord was negotiated. Elections in New Brunswick, Manitoba, and Newfoundland produced provincial governments critical of or opposed to the Accord. Last-minute negotiations produced a supplementary deal signed by all premiers, but the original Accord had to be ratified in the provincial legislative assemblies. Because of the national amending formula's three-year limit, the deadline for ratification was June 23, 1990. On June 22, 1990, Aboriginal MLA Elijah Harper blocked the consent needed to cut short debate in the Manitoba Legislative Assembly and to vote. The Assembly adjourned for the weekend without any vote. Learning of the adjournment in Manitoba, Newfoundland Premier Wells refused to hold a vote in that province, on the ground that the action in Manitoba made this unnecessary. Midnight, June 23, 1990 came, and the Accord had not been ratified in two provinces. That was the end of it.

POST-MEECH QUEBEC DEMANDS AND FEDERAL INITIATIVES

After the collapse of Meech Lake, the Quebec government said it would no longer attend any multilateral federal–provincial meetings. In future, Quebec would take part only in bilateral talks with the federal government.

In January 1991, the Quebec Liberal Party's Allaire Report called for massive decentralization. Quebec's Bill 150 provided for a referendum on Quebec sovereignty by October 26, 1992. After setting up numerous committees and consultative bodies, the federal government issued *Shaping Canada's Future* in September 1991. These proposals incorporated most of the Meech Lake provisions, but also provided for more decentralization, self-government for Aboriginal peoples, an elected but not equal Senate, and stronger federal powers over the economy. After more consultative exercises, revised federal proposals were negotiated by the first ministers and Aboriginal leaders in the summer of 1992. Quebec joined the negotiations in August, and an agreement was signed on August 28, 1992.

CHARLOTTETOWN ACCORD

On provisions that deal with the veto and the opting out amendment, the federal spending power, the selection of Supreme Court judges, and immigration, the Charlottetown Accord was very similar to the Meech Lake Accord. However, the Charlottetown Accord's distinct society provision was more restricted and was included in a complex "Canada clause". Charlottetown also went beyond Meech Lake in providing for

(i) a massive decentralization in areas that had been occupied through the federal spending power, such as tourism, mining, and forestry;
(ii) an elected and equal Senate with Aboriginal and territorial representation as well;
(iii) a permanent guarantee to Quebec of at least 25% of the seats in the House of Commons;
(iv) an entrenched annual First Ministers' Conferences;
(v) a non-justiciable "Social and Economic Union";
(vi) a less stringent procedure by which the territories could become provinces; and
(vii) massive new powers to Aboriginal peoples, including
   (a) constitutional recognition of an inherent right of self-government, justiciable in five years' time;
   (b) provision for negotiation of self-government agreements;
   (c) recognition of Aboriginal peoples and their governments in the Canada clause;

(d) guaranteed Aboriginal representation in the new Senate;

(e) an Aboriginal gender equality guarantee;

(f) freedom for Aboriginal governments from the *Charter* right to vote;

(g) a guarantee of at least four more Aboriginal constitutional conferences; and

(h) the right to prior consultation and an Aboriginal veto over proposed Aboriginal constitutional amendments.

CHARLOTTETOWN ACCORD: CRITICISM AND FATE

The Meech Lake Accord had been criticized for focusing too narrowly on Quebec. To rectify this, the Charlottetown Accord tried to constitutionalize the concerns of a wide range of other major interest groups, and ended up with an unwieldy package of conflicting guarantees. Many of the packages of guarantees were criticized as insufficient by their beneficiaries and attacked as excessive by those who were left out. For example, critics inside Quebec said the diluted distinct society provision gave Quebec too little; those outside Quebec said the 25% guarantee of the House of Commons gave Quebec too much. There were concerns about the meaning of the Aboriginal provisions, and their implications for native women. Some worried that decentralization was being carried too far. Although there had been substantial consultation in earlier stages, the later stages had reverted to the closed-door negotiation format that had caused so much concern with Meech Lake. Some key provisions, such as Quebec's 25% guarantee, had been agreed to behind closed doors, after all the consultative processes had ended. Many people felt they had been given inadequate time to understand the Accord's 51-page *Draft Legal Text.* It was released on October 9, less than three weeks before the October 26 referendum date. In the referendum (there were actually two, one for Quebec, and an identical one for the rest of Canada), Canadians rejected the Accord by a majority of 54.4%. Quebec, five English-speaking provinces, one territory, and a large proportion of the Aboriginal population voted against the Accord.

MEECH LAKE AND CHARLOTTETOWN

How did the key provisions of the Charlottetown Agreement compare with Quebec's original five demands and the Meech Lake Accord? First, both accords would have recognized Quebec as a distinct society. However, the Charlottetown Agreement would have (i) defined it to include language, civil law, and culture, and (ii) included it in a Canada Clause recognizing seven other fundamental Canadian characteristics. Second, both accords would have responded to Quebec's demand for more immigration powers by permitting immigration agreements with all the provinces. However, the Charlottetown Agreement would have responded to the Allaire Committee's demand for 31 powers by permitting labour market training and seven other powers to be transferred by agreement to provinces who wanted them. Third, both accords would have limited the federal spending power in very similar language, allowing provinces to opt out with compensation from future shared-cost programs if they provided comparable replacement programs. Fourth, both accords would have responded to Quebec's traditional demand for a veto. Most of the provisions present in s. 42 of the *Constitution Act, 1982* would have been subject to the requirement of unanimity, except that the Charlottetown Agreement would permit the creation of new provinces by federal legislation, following a first ministers' conference, but would require unanimity for increases in their Senate seats and for their participation in the amending formula. Both accords would have compensated provinces for opting out of any amendment transferring powers to the federal government. Finally, both accords would have responded to the demand for a role in selecting Supreme Court judges by allowing provinces to nominate candidates, and recognizing Quebec's special nominating role for civil law judges. In a sense, then, the Charlottetown Agreement followed the Meech Lake pattern of giving all provinces what Quebec had asked for, thus attempting to meet regional and provincial equality concerns as well.

However, in several important areas the Charlottetown Agreement went well beyond Meech Lake. First, while Meech Lake merely arranged for provincial nomination of possible Senators, the Charlottetown Agreement would have created an elected and equal Senate with special blocking, delaying, and ratifying powers.[4] Second, the Charlottetown Agreement would have made major changes to the House of Commons, increasing seats for Ontario and Quebec,[5] and guaranteeing Quebec at least 25% of Commons seats. Third, a very large part of the Charlottetown Agreement would have involved special powers and guarantees for Aboriginal peoples, ranging from a guarantee of an inherent right of Aboriginal self-government[6] to special guaranteed Aboriginal Senate seats, to an Aboriginal veto over constitutional amendments in Aboriginal matters. Fourth, the Charlottetown Agreement would have contained a new Canada Clause. It would have accompanied the distinct society provision with not only a linguistic duality provision similar to that in Meech Lake, but with recognitions of Aboriginal governmental powers, concepts such as democracy and the rule of law, racial equality and human rights, gender equality, and equality of the provinces. Fifth, the Charlottetown Agreement contained a non-justiciable Social and Economic Union provision, stating a number of social and economic goals.

Notes

1. In a clause providing for immigration agreements, for example, the Accord gave Quebec the right to exceed its share of immigrants by 5%, "for demographic reasons": *1987 Constitutional Accord*, June 3, 1987, clause 2(b).
2. *Ibid.*, Schedule: *Constitution Amendment, 1987*, s. 1, referring to proposed new s. 2 of *Constitution Act, 1867*.
3. *Ibid.*, Schedule: *Constitution Amendment, 1987*, s. 2. See also *ibid.*, s. 16: "Nothing in Section 2 of the *Constitution Act, 1867* affects s. 25 or 27 of the *Canadian Charter of Rights and Freedoms*, s. 35 of the *Constitution Act, 1982* or class 24 of s. 91 of the *Constitution Act, 1867.*"
4. The voting would have been by majority (except a double majority for French culture and language matters), and a negative vote would refer an ordinary bill to a joint sitting of House and Senate. The Senate could block important bills regarding taxation of natural resources.
5. Alberta would have received two more, and British Columbia, four more, but their proportionate representation in the House of Commons would have declined.
6. Aboriginal self-government would have to be consistent with federal and provincial laws for peace, order, and good government, and must not create new land rights. Aboriginal laws could include matters such as language, culture, economy, identity, traditions, relationship with environment, and integrity of Aboriginal societies. Courts would be required to exhaust of all negotiated remedies before acting.

(d) Barriers to Constitutional Renewal in Canada: The Role of Constitutional Culture[†][1]

Alan C. Cairns

NOTE

In a 1990 book, Andrew Cohen blamed the failure of the Meech Lake Accord on: lack of consultation with the public; the fact that the Accord could not be reopened selectively without unravelling altogether; delays in ratifying the Accord; Mr. Bourassa's use of the override in 1986; widespread distrust of the Prime Minister; and resentment by groups — such as Aboriginal peoples — who felt they had been left out of the Accord's benefits: *A Deal Undone: The Making and Breaking of the Meech Lake Accord* (Vancouver: Douglas and McIntyre, 1990).

Another writer, Patrick Monahan, argued that the main reason for the Accord's failure was not inadequate consultation, a cumbersome ratifying process, or even specific substantive provisions.

Instead, said Monahan, the key problem was that the Accord took on a symbolic and emotional character, and became associated with participants' feelings about the value of their own places in Confederation: *Meech Lake: The Inside Story* (Toronto: University of Toronto Press, 1991).

Compare these perspectives with that of Cairns. What is your view? Cairns wrote this article after the collapse of Meech Lake. How much of what he says is still relevant after the collapse of the Charlottetown Accord?

EXTRACT

INTRODUCTION

. . . .

---

† From *Canadian Politics: Past, Present and Future* (St. Catharines, Ont.: Brock University, Department of Politics, 1992) at 17–30. Reproduced with permission of the author and the Department of Politics, Brock University.

Explanations for the failure of Meech Lake flourish. Often, of course, they are the servants of unrealized constitutional ambitions as the actors in our constitutional drama position themselves for the next round. Those who play the constitutional game, whether governments or interest groups, know full well that if they can get their 'explanation' accepted the likelihood of their future success is enhanced. Accordingly, the responsibilities of constitutional scholars and constitutional players differ. The former should be less partisan, less involved, more concerned with the whole, more attentive to deeper underlying social forces, and in general simply more academic. What is the point of having a division of labour between scholars in their study and the active players on the field if the former simply duplicate the often self-serving analyses of the latter, without the benefit of equivalent insider knowledge.

For the players, the search for a way out of our constitutional impasse naturally tends to focus on rules and procedures — should the three year ratification period be changed? Is unanimity a constitutional albatross? — for they are manipulable. Modified rules can change the structure of incentives and thus increase or decrease the chance of getting an agreement.

Such a focus is unquestionably important, but it needs to be supplemented by a searching consideration of the changing constitutional culture within which the rules operate. In fact, of course, as all good institutionalists know, there is an unending reciprocity of mutual influence between the applicable rules, the performing players and the social forces that buffet both rules and players, by broad cultural changes, and by the constrained creativity of such constitutional guardians as the judiciary. Concurrently, however, the rules shape the identities of the actors, distribute advantages and disadvantages unequally, determine who is in the game and who is not, and affirm some social forces and cultural tendencies and stigmatize others. Thus, our constitutional culture is an ever changing evolutionary creation, not a static historical given.

The focus of this paper on constitutional culture, therefore, is not intended to privilege attitudes, values and identities over the institutions, constitutional arrangements, and official rules with which they are symbiotically linked. It is, instead, a simplifying [stratagem], and an attention-getting device designed to highlight one of the diffuse, background sources of our constitutional malaise. Accordingly, it pays less attention to governments and more to society than is customary in analyses of constitutional change.

CHANGE IN THE IMPLICIT CONSTITUTION

... Surrounding or pervading the sparse unemotional text of the B.N.A. Act and the conventions of responsible government, therefore, there was an implicit constitution that can now, in retrospect, be read between the lines of the written rules and established constitutional practices. Many of the implicit understandings of yesterday's constitution are now explicit, and they are challenged by the new constitutional actors. Yesterday's taken-for-granteds are no longer part of the natural order. They are contested territory.

The constitution we are leaving behind was traditional, derivative, colonial and British. Its roots, "a Constitution similar in Principle to that of the United Kingdom," were across the oceans in the Mother country. Until 1949 final constitutional interpretation was entrusted to a British judicial body, the Judicial Committee of the Privy Council. Until 1982, formal constitutional amendments in key areas remained the responsibility of the British Parliament. The ethos of constitutional Britishness was viewed as a priceless heritage of anglo-Canadian scholars up to the fifties.

Ordinary Canadians of British background received an unearned increment of status and prestige from living under a British constitution, and from surveying a global map so much of which was painted a reassuring red. Psychologically, the civic identity of many British Canadians linked them simultaneously and harmoniously to the 'old country' and to its Canadian offshoot. Their attitudes might best be summed up as diaspora constitutionalism. Further, up to at least the middle of the twentieth century, before the upsurge of modernizing Quebec nationalism, British Canadians could think — automatically assume would be more accurate — that the federal government was essentially theirs, even although their hegemony was not total.

Although the constitution responded to two European founding peoples, French as well as English, the former were accommodated by rather than dominant in the overall constitutional order, a status reserved for the latter. Quebec might not be a province like the others, but until the last three decades it was constitutionally of greater importance that the British were not a founding people like the other. From the perspective of the two founding European peoples, the major challenge in recent decades has been to refashion the constitutional order in the interest of the historically weaker French partner. This was the driving theme of the two great state papers on the constitution of the fifties and sixties, the Quebec Tremblay Report[3] and the Report of the Royal Commission on Bilingualism and Biculturalism.[4] It was the guiding premise from which competing conclusions were drawn by the Trudeau federalists and the Quebecois nationalists.

Until comparatively recently, another founding people existed on the constitutional sidelines. Status Indians had a form of constitutional recognition in the s. 91(24) allocation of "Indians, and Lands reserved for the Indians" as a federal jurisdiction. This, however, was not a badge of honour, but a vehicle for wardship status and a separate system of administration that implicitly defined Indians as constitutional outsiders, as subjects rather than fully participant citizens. They did not receive the federal vote until 1960.

Canadians who were neither French, British, nor indigenous were numerically insignificant at Confederation and existed in the constitutional shadow of the French and English founding peoples until the middle of the twentieth century. Particular ethnic groups, especially Asians, were subjected to various forms of discriminatory, stigmatizing treatment.

The working constitution was also, at its beginnings, a male constitution. Women received the vote belatedly, and participated minimally in the representative structures of the Canadian state. The first woman was elected to the House of Commons in 1921, appointed to the Senate in 1930, became a federal cabinet minister in 1957, was made a Lieutenant Governor in 1974, a Supreme Court judge in 1982, and Governor-General in 1984.

Finally, the constitution we are leaving behind was a governments' constitution. Its two basic pillars — federalism and parliamentary government — divided the power to govern between two orders of government reflecting the Canadian and provincial dimensions of our existence, and laid out the pattern of relationships between the executive and legislative branches of governments. That dominance, or priority, of governments in the constitutional order was strikingly revealed in the long search for a domestic amending formula, that until the late seventies automatically assumed that governments would decide how to distribute formal power in the amending process amongst themselves.

Yesterday's constitution, accordingly, privileged the British-French dimension of Canada's existence, especially the former, over those of all other backgrounds, including indigenous peoples, implicitly defined the constitutional world as primarily a male prerogative, accorded extensive attention to the concerns of governments by means of federalism and responsible government, and paid minimum explicit attention to the citizen-state dimension.

For the last half-century, Canadians have attempted to redress these founding biases with varying degrees of success. The Parti Quebecois pursuit of sovereignty-association, Meech Lake, the distinct society, and the Belanger-Campeau Commission are the most recent attempts to deal with the eighteenth century heritage of French-English duality in the interest of the no-longer acquiescent junior founding partner. A third of a century ago, Duplessis and the Tremblay Report pleaded with the rest of Canada to adhere strictly to the Confederation agreement and to remain faithful to the principles of federalism. Now we are told that existing federalism is dead, and the most that can be hoped for is an asymmetrical federalism in which Quebec wields extensive jurisdictional powers unavailable to the other provinces. The allegiance of the majority of Quebecois in the early days of the post-Meech Lake era to whatever can be salvaged from the existing system appears to be essentially conditional, contingent, and calculated.

Status Indians are no longer voteless and voiceless. They employ the rhetoric of First Nations in the service of a greater autonomy that, in words at least, often verges on sovereignty. They do not dispute, they simply deny the Mayflower claim of the British and French to be founding peoples, with the caustic reminder that they were waiting on the beach when these early European immigrants arrived. They have been joined in the constitution by the Metis and the Inuit under the new constitutional rubric of "aboriginal people."[5]

Non-founding peoples have gained their own constitutional recognition in the s. 27 multicultural clause of the Charter and in several of the categories of the s. 15 equality rights clause. Demographic projections, they incessantly remind their fellow citizens, support the claims of ethnocultural Canadians of European background other than French and British, and of the rapidly growing metropolitan population of Visible Minorities, that the constitution cannot restrict its sensitivities to the shrinking British and French proportion of the population.[6] Hence their recurrent and telling labelling of the Meech Lake Accord as backward looking, as seeing Canada through a rear view mirror.

Women too have come of constitutional age. They have tasted constitutional recognition; they have their own constitutional interest groups and their own well-trained lawyers to defend their constitutional concerns. They lay claim to several constitutional clauses, s. 15 and s. 28, in the making of which they played a key role. Feminist groups in particular view these clauses as weapons in their ongoing assault on a society that some of them view as a massive affirmative action program for men.

Finally, the Charter sends a powerful message to its many believers, especially in English-speaking Canada, that the constitution no longer belongs to governments, indeed that citizens are now part of the constitutional order, and thus that deference to the leadership role of the governments in constitutional matters is not any more an unquestioned constitutional norm. The fact that aboriginal, female, ethnocultural, visible minority, the disabled and other Canadians successfully wielded the phrase "eleven able-bodied white males" to underline the illegitimacy of the Meech Lake process cogently confirms the decline of deference among the new constitutional players. A quarter of a century ago, such a phrase, deprived of its contemporary message of cultural arrogance, would have been virtually meaningless.

Now, at the beginning of the last decade of the twentieth century, Canadians can look back on a range of once-sacred constitutional hierarchies that have either crumbled or are under attack — an ethnic, racial hierarchy with the British at the top, and a sexual division of constitutional and political labour that privileged Ernest Hemingway over Virginia Woolf. Finally, the hierarchy of authority and elitism sustained by deference that assumed formal constitutional change was a matter for responsible governments to handle has been badly shaken by the insouciant response of a society that would not accept a Meech Lake package that commenced its life with the support of eleven governments and all three major parties in the House of Commons.

This new constitutional culture, sustained by the Charter and aboriginal constitutional clauses, greatly reduces the flexibility of the governments outside of Quebec in responding to Quebec claims for some form of distinctive treatment. In functional terms, the Charter, its allies and supporters, restrain the federal government and the remaining provinces in the same way that Quebec nationalism keeps the Quebec government tightly leashed in the constitutional bargaining arena. Quebec nationalism led to the withdrawal of support for the Fulton-Favreau formula by Jean Lesage, to the later unwillingness of Premier Bourassa to proceed with the Victoria Charter, and to his posture of rigid inflexibility two decades later in the Meech Lake negotiations. It appears, then, that changes in the constitutional culture of English-speaking Canada, combined with the nationalist restraints on the government of Quebec, increase the likelihood that intergovernmental agreements will be repudiated if public opinion is given time to mobilize. Once that mobilization has occurred, the flexibility necessary for compromise is redefined by the purists as weakness.

THE INTERNATIONAL DIMENSION OF OUR CONSTITUTIONAL DIFFICULTIES

It is tempting, even natural, to locate the roots of our contemporary constitutional malaise in domestic factors, to assess our difficulties as the product of an inadequate response to the evolution of those domestic cleavages that have constitutional consequences. Such explanations, however, flounder as we soon discover that many of the constitutional pressures playing on us have international roots. Francophone Quebec nationalism, the assertiveness of indigenous peoples, and the claims of multiracial and multicultural Canada for constitutional recognition all draw on global trends of ethnic revival, the post World War II attack on imperialist racial hierarchies, and a growing international consciousness of indigenous peoples. Further, the emergence of numerous small states encourages concentrated minorities of national, ethnic and indigenous peoples to view independence or self-government as much more feasible, as more in accord with the nature of things, than was true in the immediate aftermath of World War II.

These global trends are supplemented and reinforced by an international explosion of rights consciousness stimulated in part by the United Nations. Its many consequences include a reduction in the deference accorded elites, pressures for Charters and Bills of Rights, and redefinition of the relative significance of governments and citizens in democratic constitutional orders to the benefit of the latter. Specifically, and as examples only, the women's movement, and the activism of the disabled are inexplicable if external social forces, international intellectual climates, and a multitude of international organizations, both governmental and non-governmental, are not considered central links in any chain of causation.

. . . . .

In a country like Canada, democratic assumptions incline the student to see constitutional change as shaped by a domestic dialectic between citizens and their governments. This, however, is to forget that the state is in constant interaction with other states and that its citizens are bombarded by values, identities, and social forces that transcend frontiers.

259

The international environment is a depository of resources that can be skilfully deployed at home. Aboriginal organizations bring the papacy and the United Nations to the support of the causes. The heroines of the feminist movement are international.

DISARRAY ABOUT THE FORMAL RULES AND THE POLITICS OF THE AMENDING PROCESS

The 1982 achievement of an amending formula that can be operated entirely in Canada no longer appears as a triumph, but rather as an interim agreement. At a minimum, Meech Lake suggests that Canadians are still painfully learning how to work the new 1982 formula. More plausibly, I would argue that the formula's guiding philosophies verged on obsolescence before the constitutional ink was dry. The formula was devised as a response to the requirements of federalism, viewed as an affair of governments, albeit modified by the concession to responsible government involved in the new requirement of legislative ratification. Given the fashioning of the formula by the 'Gang of Eight' provincial governments, who were adamantly opposed to Trudeau's competing formula with a referendum component, it was to be expected that the formula would be sensitive to governments not to citizens. Further, the history of the search for a made-in-Canada amending formula had focused almost exclusively on the respective roles of the federal and provincial governments once the United Kingdom Parliament's role had been rendered obsolete by patriation. Indeed, the eventual sorting out of those roles among governments was viewed as *the* amending problem requiring solution. Accordingly, the amending formula was not fashioned with a view to its congruence with the Charter or with a Charter-influenced constitutional culture.

However, no sooner had the new amending formula been installed than the constitutional culture in which it was to operate began to diverge from the formula's implicitly elitist assumptions. The basic premise that governments were the key, and virtually the exclusive players in generating and implementing formal constitutional change, was challenged by a new cadre of constitutional actors who denied legitimacy to a process that left them in the audience.

In that sense Meech Lake reiterated one of the recurrent lessons of our past efforts at constitutional reform. It is the most recent illustration of the inveterate Canadian tendency for the substantive issues of constitutional change to be embroiled in a debate about the legitimacy of the process of their attempted resolution. Indeed, fundamental disagreement about the rules that should govern the process of constitutional change has acquired the status of a Canadian tradition, dysfunctional though it may be.

Prior to Meech Lake, the proposed unilateralism route threatened by Prime Minister Trudeau in 1980–81 was fought before Canadian courts and before the British public and parliamentarians by provincial governments and aboriginal peoples. After the passage of the 1982 Constitution Act, the government of Quebec unsuccessfully challenged the constitutionality of the process on the ground that it had not respected a constitutional veto claimed by the Quebec government. Just a few years earlier, the Senate proposals of the federal government's Bill C–60 reform package in 1978 were successfully challenged in court as exceeding the federal government's amending jurisdiction under the 1949 British North America Act (No. 2) allocating specified powers of unilateral amendment to the federal government.

Any belief that the 1982 amending formula, especially if employed in the attempted fashion of Meech Lake, would provide the long-awaited answer to the need for a legitimate formula has been belied by the reaction to Meech Lake. Polls indicate that most Canadians, Quebecois included, support the idea of referenda by large majorities.[7] After the week-long First Ministers' Conference in June 1990 there was virtual unanimity among the exhausted political leaders that never again would they participate in such an isolated and secretive executive federalism bargaining session from which constitutional fait accompli were supposed to emerge.[8]

The federal government discussion paper "Amending the Constitution of Canada" (1990) underlines the now recognized need for "public participation," "public involvement," and "public hearings." The key process criticism throughout the Meech Lake period, it concluded, was that the amending "procedures have not provided for public involvement in the examination and determination of constitutional amendment proposals prior to the formal amendment text being put forward for acceptance or rejection."[9]

The Citizens' Forum, whose hearings are now under way, is described and justified as a medium through which the people can speak and Commissioners can listen.[10] A press release describes the Forum as providing a "framework for an unprecedented exercise in democracy," and as "reaching out for the insights and inherent wisdom of the citizens of Canada."[11] A more dramatic contrast with the philosophy of executive dominance that First Ministers sought, ultimately without success, to apply to the Meech Lake process could scarcely be imagined. Prime Minister Mulroney's rhetoric suggests that he will consult and listen ad nauseam from now on, until the last voice has been heard.[12] The Charter constituencies and aboriginal peoples presumably will resist any attempted repeat of the government monopolization of the process that characterized the early stages of Meech Lake.

Some of these reactions are, no doubt, the bitter or chastened responses of individuals, groups and governments still reeling from the debacle so recently behind us. It would be wrong, however, to write them off as ephemeral, driven by momentary passions of despair or enthusiasm that will not survive the cold light of day. Meech Lake provides us with insights into our constitutional existence that could remain hidden through decades of constitutional placidity. The Meech Lake outcome can be explained in various ways — as a conflict between older and newer definitions of the constitution that I have elsewhere somewhat grandiosely described as the Governments' constitution versus the Citizens' constitution,[13] as executive federalism versus the Charter, as the old duality of founding peoples versus the new ethnic, racial and indigenous complexity of contemporary Canada, or as the culture of deference and authority versus an emergent culture of constitutional participation.

These antitheses — and others could be constructed by those who are dichotomously inclined — reveal how far we are from agreement on how we should proceed with the task of formal constitutional change, or who should participate and how. Even if we were to try and exclude the citizenry again in Meech Lake II, Premier Bourassa has made it clear that he rejects intergovernmental bargaining on constitutional reform among eleven governments. From now on he will negotiate only on a one-to-one basis with the federal government — nation to prospective nation.[14] However, we have neither constitutional theory nor procedures to guide the legitimate one-on-one Quebec-Ottawa bargaining directed to fundamental constitutional change. To structure the bargaining in such a way assumes the existence of an English-speaking Canada equated with the rest of Canada (TROC), and represented by the federal government, an assumption that could not withstand the most cursory examination. In a corporate, institutional, or governmental sense, English-speaking Canada does not exist. It is voiceless and headless. If, therefore, we are playing the two-nations game

rather than the federalism game, our disarray is little short of paralysing.

Our lack of consensus on the process of formal constitutional change is not restricted to a few minor details to be tidied up by legal draftsmen; rather, it is one of the paramount constitutional issues, for to agree on the participants and their roles is to structure the outcome. If the game is to be a two-nations version of the intergovernmental game restricted to two actors, Quebec City and Ottawa, presiding over the demise of federal Canada, the federal government is not symmetrically related to the rest-of-Canada constituency for which it would, de facto, be speaking. If the game is still a federalism game, the other nine provincial governments will not be willing to delegate the refashioning of Canada to Quebec and a federal government facing the erosion of its own power in Quebec, even if the formal rules sanctioned such a procedure, which they do not.[15]

In any event, Meech Lake makes clear that governments do not exhaust the cast of constitutional actors. We need, accordingly, to find a process that is sensitive to the participant constitutional culture that the Charter and aboriginal aspirations have stimulated, and that has been legitimated, at least for its believers, by the role of Charter supporters and aboriginal leaders in fashioning parts of the 1982 Constitution act, and by their role in the defeat of Meech Lake. The amending process, in other words, must be moved in the direction of reconciling the traditional dominance of governments with the emerging challenge of a no longer-deferential citizen-body.

That the governments of Canadian federalism will continue to be central players is obvious, for federalism and the Canadian and provincial communities it reflects and nourishes, remain crucial to our identities. That the government and people of Quebec, if a revised constitution can contain their ambitions, might require some unique status in the amending process is also evident. But the accommodation of Quebec, the federal government and the other nine provinces is no longer enough.

The necessary rearranging of the respective roles of citizens and governments in the amending process would be difficult at the best of times. It is doubly so when the Quebec government is driven by a desire for national self-affirmation, following on the perceived humiliation of Meech Lake, that precludes a return to federalism's intergovernmental constitutional bargaining table. It is trebly difficult when put in the context of the widespread suspicion so many of the constitutional actors have for each other, to which I now turn.

THE ABSENCE OF TRUST

The constitutional amendment process is profoundly hampered by the pervasive distrust of so many of the participants for each other. The evidence is lengthy and discouraging. The widespread resort to the courts to challenge the legality of particular constitutional reform packages, noted previously, is one telling illustration.

Distrust lies behind the progressive introduction of rigidities into the amending formula, from the relatively flexible Victoria Charter 1971 proposals, to the unanimity provisions in the 1982 Constitution Act, and their further extension in the Meech Lake package. The assumption that a central criterion of a good amending formula is to alleviate insecurities, to reduce the possibility that a particular government might be a loser, was the implicit assumption behind Mulroney's reiterated defence of the Meech Lake unanimity requirement for Senate reform. Unanimity, he claimed, doubtless for the benefit of Premier Getty of Alberta, would guarantee Alberta against having the wrong kind of Senate reform imposed on it. This was a protection that Quebec had not had when the 1982 Constitution Act was fashioned and implemented.

Those who forged ahead with the Constitution Act in 1982 without Quebec's participation did so in the belief that the Parti Quebecois could not be trusted to bargain honourably for renewed federalism. The Parti Quebecois government and the nationalist elite responded by accusing the Trudeau Liberal government of betrayal, of a breach of trust, for failing to deliver the kind of renewed federalism they claimed that Quebecers justifiably assumed as inherent in Trudeau's referendum campaign commitments.[16]

The interpretations of our recent constitutional evolution by feminists, aboriginal leaders, non-founding European ethnic groups and visible minorities are a litany of bitterness, accusation, and distrust of governments. This bitterness, which has historic roots, burst forth in the Meech Lake episode in a battery of recriminations against an executive federalism First Ministers' process dominated, as we were repeatedly reminded, by eleven able-bodied white males.

The absence of trust lies behind the widespread implicit acceptance of a mirror theory of representation that presupposes a decline of deference and suggests that only representatives cloned from the same stock as the groups that felt excluded could be trusted to speak for women and aboriginals, for example. The implicit thesis that you have to be one to know one and to represent one draws powerful support from moral and intellectual trends in contemporary culture.[17] In the Meech Lake process it gained additional justification from the widespread view that the federal government failed in its duty to defend the Canadian community, Charter interests, and its own future status as a government.[18] In the absence of evidence that the federal government was a reliable proxy for their concerns, Meech Lake opponents simply denied the legitimacy of a process that tried to exclude their participation.

Mistrust leads to a constitutional paranoia ever on the lookout for slights and indignities, fearful that one's fate will be decided in a bargaining session to which one was not invited, when one was sleeping in Hull for example, or apprehensive that the male bargainers will simply forget about women's constitutional concerns, as feminists assert, or convinced that the commitment to hold a constitutional conference on aboriginal matters can only be relied on if it is written into the constitution itself.

This lack of trust, this ubiquitous paranoia, has major constitutional consequences, not only for the constitutional reform process itself, but for the objectives of the participants. It easily gets translated into an unceasing search for the maximum constitutional protection. Hence, the successful efforts of women's groups to exempt s. 28[19] from the ambit of the s. 33 notwithstanding clause.[20] The women's s. 28 clause contained its own "notwithstanding anything in this Charter," partly to ensure that the s. 27 multicultural heritage clause[21] could not be used to justify sexual inequalities on the ground they were sanctioned by traditional cultural practices. The desire of anglophone women's groups to protect s. 28 and s. 15[22] of the Charter from the distinct society clause was based on the same fear that cultural imperatives could be used on some future occasion to subject Canadian women living in Quebec to an inferior rights regime in the interest of cultural and linguistic survival.

In the constitutional politics between the Meech Lake and Langevin House meetings, ethnic and aboriginal groups succeeded in exempting their constitutional clauses from the ambit of the distinct society clause.[23] Aboriginal groups had earlier sought and gained in s. 25[24] protection of their aboriginal, treaty or other rights or freedoms from abrogation or derogation by the Charter. The Assembly of First Nations tried without success in 1983 to gain a right of veto over constitutional amendments that might affect the rights of First Nations.[25]

The lack of trust is driven by disagreement over the formal rules and the accompanying political process for amending the constitution. The 1982 amending formula presupposes the dominance of governments, modified by the requirement of legislative ratification, in the amending process. The Charter, however, generates a new set of constitutional interests, as do aboriginal constitutional clauses and the ambitions they sustain, that convinces their advocates that they should be more than onlookers when the constitution is being amended. The Quebec government, based on its francophone majority, assumed that its turn had come, following its 1982 exclusion. In addition, the Charter had a weaker hold on Quebecois, outside of anglophones and allophones, than was true elsewhere in the country, and this hampered the Bourassa government's appreciation of Charterism in the rest of Canada. In any event, the fundamental social force that the Quebec government had to represent, or gingerly not offend, was nationalism, not the Charter and its pan-Canadian ideology. Meech Lake floundered on these competing understandings, with the Quebec government assuming it had a priority claim, all governments assuming the constitution was theirs to amend, and resenting the interference of the new constitutional stakeholders, and the latter truculently non-deferential and insisting that their concerns also had to be met.

A constitutional amendment process built on mistrust is likely to display the following biases: (1) it multiplies the number of would-be constitutional players by undermining the belief that X can be trusted to represent the concerns of Y; (2) it generates a competitive search for ironclad constitutional protection in the form of vetoes, notwithstanding clauses, etc.; (3) on the flexibility/rigidity scale it will be heavily biased towards the latter; (4) it will encourage the search for loopholes and unilateralism options to break out of its confines; (5) it will lead to ingenious attempts to work the constitution, to achieve by political processes what cannot be achieved by formal amendments. However, for many of the constitutional objectives that Canadians now pursue the less constraining political process cannot be substituted for change by formal amendment.

CONCLUSION

The constitution we have left behind was sustained by an ethnic hierarchy in which the British assumed pride of place, the French a close second, and those communities that came to be labelled multicultural and multiracial in recent decades were clearly above the aboriginal peoples, although not in the charmed circle of European founding peoples restricted to French and English. From a different perspective, a gender aristocracy of males monopolized the affairs of state at our beginnings, and even now wields vastly disproportionate numerical power.

The constitutional culture that lay behind a constitution similar in principle to that of the United Kingdom has been convulsed by Quebecois nationalism, by a changing ethnic demography and the politicization of ethnicity, by the awakening of the indigenous peoples, by the rights revolution and the Charter that is its most visible instrument, and by the attack on the constitutional and political role hitherto granted to men. Many of these trends derive support from an international environment that is broadly sympathetic to what I have elsewhere called 'constitutional minoritarianism.'[26] The Charter and aboriginal constitutional clauses have been crucial catalysts in reducing deference and challenging the dominance of governments in the constitutional reform process.

We have more constitutional players than ever. Many of them speak the uncompromising language of rights, nationalism and sovereignty. Governments and citizen groups disagree on what the constitution is about, and hence on how it should be changed. Even among governments, the criteria for formal amendment that were fashioned in 1980–81 are discredited. We look back on a succession of failed efforts interspersed with isolated successes before 1982. The 1982 achievement now seems [a] Pyrrhic victory, as the exclusion of Quebec became a political resource to [delegitimize] the Constitution Act 1982, and thus open the way for the mismanaged Meech Lake affair which has grievously damaged the constitutional order.

The somewhat antiseptic language of jurisdictional conflict has been overtaken by a passionate language of identity, honour, shame, betrayal and status. This language of pride and affirmation gets in the way of compromise. A pervasive suspicion and distrust that feeds on historical grievances compounds the difficulties of constitutional reform.

We are caught in a vicious circle. While some of my observations can be characterized as disputes about rules and procedures, they are in fact reflections of a much deeper and more profound malaise. The crisis we face is one of community and identity. Our constitutional behaviour lacks fraternity, sorority, mutuality and trust. Our multiple fragmentations corrode the process we employ in the search for an accommodation that will overcome them.

We would be better off if we had a clean slate on which to write our constitutional future, for then the compulsion of necessity would drive us towards agreement. Situated, however, as we are, in the midst of an incomplete constitutional experiment, and surveying our condition as an unfinished people, we are hindered in our efforts to escape by the inertia of a decaying constitutional order.

Notes

...

3. An abridgement of the five volumes of the Tremblay Report is available. See David Kwavnick, ed., *The Tremblay Report: Report of the Royal Commission of Inquiry on Constitutional Problems* (Carleton Library No. 64) (Toronto: Carleton University Press, 1973).

4. *Report of the Royal Commission on Bilingualism and Biculturalism* (Ottawa, 1967–70).

5. *Constitution Act, 1982*, s. 35(2) "In this Act, 'aboriginal peoples of Canada' includes the Indians, Inuit and Metis peoples of Canada."

6. See Shiva S. Halli, et al., eds., *Ethnic Demography: Canadian Immigrant, Racial and Cultural Variations* (Ottawa: Carleton University Press, 1990) for up-to-date data and analysis.

7. In a "Globe and Mail — CBC News/Poll," *Globe and Mail*, July 9, 1990, two out of three Quebec residents, and an even higher ratio outside of Quebec, believe that "[c]hanges to the constitution should only be decided by the people voting directly in a referendum." In a slightly earlier pool, 71 percent of Canadians supported having a referendum on Meech Lake, including 58 percent Quebec support. Julian Beltrame, "Canadians want Meech referendum, poll finds," *Globe and Mail*, April 7, 1990.

8. *First Ministers' Conference on the Constitution*, verbatim transcript, Ottawa, Ontario, June 9–10, 1990 (Document: 800–029/004 Canadian Intergovernmental Conference Secretariat), pp. 3, 9, 24, 33, 44.

9. Federal-Provincial Relations Office, Government of Canada, *Amending the Constitution of Canada: A Discussion Paper* (Ottawa: Supply and Services Canada, 1990), pp. 1, 13, 20.

10. P.C. 1990–2347, Privy Council Minute of November 1st, 1990, establishing the Forum, instructed the Chairman and Advisory Group "to lead a process of public discussion and dialogue," and to ensure "the participation of a broad spectrum of Canadians of all ages, backgrounds, regions, and walks of life...."

11. Citizens' Forum on Canada's Future, "Getting Under Way, Mandate and Consultative Process," December 5, 1990, pp. 5–6.

12. "You will not be able to get me to ever cut off debate on a constitutional resolution. They can go on for as long as they want, years. I want to hear everybody. I want them recorded. I want them filmed. I want documents. I want (pause) and if I've missed anybody I'm going to reopen it." Robert Sheppard, "Searching for a card Mulroney can play," *Globe and Mail*, November 5, 1990, reporting an earlier June 11, 1990, *Globe and Mail* parliamentary bureau interview with Brian Mulroney.

13. Alan C. Cairns, "The Limited Constitutional Vision of Meech Lake," in Katherine E. Swinton and Carol J. Rogerson, eds., *Competing Constitutional Visions: The Meech Lake Accord* (Toronto: Carswell, 1988), p. 248.

14. Immediately after the demise of Meech Lake, Premier Bourassa stated, in a television address: "[I]t is the position of my government to negotiate henceforth with two, not 11, to negotiate with the Canadian government, which represents the whole of the population of Canada, bilateral negotiations between the government of Quebec and the federal government ... [W]e can decide to participate in certain conferences in which Quebec's interests are involved, but never at the constitutional level." "A critical moment in Quebec's history," *Globe and Mail*, June 15, 1990.

15. For a discussion, see Alan C. Cairns, "Constitutional Change and the Three Equalities," pp. 93–7, in Ronald L. Watts

and Douglas M. Brown, eds., *Options for a New Canada* (Toronto: University of Toronto Press, 1991).

16. The raw materials for the debate are available in the exchanges in Appendices A of Donald Johnston, ed., *Lac Meech: Trudeau parle ... Textes reunis et presentes par Donald Johnston* (Ville LaSalle, Quebec: Hurtubise, 1989).

17. I have explored this and related issues in "Constitutional Minoritarianism in Canada," in Ronald L. Watts and Douglas M. Brown, eds., *Canada: The State of the Federation 1990* (Kingston: Queen's University, Institute of Intergovernmental Affairs, 1990).

18. "My unease ... springs from the fact that the Accord fails to embody any vision of the national community, of Canada. It appears to be a document drawn up by provincial governments for provincial governments, the result of a constitutional contest in which the federal government was a referee but not a player aggressively pursuing its own interest and vision." Roger Gibbins, "A Sense of Unease: The Meech Lake Accord and Constitution-Making in Canada," in Roger Gibbins, et al., eds., *Meech Lake and Canada: Perspectives from the West* (Edmonton: Academic Printing and Publishing, 1988), p. 129.

19. S. 28 "Notwithstanding anything in this Charter, the rights and freedoms referred to in it are guaranteed equally to male and female persons."

20. S. 33 "(1) Parliament or the legislature of a province may expressly declare in an Act of Parliament or of the legislature, as the case may be, that the Act or a provision thereof shall operate notwithstanding a provision included in section 2 or sections 7 to 15 of this Charter.... (3) A declaration made under subsection (1) shall cease to have effect five years after it comes into force or on such earlier date as may be specified in the declaration. (4) Parliament or a legislature of a province may re-enact a declaration made under subsection (1)."

21. S. 27 "This Charter shall be interpreted in a manner consistent with the preservation and enhancement of the multicultural heritage of Canadians."

22. S. 15 "(1) Every individual is equal before and under the law and has the right to the equal protection and equal benefit of the law without discrimination and, in particular, without discrimination based on religion, sex, age or mental or physical disability. (2) Subsection (1) does not preclude any law, program or activity that has as its object the amelioration of conditions of disadvantaged individuals or groups including those that are disadvantaged because of race, national or ethnic origin, colour, religion, sex, age, or mental or physical disability."

23. S. 16 "Nothing in section 2 of the *Constitution Act, 1867* affects section 25 or 27 of the *Canadian Charter of Rights and Freedoms*, section 35 of the *Constitution Act, 1982* or class 24 of section 91 or the *Constitution Act, 1867*."

24. S. 25 "The guarantee in this Charter of certain rights and freedoms shall not be construed so as to abrogate or derogate from any aboriginal, treaty or other rights or freedoms that pertain to the aboriginal peoples of Canada including: (a) any rights or freedoms that have been recognized by the Royal Proclamation of October 7, 1763; and, (b) any rights or freedoms that may be acquired by the aboriginal peoples of Canada by way of land claims settlement."

25. See Bryan Schwarts, *First Principles, Second Thoughts: Aboriginal Peoples, Constitution Reform and Canadian Statecraft* (Montreal: Institute for Research on Public Policy 1986), chap. vi, "Consent to Constitutional Amendments" for the complexities of the veto proposal, and of a paralleled opting out proposal.

26. Cairns, "Constitutional Minoritarianism in Canada."

(e) Charlottetown Accord Draft Legal Text

[NOTE: The Accord was signed on August 28, 1992; the 51-page Draft Legal Text which contains the extracts reproduced here was released on October 9, 1992, just 17 days before the referendum, hardly a shining model of public consultation!]

PREFACE

The attached draft legal text is based on the Charlottetown Accord of August 28, 1992. It is a best efforts text prepared by officials representing all First Ministers and Aboriginal and Territorial Leaders. This draft includes amendments to the following constitutional acts:

- *Constitution Act, 1867*
- *Constitution Act, 1871*
- *Alberta Act*
- *Constitution Act, 1982* (including section 16.1, a bilateral amendment by New Brunswick and Canada).

This draft is subject to final review and approval by First Ministers and Leaders to ensure its consistency with the Charlottetown Consensus Report. Officials have made best efforts to ensure that the policy decisions summarized in the Consensus Report on the Constitution of August 28, 1992 have been translated as accurately as possible, in both official languages, into legal text that will serve as the basis for formal constitutional amendments to be presented to Parliament and the provincial legislatures.

. . . .

TABLE OF CONTENTS

. . . .

CONSTITUTION ACT, 1867

1. The Constitution Act, 1867 is amended by adding thereto, immediately after section 1 thereof, the following section:

Canada Clause

"**2.**(1) The Constitution of Canada, including the *Canadian Charter of Rights and Freedoms*, shall be interpreted in a manner consistent with the following fundamental characteristics:

(a) Canada is a democracy committed to a parliamentary and federal system of government and to the rule of law;

(b) the Aboriginal peoples of Canada, being the first peoples to govern this land, have the right to promote their language, cultures and traditions and to ensure the integrity of their societies, and their governments constitute one of the three orders of government in Canada;

(c) Quebec constitutes within Canada a distinct society, which includes a French-speaking majority, a unique culture and a civil law tradition;

(d) Canadians and their governments are committed to the vitality and development of official language minority communities throughout Canada;

(e) Canadians are committed to racial and ethnic equality in a society that includes citizens from many lands who have contributed, and continue to contribute, to the building of a strong Canada that reflects its cultural and racial diversity;

(f) Canadians are committed to a respect for individual and collective human rights and freedoms of all people;

(g) Canadians are committed to the equality of female and male persons; and

(h) Canadians confirm the principle of the equality of the provinces at the same time as recognizing their diverse characteristics.

265

Role of legislature and Government of Quebec

(2) The role of the legislature and Government of Quebec to preserve and promote the distinct society of Quebec is affirmed.

Powers, rights and privileges preserved

(3) Nothing in this section derogates from the powers, rights or privileges of the Parliament or the Government of Canada, or of the legislatures or governments of the provinces, or of the legislative bodies or governments of the Aboriginal peoples of Canada, including any powers, rights or privileges relating to language.

Aboriginal and treaty rights

(4) For greater certainty, nothing in this section abrogates or derogates from the aboriginal and treaty rights of the Aboriginal peoples of Canada."

. . . .

4. Sections 21 to 36 of the said Act are repealed and the following substituted therefor:

Constitution of Senate

"**21.**(1) The Senate shall consist of sixty-two senators of whom

(a) six shall be elected for each province, namely, Ontario, Quebec, Nova Scotia, New Brunswick, Manitoba, British Columbia, Prince Edward Island, Alberta, Saskatchewan and Newfoundland;

(b) one shall be elected for each territory, namely, the Yukon Territory and the Northwest Territories; and

(c) [aboriginal representation]"

[NOTE: The number 62 is subject to future decisions on the number of guaranteed Aboriginal seats. The issue of Aboriginal representation and voting powers of Aboriginal senators is to be discussed in the autumn of 1992, according to the Consensus Report.]

New provinces

(2) Notwithstanding subsection (1), where a new province is established from the Yukon Territory or the Northwest Territories, the new province shall be entitled to the same representation in the Senate as the territory had.

. . . .

[The Text provides for an elected Senate with powers that vary with the subject matter. For most subjects, if the Senate rejects a House of Commons bill (other than a revenue or expenditure bill, which can only be delayed), it may go eventually to a vote by a joint session of both Houses. Subjects materially affecting French language or culture must be passed by a special majority of French-speaking Senators. Natural resources tax policy bills can be vetoed by the Senate.]

. . . .

Special rules relating to the constitution of the House of Commons

(2) Notwithstanding anything in this Act,

. . . .

(b) Quebec shall always be entitled to a number of members in the House of Commons that is no fewer than twenty-five per cent of the total number of members in the House of Commons;

. . . .

8. The said Act is further amended by adding thereto, immediately after section 91 thereof, the following section:

Application of class 24 of section 91

"**91A.** For greater certainty, class 24 of section 91 applies, except as provided in section 95E, in relation to all the Aboriginal peoples of Canada."

. . . .

(2) Section 92 of the said Act is further amended by adding thereto, immediately after class 12 thereof, the following:

"**12A.** Labour market development and training in the Province."

. . . .

10. The said Act is further amended by adding thereto, immediately after section 92A thereof, the following heading and sections:

"CULTURE

Laws in relation to culture

92B.(1) The legislature of each province may exclusively make laws in relation to culture in the province.

National cultural matters

(2) The Government of Canada retains its role in relation to national cultural matters, including national cultural institutions and grants and contributions delivered by such institutions.

Authority not extended

(3) Nothing in subsection (2) extends the authority of the Parliament of Canada.

Agreements on culture with provinces

92C.(1) The Government of Canada shall negotiate with the government of any province that so requests an agreement on culture for the purpose of ensuring that both governments work in harmony, recognizing the lead responsibility of the province for culture in the province.

Agreements on culture with territories

(2) The Government of Canada shall negotiate with the government of any territory that so requests an agreement on culture for the purpose of ensuring that both governments work in harmony.

· · · ·

[The Text makes provision for the negotiation of other agreements relating to telecommunications, urban and municipal affairs, tourism, recreation, housing, mining, forestry, labour market development and training, unemployment insurance, regional development, immigration, and aliens.]

· · · ·

15. *The said Act is further amended by adding thereto, immediately after section 101 thereof, the following heading and sections:*

"SUPREME COURT OF CANADA

Supreme Court continued

101A.(1) The court existing under the name of the Supreme Court of Canada is hereby continued as the general court of appeal for Canada, and as an additional court for the better administration of the laws of Canada, and shall continue to be a superior court of record.

Composition

(2) The Supreme Court of Canada shall consist of a chief justice, to be called the Chief Justice of Canada, and eight other judges who shall be appointed by the Governor General in Council.

Who may be appointed Judges

101B.(1) Any person may be appointed a judge of the Supreme Court of Canada who, after having been admitted to the bar of a province or territory, has, for a total of at least ten years, been a judge of any court in Canada or a member of the bar of any province or territory.

Three judges from Quebec

(2) At least three of the judges shall be appointed from among persons who, after having been admitted to the bar of Quebec, have, for a total of at least ten years, been judges of any court of Quebec or of any court established by the Parliament of Canada, or members of the bar of Quebec.

Names of candidates

101C.(1) Where a vacancy occurs in the Supreme Court of Canada, the government of each province or territory may submit to the Minister of Justice of Canada the names of at least five candidates to fill the vacancy, each of whom is qualified under section 101B for appointment to the Court.

Appointment from names submitted

(2) Where an appointment is made to the Supreme Court of Canada, the Governor General in Council shall, except where the Chief Justice is appointed from among members of the Court, appoint a person whose name has been submitted under subsection (1) and who is acceptable to the Queen's Privy Council for Canada.

Appointment from Quebec

(3) Where an appointment is made under subsection 101B(2), the Governor General in Council shall appoint a person whose name is submitted by the Government of Quebec.

· · · ·

16. The said Act is further amended by adding thereto, immediately after section 106 thereof, the following section:

Shared-cost program

"**106A.**(1) The Government of Canada shall provide reasonable compensation to the government of a province that chooses not to participate in a national shared-cost program that is established by the Government of Canada after the coming into force of this section in an area of exclusive provincial jurisdiction, if the province carries on a program or initiative that is compatible with the national objectives.

. . . .

17. The said Act is further amended by adding thereto, immediately after Part VIII thereof, the following Part:

"PART VIII.1
INTERGOVERNMENTAL AGREEMENTS

No inconsistent laws

126A.(1) Where the Government of Canada and the government of one or more provinces or territories enter into an agreement that is approved under this section, no law made by or under the authority of the Parliament of Canada or of any legislature of a province or legislative authority of a territory that is a party to the agreement and has caused it to be approved under this section may amend, revoke or otherwise supersede the agreement while the approval of the agreement remains in force.

. . . .

19.(2) Rules 1 and 2 in subsection 51(1) of the Constitution Act, 1867 are repealed and the following substituted therefor:

Rule

"**1.** After the completion of the 1991 decennial census, the House of Commons shall consist of three hundred and thirty-seven members and there shall be assigned to each of the provinces and territories the following number of members: one hundred and seventeen for Ontario; ninety-three for Quebec; eleven for Nova Scotia; ten for New Brunswick; fourteen for Manitoba; thirty-six for British Columbia; four for Prince Edward Island; twenty-eight for Alberta; fourteen for Saskatchewan; seven for Newfoundland; one for the Yukon Territory; and two for the Northwest Territories."

Adjusted representation

(3) After the completion of the 1996 census, the representation of the provinces in the House of Commons shall be readjusted by adding eight members, of which three shall be for Ontario, three for British Columbia and two for Alberta.

. . . .

CONSTITUTION ACT, 1871

21. Section 2 of the Constitution Act, 1871, is repealed and the following substituted therefor:

Establishment of new provinces in territories in Canada

"**2.**(1) The Parliament of Canada may from time to time establish a new province in any territory forming for the time being part of the Dominion of Canada, but not included in any province thereof, at the request of the legislative authority of the territory, and may, at the time of such establishment, make provision for the constitution and administration of any such province, and for the passing of laws for the peace, order and good government of the province, and for its representation in the House of Commons.

First Ministers' Conference

(2) Before a new province is established under subsection (1), a conference of the Prime Minister of Canada and the first ministers of the provinces shall be convened to take into account the views of the provinces."

. . . .

CONSTITUTION ACT, 1982

. . . .

27. The said Act is further amended by adding thereto, immediately after section 33 thereof, the following section:

Application of section 33 to Aboriginal legislative bodies

"**33.1** Section 33 applies to legislative bodies of the Aboriginal peoples of Canada with such modification, consistent with the purposes of the requirements of that section, as are appropriate to the circumstances of the Aboriginal peoples concerned."

. . . .

29. Section 35.1 of the said Act is repealed and the following substituted therefor:

Inherent right of self-government

"35.1(1) The Aboriginal peoples of Canada have the inherent right of self-government within Canada.

Three orders of government

(2) The right referred to in subsection (1) shall be interpreted in a manner consistent with the recognition of the governments of the Aboriginal peoples of Canada as constituting one of three orders of government in Canada.

. . . .

Delay of justiciability

35.3(1) Except in relation to self-government agreements concluded after the coming into force of this section, section 35.1 shall not be made the subject of judicial notice, interpretation or enforcement for five years after that section comes into force.

. . . .

Application of laws

35.4(1) Except as otherwise provided by the Constitution of Canada, the laws of Canada and the laws of the provinces and territories continue to apply to the Aboriginal peoples of Canada, subject nevertheless to being displaced by laws enacted by legislative bodies of the Aboriginal peoples according to their authority.

Peace, order and good government in Canada

(2) No aboriginal law or any other exercise of the inherent right of self-government under section 35.1 may be inconsistent with federal or provincial laws that are essential to the preservation of peace, order and good government in Canada.

. . . .

Rights of the Aboriginal peoples of Canada guaranteed equally to both sexes

35.7 Notwithstanding any other provision of this Act, the rights of the Aboriginal peoples of Canada referred to in this Part are guaranteed equally to male and female persons.

Commitment to participate in constitutional conference

35.8 The government of Canada and the provincial governments are committed to the principle that, before any amendment described in section 45.1 is made,

(a) a constitutional conference that includes in its agenda an item relating to the proposed amendment, composed of the Prime Minister of Canada and the first ministers of the provinces will be convened by the Prime Minister of Canada; and

(b) The Prime Minister of Canada will invite representatives of the Aboriginal peoples of Canada to participate in the discussions on that item.]

. . . .

Constitutional conferences

35.9(1) At least four constitutional conferences on aboriginal issues composed of the Prime Minister of Canada, the first ministers of the provinces, representatives of the Aboriginal peoples of Canada and elected representatives of the governments of the territories shall be convened by the Prime Minister of Canada, the first to be held no later than 1996 and the three subsequent conferences to be held one every two years thereafter.

Agenda

(2) Each conference convened under subsection (1) shall have included in its agenda such items as are proposed by the representatives of the Aboriginal peoples of Canada.

. . . .

31. The said Act is further amended by adding thereto, immediately after Part III thereof, the following Parts:

"PART III.1
THE SOCIAL AND ECONOMIC UNION

Commitment respecting social and economic union

36.1(1) Without altering the authority of Parliament, the provincial legislatures or the territorial legislative authorities, or of the government of Canada or the governments of the provinces or territories, or the rights of any of them with respect to the exercise of their authority, Parliament, the provincial legislatures and the territorial legislative authorities, together with the government of Canada and the provincial and territorial governments, are committed to the principle of the preservation and development of the Canadian social and economic union.

Social union

(2) The preservation and development of the social union includes, but is not limited to, the following policy objectives:

(a) providing throughout Canada a health care system that is comprehensive, universal, portable, publicly administered, and accessible;

(b) providing adequate social services and benefits to ensure that all individuals resident in Canada have reasonable access to housing, food and other basic necessities;

(c) providing high quality primary and secondary education to all individuals resident in Canada and ensuring reasonable access to post-secondary education;

(d) protecting the rights of workers to organize and bargain collectively; and

(e) protecting, preserving and sustaining the integrity of the environment for present and future generations.

Economic union

(3) The preservation and development of the economic union includes, but is not limited to, the following policy objectives:

(a) working together to strengthen the Canadian economic union;

(b) the free movement of persons, goods, services and capital;

(c) the goal of full employment;

(d) ensuring that all Canadians have a reasonable standard of living; and

(e) ensuring sustainable and equitable development.

Interpretation of Charter rights and freedoms not modified

(4) This Part does not have the effect of modifying the interpretation of the rights and freedoms referred to in the *Canadian Charter of Rights and Freedoms*.

. . . .

PART IV.1
FIRST MINISTERS' CONFERENCES

First Ministers' Conferences

37.1 A conference of the Prime Minister of Canada and the first ministers of the provinces shall be con-

vened by the Prime Minister of Canada at least once each year, the first within twelve months after this Part comes into force."

. . . .

32. Sections 40 to 42 of the said Act are repealed and the following substituted therefor:

Compensation

"40. Where an amendment is made under subsection 38(1) that transfers legislative powers from provincial legislatures to Parliament, Canada shall provide reasonable compensation to any province to which the amendment does not apply.

Amendment by unanimous consent

41. An amendment to the Constitution of Canada in relation to the following matters may be made by proclamation issued by the Governor General under the Great Seal of Canada only where authorized by resolutions of the Senate and House of Commons and of the legislative assembly of each province:

(a) the office of the Queen, the Governor General and the Lieutenant Governor of a province;

(b) the powers of the Senate and the selection of senators;

(c) the number of senators by which a province or territory is entitled to be represented in the Senate and the qualifications of senators set out in the *Constitution Act, 1867*;

[(c.1) the number of senators by which the Aboriginal peoples of Canada are entitled to be represented in the Senate and the qualifications of such senators;]

[NOTE to c.1: The issue of Aboriginal representation is to be discussed in the autumn of 1992, according to the Consensus Report.]

(d) an amendment to section 51a of the *Constitution Act, 1867*;

(e) subject to section 43, the use of the English or the French language;

(f) subject to subsection 42(1), the Supreme Court of Canada;

(g) an amendment to section 2 or 3 of the *Constitution Act, 1871*; and

(h) an amendment to this Part.

Amendment by general procedure

42.(1) An amendment to the Constitution of Canada in relation to the method of selecting judges of the

Supreme Court of Canada may be made only in accordance with subsection 38(1).

Exception

(2) Subsections 38(2) to (4) do not apply in respect of amendments in relation to the matter referred to in subsection (1).

New provinces

42.1 Subsection 38(1) and sections 41 and 42 do not apply to allow a province that is established pursuant to section 2 of the *Constitution Act, 1871* after the coming into force of this section to authorize amendments to the Constitution of Canada and, for greater certainty, all other provisions of this Part apply in respect of such a province."

[**33.** The said Act is further amended by adding thereto, immediately after s. 45 thereof, the following section:

Amendments where Aboriginal peoples of Canada directly referred to

"**45.1**(1) An amendment to the Constitution of Canada that directly refers to, or that amends a provision that directly refers to, one or more of the aboriginal peoples of Canada or their governments [NOTE: A mechanism for obtaining Aboriginal consent would be worked out prior to the tabling of a Constitution resolution in Parliament], including

(a) section 2, as it relates to the Aboriginal peoples of Canada [NOTE: A reference to any provision relating to Aboriginal representation in the Senate would be added here], class 24 of

section 91, and sections 91A, 95E and 127 of the Constitution Act, 1867, and

(b) section 25 and Part II of this Act and this section,

may be made by proclamation issued by the Governor General under the Great Seal of Canada only where the amendment has been authorized in accordance with this Part and has received the substantial consent of the Aboriginal peoples so referred to.

Initiation of amendment procedures

(2) Notwithstanding section 46, the procedures for amending the Constitution of Canada in relation to any matter referred to in subsection (1) may be initiated by any of the Aboriginal peoples of Canada directly referred to as provided in subsection (1)."]

34. *Subsection 52(2) of the said Act is amended by striking out the word "and" at the end of paragraph (b) thereof, by adding the word "and" at the end of paragraph (c) thereof and by adding thereto the following paragraph:*

"(d) any other amendment to the Constitution of Canada."

35. *Section 61 of the said Act is repealed and the following substituted therefor:*

References

"**61.** A reference to the *Constitution Act, 1982* or a reference to the Constitution Acts, 1867 to 1982 shall be deemed to include a reference to any amendments thereto."

(f) The Referendum and Its Aftermath†

Jeffrey Simpson

NOTE

Compare this analysis with Patrick J. Monahan, "The Sounds of Silence" in Kenneth McRoberts & Patrick Monahan, eds., *The Charlottetown Accord, the Referendum, and the Future of Canada* (Toronto: University of Toronto Press, 1993) at 239–41. Which account best explains the failure of

† From Kenneth McRoberts & Patrick Monahan, eds., *The Charlottetown Accord, the Referendum, and the Future of Canada* (Toronto: University of Toronto Press, 1993) at 196–99. Reproduced with permission of University of Toronto Press, Incorporated.

the Charlottetown Accord? Are there any lessons here for the future?

EXTRACT

Clearly, much criticism could be made of the tactics and strategy of the Yes side's campaign — that the campaign reflected the secular equivalent of Noah's Ark goes without saying. People of different political persuasions tried to work together with indifferent results. The advertising was uninspired when it was not wrongly inspired. The prime minister's theatrics and threats, including the ripping up of the text of the accord in Sherbrooke, did not help, nor did the intervention of the Royal Bank. The Yes campaign in Quebec was sandbagged by the Wilhelmy tapes affair and the publication in *L'Actualité* of memoranda written by civil servants that reflected their negative assessments of Premier Robert Bourassa's negotiating tactics. Former prime minister Pierre Trudeau's intervention proved an important fillip to the No side. It legitimized dissent in the rest of Canada, especially among those unfavourably disposed towards Quebec. Although isolated in his opposition from all his former political colleagues in Quebec, Trudeau still commands an important and diverse following outside his native province.

These and other myriad details of a failed campaign, however, were less consequential by way of explaining the result, I believe, than the inherent difficulties of winning any referendum on constitutional amendments. Some of these factors have been touched upon above, but the cardinal one follows.

Canadian politicians' persistence in seeking formal constitutional amendments acceptable to all governments and interest groups has been matched only by their failure. For almost three decades, prime ministers and premiers, and now Aboriginal and territorial leaders, have wrestled with the Constitution, trying to reshape it to everyone's satisfaction. Though the putative explanation was the search for unity, the practical effect was the deepening of division.

Ingenuity has not been lacking. Politicians have tried small amendments and large ones. They have tried to proceed sequentially — Meech Lake first followed by other negotiations. They have tried to proceed globally with many changes rolled into one package, as in the Charlottetown Accord. They have tried classic executive federalism. They have tried executive federalism embellished with extensive public consultation, and now they have tried a referendum.

Four prime ministers, dozens of provincial premiers, and hundreds of advisers have been engaged and sometimes consumed by these efforts. There have been intellectual titans and deadbeats, people of strong and weak character, Liberals, Conservatives, New Democrats, Social Crediters, Péquistes. The results? Failure, in whole or in large part.

The closest Canada came to achieving formal changes to the satisfaction of all governments was Mr. Trudeau's patriation package of 1981–2. This is not the place to rehash that exercise, nor to engage in the ongoing interpretations as to its desirability, wisdom, and legitimacy. All that can be said as a matter of political fact is that patriation was opposed by the Parti Québecois government, predictably in my view, but also by a majority of the Liberal members of the National Assembly. My understanding of federalism as a system of divided sovereignty means that constitutional change must be approved by both levels of government, or at least by a majority of the provinces including the large ones. (I leave the detailed debate over the precise amending formula to rest in peace.) Therefore, by this standard, adding up the massive majority of federal MPs from Quebec to the handful who agreed with them in the National Assembly to assert that Quebec as a constituent part of the federation endorsed patriation and should be forever thankful for its arrival strains my understanding of federalism. At some point, if not in 1981–2, then later, a federalist government of Quebec would demand certain changes to the constitutional fabric of Canada and these would have to be considered.

However, let us saw off the interpretive differences that still abound about 1981–2, differences that, like Mr. Trudeau himself, 'haunt us still' and argue that patriation was not all that its principal architect could have wished. It was certainly not a complete success. Whole or partial failures then are the legacy of three decades of attempting to change formally the Canadian constitution.

In the wake of the referendum, two wrong conclusions commended themselves. One camp argued that if only Canadians went about formal amendments a different way, perhaps the next time they might be successful. If only this or that clause had been changed or added; if only this or that group had been present to represent additional 'interests'; if only the timing had been different; if only the personalities had been changed — the if-onlys are magnificent in their complexity and almost completely oblivious to the lessons of recent history.

The if-only school invites the country to yet another attempt to amend the Constitution formally in the hope that the next time success can replace repeated failure. The if-only school, of course, has been around for three decades in various guises, always giving the same advice. Politicians have repeatedly taken, or been tempted by, the advice and, therefore, launched fresh attempts to find a solution to Canada's tensions through formal constitutional amendments. After repeated failures, the cliché springs to life: 'Those who ignore the lessons of history are condemned to repeat them.' The most urgent lesson from the referendum, the previous constitutional failures, and the cleavages these efforts exposed is not that a new process, or this or that wording change, or some new constitutional formula, or a rehash of an old one will produce constitutional peace, but that the search itself through the venue of formal constitutional changes is too difficult, treacherous, and divisive to be attempted yet again.

Another school comprises those who counsel an extended reprieve from all constitutional debate. The most frequently heard comment following the referendum was that the issue would now be placed on the 'back burner.' This comment had the virtue of being true, but not for long. The social and economic pressures that gave rise to the constitutional debates will not disappear, nor will interest groups be silent. Western alienation, Aboriginal discontent, and Quebec restlessness will not go away simply because the Charlottetown Accord died. Pressures, therefore, will remain with us, mocking those who believe that in moving the Constitution to the 'back burner,' these pressures will likewise be shifted.

What the referendum ought to have taught the country, and especially those of us who have spent some of the best years of our lives labouring in the national-unity industry, is that these and other pressures are manifestly ill-suited for relief by formal constitutional amendments. Many of these pressures do not have their roots in the Constitution, although their relief has been wrongly described as running through the Constitution. The task, therefore, for concerned citizens is to recast the entire debate towards the alleviating of these pressures and to deal with real grievances by other means than formal constitutional amendments.

If Charlottetown and the thirty years of failure that preceded it teach the country nothing else, let it

be that the practice of enlightened politics and the delivery of sound government are better responses to national tensions than formal constitutional amendments. If that is the lesson taken from the Charlottetown debate, the country will save itself future grief and direct its energies into solutions that lie in the territory of the possible rather than search for constitutional castles in the sky.

I suspect that such a conclusion would produce a polarization of debate in Quebec, a polarization that many Quebeckers do not want. The defeats of Meech Lake and Charlottetown demonstrated that the rest of Canada is not impressed by Quebec's demands to change the constitutional status quo by formal amendments, particularly since such debates summon up the demons of regional grievances and highly symbolic issues in a country without a consensus on symbols of national life.

A few intellectuals believe that asymmetrical federalism enshrined in the Constitution can satisfy everyone: Quebeckers looking for quasi-independence, English Canadians searching for a strong central government, and Aboriginal Canadians demanding their own governments. The scarcity of common purpose upon which such a vision is built ensures that this model of federalism would not long survive and, anyway, the English-speaking part of Canada, having demonstrated its opposition to Quebec's more modest demands in Meech Lake and Charlottetown, is unlikely to accept Quebec's demands for something considerably more, up to and including asymmetrical federalism, as an operating and organizational principle of our national life. The rest of the country, having rebuffed Meech Lake and Charlottetown, is insisting that Quebec take the current constitutional arrangements and put them to the test in the confrontation with secession. It may be possible to bring administrative and pragmatic changes to the Canadian constitutional arrangements in the years before the showdown occurs, but these will not take the form of formal and sweeping constitutional changes.

The lesson from Charlottetown and Meech Lake is, therefore, that the rest of Canada would prefer Quebeckers to choose, but, of course, Quebeckers, with their innate preference for playing the angles and keeping options open, do not wish to make such a firm choice if they can avoid it.

(g)   Informal Changes[1]

As we have seen, formal constitutional amendments requiring the national or unanimity formulae are rare occurrences. They were difficult to implement in 1982, and are probably even more so now.[2] They are macro-scale national events, with multiple players and symbolic overtones. Change under the regional formula has been more common, but it is hardly an everyday event. Change under the internal formula is much easier, but many important constitutional topics lie beyond its reach.

In contrast, informal constitutional change[3] tends to be more ongoing, more gradual, lower in public profile, and easier to implement. The main informal means of bringing about constitutional change in Canada are judicial interpretation of the constitution, constitutional conventions, and (indirectly) political practice.

The work of the Judicial Committee provides a good example of the power of judicial interpretation to effect constitutional change.[4] Working from a framework document that left much unsaid, the Judicial Committee developed the foundations of Canadian federalism. In the process, they replaced Sir John A. Macdonald's centralized federalism with their own concept of coordinate federalism.

Subsequently, the Supreme Court of Canada has played an equally significant role.[5] Since becoming the highest judicial tribunal in 1949, the Supreme Court has moved federalism in a more flexible and more centralist direction. On at least two specific occasions, the court has set ground rules in major national political-constitutional debates. As well, the Court has made the *Canadian Charter of Rights and Freedoms* a leading element of Canadian public law.

Constitutional conventions[6] have played an important historic role in moving control of Canadian government from Great Britain, and from appointed officials to elected politicians. In the federal system, they have brought an end to top-down mechanisms of executive federalism and disallowance, making room for relationships based more on consultation and agreement. Regular first ministers' conferences, the practice of alternating between francophone and anglophone Supreme Court chief justices, and the regional representation in the federal Cabinet, are examples of political practices that have probably developed into

modern constitutional conventions. As noted in Chapter 10, a convention of public consultation may have emerged recently as a prerequisite to formal amendments with national scope.

Although political practice does not change the constitution directly, it can mature into constitutional conventions or lead to formal amendments that do produce this change. Much political practice with this potential is in the form of federal–provincial agreements. These include agreements on taxation,[7] immigration,[8] and labour market training,[9] the 1994 *Agreement on Internal Trade*,[10] the *Canada Wide Accord on Environmental Harmonization*,[11] and the 1999 *Framework Agreement on the Social Union*,[12] reproduced in Chapter 7.

Differences between the formal and informal means of constitutional change are sometimes matters of degree rather than kind. We have seen that formal changes range from the rigorous unanimity and national formula to the internal formula that requires nothing more than a federal or provincial statute. Conversely, some kinds of informal constitutional change may approach the macro, high-profile, or legislative quality of the higher-level formal amendments. Examples here are the Supreme Court's decisions in *Re Amendment to Constitution of Canada* and the *Quebec Secession Reference*, and the *Social Union* agreement. As in many areas of public law, the better model is not the dichotomy, but the spectrum.

Notes

1. See generally Garth Stevenson, "Canadian Federalism: The Myth of the Status Quo" in Janine Brodie & Linda Trimble, eds., *Reinventing Canada: Politics of the 21st Century* (Toronto: Prentice Hall, 2003) at 204; S.D. Schwendt, *Federal Constitutional Approaches to Quebec Nationalism and Litigation Approaches Since 1982* (M.A. Thesis, Carleton University, 1999) [unpublished]; Harvey Lazar, ed., *Canada and the State of the Federation 1997: Non-Constitutional Renewal* (Kingston: Queen's University Institute of Intergovernmental Relations, 1997).
2. Because of factors such as the emerging constitutional conventions of wide public consultation and the requirements of the federal *Constitutional Amendments Act*.
3. (That is, change that does not require procedures stipulated in Part V of the *Constitution Act, 1982*.)
4. See generally, Chapter 5.
5. See generally, Chapter 6.
6. See generally Andrew Heard, *Canadian Constitutional Conventions: The Marriage of Law and Politics* (Toronto: Oxford University Press, 1991); *Reference re Resolution to Amend the Constitution*, [1981] 1 S.C.R. 753; and Chapters 8 and 9.
7. See Hogg 2007, ch. 6.

8. See Kenneth McRoberts, *Misconceiving Canada: The Struggle for National Unity* (Don Mills, Ont.: Oxford University Press, 1997) at 152–53; H. Adelman, "Canada, Quebec, and Refugee Claimants" in Joseph H. Carens, ed., *Is Quebec Nationalism Just? Perspectives from Anglophone Canada* (Montreal & Kingston: McGill-Queen's University Press, 1995); and J. Carens, "Immigration, Political Community, and the Transformation of Identity: Quebec's Immigration Policies in Critical Perspective" in Carens, *ibid.*; K. McRoberts, "Unilateralism, Bilateralism, and Multilateralism: Approaches to Canadian Federalism" in Richard Simeon, *Intergovernmental Relations*, Collected Research Studies of the Royal Commission on the Economic Prospects for Canada, vol. 63 (Ottawa: Supply and Services Canada, 1985) at 90.

9. See H. Bakvis, "Federalism, New Public Management, and Labour Market development" in P. Fafard & D. Brown, eds., *Canada: State of the Federation 1996* (Kingston: Institute of Intergovernmental Relations, 1996), and Harvey Lazar, "The Federal Role in a New Social Union: Ottawa at a Crossroads" in Lazar, *supra* note 1, 104 at 114–118.

10. See R.H. Knox, "Economic Integration in Canada through the Agreement on Internal Trade" in Lazar, *supra* note 1 at 137. The Agreement came into effect on July 1, 1995.

11. In force January 29, 1998.

12. See J.-D. Bellavance, "Ministers sign deal without Bouchard" *National Post* (5 February 1999) A1.

(h)   Distinct Society and Nationhood Resolutions[†]

NOTE

After the *Constitution Act, 1982*, the province of Quebec demanded, among other things, that Quebec should be recognized as a distinct society. Formal distinct society provisions in the Meech Lake and Charlottetown accords were among the most controversial parts of those ill-fated initiatives. In the wake of the extraordinarily close vote in the Quebec secession referendum of 1995, the Chrétien government decided to address this demand by less formal means. To what extent was Quebec's demand met by the 1995 resolution below, and its companion resolution in the Canadian Senate?

On November 27, 2006, the House of Commons passed another special status resolution that appeared to go even further. Earlier that month, the Bloc Québécois party had moved that the House of Commons recognize Quebeckers "as a nation". In response, Prime Minister Harper introduced the motion, in the second extract below, that it be recognized that "the Québécois form a nation within a united Canada." The controversial resolution passed by 266 to 16. It prompted the resignation of the Conservative intergovernmental affairs minister, and was opposed by 15 opposition Liberal MPs. Academics said the motion would have no legal effect.[1] Some commentators consid-

ered the resolution a masterful strategic tactic. Others noted that it singled out an ethnic group and not the entire geographical entity of Quebec. Still others worried that it could raise expectations for formal moves toward secession in future.[2]

The 1995 and 2006 initiatives raise interesting questions about informal constitutional change. When does this kind of change accommodate and defuse constitutional conflict, and when does it buy time at the cost of greater conflict at a later date? The content of the initiatives raises questions as well. In particular, where should a society set the balance between accommodating difference and highlighting common concerns? This is an issue that underlies other majority–minority relationships as well.[3]

Notes

1. See, for example, Daniel LeBlanc, "Tories play down constitutional fall out[;] Nation motion lacks 'legal consequence,' minister, experts say" *The Globe and Mail* (24 November 2006) A4, online: Osgoode Hall Law School <http://osgoode.yorku.ca/media2.nsf/83303ffe5af03ed585256ae6005379c9/cfcfbf1cb4ebeddb852572300061a7ad!OpenDocument>.

2. See In Depth, "Québécois Nationhood? Canada Reacts" *CBC News* (23 November 2006), online: cbc.ca <http://www.cbc.ca/news/background/parliament39/quebecnation-reaction.html>.

3. See, for example, Alan Cairns, *Citizens Plus: Aboriginal Peoples and the Canadian State* (Vancouver: UBC Press, 2000); Will Kymlicka & Wayne Shapero, eds., *Citizenship in Diverse Societies* (New York: Oxford University Press,

---

† Tabled in the House of Commons by Prime Minister Jean Chrétien on 24 November 1995, and adopted by the House of Commons on 11 December 1995. An analogous resolution was adopted unanimously by the Senate on 14 December 1995.

2000), and Charles Taylor, "Democratic Exclusion (and its Remedies?)" in Alan Cairns *et al.*, eds., *Citizenship, Diversity and Pluralism: Canadian and Comparative Perspectives* (Montreal & Kingston: McGill-Queen's University Press, 1999).

EXTRACT

Distinct Society Resolution, adopted by House of Commons 11 December 1995

Whereas the people of Quebec have expressed the desire for recognition of Quebec's distinct society:

(1) the House recognize that Quebec is a distinct society within Canada.

(2) the House recognize that Quebec's distinct society includes its French-speaking majority, unique culture and civil law tradition.

(3) the House undertake to be guided by this reality.

(4) the House encourage all components of the legislative and executive branches of government to take note of this recognition and be guided in their conduct accordingly.

Nationhood Resolution, adopted by House of Commons 27 November 2006

That this House recognize that the Québécois form a nation within a united Canada.

(i) Incrementalism[†]

Roger Gibbins and Katherine Harmsworth

NOTE

Most informal constitutional and quasi-constitutional change is specific, gradual, and interstitial in nature. It could be described as incrementalism, in contrast to the wholesale macro formal change that was implemented in 1982, and was attempted unsuccessfully in 1987–90 and 1992. Is incrementalism a viable alternative to formal constitutional change? Like formal constitutional change, incrementalism has some characteristic strengths and weaknesses. Do you agree with those identified by Gibbons and Harmsworth? For example, does "incrementalist" necessarily equal "decentralist"? Do you agree with the claim by Gibbons and Harmsworth that "incrementalism may be the only game in town"? Assuming that this was true when they wrote, does it remain so today?

EXTRACT

Canadians face a perplexing dilemma in coming to grips with the results of the 1995 sovereignty refer-

endum in Quebec. Given the closeness of the result and the absence in subsequent polls of any signal of a significant decline in support for sovereignty,[1] there is a growing national consensus that the federal status quo must change. Bluntly put, the federalists will lose the next referendum unless they put something on the table other than the status quo and threats about the dire economic consequences of a 'yes' vote.

Yet belief in the need for change is coupled with pessimism about the possibility of achieving change, or at least constitutional change. This pessimism springs in part from the failure of past efforts at what Peter Russell has called 'mega-constitutional change.'[2] Here, the Meech Lake and Charlottetown Accords loom large, although the *Constitution Act, 1982* counts among the failures for Quebec nationalists and Charter-skeptics in English Canada. These failures — particularly the referendum rejection of the Charlottetown Accord — also undermined public confidence in executive federalism as a vehicle for constitutional renewal, and thereby appear to have left Canada without a viable constitutional process.[3]

---

† Excerpts from "Time Out: Assessing Strategies for Enhancing the Canadian Political Union," in D.R. Cameron, *The Referendum Papers: Essays on Secession and National Unity* (Toronto: University of Toronto Press, 1999) at 49, 51–52, 56–59, 61, 77–82. Reproduced with permission of C.D. Howe Institute.

There is, then, a sense that Canada 'can't get there from here' because the constitutional process has broken down and nothing has been put in its place. As a consequence, the belief in the need for change, combined with pessimism about the possibility of change, has given birth to a renewal strategy based on cautious incrementalism. If mega-constitutional change is impossible and the status quo is unacceptable, the only option appears to be incrementalism pursued through conventional political processes. As a recent editorial in the *Calgary Herald* concluded, '[Canadians] need to seek smaller, more realistic compromises rather than attempting to take giant steps forward together into the unknown.'[4]

. . . .

The results of the Quebec referendum have sparked another round in the ongoing debate on redesigning the Canadian federal state: from this round, a rough-and-ready consensus is emerging on the components of an incremental strategy. This consensus is anchored by a commitment to greater decentralization, including a respect for provincial legislative autonomy and the rollback of federal intrusions stemming from the spending power. The consensus is also anchored by a reliance on intergovernmentalism, by the faith that executive provincialism can replace many of the integrative functions performed in the past by the central government. While decentralization and intergovernmentalism are not always linked in the renewal debate, it is the thesis of this *Commentary* that they are yoked in the incremental strategy.

Rebalancing the Federation

Decentralization is generally addressed under the rubric of rebalancing, which is seen as the means to create a new partnership between the provincial and federal governments. For example, taking an approach that is typical among proponents of decentralization, the participants at the Confederation 2000 conference observed that the purpose of rebalancing would be to provide greater clarity in the functions of the two orders of government and to reduce overlap and duplication, thereby allowing governments to focus more effectively on their respective roles and responsibilities.[10] The participants recommended that rebalancing be achieved through devolving powers to the provinces, curtailing the federal spending power, and increasing provincial input with regard to national standards, new national programs, and national economic management. In these respects,

the Confederation 2000 participants were also typical of decentralization's proponents: with very few exceptions (discussed below), rebalancing is sought through a uni-directional shift in responsibility from Ottawa to the provinces. Overlap and duplication are to be pruned by cutting back on the activities of the federal government, not on those of the provinces.

Proponents of this approach usually call for greater decentralization in at least the following areas: labor market training: natural resources (such as forestry and mining); recreation; tourism; housing; and municipal and urban affairs. There is also moderate support among participants in the informal renewal debate for some measure of decentralization in other jurisdictional domains. Jean Chevrier, for instance, draws on 30 years of constitutional analysis to recommend that language, culture, and communications be managed concurrently, with federal or provincial paramountcy being stipulated.[11] Others support the expanded use of concurrent powers in a renewed federation, but with the specific intent of extending provincial influence.[12] A default legislative role for the federal government would be retained, albeit one tied to a more restricted spending power. In a similar vein are suggestions to curb the federal spending power by replacing transfer payments with tax points. For example, the Reform Party recommends that federal block grants to the provinces be replaced with tax points, established as a fixed percentage of federal tax revenue.[13] Thomas Courchene sees tax point replacements as an indispensable element of a reformed federal state.[14]

. . . .

All of the above feeds into the inevitable debate on national standards. As earlier constitutional debates were opened up to a wider range of participants, the protection of national standards and the role of the federal government in so doing provoked major controversy. However, in the more constrained intergovernmental environment that shapes the current debate, incremental reform proposals are pursuing a different theme: *national standards need not be federal government standards.* Indeed, in the more radical of the recent Courchene recommendations, the federal government would not even be involved in setting or enforcing national standards. Jim Gray, in line with the less radical of Courchene's proposals, has commented on the need to create minimum standards that would be mutually agreed on by Ottawa and the provinces. National standards unilaterally imposed by Ottawa, he argues, contribute to national disunity.[31]

. . . .

It must be stressed that greater provincial asymmetry with respect to social programs and standards is not only the inevitable result of greater decentralization; it is the very goal of such a shift. As Courchene points out, 'any notion of identical standards across all provinces is a non-starter.'[40] Decentralization makes sense if one recognizes that provinces *are* and *should be* significantly different with respect to social programs and economic management. Only then is federalism's potential for policy innovation and experimentation fully unleashed. Formal constitutional symmetry might be maintained in a more decentralized federation, but symmetry of result is incompatible with the logic of decentralization....

. . . .

If Canada is to move beyond its current crisis to a renewed federation, some mechanism must aid the transition....

. . . .

[Gibbons and Harmsworth say that incremental reform strategy relies heavily on the use of intergovernmental coordinating and decision-making bodies].

... We would argue ... that a greater reliance on intergovernmental mechanisms would erode the role of legislative assemblies and weaken democratic accountability. The result — if not necessarily the intention — of intergovernmentalism is to remove government from public forums rather than to increase democratic participation. We would also argue, although Chevrier disagrees, that intergovernmentalism will increase the complexity of government by imposing a new layer of government forums and their attendant bureaucracies between the federal and provincial governments.

Despite such concerns, there is no question that a greater reliance on intergovernmentalism forms one of the two principal anchors for the incremental strategy. Decentralization forms the other. What is interesting to note, however, is that some tension exists between the two. If intergovernmentalism is taken too far, if it includes decision rules that can force compliance on dissenting provinces, then intergovernmentalism may constitute a new variant of centralism that could negate the policy flexibility associated with decentralization. Thus, the gains accruing to the provinces through decentralization could be lost to new intergovernmental agreements and councils. It is not surprising, therefore, that strong proponents of decentralization like Premier Klein are uneasy about having compliance mechanisms attached to intergovernmental councils or agreements. But without compliance mechanisms, intergovernmentalism may prove to be a hollow shell rather than an effective means of governance for the next century....

. . . .

The heavy reliance on intergovernmentalism found in the federal vision that is embedded within the incremental strategy is not alien to Canadian political practice. Furthermore, the incremental strategy's symmetrical approach and its avoidance of formal constitutional change will appeal to many Canadians and to their governments. It must also be kept in mind, as the proponents of decentralization are quick to point out, that national standards and the internal common market might be sustained through interprovincial cooperation: intergovernmentalism might replace the heavy hand of Ottawa. While this latter scenario must be seen not as a conclusion well anchored in Canadian political experience but as an article of faith, it is not an unreasonable one.

For the reasons outlined in this *Commentary*, the incremental strategy may be the only game in town — particularly so long as

- the reform debate remains a relatively muted concern of governments that is not subjected to wide-ranging public scrutiny; and
- the debate remains directed toward the next referendum in Quebec and is therefore tightly constrained by the options palatable to federalist forces in Quebec.

Nonetheless, or perhaps as a consequence, a number of important questions should be addressed before Canadians fully embrace the incremental strategy and its twin pillars, decentralization and intergovernmentalism.

First, does the incremental strategy offer a *stable* solution with respect to Quebec, one that takes Canada past the upcoming federal election and even past the next sovereignty referendum? Can symmetrical decentralization go far enough to derail the sovereignty movement? More important, can intergovernmentalism be structured in a way that provides effective political space for Quebec sovereignty? If the answer to any of these questions is no, Canada may not be heading for a stable situation. If the incremental strategy does not offer some reasonable assurance of keeping Quebec in Canada, its outcomes must be assessed on another criterion: as an appropriate blueprint for a Canada without Quebec. Failure to assess decentralization and intergovernmentalism against this criterion would leave the rest of Canada ill-prepared should Quebec nationalists decide that they are not prepared to submerge their province in new intergovernmental forums within which they might exercise less influence than they do in Parliament today.

Second, can the combination of decentralization and intergovernmentalism sustain citizenship ties between individual Canadians and their federal government? If such ties are increasingly mediated through intergovernmental forums and agreements, with federal representatives exercising less autonomous and accountable political authority, will Canadians come to see the federal government *and the national community for which it speaks* as less relevant for their lives? In that case, will there also be a weakening of citizen support for the principle of equalization, for the protection of mobility rights, or for the reduction of interprovincial trade barriers?

Third, does the *combination* of decentralization and intergovernmentalism produce a significant democratic deficit? Does it move decisionmaking to those forums least open to public participation, thereby diluting electoral accountability with forums that answer to no single electorate? If the answer to each of these [questions] is yes, it might be wise to consider the advantages of decentralization without the encumbrances of intergovernmentalism. Maybe Premier Klein is right in arguing that decentralization should mean provincial control without the imposition of national standards. While this option would inevitably produce greater regional diversity, it would also maintain electoral accountability. If the destination of decentralization is government that is closer to the people, intergovernmentalism may be the wrong route to follow. A large dose of intergovernmentalism may be inevitable and essential in complex federal states, but intergovernmentalism must also be recognized as a new form of centralism that could potentially reduce democratic control while negating many of the advantages of decentralization.

Fourth, will the incremental strategy preclude rather than establish the preconditions for significant constitutional and institutional reform? If so, will the Canadian federal state be well equipped to handle the political challenges of the next century? The incremental strategy is likely to be an alternative to rather than a step toward intrastate reform. However, to assume that parliamentary institutions should remain untouched, that all Canada needs to do is impose an additional layer of intergovernmental institutions between the federal and provincial governments, seems unimaginative and premature.

Fifth, can a way be found to bring Canadians back into a renewal debate that is cast in incrementalist terms? If the renewal debate withdraws once again behind closed doors, if it becomes the fodder for intergovernmental discussions rather than public debate, there is some risk that the final product will face public repudiation should Canadians find the opportunity to express themselves.

Finally, will the incremental strategy enhance the political union? The answer to this last question depends on how one positions oneself on the contemporary political landscape. In many respects, incrementalism will reinforce more than threaten the status quo. It builds on constitutional principles rejected by the Canadian public but embraced as dogma by political elites; it enhances the influence of governments at the expense of citizens; and it retains federalist support in Quebec as the criterion against which the health of the Canadian political community is to be assessed. Some will equate these effects with enhancing the political union. However, those whose primary political identity is not to be found in provincial communities, who seek greater citizen leverage on Canada's constitutional evolution, and who desire to transcend rather than consolidate duality may be excused a good measure of skepticism. As in most situations, where one stands on incrementalism depends on where, and how comfortably, one sits.

None of this is to say that the products of the incremental strategy — decentralization and intergovernmentalism — are ill conceived or necessarily pernicious in their effects. Indeed, they may simply be inevitable. Nonetheless, the questions posed above should be addressed before Canada moves too far and too quickly down the incremental path. Incrementalism is more than a process. It is also a destination that must be held up to careful *public* debate before Canada has gone too far down the path to change direction.

Notes

1. In a poll of 1,001 Quebec voters conducted by Groupe Léger between September 20 and 29, 1996, 49.4 percent of decided voters said they would vote 'yes' in a referendum on sovereignty, while 50.6 percent would vote 'no' (Richard Mackie, 'Quebecers want votes delayed,' *Globe and Mail* [Toronto], October 4, 1996, p. A1).

2. Peter H. Russell, *Constitutional Odyssey: Can Canadians Become a Sovereign People?* 2nd ed. (Toronto: University of Toronto Press, 1993).

3. This lack of confidence was symbolized at the June 1996 First Ministers' Conference by Alberta Premier Ralph Klein's refusal to address constitutional matters behind closed doors. Klein's resolve on this point was not severely tested, but there is little doubt that his refusal captured the public mood.

4. 'Disunity train.' *Calgary Herald*, August 23, 1996, p. A16.

...

10. Confederation 2000, *Today and Tomorrow: An Agenda for Action* (May 3–4, 1996), p. 6.

11. Jean Chevrier, 'What Commissions and Task Forces Have Said about Renewing Canada.' *The New Federation* 5 (July/August 1996): 13.

12. Thomas Courchene, for example, has proposed that concurrent powers be associated with provincial paramountcy (*In Praise of Renewed Federalism*, The Canada Round 2 [Toronto: C.D. Howe Institute, 1991], p. 89).

13. Reform Party of Canada, *Twenty Proposals for a New Confederation* (Calgary: Reform Party of Canada, 1996), p. 10.

14. Thomas J. Courchene. *ACCESS: A Convention on the Canadian Economic and Social Systems* (working paper prepared for the Ontario Ministry of Intergovernmental Affairs, August 1996), p. 18.

...

31. Canada West Foundation, *Realizing Change '96–'97* (Calgary: Canada West Foundation, 1996), p. 4.

...

40. Courchene, *ACCESS*, p. 5.

12 Secession, Unity, and the Future

(a) Introduction

Canada's constitutional journey through the 1990s was as turbulent as in the decades before. Brief moments of hope alternated with crises that threatened to end the country. In 1995, the residents of Quebec, the second most populous province, defeated a secession proposal by a majority of only 50.6%. The province's Parti Québécois party vowed to conduct another referendum on secession as soon as "winning conditions" permitted, a promise that was reaffirmed in the years that followed.[1]

On the other hand, United Nations surveys repeatedly ranked Canada as one of the best countries in which to live.[2] Refugees and immigrants continued to move to Canada from all corners of the world. In 1996–97, all Canadian first ministers, including the Premier of Quebec, took part in a joint trade mission to Asia. Despite the unresolved constitutional differences, many individuals retained the traditional Canadian qualities of tolerance and goodwill.[3]

Rather than trying to explain this paradox[4] or predict its outcome, this chapter notes some key recent constitutional developments and issues in regard to secession, Canadian unity, the role of law and courts, and the future.

Notes

1. Premier Bouchard said in 1995 that another secession referendum would be held when the "winning conditions" were in place. In 2005, Premier Bouchard's successor Bernard Landry said there would be a referendum only if the government had the "moral reassurance" of winning it. The Parti Québécois was defeated in the 2003 provincial election and reduced to third party status in the election of March 2007. The new P.Q. leader, Pauline Marois,

said there would be a referendum when Quebeckers were "ready" for sovereignty: "The referendum paradigm" *The Globe and Mail* (15 May 2007) A4. Although the federalist Liberals were reelected in the spring of 2007, there was a sharp rise in support for the Action démocratique du Québec. This party was committed to Quebec "autonomy" — an uncertain stage between federalism and outright independence: see Carole Beaulieu & Michel Vastel, "Le Nouveau Pouvoir du Mario" *L'actualité* 32:8 (15 May 2007) 18 at 20.

2. In the 2006 United Nations Human Development Index, Canada ranked in sixth place out of 177 countries in terms of living conditions, topped only by Norway (first place), Australia, Iceland, Ireland, and Sweden: United Nations, *Human Development Report 2006: Human Development Index* <http://hdr.undp.org/hdr2006/statistics/indicators/indicators_table.cfm>. Over the past 10 years, Canada has ranked among the top 10 countries in the world, sometimes standing in first place. See also D. Bueckert, "UN report cause for both pride and pain" *CP Newstext* (11 July 1999, 16.09 EST): "For the sixth consecutive year, Canada was first in the UN Human Development Index, the most sophisticated measure of a country's well-being. However, it didn't do as well when it came to dealing with poverty [where Canada was in ninth place]. The index measures quality of life in different countries by combining data on life expectancy, per-capita income and access to education." The Index includes life expectancy, educational attainment, and adjusted real incomes. On another front, the World Economic Forum ranked Canada as standing fourth in the world in international economic competitiveness: J. McFarland, *The [Toronto] Globe and Mail*, "Canada changed to get into top ranks" *Canadian Press Newstext* (25 May 1997) (QL).

3. Note, for example, the outpouring of support and sympathy across the country for former separatist leader Lucien Bouchard during his near-fatal bacterial infection in December 1995: "Bouchard symposium" *Canadian Press* (3 December 1996).

4. For a discussion of the historic concerns of French-speaking people, see Chapter 9. Chapters 10 and 11 address constitutional developments and issues in the post-1982 period. As the material in the present chapter suggests, the grievances did not disappear after 1982.

(b)   From Referendum to *Reference*[†]

REFERENDUMS:[1] HISTORY

The immediate impetus behind the constitutional reforms of 1982, which led in turn to the reform attempts of 1987 and 1992, was a constitutional referendum in the province of Quebec. What exactly is a referendum? What role have referendums played in Canadian constitutional history? A brief look at these issues will provide some background to the Quebec secession referendum of 1995.

A referendum is a direct vote on a public issue by the public at large. It can be contrasted with a vote on a resolution or bill by an elected legislator. Although technically referendums are more specific in content and more likely to be binding than plebiscites,[2] in Canada the terms tend to be used interchangeably.[3] Referendums may involve constitutional or non-constitutional issues. We will focus here on referendums with constitutional content or implications, especially those that relate to the issue of the province of Quebec's possible secession from Canada.

Although there have been three national referendums in Canada, only the most recent involved a constitutional issue. The first, in 1898, was on prohibition;[4] the second, in 1942, was on conscription;[5] and the third, in 1992, was on the proposed Charlottetown Accord. Technically, the latter referendum canvassed residents of all provinces except Quebec. However, it was conducted jointly and simultaneously with an identical referendum under Quebec law, and the results of the two were tabulated on a national basis.[6]

At the provincial level, in addition to the Quebec component of the Charlottetown referendums, there have been three constitutional referendums in Newfoundland (two in 1948 about entry into Confederation,[7] and one in 1996 about changes to denominational schools),[8] and also two Quebec referendums on the secession of Quebec from Canada held in 1980 and 1995. The Parti Québécois of Quebec has promised to hold a third referendum on secession.

STATUS AND EFFECT

Referendums may be required legally by statute, and they might be required politically, in some cases, as a matter of constitutional convention. At the statutory level, two provinces have laws that require referendums prior to the adoption of constitutional amendments.[9] Nationally, the Meech Lake and Charlottetown experiences may have given rise to a constitutional convention regarding referendums. It may be that before trying to implement major formal constitutional change in future, governments will be expected to obtain public approval by way of referendums.

What is the effect of a referendum? Subject to the Constitution, a referendum is a consultative mechanism. Normally, then, its results are only binding if a statute so provides. Even in this situation, the Constitution can limit the effect of a referendum. For example, a referendum cannot bypass the need for the Lieutenant Governor's assent to legislation.[10]

Can the Constitution give binding legal effect to referendums? Prior to the Supreme Court's 1998 decision in the *Quebec Secession Reference*,[11] the answer to this was, clearly, "No". Even today, no referendum can constitutionally impose a particular kind of result. Nevertheless, as will be seen, certain kinds of constitutional referendums and positive referendum results can give rise to more indirect legal obligations.

To the extent that legal obligations are attached to referendums, it is especially important to be able to determine what constitutes a positive referendum result. Fifty percent plus one? A higher threshold? A threshold that varies with the circumstances? As will be seen, this issue was raised,

---

[†]   Dyck, at 389–96; MacIvor, ch. 2: "Representative Democracy vs. Direct Democracy"; Monahan, ch. 13; Craig Forcese & Aaron Freeman, *The Laws of Government: The Legal Foundations of Canadian Democracy* (Toronto: Irwin Law, 2005), ch. 3(E)7; Brooks, ch. 5: "Citizen Participation in Constitutional Reform"; and Patrick J. Boyer, *Direct Democracy in Canada: The History and Future of Referendums* (Toronto: Dundurn Press, 1992). See also Peter H. Russell, *Constitutional Odyssey: Can Canadians Become a Sovereign People?*, 2d ed. (Toronto: University of Toronto Press, 1993) at ch. 11. For very recent developments, it is especially important to supplement readings in standard texts with journal, Internet, and media sources.

but not answered, in the *Quebec Secession Reference*.[12]

THE 1980 QUEBEC REFERENDUM

The wording of a referendum can have an important effect on its outcome. For example, polls have indicated that the residents of Quebec are much less likely to respond positively to a question about complete independence than to a more modest proposal for Quebec independence with economic and other ties to the rest of Canada. Similarly, a question about a mandate to negotiate a change asks less than a question seeking a mandate to make that change outright. The wording of the 1980 Quebec secession referendum reflected this fact. It said:

> The government of Quebec has made public its proposal to negotiate a new agreement with the rest of Canada, based on the equality of nations.
>
> This agreement would enable Quebec to acquire the exclusive power to make its laws, administer its taxes and establish relations abroad — in other words, sovereignty — and at the same time, to maintain with Canada an economic association including a common currency.
>
> Any change in political status resulting from these negotiations will be submitted to the people through a referendum.
>
> On these terms, do you agree to give the government the mandate to negotiate the proposed agreement between Quebec and Canada?

The referendum was held on May 20, 1980. Eighty percent of Quebec's 4.4 million voters voted. Of these, 59.5% voted "no", and 40.5% voted "yes". During the referendum campaign federal Liberals had campaigned strenuously in favour of the "no" vote. They promised massive constitutional change to accommodate Quebec's concerns, in the event of a "no" vote. There was a "no" vote, and the result was the *Constitution Act, 1982*, agreed to, ironically, by every province except Quebec.

THE 1995 QUEBEC REFERENDUM

A year after the failure of the Charlottetown Accord on October 26, 1992, a federal election returned a massive Liberal majority. The new Prime Minister, Mr. Jean Chrétien, said he was in no hurry to try more formal constitutional change. However, the election also produced a precedent in Canadian history: an official opposition party dedicated officially to secession. Ironically, the leader of the pro-separatist Bloc Québécois was the charismatic former federal Cabinet minister, Mr. Lucien Bouchard. The following year, in 1994, the pro-separatist Parti Québécois were elected to power in Quebec.

On December 6, 1994, Premier Jacques Parizeau proposed a second referendum on Quebec sovereignty.[13] It would ask Quebekers, "Are you in favour of the Act passed by the National Assembly declaring the sovereignty of Quebec?" The "Act" referred to was a draft bill on Quebec sovereignty,[14] to come into effect after a positive referendum vote. After the achievement of sovereignty, the government of Quebec would be authorized to conclude an economic association agreement with the rest of Canada. On June 12, 1995, the leaders of the Parti Québécois, the Bloc Québécois, and the Action Démocratique came to a tripartite agreement[15] on a revised secession plan.

On September 7, the Parti Québécois tabled Bill 1, *An Act respecting the future of Quebec*,[16] in the National Assembly. Bill 1 was accompanied by the following referendum question:

> Do you agree that Québec should become sovereign, after having made a formal offer to Canada for a new Economic and Political Partnership, within the scope of the Bill respecting the future of Québec and of the agreement signed on June 12, 1995?

There was much more emphasis on association with the rest of Canada than in the earlier version. After a positive referendum result, the government of Quebec would be required to propose a treaty on economic and political partnership with the rest of Canada *before* declaring the sovereignty of Quebec. The stress throughout was on partnership, trade, joint institutions, and preserving the benefits of the *status quo*. Buried in this wording, though, was an important provision. If the treaty negotiations proved fruitless — in the view of the National Assembly after consulting a Quebec government-appointed committee — the National Assembly could declare the sovereignty of Quebec. This amounted to a claim to be able to unilaterally declare independence.

The referendum debate was an emotional affair. The Parti Québécois suggested that their proposal offered Quebekers the best of both worlds. The fact that secession-and-partnership assumed the agreement of the rest of Canada was treated as a detail. The federal finance minister warned that citizens of a separate Quebec state would lose their Canadian passports, and the right to the benefits of the Canadian economic union. Bloc Québécois leader Lucien Bouchard responded by suggesting that if the rest of Canada did not negotiate with Quebec, Quebec might not pay its share of the national debt.

As the campaign wore on, the "No" side began to trail in the opinion polls. Then, at a "No" rally speech on October 24, Prime Minister Chrétien promised to keep open all avenues of change, including constitutional and administrative change.[17] On October 30, 1995, Quebekers said "No" to the sovereignty referendum question. However, they said no by a much narrower margin than in 1980:[18] by 50.58% to 49.42%.[19]

Just over 50,000 votes — less than the number of spoiled ballots — separated the two sides. All regions of Quebec except Montreal, the eastern townships, the Outaouais, and far northern Quebec voted "yes".[20] Although non-French-speaking voters voted overwhelmingly "no", about 60% of French-speaking voters voted "yes".[21]

Premier Parizeau resigned shortly after the referendum and was replaced by the Bloc Québécois leader Lucien Bouchard. Both said there would be another referendum.[22] Meanwhile, the federal government announced specific measures to implement the Prime Minister's referendum campaign promise of change.[23] In December 1995, the Senate and the House of Commons passed distinct society resolutions[24] that recognized "that Quebec is a distinct society within Canada" and that "Quebec's distinct society includes its French-speaking minority, unique culture and civil law tradition." In February 1996, Parliament enacted a statute providing that the federal government would not propose an amendment to the Constitution of Canada (other than an amendment that a province could veto or dissent from) without the support of Ontario, Quebec, British Columbia, at least two Atlantic provinces with a combined population of more than 50% of that of all the Atlantic provinces, and at least two Prairie provinces with a combined population of more than 50% of that of all the Prairie provinces.[25] By the first part of 1997, the federal government had entered into federal–provincial agreements devolving control of labour market training to eight provinces including Quebec.[26]

The Quebec Liberal party claimed that these measures were not enough, that there must be a constitutional recognition of Quebec's position as a distinct society, and a constitutional veto for Quebec. Outside Quebec, polls indicated that a majority of Canadians opposed constitutional recognition of distinct society status for Quebec. Once again, formal constitutional change was being proposed, and once again there was the prospect that what might be too little for Quebec could be too much for the rest of Canada.

BERTRAND LITIGATION

A month before the introduction of Quebec's Bill 1, former sovereigntist-turned-federalist, Mr. Guy Bertrand, began a court challenge against the draft bill and the proposed sovereignty process.[27] Mr. Bertrand won an interim victory on August 31, 1995, when the Quebec Superior Court rejected an attempt by the Quebec government to stop the court action.[28] Lesage J. said that the legislature was not wholly immune to the *Charter* by virtue of parliamentary privilege; that it was not clear that the province's unilateral secession would be recognized in international law; and that there were some important constitutional questions here that merited an answer. When court proceedings resumed on September 5, the Quebec government withdrew from them.

Meanwhile, on September 8, 1995, Mr. Bertrand failed in his Superior Court effort to halt the referendum by means of an interim injunction.[29] Lesage J. said courts should not interfere with the right of the people to express themselves or intrude unduly into the legislative branch of government. On the other hand, Lesage J. did grant Mr. Bertrand a declaration that the proposed sovereignty bill, which would permit a proclamation of Quebec sovereignty outside the amending procedure in the *Constitution Act, 1982*, "constitutes a serious threat to the rights and freedoms of the plaintiff guaranteed by the *Canadian Charter of Rights and Freedoms*." A week before the vote, there was another constitutional challenge to the sovereignty legislation and process, this time by members of a Canadian unity group.[30]

As seen, the referendum went ahead, and was defeated by the narrowest of margins. Although Bill 1 died on the order paper after the referendum defeat, the Parti Québécois said there would be another referendum when the conditions were right. Meanwhile, Mr. Bertrand continued his battle, seeking declarations and permanent injunctions.

FEDERAL INTERVENTION

Pressure mounted on the federal government either to participate in further stages of the *Bertrand* litigation, or to refer its own questions about the legality of Quebec secession to the Supreme Court of Canada. On May 10, 1996, the federal Minister of Justice announced that the federal government would be represented in the motion to dismiss the *Bertrand* action.[31] On August 30, 1996, Mr. Pidgeon J. of the Quebec Superior Court rejected the Quebec Attorney General's motion to dismiss.[32]

After explaining the role of the courts in protecting the rule of law, Pidgeon J. decided that Quebec had not made the case that the action should be dismissed at this preliminary stage of the proceedings. In response to the Quebec government's argument that the issue was now moot, Pidgeon J. noted that the Legislative Assembly had treated the sovereignty project as still very much alive after the referendum. He said that even if the issue had become moot, on constitutional issues a trial judge would have a discretion to proceed. Pidgeon J. said that in this case, Mr. Bertrand had raised some constitutional questions that merited resolution on the merits:

- Is the right to self-determination synonymous with the right to secede?
- Can Quebec secede from Canada unilaterally?
- Is the process of Quebec's accession to sovereignty sanctioned by international law?
- Does international law have precedence over domestic law?

In September 1996, yet another sovereignty referendum seemed possible. The federal Justice Minister said that the federal government would refer the question of the constitutional or international law validity of unilateral Quebec secession to the Supreme Court of Canada.[33] On September 30, 1996, acting pursuant to s. 53 of the *Supreme Court Act*, the Governor in Council submitted the following reference questions to the Supreme Court of Canada:

> Under the Constitution of Canada, can the National Assembly, legislature or government of Quebec effect the secession of Quebec from Canada unilaterally?
>
> Does international law give the National Assembly, legislature or government of Quebec the right to effect the secession of Quebec from Canada unilaterally? In this regard, is there a right to self-determination under international law that would give the National Assembly, legislature or government of Quebec the right to effect the secession of Quebec from Canada unilaterally?
>
> In the event of a conflict between domestic and international law on the right of the National Assembly, legislature or government of Quebec to effect the secession of Quebec from Canada unilaterally, which would take precedence in Canada?[34]

Once again, the judiciary was drawn to the centre of Canada's troubled public law.[35]

Notes

1. See, for example, Richard Johnston, *The Challenge of Direct Democracy: The 1992 Canadian Referendum* (Montreal & Kingston: McGill-Queen's University Press, 1996); Pierre Marquis for Library of Parliament Research Branch, *Referendums in Canada* (Ottawa: Supply and Services Canada, 1994); Patrick Boyer, *The People's Mandate: Referendums and a More Democratic Canada* (Toronto: Dundurn Press, 1992); Mollie Dunsmuir for Library of Parliament Research Branch, *Referendums: the Canadian Experience in an International Context* (Ottawa: Supply and Services Canada, 1992); J. Patrick Boyer, *Lawmaking by the People: Referendums and Plebiscites in Canada* (Toronto: Butterworths, 1982).
2. For contrasting distinctions, see Boyer, *ibid.*, 1992, at 23–26.
3. A point conceded by Boyer.
4. Forty-four percent of eligible Canadian voters participated. Of these, 51% voted "yes", and 49% voted "no": V. Lemieux, revised by S.J.R. Noel, "Referendum" in James H. Marsh, ed., *The Canadian Encyclopedia*, Year 2000 ed. (Toronto: McClelland & Stewart, 1999).
5. Over 60% of the voters who participated voted "yes", and under 40% voted "no". In Quebec, the proportions were more than reversed. Over 70% of Quebekers opposed conscription: *ibid.*
6. Altogether, 75% of eligible voters participated. Of these, 54.4% voted against the Accord, and 44.6% voted for it: *ibid.*
7. The referendums were held on June 23, 1948, and July 22, 1948. In the first, none of the options produced an absolute majority. In the second, 52.3% voted in favour of Confederation, and 46.7% voted against it: *ibid.*
8. A majority of those who participated supported the proposed changes: *ibid.*
9. See B.C. *Constitutional Amendment Approval Act*, R.S.B.C. 1996, c. 67; Alberta *Constitutional Referendum Act*, R.S.A. 1980, c. 25.
10. *Re Initiative and Referendum*, [1919] A.C. 103 at 111, 112 (J.C.P.C.).
11. *Reference re the Secession of Quebec*, [1998] 2 S.C.R. 217.
12. *Ibid.*
13. Note: For many of the legal elements of the chronology that follows, the writer is indebted to the detailed account in the Statement of Facts of the "Factum of the Attorney General of Canada" filed with the Supreme Court of Canada on February 28, 1997, in connection with the federal Cabinet's reference to the Supreme Court of questions relating to Quebec's unilateral secession.
14. *An Act respecting the sovereignty of Québec*. The Explanatory Notes accompanying the draft bill said its goal was that Quebec become a "sovereign country".
15. Agreement between Parti Québécois, Bloc Québécois, and Action Démocratique ratified by Messrs. Jacques

Parizeau, Lucien Bouchard, and Mario Dumont on June 12, 1995.

16. Bill 1, *An Act respecting the future of Québec*, 1st Sess., 35th Leg., Quebec, 1995.

17. B. Cox, "Chrétien upbeat, urged calm as he prepared to address nation" *Canadian Press* (25 October 1995). (The Prime Minister's televised October 25 speech to the nation did not repeat his earlier promise of possible constitutional change.)

18. As seen above, the vote in 1980 was 59.5% to 40.5% against a more tentatively worded referendum proposal — for a mandate to negotiate a sovereignty-association agreement with the rest of Canada. By way of comparison, in the Charlottetown Accord referendum of October 26, 1992, 72% of the Canadian electorate cast ballots, with 54.3% voting "no" and 44.7% voting "yes". Four provinces and one territory voted "yes", but in Ontario the "yes" side had a majority of only 50.1%. Six provinces, including Quebec, voted "no": Curtis Cook, "Introduction: Canada's Predicament" in Curtis Cook, ed., *Constitutional Predicament: Canada after the Referendum of 1992* (Montreal & Kingston: McGill-Queen's University Press, 1994), Table 1, at 7.

19. Quebec, *Rapport des résultats officiels du scrutin: référendum du 30 octobre 1995* (Quebec: Directeur général des élections du Québec, November 1995). For a general account of the referendum campaign and its immediate outcome, see Robert J. Jackson & Doreen Jackson, *Canadian Government in Transition: Disruption and Continuity* (Scarborough, Ont.: Prentice Hall, 1996) at 105–15.

20. *Ibid.* at 110. In separate non-governmental referendums held earlier, the Cree and Inuit of the northwestern part of the province voted — heavily — against the secession proposal.

21. *Ibid.*

22. Speeches by Messrs. Parizeau and Bouchard on October 30, 1995.

23. See B. Cox, "Ottawa to give Quebec distinct society status, provide regional veto" *Canadian Press* (27 November 1995), referring to a federal announcement on that day. In November the federal government also made a commitment to withdraw from labour market training.

24. The House of Commons distinct society resolution was passed on December 11, 1996, with both the Bloc Québécois and the Reform Party voting against it. A similar resolution was passed unanimously by the Senate on December 14, 1995.

25. *An Act Respecting Constitutional Amendments*, S.C 1996, c. C-1.

26. By the end of April 1997, agreements had been signed with all provinces except Saskatchewan and Ontario. The agreement with Quebec was signed on April 21, 1997.

27. Mr. Bertrand filed an action in the Quebec Superior Court for a declaration, a permanent injunction, and interlocutory relief to challenge and stop the 1994 Draft Bill and the proposed process for moving to sovereignty: *Bertrand v. Bégin* (10 August 1995) Québec 200-05-002117-955 (Q.C.S.). The Quebec Attorney-General, Mr. Paul Bégin, responded by filing a motion to dismiss the *Bertrand* motion for interlocutory relief: *Bertrand v. Bégin* (24 August 1995) Québec 200-05-002117-955 (Q.C.S.).

28. Lesage J. rejected the Quebec Attorney General's motion to dismiss, and agreed to hear Mr. Bertrand's motion for an interlocutory injunction and declaration: *Bertrand v. Quebec (A.G.)* (1995), 127 D.L.R. (4th) 408 (S.C.C.).

29. On August 10, 1995, Mr. Bertrand filed an action in the Quebec Superior Court for a declaration, a permanent injunction, and interlocutory relief to challenge and stop the 1994 Draft Bill and the proposed process for moving to sovereignty: *Bertrand v. Bégin* (10 August 1995) Québec 200-05-002117-955 (Q.C.S.). The Quebec Attorney-General, Mr. Paul Bégin, responded by filing a motion to dismiss the *Bertrand* motion for interlocutory relief: *Bertrand v. Bégin* (24 August 1995) Québec 200-05-002117-955 (Q.C.S.). On August 31, 1995, Lesage J. rejected the Quebec Attorney-General's motion to dismiss, and agreed to hear the motion for an interlocutory injunction and declaration presented by Mr. Bertrand: *Bertrand v. Quebec (A.G.)* (1995), 127 D.L.R. (4th) 408 (S.C.C.).

30. Motion by Dr. Roopnarine Singh and others, members of the Special Committee on Canadian Unity, for a declaratory judgment: *Singh v. Attorney General of Quebec* (23 October 1995) Montreal 500-05-11275-953.

31. Attorney General of Canada, News Release, "Federal Government to Respond to Quebec's Position in Court Case" (10 May 1996), online: Department of Justice <http://canada.justice.gc.ca/en/news/nr/1996/bert.html>.

32. *Bertrand v. Quebec (A.G.)* (1996), 138 D.L.R. (4th) 481 (Q.S.C.). As a result, the Quebec government withdrew from the litigation.

33. Statement of Minister of Justice and Attorney General of Canada to the House of Commons, 26 September 1996.

34. P.C. 1996-1497. The order in council also included a six-paragraph preamble.

35. For its part, the Quebec government refused to participate in the reference litigation. Therefore, the Supreme Court appointed an *amicus curiae* to argue the case for secession. The *amicus* was Mr. André Joli-Coueur, a well-known Quebec lawyer.

(c)   1995 Referendum Question and Quebec Bill 1†

Referendum Question

The official translation of the referendum question on which Quebeckers voted on October 30 reads: "Do you agree that Québec should become sovereign, after having made a formal offer to Canada for a new Economic and Political Partnership, within the scope of the Bill respecting the future of Québec and of the agreement signed on June 12, 1995?"

---

† *Bill 1, An Act Respecting the Future of Québec, tabled at the National Assembly September 7, 1995.* [Translated from French. The Bill's forty-three paragraph preamble is omitted.]

BILL 1, AN ACT RESPECTING THE FUTURE OF QUÉBEC

. . . .

[Preamble]

. . . .

The Parliament of Québec enacts as follows:

Self-Determination

1. The National Assembly is authorized, within the scope of this Act, to proclaim the sovereignty of Québec.

The proclamation must be preceded by a formal offer of economic and political partnership with Canada.

Sovereignty

2. On the date fixed in the proclamation of the National Assembly, the Declaration of sovereignty appearing in the Preamble shall take effect and Québec shall become a sovereign country; it shall acquire the exclusive power to pass all its laws, levy all its taxes and conclude all its treaties.

Partnership Treaty

3. The Government is bound to propose to the Government of Canada the conclusion of a treaty of economic and political partnership on the basis of the tripartite agreement of June 12, 1995 reproduced in the schedule.

The treaty must be approved by the National Assembly before being ratified.

4. A committee charged with the orientation and supervision of the negotiations relating to the partnership treaty, composed of independent personalities appointed by the Government in accordance with the tripartite agreement, shall be established.

5. The Government shall favour the establishment in the Outaouais region of the seat of the institutions created under the partnership treaty.

New Constitution

6. A draft of a new constitution shall be drawn up by a constituent commission established in accordance with the prescriptions of the National Assembly. The commission, consisting of an equal number of men and women, shall be composed of a majority of non-parliamentarians, and shall include Quebeckers of various origins and from various backgrounds.

The proceedings of the commission must be organized so as to ensure the fullest possible participation of citizens in all regions of Québec, notably through the creation of regional sub-commissions, if necessary.

The commission shall table the draft constitution before the National Assembly, which shall approve the final text. The draft constitution shall be submitted to a referendum and shall, once approved, become the fundamental law of Québec.

7. The new constitution shall state that Québec is a French-speaking country and shall impose upon the Government the obligation of protecting Québec culture and ensuring its development.

8. The new constitution shall affirm the rule of law, and shall include a charter of human rights and freedoms. It shall also affirm that citizens have responsibilities towards their fellow citizens.

The new constitution shall guarantee the English-speaking community that its identity and institutions will be preserved. It shall also recognize the right of the aboriginal nations to self-government on lands over which they have full ownership and their right to participate in the development of Québec; in addition, the existing constitutional rights of the aboriginal nations shall be recognized in the constitution. Such guarantee and such recognition shall be exercised in a manner consistent with the territorial integrity of Québec.

Representatives of the English-speaking community and of each of the aboriginal nations must be invited by the constituent commission to take part in the proceedings devoted to defining their rights. Such rights shall not be modified otherwise than in accordance with a specific procedure.

9. The new constitution shall affirm the principle of decentralization. Specific powers and corresponding fiscal and financial resources shall be attributed by law to local and regional authorities.

Territory

10. Québec shall retain its boundaries as they exist within the Canadian federation on the date on which Québec becomes a sovereign country. It shall exercise its jurisdiction over the land, air and water forming its territory and over the areas adjacent to its coast, in accordance with the rules of international law.

Citizenship

11. Every person who, on the date on which Québec becomes a sovereign country, holds Canadian citizenship and is domiciled in Québec acquires Québec citizenship.

Every person born in Québec who, on the date on which Québec becomes a sovereign country, is domiciled outside Québec and who claims Québec citizenship also acquires Québec citizenship.

In the two years following the date on which Québec becomes a sovereign country, any person holding Canadian citizenship who settles in Québec or who has established a substantial connection with Québec without being domiciled in Québec may claim Québec citizenship.

12. Québec citizenship may be obtained, once Québec has become a sovereign country, in the cases and on the conditions determined by law. The law must provide, in particular, that Québec citizenship shall be granted to every person born in Québec, or born outside Québec to a father or mother holding Québec citizenship.

13. Québec citizenship may be held concurrently with Canadian citizenship or that of any other country.

Currency

14. The currency having legal tender in Québec shall remain the Canadian dollar.

Treaties and International Organizations and Alliances

15. In accordance with the rules of international law, Québec shall assume the obligations and enjoy the rights set forth in the relevant treaties and international conventions and agreements to which Canada or Québec is a party on the date on which Québec becomes a sovereign country, in particular in the North American Free Trade Agreement.

16. The Government is authorized to apply for the admission of Québec to the United Nations Organization and its specialized agencies. It shall take the necessary steps to ensure the participation of Québec in the World Trade Organization, the Organization of American States, the Organization for Economic Cooperation and Development, the Organization for Security and Co-operation in Europe, the Francophone, the Commonwealth and other international organizations and conferences.

17. The Government shall take the necessary steps to ensure the continuing participation of Québec in the defence alliances of which Canada is a member. Such participation must, however, be compatible with Québec's desire to give priority to the maintenance of world peace under the leadership of the United Nations Organization.

Continuity of Laws, Pensions, Benefits, Licences and Permits, Contracts and Courts of Justice

18. The Acts of the Parliament of Canada and the regulations thereunder that apply in Québec on the date on which Québec becomes a sovereign country shall be deemed to be laws and regulations of Québec. Such legislative and regulatory provisions shall be maintained in force until they are amended, replaced or repealed.

19. The Government shall ensure the continuity of the unemployment insurance and child-tax benefit programs and the payment of the other benefits paid by the Government of Canada to individuals domiciled in Québec on the date on which Québec becomes a sovereign country. Pensions and supplements payable to the elderly and to veterans shall continue to be paid by the Government of Québec according to the same terms and conditions.

20. Permits, licences and other authorizations issued before October 30, 1995, under the Act of the Parliament of Canada that are in force in Québec on the date on which Québec becomes a sovereign country shall be maintained. Those issued or renewed on or after October 30, 1995, shall also be maintained unless they are denounced by the Government within one month following the date on which Québec becomes a sovereign country.

Permits, licences and other authorizations that are so maintained will be renewable according to law.

21. Agreements and contracts entered into before October 30, 1995, by the Government of Canada or its agencies or organizations that are in force in Québec on the date on which Québec becomes a sovereign country shall be maintained, with the Government of Québec substituted, where required, for the Canadian party. Those entered into on or after October 30, 1995, shall also be maintained, with the Government of Québec substituted, where required, for the Canadian party, unless they are denounced by the Government within one month following the date on which Québec becomes a sovereign country.

22. The courts of justice shall continue to exist after the date on which Québec becomes a sovereign country. Cases pending may be continued until judgment. However, the law may provide that cases pending before the Federal Court or before the Supreme Court shall be transferred to the Québec jurisdiction it determines.

The Court of Appeal shall become the court of highest jurisdiction until a Supreme Court is established under the new constitution unless otherwise provided for by law.

Judges appointed by the Government of Canada before October 30, 1995, who are in office on the date on which Québec becomes a sovereign country shall be confirmed in their functions and shall retain their jurisdiction. The judges of the Federal Court and of the Supreme Court of Canada who were members of the Québec Bar shall become, if they so wish, judges of the Superior Court and of the Court of Appeal, respectively.

Federal Public Servants and Employees

23. The Government may, in accordance with the conditions prescribed by law, appoint the necessary personnel and take appropriate steps to facilitate the application of the Canadian laws that continue to apply in Québec pursuant to section 18. The sums required for the application of such laws shall be taken out of the consolidated revenue fund.

The Government shall ensure that the public servants and other employees of the Government of Canada and of its agencies and organizations, appointed before October 30, 1995, and domiciled in Québec on the date on which Québec becomes a sovereign country, shall become, if they so wish, public servants or employees of the Government of Québec. The Government may, for that purpose, conclude agreements with any association of employees or any other person in order to facilitate such transfers. The Government may also set up a program of voluntary retirement; it shall honour any retirement of voluntary departure arrangement made with a transferred person.

Interim Constitution

24. The Parliament of Québec may adopt the text of an interim constitution which will be in force from the date on which Québec becomes a sovereign country until the coming into force of the new constitution of Québec. The interim constitution must ensure the continuity of the democratic institutions of Québec and of the constitutional rights existing on the date on which Québec becomes a sovereign country, in particular those relating to human rights and freedoms, the English-speaking community, access to English-language schools, and the aboriginal nations.

Until the coming into force of the interim constitution, the laws, rules and conventions governing the internal constitution of Québec shall remain in force.

Other Agreements

25. In addition to the partnership treaty, the Government is authorized to conclude with the Government of Canada any other agreement to facilitate the application of this Act, in particular with respect to the equitable apportionment of the assets and liabilities, of the Government of Canada.

Coming into Force

26. The negotiations relating to the conclusion of the partnership treaty must not extend beyond October 30, 1996, unless the National Assembly decides otherwise.

The proclamation of sovereignty may be made as soon as the partnership treaty has been approved by the National Assembly or as soon as the latter, after requesting the opinion of the orientation and supervision committee, has concluded that the negotiations have proved fruitless.

27. This Act comes into force on the day on which it is assented to.

SCHEDULE
TEXT OF THE AGREEMENT BETWEEN THE PARTI QUÉBÉCOIS, THE BLOC QUÉBÉCOIS AND THE ACTION DÉMOCRATIQUE DU QUÉBEC

Ratified by
Messrs. Jacques Parizeau, Lucien Bouchard and Mario Dumont
Québec City
June 12, 1995

A Common Project

As the representatives of the Parti Québécois, the Bloc Québécois and the Action démocratique du Québec, we have reached agreement on a common project to be submitted in the referendum, a project that responds in a modern, decisive and open way to the long quest of the people of Québec to become masters of their destiny.

We have agreed to join forces and to coordinate our efforts so that in the Fall 1995 referendum, Quebecers can vote for a real change: to achieve sovereignty for Québec and a formal proposal for a new economic and political partnership with Canada, aimed among other things at consolidating the existing economic space.

The elements of this common project will be integrated in the bill that will be tabled in the Fall and on which Quebecers will vote on referendum day.

We believe that this common project respects the wishes of a majority of Quebecers, reflects the historical aspirations of Québec, and embodies, in a concrete way, the concerns expressed before the Commissions on the future of Québec.

Thus, our common project departs from the Canadian status quo, rejected by an immense majority of Quebecers. It is true to the aspirations of Quebecers for autonomy and would allow Québec to achieve sovereignty: to levy all of its taxes, pass all of its laws, sign all of its treaties. Our project also reflects the wish of Quebecers to maintain equitable and flexible ties with our Canadian neighbours, so that we can manage our common economic space together, particularly by means of joint institutions, including institutions of a political nature. We are convinced that this proposal is in the interests of both Québec and Canada, though we cannot of course presume to know what Canadians will decide in this regard.

Finally, our project responds to the wish so often expressed in recent months that the referendum unite as many Quebecers as possible on a clear, modern and open proposal.

The referendum mandate

Following a Yes victory in the referendum, the National Assembly, on the one hand, will be empowered to proclaim the sovereignty of Québec, and the government, on the other hand, will be bound to propose to Canada a treaty on a new economic and political Partnership, so as to, among other things, consolidate the existing economic space.

The referendum question will contain these two elements.

Accession to sovereignty

Insofar as the negotiations unfold in a positive fashion, the National Assembly will declare the sovereignty of Québec after an agreement is reached on the Partnership treaty. One of the first acts of a sovereign Québec will be ratification of the Partnership treaty.

The negotiations will not exceed one year, unless the National Assembly decides otherwise.

If the negotiations prove to be fruitless, the National Assembly will be empowered to declare the sovereignty of Québec without further delay.

The treaty

The new rules and the reality of international trade will allow a sovereign Québec, even without a formal Partnership with Canada, continued access to external markets, including the Canadian economic space. Moreover, a sovereign Québec could, on its own initiative, keep the Canadian dollar as its currency.

However, given the volume of trade between Québec and Canada and the extent of their economic integration, it will be to the evident advantage of both States to sign a formal treaty of economic and political Partnership.

The treaty will be binding on the parties and will specify appropriate measures for maintaining and improving the existing economic space. It will establish rules for the division of federal assets and management of the common debt.

It will create the joint political institutions required to administer the new Economic and Political Partnership, and lay down their governing rules. It will provide for the establishment of a Council, a Secretariat, an Assembly and a Tribunal for the resolution of disputes.

As a priority, the treaty will ensure that the Partnership has the authority to act in the following areas:

- customs union;
- free movement of goods;
- free movement of individuals;
- free movement of services;
- free movement of capital;
- monetary policy;
- labour mobility;
- citizenship.

In accordance with the dynamics of the joint institutions and in step with their aspirations, the two member States will be free to make agreements in any other area of common interest, such as:

- trade within the Partnership, so as to adapt and strengthen the provisions of the Agreement on Internal Trade;

- international trade (for example, to establish a common position on the exemption with respect to culture contained in the WTO Agreement and NAFTA);
- international representation (for example, the Council could decide, where useful or necessary, that the Partnership will speak with one voice within international organizations);
- transportation (to facilitate, for example, access to the airports of the two countries or to harmonize highway, rail or inland navigation policies);
- defence policy (for example, joint participation in peace-keeping operations or a coordinated participation in NATO and NORAD);
- financial institutions (for example, to define regulations for chartered banks, security rules and sound financial practices);
- fiscal and budgetary policies (to maintain a dialogue to foster the compatibility of respective actions);
- environmental protection (in order to set objectives in such areas as cross-border pollution and the transportation and storage of hazardous materials);
- the fight against arms and drug trafficking;
- postal services;
- any other matters considered of common interest to the parties.

Joint Institutions

1. THE COUNCIL

The Partnership Council, made up of an equal number of Ministers from the two States, will have decision-making power with regard to the implementation of the treaty.

The decisions of the Partnership Council will require a unanimous vote, thus each member will have a veto.

The Council will be assisted by a permanent secretariat.

The Secretariat will provide operational liaison between the Council and the governments and follow up on the implementation of the Council's decisions. At the request of the Council or the Parliamentary Assembly, the Secretariat will produce reports on any matter relating to the application of the treaty.

2. THE PARLIAMENTARY ASSEMBLY

A Partnership Parliamentary Assembly, made up of Québec and Canadian Members appointed by their respective Legislative Assemblies, will be created.

It will examine the draft text of Partnership Council decisions, and forward its recommendations. It will also have the power to pass resolutions on any aspect of its implementation, particularly after receiving the periodical reports on the state of the Partnership addressed to it by the Secretariat. It will hear, in public sessions, the heads of the bipartite administrative commissions responsible for the application of specific treaty provisions.

The composition of the Assembly will reflect the population distribution within the Partnership. Québec will hold 25% of the seats. Funding for Partnership institutions will be shared equally, except for parliamentarians' expenses, which will be borne by each State.

3. THE TRIBUNAL

A tribunal will be set up to resolve disputes relating to the treaty, its implementation and the interpretation of its provisions. Its decisions will be binding upon the parties.

The working procedures of the Tribunal could be modeled on existing mechanisms, such as the panels set up under NAFTA, the Agreement on Internal Trade or the World Trade Organization Agreement.

The Committee

An orientation and supervision committee will be set up for the purposes of the negotiations. It will be made up of independent personalities agreed upon by the three parties (PQ, BQ, ADQ). Its composition will be made public at the appropriate time. The Committee will

1. take part in the selection of the chief negotiator;
2. be allowed an observer at the negotiation table;
3. advise the government on the progress of the negotiations;
4. inform the public on the procedures and on the outcome of the negotiations.

The democratically appointed authorities of our three parties, having examined and ratified the present agreement yesterday, Sunday, June 11, 1995 — the Action démocratique du Québec having met in Sherbrooke, the Bloc Québécois in Montréal, and the Parti Québécois in Québec — we hereby ratify this common project and we call upon all Quebecers to endorse it.

(d) Quebec Secession Reference[†]

NOTE

On September 30, 1996, pursuant to s. 53 of the *Supreme Court Act*, the Governor in Council referred the following questions to the Supreme Court of Canada:

Question 1: Under the Constitution of Canada, can the National Assembly, legislature or Government of Quebec effect the secession of Quebec from Canada unilaterally?

Question 2: Does international law give the National Assembly, legislature or government of Quebec the right to effect the secession of Quebec from Canada unilaterally? In this regard, is there a right to self-determination under international law that would give the National Assembly, legislature or government of Quebec the right to effect the secession of Quebec from Canada unilaterally?

Question 3: In the event of a conflict between domestic and international law on the right of the National Assembly, legislature or government of Quebec to effect the secession of Quebec from Canada unilaterally, which would take precedence in Canada?

Because the Quebec government refused to take part, the Court appointed an *amicus curiae*, Mr. André Joli-Coeur, to argue the case for secession. The *amicus* said the Supreme Court had no jurisdiction to answer these issues. However, he said that if there was jurisdiction, Question 1 should be answered "yes" because the Constitution contained no prohibition against secession, and because a referendum vote for secession should be respected as an expression of democracy. The *amicus* said the second question should also be answered "yes" because international law will give legitimacy to a government that exercises effective control over the relevant territory. On the issue of self-determination, the *amicus* said that although the Quebec people have an international law right of self-determination, he would not rely on this right in support of secession, since Quebekers' fundamental rights had not been violated in a grave manner.

The Court's answer to Questions 1 and 2 (both parts) was "no". Thus, it was unnecessary to answer Question 3. On Question 1, the Court said unilateral secession would violate the Constitutional principles of federalism, the rule of law and constitutionalism, individual and minority rights, and democracy (in Canada as a whole, and outside Quebec). On the other hand, the Court also found that the principle of democracy would be satisfied within Quebec if a clear majority of the population of Quebec voted on a clear referendum question to pursue secession. In this situation, said the Court, the federal government and the other provincial governments would be required to participate in negotiating constitutional changes to respond to that desire.

The *Reference* raised some important questions. What is the basis of the legal-constitutional status of the principles of federalism, constitutionalism and the rule of law, individual and minority rights, and democracy? What other unwritten principles will be found to be part of the formal s. 52(1) Constitution of Canada? How do these principles relate to constitutional texts, to each other, and to non-legal unwritten constitutional principles? If none of these four sets of principles can trump the others, just how do these principles interrelate? Is the general principle of democracy now legally enforceable, while its more specific supporting principles — such as representative and responsible government — are not? How will the Court be able to distinguish legally enforceable "framework" issues from political "content" issues?

[†] *IN THE MATTER OF Section 53 of the Supreme Court Act, R.S.C., 1985, c. S-26; AND IN THE MATTER OF a Reference by the Governor in Council concerning certain questions relating to the secession of Quebec from Canada, as set out in Order in Council P.C. 1996-1947, dated the 30th day of September, 1996*, [1998] 2 S.C.R. 217; [1998] S.C.J. No. 61 (argument: 16, 17, 18, and 19 February 1998; decision: 20 August 1998). The decision can also be accessed at <http//www.lexum.umontreal.ca/csc-scc/en/index.html>. The factums and other background information can be found in A.F. Bayesky, ed., *Self-Determination in International Law: Quebec and Lessons Learned* (The Hague, Netherlands: Kluwer Law International, 2000).

What is a "clear" majority? A "clear" question? Who determines this when the parties can't agree? If a party refuses to negotiate, what sanctions follow? When, if at all, will courts intervene? Can "clear" referendum results trigger duties to negotiate subjects other than secession? What is the duration of the duty to negotiate? What happens if negotiations break down? What link did the Court draw between domestic and international law? At a more general level, was this a cautious or activist decision? Did it advance or diminish the prospect of Quebec secession? Did it strengthen or weaken the role of Canadian courts and law?

EXTRACT

[THE COURT (Lamer C.J. and L'Heureux-Dubé, Gonthier, Cory, McLachlin, Iacobucci, Major, Bastarache and Binnie JJ.):

The Court first addressed some preliminary questions about its own jurisdiction in this *Reference*. It held that: (i) s. 53 of the *Supreme Court Act* is not unconstitutional; (ii) a court of appeal can exercise original jurisdiction on an exceptional basis, if it is not incompatible with its appellate jurisdiction; (iii) the Supreme Court of Canada can exercise an advisory jurisdiction, even if it is not expressly authorized; (iv) the questions submitted in this reference were within the scope of s. 53 of the *Supreme Court Act*; (v) the Court could consider matters of international as well as domestic law; and (vi) the issues here were not too speculative, too political, or too premature to be considered. Paragraphs 6 to 28 highlight some of the reasoning behind these findings.]

. . . .

[6] In *Re References by Governor-General in Council* (1910), 43 S.C.R. 536, affirmed on appeal to the Privy Council, [1912] A.C. 571 (*sub nom. Attorney-General for Ontario* v. *Attorney-General for Canada*), the constitutionality of this Court's special jurisdiction was twice upheld. The Court is asked to revisit these decisions. In light of the significant changes in the role of this Court since 1912, and the very important issues raised in this Reference, it is appropriate to reconsider briefly the constitutional validity of the Court's reference jurisdiction.

. . . .

[9] The words "general court of appeal" in s. 101 [of the *Constitution Act, 1867*] denote the status of the Court within the national court structure and should not be taken as a restrictive definition of the Court's functions. In most instances, this Court acts as the exclusive ultimate appellate court in the country, and, as such, is properly constituted as the "general court of appeal" for Canada. Moreover, it is clear that an appellate court can receive, on an exceptional basis, original jurisdiction not incompatible with its appellate jurisdiction.

. . . .

[12] The *amicus curiae* submits that

> [translation] [e]ither this constitutional power [to give the highest court in the federation jurisdiction to give advisory opinions] is expressly provided for by the Constitution, as is the case in India (*Constitution of India*, art. 143), or it is not provided for therein *and so it simply does not exist*. This is what the Supreme Court of the United States has held. [Emphasis added.]

[13] However, the U.S. Supreme Court did not conclude that it was unable to render advisory opinions because no such express power was included in the U.S. Constitution. Quite the contrary, it based this conclusion on the express limitation in art. III, s. 2 restricting federal court jurisdiction to actual "cases" or "controversies". See, e.g., *Muskrat* v. *United States*, 219 U.S. 346 (1911), at p. 362. This section reflects the strict separation of powers in the American federal constitutional arrangement. Where the "case or controversy" limitation is missing from their respective state constitutions, some American state courts do undertake advisory functions (e.g., in at least two states — Alabama and Delaware — advisory opinions are authorized, in certain circumstances, by statute: see Ala. Code 1975 s. 12-2-10; Del. Code Ann. tit. 10, s. 141 (1996 Supp.)).

. . . .

[27] As to the "proper role" of the Court, it is important to underline, contrary to the submission of the *amicus curiae*, that the questions posed in this Reference do not ask the Court to usurp any democratic decision that the people of Quebec may be called upon to make. The questions posed by the Governor in Council, as we interpret them, are strictly limited to aspects of the legal framework in which that democratic decision is to be taken. The attempted analogy to the U.S. "political questions" doctrine therefore has no application. The

legal framework having been clarified, it will be for the population of Quebec, acting through the political process, to decide whether or not to pursue secession. As will be seen, the legal framework involves the rights and obligations of Canadians who live outside the province of Quebec, as well as those who live within Quebec.

[28] As to the "legal" nature of the questions posed, if the Court is of the opinion that it is being asked a question with a significant extralegal component, it may interpret the question so as to answer only its legal aspects; if this is not possible, the Court may decline to answer the question. In the present Reference the questions may clearly be interpreted as directed to legal issues, and, so interpreted, the Court is in a position to answer them.

. . . .

[The Court surprised many observers by relying on "unwritten" principles outside the text of the Canadian constitution for much of its answer to Question 1. In the following paragraphs the Court developed the idea that the formal Constitution of Canada referred to in s. 52(2) of the *Constitution Act, 1982* comprises principles as well as texts, and went on to discuss the nature and application of the principles it considered relevant here.]

[32] ... The "Constitution of Canada" certainly includes the constitutional texts enumerated in s. 52(2) of the *Constitution Act, 1982.* Although these texts have a primary place in determining constitutional rules, they are not exhaustive. The Constitution also "embraces unwritten, as well as written rules"....

. . . .

[49] ...Our Constitution is primarily a written one, the product of 131 years of evolution. Behind the written word is an historical lineage stretching back through the ages, which aids in the consideration of the underlying constitutional principles. These principles inform and sustain the constitutional text: they are the vital unstated assumptions upon which the text is based. The following discussion addresses the four foundational constitutional principles that are most germane for resolution of this Reference: federalism, democracy, constitutionalism and the rule of law, and respect for minority rights. These defining principles function in symbiosis. No single principle can be defined in isolation from the others, nor does any one principle trump or exclude the operation of any other.

[53] Given the existence of these underlying constitutional principles, what use may the Court make of them? In the *Provincial Judges Reference*, [1997] 3 S.C.R. 3 at paras. 93 and 104, we cautioned that the recognition of these constitutional principles (the majority opinion referred to them as "organizing principles" and described one of them, judicial independence, as an "unwritten norm") could not be taken as an invitation to dispense with the written text of the Constitution.... However ... [i]n the *Provincial Judges Reference*, at para. 104, we determined that the preamble "invites the courts to turn those principles into the premises of a constitutional argument that culminates in the filling of gaps in the express terms of the constitutional text".

[54] Underlying constitutional principles may in certain circumstances give rise to substantive legal obligations (have "full legal force", as we described it in the *Patriation Reference, supra,* at p. 845), which constitute substantive limitations upon government action....

. . . .

[57] ... [T]he principle of federalism remains a central organizational theme of our Constitution. Less obviously, perhaps, but certainly of equal importance, federalism is a political and legal response to underlying social and political realities.

. . . .

[The Court said that federalism recognizes the diversity and autonomy of the component parts of Confederation [para. 58], and facilitates the pursuit of collective goals by cultural and linguistic minorities that form the majority within a particular province, such as Quebec [para. 59]].

. . . .

[61] Democracy is a fundamental value in our constitutional law and political culture. While it has both an institutional and an individual aspect, the democratic principle was also argued before us in the sense of the supremacy of the sovereign will of a people, in this case potentially to be expressed by Quebecers in support of unilateral secession....

. . . .

[64] Democracy is not simply concerned with the process of government. On the contrary..., democracy is fundamentally connected to substantive goals, most importantly, the promotion of self-government. Democracy accommodates cultural and group identities....

[65] In institutional terms, democracy means that each of the provincial legislatures and the federal Parliament is elected by popular franchise.... Historically, this Court has interpreted democracy to mean the process of representative and responsible government and the right of citizens to participate in the political process as voters.... In addition, the effect of s. 4 of the *Charter* is to oblige the House of Commons and the provincial legislatures to hold regular elections and to permit citizens to elect representatives to their political institutions....

[66] It is, of course, true that democracy expresses the sovereign will of the people. Yet this expression, too, must be taken in the context of the other institutional values we have identified as pertinent to this Reference. The relationship between democracy and federalism means, for example, that in Canada there may be different and equally legitimate majorities in different provinces and territories and at the federal level. No one majority is more or less "legitimate" than the others as an expression of democratic opinion, although, of course, the consequences will vary with the subject matter....

[67] The consent of the governed is a value that is basic to our understanding of a free and democratic society. Yet democracy in any real sense of the word cannot exist without the rule of law.... Equally, however, a system of government cannot survive through adherence to the law alone. A political system must also possess legitimacy, and in our political culture, that requires an interaction between the rule of law and the democratic principle. But there is more. Our law's claim to legitimacy also rests on an appeal to moral values, many of which are imbedded in our constitutional structure. It would be a grave mistake to equate legitimacy with the "sovereign will" or majority rule alone, to the exclusion of other constitutional values.

[68] Finally, we highlight that a functioning democracy requires a continuous process of discussion. A democratic system of government is committed to considering ... dissenting voices, and seeking to acknowledge and address those voices in the laws by which all in the community must live.

[69] The *Constitution Act, 1982* gives expression to this principle, by conferring a right to initiate constitutional change on each participant in Confederation. In our view, the existence of this right imposes a corresponding duty on the participants in Confederation to engage in constitutional discussions in order to acknowledge and address democratic expressions of a desire for change in other provinces. This duty is inherent in the democratic principle which is a fundamental predicate of our system of governance.

[70] The principles of constitutionalism and the rule of law lie at the root of our system of government....

[71] In the *Manitoba Language Rights Reference*, [1985] 1 S.C.R. 721 at pp. 747–52, this Court outlined the elements of the rule of law. We emphasized, first, that the rule of law provides that the law is supreme over the acts of both government and private persons. There is, in short, one law for all. Second, we explained, at p. 749, that "the rule of law requires the creation and maintenance of an actual order of positive laws which preserves and embodies the more general principle of normative order".... A third aspect of the rule of law is, as recently confirmed in the *Provincial Judges Reference*, *supra*, at para. 10, that "the exercise of all public power must find its ultimate source in a legal rule". Put another way, the relationship between the state and the individual must be regulated by law....

[72] ... The constitutionalism principle ... requires that all government action comply with the Constitution. The rule of law principle requires that all government action must comply with the law, including the Constitution. This Court has noted on several occasions that with the adoption of the *Charter*, the Canadian system of government was transformed to a significant extent from a system of Parliamentary supremacy to one of constitutional supremacy. The Constitution binds all governments, both federal and provincial, including the executive branch....

[73] An understanding of the scope and importance of the principles of the rule of law and constitutionalism is aided by acknowledging explicitly why a constitution is entrenched beyond the reach of simple majority rule. There are three overlapping reasons.

[74] First, a constitution may provide an added safeguard for fundamental human rights and individual freedoms which might otherwise be susceptible

to government interference.... Second, a constitution may seek to ensure that vulnerable minority groups are endowed with the institutions and rights necessary to maintain and promote their identities against the assimilative pressures of the majority. And third, a constitution may provide for a division of political power that allocates political power amongst different levels of government. That purpose would be defeated if one of those democratically elected levels of government could usurp the powers of the other simply by exercising its legislative power to allocate additional political power to itself unilaterally.

[75] The argument that the Constitution may be legitimately circumvented by resort to a majority vote in a province-wide referendum is superficially persuasive, in large measure because it seems to appeal to some of the same principles that underlie the legitimacy of the Constitution itself, namely, democracy and self-government. In short, it is suggested that as the notion of popular sovereignty underlies the legitimacy of our existing constitutional arrangements, so the same popular sovereignty that originally led to the present Constitution must (it is argued) also permit "the people" in their exercise of popular sovereignty to secede by majority vote alone. However, closer analysis reveals that this argument is unsound, because it misunderstands the meaning of popular sovereignty and the essence of a constitutional democracy.

[76] Canadians have never accepted that ours is a system of simple majority rule. Our principle of democracy, taken in conjunction with the other constitutional principles discussed here, is richer. Constitutional government is necessarily predicated on the idea that the political representatives of the people of a province have the capacity and the power to commit the province to be bound into the future by the constitutional rules being adopted. These rules are "binding" not in the sense of frustrating the will of a majority of a province, but as defining the majority which must be consulted in order to alter the fundamental balances of political power (including the spheres of autonomy guaranteed by the principle of federalism), individual rights, and minority rights in our society. Of course, those constitutional rules are themselves amenable to amendment, but only through a process of negotiation which ensures that there is an opportunity for the constitutionally defined rights of all the parties to be respected and reconciled.

[77] In this way, our belief in democracy may be harmonized with our belief in constitutionalism.

Constitutional amendment often requires some form of substantial consensus precisely because the content of the underlying principles of our Constitution demand it. By requiring broad support in the form of an "enhanced majority" to achieve constitutional change, the Constitution ensures that minority interests must be addressed before proposed changes which would affect them may be enacted.

[79] The fourth underlying constitutional principle we address here concerns the protection of minorities....

. . . .

[83] Secession is the effort of a group or section of a state to withdraw itself from the political and constitutional authority of that state, with a view to achieving statehood for a new territorial unit on the international plane. In a federal state, secession typically takes the form of a territorial unit seeking to withdraw from the federation. Secession is a legal act as much as a political one....

[84] The secession of a province from Canada must be considered, in legal terms, to require an amendment to the Constitution, which perforce requires negotiation.... It is of course true that the Constitution is silent as to the ability of a province to secede from Confederation but, although the Constitution neither expressly authorizes nor prohibits secession, an act of secession would purport to alter the governance of Canadian territory in a manner which undoubtedly is inconsistent with our current constitutional arrangements. The fact that those changes would be profound, or that they would purport to have a significance with respect to international law, does not negate their nature as amendments to the Constitution of Canada.

[85] The Constitution is the expression of the sovereignty of the people of Canada. It lies within the power of the people of Canada, acting through their various governments duly elected and recognized under the Constitution, to effect whatever constitutional arrangements are desired within Canadian territory, including, should it be so desired, the secession of Quebec from Canada.... The manner in which such a political will could be formed and mobilized is a somewhat speculative exercise, though we are asked to assume the existence of such a political will for the purpose of answering the question before us. By the terms of this Reference, we have been asked to consider whether it would be constitutional in such a circumstance for the National

Assembly, legislature or government of Quebec to effect the secession of Quebec from Canada unilaterally.

[86] ... [W]hat is claimed by a right to secede "unilaterally" is the right to effectuate secession without prior negotiations with the other provinces and the federal government. At issue is not the legality of the first step but the legality of the final act of purported unilateral secession. The supposed juridical basis for such an act is said to be a clear expression of democratic will in a referendum in the province of Quebec. This claim requires us to examine the possible juridical impact, if any, of such a referendum on the functioning of our Constitution, and on the claimed legality of a unilateral act of secession.

[87] Although the Constitution does not itself address the use of a referendum procedure, and the results of a referendum have no direct role or legal effect in our constitutional scheme, a referendum undoubtedly may provide a democratic method of ascertaining the views of the electorate on important political questions on a particular occasion. The democratic principle identified above would demand that considerable weight be given to a clear expression by the people of Quebec of their will to secede from Canada, even though a referendum, in itself and without more, has no direct legal effect, and could not in itself bring about unilateral secession.... In this context, we refer to a "clear" majority as a qualitative evaluation. The referendum result, if it is to be taken as an expression of the democratic will, must be free of ambiguity both in terms of the question asked and in terms of the support it achieves.

[88] The federalism principle, in conjunction with the democratic principle, dictates that the clear repudiation of the existing constitutional order and the clear expression of the desire to pursue secession by the population of a province would give rise to a reciprocal obligation on all parties to Confederation to negotiate constitutional changes to respond to that desire.... The corollary of a legitimate attempt by one participant in Confederation to seek an amendment to the Constitution is an obligation on all parties to come to the negotiating table. The clear repudiation by the people of Quebec of the existing constitutional order would confer legitimacy on demands for secession, and place an obligation on the other provinces and the federal government to acknowledge and respect that expression of democratic will by entering into negotiations and conducting them in accordance with the underlying constitutional principles already discussed.

[89] What is the content of this obligation to negotiate? ...

[90] The conduct of the parties in such negotiations would be governed by the same constitutional principles which give rise to the duty to negotiate: federalism, democracy, constitutionalism and the rule of law, and the protection of minorities. Those principles lead us to reject two absolutist propositions. One of those propositions is that there would be a legal obligation on the other provinces and federal government to accede to the secession of a province, subject only to negotiation of the logistical details of secession....

[91] ... We hold that Quebec could not purport to invoke a right of self-determination such as to dictate the terms of a proposed secession to the other parties: that would not be a negotiation at all.... The democracy principle, as we have emphasized, cannot be invoked to trump the principles of federalism and rule of law, the rights of individuals and minorities, or the operation of democracy in the other provinces or in Canada as a whole. No negotiations could be effective if their ultimate outcome, secession, is cast as an absolute legal entitlement based upon an obligation to give effect to that act of secession in the Constitution. Such a foregone conclusion would actually undermine the obligation to negotiate and render it hollow.

[92] However, we are equally unable to accept the reverse proposition, that a clear expression of self-determination by the people of Quebec would impose no obligations upon the other provinces or the federal government. The continued existence and operation of the Canadian constitutional order cannot remain indifferent to the clear expression of a clear majority of Quebecers that they no longer wish to remain in Canada.... The rights of other provinces and the federal government cannot deny the right of the government of Quebec to pursue secession, should a clear majority of the people of Quebec choose that goal, so long as in doing so, Quebec respects the rights of others. Negotiations would be necessary to address the interests of the federal government, of Quebec and the other provinces, and other participants, as well as the rights of all Canadians both within and outside Quebec.

[93] The negotiation process precipitated by a decision of a clear majority of the population of Quebec on a clear question to pursue secession would require the reconciliation of various rights and obligations by the representatives of two legitimate majorities, namely, the clear majority of the popula-

tion of Quebec, and the clear majority of Canada as a whole, whatever that may be. There can be no suggestion that either of these majorities "trumps" the other. A political majority that does not act in accordance with the underlying constitutional principles we have identified puts at risk the legitimacy of the exercise of its rights.

. . . .

[95] Refusal of a party to conduct negotiations in a manner consistent with constitutional principles and values would seriously put at risk the legitimacy of that party's assertion of its rights, and perhaps the negotiation process as a whole.

[96] No one can predict the course that such negotiations might take. The possibility that they might not lead to an agreement amongst the parties must be recognized. Negotiations following a referendum vote in favour of seeking secession would inevitably address a wide range of issues, many of great import. After 131 years of Confederation, there exists, inevitably, a high level of integration in economic, political and social institutions across Canada. The vision of those who brought about Confederation was to create a unified country, not a loose alliance of autonomous provinces. Accordingly, while there are regional economic interests, which sometimes coincide with provincial boundaries, there are also national interests and enterprises (both public and private) that would face potential dismemberment. There is a national economy and a national debt. Arguments were raised before us regarding boundary issues. There are linguistic and cultural minorities, including aboriginal peoples, unevenly distributed across the country who look to the Constitution of Canada for the protection of their rights. Of course, secession would give rise to many issues of great complexity and difficulty. These would have to be resolved within the overall framework of the rule of law, thereby assuring Canadians resident in Quebec and elsewhere a measure of stability in what would likely be a period of considerable upheaval and uncertainty. Nobody seriously suggests that our national existence, seamless in so many aspects, could be effortlessly separated along what are now the provincial boundaries of Quebec....

[97] In the circumstances, negotiations following such a referendum would undoubtedly be difficult. While the negotiators would have to contemplate the possibility of secession, there would be no absolute legal entitlement to it and no assumption that an agreement reconciling all relevant rights and obligations

would actually be reached. It is foreseeable that even negotiations carried out in conformity with the underlying constitutional principles could reach an impasse. We need not speculate here as to what would then transpire. Under the Constitution, secession requires that an amendment be negotiated.

[98] The respective roles of the courts and political actors in discharging the constitutional obligations we have identified follows ineluctably from the foregoing observations. In the *Patriation Reference*, a distinction was drawn between the law of the Constitution, which, generally speaking, will be enforced by the courts, and other constitutional rules, such as the conventions of the Constitution, which carry only political sanctions. It is also the case, however, that judicial intervention, even in relation to the law of the Constitution, is subject to the Court's appreciation of its proper role in the constitutional scheme.

. . . .

[100] The role of the Court in this Reference is limited to the identification of the relevant aspects of the Constitution in their broadest sense. We have interpreted the questions as relating to the constitutional framework within which political decisions may ultimately be made. Within that framework, the workings of the political process are complex and can only be resolved by means of political judgments and evaluations. The Court has no supervisory role over the political aspects of constitutional negotiations. Equally, the initial impetus for negotiation, namely a clear majority on a clear question in favour of secession, is subject only to political evaluation, and properly so....

[101] If the circumstances giving rise to the duty to negotiate were to arise, the distinction between the strong defence of legitimate interests and the taking of positions which, in fact, ignore the legitimate interests of others is one that also defies legal analysis. The Court would not have access to all of the information available to the political actors, and the methods appropriate for the search for truth in a court of law are ill-suited to getting to the bottom of constitutional negotiations. To the extent that the questions are political in nature, it is not the role of the judiciary to interpose its own views on the different negotiating positions of the parties, even were it invited to do so ... [The judiciary h]aving established the legal framework, it would be for the democratically elected leadership of the various participants to resolve their differences.

[102] The non-justiciability of political issues that lack a legal component does not deprive the surrounding constitutional framework of its binding status, nor does this mean that constitutional obligations could be breached without incurring serious legal repercussions. Where there are legal rights there are remedies, but as we explained in the *Auditor General's* case, *supra*, at p. 90, and *New Brunswick Broadcasting*, *supra*, the appropriate recourse in some circumstances lies through the workings of the political process rather than the courts.

[103] To the extent that a breach of the constitutional duty to negotiate in accordance with the principles described above undermines the legitimacy of a party's actions, it may have important ramifications at the international level. Thus, a failure of the duty to undertake negotiations and pursue them according to constitutional principles may undermine that government's claim to legitimacy which is generally a precondition for recognition by the international community. Conversely, violations of those principles by the federal or other provincial governments responding to the request for secession may undermine their legitimacy. Thus, a Quebec that had negotiated in conformity with constitutional principles and values in the face of unreasonable intransigence on the part of other participants at the federal or provincial level would be more likely to be recognized than a Quebec which did not itself act according to constitutional principles in the negotiation process. Both the legality of the acts of the parties to the negotiation process under Canadian law, and the perceived legitimacy of such action, would be important considerations in the recognition process. In this way, the adherence of the parties to the obligation to negotiate would be evaluated in an indirect manner on the international plane.

[104] Accordingly, the secession of Quebec from Canada cannot be accomplished by the National Assembly, the legislature or government of Quebec unilaterally, that is to say, without principled negotiations, and be considered a lawful act. Any attempt to effect the secession of a province from Canada must be undertaken pursuant to the Constitution of Canada, or else violate the Canadian legal order. However, the continued existence and operation of the Canadian constitutional order cannot remain unaffected by the unambiguous expression of a clear majority of Quebecers that they no longer wish to remain in Canada. The primary means by which that expression is given effect is the constitutional duty to negotiate in accordance with the constitutional principles that we have described herein. In the event

secession negotiations are initiated, our Constitution, no less than our history, would call on the participants to work to reconcile the rights, obligations and legitimate aspirations of all Canadians within a framework that emphasizes constitutional responsibilities as much as it does constitutional rights.

[105] It will be noted that Question 1 does not ask how secession could be achieved in a constitutional manner, but addresses one form of secession only, namely unilateral secession. Although the applicability of various procedures to achieve lawful secession was raised in argument, each option would require us to assume the existence of facts that at this stage are unknown. In accordance with the usual rule of prudence in constitutional cases, we refrain from pronouncing on the applicability of any particular constitutional procedure to effect secession unless and until sufficiently clear facts exist to squarely raise an issue for judicial determination.

[106] ... Although under the Constitution there is no right to pursue secession unilaterally, that is secession without principled negotiation, this does not rule out the possibility of an unconstitutional declaration of secession leading to a *de facto* secession. The ultimate success of such a secession would be dependent on effective control of a territory and recognition by the international community. The principles governing secession at international law are discussed in our answer to Question 2.

[107] In our view, the alleged principle of effectivity has no constitutional or legal status in the sense that it does not provide an *ex ante* explanation or justification for an act. In essence, acceptance of a principle of effectivity would be tantamount to accepting that the National Assembly, legislature or government of Quebec may act without regard to the law, simply because it asserts the power to do so. So viewed, the suggestion is that the National Assembly, legislature or government of Quebec could purport to secede the province unilaterally from Canada in disregard of Canadian and international law. It is further suggested that if the secession bid was successful, a new legal order would be created in that province, which would then be considered an independent state.

[108] Such a proposition is an assertion of fact, not a statement of law. It may or may not be true; in any event it is irrelevant to the questions of law before us. If, on the other hand, it is put forward as an assertion of law, then it simply amounts to the contention that the law may be broken as long as it

can be broken successfully. Such a notion is contrary to the rule of law, and must be rejected.

. . . .

[The Supreme Court's reasoning on Question 2 is summarized in the following propositions:

At international law there is no specific right of component parts of sovereign states to secede unilaterally [para. 111]. Although international law does not specifically deny such a right, it attaches great importance to territorial integrity [para. 112]. If unilateral secession is incompatible with the domestic Constitution, it is likely to be forbidden at international law [para. 112], unless there are exceptional circumstances 122].

In very extreme cases, the principle of self-determination can give rise to a right of unilateral secession [para. 126]. There are two aspects to the principle of self-determination, one external and the other internal [para. 126]. The external aspect gives component parts of parent states the right to secede unilaterally (a) if these parts constitute "peoples" [para. 123], and (b) if they have been denied internal self-determination, which is the right to be free of colonial domination [para. 132] or from alien subjugation, domination, or exploitation [para.

133]. This secession right may extend to other cases of a complete blockage of the meaningful exercise of internal self-determination, but international law is not clear on this point [paras. 134–35].

Assuming without deciding that the Quebec population are a "people" [para. 125], they have not been denied internal self-determination [para. 136] and therefore have no international law right to external self-determination or unilateral secession [para. 138]. Although the issues of the rights of Aboriginal peoples and boundaries are important, it is unnecessary to address them [para. 139].

Although the principle of effectivity may eventually give legal status to an illegal act, this is irrelevant to the question of the international law legality of unilateral secession in the first place [para. 146]. In any event, the illegality of a secession, including the lack of a right of external self-determination, could have the effect of denying the international recognition on which *de facto* secession partly depends [para. 143].

Because of its finding that there was no right to unilateral secession under either domestic constitutional law or international law, the Court found it unnecessary to answer *Reference* Question 3.]

(e) *Clarity Act*†

NOTE

Claiming that it was only following the guidelines set out in the *Quebec Secession Reference*, the federal government introduced the following legislation on a future Quebec secession referendum. The federal government felt that legislation was needed to make it clear just what would be required (for example, a straightforward question about secession and more than a simple majority result on a referendum) before there could be any federal participation in secession negotiations.

Predictably, Senators argued that the legislation's proposed process was wrong to bypass the Senate. Some federalists argued that the legislation conceded too much, providing sovereigntists with a road map to separation. Others worried that it would provoke more moderate Quebec nationalists. The Quebec government called the statute an arrogant interference with the affairs of Quebekers, and with their inherent right of self-determination. The Quebec government responded with a *Fundamental Rights Act*,‡ asserting the right of Quebekers to decide their own future, by a simple majority referendum vote.

---

† *An Act to give effect to the requirement for clarity as set out in the opinion of the Supreme Court of Canada in the Quebec Secession Reference*, S.C. 2000, c. 26.

‡ *An Act respecting the exercise of the Fundamental Rights and Prerogatives of the Québec People and the Québec State*, S.Q. 2000, c. 46.

Would some of these issues be returning to the courts?

EXTRACT

PREAMBLE

WHEREAS the Supreme Court of Canada has confirmed that there is no right, under international law or under the Constitution of Canada, for the National Assembly, legislature or government of Quebec to effect the secession of Quebec from Canada unilaterally;

WHEREAS any proposal relating to the break-up of a democratic state is a matter of the utmost gravity and is of fundamental importance to all of its citizens;

WHEREAS the government of any province of Canada is entitled to consult its population by referendum on any issue and is entitled to formulate the wording of its referendum question;

WHEREAS the Supreme Court of Canada has determined that the result of a referendum on the secession of a province from Canada must be free of ambiguity both in terms of the question asked and in terms of the support it achieves if that result is to be taken as an expression of the democratic will that would give rise to an obligation to enter into negotiations that might lead to secession;

WHEREAS the Supreme Court of Canada has stated that democracy means more than simple majority rule, that a clear majority in favour of secession would be required to create an obligation to negotiate secession, and that a qualitative evaluation is required to determine whether a clear majority in favour of secession exists in the circumstances;

WHEREAS the Supreme Court of Canada has confirmed that, in Canada, the secession of a province, to be lawful, would require an amendment to the Constitution of Canada, that such an amendment would perforce require negotiations in relation to secession involving at least the governments of all of the provinces and the Government of Canada, and that those negotiations would be governed by the principles of federalism, democracy, constitutionalism and the rule of law, and the protection of minorities;

WHEREAS, in light of the finding by the Supreme Court of Canada that it would be for elected representatives to determine what constitutes a clear question and what constitutes a clear majority in a referendum held in a province on secession, the House of Commons, as the only political institution elected to represent all Canadians, has an important role in identifying what constitutes a clear question and a clear majority sufficient for the Government of Canada to enter into negotiations in relation to the secession of a province from Canada;

AND WHEREAS it is incumbent on the Government of Canada not to enter into negotiations that might lead to the secession of a province from Canada, and that could consequently entail the termination of citizenship and other rights that Canadian citizens resident in the province enjoy as full participants in Canada, unless the population of that province has clearly expressed its democratic will that the province secede from Canada;

NOW, THEREFORE, Her Majesty, by and with the advice and consent of the Senate and House of Commons of Canada, enacts as follows:

House of Commons to consider question

1.(1) The House of Commons shall, within thirty days after the government of a province tables in its legislative assembly or otherwise officially releases the question that it intends to submit to its voters in a referendum relating to the proposed secession of the province from Canada, consider the question and, by resolution, set out its determination on whether the question is clear.

Extension of time

(2) Where the thirty days referred to in subsection (1) occur, in whole or in part, during a general election of members to serve in the House of Commons, the thirty days shall be extended by an additional forty days.

Considerations

(3) In considering the clarity of a referendum question, the House of Commons shall consider whether the question would result in a clear expression of the will of the population of a province on whether the province should cease to be part of Canada and become an independent state.

Where no clear expression of will

(4) For the purpose of subsection (3), a clear expression of the will of the population of a province that the province cease to be part of Canada could not result from

(a) a referendum question that merely focuses on a mandate to negotiate without soliciting a direct expression of the will of the population of that province on whether the province should cease to be part of Canada; or

(b) a referendum question that envisages other possibilities in addition to the secession of the province from Canada, such as economic or political arrangements with Canada, that obscure a direct expression of the will of the population of that province on whether the province should cease to be part of Canada.

Other views to be considered

(5) In considering the clarity of a referendum question, the House of Commons shall take into account the views of all political parties represented in the legislative assembly of the province whose government is proposing the referendum on secession, any formal statements or resolutions by the government or legislative assembly of any province or territory of Canada, any formal statements or resolutions by the Senate, and any other views it considers to be relevant.

No negotiations if question not clear

(6) The Government of Canada shall not enter into negotiations on the terms on which a province might cease to be part of Canada if the House of Commons determines, pursuant to this section, that a referendum question is not clear and, for that reason, would not result in a clear expression of the will of the population of that province on whether the province should cease to be part of Canada.

House of Commons to consider whether there is a clear will to secede

2.(1) Where the government of a province, following a referendum relating to the secession of the province from Canada, seeks to enter into negotiations on the terms of which that province might cease to be part of Canada, the House of Commons shall, except where it has determined pursuant to section 1 that a referendum question is not clear, consider and, by resolution, set out its determination on whether, in the circumstances, there has been a clear expression of a will by a clear majority of the population of that province that the province cease to be part of Canada.

Factors for House of Commons to take into account

(2) In considering whether there has been a clear expression of a will by a clear majority of the population of a province that the province cease to be part of Canada, the House of Commons shall take into account

(a) the size of the majority of valid votes cast in favour of the secessionist option;

(b) the percentage of eligible voters voting in the referendum; and

(c) any other matters or circumstances it considers to be relevant.

Other views to be considered

(3) In considering whether there has been a clear expression of a will by a clear majority of the population of a province that the province cease to be part of Canada, the House of Commons shall take into account the views of all political parties represented in the legislative assembly of the province whose government proposed the referendum on secession, any formal statements or resolutions by the government or legislative assembly of any province or territory of Canada, any formal statements or resolutions by the Senate, and any other views it considers to be relevant.

No negotiations unless will clear

(4) The Government of Canada shall not enter into negotiations on the terms on which a province might cease to be part of Canada unless the House of Commons determines, pursuant to this section, that there has been a clear expression of a will by a clear majority of the population of that province that the province cease to be part of Canada.

Constitutional amendments

3.(1) It is recognized that there is no right under the Constitution of Canada to effect the secession of a province from Canada unilaterally and that, therefore, an amendment to the Constitution of Canada would be required for any province to secede from Canada, which in turn would require negotiations involving at least the governments of all of the provinces and the Government of Canada.

Limitation

(2) No Minister of the Crown shall propose a constitutional amendment to effect the secession of a province from Canada unless the Government of Canada has addressed, in its negotiations, the terms

of secession that are relevant in the circumstances, including the division of assets and liabilities, any changes to the borders of the province, the rights, interests and territorial claims of the Aboriginal peoples of Canada, and the protection of minority rights.

(f)   The Clarity and Fundamental Rights Acts: Colliding Paths?[†]

Daniel Turp

NOTE

Prominent Quebec secessionist Daniel Turp sees the federal *Clarity Act* as a direct attack on Quebekers' capacity to choose their own political future. Patrick Monahan, on the other hand, argues that the *Clarity Act* is constitutionally valid (under either s. 44 of the *Constitution Act, 1982* or s. 91 of the *Constitution Act, 1867*; is not inconsistent with the requirements in the *Quebec Secession Reference*; is limited to the question of *federal* government participation in secession negotiations or a possible secession amendment; and is entirely appropriate in contemplating a key role for political actors, especially the House of Commons: Monahan, at 223–29. With whom do you agree? Whatever your conclusion on these issues, it is hard to disagree with Turp's suggestion that the *Clarity Act* and the *Fundamental Rights Act* are on a collision course.

EXTRACT

THE *CLARITY ACT* AND QUÉBEC: IDEAS IN COLLISION

.   .   .   .

The *Clarity Act* attempts essentially to define the wording of the question in a future referendum on Québec's sovereignty and to determine the majority threshold that would allow the Canadian government to shirk its obligation to negotiate. By doing so, it collides headlong with ideas that have prevailed for decades and guaranteed the Québec nation a freedom the government is now trying to take away.

Under the auspices of Québec's *Referendum Act*,[12] the government of Québec initiated referendums on Québec's political and constitutional future. In both the 1980 and 1995 referendums,[13] the participation in the debate of the government of Canada and the Parliament as well as many provincial prime ministers and federalist forces in Québec for the "No" camp, [legitimizes] the democratic process of the referendums[14] and to a certain extent indicates "a tacit acceptance of the possibility for Québec to secede."[15]

In the organization of these referendums, Québec's elected representatives would decide the wording of the referendum question.[16] This notion has been challenged by the *Clarity Act*, which grants the House of Commons with the power to determine the clarity of a referendum question,[17] The House of Commons of Canada — where only 25% of the members are from Québec (75 of 301) — is to be given, in the name of clarity, the right to reject a question formulated by the National Assembly and the elected [representatives] of the people of Québec. According to the *Clarity Act*, a clear question appears to be solely a question that would ask whether a province should cease to be part of Canada and become an independent state[18] leaving no other constitutional option for the National Assembly without intrusion from the federal government.

The idea that a referendum is won with a majority of 50% plus one of the valid votes cast seemed also to have prevailed in all referendums organized with respect to the political and constitutional future in Québec and Canada. Here too, ideas

---

[†] From "Quebec's Right to Secessionist Self-determination: The Colliding Paths of Canada's *Clarity Act* and Quebec's *Fundamental Rights Act*" in D. Turp, *The Right to Choose: Essays on Quebec's Right of Self-Determination* (Montreal: Les Éditions Thémis Inc., 2001) 731 at 737–46. Reproduced with permission.

are in collision, since the intent of the *Clarity Act* is to give the House of Commons the power to decide that a majority of 50% plus one of valid votes cast is not enough to compel the federal government to assume its constitutional and mandatory duty to negotiate.

On this point, the collision is all the more real and the undemocratic nature of the bill all the more obvious in the light of Canadian practice on the subject of majority rule. All referendums in Canada have been held on the basis of majority rule. Newfoundland joined Confederation (on [its] third try) with 52% of the valid votes cast. All referendums on Québec's and Canada's political and constitutional future — on sovereignty-association of 1980, on the Charlottetown Accord in 1992 or on sovereignty and partnership in 1995 — were all governed by majority rule of 50% plus one of the valid votes cast.

To cast doubt on the rule of 50% plus one is also to contravene the fundamental principle of the equality of voters. The vote of some must have the same value as the vote of others. This is a matter of equity and justice the Supreme Court of Canada recognized in its 1991 decision on electoral boundaries in Saskatchewan: "[...] dilution of one citizen's vote as compared with another's should not be countenanced."[19]

. . . .

The *Fundamental Rights Act* and Canada: interests in collision

In reaction to such a serious threat to the freedom of the people of Québec to determine their future, the government of Québec tabled, on December 15, 1999, two days after the tabling of the *Clarity Bill*, a bill entitled *An Act respecting the fundamental rights and prerogatives of the Québec people and of the Québec State*. It was adopted by the National Assembly on December 7, 1999, assented to on December 13 and came into force on February 28, 2001. With this bill, the government called on the National Assembly of Québec to reaffirm Québec's freedom to determine its future and to adopt measures to establish this freedom on solid legal grounds.

. . . .

The *Fundamental Rights Act* has a much broader scope than the *Clarity Act* and was described by the Prime Minister of Québec as a charter of collective rights for Québec. As such, it is in collision not only with the *Clarity Act* but with the vision of Canada

held by its leaders and the interests they appear to promote.

One of the dominant features of the *Fundamental Rights Act* is its unreserved affirmation of the existence of the Québec people in the first chapter. This affirmation was necessitated by Canada's inability to recognize such an existence. After consistently refusing to consider that Quebecers constituted a people, albeit a nation, the attempt to affirm the existence of a "distinct society" in Québec was also challenged by the rest of Canada and its representatives.[22]

The affirmation of the existence of the people of Québec is therefore necessary in this context and permits the bill to enshrine the right to self-determination and the right to choose a political system and a legal status for Québec. In the particular case of section 4 of the *Fundamental Rights Act*, it means choosing the instrument and the rules that will best represent the will of the population and actually gives effect to [Québec's] right to freely determine [its] future. This section provides clearly that "[w]hen the Québec people [are] consulted by way of a referendum under the Referendum Act, the winning option is the option that obtains a majority of the valid votes cast, namely fifty percent of the valid votes cast plus one."

Section 5 of the *Fundamental Rights Act* rightly provides that the Québec state derives its legitimacy from the will of the people inhabiting its territory and contains an affirmation fully consistent with the third paragraph of article 21 of the *Universal Declaration of Human Rights*, which provides that "[t]he will of the people shall be the basis of the authority of government." The subsequent reference to the fact that the will of the people is expressed through the election of members to the National Assembly by universal suffrage, by secret ballot, under the one person, one vote system, pursuant to the *Election Act*[23] and through referendums[24] held pursuant to the *Referendum Act* is also consistent with the requirements of this international instrument and sets out the two Québec laws whose democratic nature is incontrovertible.

The objective of protecting Québec's internal and international jurisdictions is apparent in the other sections of chapter II of the Act and is set to collide with the interests of the federal government, which has tried to progressively expand its jurisdiction. Accordingly, section 6 of the *Fundamental Rights Act* states that "[t]he Québec State is sovereign in the areas assigned to its jurisdiction by laws and constitutional conventions." There are recent examples to support the argument that

Québec's jurisdiction has been infringed by federal authorities, whether it be in the case of the millennium scholarship institution or of the passage, without Québec's approval, of a framework agreement on Canada's social union.[25]

This sort of attitude reflects an increasing and obvious desire on the part of these federal authorities to assume a determinant role in all spheres of activity and to use their spending power to this end. Québec has consistently disputed the exercise of this power, but its pleas have been ignored. Accordingly, the government decided to remind Parliament and the government of Canada of Québec's profound commitment to its areas of jurisdiction and to their integrity and of its intention to resist any attempt to further usurp these areas that were given to Québec by law and constitutional convention.

In addition, Québec's exercise of international jurisdiction has consistently been disputed by the federal government of Canada. Here again the differing interests of Canada and Québec collide. Arguing that only the federal government had international jurisdiction as granted by royal prerogative, successive Canadian governments have rejected the doctrine formulated in 1965 by minister Paul Gérin-Lajoie to the effect that Québec could extend its internal jurisdiction internationally. Under these conditions, the principle [is] enshrined in the first paragraph of section 7 of the *Fundamental Rights Act* whereby "[t]he Québec State is free to adhere to any treaty, convention or international agreement in matters under its constitutional jurisdiction" and "[t]he Québec State is not bound by any treaty, convention, agreement or Act in the areas under its jurisdiction unless it has formally adhered to it by a decision of the National Assembly or the government, subject to the applicable legislative provisions."

. . . .

[T]he government of Québec wanted to affirm in the third paragraph of section 7 that Québec "may, in areas under its jurisdiction, transact with foreign states and ensure its representation outside Québec." In this era of globalization, such an affirmation seems all the more compelling in the light of what the Québec minister for Canadian Intergovernmental Affairs, Joseph Facal, called [a] "federative deficit",[26] which aims to prevent Québec from reaching out to the international community.

Added following the hearings of the National Assembly's Committee on Institutions, section 8 of the *Fundamental Rights Act* reiterates Québec's jurisdiction over language issues and reiterates that

French is the official language of Québec. It also emphasizes the fact that the "Québec State must promote the quality and influence of the French language" and that it "shall pursue those objectives in a spirit of fairness and open-mindedness, respectful of the long-established rights of Québec's English-speaking community." This desire to preserve and promote Québec's French language also conflicts with another desire, that of the federal government to promote two official languages in Canada.

In the chapter on the territory of Québec, the National Assembly of Québec reaffirmed that "[t]he territory of Québec and its boundaries cannot be altered except with the consent of the National Assembly." This provision is intended to ensure that the existing boundaries of Québec are respected and maintained and to counter the partitionist reveries in paragraph 3(2) of the *Clarity Act*. This provision is intended primarily to limit the right of the Québec people to choose freely their political future and status. Québec's territorial integrity, the intangibility of its borders and the rule of law ... form the cornerstone of a very broad consensus emerging in Québec.[27]

The *Fundamental Rights Act* assures the Abenaki, Algonquin, Attikamek, Cree, Huron, Innu, Malecite, Micmac, Mohawk, Naskapi and Inuit Nations of a rightful place and sets forth, in the fifth clause of the preamble, the principles associated with the recognition of the aboriginal nations including their right to autonomy within Québec. In addition, in sections 11 and 12 of the Act, the National Assembly recognizes, in exercising its constitutional jurisdiction, the existing rights — aboriginal and treaty — of the aboriginal nations of Québec, and the government undertakes to promote the establishment and maintenance of harmonious relations with these nations and to foster their development and improvement of their economic, social and cultural conditions. All these principles reaffirm the motion passed in 1985 by the National Assembly.[28]

On all these matters, the *Fundamental Rights Act* and the *Clarity Act* differ in their concepts of the future. However, with the final provision of the *Fundamental Rights Act*, the collision becomes headlong. Section 13 of this act provides that "[n]o other parliament or government may reduce the powers, authority, sovereignty or legitimacy of the National Assembly, or impose constraint on the democratic will of the Québec people to determine [their] own future." This provision is fundamental and is designed to nullify any effect of the *Clarity Act* in Québec.

305

* * *

In this pivotal year 2001, the right of peoples and nations to self-determination remains as relevant as ever. It underlies claims to autonomy and independence and the calls for freedom heard on every continent. This right rests on the guarantee of rights to national and ethnic, cultural or religious minorities and on the recognition of the right of peoples and nations to self-determination. It should notably evolve towards the recognition that political independence is a means to implement such a right in a democratic context, such as the context of Québec's claim for independence.

So long as governments and international institutions continue to question the right to self-determination and refuse to give it effect, they exacerbate conflicts and promote neither political

harmony nor cultural diversity. However, their democratization is essential and cannot be achieved at a cost to the minorities, peoples and nations that fashion this international system and give meaning to the concept of international community. This democratization must, however, be based on principles that neither threaten freedom nor impose trusteeship regimes on minorities, peoples or nations. It must never be based on the principles that gave rise to the *Clarity Act* recently enacted by the House of Commons of Canada, which represents the antithesis of the process of democratization that springs from true recognition of the right to self-determination.[29] This democratization must be based on a real desire to recognize minorities, peoples and nations which will continue to enrich the international community and the heritage of humankind.

(g) Constitutional Reform and the Future

CONCERNS

At the beginning of a new century, Canada remains a place of extraordinary opportunity and daunting challenges. A vast country, rich in resources, with one of the best living standards in the world,[1] faces a serious threat to its survival. Decades of turbulence promise still more upheaval. The poet's old lament that "the centre cannot hold"[2] is more than a concern of Ottawa mandarins fussing about their jobs. The ties that hold Canadians together have been fraying, and they are threatening to unravel.

By the late 1990s and the start of the new century, the old problems persisted, and new discontents clamoured for action. Overshadowing all else were the concerns of French-speaking Quebeckers. Alarmed that their culture, language, and way of life was submerging in an English-speaking sea, many French-speaking Quebeckers demanded more powers, more special status, even complete sovereignty, for their province. These demands could not be ignored. Quebec is Canada's largest province, with the second-largest population, and many of the country's natural resources. French-speaking Quebeckers are one of the country's major founding cultural groups. Their rich history pre-dates that of Canada itself.

There were other serious concerns. Aboriginal people, the land's first occupants, sought constitutionally entrenched Aboriginal self-government to combat the massive social and economic challenges that confront them — products, in their view, of centuries of oppression by non-Aboriginals. Western and Atlantic region residents wanted more influence in shaping decisions that affect Canada as a whole. People in the northern territories wanted more influence for their governments, and provincial status when they were ready for it.[3]

Women, more than half the Canadian population, led the struggle to bring formal equality for disadvantaged groups closer to substantive equality. In the wake of the *Charter*, new gaps were appearing before old and young, west and east, homeowners and the homeless, and Internet travellers and those left behind. While health costs climbed, and the poor fell behind, governments privatized services and chipped at the foundations of the welfare state. While some provinces prospered from oil revenues and mineral exports to China, others struggled to pay for aging roads and programs for unemployed youth. Technological change revolutionized communications for some, and put others out of work. Other major changes, such as the working mother trend and the reshaping of the modern Canadian family, generated major new needs and demands. The land and its resources were being re-shaped too, as glaciers receded, species vanished, and forests and farm plots became clear-cuts and parking lots. Summer winds brought ozone and particulates, and in the country with 20% of the world's freshwater stores, the water was being threatened by high-level consumption, untreated sewage, and underregulated industrial waste.

THE RESPONSE SO FAR

In the past several decades, Canadians have tried to resolve some of their most serious concerns through changes to the Constitution. In the late 1970s and early 1980s, mainly to address the demands of French-speaking Quebeckers, the Trudeau government enacted the *Constitution Act, 1982*. At the same time, the Act promised help for disadvantaged groups and Aboriginal peoples.

Several decades later, the verdict is still open on how much the latter have benefited from the constitutional guarantees, and Quebec's secession is still a threat. For those whose concerns it "constitutionalized", there was disappointment when court-enforced legal guarantees let them down. This prompted demands for even stronger constitutional protection. For those who felt their interests were left out, the enactment of the *Constitution Act, 1982* fuelled a desire for a place in the constitutional sun. The *Constitution Act, 1982* was enacted without the consent of the Quebec provincial government, generating a grievance that is still unresolved.

Since 1982, two full-scale constitutional attempts to accommodate the concerns of Canadians both failed dramatically. Meech Lake, an attempt to redress the feeling that the *Constitution Act, 1982* ignored Quebec's interests, foundered on the basis of opposition from *Constitution Act, 1982* rights-holders who felt that Meech Lake threatened or neglected *their* interests. Then the Charlottetown Accord tried to accommodate the concerns of Meech Lake outsiders such as Aboriginal peoples. In doing so, it created a hodge-podge of special rights and rights hierarchies that troubled others. The size and range of the Charlottetown Accord led many Quebeckers to conclude that their own special interests had been diluted. Yet provisions designed to combat this feeling, such as Quebec's permanent guarantee of 25% of the seats in the House of Commons, were regarded outside Quebec as unfair special treat-

ment. After both Meech Lake and Charlottetown, there was a general concern that the public had been unable to participate effectively in approving the changes.[4]

Today, after a period of constitutional exhaustion, there are some calls again for major constitutional change. In light of what has happened so far, these calls should be treated with caution.

SOME STRUCTURAL OPTIONS

At the same time, the concerns and demands described above must be addressed. In particular, a third Quebec referendum on secession is still a possibility. What, then, are some of the main structural options that are available? Although the list below[5] focuses mainly on possible responses to the concerns of French-speaking Quebeckers, even this basic challenge cannot be considered in a vacuum. One caveat is necessary: most of these options assume that a significant majority of Quebeckers do not vote "yes" on a referendum to secede from Canada — if they do, Quebeckers and other Canadians will be in uncharted land.

The Status Quo

The *status quo* in Canada is a relatively decentralized federal system that unites over 30 million people in 13 provinces and territories of widely differing sizes and resources, in a form of economic union.[6] One province, Quebec, is unique because of its French-speaking majority. A number of constitutional provisions relate specially to Quebec's legal system and languages. For the most part, though, Quebec is treated formally as an ordinary province. In the far north, Canada's three huge territories have tiny populations and limited provincial-type powers. Under provincial control are thousands of municipal and regional governments that range from villages to metropolitan bodies for city populations in the millions. Canada's one million Aboriginal peoples are subject to public governments, but have a number of special self-government structures as well. Beyond this, the country's constitution includes a *Charter* of individual and some group rights[7] and a constitutional amending formula that is controlled formally by the federal and provincial governments.[8]

The *status quo* appears to offer a default option, available when or if others fail.[9]

But many Canadians have expressed dissatisfaction with this option in the past. For some, at least, we need major structural constitutional changes to the protection of rights or to the operation of the federal system.

Group Rights Protection

The *Charter* attempted to protect minority, ethnic, and other group private rights by entrenching them in the formal part of our constitution. Pluralist pressures might be accommodated by additional rights protection, such as entrenchment of specific Aboriginal rights to self-government. For Quebec, this approach could involve constitutional recognition of the people of that province as a distinct society. On the other hand, this approach could transfer more power to an unelected judiciary, could provoke opposition from those it left out, could exacerbate inequalities between individual Canadians or provinces, and would do little to address economic inequalities.[10] Outside Quebec, distinct society recognition might be palatable if it involved no special legal powers or privileges; inside Quebec, this might not be good enough.

Centripetal Federalism

Centripetal federalism involves the participation of regional governments in institutions at the national level. This approach would enhance provincial and regional representation in federal government institutions such as the Senate and the Supreme Court of Canada. Although it might meet many regional concerns, especially in western Canada, this approach would do relatively little to address concerns in Quebec. Many Quebeckers have sought more power or sovereign status *for that province*. Moreover, if centripetal federalism is implemented on the basis of equal provincial representation,[11] it requires less than equal federal representation for individual residents in the more populous provinces.[12]

Decentralized Federalism

Another option is constitutional amendments to give the provinces greater jurisdiction over a range of subjects from labour training to telecommunications and culture. This could respond to Quebec's desire for more powers by offering similar powers to all provinces. This approach was a key aspect of the Meech Lake and Charlottetown accords.

However, too much decentralization could lead to extreme regional inequality, internal population and economic immobility, and a cultural void at the national level. Moreover, not all provinces may desire the same degree of decentralization. What may be thought necessary in Quebec or desirable in Alberta might be financially unworkable in Newfoundland.

Asymmetrical Federalism

This would give greater powers or rights only to the provinces that desire them. The approach might be carried further to confer very distinct status and powers on the province of Quebec. It might accommodate many concerns in Quebec, but could also exacerbate inequalities in basic public services of different provinces. Unless every province could take advantage of a special arrangement, special benefits for some could provoke resentment by others. Provincial egalitarianism was an important factor in influencing and ultimately helping to defeat the Meech Lake and Charlottetown accords; in the 1997 federal election the Reform Party attracted considerable support outside Quebec by insisting on equality of the provinces as well as equality of individuals.

Dualist Federalism

This approach would emphasize a French-speaking/English-speaking duality, or a combination of the two. However, it could provoke opposition from groups (such as Aboriginal peoples, ethnic groups other than those with English or French roots, or others) or provinces not specifically associated with these dualities.

Provincial Confederation

A federal system shares the powers of a single state between two levels of government, each sovereign in its own sphere. A true confederation, on the other hand, is an association of two or more states united through a central government that exercises delegated powers on behalf of sovereign provinces. A simple provincial confederation would involve a nominal federal government exercising powers on behalf of sovereign provinces, each with a veto over constitutional changes. The delegated powers might include some areas of common concern, such as defence, transportation, currency, trade and environmental protection, and immigration, or might be limited to economic matters. Provincial confederation would be a flexible but highly unstable arrangement, with all the disadvantages of extreme decentralized federalism. At the economic level, it would likely involve something like a common market,[13] or customs union,[14] rather than a full economic union.[15] Outside some sovereigntist and autonomist circles in Quebec,[16] there appears to be little support for this approach.

Sovereignty-association

This concept involves a sovereign Quebec and a sovereign body comprising Canada outside Quebec, associated for economic and other specific purposes. Such an arrangement might involve a customs union with a common currency, as between Slovakia and the Czech Republic,[17] or it might amount to no more than a free trade area.[18] The concept is strongly supported by the Parti Québécois. It has little support outside Quebec.

Separate Sovereign Status

This would involve a wholly separate, sovereign Quebec, or (in the case of Aboriginal peoples), separate, sovereign Aboriginal communities. While responding to the demands of some Quebeckers and some Aboriginal people, this option would be difficult to implement as a practical matter. It could involve considerable social unrest, and major economic and political disruption. There would be no likelihood of any special economic links, especially in the short term. Outside Quebec, and apart from some more militant Aboriginal associations, this option appears to have little support as a first preference.[19]

COMMON ELEMENTS

Four general comments can be made about these options. First, many of the alternatives are not mutually exclusive, and many other arrangements are conceivable. Second, none of these options is without problems. Third, most of the options focus on the problem of discontent in Quebec, without addressing the many other concerns described earlier. Fourth, most of the non-sovereigntist options above can be pursued by informal or even non-constitutional means.

THE FUTURE

Despite past failures, it would be rash to set aside all our efforts at formal constitutional change. Fundamental challenges can require significant responses, and at some point formal ground rules must be updated to reflect social realities. But formal documents with entrenched rights are only one part of the Canadian constitution. For over a hundred years this country managed to accommodate most differences, diversity, and reform through ordinary statutes, intergovernmental agreements, and political conventions. There were lapses and inequities, but change was possible, and the country survived.

Informal and non-constitutional change has a lower profile, is less dramatic, less rigid, and more responsive to electoral control than formal constitutional amendments. Most of the concerns and problems considered at the beginning of this discussion have cultural, economic, environmental, or political roots — they do not necessarily require constitutional solutions. Constitutional rights are unlikely to provide jobs, relieve poverty, or generate cultural respect. Even where it might make a difference, constitutional change is powerful medicine. Its side-effects may outweigh its benefits.

Where net benefits do seem likely, most options can be accomplished by ordinary statutes, common law presumptions, and executive agreements.[20] Openness can be secured by more effective consultation, perhaps by plebiscite, before important agreements are signed. Then mistakes can be rectified, and politicians can be held fully accountable.

Beyond this, we need the qualities that have served Canadians for over a century and a quarter — tolerance, respect for others, and an awareness that not all problems need be constitutional problems. Is this too high a price for the privilege of living in one of the most fortunate countries in the world?

Notes

1. As noted earlier in this chapter, the United Nations Development Program has consistently ranked Canada as one of the best countries in the world in which to live: see, for example, P. Knox, "Canada still best place to live, UN says — Best in world 4th year in a row" *The [Toronto] Globe and Mail* (12 June 1997) A1.
2. "Things fall apart, the centre cannot hold;

    Mere anarchy is loosed upon the world,
    The blood-dimmed tide is loosed, and everywhere
    The ceremony of innocence is drowned...."

W.B. Yeats, "The Second Coming" in A.N. Jeffares, ed. *W.B. Yeats' Selected Poetry* (London: Pan Books, 1962) at 99.

3. The planned creation of the new northern territory of Nunavut reflected both Inuit and general northern desires for greater self-control.

4. Although the Charlottetown process was (unlike that in Meech Lake) preceded by massive consultation, the 51-page final legal text of the complex agreement was released only weeks before the referendum, with little opportunity for public discussion and virtually none for alteration.

5. This list was adopted in part from R.M. Lee, "A Brief Guide to What's Watts" *Ottawa Citizen*, 1991, B-1, summarizing options considered by Ronald L. Watts, "Options for the Future of Canada: The Good, the Bad, and the Fantastic" in Ronald L. Watts & Douglas M. Brown, eds., *Options for a New Canada* (Toronto: University of Toronto Press, 1991) at 123. Watts stressed that the constitutional options should not be regarded as mutually exclusive or assumed to be equally attainable.

6. For a succinct description of "economic union", see Robert A. Young, *The Secession of Quebec and the Future of Canada* (Montreal & Kingston: McGill-Queen's University Press, 1995) at 30–33.

7. The *Charter* is by no means comprehensive. It says little, for example, about the wide economic gaps between many individual Canadians. The equality guarantees in ss. 15 and 28 do not refer to economic inequality, and the equalization and regional disparity provisions in s. 36 fall short of constituting guarantees.

8. This formal control may now be subject to a developing constitutional convention that requires that major amendments be approved directly by the Canadian public.

9. See, however, Garth Stevenson, "Canadian Federalism: The Myth of the Status Quo" in Janine Brodie and Linda Trimble, eds., *Reinventing Canada: Politics of the 21st Century* (Toronto: Prentice Hall, 2003) at 204–16. Stevenson argues that significant changes have been occurring in Canadian federalism recently, even in the absence of major formal amendments. As a result, he says the idea of a fixed status quo is a myth.

10. Arguably, a *Charter* — which is enforced by judges — *can* do relatively little to make the budgetary and administrative changes necessary to significantly reduce economic inequalities.

11. As it was in the "Triple-E" Senate proposal supported by many Westerners during the Meech Lake and Charlottetown talks.

12. For example, if Prince Edward Island were given the right to elect or nominate the same number of Senators as Ontario, Ontario would have far less *per capita* Senate representation than Prince Edward Island.

13. That is, with common external trade controls, but only limited central economic regulation: see the comparison between economic union, common market, customs union, and free trade area in Young, *supra* note 6, ch. 3.

14. That is, with common external trade controls, but no central economic regulation: *ibid.*

15. With common external trade controls and policy and central economic regulation to prevent internal trade barriers, encourage internal economic exchange: *ibid.*

16. See the Economic and Political Partnership structure proposed by the Parti Québécois in the 1995 referendum on secession. As well, the "autonomy" contemplated by the Action démocratique du Québec might involve some kind of strict confederal arrangement: see Carole Beaulieu and Michel Vastel, "Le Nouveau Pouvoir du Mario" *L'actualité*, 32:8 (15 May 2007) 18.

17. Young, *supra* note 6, ch. 11.

18. That is, with minimal or non-existent internal tariffs, but independent internal and external economic policies: *ibid.*, ch. 3.

19. However, if Quebeckers did vote clearly and unequivocally in favour of secession, this sentiment could change. Many non-Quebeckers might then advocate a "clean break" rather than negotiating economic ties as close as those at present.

20. For example, of the five constitutional demands made by Quebec in the wake of the *Constitution Act, 1982*, nearly all have been addressed to some extent by informal means. While the wide-ranging Aboriginal provisions of the Charlottetown Accord came to nothing, concrete changes were being negotiated — although with agonizing slowness — in the form of Aboriginal land claims agreements. Critics might decry informal change as a tool of "rachet federalism", in which one accommodation simply paves the way for another. But that argument could be made of any change, and it may underestimate intangible qualities such as good will, generosity, and the will to live together.

(h) Constitutionalism and the Crisis of the Nation-State[†]

Peter Emberley

NOTE

Peter Emberley's article recalls our examination of public law and the state at the beginning of the sourcebook. Emberley suggests that it is not only Canada, but the very concept of the nation-state, that is under siege in the modern world. What are the forces that the author says are acting on the nation-state? What are the consequences for the process of future constitutional

† From "Globalism and Localism: Constitutionalism in a New World Order," in C. Cook, ed., *Constitutional Predicament: Canada after the Referendum* (Montreal & Kingston: McGill-Queen's University Press, 1994) at 199–217, 285–87. Reproduced with permission.

change in Canada? For the role of courts in this process? Is the nation-state as endangered as Emberley suggests? Compare Emberley's portrait of the nation-state with that of Jürgen Habermas in Chapter 1. Which portrait best describes Canada in the 21st century?

EXTRACT

"The constitutional odyssey must end," Peter Russell argued in a recent article in the *Globe and Mail* (4 October 1992), "to secure Canada's sovereignty." There is really only one essential question, Russell contends, underlying our constitutional wrangles: whether we can be a people sharing a common constitution. "Is it too much." he challenges, "to seek closure on that question?"

Seek *closure*? Is it accidental that one of Canada's most respected political scientists would express his desire for unity with a term that resonates deeply with the deconstructive tactics of progressive intellectuals all over Europe and North America? And though Russell *seeks* closure while those intellectuals *vilify* closure, is it not curious that each sees the task of politics in relation to the closure of discourse? And does Russell's desire for closure not finally vitiate his own liberal politics?

In this essay, I am suggesting that the convergence of language is neither accidental nor merely semantic. I shall argue that the *problematique* of contemporary politics is one necessarily characterized by ambiguity, paradox, and disjunction. Russell's malapropism is repeated by many, from those who are committed to democratic pluralism but use the language of Derridean difference, to environmentalists who, in the interests of a less destructive relation to nature, desire more effectual "resource management"; to Aboriginal people who wish to live by their ancestral traditions, which they have come to know as their "cultural values"; to marginal populations who seek political recognition but denounce Western power; and to legislators who cannot distinguish between political, social, and administrative issues, reckoning that each has a place in the constitution.

The obvious difficulty of these positions is that each is composed of metaphysical postulates contesting with one another, rendering the amalgam incoherent and even comical: early modern (Newtonian) liberalism with postmodernist renunciation of the subject; traditional metaphysics of nature with the technological act of seeing the world as object; premodern cosmologies with the radical historicist denial of order; a humanist desire for "self-empowerment" with Heidegger's anti-humanist "fundamental ontology"; and premodern and modern *diaresis* of different dimensions of reality with contemporary suspicion of distinctions.

These strange fusions are indicative of the fact that we are living through a complex time. The paradoxes betray a deep crisis in the self-interpretation of contemporary man: we are attempting in a seminal manner to express the experience of participating in a dynamic that is radically transforming the bearings defining us as modern beings, while having as compass points only the political language of that modern period. Part of us is gravitating towards a centre while as great a part is shifting to multiple peripheries. Some explanations of this motion even suggest that the present dynamism is exploding centre-periphery relations.[1] In desperation to express what it is we are experiencing, we are grasping into the vocabularies of the premodern and non-Western. But what is peculiarly contemporary about these combinations is not simply their inconsistency — for when has the everyday world ever been free of contradictions and paradoxes? — but that these inconsistencies are wholly acceptable to us. Indeed, they are not seen as inconsistencies, nor do we question their coherence because the difference between surface and ground is becoming obscure to us. We live in a time when the demand for consistency and coherence no longer has any standing and when the simple fact that we are aroused, agitated, or tantalized by images and signs is sufficient justification for these pastiches of political declaration to be the mainstay of our political debate.[2]

Permit me to establish the parameters of this paper's argument as follows: decisive watersheds in the history of the West are marked by a dissolution in the primary political unit. This dissolution coincides with efforts to resymbolize order, efforts which can occur across the spectrum of human activity. Our times, it has been suggested, are reproducing the form of the political mobilization, intellectual realignment, and spiritual perplexity occasioned by the decline of the Greek polis in the fourth century B.C. and the ecumenic empire in the thirteenth century. In our case it is the nation-state that is losing its status as the symbol of order, as the symbol that focuses our ambitions and hopes, our desires and thoughts. Its dissolution has both a theoretical and a pragmatic dimension.

Let us look first at the theoretical dimension. Modern constitutionalism, and the moral principles it safeguarded, was sustained by a theoretical foundation that had its birth in the symbolic reconstellation of the Renaissance and Reformation. However, at its core, modern constitutionalism also reaches back to the metaphysic of Plato and Aristotle. In the new science projected by Francis Bacon and René Descartes, which built on the achievements of the Renaissance and the Reformation and whose theoretical conceptualization underscores modern constitutionalism, that metaphysic is still present. However, in the desire to give that metaphysic an immediate political efficacy, early modern thinkers dogmatized certain features of it. In Hobbes and Locke, for example, the symbols "rational man" and "social man," which in the past articulated complex and fluid tensions within human existence, could become the authoritative bases for concepts of political sovereignty, political power, and the juridical person. In application, these ideas historically lent themselves far too conveniently to harsh, crude, and oppressive practices. Many have pointed out how, in the interests of efficacy, these thinkers offered reductionist and vulgar accounts of human longing. However, there was also a restraining feature to modern thought: it has to be admitted that these modern thinkers retained the restrained anthropomorphism of the ancient metaphysic: man, for Plato as for Hobbes, is the measure of all things.[3] This meant that reflection on the whole — nature, the universe, the world — was mediated by a conception of what was good and useful for man.

But four hundred years of subsequent deconstruction of these dogmatisms, in the hands of Kant, Hegel, and Nietzsche, has led to a progressive, and finally, radical repudiation of all the forms of the traditional metaphysic, the denunciation of the humanism it had sanctioned, and the rise of a situation in which traditional moral and political categories of analysis increasingly no longer have standing. The ease with which individuals feel they can jettison or creatively manipulate their identity — regardless of historical or cultural matrices, not to say natural ones — as well as the evident impotence individuals experience in affecting the essential features of mass society (evident both at a pragmatic level and in intellectual fashion) and the widespread acceptance of a self-interpretation that sees human beings as part of a universal process signal that what we take persons and society to be is under radical revision. In an age in which tremendous technological forces can be unleashed, whose power exceeds human measure, and in which many see the "person" less as an initiator of action than as an effect (often an accidental or arbitrary one), a fundamental reassessment of the modern self-interpretation seems to be occurring. My view is that the current situation is one where central modern concepts such as agency, intentionality, power, identity, and causality — which had been keyed in to an epistemological structure whose source was Newtonian physics and Cartesian subjectivism and rationalism — no longer appear to have sufficient explanatory power. An atavistic residue of these remains in legal and political speech, where the fiction of sovereignty, responsibility, and representation is maintained but the concrete evidence of social life, I suggest, belies this speech.

Simultaneously, the organization of independent nation-states is being replaced by a system of interdependencies whose "anarchic" form of power defies control or regulation by single actors, be they individuals, groups, institutions, or governments. The web of power has neither centre nor periphery; its relations are neither continuous nor causal; its motions are neither sequential nor uniform. We are witnessing complex and contradictory forces, which on the one hand are apparently integrating and homogenizing global culture, social policy, and technological programs and, on the other hand, are evidently disseminating production processes, proliferating social identities, and valourizing localized initiative. A situation is emerging where concerted, globally cooperative participation is required (in response to an increasingly fragile ecosystem, to potential nuclear terrorism, to the threat of regional wars) and yet where the possibility of agreement on criteria or measures of what is reasonable, just, or appropriate is being flatly rejected under the guise of a new pluralism. I suggest, however, that this pluralism has none of the substance or critical potential of classic democratic pluralism (as is still evident in C.B. Macpherson, Carole Pateman, and Robert Dahl). It is instead a mere multiplicity or heterogeneity of deracinated voices (or "discourses"), constituted in great part through the communications media, and distanced from any reality commonly attested to, other than that which is the product of subjective grievance or private fantasy. This radical heterogeneity and fragmentation is the context in which contemporary efforts to reappraise and renew constitutions is taking place, and it is placing burdens upon courts and legislators which the "metaphysic" of modern constitutionalism cannot bear.

The Canadian discord is an example of this world crisis. From Meech Lake to the Charlottetown Constitutional Accord, a plethora of recommendations and detractions, options and grievances, has been aired; each voice has been granted legitimacy and been permitted to be fully recognized as necessary to the political debate. The new constitution was to speak authentically to different voices, and it was to resonate with the radically transforming dynamics of contemporary life. The language of this amalgam is confusing and discontinuous: "founding nations," "empowerment," "global competitiveness," "distinct society," "effectiveness," "parliamentary supremacy," "managing culture," "special responsibility," "asymmetry," "affirmative action," and so on. It is remarkable that anyone would assume that all these voices could and should be accommodated. The debate quintessentially exemplifies the novelty of the contemporary world. Images and signs of ancient Greek practice, Roman theory, medieval organization, early modern reform, and late modern praxis float and circulate around; politics (which, incidentally, is no longer differentiated from legal, social, economic, or administrative dimensions) is a grand play of the surface. What is absent is the assumption, which governed both the ancient and the modern world, that politics needs a ground; or better, that political reform should be grounded in rational justification, or experience, or a philosophy of history, or the self-evidentness of political or moral principle.

Perhaps we should not be surprised. That we would proceed in the absence of a ground has been prepared for us by predominant philosophers of this century, who witnessed, participated in, and attempted to symbolize the dynamic of world transformation that is currently underway. In a lecture given in 1956, Martin Heidegger undertook a radical deconstruction of Leibniz's principle of sufficient reason. The lecture, entitled "Der Satz vom Grund," or "The Principle of Ground," was an effort to shift subsequent philosophy away from the traditional premises of rational inquiry: namely that everything has a ground, everything that is real has a ground for its reality, every behaviour has a foundation, no judgment without justification, no truth without proven correctness, no event without a cause that is a kind of ground; in sum, nothing without ground. Leibniz's principle of sufficient reason, the principle that nothing exists for which the ground of its existence cannot be sufficiently presented, he argued, only encapsulates what is expressed in all philosophy to date. But there is a more authentic relation, Heidegger challenged, that the essence of man can have to Being. Calling that thinking which requires a ground a "madness," Heidegger looked to a future in which the Western error would be overcome.

Thirty-six years later, I want to argue, we are participating in such an overcoming and are beginning to catch the faint outlines of an era that finds its self-interpretation in that primordial genesis of perpetual becoming which Heidegger took to be the more authentic resonance with Being. What was meant to be an ontological analytic — or, to give it the most generous recognition, a reformulation of human consciousness — has become for us the concrete actuality of our everyday lives. I suggest that if we wish to understand the distinctive modalities of contemporary constitutionalism, and the Canadian situation in particular, it is to Heidegger and his epigone that we must turn to observe with them the unfolding of the dynamic to which they were witness.[4]

I would like to focus my discussion on the crisis of the nation-state. To understand the character of the nation-state thoroughly, one must attend not only to its pragmatic historical reality but also to both the logic of its conceptual organization — as this is elaborated in the works of Thomas Hobbes and John Locke and completed in the thought of Immanuel Kant — and to the perception of the order of reality it was meant to represent. In her book *The Origins of Totalitarianism*, Hannah Arendt has set out the former with great clarity. I shall summarize this account only briefly before turning to the latter topic.

Throughout the seventeenth and eighteenth centuries, nation-states developed under the direction of absolute sovereigns. These forms of political association were highly unstable, because they linked together two opposing forces: the state, with its focus on freedom of the legal person and equality before the law, and the nation, with its demand for conformity to its ethos and exclusivity. The recurring conflicts within them [were] a consequence of attempting to graft national interest onto legal institutions. Either the state was an instrument of the law or it was an instrument of the nation. Conceptually, the nation-state was organized, on the one hand, around the ideas of sovereignty and the juridical person and, on the other hand, on the principle of the equal recognition of particularistic or ascriptive relations under the law and the act of representation whereby these relations could acquire a public persona.

The state is an enactment of sovereign legislation, and its form assumes the existence of autonomous individuals who can reproduce the act of sovereign legislation within themselves. The principle of the state's authority is not bonds of family or blood ties, but consent to the enactment of the rule of law. The sovereign establishes a public domain regulated not by a substantive vision of what humans think good, for on that no agreement is possible, but by certain procedural criteria of right, which safeguard the security and rights of the person. The authority held by the state is legitimate by virtue of each individual's rational ratification of the contractual relation he or she has to the state. This is either a calculation of how one's rational self-interest is preserved by obliging oneself to the principle of contractual relations; or it is a situation where the political contract is dignified by the moral act of affirming the law as the universal form of respect for all rational persons. In either case, no primordial or innate bonds to one's people, or land, or tribe provides the distinctly rational principle of obligation. In other words, political organization rests on the distinctions between state and society, and between the political and the social. The understanding of equality, identity, and freedom are all defined by these distinctions. The individual recapitulates the form of political sovereignty in the act of self-division: his particular will is surmounted by a general will that is the expression of rational calculation. Sovereignty at the level of world organization means that the world is a system of states, a collection of distinct powers, whose legislative enactments give them absolute control of the territory and people within their boundaries, and who in principle are independent of each other. The world situation is one of a tenuous and fragile balance of powers.

The imperative of formal equality under the law means that the task of government is to ensure a homogeneous population. It must integrate distinct individuals to accept and respect one another as legal persona and to see the rational necessity of a common law. The only way that government will be able to integrate a differentiated body politic is by enforcing consent to principles of right rather than to substantive notions of justice. Its legitimacy will nevertheless recurringly be questioned. This is why a civil service that is economically independent and politically neutral is central to a state's persistent ability to legitimate itself. The state's authority depends on it. To speak of "authority" is to recognize a power above the state: its constitution, a paradigm of order that stipulates the character and accompanying procedures for the maintenance of political liberty and sovereignty and is the rational standard for all political practice.

The second term of the "nation-state" hybrid pulls in the opposite direction. The nation is partial and exclusive. It grounds the legitimacy of its principles on a commonality of innate characteristics, or tribal allegiances, or a shared destiny, which is to say that it defines human essence by its rootedness and irreducible belongingness to a place and to a history. Human experience is not simply within universal space and time; these are instead invested with human meaning, located and dignified by stories of memorable events and exemplary persons. A nation operates by a substantive vision of virtue and the good, and finds the principle of obligation in culture, language, religion, or race. Integral to the nation's principle, then, is privilege. It sees the law as the outgrowth of its unique national substance and as something that is not valid beyond its own people and the boundaries of its own territory. The nation is a contained entity; it has to be added that expansion is not inherent to its principle.

When nation and state combine, the result is obviously unstable. The nation-state must balance rootedness and belongingness with equality under the law. It must balance exclusivity with fairness, substantive justice with respect for difference. The two poles between which the nation-state is situated produce a field of tension structured by forces tending on the one hand to identity and on the other hand to difference. Another way of saying this is that one of its forces pushes for universality; the other, for particularity. As state, it must maintain equality of rights for all, even beyond its own boundaries, but as nation, it will make nationality a prerequisite of citizenship. The state machinery must rule above nationalities, but its legitimation depends on consciousness of national identity. Internally, the nation-state will be subject to conflict in which its efforts to establish national consciousness will splinter, and a multiplicity of nationalities will desire distinctive sovereignty. Every group must be respected as equal, but there are inevitable conflicts between different groups, each reluctant to grant the other this basic recognition of equality. The nation-state will have to make continuous efforts to assimilate, rather than integrate, the population in order to ensure active consent to its government. It cannot allow things to degenerate into simple facts of birth, and it has to maintain the elaborate artifice of the political state; but the substance of the regime comes from forces denying these efforts. The contradiction between equality and privilege can be resolved only by an ideology of respect and self-respect. Even if that result can be produced, the nation-state cannot avoid tension, political agitation towards one pole or the other, the recurring threat of dispersion of national focus, and the mobilization of support behind either extreme unity or extreme divisiveness and fragmentation.

Historically, this tension and unrest were not always a bad thing. For one, they ensured a politics of continual self-questioning. More importantly, they constituted the ingredients of the most essential character of a body politic — plurality. Where the nation-state could balance its contradictory forces, it produced a politics of reciprocity, in which identity was harmonized with difference. A politics of plurality, which is more than simple multiplicity of the same view countless times over, testified to the uniqueness of essentially different perspectives.

The nation-state was an historical achievement. That is to say that the nation-state was a chance combination of political expedience and insight into the grounds of human order. Now, as even Plato understood, these chance combinations cannot be expected to be everlasting. Arendt is particularly vivid in her demonstration of how its contradictions have torn the nation-state apart; it cannot be said to be our primary political unit, for the nation-state increasingly now fails to focus our self-understanding.[5] Two processes emanate from our historical experience of the nation-state: the aggregation of some phenomena into a universal pattern and the dissemination of others towards the minutely particular. Released from the limits imposed by the humanist science of politics that attempted to harmonize them — and to ground them in a science of order — these processes are now producing a wholly novel array of identities and interdependencies which are quite outside the practices, institutions, and ethos of the nation-state.

THE DISRUPTION OF MODERN CONSCIOUSNESS

The historical particulars of the gradual inanition of the nation-state [have] been widely documented by international-relations theorists. The names Richard Ashley, James Der Derian, Michael Shapiro, Rob Walker, and Henry Kariel are well known, as are the general arguments made by many writers in the journals *Alternatives* and *Millennium*. These theorists have argued that such phenomena as direct foreign investment, trade liberalization, tied capital and debt flows, the international division of labour, the dissemination of production processes, the disappearance of dominant poles structuring central and peripheral relations, the growing presence of multilateral institutions such as GATT, the proliferation of a vast array of old and new nationalisms, and the effect of mass culture have significantly diminished the sovereignty, territorial integrity, and symbolic order of the nation-state, not only vis-à-vis other states but also domestically. In a global economy, it is argued, management and administration of system-norms are gradually replacing traditional nation-state performance.[6] Moreover, as these international-relations theorists also point out, the unfolding reality is making mockery of modern forms of political analysis: developmental theories, group theory, rational actor models, deterrence theory, and interpretations of structures of dominance and subordination. In the absence of those visible poles which, during the modern period, structured the various political terrains — two distinct empires, East and West, state and society, centre and margin — and in the emergence of mass, global society interconnected by sophisticated information and communications technologies, modern concepts seem to be faltering. The new world "order," it is argued, is a radical disruption of the modern organization of power and ideas, a revolutionary sweep of the ground upon which modern practice and theory stood.

We need, however, to add a further element to this account by international-relations theorists. The organization of power under the symbol "nation-state" was more than the conjunction of social/economic relations and ideas. It was also the expression of a perception of the order of reality. The construct of reality upon which the nation-state's distribution of political actors, social relations, and authorized knowledges rested can be apprehended by an audit of its epistemological presuppositions.[7] What held the symbolic structure of the nation-state together was a specific ordering of human consciousness, distinctive to the modern era, namely, the coordinates of space and time derived from the Newtonian-Cartesian paradigm. The understandings of politics, culture, and power of the modern period are based on notions of space as enclosed, homogeneous, and exclusive, and on notions of time as linear, successively durational, and irreversible, constituting the human experiences of sequentiality, causality, and continuity. This is a view of the world which sees its forces as mechanical and its phenomena as mutually exclusive. Each compartment or departmental boundary is seen as having a separate order of constitutionality, a regime understood as having a singular purpose or end.

Politically, a consciousness ordered by the Newtonian-Cartesian perspective will identify the relevant phenomena as structured by the problems of sovereignty and freedom of self-definition. How is power distilled into authority? What vector of force causes the effect of constraint? How can human relations be seen within the series of objectification, alienation, resistance, and reconciliation? The traditional causalities and sequences constituting the activity of autonomous states, the contract relations between self-interested agents and groups, the coordination of centres and peripheries of control, or the composition of political personae are recognized to be stable and secure. The durable coordinates of uniformity and repeatability, homogeneity, and distance, which constitute distinctive "points of view," underlie the formal equality and recognition of plurality of legal persons under the law.

It is within this paradigm, which sees the world as a taxonomic grid of distinct and separate entities, each structured by the idea of independent sovereignty and each located at a specific conjuncture of history and place, that the questions of ethnicity, nationalism, cultural right to self-determination, economic control, and ideology — and the constitutional separating out and uniting together of these elements — are still, in great part, being posed. Seeing the world as a mechanical interaction of spaces and durations legitimates certain types of questions while ignoring others. In an important way, it sees the problems of politics and culture exclusively as being confined within specifiable boundaries and as being characterized as a specific, localizable set of phenomena and a logic distinctive to an established form of social existence, such as labour, class, religion, or art.

This problematization of culture and politics assumes that power is something held, appropriated, transferred, and exchanged; in other words, that there is a fixed quantum of power within which political relations are formed. Power, in this perspective, is an opaque force emanating from a subject (an individual, group, class, state, or nation) through knowable dramas of history within the evident experience of a place. The task is to acquire power and to turn it to one's advantage. This same problematization also assumes that there are reasons and justifications that legitimate action, that any rational person could be brought to recapitulate for himself. There are forms of inquiry and objects of cognition that can rationally substantiate the exercises of power. Power and knowledge (as Michel Foucault depicts in *Discipline and Punish*, his study of lawlessness within and beyond the juridical state) articulate themselves on one another, forming the distinctive tensions and ambiguities of this political history.[8]

The dynamic in which we find ourselves today, however, cannot be confined conveniently by this Newtonian-Cartesian system of boundaries. The world in which the problems of identity and difference arise is one that is traversed by a new form of power whose fluidity, non-localizable episodes, and non-linear generative order is breaking apart centre/margin relations, cause/effect sequences, and traditional models of intentionality, agency, and responsibility. At a pragmatic level, once the ascending forces of existence manifest themselves as global information networks, disseminated production modes,

bio-technological interventions and simulations, and optimalizations of life forms, the regulative parameters and symbolizations of order of modern constitutionalism are left far behind. The projected scope of the new developments is even taking us beyond an era of *international* political economy or *multinational* corporate enterprise, at least as these have traditionally been mediated through the interests of a sovereign nation-state, to a global and mass process with its own internal dynamic. The current realignments and unending readjustments of the defined limits of what we have taken the human to be — singularly, politically, economically, socially — simply exceeds the still considerably "humanistic" boundaries of an industrial, materials-based society. Indeed, the "personal," "political," "economic," and "social" can hardly be kept conceptually distinct. We are required to think of a globally transformative process of a new "order."

What is this new process? From within liberalism and from within the regulative principles of modern constitutionalism has emerged a dynamic (variously called global realignment, systems-management, the consumer age, the information and communications process) whose vitality, I wish to argue, is corroding those political and economic parameters of modernity which, since the Industrial Revolution, have limited that dynamic. The era of the nation-state and the confinement of questions of economics and social existence to the political form of sovereignty is nullified under the realignment effected by the globalizing transformation of this dynamic, which, to give it its most general name, is technology.

This needs explanation by our expanding on what is meant by "technology." Technology is more than an aggregate of techniques, instruments, machines, and organizational procedures. It is a way of seeing human and non-human nature as something to be controlled and managed. It is not even just a perspective or mind-set; increasingly, it is the ontological basis of our being, a development that can be thoroughly thought through only by bringing together the work of Hegel and Heidegger, a task that can be started by reading Jacques Ellul's seminal work, *The Technological Society*.

For our present purposes, technology (that is, the appropriation, mastery or domination, and correction of human and non-human nature) is not merely applied science but is the modern form of science and thus our sole mode of legitimate rationality. Prior to modernity, knowledge came from practical experience or through thoughtful wonder at, and consent to, the eternity of what is, but since Galileo and Descartes modern knowledge has been a type of making: the world must be reordered to reveal its inner structure and laws. Instruments must disturb and break down the compounds in which existence appears in the everyday. Knowing requires an extracting of phenomena as objects. Reason is technical, regulative, and interventionist, rather than receptive. Science itself has become inherently technological — to know is to control and master ambiguity, contradiction, and tension in existence. Technology is increasingly our way of revealing and understanding our being — displacing philosophy, art, religion, and politics, which were the traditional indices of what human limit and possibility are. In technology we expect to find both the fullest expression of our freedom and the highest form of our rationality.[9]

Now, technology, as reading Descartes and Bacon makes clear, is also an interventionist and regulative mode of world organization. Our hopes for freedom and understanding can advance by this account only through constant re-creation and experimentation with reality. Descartes' method, whose imperative of world-denial and world reconstruction leads to this, is important for another reason: the resolutive-compositive method demands universality and homogeneity, not only because Descartes understood it to be applicable transculturally, but because it assumes a reality that is essentially unidimensional, clear, and simple, its parts equally commensurable to one another. World events are subject to universally valid laws. The suspension of trust in the senses and their images is at once the occlusion of the entire existing intellectual tradition, popular opinion, and common sense. Henceforth, man would see himself as a universal being, with no fixed centre.

This universality means a number of things. Technology refers to a "systematic" deployment of instruments, procedures, and skills under organized rules to achieve the effect of optimal efficiency. "System" suggests a process of growing interdependence of controlled environments whereby single components are "rationalized" and thereby rendered equivalent and substitutable. Industrial, social, cultural, and psychological phenomena are ordered into subsystems and installed within an interrelated and interdependent web. Separate and distinctive techniques tend to integrate and function within continuous processes. The emergence of supply networks, multinational production cooperatives, and information networks indicates a correlation of manifold technologies in which diverse techniques are coordinated to function according to overall processes of development that are internal to the system. The density and complexity of the world is reduced and contracted to resemble the perfect workings of a machine and the mathematical logic of perfect relations and proportions. Moreover, all systems function by the process of "dynamic disequilibrium": as long as they continue to be challenged by countervailing tendencies and by margins of indetermination they are vital, for the system's strength is measured by its capacity to grow in power. Thus, such systems are expansionary: to avoid internal dissonance, a system, coming up against other systems, will enhance itself by competition and then incorporate these or demand their realignment in conformity with its own logic. "Organization" refers to the progressive deployment of a single logic of abstraction, optimalization, and idealized reconstruction at every level to maximize management. The conjunction of systematization and organization universalizes all internal processes to a single logic and then expands the system to incorporate other ensembles.

When systematization and organization proceed together and maintain the dynamic self-modification of recurring innovation, technology displays a single end: efficiency. "Efficiency" suggests the *telos* of technological development: taking the plurality of ends and means and reducing them to one system of means — the most efficient. When this is achieved, all dissonance and asymmetry has been eliminated, a situation we now term "user-friendly." User-friendly technology is an example of pure efficiency, a state in which all the components are in tensionless coordination.

This systematization and rationalization of all the dimensions of human reality, where even the characteristically human experiences of the self, politics, social life, and reason become technicized and optimalized through the medium of technology, leads Jacques Ellul to write that technology is "the totality of methods rationally arrived at and having absolute efficiency (for a given stage of development) in every field of human activity." Technology, he claims, has become automatic, self-augmenting, monistic, universal, and autonomous.[10] Wherever man goes, he sees and participates only in a technological system whose imperatives proceed by their own accord.

This process entails more, though, than the mere replication of the same thing worldwide. In its current phase, technology is producing what Marshall McLuhan has called a "global village." McLuhan does not mean by this that the world has simply been homogenized. He is instead pointing to a development within technology which brings wholly new fusions and interdependencies into existence, modalities which decisively shatter the Newtonian-Cartesian order of reality. The new communication and information technology, he argues, is underwriting novel forms of power, relations, senses of identity, conceptions of action, and entanglements of social, economic, and political force. What makes McLuhan's characterization of the global village unique is that he writes of *isolated* individuals simultaneously and multidimensionally connected with every other being through the medium of electronics and information transmission. For example, in *The Gutenberg Galaxy* he writes of a new global embrace which "abolishes both time and space," in which a new mythic tribalism has emerged. Boundaries and separations, fixed points of view, and sequential causality will be dissolved. In a world of circuits and integral patterns, of total environments and fused interdependencies, the space between individuals will be overcome, he predicts. McLuhan does not see this as merely a vast universal homogeneity or as something that modern science can explain. He claims "our speed-up is not a slow expansion outward from centre to margins but an instant implosion and an interfusion of space and functions." An "implosion" means a "bursting inwards" in which each person withdraws from the mediated relations and forms of everyday life and, with perhaps a small band of like-minded fellows, experiences via the electronic communications network an immediate affectivity with the whole globe. "General cosmic consciousness," as McLuhan identifies it, is at the same time isolation and universal resonance.[11]

Earlier, I referred to the pattern of contemporary motion as simultaneous gravitation towards a centre and towards multiple peripheries. Nowhere is this more evident than in politics, where the conjunction of highly sophisticated executive-management skills on behalf of "global competitiveness" and the activation of a plethora of nationalisms or "identities" (based on ethnicity, gender, religion, race, and sexual preference) is redefining political action. The phenomena produced by these processes do not seem to be explained readily by modern notions of causality, of representation and reiteration, of localizable power, or of direction. What we are observing instead is, I think, the emergence of a new paradigm of interaction and energy, of nonlocal connections and simultaneity. Speaking very generally, the network that is emerging has an uncanny resemblance to what one might speculate is a practical application of Heidegger's "fundamental ontology," or of the postmodernist's "philosophy of difference." Needless to say, the effort to characterize what this means must usually have recourse to metaphor, though modern science is attempting to find a vocabulary to express "nongenerative order." Looked at in terms of its political appearance, the network is one

that links a kind of retribalized existence with instantaneous reactivity to the whole globe. This situation is one in which the imploded "identity" confronts directly and without mediation the powerful dynamics of the global environment. Monad and global force resonate with one another without any dialectical intervention, without any of the everyday forms of political or social causality, and without political or legal protection. No distinctive modalities of mediation arise in this pure affectivity. Jean Baudrillard is one who has tried to express what the implication of this is. In his *In the Shadow of the Silent Majorities — or The End of the Social and Other Essays*, he writes:

> The medium also falls into that indefinite state characteristic of all our great systems of judgment and value. A single model, whose efficacy is immediacy, simultaneously generates the message, the medium, and the "real." In short, *the medium is the message* signifies not only the end of the message, but also the end of the medium. There are no longer media in the literal sense of the term ... — that is to say, a power mediating between one reality and another, between one state of the real and another — neither in content nor in form. Strictly speaking, that is what implosion signifies: the absorption of one pole into another, the short-circuit between poles of every differential system of meaning, the effacement of terms and of direct oppositions, and thus that of the medium and the real. Hence the impossibility of any mediation ... circularity of all media effects. Hence the impossibility of a sense (meaning), in the literal sense of a unilateral vector which leads from one pole to another.[12]

The implication of this is that in the context of making and revising constitutions, it now becomes increasingly inappropriate to speak of the questions of sovereignty, commonality, political power and economic control, and the recognition of identity as if these were phenomena still linked to political entities defined within the boundaries and the political *problematique* of the juridical nation-state. The new empowerments, fusions and interdependencies, experiments, and strategies that we are witnessing are taking place within a field of energy which, linking enormous technological capacity (nuclear power, recombinant DNA engineering, and simulation technology) and intense commitment to images of identity (the "black-Athena" movements, the "age of the goddess" movements, the "men's rights" movements) produce motions which exceed the measures of modernity (its humanism, its standards of utility and protection of the individual) and which perhaps cannot be predicted or controlled.

Since it is germane to the issue of the Canadian constitutional debate, permit me to focus briefly on the trajectory which some are calling the "new pluralism." From the perspective outlined above, what characterizes the distinctiveness of the contemporary appeals to religion, race, locality, and gender is twofold: first, that the juridical and political parameters within which these had been defined as issues associated with pluralism are evaporating, leaving these allegiances and commitments as free-floating phenomena that can be attached to any globally mobilized movement. Secondly, they are increasingly defined through technology. By this I mean that they are highly technicized phenomena — emanations of communications technology, signs manipulated by those who have access and resources to mobilize masses, forms not so much of particular culture but rather of marketing strategy and effective communication.

I do not think that we can see the regional activation of tribal allegiances as genuine forms of attachment and obvious options and points of resistance to the age of globalizing transformations and realignments. Jean Baudrillard, in a series of devastating critiques of contemporary society, suggests that they must be understood as signs of nostalgia and simulation within the peculiar processes of the contemporary information order. He repudiates the view that the discovery of ethnic and cultural wholeness is a continuation of the humanist affirmation of enriched subjectivity in the face of technology's objectifying processes. Baudrillard suggests that the information age produces a consciousness wholly unlike that of even late capitalism. The commodity form, he challenges, no longer prevails. Instead, the environment is constituted by a constant dispersion of signs. No stable value orders the commutability of these signs. The infinite metamorphosis of signification means that there is no "real." We consume images that appear intelligible within no political horizon or rational understanding. These images are, Baudrillard suggests, "hyper-real": they are ones where the real has withdrawn and returned as highly stylized, formalized simulations. (Members of the environmentalism movement use the idea of "sacred nature" in this creative manner.) They are refurbished "copies" though the original may never have existed, or where the "original" lived — context itself is utterly refabricated. (The Puritan ethic of hard work and honesty survives because Plymouth Plantation exists.) Past cultures become eclectic signs that have lost their referents in the service of mass consumption and innovative marketing strategies. Their use and deployment in the media as circulating

signs permits of no recollection or reminiscence to a primal point, an *arche*, which would endow them with meaning. Under the global transformation which information technology activates, culture becomes wholly abstracted, reduced, and processed as manipulable data. Everything becomes a stylistic variation of the same.

Abstracted from contexts of meaning, culture then becomes an arbitrary horizon, and it can provide no substantive basis for meaningful action. Discrete and singular practices, ways of life, and understandings have been made over to participate in the overall functionalism of the system. Culture can no longer be seen as a set of practices from which resistance can proceed, or as a structure that confers meaning on the processes unleashed by technology; instead, it is seen as an ancillary to technological functionality. It is just more information that can be arranged and rearranged into repertoires. As Baudrillard suggests, the symbols of culture simply become masses of detritus and excess, dead signs where at best everything is made available to everyone.

Seen in this light, the dispersion and proliferation of identities [is] not as great an object of hope as it may at first appear to be. If we accept Baudrillard's argument that the general form of our consciousness is becoming structured by the logic of the information age, then while we may seem to be more receptive to diversity and while we encourage multiplicity, we have left no measures which would contribute to our understanding of the distinctions within that differentiation. It is the proliferation of difference in the same mode and through the same medium, namely communications. In a state of uniform heterogeneity, or mass differentiation, a more intrusive reductionism and [trivialisation] has occurred. We have before us the spectre of anonymous global processes combined with tribalism and isolationism; and the preponderant part of the initiatives being undertaken today — politically, socially, and economically — celebrates this double process.

The Charlottetown Accord cannot, of course, be accused of merely falling in line with the contemporary development. In a magisterial tone it recognizes the main structures and practices of the modern nation-state: the primacy of the rule of law, the recognition of the legal person, the supremacy of a sovereign parliament, territorial integrity, and so on. However, both within the document and during the accompanying debate, powerful dissenting voices also created the conditions for Canada's participation in the double process of globalism and localism. The agreement attempted to be all things to all people, uniting regional "empowerment" with economic competitiveness. Aboriginal demand for self-determination with effective resource management, the rule of law with the prerogatives of birth. The process was one attempting to reconcile features of the Meech Lake Accord, the Beaudoin-Dobbie Report, and the Allaire Report, while taking seriously the Bélanger-Campeau Commission, the triple-E Senate proposals, and Ontario's desire for a social charter, without recognizing that there were fundamental theoretical incompatibilities between them. The result was not a simple compromise package reflecting the give-and-take conciliation of modern pluralism. Instead, its incoherent amalgam of remnants of earlier historical periods, future possibilities, localized grievances, and global pressures reflects the contemporary quandary of constitutionalism in a new world "order." On the one hand it diversifies and fragments, disseminating cultural identities into multiple contingencies, decentralizing federal spending power and shared cost programs, and localizing constitutional entitlement on the basis of declared identity. On the other hand, it commits the new machinery of federalism to working effectively to use the institutions of government to produce a single market initiative in the interests of global competitiveness. For example, local procurement practices, agricultural supply marketing boards, local hiring policy, all "means of arbitrary discrimination" or "disguised restriction of trade across boundaries," are to be administratively regulated against, in effect, by an extension of the free trade agreement internally for a more effectual participation in the global economy. Apart from the obviously inevitable contradictory results of these two pulls (for example, what happens when Aboriginal peoples, using their resources as they see appropriate to maintaining their "traditional culture," come up against the regulations of "environmental management"?), what is apparent, in the erosion of national focus, in the evident mistrust of parliamentary federalism, and in the renunciation of the liberal democratic principles of representation and equality of political rights is that Canada is aligning itself with the powerful dynamic of the contemporary era.

The Charlottetown Accord was, of course, defeated. The No vote of the referendum was not surprising, because it simply continued the process unleashed by the accord itself: having legitimated a plethora of irreconcilable voices, it was predictable that an infinite regress down to the most minute grievance, extravagant expectation, and expression of cynicism would occur. The broadcasting of results before all the votes were in ensured that voters

acted on any number of projected scenarios. Indeed, the No was a perfect example of the peculiarities of the contemporary postmodern condition: the "global" result of radically contradictory positions created the "hyper-reality" of agreement by valourizing every particular disappointment and fantasy (by giving each media coverage) and aggregating them into a "totality." The accord did not establish or recall us to commonality: it did not testify to or evoke plurality. What it affirmed was multiplicity — many different voices under the single sign of communications.

Our future cannot be that hoped [for] by Peter Russell. There cannot but be a rise in paradox and ambiguity, because that is the modality of the process in which we are now situated. Russell's desire for closure can no longer be satisfied, short of the massive employment of social and behavioural technologies. Sovereignty and the closed world of territorial integrity are no longer options for us either. As we participate in the ascendance of a new world disorder, our only hope is that a sufficient reserve of common sense and common decency remains immune to the transformations reconfiguring our world.

Notes

1. See David B. Allison, ed., *The New Nietzsche: Contemporary Styles of Interpretations* (Cambridge, Mass.: MIT Press, 1985).
2. I have used the word "pastiche" following Frederic Jameson's essay "Postmodernism of the Cultural Logic of Late Capitalism," *New Left Review*, July/August 1984, 146.
3. Of course, as the *Protagoras* and *Laws* make clear, Plato's humanism is one that identifies the distinctively human as the impulse of transcendence towards the divine or eternal. However, these are apprehended through the human measure of the Good.
4. Simply stated, I am suggesting that the events and realignments occurring in our decade overreach the explanatory power of modern philosophies of history. My argument is not restricted to counterclaims supported by empirical fact. Rather, I am suggesting that the metaphysic of the modern analyses is increasingly irrelevant to the contemporary situation. (Nor would I deny that that metaphysic may have underwritten a safer and more decent era of human association than that upon which we are about to embark. We simply cannot know.) The viability of a metaphysic to comprehend the forms of human intercourse, I believe, is vouchsafed by the distinctive institutions, practices, ways of life, skills, forms of education, and self-interpretations of a specific society at a unique juncture of its history. I am not making a statement regarding the truth of a specific metaphysic. What I am saying is that however "true" the metaphysic may be abstractly, or even when assented to in private experience, it is an instrument for illuminating the cardinal components of a political regime only when it is concretely actuated. Modern philosophies of history (Hegelian, Marxist, liberal) — with their metaphysical assumptions of pure origins, sequential time, spatial order, teleological processes, and intelligible totalities — were vouchsafed by the power structures and ideology of the na-

tion-state. With the disintegration of the nation-state, these philosophies of history have become obsolete.

5. Historically, and especially in Europe, Arendt argues, the nation-state's fragility meant that its principle was almost immediately corrupted. The disintegration occurred internally when society emancipated itself from public concerns. The nation-state broke down when the state was overwhelmed by the dominance of one social interest defined by a single class, the bourgeoisie. The dynamic of this class's interest unleashed a process of never-ending accumulation of power to make possible its never-ending accumulation of capital. Imperialist expansion arose from an economic crisis of an overproduction of capital which could not be productively invested within national boundaries. Coming up against national limitations to its economic expansion, the bourgeoisie would not give up the capitalist system of constant economic growth, and the nation-state proved unfit for the further growth of the capitalist economy.

6. The new Canadian drug bill, c-91, which will be locked in to the North American Free Trade Agreement, is an example of the erosion of national sovereignty in the face of the imperatives pursued by multinational pharmaceutical companies.

7. Examining the "epistemology" which underscores and legitimates our contemporary self-interpretation is, however, only a first step. It is the step taken by such thinkers as Marshall McLuhan and Walter Ong. Critics of their "neo-Kantian" analyses, such as Michel Foucault and Jacques Donzelot, have directed their attention to the modality of power in contemporary society which undergirds the categories of consciousness informing contemporary self-interpretation. I would argue that even a more far-reaching perspective that examines the "psyche" in its totality would be necessary to grasp its essence fully. However, one must begin somewhere.

8. To be clear, many of the new nations, ethnic associations, and social movements (especially those asserting themselves after the experience of oppression at the hands of imperial power or illiberal regimes) are interpreting and legitimating their actions by appeal to the modern discourse. Many have no other tools at their disposal as they recapitulate the historical development of the modern nation-state. But this is simply a catch-up phase prior to being caught up by the dynamic that is overtaking the modern period.

9. See Hannah Arendt, *The Human Condition* (Chicago: University of Chicago Press, 1958); George Grant, "Knowing and Making," *Transactions of the Royal Society of Canada*, 4th series, vol. 12, 1967; Martin Heidegger, "The Question Concerning Technology," in *Basic Writings*, ed. David F. Krell (New York: Harper and Row, 1977), 287–317; and Carl Mitcham and Robert Mackey, eds., *Philosophy and Technology: Readings in the Philosophical Problems of Technology* (New York: Free Press, 1971).

10. Jacques Ellul, *The Gutenberg Galaxy* (New York: Vintage, 1964), XXV.

11. Marshall McLuhan, *The Gutenberg Galaxy* (Toronto: University of Toronto Press, 1962) and *Understanding Media* (New York: Mentor, 1964).

12. Jean Baudrillard, "Implosion of Meaning in the Media," in *In the Shadow of the Silent Majorities — or The End of the Social, and Other Essays,* (New York: Semiotexte, 1983), 102.

Bibliography

This is a selective list, with an emphasis on texts and monographs. For articles, case comments, and other materials that are not in this list, see the *Index to Canadian Periodical Literature* and the *Index to Canadian Legal Literature*. As well, most of the Canadian court decisions in this sourcebook can be accessed electronically through databases such as Quicklaw, Lexis-Nexis, or WestlaweCarswell. For post-1985 Supreme Court of Canada decisions on the Internet, see <http://www.lexum.umontreal.ca/csc-scc/en/index.html>. For additional materials, see the notes that accompany many of the sections of the text.

A. GENERAL

Bakan, Joel, *et al.*, eds., *Canadian Constitutional Law*, 3d ed. (Toronto: Emond Montgomery, 2003).

Brooks, Stephen, *Canadian Democracy: An Introduction*, 4th ed. (Toronto: Oxford University Press, 2004).

Bryant, Michael J. & Lorne Sossin, *Public Law* (Toronto: Carswell, 2002).

Dickerson, Mark O. & Thomas Flanagan, *An Introduction to Government and Politics: A Conceptual Approach*, 7th ed. (Toronto: Thomson Nelson, 2005)

Dyck, Rand, *Canadian Politics: Critical Approaches*, 5th ed. (Toronto: Thomson Nelson, 2008).

Fitzgerald, Patrick & Barry Wright, *Looking at Law: Canada's Legal System*, 5th ed. (Toronto: Butterworths Canada, 2000).

Forcese, Craig & Aaron Freeman, *The Laws of Government: The Legal Foundations of Canadian Democracy* (Toronto: Irwin Law, 2005).

Funston, Bernard W. & Eugene Meehan, *Canadian Constitutional Law in a Nutshell*, 3d ed. (Toronto: Carswell, 2003)

Haworth, Alan, *Understanding the Political Philosophers: From Ancient to Modern Times* (New York: Routledge, 2004).

Hogg, Peter W., *Constitutional Law of Canada*, 4th ed.: 2007 student ed. (Toronto: Carswell, 2007).

———, *Constitutional Law of Canada*, 4th ed. (Scarborough, Ont.: Carswell, 1997).

Jackson, Robert J. & Doreen Jackson, *Canadian Government in Transition: Disruption and Continuity*, 4th ed. (Toronto: Prentice-Hall, 2006).

———, *Politics in Canada: Culture, Institutions, Behaviour and Public Policy*, 6th ed. (Toronto: Pearson Education Canada, 2006).

Johnson, Larry, *Politics: An Introduction to the Modern Democratic State* (Peterborough, Ont.: Broadview Press, 2001).

Landes, Ronald G., *The Canadian Polity: A Comparative Introduction*, 6th ed. (Toronto: Prentice-Hall, 2002).

Lukes, Steven, *Power: A Radical View*, 2d ed. (New York: Palgrave Macmillan, 2005).

MacIvor, Heather, ed., *Canadian Politics and Government in the Charter Era*, 4th ed. (Toronto: Thomson Nelson, 2006).

———, ed., *Parameters of Power: Canada's Political Institutions* (Toronto: Thomson Nelson, 2006).

Malcolmson, Patrick & Richard Myers, *The Canadian Regime: An Introduction to Parliamentary Government in Canada*, 3d ed. (Peterborough, Ont.: Broadview Press, 2005).

Marsh, James H., ed., *The Canadian Encyclopedia*, Year 2000 ed. (Toronto: McClelland & Stewart, 1999).

Monahan, Patrick J., *Constitutional Law*, 3d ed. (Toronto: Irwin Law, 2006).

Reesor, Bayard, *The Canadian Constitution in Historical Perspective* (Scarborough, Ont.: Prentice-Hall, 1992).

Whittington, Michael, *Canadian Government and Politics: Institutions and Processes* (Toronto: McGraw-Hill, 1995).

Whittington, Michael & Glen Williams, eds., *Canadian Politics in the 21st Century*, 6th ed. (Toronto: Thomson Nelson, 2004).

B. ELEMENTS OF PUBLIC LAW (CHAPTER 1)

Political Philosophies (see also Democracy, in part C below)

Ball, Terrence, *et al.*, *Political Ideologies and the Democratic Ideal*, Canadian ed. (Toronto: Pearson Longman, 2006).

Beiner, Ronald & Wayne Norman, *Canadian Political Philosophy* (Toronto: Oxford University Press, 2001).

Benewick, Robert & Philip Green, *The Routledge Dictionary of Twentieth-Century Political Thinkers*, 2d ed. (London & New York: Routledge, 1998).

Cahn, Steven M., ed., *Classics of Political and Moral Philosophy* (New York: Oxford University Press, 2002).

Habermas, Jürgen, *Between Facts and Norms: Contributions to a Discourse Theory of Law and Democracy*, trans. by William Rehg (Cambridge, Mass.: The MIT Press, 1998).

Locke, John, *Two Treatises of Government* (Cambridge: Cambridge University Press, 1988 [1698]).

McCullough, H.B., ed., *Political Ideologies and Political Philosophies*, 3d ed. (Toronto: Thomson Nelson, 2001).

Mill, John S., *Considerations on Representative Government* (New York: Liberal Arts Press, 1962 [1859]).

———, *Utilitarianism and other Writings* (Cleveland: Meridian Books, 1962 [1861]).

Porter, Jene M., *Classics in Political Philosophy* (New York: Prentice Hall, 2000).

Russell, Bertrand A., *Contemporary History of Western Philosophy* (London: Unwin Paperbacks, 1984 [1946]).

Stewart, Gordon T., *The Origins of Canadian Politics: A Comparative Approach* (Vancouver: UBC Press, 1986).

Willoughby, Westel W., *The Political Theories of the Ancient World* (Freeport, N.Y.: Books for Libraries Press, 1969 [1903]).

Nature of the State

Emberley, Peter, "Globalism and Localism: Constitutionalism in a New World Order" in Curtis Cook, ed., *Constitutional Predicament: Canada after the Referendum of 1992* (Montreal & Kingston: McGill-Queen's University Press, 1994).

Harris, Phil, *An Introduction to Law*, 6th ed. (London: Butterworths, 2002), chs. 2 and 4.

Held, David, "Central Perspectives on the Modern State" in David Held *et al.*, *States and Societies* (Oxford: Martin Robertson in association with The Open University, 1983).

De Jasay, Anthony, *The State* (New York: Blackwell, 1985).

Knuttila, Murray & Wendee Kubik, *State Theories: Classical, Global, and Feminist Perspectives*, 3d ed. (Halifax: Fernwood Publishing, 2000).

Panitch, Leo, *Canadian State: Political Economy and Political Power* (Toronto: University of Toronto Press, 1977).

Sociological and Political Background

Brodie, Janine & Linda Trimble, eds., *Reinventing Canada: Politics of the 21st Century* (Toronto: Prentice Hall, 2003).

Carmichael, Don, Tom Pocklington & Greg Pyrcz. *Democracy, Rights, and Well-Being in Canada*, 2d ed. (Toronto: Harcourt Brace, 2000).

Cotterrell, Roger, *The Sociology of Law: An Introduction*, 2d ed. (London: Butterworths, 1992).

Dickerson, Mark O., Tom Flanagan & Neil Nevitte, eds., *Introductory Readings in Government and Politics*, 3d ed. (Toronto: Nelson, 1993).

McQuaig, Linda, *Behind Closed Doors* (Markham, Ont.: Viking, 1987).

Olsen, Dennis. *The State Elite* (Toronto: University of Toronto Press, 1980).

Porter, John, *The Vertical Mosaic* (Toronto: University of Toronto Press, 1965).

Samuelson, Les & Wayne Antony, eds., *Power and Resistance: Critical Thinking About Canadian Social Issues*, 3d ed. (Halifax: Fernwood Press).

Simpson, Jeffrey, *The Friendly Dictatorship* (Toronto: McClelland & Stewart, 2001).

C. ELEMENTS OF THE CONSTITUTION (CHAPTER 2)

See especially:

Dicey, Albert V., *An Introduction to the Study of the Law of the Constitution*, 10th ed. (London: Macmillan, 1965 [first ed., 1885; last revision by Dicey, 1915]).

Hogg, Peter W., *Constitutional Law of Canada*, 4th ed. (unabridged) (Scarborough, Ont.: Carswell, 1996) and 2007 student ed., especially ch. 1.

See also:

Bourgeois, Don J., *Public Law in Canada* (Scarborough, Ont.: Nelson, 1990).

Davis, Louis B.Z., *Canadian Constitutional Law Handbook* (Aurora: Canada Law Book, 1985).

Finkelstein, Neil, ed., *Laskin's Canadian Constitutional Law*, 5th ed. (Toronto: Carswell, 1986).

Funston, Bernard W. & Eugene Meehan, *Canada's Constitutional Law in a Nutshell*, 3d ed. (Toronto: Carswell, 2003).

Heard, Andrew, *Canadian Constitutional Conventions: The Marriage of Law and Politics* (Toronto: Oxford University Press, 1991).

Hutchinson, Allan C. & Patrick Monahan, *The Rule of Law: Ideal or Ideology* (Toronto: Carswell, 1987).

Magnet, Joseph E., *Modern Constitutionalism: Identity, Equality and Democracy* (Markham, Ont.: LexisNexis Butterworths, 2004).

———, *Constitutional Law of Canada: Cases, Notes and Materials*, 8th ed. (Edmonton: Juriliber Ltd., 2001).

———, ed., *Constitutional Law of Canada*, 5th ed. (Montreal: Blais, 1993).

Milne, David, *The Canadian Constitution* (Toronto: James Lorimer and Company, 1991).

Mishler, William, *Political Participation in Canada* (Toronto: Macmillan, 1979).

Reesor, Bayard, *The Canadian Constitution in Historical Perspective* (Scarborough, Ont.: Prentice-Hall, 1992).

Tremblay, André, *Droit constitutionnel: principes* (Montreal: Éditions Thémis, 1993).

Ward, Norman, ed., *Dawson's The Government of Canada*, 6th ed. (Toronto: University of Toronto Press, 1987).

Wheare, Kenneth C., *Modern Constitutions*, 2d ed. (London: Oxford University Press, 1966).

Democracy

Bohman, James, *Public Deliberation: Pluralism, Complexity, and Democracy* (Cambridge, Mass.: The MIT Press, 1996).

Carter, April & Geoffrey Stokes, eds., *Democratic Theory Today: Challenges for the 21st Century* (Cambridge, UK: Polity Press; Oxford & Malden, Mass.: Blackwell Publishers, 2002).

Fishkin, James S. & Peter Laslett, eds., *Debating Deliberative Democracy* (Malden, Mass. & Oxford: Blackwell, 2003).

Goodlad, Stephen J. *The Last Best Hope: A Democracy Reader* (San Francisco: Jossey-Bass, 2001).

Gutman, Amy & Dennis Thompson, *Democracy and Disagreement* (Cambridge & London: The Belknap Press of Harvard University Press, 1996).

Habermas, Jürgen, *Between Facts and Norms: Contributions to a Discourse Theory of Law and Democracy*, trans. by William Rehg (Cambridge, Mass.: The MIT Press, 1998).

Macpherson, C.B., *The Life and Times of Liberal Democracy* (Toronto & New York: Oxford University Press, 1977).

Pocklington, Tom C., *Representative Democracy: An Introduction to Politics and Government and Rights in Canada* (Toronto: Harcourt Brace, 1994).

———, "Democracy" in Tom C. Pocklington, ed., *Liberal Democracy in Canada and the United States: An Introduction to Politics and Government* (Toronto: Holt, Rinehart and Winston of Canada, Limited, 1985), ch. 1.

Rawls, John. *Political Liberalism* (New York: Columbia University Press, 1993).

Urbinati, Nadia, *Mill on Democracy: From the Athenian Polis to Representative Government* (Chicago & London: University of Chicago Press, 2002).

Valadez, Jorge N., *Deliberative Democracy, Political Legitimacy, and Self-Determination in Multicultural Societies* (Boulder: Westview Press, 2001).

D. ORIGINS AND STRUCTURE OF THE *CONSTITUTION ACT, 1867* (CHAPTER 3)

Some Historical Sources

Browne, G.P., *Documents on the Confederation of British North America* (Toronto: McClelland & Stewart, 1969).

Careless, James M.S., *Canada: A Story of Challenge* (Toronto: Macmillan, 1970), ch. 13.

Cook, Ramsay, *Canada, Quebec and the Political Uses of Nationalism*, 2d ed. (Toronto: McClelland & Stewart, 1995).

Craig, Gerald M., *Lord Durham's Report* (Toronto: McClelland & Stewart, 1963).

Creighton, Donald, *The Road to Confederation: The Emergence of Canada 1863–1867* (Toronto: Macmillan, 1964).

———, *The Dominion of the North: A History of Canada* (Toronto: Macmillan, 1962).

———, *John A. Macdonald: The Old Chieftain* (Toronto: Macmillan, 1955), 2 vols.

Evans, A. Margaret, *Sir Oliver Mowat* (Toronto: University of Toronto Press, 1992), esp. ch. 6.

Finlay, John L. & Douglas N. Sprague, *The Structure of Canadian History*, 6th ed (Toronto: Prentice-Hall Allyn and Bacon Canada, 2000).

LaSelva, Samuel V., *The Moral Foundations of Canadian Federalism: Paradoxes, Achievements and Tragedies of Nationhood* (Montreal & Kingston: McGill-Queen's University Press, 1996).

McInnis, Edgar, *Canada: A Political and Social History*, 4th ed. (Toronto: Holt, Rinehart and Winston of Canada, 1982), chs. 12 and 13.

McNaught, Kenneth, *The Pelican History of Canada* (Markham, Ont.: Penguin, 1982).

Morton, William L., *The Critical Years: The Union of British North America, 1857–1873* (Toronto: McClelland, 1964).

Oliver, Peter C. *Constitution of Independence: The Development of Constitutional Theory in Australia, Canada, and New Zealand* (Oxford; New York: Oxford University Press, 2005).

Reesor, Bayard, *The Canadian Constitution in Historical Perspective* (Scarborough, Ont.: Prentice-Hall, 1992), ch. 3.

Samuels II, Raymond, ed., *Canadian Constitutional Development Since 1535: Part I* (Ottawa: The Agora Cosmopolitan, 2002).

Saywell, John T., *The Lawmakers: Judicial Power and the Shaping of Canadian Federalism* (Toronto: Osgoode Society for Canadian Legal History, University of Toronto Press, 2002).

Silver, Arthur I., *The French-Canadian Idea of Confederation, 1864–1900*, 2d ed. (Toronto: University of Toronto Press, 1997).

Stanley, George F.G., *A Short History of the Canadian Constitution* (Toronto: Ryerson Press, 1969), chs. 3 and 4.

Stevenson, Garth, *Unfulfilled Union: Canadian Federalism and National Unity*, 4th ed. (Montreal & Kingston: McGill-Queen's University Press, 2004), ch. 2.

Wade, Mason, *The French Canadians: 1760–1967*, Rev. ed., 2 vols. (Toronto: Macmillan, 1968).

Federalism

Kincaid, John & G. Alan Tarr, eds. and John Kincaid, senior ed., *Constitutional Origins, Structure, and Change in Federal Countries* (Montreal & Kingston: McGill-Queen's University Press, 2005).

King, Preston, *Federalism and Federation* (Baltimore: Johns Hopkins University Press, 1982).

Simeon, Richard & Ian Robinson, *State, Society, and the Development of Canadian Federalism* (Toronto: University of Toronto Press, 1990).

Stevenson, Garth, *Unfulfilled Union: Canadian Federalism and National Unity*, 4th ed. (Montreal & Kingston: McGill-Queen's University Press, 2004).

———, *Ex Uno Plures: Federal–Provincial Relations in Canada, 1867–1896* (Montreal & Kingston: McGill-Queen's University Press, 1993).

———, "Federalism" in Tom C. Pocklington, ed., *Liberal Democracy in Canada and the United States: An Introduction to Politics and Government* (Toronto: Holt, 1985), ch. 6.

Watts, Ronald L., *Comparing Federal Systems in the 1990s* (Kingston: Institute of Intergovernmental Relations, Queen's University, 1996).

Wheare, Kenneth C., *Federal Government*, 4th ed. (New York: Oxford University Press, 1964).

E. THE JUDICIARY (CHAPTER 4)

See especially:

Hogg, Peter W., *Constitutional Law of Canada*, 4th ed.: 2007 student edition. (Toronto: Carswell, 2007), ch. 7 (Courts) and ch. 8 (Supreme Court of Canada).

———, *Constitutional Law of Canada*, 4th ed. (Scarborough, Ont.: Carswell, 1997), ch. 7 and ch. 8.

Howse, Paul & Peter Russell, eds., *Judicial Power and Canadian Democracy* (Montreal & Kingston: McGill-Queen's University Press, 2001).

Russell, Peter H., *Constitutional Odyssey: Can Canadians Become a Sovereign People?*, 3d ed. (Toronto: University of Toronto Press, 2004).

———, *The Judiciary in Canada: The Third Branch of Government* (Toronto: McGraw-Hill, 1987).

See also:

Bogart, W.A., *Good Government? Good Citizens?: Courts, Politics, and Markets in a Changing Canada* (Vancouver: UBC Press, 2005).

———, *Courts and Country: The Limits of Litigation and the Social and Political Life of Canada* (Don Mills, Ont.: Oxford University Press, 1994).

Brodie, Ian, *Friends of the Court: The Privileging of Interest Group Litigants in Canada* (Albany, N.Y.: State University of New York Press, 2002).

Browne, Gerald P., *The Judicial Committee and the British North America Act* (Toronto: University of Toronto Press, 1967).

Canadian Bar Association, *The Supreme Court of Canada: Legacy and Challenges: Commemorative Edition on the 125th anniversary of the Supreme Court of Canada*, in volumes 79(1) 2000 and 80(2) 2001 of *Canadian Bar Review* (Ottawa: Canadian Bar Association, 2001).

Canadian Bar Association, *The Independence of the Judiciary in Canada* (Ottawa: Canadian Bar Association, 1985).

Canadian Centre for Justice Studies, *The Juristat Reader: A Statistical Overview of the Canadian Justice System* (Toronto: Thomson Books, 1999).

Fleming, Roy B., *Tournament of Appeals: Granting Judicial Review in Canada* (Vancouver: UBC Press, 2004).

Greene, Ian, *The Courts* (Vancouver: UBC Press, 2007).

Greene, Ian, *et al.*, *Final Appeal: Decision-Making in Canadian Courts of Appeal* (Toronto: James Lorimer and Company, 1998).

MacKinnon, F., "The Establishment of the Supreme Court of Canada" in W.R. Lederman, ed., *The Courts and the Canadian Constitution* (Toronto: McClelland & Stewart, 1964), 106–24.

Martin, Robert I., *The Most Dangerous Branch: How the Supreme Court of Canada Has Undermined Our Law and Our Democracy* (Montreal & Kingston: McGill-Queen's University Press, 2003).

McCormick, Peter, *Supreme at Last: The Evolution of the Supreme Court of Canada* (Toronto: James Lorimer & Company Ltd., 2000).

McCormick, Peter & Ian Greene, *Judges and Judging* (Toronto: James Lorimer and Company, 1990).

Mellon, Hugh & Martin Westmacott, eds., *Political Dispute and Judicial Review: Assessing the Work of the Supreme Court of Canada* (Toronto: Nelson Thomson Learning, 2000).

Monahan, Patrick, *Politics and the Constitution: The Charter, Federalism and the Supreme Court of Canada* (Agincourt: Carswell, 1987).

Saywell, John T., *The Lawmakers: Judicial Power and the Shaping of Canadian Federalism* (Toronto: Osgoode Society for Canadian Legal History, University of Toronto Press, 2002).

Snell, James G. & Frederick Vaughan, *The Supreme Court of Canada: History of the Institution* (Toronto: University of Toronto Press, 1985).

Weiler, Paul C., *In the Last Resort: A Critical Study of the Supreme Court of Canada* (Toronto: Carswell, 1974).

F. DIVISION OF LEGISLATIVE POWERS (CHAPTERS 5 TO 7)

See especially:

Reesor, Bayard, *The Canadian Constitution in Historical Perspective* (Scarborough, Ont.: Prentice-Hall, 1992), ch. 7.

Russell, Peter H., *et al.*, *Federalism and the Charter: Leading Constitutional Decisions*, 5th ed. (Ottawa: University of Ottawa Press, 1989).

See also:

Bakvis, Herman & Grace Skogstad, eds., *Canadian Federalism: Performance, Effectiveness, and Legitimacy* (Toronto: Oxford University Press, 2002).

Magnet, Joseph E., ed., *Constitutional Law of Canada: Cases, Notes and Materials*, 8th ed. (Edmonton: Juriliber, 2001).

Olmsted, Richard A., Department of Justice, Canada, *Decisions of the Judicial Committee of the Privy Council Relating to the British North America Act, 1867 and the Canadian Constitution*, 3 vols. (Ottawa: Queen's Printer, 1954). Two other collections are: Neil Finkelstein, ed., *Laskin's Canadian Constitutional Law*, 5th ed. (Toronto: Carswell, 1986).

Saywell, John, *The Lawmakers: Judicial Power and the Shaping of Canadian Federalism* (Toronto: University of Toronto Press/Osgoode Society for Canadian Legal History, 2002).

For commentary, see:

Economic Council of Canada, *Constitutional Division of Powers: An Economic Perspective* (Ottawa: Supply and Services Canada, 1992).

Hogg, Peter W., *Constitutional Law of Canada*, 4th ed.: 2007 student edition. (Toronto: Carswell, 2007), Part II.

———, *Constitutional Law of Canada*, 4th ed. (Scarborough, Ont.: Carswell, 1997), Part II.

Monahan, Patrick, *Politics and the Constitution: The Charter, Federalism and the Supreme Court of Canada* (Agincourt: Carswell, 1987), Part 3.

Monahan, Patrick J., *et al.*, *A New Division of Powers for Canada*, Study No. 8, Background Studies of the York University Constitutional Reform Project (North York: York University Constitutional Reform Project, 1992).

O'Connor, William F., Parliamentary Counsel of the Senate, *Report pursuant to resolution of the Senate to the Honourable the Speaker by the Parliamentary Counsel relating to enactment of the British North America Act, 1867, any lack of consonance between its terms and judicial construction of them and cognate matters* (O'Connor Report) (Ottawa: King's Printer, 1939).

Swinton, Katherine E., *The Supreme Court and Canadian Federalism: The Laskin-Dickson Years* (Toronto: Carswell, 1990).

G. THE LEGISLATURE, THE EXECUTIVE, AND EXECUTIVE POWER (CHAPTER 8)

The Legislature

Bauman, Richard & Tsvi Kahana, ed., *The Least Examined Branch: the Role of Legislatures in the Constitutional State* (New York: Cambridge University Press, 2006).

Irvine, William, *Does Canada Need a New Electoral System?* (Kingston: Institute of Intergovernmental Relations, 1979).

Joyal, Serge, ed., *Protecting Canadian Democracy: The Senate You Never Knew* (Montreal & Kingston: McGill-Queen's University Press/ Canadian Centre for Management Development, 2003).

Kemp, Paul, *Does Your Vote Count?* (Toronto: Dundurn Press, 2002).

Law Commission of Canada, *Voting Counts, Electoral Reform for Canada* (Ottawa: Minister of Public Works and Government Services, 2004).

Law Commission of Canada, *Renewing Canadian Democracy* (Ottawa: Law Commission of Canada, 2002), online: LRC <http://www.lcc.gc.ca/en/themes/gr/er/discussion_paper/toc.asp>.

Lijphart, Arend, *Patterns of Democracy: Government Forms and Performance in Thirty-Six Countries* (New Haven: Yale University Press, 1999).

Longstaff, Bill, *Democracy Undone: The Practice and the Promise of Self-governance in Canada* (Calgary: Ballot Pub., 2001).

Mallory, J.R., *The Structure of Canadian Government*, Rev. ed. (Toronto: Gage, 1984), chs. 5–7.

Milner, Henry, ed., *Making Every Vote Count: Reassessing Canada's Electoral System* (Peterborough, Ont.: Broadview Press, 1999).

Savoie, Donald J., *Breaking the Bargain: Public Servants, Ministers, and Parliament* (Toronto: University of Toronto Press, 2003).

———, *Governing from the Centre: The Concentration of Power in Canadian Politics* (Toronto: University of Toronto Press, 1999).

Siedle, Leslie F. & David C. Docherty, eds., *Reforming Canadian Democracy* (Montreal & Kingston: McGill-Queen's University Press, 2003).

Smith, David E., *The Canadian Senate in Bicameral Perspective* (Toronto: University of Toronto Press, 2003).

Ward, Norman, ed., *Dawson's The Government of Canada*, 6th ed. (Toronto: University of Toronto Press, 1987), part V.

Wheare, Kenneth C., *Legislatures*, 2d ed. (London: Oxford University Press, 1968).

The Executive

Boadway, Robin W. & Paul A.R. Hobson, eds., *Equalization: Its Contribution to Canada's Economic and Fiscal Progress* (Kingston: John Deutsch Institute for the Study of Economic Policy, Queen's University, 1998).

Canada, Privy Council Office, *Governing Responsibly: A Guide for Ministers and Ministers of State* (Ottawa: Privy Council Office, 2004).

Chernomas, Robert & Ardeshie Sepehri, eds., *How to Choose? A Comparison of the U.S. and Canadian Health Care Systems* (Amityville, N.Y.: Baywood Publishing, 1998).

Fortin, Sarah, Alain Nöel, & France St-Hiliare, eds., *Forging the Canadian Social Union: SUFA and Beyond* (Montreal: Institute for Research on Public Policy, 2003).

Gagnon, Alain G. & Hugh Segal, eds., *The Canadian Social Union Without Quebec: Eight Critical Analyses* (Toronto: Centre for Social Management, University of Toronto, 2000).

Hogg, Peter W., *Constitutional Law of Canada*, 4th ed.: 2007 student edition. (Toronto: Carswell, 2007), ch. 6 (Financial Arrangements), ch. 9 (Responsible Government), and ch. 10 (The Crown).

———, *Constitutional Law of Canada*, 4th ed. (Scarborough, Ont.: Carswell, 1997), ch. 6, ch. 9 and ch. 10.

La Forest, Gerard V., *Natural Resources and Public Property under the Canadian Constitution* (Toronto: University of Toronto Press, 1969).

Mallory, J.R., *The Structure of Canadian Government*, Rev. ed. (Toronto: Gage, 1984), chs. 1, 2, and 3.

Marcuz, Michelle Marie, *Managing Interdependence: Federal–provincial Collaboration and the Renewal of Canada's Social Union*, M.A. Research Essay, Carleton University, 1999 (unpublished).

Noonan, Peter W., *The Crown and Constitutional Law in Canada* (Calgary, Sripnoon Publications, 1998).

Simeon, Richard & Ian Robinson, *Federalism and the Economic Union* (Toronto: University of Toronto Press, 1990).

Smiley, Donald V., "Central Institutions" in S.M. Beck & I. Bernier, *Canada and the New Constitution: The Unfinished Agenda*, vol. 1 (Montreal: Institute for Research on Public Policy, 1983).

Ward, Norman, ed., *Dawson's The Government of Canada*, 6th ed. (Toronto: University of Toronto Press, 1987), part III.

Watts, Ronald L., *Executive Federalism: A Comparative Analysis* (Kingston: Institute of Intergovernmental Relations, Queen's University, 1989).

White, Graham, *Cabinets and First Ministers* (Vancouver: UBC Press, 2005).

H. THE CONSTITUTION ACT, 1982 AND AFTER (CHAPTERS 9, 10, 11)

Prologue and General Aspects (Chapter 9)

McWhinney, Edward, *Canada and the Constitution, 1979–1982* (Toronto: University of Toronto Press, 1982).

Milne, David, *The New Canadian Constitution* (Toronto: James Lorimer and Company, 1982), chs. 1–5.

Romanow, Roy, John Whyte, & Howard Leeson, *Canada — Notwithstanding: The Making of the Constitution, 1976–1982* (Toronto: Carswell/Methuen, 1984).

Sheppard, Robert & Michael Valpy, *The National Deal: The Fight for a Canadian Constitution* (Toronto: Fleet Books, 1982).

Charter

Bakan, Joel, *Constitutional Rights and Social Wrongs* (Toronto: University of Toronto Press, 1997).

Beatty, David, *Talking Heads and the Supremes* (Agincourt: Carswell, 1990).

Beaudoin, Gérald-A. & Errol Mendes, *The Canadian Charter of Rights and Freedoms*, 4th ed. (Markham, Ont.: LexisNexis Butterworths, 2005).

Greene, Ian, *The Charter of Rights* (Toronto: James Lorimer and Company, 1989).

Hiebert, Janet L., *Charter Conflicts: What is Parliament's Role?* (Montreal & Kingston: McGill-Queen's University Press, 2002).

Hutchinson, Allan C., *Waiting for CORAF: A Critique of Law and Rights* (Toronto: University of Toronto Press, 1995).

Kelly, James B., *Governing with the Charter: Legislative Intent and Judicial Activism and Framers' Intent* (Vancouver, B.C.: UBC Press, 2005).

Knopff, Rainer & Fred L. Morton, *The Charter Revolution and the Court Party* (Peterborough, Ont.: Broadview Press, 2000).

———, *Charter Politics* (Scarborough, Ont.: Nelson, 1992).

Leishman, Rory, *Against Judicial Activism: The Decline of Freedom and Democracy in Canada* (Montreal & Kingston: McGill-Queen's University Press, 2006).

Mandel, Michael, *The Charter of Rights and the Legalization of Politics in Canada*, Rev. ed. (Toronto: Thompson Educational Publishing, 1994).

Manfredi, Christopher P., *Judicial Power and the Charter: Canada and the Paradox of Liberal Constitutionalism*, 2d ed. (Toronto: Oxford University Press, 2001).

Meehan, Eugene, *et al.*, *The 1999 Annotated Canadian Charter of Rights and Freedoms* (Scarborough, Ont.: Carswell, 1998).

Roach, Kent, *The Supreme Court on Trial: Judicial Activism or Democratic Dialogue* (Toronto: Irwin Law, 2001).

Scheiderman, David & Kate Sutherland, eds., *Charting the Consequences: The Impact of Charter Rights on Canadian Law and Politics* (Toronto: University of Toronto Press, 1997).

Sharpe, Robert J, & Kent Roach, *The Canadian Charter of Rights and Freedoms*, 3d ed. (Toronto: Irwin Law, 2005).

Swinton, Katherine E. & Carol J. Rogerson, eds., *Competing Constitutional Visions: The Meech Lake Accord* (Toronto: Carswell, 1988).

Weiler, Joseph M. & Robin M. Elliot, eds., *Litigating the Values of a Nation: the Canadian Charter of Rights and Freedoms* (Toronto: Carswell, 1986).

Aboriginal Provisions and Changes (Chapters 10 and 11)

Cairns, Alan C., *First Nations and the Canadian State: In Search of Coexistence* (Kingston: Institute of Intergovernmental Relations, Queen's University, 2005).

———, *Citizens Plus: Aboriginal Peoples and the Canadian State* (Vancouver: UBC Press, 2000).

Canada, *Report of the Royal Commission on Aboriginal Peoples*, 5 vols. (Ottawa: Minster of Supply and Services Canada, 1996).

Dickason, Olive P., *Canada's First Nations: A History of Founding Peoples from Earliest Times*, 3d ed. (Toronto: Oxford University Press, 2002).

Elliott, David W., *Law and Aboriginal Peoples in Canada*, 5th ed. (Concord, Ont.: Captus Press, 2005).

Flanagan, Tom. *First Nations? Second Thoughts* (Montreal & Kingston: McGill-Queen's University Press, 2000).

Macklem, Patrick, *Indigenous Difference and the Constitution of Canada* (Toronto: University of Toronto Press, 2001).

McNeil, Kent, *Emerging Justice?: Essays on Indigenous Rights in Canada and Australia* (Saskatoon: Native Law Centre, University of Saskatchewan, 2001).

Miller, James R., *Shingwauk's Vision; A History of Native Residential Schools* (Toronto: University of Toronto Press, 1996).

Royal Commission on Aboriginal Peoples, *Report of the Royal Commission on Aboriginal Peoples* (Ottawa: Canada Communication Group, 1996).

Amending Procedures

Hurley, James R., Privy Council Office, Government of Canada, *Amending Canada's Constitution: History, Processes, Problems and Prospects* (Ottawa: Supply and Services Canada, 1996).

Lazar, Harvey, ed., *Canada and the State of the Federation 1997: Non-Constitutional Renewal* (Kingston: Queen's University Institute of Intergovernmental Relations, 1997).

Pelletier, Benôit, *La Modification constitutionelle au Canada* (Toronto: Carswell, 1996).

Meech Lake and Aftermath

See especially:

Cairns, Alan C., "The Charlottetown Accord: Multinational Canada v. Federalism" in Curtis Cook, ed., *Constitutional Predicament: Canada after the Referendum of 1992* (Montreal & Kingston: McGill-Queen's University Press, 1994).

Milne, David, *The New Canadian Constitution* (Toronto: James Lorimer and Company, 1982).

Russell, Peter H., *Constitutional Odyssey: Can Canadians Become a Sovereign People?*, 3d ed. (Toronto: University of Toronto Press, 2004).

See also:

Behiels, Michael, ed., *The Meech Lake Primer: Conflicting Views of the 1987 Constitutional Accord* (Ottawa: University of Ottawa Press, 1989).

Campbell, Robert M. & Leslie A. Pal, "The Rise and Fall of the Charlottetown Accord" in *The Real Worlds of Canadian Politics*, 3d ed. (Peterborough, Ont.: Broadview Press, 1994), ch. 3.

Cohen, Andrew, *A Deal Undone: The Making and Breaking of the Meech Lake Accord* (Vancouver: Douglas, 1990).

Hogg, Peter W., *Meech Lake Constitutional Accord Annotated*, 2d ed. (Toronto: Carswell, 1988).

Johnston, Richard, *et al.*, *The Challenge of Direct Democracy: The 1992 Canadian Referendum* (Montreal & Kingston: McGill-Queen's University Press, 1996).

McRoberts, Kenneth, *Misconceiving Canada: The Struggle for National Unity* (Don Mills, Ont.: Oxford University Press, 1997).

McRoberts, Kenneth & Patrick J. Monahan, eds., *The Charlottetown Accord, the Referendum, and the Future of Canada* (Toronto: University of Toronto Press, 1993).

Monahan, Patrick J., *Meech Lake: The Inside Story* (Toronto: University of Toronto Press, 1991).

Smith, David E., *et al.*, *After Meech Lake: Lessons for the Future* (Kingston: Institute of Intergovernmental Relations, Queen's University, 1991).

Weaver, R. Kent, *The Collapse of Canada?* (Washington, D.C.: Brookings Institute, 1992).

Informal Changes

Doern, Bruce & Mark MacDonald, *Free Trade Federalism: Negotiating the Canadian Agreement on Internal Trade* (Toronto: University of Toronto Press, 2001).

Lazar, Harvey, ed., *Canada and the State of the Federation 1997: Non-Constitutional Renewal* (Kingston: Queen's University Institute of Intergovernmental Relations, 1997).

Trebilcock, Michael J. & Daniel Schwanen, eds., *Getting There: An Assessment of the Agreement on Internal Trade* (Toronto: C.D. Howe Institute, 1995).

I. SECESSION, UNITY, AND THE FUTURE (CHAPTER 12)

The *Secession Reference*

Bayefsky, Anne, ed., *Self-determination in International Law: Quebec and Lessons Learned: Legal Opinions Selected and Introduced by Anne Bayefsky* (The Hague, Netherlands: Kluwer International, 2000).

Newman, Warren J., *The Quebec Secession Reference: The Rule of Law and the Position of the Attorney General of Canada* (Toronto: York University Press, 1999).

Schneiderman, David, ed., *The Quebec Decision: The Supreme Court Case and Commentary* (Toronto: James Lorimer and Company, 1999).

Secession, Unity and the Future

Baker, Judith, ed., *Group Rights* (Toronto: University of Toronto Press, 1994).

Boyer, J. Patrick, *Lawmaking by the People: Referendums and Plebiscites in Canada* (Toronto: Butterworths, 1982).

Bryden, Philip, Steven Davis & John Russell, eds., *Protecting Rights and Freedoms: Essays on the Charter's Place in Canada's Political, Legal, and Intellectual Life* (Toronto: University of Toronto Press, 1994).

Cairns, Alan C., *Reconfigurations: Canadian Citizenship and Constitutional Change* (Toronto: McClelland & Stewart, 1995).

Cameron, David R., ed., *The Referendum Papers: Essays on Secession and National Unity* (Toronto: University of Toronto Press, 1999).

Carens, Joseph H., ed., *Is Quebec Nationalism Just? Perspectives from Anglophone Canada* (Montreal & Kingston: McGill-Queen's University Press, 1995).

Cook, Curtis, ed., *Constitutional Predicament: Canada after the Referendum of 1992* (Montreal & Kingston: McGill-Queen's University Press, 1994).

Department of Politics, Brock University, *Canadian Politics: Past, Present and Future* (St. Catharines: Department of Politics, Brock University, 1992).

Dunsmuir, Mollie, Library of Parliament Research Branch, *Referendums: the Canadian Experience in an International Context* (Ottawa: Supply and Services Canada, 1992).

Finkelstein, Neil, *The Separation of Quebec and the Constitution of Canada* (North York: York Centre for Public Law and Public Policy, 1992).

Gagnon, Alain-G. & James Tully, eds., *Multinational Democracies* (New York: Cambridge University Press, 2001).

Gagnon, Alain-G., Montserrat Guibernau, & François Rocher, eds., *The Conditions of Diversity in Multinational Democracies* (Montreal: Institute for Research on Public Policy, 2003).

Gibson, Gordon, *Plan B: The Future of the Rest of Canada* (Vancouver: Fraser Institute, 1994).

Gibbons, Roger & Guy Laforest, *Beyond the Impasse: Toward Reconciliation* (Montreal: Institute for Research on Public Policy, 1998).

Jackson, Robert J. & Doreen Jackson, *Stand Up for Canada: Leadership and the Canadian Political Crisis* (Scarborough, Ont.: Carswell, 1992).

Johnson, William, *A Canadian Myth: Quebec, Between Canada and the Illusion of Utopia* (Montreal: Robert Davies, 1994).

Kymlicka, Will, *Multicultural Citizenship: A Liberal Theory of Minority Rights* (Oxford: Oxford University Press, 1995).

Landry, Bernard, *La cause du Québec* (Montréal: VLB, 2002).

Lavergne, France, updated by Julien Coté, *Instruments of Direct Democracy in Canada and Québec*, 3d ed. (Québec: Le Directeur général des élections du Québec, 2001).

Lenihan, Donald G., Gordon Robertson & Roger Tassé, *Reclaiming the Middle Ground* (1994).

Marquis, Pierre, Library of Parliament Research Branch, *Referendums in Canada: The Effect of Populist Decision-Making on Representative Democracy* (Ottawa: Supply and Services Canada, 1993).

Monahan, Patrick, *Doing the Rules: An Assessment of the Federal Clarity Act in Light of the Quebec Secession Reference* (Toronto: C.D. Howe Institute, 2000).

Resnick, Philip, *Thinking English Canada* (Don Mills, Ont.: Stoddart, 1994).

Russell, Peter H., *Constitutional Odyssey: Can Canadians Become a Sovereign People?* 3d ed. (Toronto: University of Toronto Press, 2004).

Seidel, F. Leslie, ed., *Seeking a New Canadian Partnership* (Montreal: Institute for Research on Public Policy, 1994).

Turp, Daniel, *The Right to Choose: Essays on Quebec's Right of Self-Determination* (Montréal: Les Éditions Thémis Inc., 2001).

Vipond, Robert C., *Liberty & Community: Canadian Federalism and the Failure of the Constitution* (Albany, N.Y.: State University of New York Press, 1991).

Watts, Ronald L. & Douglas M. Brown, eds., *Canada: The State of the Federation 1993* (Kingston: Institute of Intergovernmental Relations, Queen's University, 1993).

———, *Options for a New Canada* (Toronto: University of Toronto Press, 1991).

Webber, Jeremy, *Reimagining Canada: Language, Culture, Community, and the Canadian Constitution* (Montreal & Kingston: McGill-Queen's University Press, 1994).

Williams, Douglas E., ed., *Reconfigurations: Canadian Citizenship and Constitutional Change* (Toronto: University of Toronto, 1995).

Young, Robert A., *The Struggle for Quebec: From Referendum to Referendum?* (Montreal & Kingston: McGill-Queen's University Press, 1999).

———, ed., *Stretching the Nation: The Art of State in Canada* (Montreal & Kingston: McGill-Queen's University Press, 1999).

———, *The Secession of Quebec and the Future of Canada* (Montreal & Kingston: McGill-Queen's University, 1995).